Communication Yearbook /13

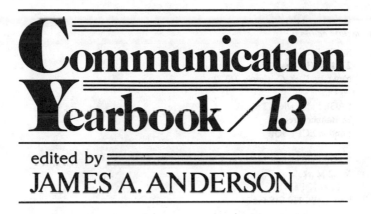

Communication
Yearbook / 13

edited by
JAMES A. ANDERSON

 Published Annually for the
International Communication
Association

 SAGE PUBLICATIONS
The Publishers of Professional Social Science
Newbury Park   London   New Delhi

For information address:

SAGE Publications, Inc.
2111 W. Hillcrest Drive
Newbury Park, California 91320

SAGE Publications Ltd.
28 Banner Street
London EC1Y 8QE

SAGE Publications India Pvt. Ltd.
M-32 Market
Greater Kailash I
New Delhi 110 048 India

Printed in the United States of America

Library of Congress: 76-45943
ISBN 0-8039-3349-5

FIRST PRINTING, 1990

CONTENTS

THE INTERNATIONAL COMMUNICATION ASSOCIATION

The *Communication Yearbook* series is sponsored by the International Communication Association, one of several major scholarly organizations in the communication field. It is composed of 2,500 communication scholars, teachers, and practitioners.

Throughout its 41-year history, the Association has been particularly important to those in the field of communication who have sought a forum where the behavioral science perspective was predominant. The International Communication Association has also been attractive to a number of individuals from a variety of disciplines who hold communication to be central to work within their primary fields of endeavor. The Association has been an important stimulant to the infusion of behavioral concepts in communication study and teaching, and has played a significant role in defining a broadened set of boundaries of the discipline as a whole.

The International Communication Association is a pluralist organization composed of ten subdivisions: Information Systems, Interpersonal Communication, Mass Communication, Organizational Communication, Intercultural and Development Communication, Political Communication, Instructional and Developmental Communication, Health Communication, Philosophy of Communication, and Human Communication Technology.

In addition to *Communication Yearbook*, the Association publishes *Human Communication Research, Communication Theory,* the *ICA Newsletter,* and *ICA Directory.* Several divisions also publish newsletters and occasional papers.

PREFACE

This preface is designed first of all to produce some anticipation for what lies within and then to discuss two metatheoretical issues that might serve as connecting schemes for the whole of the work.

THE GRAND TOUR

The first section of this volume brings together four works and accompanying commentary that examine organizational communication from an interpretive, social constructionist perspective. Stanley Deetz and Dennis Mumby begin the discussion by positing organizational control as a discursive practice and suggesting that maximizing control rather than maximizing profit has become the end of the multinational, dispersed-ownership corporation. In reclaiming the critical, they argue that such practices necessarily exploit or suppress some and are, therefore, flawed. They flirt with a Habermasian, utopian answer, but in the end settle for Foucault's solution of recurring temporary refurbishment. In her commentary, Beth Haslett adopts a pluralistic position to point out that managerial control is not that effective and that the organization is the site of many voices. Cynthia Stohl and Patty Sotirin work a specific example of the discursive practices of control and show how critical analysis can be of benefit. H. L. Goodall, Jr., develops the importance of settings and props for understanding the performances that materialize an organization's culture. Among other conclusions, he advances the claim that membership is as much in the management of costumes and props as any other. Charles Conrad, for his part, provides a thoughtful analysis of ethnographic narrative. Sandra Sanford offers us the unusual circumstance of hearing the "native's" voice in comment on an ethnography. Sonja Sackmann asks us to step back and consider the many approaches we have developed to the concept of organizational culture. Taking an action perspective, she analyzes what organizing practices can be advanced from cultural inquiry. Connie Gersick explores the tension between description and control (or management) in the study of organizational culture. Larry Greiner argues an inherent hierarchical character of organizing that modifies the expression and therefore the analytical approach to organizational culture. Mary Helen Brown concludes this section by investigating the culture-defining properties of organizational stories. She offers a lengthy comment on the utility of stories for organizational research. Gary Kreps extends Brown's analysis by applying the story as a resource for change efforts. Jill McMillan argues the relationship between organizational stories (and other symbols) and power, taking a much more optimistic position on control than either Deetz and Mumby or Greiner.

The next section explores topics in interpersonal communication, beginning with Wayne Beach's investigation of the phenomena of interaction analysis. Beach considers the use of macroconcepts and research methods in the understanding of the practical accomplishments of mundane conversational texts. Robert Hopper picks up and extends Beach's discussion of coding and its consequences for claim. Jenny Mandelbaum describes what phenomena are made apparent in interactional analysis. Renee Meyers and David Seibold direct our attention to group argument. They review cognitive-informational theory, particularly persuasive arguments theory (PAT). Finding it wanting, they advance Giddens's structuration theory as a more appropriate approach. Franklin Boster considers the nature of argument, its mechanics and effects in group discussion. Dennis Gouran works to strengthen Meyers and Seibold's critique of PAT and offers three propositions to advance analysis from structuration theory. William Cupach and Sandra Metts take on embarrassment, working through the predicament, response, remediation, and resolution of such episodes. Their conclusions are a road map for future research. Robert Edelmann comments from his own extensive research experience, interlacing analysis with evidence from that corpus of work. Sandra Petronio establishes embarrassment firmly as a communication phenomenon, showing how the predicament, remediation, and resolution are all communication practices. Steven Wilson and Linda Putnam continue their work in negotiation. In their chapter, the operant questions concern the nature of goals and their function as boundaries of practice. Pamela Benoit tests the implications of Wilson and Putnam's ontological arguments and offers her own refinements. William Donohue develops an argument of goals as interactional achievements that can be examined from both general and particular perspectives.

Youichi Ito opens the third section with a telling analysis of the difficulties in developing theory concerning the informational dependence of Third World countries. His analysis posits cultural information as a commodity that increases in value according to the relative economic success of the representative nations. Majid Tehranian sees the crucial moment as the move to industrializing status for less developed countries. Jaswant Yadava argues for a more complex process that goes beyond economic competition. Joseph Turow, while granting that the products of media are resources for audiences and not causal agents, also argues that an understanding of media in contemporary life requires an understanding of the influences that shape those products. He offers a case study from television. Charles Bantz critiques Turow's resource dependency model and offers instead the notion of industrial communities enacting their environments. Sandra Braman and Akiba Cohen work to refine Turow's definitions and point to the value of an expanded research agenda. Finally, Virginia Fry, Alison Alexander, and Donald Fry offer a fitting capstone to the volume by exploring the emergence of text from media product in the process of media consumption. They show the resource value of text for the practices of everyday life. Dennis Davis reviews the paradigmatic development of communication and sets the location of the Fry, Alexander, and Fry chapter as an element in the evolving cultural analysis perspective. Stuart Sigman applies a semiotic analysis within a social action frame to consider the fulfillment of mediated messages within the social performances of interpretation.

CONNECTIONS IN METATHEORETICAL ISSUES

From my perspective as an analyst of theories and their supporting methodologies, this volume is a particularly rich field. In developing their arguments, the authors have pressed the frontiers of a number of metatheoretical issues. I would like to discuss two of them here: how the move toward constructionism has made the critical once again visible and how interpretivism forces the question of the moral position of an argument.

Constructionism and the Critical

In keeping with the tradition of the *Yearbook*, the arguments contained herein have an empirical fundament. But this empirical foundation is being used to raise radically different arguments. In this volume, we reach from Deetz and Mumby's value-driven analysis of power and discourse in organizations to Cupach and Metts's more dispassionate analysis of the causes of embarrassment. Spread out between these poles — in more or less this order — are Goodall; Meyers and Seibold; Fry, Alexander, and Fry; Brown, Sackmann, Wilson and Putnam; Ito; Turow; and Beach. The commentators hold their own places and add that many more examples of the variety are possible. Exploring the differences within this variety invokes questions as to where the critical and the moral shall sit in empirical inquiry. If we consider the critical and the moral as elements in the larger field of ethics, then we can define the critical as arguments toward the good and (as we shall see) the moral as the strategies of and tactical choices within arguments.

Questions of value and choice have been debated in the social sciences, particularly by those members of the scientific community who have believed that our job is to describe what is *out there* and how it works, usually toward the end of suppressing such value-oriented questions. As some social theory moved away from variable atomism and/or structuralism, however, and toward the idea that the forces that influence are in some part the consequence of our collective decision making, the presumption of a value-free, transcendent science was undermined. Some of these developing theories directly implicated science and its claims in the ideological and political. Science was identified as part of the ideological apparatus that creates the political playing field. Once made, this move demands the critical turn in scientific argument, because any claim of what is also constitutes a claim of what ought to be by virtue of the reproductive effectivity of science. This issue is clearly unresolved, but it percolates throughout this volume. Deetz and Mumby, Sackmann, Ito, and Beach address it specifically in their arguments, but it is necessarily present in each of the others.

Interpretivism and the Moral

If constructionism recalls the critical into science, then interpretivism recalls the moral. Goodall, Brown, Meyers and Seibold, and Fry, Alexander, and Fry mount their arguments as insightful readers of facts. Their chapters are the product of their intuitions about how these facts can be brought into sensibility. They are professional claim makers involved in the production of their community's knowledge. The element of import for this discussion is that the claim exists only in its presentation, in this case in the writing.

There is a delicate analysis that needs to be performed here. This is not Berkeleianism, but a recognition that for intepretivists, social science claim is about collectively created relationships between and among facts and that these relationships are the product of human consciousness. It is the intuiting — the putting together — of these relationships that is the interpretive act. Each of us, therefore, is (theoretically) able to bring the collection of intersubjectively acknowledged facts to different conclusions. We are, therefore, morally responsible for the conclusions that we draw. We are morally responsible because we cannot seek refuge in the sportscaster's defense of "telling it like it is." We are telling how it is sensible to us in the collectively created world in which we live.

The significance of this moral responsibility would be greatly reduced if we were examining the circumstance of an individual giving his or her opinion about the nature of some facet of the world. Such is not the case because we are speaking of those charged by their society to produce the knowledge from which others will act. For the interpretive social scientist (who is necessarily a constructionist), the business of inquiry is not to reveal the world to us but to create some part of the world for us. Inquiry is the professional practice of the social creation of reality. We have been granted the space, time, and resources (meager though they often are) to practice this craft. It is easy to become cynical about this charge as we protect ourselves from it through various professional devices. It is, however, what every article (and preface) in this volume intends. The morality (or ethical quality, for the squeamish) of every argument contained herein, consequently, is legitimately open to analysis from this interpretive perspective. (The tag line disclaimer is important, as competent, objective claims can be falsified but cannot be immoral.)

Let me impose upon you to offer one example from the popular press: *Newsweek* of May 22, 1989, reported a story on Black fathers who have returned to take their children out from under the care of their crack-addicted mothers. Jean Seligmann writes:

> Thomas, still on welfare, works part time in a hospital mail room. "Fathers are taking their stand," he says. I'm young, I'm black and I'm male. I'm not supposed to be doing this, but I'm sure glad I am." (p. 64)

Who told Mr. Thomas that he was not supposed to care for his addicted child? We scientists, clinicians, caseworkers, and journalists who dispassionately report that men leave their families as if the decision were one of individual accountability and culpability. The facts may be clear — men, particularly Black men, do leave their families — but the argument that absolves the social system is morally suspect, as suspect as the phrase "particularly Black men." In that phrase, I chose to characterize a race because it was convenient and defensible given the data. But the phrase advances the claim that it is in being Black — not in being subordinated or in having some other related demographic characteristic (e.g., age, economic status, educational background) that I could have chosen as the descriptor — that one would find the agency of the action of paternal irresponsibility. There is, of course, no convincing evidence that the claim is true. Rather, it is a perspective that we maintain for the good of the present order.

This argument quickly becomes disconcerting because moral responsibility is invoked at the most routine moments — the surveyist's selection of demographic questions, Professor Goodall's decision of what an individual's office decor means, or Professor Brown's identification of one codifying story of an organization. How does one act morally to anticipate the consequences of those initiating decisions? How does one manage the strategic interpretation of fact so as not to reproduce the inequities in which we live? These questions have partial answers in the works of Goodall and Brown and in the others as well. I can recommend their reading with such questions in mind.

ACKNOWLEDGMENTS

There is no question of the debt this volume owes to the many who helped in its preparation. My thanks to Connie Bullis, Steve Duck, Don Faules, Fred Jablin, Christine Oravec, Sally Planalp, Phillip Tompkins, and Paul Traudt, among others, for their comments on proposals and drafts. Julie Brown came on board as the editorial associate at the end of *Yearbook 12* and has contributed in a superior fashion ever since. She is an outstanding young scholar, and the *Yearbook* has benefited immeasurably from her efforts. Finally, the University of Utah Department of Communication has freely made its resources available. The *Yearbook* could not have been produced without that support.

—*James A. Anderson*
University of Utah

SECTION 1

ORGANIZATIONS: CRITICISM AND CULTURE

1 Power, Discourse, and the Workplace: Reclaiming the Critical Tradition

STANLEY DEETZ
Rutgers University

DENNIS K. MUMBY
Purdue University

In the past ten years the critical tradition has made significant contributions to communication studies in organizations, challenging the hegemony of mainstream, functionalist approaches. As a result, issues of power and control have become legitimate areas of study for organizational researchers. This chapter assesses that critical turn and argues that, while such a move was long overdue, its effect has been diffused because of a lack of clarity in conceptualizing the relationships among power, discourse, and the workplace. As such, after delineating the seminal contributions of Marx, Braverman, and Burawoy to the question of workplace control, we suggest how this issue can be more powerfully conceptualized in modern, dispersed-ownership, managerially oriented organizations. By focusing on the relationship between power and discourse, we show how particular systems of interest representation emerge in the modern organization. Our aim is to demonstrate that the configuration of power in organizations is just as much the result of a discursive struggle over the meaning of organizational practices as it is the product of more overt struggles around economic issues.

W ORK is a central human activity not only in terms of the total amount of time spent in it, but also in its relation to social and personal identity. The workplace, and its organization, is not just a human product for the accomplishment of certain functions; it produces people as well as information, goods, and services. From a critical studies standpoint, the workplace is a potential site of conflict over the representation of differing interests in decisions regarding products, the environment, and our collective character. In order to understand the

Correspondence and requests for reprints: Stanley Deetz, Department of Communication, 4 Huntington Street, Rutgers University, New Brunswick, NJ 08903.

Communication Yearbook 13, pp. 18-47

role of communication in these conflicts and their resolution or suppression, we must understand the material and discursive structure of the workplace.

While many organizational configurations for work and the workplace exist today, none is as important as the publicly capitalized, dispersed-ownership, multiunit corporation. The corporate organization is a primary institution in modern society, in many ways overshadowing the state in its multinational influence and in its control and direction of people's lives. While the state's power is exercised in control and limitation, corporate organizations make most decisions as to technological development, utilization of resources, and working relations among people, and corporate values and practices extend into nonwork areas of life.

Despite the wide variety of social effects, corporate organizations have remained largely autocratic in form. One wonders why people so willingly consent to and support this degree of control that no modern state has seemed to be able to accomplish. While no public cry of "No merger, development, or new product without representation" is likely, the power and effect of corporate organizations must be understood. Who holds control, how and on what bases they hold control, and to what ends this control is directed are all central questions.

Organizational research often treats the modern corporation, and its managerial control, as a naturally occurring, rather than politically created, form. Consequently, questions of power and control become narrowed and understood only from a managerial point of view. To open them to fuller examination, we will first reclaim a more basic theory of power and control in organizations and of the relation of work to human identity and development through a reexamination of Marx's treatment of industrialization and later analyses of the structure of work and control. Second, we will examine the historical development of the modern corporate form to show the forces that shaped it, the historical emergence of the roles and consciousness given in it, and the development of managerial interests as dominant. Finally, we will extend the critical theory of organization to account more fully for the nature of power, knowledge, and control in the modern corporation. From this analysis, we will show how the critique of managerial domination and the exclusion of other interests might proceed. We believe that such a reformulation is necessary to enhance representation of competing interests in organizations and to respond to the dramatic changes in organizations resulting from the move from production to information work and the rapid introduction of computer-assisted communication technologies.

EXPLOITATION AND COERCION

The works of Karl Marx on the historical development of industrialization and capitalism still provide the most complete treatment of power and control in organizations and the relation of work to human identity. Marx's conceptions changed in his own writings and have continued to be reinterpreted. Despite the

changes, however, a core legacy continues to drive applications and interpretations. There are many ways to present this legacy. Because Marx's formulations as
well as many of the disputes thereafter are quite familiar, we will not belabor them
here. Rather, we briefly sketch what Marx would tell us of the workplace.

Essentially, the workplace is composed of both means and mode of production.
The *means of production* refers to processes of work itself, including available
technologies, job design, raw materials, and the skills of workers. In Marx's view,
industrialization brought with it dehumanization and alienation from work and
work products. Human identity is concretized in the making of a product. Identity
cannot be situated in mass production. Further, with capitalist industrialization,
workers no longer sold produced products, but themselves as product producers.
Hence the division of labor, the treatment of labor as a commodity, and the
separation of the individual from his or her product produced a fragmented, lost
person, estranged from his or her own production activities (Marx, 1964).

The *mode of production* refers to the complex economic and social relationships
that exist among parties of the production process. Economically, the capitalist
mode of production expropriated surplus labor from the owners of that labor. The
amount of this surplus could be calculated by determining the difference between
value of the product and that paid for the labor used to produce it (including the
labor embodied in making the equipment used in the production process and so
forth). Such calculation makes sense if you start from a labor theory of value. To
Marx, the surplus value of labor was hidden from both workers and capitalists. The
capitalist would understand the realization of profit as coming from the investment
in the plant and equipment, with the amount of profit determined by market
conditions rather than by unpaid labor. The worker being paid a wage would not
be in a position to determine the portion of the value of the product that was a result
of his or her labor and hence could not recognize unpaid labor. Labor was a
commodity, like other commodities, having an exchange value on the market
rather than being the source of all product value.

The capitalist mode of production also fixed social relations. The owners of
their own labor and the owners of capital entered into the contract differently.
Essentially, the worker was placed at a great disadvantage by his or her historical
situation. The lack of means of production and the bodily necessity for subsistence
during the time of production meant that the worker always bargained and worked
under duress (Marx, 1906, p. 80). Hence exploitation and coercion characterized
the work process. The roles of owner and worker were not of their own creation,
but were produced and reproduced out of historical forms of domination. The
means and mode of production at each historical moment form an infrastructure
determining other aspects of social relations.

While hidden, the historical situation created continued conflict between the
interests of workers and those of capitalists. These tensions were largely kept in
check by the production of a superstructure. The superstructure consisted of the
values, laws, rules, ideology, and institutions that both hid the actual conditions

under which people worked and governed people's conduct according to capitalist needs.

Marx believed that with the continuing accumulation of capital and growing gap between the living conditions of capitalists and workers, ultimately workers would realize their true interest and revolt, thus transforming the economic order. Explanations for why this did not take place range from the identification of flaws in Marx's analysis, to descriptions of the manner in which the development of the welfare state has kept the workers' condition tolerable, to the examination of the production of powerful ideological structures obscuring the conditions of exploitation. Unfortunately, this preoccupation with a determinist and political reading of Marx has led most either to overlook or to distort Marx's useful analysis of control of the labor process and its consequences for human identity formation.

Harry Braverman has been the most significant figure in reclaiming this aspect of Marx's analysis. In *Labor and Monopoly Capital* (1974), he rehabilitates Marx's theory of the labor process through an insightful analysis of the contemporary work situation. Because his work is also familiar to most, we will highlight only a few central points here.

First, the labor process is largely similar in all industrial nations, including the United States and the Soviet Union, with regard to job design and relations among different segments of the work force. Capitalist work relations hold independent of political ideologies.

Second, technological developments, the rise of the service sector, and the increased portion of the economy given to management have not created a new distinct class structure or class identity. In many respects, these expanded occupational areas structurally reproduce familiar characteristics of the production labor processes.

Third, and most significant, degradation of work is ongoing across occupational areas. Contrary to the popular perception that industrial nations are producing a more highly educated and skilled labor force and that continued technological development will require even greater skill on the part of the worker, Braverman demonstrates that "deskilling" is evident in all economic sectors. Essentially, the separation of conception from execution in production processes and increased division of labor removes knowledge from work and creates a degraded, alienated work force. With "rationalization" (the application of science to work) all modern office work becomes increasingly clerical and service occupations become laboring activities outside a physical plant. Others have documented similar changes in the professions (see Heydebrand, 1977).

To Braverman, the degradation of work and workers is an expected outcome of the drive for capital accumulation. However, while his descriptions of the changes in the nature of work are compelling, his brief analyses of how these changes are carried out are not. Viewing managerial control as motivated and accomplished by a desire for capital accumulation leaves much unanswered. In this regard, Braverman's analyses of the control by owners and the linking of upper management with monied interests is particularly strained. It is only partially true that upper levels of management come from wealthy families and probably not true that managerial decisions can be explained by family of origin. Several questions remain. Why do members of the society willingly or unwillingly participate in such a system? What are the mechanisms by which continued participation by workers is ensured? And why, if the processes of degradation and alienation are ongoing, does the reported experience of the work force only occasionally recognize this fate? Consent rather than coercion appears to characterize the modern worker's relation to the production apparatus.

IDEOLOGY AND MANUFACTURED CONSENT

Such questions as these have driven the work of Michael Burawoy. In *Manufacturing Consent* (1979), Burawoy explores two essential issues. First, how are the social relations of the capitalist enterprise produced and reproduced? As he argues, organizations are not simply given in their current form and persist through time; they have to be produced and reproduced continually. The capitalist system cannot autonomously and anonymously accomplish these tasks; they are done by somebody, somehow.

Second, the worker, both in Marx's time and even more clearly today, freely participates in the labor process, giving support and consent to existing forms of control. What are the mechanisms of organizing this consent in the activity of work? How can the experiences of the workers themselves be accounted for? This issue is organized for Burawoy around a rather unique question: quoting Lynd, "Why do workers work as hard as they do?"

Burawoy argues that both management-worker conflict and worker consent are organized in the work process itself. Understanding how this relationship occurs in the workplace requires an understanding of the political and ideological realms of the organization of production. The core issue is how people represent and try to fulfill their interests in the organization. Representation and fulfillment of interests require choices arrived at by some reasoning process. To Burawoy (1979), workers, in making their choices, can be seen neither as simply irrational nor as economically rational. Rationality itself is "a product of the specific organization of production and is part and parcel of the factory 'culture' " (p. 4). The fact that workers participate in making choices generates consent. To the extent that their choices and reasoning processes are not of their own making or in their own best interest, we have domination.

The key issue is that of reasoning and "consent." In most organizational theory, consent has been assumed to derive from something else but has not itself been subject to analysis. Burawoy, quoting Gouldner (1954, p. 223), argues:

For Weber, therefore, authority was given consent because it was legitimate, rather than being legitimate because it evoked consent. For Weber, therefore, consent is always a datum to be taken for granted rather than a problem whose sources had to be traced. In consequence, he never systematically analyzed the actual social process-es which either generated or thwarted the emergence of consent.

Consent is a far more effective means of control than coercion. How does it emerge? The answer rests in a conception of ideology and experience.

Burawoy, following Gramsci (1971), argues that the experience of a people and not just their actual situation is an active force in decision making. Experience is not a personal or subjective thing but arises out of the concrete material situation, out of the individual's position. However, the conditions for the production of experience are hidden; hence experience appears personal, natural, and inevitable. In this sense, experience can be said to be ideological. The conditions of experience production cannot be assessed. Ideology is not imposed on people as a disguise for their true interests, but both expresses and is produced out of their life activities. As Burawoy (1979) argues:

> Ideology is, therefore, not something manipulated at will by agencies of socializa-tion — schools, family, church, and so on — in the interests of a dominant class. On the contrary, these institutions elaborate and systematize lived experience and only in this way become centers of ideological dissemination. Moreover, dominant classes are shaped by ideology more than they shape it. To the extent that they engage in active deception, they disseminate propaganda, not ideology. (pp. 17-18)

Ideology is outside what is in one's head. It serves as an organizing force for theories, attitudes, values, and so forth. Individuals' and groups' realization of their interests and the reasoning process for accomplishing their interests emerge out of ideology. In this sense, interests, choices, and the giving of consent are produced out of the concrete relations in the work process held in place by a capitalist mode of production.

For Burawoy, the modern workplace differs from early industrial ones in that the worker has acquired a type of decisional autonomy and limits have been placed on the coercive power of owners and management. But this situation does not enable the worker to recognize exploitation through unpaid labor. Workers are less constrained in the pursuit of their interests, but the ideological structure of interests leads them to constrain the pursuit of their own interests spontaneously to the benefit of profit, perhaps to an extent greater than management could ever require. As Burawoy (1979) argues regarding the changes in the relations in production:

> [These changes] have offered workers a very limited but nevertheless critical freedom in their adaptation to the labor process. The rise of rules and, with them, constraints on managerial intervention, have opened up an area of choice within which workers can constitute work as a game. Workers are sucked into the game as a way of reducing the level of deprivation. But participation has the consequence of generating consent to the rules, which define both the conditions of choice and the limits of managerial discretion. Thus, it is not the rules themselves but the activities they circumscribe that generate consent. (p. 199)

TOWARD AN EXPANDED VIEW

Many of the basic concepts from the critical tradition are essential to an understanding of power and the representation of interests in the modern workplace.
Burawoy and Braverman provide an essential theoretical context from which we
can develop and interpret further analyses, but their works have limitations.

First, both authors remain preoccupied with a certain category of workers.
Without a doubt, Burawoy (1979) produced a penetrating analysis of piece-rate
laborers. While this population is significant, the nature of this work is hardly
representative of either the production relations or the production activities of the
modern work force. The demographics of the modern work force virtually demand
that an adequate theory incorporate an accounting of the activities and situation of
managerial and professional groups as well as laborers. While certainly analogies
can be drawn between different groups, each occupies a different structural place
in the organization with distinct interests. Further, class division does not exhaust
the concern with group differences in power and conditions of domination. The
modern concern with gender and women's struggle to achieve significant roles in
organizations cannot be trivialized or simply reduced to salary differences and
conditions of employment, as significant as those issues are.

Second, Burawoy's and Braverman's taken-for-granted conception of the management group does not match well with the empirical nature of modern organizations. In both their analyses, management is treated as an extension of owners,
administering and making decisions in owners' interests. Conceiving of such unity
hides distinct interest differences between the two groups and misleads the examination of the motivational foundation for many corporate decisions.

Third, both the means and relations of production have a significantly different
character from that suggested in even a revisionist Marxist analysis. If we expand
the focus of our attention to workers outside the traditional production process, we
find different constraints on the nature of the work activity. While Braverman
(1974) may be partially right that the service and information labor force is
"deskilled" and economically exploited, the technological infrastructure that supports this condition is different from that supporting the traditional labor process.
As we shall develop later, such exploitation may be better explained by the
domination of a particular cognitive interest rather than a class interest, and hence
might restrict everyone to no one's benefit.

Finally, even a weakened notion of economic determinism supplemented by an
expanded conception of ideology does not account well for the decisional structure
of most modern organizations. The image of modern corporations as driven by a
desire for profit benefiting a capitalist group does not match empirical analyses of
modern corporate life. Organizations must be understood in a complex fashion.
Economic conditions cannot be seen as an independent external force, but become
one of several competing logics or discursive practices within organizations. To
understand and utilize such a conception and to gather the full benefit of

Braverman's and Burawoy's analyses, we must rethink the nature of organizations and the relations of production in modern society.

THE RISE OF MANAGERIAL CAPITALISM

Without a doubt, the nature of the modern organization is protected from rational assessment. But its nature is not only or primarily hidden from the worker for the sake of the production of surplus value. For all groups—owners, managers, workers, and even Marxists—the concept that ownership equals control organizes both thought and action and obscures the actual relations of production. Historically, such an equation was probably accurate, and theorists have long known that management has usurped most practical owner power (Berle & Means, 1932), yet, the continued belief in the equation undoubtedly serves important functions for each group. An adequate discussion of organizations today, however, requires rethinking the relations of production.

Alfred Chandler (1977) has presented the most complete and detailed analysis of the historical development of the modern corporation in the United States. Others have duplicated this analysis in other industrial nations (Chandler & Daems, 1980). As Chandler (1977) summarizes his analysis:

> The institution [modern business organization] appeared where managerial hierarchies were able to monitor and coordinate the activities of a number of business units more efficiently than did market mechanisms. It continued to grow so that these hierarchies of increasingly professional managers might remain fully employed. It emerged and spread, however, only in those industries and sectors whose technology and markets permitted administrative coordination to be more profitable than market coordination. Because these areas were at the center of the American economy and because professional managers replaced families, financiers, or their representatives as decision makers in these areas, modern American capitalism became managerial capitalism. (p. 11)

Several portions of Chandler's analysis are significant for understanding the internal relations of corporations today and inform a critical analysis of them. Four points are key here: (a) the conditions enabling the continued corporate expansion, (b) the development of the professional manager, (c) the separation of management and ownership, and (d) the focus on long-term stability and growth rather than profit maximization.

Expansion of the Corporate Form

The corporate form developed and grew in those areas where the combination of technologically driven increases in production and expanded markets based on population growth, transportation improvements, and new communication systems increased the advantage of administrative, over market, coordination. As the multiunit organization freed itself partially from market demand, the ability to administer became the primary limit to size and expansion of control. Communication systems thus became a central determinant of the spread of control. The more sophisticated the communication technology, the less central the market conditions in determining the nature and scope of the enterprise. We see here the first step of the move from an economically driven capitalism to a communication-driven one.

The Career Manager

Chandler emphasized increased reliance on managerial training, skills, and movement up the corporate ladder. But certainly more was at stake: The development of educational programs and a professional identity transformed the character of managerial knowledge and helped foster a unique managerial ideology. As Judith Merkle (1980) shows in her tracing of the legacy of the scientific management movement, such an ideology did not spontaneously arise out of the society or as a representation of a natural class interest, but as a result of a massive and systematic attempt to create a form of organization. Even in the Soviet Union, Lenin argued strongly for utilizing scientific management as a means of keeping up with capitalist progress (Merkle, 1980, pp. 105-109). Taylorism was largely accepted in the industrial world as a material practice and an ideology.

As Weber (1978) shows more generally in his analysis of bureaucratic rationality, the impulse and initial effect of Taylor's work and the professionalization of management was emancipating. "Rational" grounds for decisions replaced traditional practices and values. The codification of procedures offered workers protection as well as managers stability and control. As membership in the management group and promotions became, at least partially, based on training and skill, upward mobility became possible for working-class individuals. The corporate organization was opened for a new kind of discourse, one based on reason and consensual rules. But, as happens often in society, capricious decision making, discrimination, and privilege are overcome by fixed procedures and rational processes that in turn contain their own hidden values that generate new forms of domination. While the actual nature of this new form of domination is the subject of the next section of the chapter, let us sum it up here by saying that as management is transformed into administration, it becomes both skilled and deskilled in Braverman's sense. The manager is a technical expert, but conception of the rules is separated from execution of them. Procedures are evoked for control and efficiency in themselves, with the ends for which they are evoked becoming both taken for granted and obscured. The desire for control because it will produce increased profit becomes a desire for control that might fortuitously increase profits, much as the professionalized student changes from seeking learning (with grades as a by-product) to seeking grades (with learning as a potential by-product).

The Separation of Ownership and Management

Not only does administration replace aspects of the marketplace in production decisions, but the control of the organizations shifts from profit-centered owners to career-centered managers. Although, structurally, owners have the potential for control through a board of directors, in practice nearly all control is in the hands of career managers. There are a number of reasons for this. The size and complexity of the modern business unit forces control of most operating decisions to an anonymous group of middle managers. Further, most owner representatives on boards of directors serve only part-time, with primary obligations elsewhere (Mintzberg, 1983). Their ability and desire to exercise control are at most occasional. Most find it far easier to sell their interest in a company than to try to exercise control in it. Even if they wish to influence major decisions, owners' power is limited. Necessary information is frequently not available to them, or is greatly influenced in its construction by the management group. Management through proxy frequently controls a majority of the votes. Significant events where owners have attempted to influence corporate policy have been failures (Mintzberg, 1983).

Thus management's decisional prerogative may be legitimized through the conception of management as an extension of ownership, but management actually functions as an independent group actualizing self-interest. A critical analysis based on a labor theory of value fails here, because the primary structure is not capitalist exploitation of surplus labor for profit. In some respects, modern diffused ownership through public stock holding partly meets Marx's ideal. Significantly, even if stock ownership were equitably distributed in the society, domination and exploitation would still prevail through administration. Such is, of course, vividly clear in industrialized communist countries, where, while ownership may be public, workplace relations are much the same as in all other industrial nations. The Yugoslavian example is as unique to Eastern bloc countries as the Scandinavian experiments are to the Western world. But the critical tradition helps greatly in identifying the obscured structural tension that remains. Managerial interests compete with and dominate the interests of other parties, including workers and owners, and do so by evoking accepted, but no longer relevant, social values.

The Corporation as an End in Itself

A new form of workplace identity and knowledge was formed as the practical interest of the entrepreneur and capitalist became transformed into a technical interest of the manager. While for the owner the corporation is a means to profit, the professional manager is interested in the long-term stability and growth of the enterprise. Certainly such a change in the basis for decisions is significant. Many have documented the move away from profit as a central focus of decision making, most notably Galbraith (1967) and Cyert and March (1963). By focusing on the implication for economics, these works, as well as Chandler's, may not do enough to develop the human implications of the shift of logic in organizations.

The reported focus on profits as well as the emergent focus on long-term growth and stability may obscure the extent to which managers make decisions based primarily on managerial ideology, including emphasis on personal career gains. Weick (1979) and Jehenson (1984), among others, clearly distinguish between the reasons *for* managerial decisions and the reasons *given for* them. Numerous values compete with economic ones. They range from interest in increased organizational size and control, to implementation of state-of-the-art technologies, to daily preference for easily justified decisions (owing to common practices) over situationally better ones.

The manager's identity and interests differ from those of owners and workers. As Marx demonstrated, with the rise of industrial capitalism, the workers' identity became fragmented as they were separated from their product, and their labor, rather than their products, became the commodity they sold. A parallel but more extreme fragmentation happens to the manager with the rise of managerial capitalism. In an idealized version, managers' primary product is themselves. Their subjectivity is embodied more in a position than in a product. The measure of accomplishment is not the self reflected in the product, but in the advancement it achieved. The produced corporate image and self-marketing become central activities of work itself and extend into nonwork areas of life. Corporate and personal identities merge. While the worker seeks freedom — from necessity and for self-fulfillment — and the owner seeks profit, the manager seeks control. Changes in the market, the environment, or others pose a threat to identity and need to be brought under administrative control. Stability and growth thus best characterize the optimal condition under which a manager works. No mission or product can be as important as the survival of the corporation itself. Both surplus labor and what might be called surplus capital are necessary to sustain the career identity of management and costs of self-marketing.

This description is, of course, an overcharacterization to show the structural force of the managerial condition. Individual managers do make decisions against their careers and the owner/manager/worker division is never totally clear. For example, many managerial groups have stock-ownership options and profit-sharing plans that partially structure their interests as ownership. Given the rather uncertain predictive relation between particular decisions and the realization of profit and the relatively more direct effects of decisions on career moves, this owner interest is quite weak.

INTERESTS AND INTEREST REPRESENTATION

Just as Marx could document the significant changes in work life based on industrialization, it is important today to understand such changes based on communication and managerial coordination. With the emergence of managerial capitalism, the modern organization is not well conceived as a site of illegitimate (or legitimate) domination of laborers by owners through managerial coordination.

Neither market conditions nor the desire for capital accumulation well explain the process of decision making.

In modern, "deindustrialized" society, the value of labor and nature of the production process are not as significant as having information and the opportunity to engage in meaningful discourse regarding decisions. Analysis of the tension between capital and labor is less significant than that of the tension within systems allocating opportunities for expression. The modern problem is not monopoly capital but a monopoly of information and dialogue chances, or what Baudrillard (1935/1975) calls the "monopoly of the code" (p. 127; see also Agger, 1985, p. 6). Marx's concept of false consciousness gives over naturally to Habermas's concept of systematically distorted communication. The development and implementation of new communication technologies for extended control supports the maintenance and reproduction of inequitable interest representation through managerial domination.

The modern organization is potentially a site of struggle by numerous competing interests. Such competition is rarely observed. The conservative position is, of course, that the potential variety of interests have come to align in the modern corporation, and while each group may have different motives for its actions, they are integrated in modern structures (Bell, 1960; Parsons, 1956). Rather than pretend that anyone is in a good position to know what anyone's (let alone everyone's) true interests are, our questions have been different. They might be summarized as follows: Are the structures of interest representation such that self-interest can be understood and articulated? Do different interests have an equal opportunity for impact on decision making? Are there processes that suppress conflict among potentially competing interests? If conditions of inequality exist, how are they justified? When and in what ways are these justifications simply disguises hiding and perpetuating dominant group interests?

We have moved to answer these questions partially by looking at the historical processes of capitalist domination and the emergence of managerial domination. What is yet needed is a detailed analysis of how conflict and consent are organized in modern corporate life. The problem is similar to, but perhaps more complex than, Burawoy's (1979) shop floor. Here we can only lay the conceptual grounds for this investigation. Our concern is with the conception of interests, the nature of power in interest representation, and the systems of interaction in which domination or representation occurs.

Conceptualizing "interests" is difficult. The failure to do so, however, creates a number of problems in organizational analysis, particularly regarding the understanding of power. Most often interests are assumed as self-evident, but subsequent analyses frequently hide more than they reveal. For example, if the conclusion is reached that coalitions are used in some organizations to keep certain groups in control, we know that someone's interest is advanced, but we know little of the content or construction of that interest. We can talk of career advancement, management of culture, or greater efficiency without knowing anything of the end or interest that is served by these. Operating with an exchange theory of value, differences among interests are hidden by their common translation to price or cost. Economic value makes the assessment of other values difficult and the fairness or quality of the deal indeterminable. Domination can be understood only with an adequate concept of interests.

As Burawoy (1979) demonstrates, interests are certainly manifest in people but are not limited to what people can explicitly know, feel, or articulate. While different in content, structurally, interests relate to the individual like grammar and culture — they are often invisible, yet they form the bases for particular forms of expression and action. Further, like grammar and culture, the individual's attempt to describe them may be quite in error, even though they are used with great efficiency. As individuals rarely know all the rules of the grammar they use, they often hardly "know" all of their interests.

However, there are further characteristics that strain the metaphor. The interest we feel and act out of may not be our own or in our own best interest. The problem is one of determination as well as expression of self-interest. A person can "live" someone else's culture (e.g., the Black man who "lives" White or the corporate woman who totally emulates her male counterparts), but in these cases there is a "real" other community to which that person can be compared, even if such a judgment is filled with conceptual and political difficulties. We have no "real" fixed empirical "interest" with which to compare manifest interests. The term thus refers more to a way of thinking about the structure of needs and desires on one hand and the structure (intention, motif) of action on the other. In this sense, an interest is not a property of someone, but a structure that anyone could take on as his or her own, to his or her benefit or detriment. Of course, a particular position cannot be taken on by just anyone, since our historical context gives a particular position to particular people and not to others.

Structurally, our analysis is aided by identifying two types of interest, which can be identified as "whose" and "what" interest (see Deetz, 1985a, 1985b). By "whose" interest we do not mean initially those simply of somebody, but the available roles in organizational life. Dahrendorf (1959) has most clearly demonstrated how participant roles generate natural vested interests and group conflict. Abrahamsson (1977), Mitroff (1983), March and Simon (1958), and Barnard (1938) have been part of a long tradition in organizational studies that identifies natural differences between the different "participants" or "stakeholders" in organizations. At a minimum, we can locate interests identified with workers, managers, investors, suppliers, consumers, and distributors, as well as the general society in their concern with the environment and general development of the work force. As we have seen, there is no necessary reason for any one of these interests to predominate, but, at this point in history, managerial interests have come to enjoy an arbitrary advantage. How this is carried out will be developed below in the discussion of power. The priority given managerial interest is the principal factor distinguishing the modern corporate form from organization patterns of the past. Core organizational issues such as efficiency and effectiveness are significantly different if looked at from other interest standpoints (see Cameron & Whetten, 1983; Jehenson, 1984).

Again, it should be emphasized that initially these are positional rather than personal interests. Any individual potentially holds several positional interests, for example, as investor and worker. To the extent that these are conceptualized simultaneously, tension is experienced. The interests of a group of people holding a position are advanced to the extent that the group both realizes and actualizes its interests. While the interests of a group might at times be represented by a dominant interest such as profit for owners or control for managers, interests are more complex than this representation indicates. The interests of the individual exceed those resulting from his or her structural position. A manager, driven by career advancement and fearing the least inefficiency owing to inconveniences from his or her body, family, co-workers, and friends, can both succeed *and* miss fulfilling other critical needs. The question we are asking is not what a person's real needs are, but how does a system of one-sidedness and domination get created and sustained so that others are denied or dismissed either by an individual or by a group? While we cannot do it here, ultimately we are interested in the effects this domination has on the type of products produced, the treatment of the environment, and the development of the citizenry.

Finally, while interests are not developed from the psyche of individuals but from historically derived structural positions, it is real people who embody them. The people who get to fill each position do not arrive there through nature but out of their chance historical placement. Nevertheless, it is through the concrete expression and action of individuals that such structures are reproduced *or* changed.

Further, we are interested not only in whose interests get represented, but in what interests these are. Here, following Habermas (1971), we can distinguish different cognitive or knowledge-producing interests. Essentially, we are arguing that there are different types of rationality that can be used to form knowledge and guide decision making. Within communication studies, these interests can be considered as communication guided by the desire for mastery and control and as communication guided by the attempt to reach understanding (Habermas, 1984). While every individual has the capacity for and probably at times utilizes each form of reasoning, at different historical moments one form may become privileged. The critical theorists have done much to document the manner in which scientific-technical (instrumental) reasoning has come to dominate modern society (e.g., Adorno & Horkheimer, 1972; Habermas, 1975, 1984). Others have shown the manifestations of this domination in organizations (Agger, 1985; Deetz, 1985a; Luke & White, 1985; Mumby, 1988).

In the modern corporation, managerial and instrumental-rational interests join together to give preference to certain forms of knowledge and particular types of decisions. Our analysis must show how these interests dominate and how that domination is reproduced. This analysis requires an examination of the relation between power and interest representation.

ORGANIZATIONAL POWER AND INTERESTS

By focusing on the question of interests, we conceive of power neither as simply a possession of individuals nor as a relationship between individuals, but rather as a structural quality of institutional life, which is chronically reproduced by the day-to-day communicative practices of its members (Giddens, 1979, 1981, 1984). We therefore make the assumption that power is a pervasive and ubiquitous characteristic of all institutional life and that, in fact, all forms of social interaction are at least partially defined by it, whether it be an explicit element in a dyadic relationship or a sedimented, routinized feature of institutional life. Power is an integral feature of all social interaction insofar as it both sets the limits of and provides the possibilities for human action or agency. It is "the origin of all that is liberating and productive in social life as well as all that is repressive and destructive" (Giddens, 1981, p. 51).

This janiform conception of power provides a useful beginning point from which to elaborate a view of the relationship between organizational power and interest representation, and also suggests how we might conceive of the relationship between communication and power. First, if power is conceived as involving a relationship of autonomy and dependence between social actors or groups, then power is exercised in the context of a struggle between domination and resistance. That is, power is not defined simply in terms of one person or group exercising control over another, but rather is conceived as the process through which competing interests exist interdependently, simultaneously vying for a privileged status in the whole constellation of interests that characterize institutional life. Second, communication and power are interrelated in a fundamental way. Rather than viewing communication as somehow causally related to the exercise of power (i.e., as representative of or reflecting antecedently existing power relations), we wish to argue that communication is more fundamentally constitutive of power than is traditionally suggested in the organizational literature (e.g., Pfeffer, 1981). In effect, we argue that one of the most important areas in which power is exercised is in the struggle over meaning (Grossberg, 1982; Hall, 1985; May, 1988). In other words, the most important site of the struggle over power in organizations is not the context of allocation of material resources and decision-making capabilities; rather, power is most successfully exercised when an individual or group has the ability to frame discursive and nondiscursive practices within a system of meanings that is commensurate with that individual's or group's own interests (Brown, 1978).

The complex relationship between communicative practices and power will be more fully articulated in the next section of the chapter. Our immediate task is to delineate the role that the concept of power plays in our overall theory of organizational communication. To that end, we will make a relatively detailed excursus into the works of Jürgen Habermas and Michel Foucault, and suggest how they might provide us with the grounds for radical organizational critique.

As indicated above, a theory of power must not only consider the existence of conflicting interests, but must also examine the process through which the relationship between these interests is maintained, reproduced, or altered. Such an approach requires that we directly confront the issues of knowledge and meaning formation and the ways in which such issues impinge on the identity of the social actor as he or she participates in the production and reproduction of organizational life.

The relationship between knowledge and the question of interests is directly addressed by Habermas. In particular, we are concerned with the ways in which Habermas's theory of communicative action can provide us with a *practical* critique of managerial capitalism as it is manifested in the workplace. Habermas's discourse on communication, knowledge, and human interests provides a useful and radical counterpart to managerial discourse, which is rooted in a particular form of rationality and thus articulates a particular set of underlying interests. In essence, through Habermas we can present the ideal conditions for the occurrence of communication freed from both internal and external constraints in order that we can see where and by what means power is enacted in the organization.

An excellent example of the way in which Habermas's work provides for a practical critique of orthodox organizational rationality is suggested by Forester's (1982a, 1982b) application of Habermas's universal pragmatics to organizational planning. Forester (1982a) argues that planners should view organizations not only as functionally goal oriented and made up of various social roles (a position that basically embodies the classical view of organizations), but also as the site of reproduction of *political* relations among citizens:

> As structures of communicative relations, then, organizations not only produce instrumental results or "ends," they also reproduce social and political relations of *knowledge* (who knows what), *consent* (who accepts whose authority and who resists), *trust* (who has established networks of cooperative contacts), and *attention* (who considers which issues and neglects which others). (p. 7)

Forester's four elements of knowledge, consent, trust, and attention correspond directly with the four validity claims that Habermas presents in his theory of universal pragmatics (respectively, truth, rightness, truthfulness, and comprehensibility). Without discussing these validity claims in depth (greater detail is provided in Habermas, 1979), Habermas maintains that together they provide the universal conditions under which all speech acts may be assessed. Each and every act of communication embodies these four claims and thus anticipates (but never attains) the ideal speech situation. As such,

> no matter how the intersubjectivity of mutual understanding may be deformed, the *design* of an ideal speech situation is necessarily implied in the structure of potential speech, since all speech, even of intentional deception, is oriented toward the idea of truth. (Habermas, 1970, p. 372)

The ideal speech situation thus provides the grounds for the critique of systematically distorted communication, that is, all forms of communication that are ideological and that therefore generate consent through means other than an intersubjectively generated rational will to truth.

Forester applies these universal conditions to planning practice by showing how certain forms of organizational behavior systematically exclude certain interest groups from participation in important decision-making processes. For example, health care organizations play a direct role in the production and reproduction of citizens' knowledge about their own health, to a large degree determining their awareness or ignorance about issues such as the causes of illness, available modes of prevention, and the health of the system to which citizens subscribe (Forester, 1982a, p. 9). In general, Forester argues that Habermas's universal pragmatics can provide the grounds upon which organizational planners can recognize the ways that organizations with which they work reproduce the social and political relations of domination in society. The recognition of such domination, Forester claims, is the first step toward countering it and providing ways to democratize organizational functioning and decision making. The major point, however, is that "organizations can be recognized to be structures of practical communicative interactions in which actors make claims upon one another's attention, beliefs, trust and sense of propriety or legitimacy" (Forester, 1982a, p. 11).

While Forester's research provides an important application of the Habermasian project to organizational critique, his analysis is limited by the focus on the principles of the ideal speech situation as the grounds upon which to critique various forms of organizational communication. Neglected is a closer analysis of the knowledge-constitutive interests that ground communicative action, whether it takes place in an organizational context or not. It is to Habermas's notion of interests that we now turn.

Habermas conceptualizes interests in two largely distinct yet related ways. We would argue that his formulation is directly applicable to the process by which managerial rationality has come to hold sway in organizational life. First, interests are discussed in the context of the ways in which humans generate knowledge about themselves and the world in which they live. Second, interests also refer to the constellation of different and competing social groups, each of which has its own agenda in the ongoing process of structuring institutional life. These two conceptions are explicated below.

Habermas argues that there are three fundamental realms that make up the human life-world: work/labor, social interaction, and power. Associated with each of these realms is a corresponding definition of what constitutes knowledge. Habermas argues that the work realm is characterized by instrumental action that produces knowledge aimed at the technical control of that realm. This form of knowledge is therefore derived out of what he refers to as a "technical" knowledge-constitutive (or cognitive) interest. On the other hand, the realm of interaction is characterized by a practical cognitive interest that aims at generating mutual understanding between individuals through communicative action.

As such, the empirical-analytic sciences are fundamentally grounded in a technical interest, while the hermeneutic sciences are grounded in a practical interest aimed at "maintaining the intersubjectivity of mutual understanding in ordinary-language communication and in action according to common norms" (Habermas, 1971, p. 176). Of course, research in organizations is by no means freed from participation in these knowledge-constitutive conditions, and for the most part reproduces the hegemony of the technical interest.

The modern organization itself, however, embodies both kinds of knowledge. Organization members are defined at least in part by their ability both to technically transform the world around them and to communicate with each other such that a common sense of organizational community is formed. However, the production and reproduction of managerial rationality depends heavily on the privileging of the technical cognitive interest, such that all forms of organizational interaction are subsumed by it and thus defined in terms of it. This ideology of technical rationality obscures not only the legitimacy of the practical interest, but also the knowledge connected with Habermas's third realm of human existence, which he refers to as the emancipatory cognitive interest. This interest is grounded in the realm of power. He argues that self-reflection is a defining quality of the individual's movement toward autonomy and responsibility (*Mündigkeit*). This self-reflective process is emancipatory in that it frees "consciousness from its dependence on hypostatized powers" (Habermas, 1971, p. 313).

Placed in a communicative context, the emancipatory interest is predicated upon the possibility of discourse that is free from the distortion of coercive practices and thus contributes to the growth of both individual and social autonomy and responsibility. One could therefore argue that Forester's work in organizational planning exemplifies the emancipatory interest in the sense that he appropriates Habermas's universal pragmatics and the ideal speech situation as a means of moving toward democratization of the workplace and away from the arbitrary privileging of the interests of certain groups.

There is thus a clear connection between Habermas's conception of the three knowledge-constitutive interests and his formulation of the ideal speech situation, the latter providing the conditions under which emancipation through self-reflection can truly occur (while simultaneously embodying both the technical and practical interests, in the claims to truth and appropriateness, respectively).

Habermas's conception of knowledge-constitutive interests provides a useful way of reconceptualizing, in a communication context, our earlier discussion of Braverman (1974) and his polemic on the labor process in the age of monopoly capitalism. Citing Taylor and his scientific management theory as the midwife of modern conceptions of management, Braverman argues that Taylorist principles have become the mainstay of current relations of production in the modern organization. These principles are as follows: (a) "the dissociation of the labor process from the skills of the workers"; (b) "the separation of conception from execution" of the labor process; and (c) "the use of ... monopoly over knowledge [by management] to control each step of the labor process and its mode of execution" (pp. 112-120).

The implementation of these principles has resulted not only in a largely alienated and deskilled working class, but also in the privileging of a managerial system of (scientific) rationality in which all forms of interaction are made sense of in the context of issues such as efficiency, productivity, and profit seeking. Thus "the more science is incorporated into the labor process, the less the worker understands the process; the more sophisticated an intellectual product the machine becomes, the less control and comprehension of the machine the worker has" (Braverman, 1974, p. 428).

Articulated in Habermasian terms, Braverman's modern corporation exemplifies the hegemony of the technical interest over other interests. Managerial capitalism, as manifest in modern organizations, embodies the fundamental principle that decision-making power must lie in the hands of those who have the knowledge to make (rational) decisions based upon all available information. In terms of the technical interest, such decisions can, by definition, be made only by the managerial class. Other groups are automatically defined out of the decision-making process.

From Habermas's perspective this defining of organizational reality in terms of the technical interest is a product of distorted communication insofar as it systematically excludes certain groups from fully participating in organizational life. Deskilling, as defined by Braverman, is therefore an ideological and systematically distorted process in that it is based on a fundamental contradiction — that is, the ever-increasing sophistication of management methods and the technological hardware that accompanies it, and the ever-decreasing involvement of workers in the conception of the labor process in which they are engaged.

In sum, the legitimation of managerial rationality through the dominance of the technical interest necessarily produces systematically distorted communication insofar as all forms of discourse are made sense of (i.e., judged as valid) via the interpretive template of technical-rational knowledge. In this sense, all organizational communication is potentially reducible to its role in the reproduction of managerial technocracy. The arbitrary dominance of this group's interests negates the possibility for a rational consensus based on self-reflection and a collective will. One could thus make the claim that Habermas separates knowledge and power relations; truth can emerge only in discursive situations that are free from all exercise of power (except that implicitly embodied in the ideal speech situation as the will to reason).

Habermas's view of the relationship between knowledge and power has strong implications for the theory of organizational communication developed in this chapter. First, his theory clearly articulates a close relationship between discourse and the social construction of organizational knowledge. Discourse is not seen as incidental to such knowledge, but is indeed constitutive of it. For our purposes this view is important given the central role that discourse will play in our development of a critical theory of communication. We will argue not only that discourse is constitutive of knowledge, but that its analysis is integral to an examination of the relations of power that characterize organizations.

Second, Habermas (1970, 1975) claims that knowledge in contemporary society is overwhelmingly defined in terms of the technical interest, and that technical efficiency and rationality constitute one of the main guiding principles in measuring the success of institutional behavior. This position has implications for our own study in that the legitimation of technical rationality induces a particular view of human interaction, especially in the workplace. Technical rationality collapses that distinction between work and interaction and reduces all modes of organizational behavior to variations around a particular definition of organizational rationality, that is, technical efficiency.

Habermas's development of the notion of knowledge-constituting interests therefore enables the development of a particular conception of power that is radically bifurcated from the process of knowledge construction, at least in the ideal sense. In other words, the exercise of power is seen as inimical to the emergence of knowledge in a discursive context free from coercion and ideological distortion. However, this position is problematic for our own conception of power, particularly in its implicit suggestion that individuals are potentially able to establish a position outside of power relations in order to critique their ideological nature.

Our own position is that power is an inevitable and constitutive element in all social and institutional interaction, and must therefore be analyzed as such. As indicated at the beginning of this section, all communication necessarily involves the use of power, and the role of a radical theory of organizational communication is to explicate the processes through which power is manifested and thus shapes organizational reality. So while Habermas provides a useful way of showing how the technical interest functions ideologically to disenfranchise certain interest groups, his transcendental move to a set of universal conditions by which to judge discourse causes difficulties for examining the ways in which power interacts with knowledge and meaning in concrete organizational contexts.

Foucault's corpus of work indicates how we might obviate this problem and more fruitfully conceptualize the power-knowledge relationship. Foucault represents an important way in which we can further delineate the exercise of power in organizations, based on a perspective that conceives of power as an integral component of the construction of knowledge in society. For Foucault, Habermas's project of ideology-critique (in the form of critiquing systematically distorted communication) "deludes itself if it posits the possibility of knowledge emancipated from power relations, or if it thinks that it could decide what our interests would necessarily be in the absence of any social coercion" (Hoy, 1986, p. 133).

Habermas's position on power and knowledge and others like it are termed the "Repressive Hypothesis" by Foucault (1980, pp. 15-49). In this view, power is perceived simply as a constraining mechanism that represses truth through a systematic distortion of reality. Habermas's work is thus an exemplary case of the power of repression being opposed by the discourse of truth. For Foucault (1982), on the other hand, power and freedom function in what he terms an "agonistic" relationship:

> At the very heart of the power relationship, and constantly provoking it, are the recalcitrance of the will and the intransigence of freedom. Rather than speaking of an essential freedom, it would be better to speak of an "agonism" — of a relationship which is at the same time reciprocal incitation and struggle; less of a face-to-face confrontation which paralyzes both sides than a permanent provocation. (pp. 221-222)

Thus, by definition, all relations of power are necessarily reciprocal in nature, a principle similarly embodied in Giddens's (1979) notion of the "dialectic of control," in which he maintains that "an agent who does not participate in the dialectic of control, in a minimal fashion, ceases to be an agent" (p. 149). This view of power is more fruitful for our purposes in that it can be effectively applied to the struggle over meaning, referred to earlier in this section. Foucault's articulation of an agonistic relationship between power and freedom permits a focus on the ways in which different discourses compete among each other to define the terrain of signification upon which the struggle over meaning occurs.

Foucault's conception of power replaces the juridical view (such as that of Habermas) with one that is rooted in the politics of everyday life. Foucault (1980) adopts a technical and strategic approach to power in which the goal is to delineate the growth of disciplinary techniques that serve to construct a body of knowledge about (and hence define) the individual. Thus power over the individual is linked to a "regulated and polymorphous incitement to discourse" (p. 34). There is no single locus of power, such as the state, or the monarchy; rather, power is "capillary" in nature, being dispersed among the practices and discourses of everyday life. Indeed, much of the corpus of Foucault's work is devoted to documenting the various kinds of disciplinary practices that have emerged in the past 200 years or so in various institutional forms, and that function to constitute the subject within various discursive and nondiscursive strategies. Thus discourses (and the practices associated with them) have developed in the areas of punishment, mental health care, sexuality, the labor process, and so on, that meticulously define a set of disciplinary techniques, or micropractices, which, in turn, carefully delineate a political technology of the body. The result is a vast archive of discourse that attempts to define what it means to be an individual.

Applied to the relationship between power and organizational communication, Foucault's position becomes particularly germane. We have already argued that a view of organizations exclusively characterized in terms of the exploitation and regression of labor by the capitalist class is outmoded. Rather than the principal issue being one of critiquing the capitalist enterprise, we have redefined it as being one of delineating the modes of discourse that have emerged out of what we have called "managerial capitalism." Our concern is to show how such discourse functions to create a particular form of (managerial) rationality that structures the

experience of organizational identity in a particular way. We would argue, therefore, that the social construction of organizational reality is characterized not by
the straightforward repression of one group by another, but rather by the complexity of various discursive practices that define what it means to be an organization member. It is these discursive practices that both articulate and instantiate the
constellation of power interests that characterize organizations, and that allow for
the privileging of managerial interests over others.

Certainly it is the case that in the last hundred years the amount of discourse
associated with the management of organizations has increased almost exponen-
tially. Beginning with Frederick Taylor, one can trace a lineage through Mayo,
Barnard, Simon, and Argyris to the present preoccupation with "corporate culture."
In each case, the discourse emerges around a managerial concern with situating the
worker in a particular way in the organization. With Taylor, the concern was to
develop work methods developed along scientific principles in order to minimize
the amount of physical and mental control the worker has over the labor process.
There is probably no better example of a disciplinary technology in the realm of
the labor process than Taylor's (1911) meticulous delineation of the nature of work
tasks. Similarly, Mayo's Hawthorne studies led to the emergence of a whole body
of discourse that focused on the relational aspects of the work process. Here,
control was embodied in the attempt to regulate the emergent social norms of
worker interaction. Even the current discourse on corporate culture is oriented
toward exercising control over organization members through the shaping of the
organization's cultural reality.

The common elements among the modes of organizational discourse mentioned
above are that each implicitly recognizes the tension that characterizes the relationship between the individual and the organization, and each attempts to resolve that
tension differently. In each instance, however, the resolution is sought through the
implicit assumption of managerial rationality. In different ways, the concern is
with developing a mode of discourse that will configure the individual within the
organization in such a way that the primacy of technical rationality will be
affirmed. Taylorism achieves this affirmation by developing an organizational
discourse that simply subjugates the worker to the mechanics of his or her task,
while, at the other extreme, the corporate culture theorists recognize that managerial rationality must be inculcated through the careful control of organizational
members' perceived reality.

Thus in the organizational sphere there has occurred a tremendous flourishing
of discursive techniques aimed at controlling the very way in which the individual
as subject is inserted into the organization. We would argue that all of these forms
of discourse function to reproduce the conditions under which managerial capitalism maintains its hegemony. The very notion of what it means to be an organization member is defined by the emergence of discourse around the dominant
technical knowledge-constituting interest.

Foucault's conception of power as a pervasive characteristic of human social
life thus provides an effective tool for use in delineating the discursive practices

that constitute human subjectivity, particularly in the realm of organizational communication. The next section provides a more explicit discussion of the ways in which discourse actually functions to construct the subject as organization member.

Let us preface this discussion, however, by indicating that Foucault would probably disavow the kind of critical, emancipatory turn that we make. Certainly his position diverges considerably from Habermas's attempt to posit quasi-transcendental conditions for the critique of and emancipation from coercive social forces. The two overlap, however, in that both attempt to explicate the privileging of the forms of discourse related to technorational knowledge systems. While Habermas views this privileging as ideological in nature (and thus subject to critique and an emancipatory move), Foucault is content simply to delineate the construction of knowledge through disciplinary technologies and pointedly avoids any kind of emancipatory turn. In effect, Foucault avoids offering any foundational principles upon which knowledge can be built. There is no "essence" to the human condition; rather, it is the product of the epistemic practices that characterize a particular age.

For our purposes, Foucault can be appropriated in a critical fashion in that he provides the opportunity to develop a position from which one can engage in perpetual critique. Rather than arguing that a critical impulse requires the kind of normative foundation suggested by Habermas, we can say that the purpose of critique is to draw attention to the "social multiaccentuality of the ideological sign" (Volosinov, 1973, p. 23). In other words, critique involves a process of resistance to hegemonic discursive practices leading to an opening up of the discourses articulated in a particular social domain.

Our concern therefore lies with the ways in which different interest groups attempt to appropriate the sign (discourse) for their own purposes. The next section of this chapter thus tries to demonstrate how discourse functions ideologically to disguise its "multiaccentuality," thereby privileging certain discursive practices. Our own discourse, however, does not intend to replace one privileged form with another, but rather to resist the "eternalization" of the ideological sign and thus open up its discursive possibilities. In this context, it is necessary to delineate further the relationship between discourse and ideology.

DISCOURSE, MEANING, AND POWER

Thus far we have argued that a critical theory of organizational communication is enriched by a return to and reconsideration of some of the fundamental tenets of Marxist social theory. The work of Marx, along with that of more contemporary theorists such as Gramsci, Braverman, and Burawoy, provides a rich analytic perspective through which to examine the ways in which organizational life plays itself out. Implicit in this framework is the notion that the concrete, material practices in which social actors engage are intrinsic to the production of meaning in organizations. In this section, we want to describe a relationship between discourse and organizational practice that is nonrepresentational in nature and that recognizes the constitutive role that communication plays in the ongoing creation of organizational reality. The development of a nonrepresentational (i.e., material) view of discursive practices means that discourse is not assigned an auxiliary role in the process of organizing, but is rather viewed as isomorphic with organizing itself.

This position has several implications. First, organizational discourse is conceived as simultaneously derived from and constitutive of the process of organizational knowledge and meaning formation. The cognitive interests of the social actor are thus inextricably tied up with the discourse in which he or she engages. As Schrag (1986) states, "We thus rather quickly learn the truth that we never stand at a beginning but are always somehow already begun, held within a web of delivered discourse, social practices, professional requirements, and the daily decisions of everyday life" (p. 4). In other words, the process of identity formation through which each individual goes is inseparable from the communicative practices within which everyone is embedded.

The second implication of this position, and one that is closely tied to the first, is that discourse and power are integral to each other and thus interdependent. We have already shown how both Habermas and Foucault, in different ways, make a direct link between the discursive practices in which people engage and the power relations that evolve in particular social structures. We argue that discourse is both medium and product of the power relations that characterize organizational behavior. We suggest that a critical view of communication must be not only nonrepresentational in nature, but *political*; that is, it must be able to show the ways in which discourse can function ideologically to produce, maintain, and reproduce certain kinds of power relations within organizational structures.

The third and final implication of this position is again closely connected to the previous two, and it relates to the idea of a *material* conception of discourse. Several theorists in organization studies have argued the case for discourse, or language, playing a central role in constituting the relationship between the individual and organizational reality (Frost, Moore, Louis, Lundberg, & Martin, 1985; Putnam & Pacanowsky, 1983; Smircich, 1983). Similarly, we would argue that, while discourse performs a referential (informational) function in organizations, more important, it makes certain behaviors possible. For example, the kinds of storytelling that organization members engage in do not merely express a certain kind of organizational reality; rather, they actually *constitute* that organization's reality (Mumby, 1987). Similarly, research into organizational metaphors seems to suggest that the metaphors that organization members use structure their experience of the organization in fundamental ways (Deetz, 1986; Deetz & Mumby, 1985; Morgan, 1986; Smith & Eisenberg, 1987). Metaphors are not simply useful ways in which members can describe their organization; they actually create the possibility for the adoption of certain interpretive schemata. Thus the frequently exercised bifurcation of the symbolic realm and the realm of practical activity

(Pfeffer, 1981) does not serve the fruitful analysis of communicative practices or power relations and, indeed, serves only to position communication as peripheral to issues of power.

A material conception of discourse, then, focuses on the concrete practices in which people engage in the process of constituting the meaning systems of their everyday world. People not only communicate things about their social world, they also create their social world in communicating. As we have seen, the process of communicating necessarily takes place in the context of power relations; communication is both defined by and defines the structure of those relations. In this sense, communication can be said to function ideologically in that it produces and reproduces (i.e., legitimates) a particular structure of power relations (i.e., system of interests) to the arbitrary exclusion of other possible configurations of interests.

The concept of ideology serves as a useful construct to help explain the ways in which patterns of discourse can be linked to the power relations that are a structural aspect of organizations. In this context, ideology can be viewed as both the medium and the product of discursive practices; that is, it is through ideology that individuals contextualize and make sense of various discourses, while at the same time it is only through discourse that particular ideological meaning formations can be produced and reproduced.

Rosen's (1985) analysis of the ritual aspects of a corporate breakfast serves to exemplify this process, illustrating how this organizational event (constituted through discourse) makes sense only within the context of a particular set of ideological frames of reference (meanings); simultaneously, the event is a material manifestation and instantiation of those ideological meanings that provide a frame for interpretation. Thus the breakfast is framed not simply as a social event, but as a discursive site for the reaffirmation of the company's managerial hierarchy and the goals associated with it. In this context, organizational members can publicly engage in discourse that situates them in a particular way in the organizational meaning system. Each individual announces his or her commitment to the organization and to the technical rationality that underlies the organization's corporate reality. Through the ideological structuring of discourse, therefore, the breakfast reproduces the existing relations of domination that structure that particular organization.

We can say, then, that ideology is not simply a set of beliefs or values that are taken on by particular individuals; rather, it is that which creates the very possibility of having certain beliefs or values. In other words, ideology plays a constitutive role in the creation of individual identity. In Althusserian terms, it is what "hails" or interpellates the individual as a conscious subject. As Althusser (1970) states:

> The category of the subject is constitutive of all ideology, but at the same time and immediately I add that *the category of the subject is only constitutive of all ideology insofar as all ideology has the function (which defines it) of "constituting" concrete individuals as subjects.* (p. 171)

Given the materialist conception of discourse adopted in this chapter, we can say that discursive practices can function ideologically to create a particular kind of situated identity and understanding of self-interest. If Althusser is correct, then ideology exists only in its material, practical form as a process through which the power relations of a particular social structure are realized. As such, ideology circumscribes the parameters of identity for people who exist within the framework of such power relations.

Ideology functions to articulate the connection between communication and power; it is what makes possible their coterminous character. In this sense, ideology is the interpretive frame within which each social actor is able to make sense of the practices in which he or she and others engage in the process of social interaction. At the same time, of course, the ideologically produced interpretive frame is itself produced and reproduced in the material communicative practices of social actors, which, in turn, are framed by the sedimented power relations of the institutional structure. Thus, as Volosinov (1973) states, "without signs [communication] there is no ideology" (p. 9).

The above conceptual schema provides a radical framework with which to examine the process of meaning construction as it occurs in organizational settings. It allows us to go beyond rather simplistic notions of meaning that revolve around either subjective or objective criteria. Instead, we can argue that meaning is a function of the complex interaction among communication, ideology, and power that has been delineated above. Meaning, therefore, is necessarily *political* in nature. Such is the case by virtue of the inevitable "dialectic of control" that is characteristic of all social interaction, institutional or otherwise.

A FINAL GLANCE

Our argument has been that the critical tradition has drawn attention to arbitrary systems of domination in modern corporations. Certain social groups and certain interests are far more completely represented in decision making than are others. These advantages are not based on a rational or consensual value foundation but on historical material conditions produced and reproduced by human actors. While authors in the critical tradition have enabled a deeper analysis of power relations than possible in other organization study traditions, their focus on economic determinants and the capitalist group has failed to account for central features of the modern corporation.

The rise of managerial capitalism has changed the site of potential conflict in interest representation. A logic of control has replaced profit in the decision-making process, and extension of control has replaced capital accumulation in corporate development. Management coupled with "technical reasoning" producing technorational knowledge is clearly privileged over all other groups with equally legitimate interests in corporate decisions.

By looking at power and discourse in organizations, we have attempted to show the nature of this privilege and how continued domination is accomplished. Power is not generally coercive in modern organizations but represented by freely given consent, frequently to someone else's benefit. As we have shown, discursive practices are always political in form and content. Specific practices both produce and reproduce particular power configurations. These practices are neutralized, naturalized, and legitimated through their specific forms of appearance (Deetz, 1985a).

Within the critical tradition, our interest has been not only with describing systems of domination, but also with critique and reform. In this regard, we recognize the inherent pitfalls associated with any kind of emancipatory position, which inevitably runs the risk of replacing one privileged form of discourse with another. We have tried to mitigate this difficulty by arguing for a position of perpetual critique in which we do not privilege critical discourse per se, but rather indicate how *any* discourse is necessarily the product of an arbitrary structure of interests. In this context, Habermas's work demonstrates how these interests function in a knowledge-constitutive way, while Foucault's insight is to show the pervasiveness of power relations, and to indicate how essential it is that we understand how inextricably linked power and knowledge really are. Only through an understanding of this process can we begin to get a sense of human identity formation in modern organizations.

We have not been able to deal in depth with the extraordinarily important issue of the rapid development and implementation of computer-assisted communication systems, but it is our hope that we have laid a clear foundation for this analysis. Considerable work needs to be done to see how new communication systems alter power relationships in specific corporate contexts. Kling (1980) provides a theoretical frame for such a beginning. The issue of differing access to communication systems is perhaps the most obvious concern; deeper concerns also exist (see Deetz, in press). Do new information and communication systems extend the privilege of certain forms of knowledge? Independent of access, are certain groups' interests and human needs better or less well represented in these systems?

There are also broader social issues. Chandler's historical analysis suggests that the development of expanded communication systems was a central determinant in the development of managerial capitalism. As early as the late nineteenth century, new communication systems enabled the expanded creation of social needs and subsequent markets and enabled administrative coordination to take control over market coordination. Contemporary information and communication systems become material conditions for greatly extending these processes. As communication systems have become more sophisticated, growth in administrative coordination has become possible. The situation is not one of greater economies of scale (for acquisitions and mergers have mixed balance sheets) but greater managerial control. Greater size in turn demands greater systems of coordination and control. Representation of nonmanagerial interests in upsized corporations itself requires managerial coordination. The illusion of freedom in the satellite plant obscures the impossibility of directing corporate decisions. Antitrust legislation based on limiting market monopoly and price fixing does little to limit the increased monopoly of control and dialogic opportunity. These and a host of other concerns provide an important agenda for the future.

REFERENCES

Abrahamsson, B. (1977). *Bureaucracy or participation: The logic of organization.* Beverly Hills, CA: Sage.

Adorno, T., & Horkheimer, H. (1972). *Dialectic of enlightenment.* New York: Herder & Herder.

Agger, B. (1985). The dialectic of deindustrialization: An essay on advanced capitalism. In J. Forester (Ed.), *Critical theory and public life* (pp. 3-21). Cambridge: MIT Press.

Althusser, L. (1970). *Lenin and philosophy and other essays* (B. Brewster, Trans.). New York: Monthly Review Press.

Barnard, C. (1938). *The function of the executive.* Cambridge, MA: Harvard University Press.

Baudrillard, J. (1975). *The mirror of production* (M. Poster, Trans.). St. Louis: Telos. (Original work published 1935)

Bell, D. (1960). *The end of ideology.* New York: Free Press.

Benson, J. (1977). *Organizational analysis: Critique and innovation.* Beverly Hills, CA: Sage.

Berle, A., & Means, G. (1932). *The modern corporation and private property.* New York: Harcourt, Brace & World.

Braverman, H. (1974). *Labor and monopoly capital: The degradation of work in the twentieth century.* New York: Monthly Review Press.

Brown, R. H. (1978). Bureaucracy as praxis: Toward a political phenomenology of formal organizations. *Administrative Science Quarterly, 23,* 365-382.

Burawoy, M. (1979). *Manufacturing consent: Changes in the labor process under monopoly capitalism.* Chicago: University of Chicago Press.

Cameron, K., & Whetten, D. (Eds.). (1983). *Organizational effectiveness: A comparison of multiple models.* New York: Academic Press.

Chandler, A. (1977). *The invisible hand: The managerial revolution in American business.* Cambridge, MA: Harvard University Press.

Chandler, A., & Daems, H. (Eds.). (1980). *Managerial hierarchies: Comparative perspectives on the rise of the modern industrial enterprise.* Cambridge, MA: Harvard University Press.

Cyert, R., & March, J. (1963). *A behavioral theory of the firm.* Englewood Cliffs, NJ: Prentice-Hall.

Dahrendorf, R. (1959). *Class and class conflict in industrial society.* Stanford, CA: Stanford University Press.

Deetz, S. (1985a). Critical-cultural research: New sensibilities and old realities. *Journal of Management, 11,* 121-136.

Deetz, S. (1985b). Ethical considerations in cultural research in organizations. In P. Frost, L. Moore, M. Louis, C. Lundberg, & J. Martin (Eds.), *Organizational culture* (pp. 251-269). Beverly Hills, CA: Sage.

Deetz, S. (1986). Metaphors and the discursive production and reproduction of organization. In L. Thayer (Ed.), *Organization-communication: Emerging perspectives I* (pp. 168-182). Norwood, NJ: Ablex.

Deetz, S. (in press). Representation of interests and the new communication technologies. In M. Medhurst (Ed.), *Communication and the culture of technology.* Pullman: Washington State University Press.

Deetz, S., & Kersten, A. (1983). Critical models of interpretive research. In L. Putnam & M. Pacanowsky (Eds.), *Communication and organization: An interpretive approach* (pp. 147-171). Beverly Hills, CA: Sage.

Deetz, S., & Mumby, D. K. (1985). Metaphors, information, and power. *Information & Behavior, 1*, 369-386.

Forester, J. (1982a). Know your organizations: Planning and the reproduction of social and political relations. *Plan Canada, 22*, 3-13.

Forester, J. (1982b). *Critical theory and organizational analysis* (Working paper, Department of City and Regional Planning). Ithaca, NY: Cornell University.

Foucault, M. (1980). *The history of sexuality* (R. Hurley, Trans.). New York: Vintage.

Foucault, M. (1982). The subject and power. In H. Dreyfus & P. Rabinow (Eds.), *Michel Foucault: Beyond structuralism and hermeneutics* (pp. 208-226). Sussex, UK: Harvester.

Frost, P. J., Moore, L. F., Louis, M. R., Lundberg, C. C., & Martin, J. (Eds.). (1985). *Organizational culture*. Beverly Hills, CA: Sage.

Galbraith, K. (1967). *The new industrial state*. New York: New American Library.

Geuss, R. (1981). *The idea of a critical theory*. New York: Cambridge University Press.

Giddens, A. (1979). *Central problems in social theory*. Berkeley: University of California Press.

Giddens, A. (1981). *A contemporary critique of historical materialism* (Vol. 1). London: Macmillan.

Giddens, A. (1984). *The constitution of society*. Berkeley: Campus.

Gouldner, A. (1954). *Patterns of industrial bureaucracy*. Glencoe, IL: Free Press.

Gramsci, A. (1971). *Selections from the prison notebooks* (Q. Hoare & G. Nowell Smith, Trans.). New York: International.

Grossberg, L. (1982). The ideology of communication: Post-structuralism and the limits of communication. *Man and World, 15*, 83-101.

Habermas, J. (1970). Toward a theory of communicative competence. *Critical Inquiry, 13*, 360-375.

Habermas, J. (1971). *Knowledge and human interests* (J. Shapiro, Trans.). Boston: Beacon.

Habermas, J. (1975). *Legitimation crisis* (T. McCarthy, Trans.). Boston: Beacon.

Habermas, J. (1979). *Communication and the evolution of society* (T. McCarthy, Trans.). Boston: Beacon.

Habermas, J. (1984). *The theory of communicative action: Vol. 1. Reason and the rationalization of society* (T. McCarthy, Trans.). Boston: Beacon.

Hall, S. (1985). Signification, representation, ideology: Althusser and the post-structuralist debates. *Critical Studies in Mass Communication, 2*, 91-114.

Heydebrand, W. (1977). Organizational contradictions in public bureaucracies. In T. Benson (Ed.), *Organizational analysis: Critique and innovation* (pp. 85-109). Beverly Hills, CA: Sage.

Hoy, D. C. (1986). Power, repression, progress: Foucault, Lukes, and the Frankfurt school. In D. C. Hoy (Ed.), *Foucault: A critical reader* (pp. 123-148). Oxford: Basil Blackwell.

Jehenson, R. (1984). Effectiveness, expertise and excellence as ideological fictions: A contribution to a critical phenomenology of the formal organization. *Human Studies, 7*, 3-21.

Kling, R. (1980). Social analyses of computing: Theoretical perspectives in recent empirical research. *Computing Surveys, 12*, 61-110.

Luke, T., & White, S. (1985). Critical theory, the information revolution, and an ecological path to modernity. In J. Forester (Ed.), *Critical theory and public life* (pp. 22-53). Cambridge: MIT Press.

March, J., & Simon, H. (1958). *Organizations*. New York: John Wiley.

Marx, K. (1906). *Capital: A critique of political economy* (S. Moore & E. Aveling, Trans.). New York: Modern Library.

Marx, K. (1964). *Economic and political manuscripts of 1844* (M. Milligan, Trans.). New York: International.

May, S. (1988, November). *A critical examination of organizational culture: Power, history, agency-structure, and the researcher*. Paper presented at the annual meeting of the Speech Communication Association, New Orleans.

Merkle, J. (1980). *Management and ideology: The legacy of the international scientific management movement*. Berkeley: University of California Press.

Mintzberg, H. (1983). *Power in and around the organization*. Englewood Cliffs, NJ: Prentice-Hall.

Mitroff, I. (1983). *Stakeholders of the organizational mind*. San Francisco: Jossey-Bass.

Morgan, G. (1986). *Images of organization*. Beverly Hills, CA: Sage.

Mumby, D. K. (1987). The political function of narrative in organizations. *Communication Monographs, 54*, 113-127.

Mumby, D. K. (1988). *Communication and power in organizations: Discourse, ideology, and domination*. Norwood, NJ: Ablex.

Parsons, T. (1956). *Economy and society: A study in the integration of economic and social theory*. Glencoe, IL: Free Press.

Pfeffer, J. (1981). *Power in organizations*. Marshfield, MA: Pitman.

Putnam, L., & Pacanowsky, M. (Eds.). (1983). *Communication and organizations: An interpretive approach*. Beverly Hills, CA: Sage.

Rosen, M. (1985). Breakfast at Spiro's: Dramaturgy and dominance. *Journal of Management, 11*(2), 31-48.

Schrag, C. (1986). *Communicative praxis and the space of subjectivity*. Bloomington: Indiana University Press.

Smircich, L. (1983). Concepts of culture and organizational analysis. *Administrative Science Quarterly, 28*, 339-358.

Smith, R., & Eisenberg, E. (1987). Conflict at Disneyland: A root metaphor analysis. *Communication Monographs, 54*, 367-380.

Taylor, F. (1911). *Scientific management*. New York: Harper & Row.

Thompson, J. B. (1984). *Studies in the theory of ideology*. Berkeley: University of California Press.

Volosinov, V. N. (1973). *Marxism and the philosophy of language* (L. Matejka & I. R. Titunik, Trans.). Cambridge, MA: Harvard University Press.

Weber, M. (1978). *Economy and society* (G. Roth & C. Wittich, Eds.). Berkeley: University of California Press.

Weick, K. (1979). *The social psychology of organizing* (2nd ed.). Reading, MA: Addison-Wesley.

Discourse, Ideology, and Organizational Control

BETH HASLETT

University of Delaware

EETZ and Mumby provide a very provocative, thoughtful essay on the interrelationships among ideology, power, and discourse. The essay is impressive in its scope, and assumes a critical stance that calls for a perpetual critique of the way in which political ideology influences power and discourse in organizations.

Briefly, Deetz and Mumby offer a radical critique of modern organizations. The exploitation of surplus labor has now been replaced by managerial capitalism. Managerial capitalism, they argue, through its control of information and emphasis on technological rationality, dominates organizational decision making and arbitrarily excludes the representation of others' interests. They go on to point out:

> Within the critical tradition, our interest has been not only with describing systems of domination, but also with critique and reform. In this regard, we recognize the inherent pitfalls associated with any kind of emancipatory position, which inevitably runs the risk of replacing one privileged form of discourse with another. We have tried to mitigate this difficulty by arguing for a position of perpetual critique in which we do not privilege critical discourse per se, but rather indicate how *any* discourse is necessarily the product of an arbitrary structure of interests. (pp. 44)

While I agree with Deetz and Mumby that both organizations and discourse are political in nature, I question the particular political ideology driving this essay — namely, the domination of organizations by managerial capitalism. My commentary will focus on three broad concerns: first, reservations concerning the political

AUTHOR'S NOTE: I wish to thank Charles Pavitt for his comments on an earlier draft of this commentary.

Correspondence and requests for reprints: Beth Haslett, Department of Communication, University of Delaware, Newark, DE 19711.

Communication Yearbook 13, pp. 48-58

view of organizations developed by Deetz and Mumby; second, an expanded analysis of discourse, power, and ideology; and, finally, reservations concerning the linkage between political ideology and organizational discourse suggested by Deetz and Mumby.

ORGANIZATIONS AS POLITICAL ENTITIES

The political ideology of managerial capitalism, according to Deetz and Mumby, dominates organizational discourse and organizational decision making. This domination necessarily excludes the expression of other interests. Although Deetz and Mumby fail to specify what effects flow from this, they imply that these effects are negative. What is needed here is a more detailed analysis of what impact managerial capitalism, if it exists, has on modern organizations. If other interests are excluded, what harm or influence does this have on modern organizations?

The Nature of Modern Organizations

In what follows, I will discuss four aspects of modern organizations that Deetz and Mumby focus on as entailing managerial capitalism. Although Deetz and Mumby seem to regard managerial capitalism as an inevitable outcome of (evolution from) these characteristics of modern organizations, such a deterministic stance seems unwarranted. In a nutshell, modern organizations are too complex and diverse to be subsumed under one political ideology, that of managerial capitalism (Burns & Stalker, 1961; Morgan, 1986). For example, complexity in terms of size, type of industry, volatility and uncertainty in the environment, and organizational structure as well as diversity in terms of patterns of decision making and access to power are just a few factors that would create substantive differences in how managers operate. Because of such diversity across organizations, it seems likely that managers will have diverse interests, points of views, and access to power. Furthermore, conflict across managers in view of their diverse interests and perspectives seems likely as well.

Expansion of Corporate Form

After Chandler, Deetz and Mumby suggest that administrative coordination has replaced market coordination. Administrative coordination, carried out by professional managers, could expand control over workers significantly through the use of communication technology. According to Deetz and Mumby, economically driven capitalism is now replaced by a communication-driven managerial capitalism.

However, the use of communication technology does not necessarily support managerial capitalism. Woodward (1965) found that different technologies impose different conditions on individuals and organizations, and thus no one single model of organizing seems appropriate. Furthermore, any technology may be used to support a diverse array of organizational structures. It is important to have a "good fit" between technologies and organizations, and this is a *strategic* choice to be made. Morgan (1986) suggests that communication technologies may spawn new forms of organizations as organizations seek to balance structure, technology, the needs of individuals and organizations, and the demands of the external environment.

Diversity in Modern Organizations

Beyond concerns for communication technology and expansion of managerial control, more specific questions can be raised about managerial capitalism. First, Deetz and Mumby suggest that managerial capitalism is so pervasive that it is a universal condition of modern organizations. Such a claim, I believe, fails to take account of cultural differences across nations.

The linkages Deetz and Mumby themselves articulate among ideology, power, and discourse suggest that cultural differences (here, specifically, ideological differences across nations) would *necessarily* imply different relationships across these concepts. For example, the values placed on human resources and a strong set of core values result in a Japanese management style that emphasizes group decision making and strong lateral communication networks throughout the organization (Hatvany & Pucik, 1981). Burns and Stalker (1961) suggest that organizations may be either mechanistic or organic: Mechanistic organizations have strong formal lines of authority and communication, whereas organic organizations have very diffuse, specialized lines of authority and communication as a function of task demands. Euske and Roberts (1987) discuss models of organizations that emphasize the importance of environmental influences on organizations. Cultural differences in ideologies and values create different environments and thus, by implication, differences across organizations. Therefore, on a number of different levels, differences in ideology would necessitate organizational differences in the configuration of discourse and power because the interpretive frame (ideology) unifying them will differ across cultures.

Moreover, Deetz and Mumby's analysis does not appear to take organizational complexity into account. Their view seems to be that modern organizations are inevitably subject to managerial capitalism irrespective of culture and complexity. However, modern organizations may differ significantly in their structural configurations (e.g., internal structure, such as matrix or lattice management, size, complexity, type of industry) and power configuration (e.g., centralized or decentralized, leadership style and influence).

Different configurations — of structure and of power — have different effects on the flow of information within organizations and, consequently, on managerial power. Given different configurations, then, it seems unlikely that only one voice — that of managerial capitalism with its emphasis on scientific/technological rationality — would be expressed within an organization. For example, over the life span of an organization, different interests and groups favoring those interests will possess the most power in organizations (Schein, 1985). But as different crises arise, disruptions in organizational power may occur and create new power coalitions in which different sets of interests may predominate (Morgan, 1986). If managerial capitalism is a universal influence, its influence in organizations would appear to vary as a result of organizational diversity.

Individuals and Organizations

The remaining three aspects of modern organizations emphasized by Deetz and Mumby can be subsumed under the general rubric of how individuals are integrated into the organization. This discussion addresses career managers, managerial control, and managerial identification with the organization.

Managerial capitalism implies that managers speak with one voice, that of technological rationality. This view ignores the inherent conflict within organizations as a function of hierarchy and the specialization of labor (and, by implication, across managers as well). Morgan (1986) views organizations as political systems that create order and direction among diverse, conflicting groups. Organizational members' interests are simultaneously task oriented, career oriented, and personally oriented.

Conflict occurs whenever interests are at odds and may be built into the nature of the task. Power, according to Morgan, resolves conflicts. However, the sources of power and access to power are spread across groups and individuals, rather than limited to managers espousing technological rationality. Morgan (1986) suggests that the following sources of power play an important role in organizations: formal authority, control of scarce resources, decision processes, knowledge and information, boundaries, technology and counterorganizations, use of organizational rules and regulations, interpersonal alliances and coalitions, management of gender relations, one's current power base, and the capacity to establish meanings and define the stage of action (p. 159). Conflict is presented as a natural state in organizations due to competing interests. This claim implies, of course, that competing interests are expressed in the organization, rather than suppressed by the domination of managerial capitalism. Even if we assume that managerial capitalism is indeed dominant, observable conflict still exists between "management" and "labor" and, clearly, at least two distinct, competing voices can be heard (the Eastern Airlines strike being a recent notable case in point).

Burrell and Morgan's (1979) analysis distinguishes among unitary, radical, and pluralist views of individuals and their relationship to organizations. Each perspective has a distinct ideology, a distinctive view of interests and conflict, and a different assessment of power. Briefly, a unitary view of organizations conceives of interests as being united by common objectives and goals; conflict is rare and produced by deviants, and power is exercised by managerial prerogative. In contrast, the pluralist perspective views interests as being diverse and thus the organization represents a loose coalition that has limited interest in organizational goals; conflict is inherent and ineradicable, and power is exercised by different power holders using multiple sources of power. Finally, the radical view emphasizes interests in terms of rival forces; conflict is inevitable and reflects larger social conflicts, and power is unequally distributed across the organization.

Deetz and Mumby clearly fall within the radical perspective. The opposing interests are managerial capitalism versus other, unspecified, suppressed interests; conflict is inevitable, and the power controlling organizations is held by managers through technological rationality. My own view is a pluralistic one that acknowledges a diversity of organizational forms and structures, rather than characterizing modern organizations in global terms that obscure significant cultural variation and conflict within and across organizations (see also Gudykunst, Stewart, & Ting-Toomey, 1985). The view of managerial domination through technological rationality ignores the prevalence and severity of conflicts of interest within organizational members themselves, across organizational subgroups, and across counterorganizations (Morgan, 1986). Finally, it should be noted that top managers themselves believe their power to be seriously limited (Morgan, 1986; Smith & Grenier, 1982) and that people in low-authority positions may exercise significant power (Mechanic, 1962).

Deetz and Mumby suggest that owners exercise little control in organizations, and that professional managers dominate the decision-making process. This again seems to be a broad generalization that obscures the variety of organizational decision-making processes and the fact that decision making occurs at multiple levels in the organization. A variety of interests seem to be represented in organizational decision making (Morgan, 1986). Furthermore, given the increasing interconnectedness of economic markets, more diversity of interests and more diversity in the exercise of power seem likely. Much of this influence may come from outside organizational boundaries (e.g., competition, available resources).

In addition, decision making must occur at multiple levels throughout the organization, especially when we argue, as do Deetz and Mumby, that information flow is central in decision making. Many people control, add to, subtract from, and alter (distort?) the information and knowledge that are shared in organizational decision making (Blankenship & Miles, 1986; March & Simon, 1958; Tushman, 1979).

According to Deetz and Mumby, managers focus mainly on their image and self-marketing within the organization. However, if indeed this is the case, they overlook the fact that in order to "look good" managers probably facilitate the goals of the organization as well as their own. Finally, there seems little support for their view that managers subsume so much of their identity to the organization: That move would seem to be a function of individual needs and goals, only *some* of which would be work related.

Power in Organizations

Deetz and Mumby emphasize power as a function of position. However, power — as authority that stems from one's position in the organization — is but one source of power, albeit a very valuable one. This view of power, like Deetz and Mumby's view of modern organizations, fails to acknowledge the complexity of power. Influence, for example, is another dimension of power that is not necessarily tied to hierarchical position (Bacharach & Lawler, 1980). Morgan's analysis of power, mentioned above, incorporates sources of power that are not tied to hierarchical position.

Furthermore, many organizational theorists emphasize the interactive nature of power: Power reflects an interdependency across actors or units (Bacharach & Lawler, 1980; Pfeffer, 1981; Thibaut & Kelley, 1959; Weick, 1979). Deetz and Mumby appear to look at power from a monolithic managerial view that does not assess the interactive dimension of power or power sources not related to hierarchical position. As previously discussed, power may be dispersed throughout the organization, both horizontally and vertically, and even those viewed as being in low power positions may exert considerable control over decisions (Brass, 1984; Mechanic, 1962).

Decision Making in Organizations

Deetz and Mumby's view of decision making concentrates on the control allegedly held by managers in modern organizations. To suggest that decision making rests exclusively on this level is to deny the multiple levels of decision making that may occur in organizations (Frost, 1987; Hatvany & Pucik, 1981). Even within managers themselves, significant conflict among interests suggests that managers, even if they do have such control, do not speak with one voice, that of technological rationality (Morgan, 1986).

In addition, Deetz and Mumby's model of decision making suggests that decisions are rationally structured and proceed from careful gathering of information. This view seems contradictory to other views of organizational decision making that emphasize the retrospective sense-making of organizations (Weick, 1979) and the use of information to *confirm* previously arrived-at decisions (Daft & Lengel, 1984; Huber & Daft, 1987). Pfeffer (1982) also observes that managers may legitimate decision making to outsiders in terms that have little or no impact on how work is actually done in the organization. Thus, for a variety of reasons, decision making, as a process, does not seem as straightforward and deterministic as Deetz and Mumby suggest.

Representation of Interests in Organizations

Deetz and Mumby argue that managerial capitalism suppresses the equal representation of diverse interests in an organization. In order to participate in organizations, members must have the information and the opportunities to engage in meaningful discussion regarding decisions. Further, Deetz and Mumby suggest that interests are only partially knowable and that some may be in conflict with others. They also point out that the interests we act out may not be our own or in our own best interests. Given this vagueness about interests and the difficulty in knowing one's own interests, the whole issue of interest representation may be moot. Interests can never be fully known, and thus we have no standard of judgment for whether they have been expressed or given equal consideration in organizational discussions.

In part, Deetz and Mumby circumvent some of these problems by arguing that interests are structures that relate needs and actions. Thus interests are not personal, but rather positional. Within organizations, one's interests are vested in the position one holds, and managers have an arbitrary advantage in terms of their position for expressing their interests. However, competition across managers and departments in organizations suggests that positional interests, *even if dominant*, are not that simple or deterministic (Morgan, 1986; Pfeffer, 1981).

In their discussion of what interests may dominate, Deetz and Mumby suggest that cognitive interests may be either to control or to understand. In their view, managers seek control through scientific/technological rationality. However, it can be argued that managers are concerned with understanding as well—not just control. Managers may also have other interests—in personal development and growth, facilitating others' careers, serving as spokespersons, and the like—that are not explicitly tied to control (Mintzberg, 1973). While I agree that management, by nature and by definition, implies control, I think the key issue here is the *extent* of managerial control. From a pluralist perspective, in which many voices in an organization compete for power and control, managers do not *dominate*; rather, they *compete* for power. Thus the picture Deetz and Mumby paint of managerial domination is fundamentally inaccurate because it fails to take into account competing interests, both within managers themselves and across managers in the organization.

Finally, Deetz and Mumby's essay does not explicitly point out whose interests are being suppressed and what negative effects occur as a result of this suppression. Since individuals in organizations are involved in multiple relationships, it seems reasonable to suggest that they have multiple interests, which may sometimes conflict with one another. Deetz and Mumby seem to obscure conflicts among interests, assuming, of course, that one's interests are sufficiently knowable.

In summary, I believe that viewing organizations as political is a very valuable and insightful way to approach understanding them. However, I do not find the particular critical, radical perspective outlined by Deetz and Mumby to be a compelling analysis. Although Deetz and Mumby might argue that all of my reservations themselves may be subsumed under an ideology of technological rationality, I am not convinced that such is the case. To suggest that a political ideology, such as technological rationality, is so pervasive as to be a universal organizational ideology fails to take into account profoundly different cultural and value orientations in technologically developed countries (Geertz, 1973; Schein, 1985).

In general, while Deetz and Mumby's chapter has impressive scope, this breadth is also a weakness. Questions inevitably arise—for instance: What are modern organizations? Are they mechanistic structures of the type discussed by

Burns and Stalker (1961)? Are they restricted to mass-production industries? What is technological rationality? What values drive this ideology? What is managerial capitalism as a value system and as a control system? What are the relevant interests that Deetz and Mumby suggest need to be involved in organizational decision making?

Despite these shortcomings, Deetz and Mumby succeed in their aim of expanding the dialogue on the nature of organizations and what it means to be a member of a modern organization. In this sense their essay is thought provoking, because it compels us to look at fundamental assumptions underlying our thinking about organizations. From this analysis, I am led to consider the interrelationships among ideology, power, and communication.

THE INTERRELATIONSHIPS AMONG
IDEOLOGY, POWER, AND COMMUNICATION

I believe the interrelationships Deetz and Mumby suggest among ideology, power, and communication are valid and important, and tap a level of analysis ignored by many organizational scholars. There are four important points I wish to emphasize here:

- All interaction involves power.
- Through interaction, organizational members socially construct organizational reality and make sense of organizational activities.
- Discourse is isomorphic with organizing itself.
- Organizational discourse formulates organizational meaning and knowledge.

Taken together, these points emphasize the centrality of communication in any social activity, not just the activity of organizing. Discourse, through the formulation of meaning and knowledge, defines an organization and what it means to be a member of an organization. This view is not unique to a material conception of discourse, but is reflected in the work of organizational theorists such as Weick (1979), Poole and McPhee (1983), and Pondy, Frost, Morgan, and Dandridge (1985) as well as the work of scholars representing the organizational culture perspective (Putnam & Pacanowsky, 1983; Smircich, 1983) and those interested in organizational symbolism (Dandridge, Mitroff, & Joyce, 1980; Wilkins, 1985). More generally, this view would also be compatible with conversational and discourse-analytic perspectives as well.

In my view, these perspectives focus attention on the fact that organizing is communicating, irrespective of which particular organizational perspective one might adopt (i.e., structural, interpretive, systems, or critical). Deetz and Mumby highlight the role of discourse in knowledge formation and power, which are linkages typically underdeveloped in most organizational communication research. However, their analysis is limited in that they deal only with the structural aspects of power and ignore other dimensions of power. I also disagree with their claim that all organizational communication can be subsumed under a managerial emphasis on instrumental action and technological control. In contrast, after Foucault, I believe power (and knowledge) are dispersed throughout everyday life; thus I reject the critical move made by Deetz and Mumby in their essay.

Finally, since new technologies vary in their functions (Huber & Daft, 1987), it seems unreasonable to assume that managerial domination is an inevitable outcome of the new technologies. Evidence thus far indicates that organizations are using these technologies in a variety of ways, creating in some instances more sharing of decision making and in other cases supporting more centralized decision making (Morgan, 1986). Given the innovativeness with which organizations are using the new communication technologies (Rogers & Picot, 1983), their effects appear as diverse as organizations themselves.

LINKING IDEOLOGY AND DISCOURSE

Underlying Deetz and Mumby's analysis is the assumption that any ideology limits discourse such that only one "privileged voice" is heard. In principle, it may be possible for an ideology to be so compelling that literally only one voice is heard. Given today's world of global interconnectedness, however, it seems reasonable that members of modern organizations (in technologically developed countries) are aware of competing ideologies and that debate and discussion across ideologies and forms of discourse is possible, as opposed to the view that one privileged voice necessarily excludes others from being heard. Research on cognitive processing and schema theories suggests that people in fact do switch routinely among different frames of interpretation (i.e., ideology). Also, the ability to critique other viewpoints presupposes the ability to take the perspective of another. Thus I believe that discourse across competing frames of interpretation is possible, albeit very difficult (see also Kuhn, 1962).

CONCLUSION

Deetz and Mumby's essay provides a mix of pluses and minuses. On the minus side, their political view of organizations seems too mechanistic and deterministic, and thus fails to take into account adequately the complexity and diversity of modern organizations. Their views concerning power, communication, and ideology in organizations, however, are useful because they highlight the importance of communication in organizations. Nonetheless, this is only *one* view of the multiple ways in which these constructs may be interrelated. Finally, their essay is useful in that it broadens the ways in which scholars (and organizational members) may look at organizations and thus engage in a "perpetual critique." Such dialogue, in my view, can only strengthen our understanding of how organizations function.

REFERENCES

Bacharach, S., & Lawler, E. (1980). *Power and politics in organizations*. San Francisco: Jossey-Bass.

Blankenship, L., & Miles, R. (1986). Organizational structure and managerial decision behavior. *Administrative Science Quarterly, 13*, 106-120.

Brass, D. (1984). Being in the right place: A structural analysis of individual influence in an organization. *Administrative Science Quarterly, 29*, 518-539.

Burns, T., & Stalker, G. (1961). *The management of innovation*. London: Tavistock.

Burrell, G., & Morgan, G. (1979). *Sociological paradigms and organizational analysis*. London: Heineman Educational Books.

Daft, R., & Lengel, R. (1984). Information richness: A new approach to information processing and organization design. In B. Staw & L. Cummings (Eds.), *Research in organizational behavior.* Greenwich, CT: JAI.

Dandridge, D., Mitroff, I., & Joyce, W. (1980). Organizational symbolism: A topic to expand organizational analysis. *Academy of Management Review, 5*, 77-82.

Euske, N., & Roberts, K. (1987). Evolving perspectives in organization theory: Communication implications. In F. Jablin, L. Putnam, K. Roberts, & L. Porter (Eds.), *Handbook of organizational communication* (pp. 41-69). Newbury Park, CA: Sage.

Frost, P. (1987). Power, politics, and influence. In F. Jablin, L. Putnam, K. Roberts, & L. Porter (Eds.), *Handbook of organizational communication* (pp. 503-548). Newbury Park, CA: Sage.

Geertz, C. (1973). *The interpretation of cultures*. New York: Basic Books.

Gudykunst, W., Stewart, L., & Ting-Toomey, S. (1985). *Communication, culture and organizational processes*. Beverly Hills, CA: Sage.

Hatvany, N., & Pucik, V. (1981). Japanese management practices and productivity. *Organizational Dynamics, 13*, 5-21.

Huber, G., & Daft, R. (1987). The information environments of organizations. In F. Jablin, L. Putnam, K. Roberts, & L. Porter (Eds.), *Handbook of organizational communication* (pp. 130-164). Newbury Park, CA: Sage.

Kuhn T. (1962). *The structure of scientific revolutions*. Chicago: University of Chicago Press.

March, J., & Simon, H. (1958). *Organizations*. New York: John Wiley.

Mechanic, D. (1962). Sources of power and power participants in complex organizations. *Administrative Science Quarterly, 7*, 349-364.

Mintzberg, H. (1973). *The nature of managerial work*. New York: Harper & Row.

Morgan, G. (1986). *Images of organization*. Beverly Hills, CA: Sage.

Pfeffer, J. (1981). *Power in organizations*. Marshfield, MA: Pitman.

Pfeffer, J. (1982). *Organizations and organizational theory*. Boston: Pitman.

Pondy, L., Frost, P., Morgan, G., & Dandridge, T. (Eds.). (1985). *Organizational symbolism*. Greenwich, CT: JAI.

Poole, M. S., & McPhee, R. (1983). *A structurational theory of organizational climate*. Beverly Hills, CA: Sage.

Putnam, L., & Pacanowsky, M. (Eds.). (1983). *Communication and organizations: An interpretive approach*. Beverly Hills, CA: Sage.

Rogers, E., & Picot, A. (1983). The impacts of new communication technologies. In E. Rogers & F. Balle (Eds.), *The media revolution in America and Western Europe*. Norwood, NJ: Ablex.

Schein, E. (1985). *Organizational culture and leadership*. San Francisco: Jossey-Bass.

Smircich, L. (1983). Organizations as shared meanings. In L. Pondy, P. Frost, G. Morgan, & T. Dandridge (Eds.), *Organizational symbolism*. Greenwich, CT: JAI.

Smith, H., & Grenier, M. (1982). Sources of organizational power for women: Overcoming structural obstacles. *Sex Roles, 8*, 733-746.

Thibaut, J., & Kelley, H. (1959). *The social psychology of groups*. New York: John Wiley.

Tushman, M. (1979). Impacts of perceived environmental variability on patterns of work related communication. *Academy of Management Journal, 22*, 482-500.

Weick, K. (1979). *The social psychology of organizing* (2nd ed.). New York: Random House.
Wilkins, A. (1985). Organizational stories as symbols which control the organization. In L. Pondy,
    P. Frost, G. Morgan, & T. Dandridge (Eds.), *Organizational symbolism.* Greenwich, CT: JAI.
Woodward, J. (1965). *Industrial organization: Theory and practice.* London: Oxford University Press.

Absence as Workplace Control: A Critical Inquiry

CYNTHIA STOHL
PATTY SOTIRIN
Purdue University

ORGANIZATIONAL communication scholars may not agree on much, but today even the most managerially biased of us would agree that power, knowledge, and control are essential features of life in modern corporations. In their provocative and intriguing article, Deetz and Mumby attempt to provide a communicative reformulation of critical theory to better account for the nature of these essential features.

Their "reclaiming" of critical theory traditions provides the conceptual foundation for three basic assertions about organizational communication:

(1) Communicative practices are inseparable from identity, meaning, and knowledge formation.
(2) Discourse and power are interdependent.
(3) Discourse is nonrepresentational, that is, material.

In accord with these assertions, Deetz and Mumby direct research attention to the construct of ideology as a mediating link between relations of power and communicative practices. Critical analysis of ideology focuses on the ways in which patterns of organizational discourse produce and reproduce a dominant order of power and meaning privileging managerial and technical interests. The researcher seeks to resist such domination and privilege in order to "open discursive possibilities" (p. 40).

AUTHORS' NOTE: We would like to express our appreciation to Tara Sotirin for her brief moments of absence and to Susan Schell for the moments of her presence in our text.

Correspondence and requests for reprints: Cynthia Stohl, Department of Communication, Purdue University, West Lafayette, IN 47907.

Communication Yearbook 13, pp. 59-68

With these formulations, Deetz and Mumby have provided for the potential accomplishment of two of the three essential tasks critical research has defined for itself: description and critique (Deetz, 1982; Deetz & Kersten, 1983; Steffy & Grimes, 1986). The third task — organizational reform — remains unfulfilled.

Organizational reform involves the development of the emancipatory conditions for organizational praxis. Organizational praxis, according to Heydebrand (1983), "refers not only to the technical transformation of the environment and to the solution of practical problems, but also to the conscious self-transformation of collective actors" (p. 306). The aim of such reform is the elimination of closure, or "the undermining of the conditions leading to false consensus" and the reopening of organizational discourse by bringing individuals to an awareness of unnecessary distortions and providing forms for overcoming unnecessary blockages and systematic repression (Deetz, 1982, p. 140).

Deetz and Mumby do not deal with this third task because their essay does not descend to the level of situated communicative practice (Forester, 1983). The general lack of empirical level analysis is reflective of a serious deficiency in the corpus of critical work in our field (Kersten, 1986). In this response, we seek to redress the omission of empirical evidence by examining specific communicative practices associated with absence of workers in certain contemporary organizations. We offer our own inquiry into the ideological functions of absence as a limited demonstration of the potential viability of Deetz and Mumby's critical perspective.[1]

TEAMS, ABSENCE, AND IDEOLOGY

Why select absence as the focus of our discussion? First, it has become a signifier of the new team approach in organizations. Second, it is critical to the emergence of new forms of organization. Third, absence embodies a traditional domain of conflict between management and workers. Fourth, the set of practices surrounding absence exacerbates the contradictions in the new order.

Our examples are based on the prototype team design used at New United Motors Manufacturing, Incorporated (NUMMI), and our own interviews and experiences within similar plants. The NUMMI plant in Fremont, California, is described in detail by Parker and Slaughter (1988a, 1988b).[2] In this type of plant, each team is composed of a small group of line workers who have primary responsibility for maintaining productivity levels, continuing improvement of the production process, and the quality of the product. Team members are expected to participate in making decisions about scheduling, overtime, and job rotation. The organization is tightly designed; narrow job classifications are replaced with broadly defined multiple skill levels supported by pay-for-knowledge schemes. There are no regular absentee replacement workers; instead, multiskilled team members take up the slack for employees who are ill or absent.

The centrality of absence as a managerial concern stems from its ramifications for work force control, production efficiency, and profitability. Indeed, Volvo cited the costs of absenteeism as the instigating factor in its experiments with work reforms, arguing that absenteeism involves not only administrative and production costs, but also costs to society in terms of "the impact on consumption spending, the balance of payments, compensation benefits, demand for scarce capital resources, and possible criminal behavior" (Lindholm & Norstedt, 1975, p. 7). In the new team design, these costs are leveraged down to the group level by eliminating absentee replacement operators (AROs). This practice changes the meaning of absence within the production process. In its conventional definition, absenteeism is an input problem impairing system efficiency and productivity capabilities. In the new team design, absenteeism is an input problem at the group level but an opportunity at the organizational level to force the system to operate at maximal levels of stress (Parker & Slaughter, 1988a). Thus absence is interpreted in ways that further managerial and technical interests to the detriment or inconvenience of group and individual interests.

This brief introduction indicates the way absence in the new team design instantiates a particular configuration of interests. We feel that absence thus offers an appropriate focus for our pragmatic exploration of the construct of ideology as explicated by Deetz and Mumby. In their theoretical schema, ideology helps explain the ways in which patterns of discourse can be linked to power relationships. Their discussion directs our attention to two domains of ideological function. Ideology (a) plays a constitutive role in the creation of identity (*interpellation*) and (b) provides the basis for the privileging of particular interpretive schemes and interest configurations (*legitimation*). In addition, ideology embraces the political struggle to appropriate or resist particular meanings and the possibilities they circumscribe (*dialectic of control*). Our analysis of situated communicative practice highlights the following questions: What patterns of expression and interest representation characterize the way such practices articulate particular workplace identities such as the cooperative co-worker, the sympathetic team leader, the loyal organizational/team member, or the freeloader? Do such practices protect and perpetuate the dominance of certain interests? What alternative identities and techniques of control emerge from the contradictions between practices and meanings of absence?

Interpellation

Interpellation refers to ideology's constitutive role in the formation of situated identities and understandings of self-interest. Deetz and Mumby lead us to expect a complex of constitutive communicative practices that "circumscribe the parameters of identity" for team workers in ambiguous and often contradictory ways (p. 43). We will limit our analysis to discourses of absence (absenteeism, vacation, break, and lunch time, personal leave, and tardiness), nonpresence (idle time, daydreaming, or mindlessness), and attendance. Through such discourses the quality, value, and dignity of workers are framed in accord with system demands, and team membership is deployed as a coercive technique of control. Our analysis reveals a variety of discursive and nondiscursive practices that cast absence as communal betrayal and paradoxically undermine the solidarity of peer relationships. Examples range from public displays of absence records, sanctions against workstation nonpresence (restrictions on bathroom, vacation, or lunch breaks), and the social organization of work.

We contend that these practices delimit the meanings of absence in ways that subordinate the workers' interests and constrain their exercise of choice. The dominant meanings in the use of absence as a technique of control appear to be those of absence as a problem in need of solution or a pathology in need of cure. At the system level, absence "means" lack of worker commitment and involvement, poor work attitude, lack of responsibility, and failure to fulfill contractual obligations. At the group level, absence "means" added stress on team members, a betrayal of communal obligations, and a threat to the exclusiveness of group "we-ness." At the individual level, absence "means" guilt and/or deviance. To the extent these "meanings" dominate organizational life, choice is abdicated: The individual becomes bound as a team member to be present at the workplace; the group is bound to humiliate and/or punish the absent member; the system is bound to rehabilitate or exorcise the absent worker. Absence as the exercise of choice becomes mere illusion. In this way, team member identity is constituted through the worker's participation in the ongoing instantiation of a set of values dictated by group and system needs, namely, diligence, loyalty, conformity, and obedience — in other words, presence.

These meanings and values appear to mark the parameters of team worker identity. But Deetz and Mumby caution that ideology is more than a system of beliefs and values (see Beyer, Dunbar, & Meyer, 1988; Weiss & Miller, 1988). It is "that which creates the very possibility of having certain beliefs or values" (p. 42). Further, they argue that ideology is both the medium and the product of communicative practices. Therefore, it remains for us to examine the materiality of absence. To do so, we turn to specific practices characterizing the new team design.

Typical of the new team design is a "no-fault" absence policy. Through a series of calculations, all absences except those contractually allowable (e.g., absence for jury duty but not for personal or family illness) culminate in offenses that may result in eventual firing (Parker & Slaughter, 1988a). Imposing a quantitative measure on absences suppresses the qualitative dimension, reducing the life experiences represented by an absence to a quantitative "fact." The neutrality of such "facts" supports the dominant interpretation of absence as a problem of the individual, a pathology needing cure. Thus it is not surprising that many plants retain "counselors" or company nurses to help chronic absentees with their "problem."

A second practice that circumscribes identity is the ideological equation of attendance and productivity with human worth and dignity. At Toyota, the new team design is called the "respect-for-human" system; more blatantly, a manual from the Michigan Mazda plant warns, "If you are standing in front of your machine doing nothing, you yourself are not gaining respect as a human being" (quoted in Parker & Slaughter, 1988b, p. 43). In this sense, nonpresence in the production process through idle time, daydreaming, or even socializing constitutes the worker as a worthless entity.

Finally, the practice of eliminating absentee replacement workers has consequences for the meaning of absence at organizational and group levels. This practice invokes peer pressure and social obligation in which the absentee team member becomes the object of blame and resentment. Because there are no replacement workers to perform an absent worker's tasks, team leaders or coworkers must do so. Parker and Slaughter (1988a) observe that the increased pressure experienced in such a situation leads "workers [to] blame each other for missing work rather than blaming management for not providing enough workers" (p. 46). Thus the immediate expressions of worker self-interest contribute to the managerial interest in work force control; the sociability and camaraderie that emerges spontaneously in natural work groups are appropriated as techniques of control.

Legitimation

Along with attention to the ideological constitution of identity, Deetz and Mumby advise us to focus on the ways communication legitimates a particular structure of power relations while excluding alternative configurations of interest as impossible, mere fantasy, or undesirable (Therborn, 1980). Our inquiry focuses on the way particular interests in the new team design use certain forms of public expression — recognition and accounts — and why such uses instantiate and perpetuate the logic of control characterizing the alignment of managerial group and technorational cognitive interests.

Our first example is a form of public display that participates in a collusion of interests. In some team design plants, the local union newsletters regularly devote up to one-fourth of their space to the recognition of workers with perfect attendance, complete with photographs. Through this practice, the union legitimates the managerial distinction between a "good" worker and a "bad" worker ("Good workers come in everyday, do their jobs without complaint or error and go home, bad workers require constant supervision and harsh penalties to curb absenteeism"; Parker & Slaughter, 1988a, p. 40). The "good" worker exemplars may or may not be top production workers; what is marked as important is the priority of their commitment to the workplace, legitimating the subordination of any and all other claims on their presence.

In addition, this practice has larger communicative significance; it implies a convergence between worker and managerial interests and a shift in the union's role. Traditionally, the union has represented the interests of labor against managerial interests. However, unions are considered partners in the new team design and, consequently, their role has shifted to that of mediator between management and labor (Parker & Slaughter, 1988a). Many observers argue that the shift to partnership between union and management legitimates managerial concerns and perverts cooperation into the ultimate strategy of control (Kochan, Katz, & McKersie, 1987). While absence has traditionally been a powerful tactic of labor resistance, the celebration of perfect attendance in union newsletters upholds managerial interests in both substantive and formal dimensions: It legitimates the primacy of cooperation in a public display that serves as both reward and sanction toward the control of absenteeism.

The control of absenteeism is also central to another set of communicative practices characteristic of the new team design: The performance and evaluation of accounts for absences. Under the no-fault absence policy discussed above, workers are required to account for their absences. They must fill out forms in triplicate and submit their excuses to team leaders for assessment. Returning absentees are often called to account at team meetings and their excuses evaluated by the team. Frequently, they are called to account by management as well.

Perhaps the most striking formal feature in the performance of accounts of absence is the guilt of the speaker. The situation in which workers render accounts of their absences is structured by guilt—premised on a violation necessitating penalty, punishment, or forgiveness. The speaker speaks from a position of culpability; the audience listens secure in the righteousness and rightfulness of communal condemnation and evaluation; and the situation itself is orchestrated as a concerted reassertion of the social norms governing proper conduct. Rosen (1985) suggests that the performance of accounts can be thought of as public displays of "repentance" that reaffirm the importance of corporate values or standards. Scott and Lyman (1968, p. 50) argue that "Every account is a manifestation of the underlying negotiation of identities." Tompkins and Cheney (1983) suggest that accounts reveal the nature of the identification process. In this sense, the monolithic nature of the team worker identity constrains the latitude for negotiation by denying the legitimacy of alternative identities. Under the quise of neutrality, accounts of absence are evaluated primarily on technical criteria. The narrow latitude of acceptable and appropriate accounts rules out the reasons typical of absences among working mothers, the handicapped, and older workers; thus traditional patterns of discrimination are reproduced.

Under this system, then, teams are "authorized" to demand and evaluate absence accounts within the framework of necessity and neutrality in which absence is defined as deviant behavior. The autonomy and responsibility of the group does not extend to an interrogation of that framework itself. In this sense, the situation in which accounts are demanded, performed, and evaluated is itself a message that legitimates and reifies a particular social structure and configuration of interests.

Dialectic of Control

Interpellation and legitimation appear somewhat deterministic without consideration of ideology as a site of contestation. To examine the reciprocal nature of power relationships and the possibility for emancipatory practice, we have extracted from Deetz and Mumby's discussion Giddens's notion of a "dialectic of control." Giddens (1979, pp. 198-199, 212; 1984, p. 16) argues that relations of autonomy and dependence (power relations) are never fixed; that is, subordinates can always exercise some degree of control over the conditions of hegemonic reproduction. Deetz and Mumby advise that research into the dialectic of control involves inquiry into the political nature of meaning. Their emancipatory task is twofold: resisting ideological closure and privilege as well as opening discursive possibilities.

The scope and nature of "discursive penetration" among social actors is important to the dialectic of control. *Discursive penetration* refers to the ability of social actors to express insights about the circumstances of their action. Discursive penetration can both reinscribe team members within the particular identities and meanings that reproduce the privilege of managerial interests and make it possible to resist reinscription and assert absence as an instantiation of human and social interests.

An example of the ideological restrictions on the emancipatory potential of discursive penetration is the petition effort mounted by more than a thousand workers at the NUMMI plant to protest management's failure to address the problem of absenteeism (Parker & Slaughter, 1988a). The lack of AROs made even the low level of absenteeism (three days per year) a tremendous source of pressure. According to Parker and Slaughter, workers "thought they were politely asking management to provide replacement workers at least for long term absences" (p. 105). Instead, management and the union hired an attendance counselor to help absentees overcome their problems.

In this example, workers' expression of self-interest was framed by the definition of absence as a problem or pathology of the individual. Our contention is that even hiring AROs would not catalyze significant reformation of the power and meaning structures at NUMMI. The form of the request (petition), its advocated solution (hire AROs), and management's response (attendance counselor) articulate a particular configuration of interests and meanings that protect and perpetuate managerial privilege and prerogative.

We turn now to an example of the ways discursive penetration might open possibilities for organizational reform. In this example, we contend that the experiences of communality and solidarity within a new team design mark a potential challenge to corporate practices and meanings that constitute the team and absence as techniques of control. In this sense, team experiences and activities may provide modes of resistance and produce alternative practices, configurations of interests, identities, and meanings.

In a short-lived experiment at General Motors in the mid-1970s, the production process itself was ceded to a four-member team that assembled an entire van in one location over a two-day period, using the flexibility of automated assembly carriers. Team members engaged in concertive decision making, even meeting on weekends to resolve production problems, and when the product was completed included a picture of themselves along with their names and phone numbers (Parker & Slaughter, 1988b).

The technological innovations associated with this experiment were patterned after the Kalmar Volvo plant in Sweden (Aguren, Bredbacka, Hansson, Ihregren, & Karlsson, 1985) and are similar to those at NUMMI. However, besides freeing workers from the technical control of the assembly line itself, the team was given expanded responsibility and control over the technology. Although we do not suggest that this team design is free from managerial authority, we do contend that because it offers workers greater control over their immediate production practices, they can appropriate this control to accommodate a larger spectrum of interests. For example, computer capabilities could be used to assist in the arrangement of flextime for even the most complicated production operations, thereby honoring complex sets of preferences among multiple interests both within and outside the organization. Absence, then, could be constituted not as a production problem but as a dimension of work design.

It would be naive, however, to ignore the way the political economy of the factory subverts the realization of such a possibility. The dominant configuration of interests (managerial and technical) retains control over necessary training and computer access, making any such use of organizational resources in the service of alternative interests a managerial prerogative. We suggest that it is this very arrangement framing team design that opens the possibility for workers' insight into the contradictions of their team experience. It is through such insight that social actors come to engage in organizational self-reformation (Heydebrand, 1983; Mumby, 1988). Specifically, the disjuncture among the experience of teamwork as communal responsibility, the ideology of teamwork as synergism in the service of organizational interests, and the political economy of the factory context in which the team itself is but a subunit in the administrative hierarchy punctuate the conditions of domination and repression that contextualize team designs.

While we can only speculate on the ways the team organization of the experiment changed relationships and understandings for members, the team concept clearly offers emancipatory possibilities. The practice of team meetings in which returning absentees are called to account might be reconstituted as forums for the expression of diverse and divisive interests and ideas rather than puppet courts where communication patterns are dominated by hierarchical authority systems. An absent member need not necessarily be constituted in terms of system needs or managerial interests but as an absent person whose absence is understood within a broader configuration of interests structured around experiences of interdependence, sociability, and community.

SUMMARY

Our critical inquiry has shown how cooperation and teamwork have become techniques of coercion in the new team design and how the communality and sociability of groupness are deformed in the service of technical and managerial interests.

In themselves, these insights seemingly do little to extend what the conventional labor relations perspective suggests: that the new team designs undermine the threat of workers' absence (i.e., strikes) as the ultimate assertion of workers' interests (Kochan, Katz, & McKersie, 1987). The dialectic conceptions of power and control in our critical analyses, however, have also indicated the potential of the team as a practical/political strategy of collective activism and self-transformation operating through the contradictions and ambiguities generated among multiple levels, interests, practices, and discourses.

We offer our commentary as an affirmation of the potential in Deetz and Mumby's work and as our own "speech act with practical consequences" (Steffy & Grimes, 1986, p. 334). The viability to inform practical/political strategies for organizational change, a stance of critique in organizational communication practice, and an ethical commitment to human reflexivity, autonomy, and responsibility are important practices of scholarship. Even if the work of Deetz and Mumby is not wholeheartedly embraced, they have provided the impetus for a moment of self-reflection on the absence of a critical stance in most organizational communication research.

NOTES

1. There are textual limitations that complicated our efforts to utilize Deetz and Mumby's reclamation effort. First, the adumbrated rendition of that tradition as a Marx-Braverman-Burawoy trilogy is an incomplete and inadequate reduction. The eclectic mélange of perspectives cited to supplement this trilogy — including phenomenological (Jehenson, 1984), cognitive (Weick, 1979), postmodern (Baudrillard, 1975), and Marxist perspectives — renders the rendition being reclaimed ambiguous rather than elucidates it. Conversely, there is a critical tradition in organizational research and theory that Deetz and Mumby ignore, that is, the self-proclaimed "critical" work of the institutional school (Scott, 1987; Selznick, 1957) and the neo-Weberian school (March & Simon, 1958; Perrow, 1972). Hence they fail to contextualize their reclamation effort within the traditions most familiar to the organizational scholars ostensibly addressed in their text. Finally, their use of the term *discourse* as the unit of analysis remains unspecified. For example, it is unclear how discursive and nondiscursive activities are related: How are we to recognize and account for the differences between intended communicative activities, such as accounts, and those that have communicative effect, such as situations (Stohl & Redding, 1987)?

2. Based on their own experiences as auto workers and union activists, Parker and Slaughter have produced texts that are both critical and hopeful. Although they do not use the terminology of critical theory, they clearly demonstrate a commitment to emancipatory elucidation of oppressive conditions and practices. We appropriate and expand upon their insights in order to develop an empirically based exploration of the critical communicative perspective proposed by Deetz and Mumby.

REFERENCES

Aguren, S., Bredbacka, C., Hansson, R., Ihregren, K., & Karlsson, K. (1985). *Volvo Kalmar revisited: Ten years of experience* (S.A.R.L. Social and Economic Studies, Trans.). Stockholm: Efficiency and

Participation Development Council, Swedish Employers' Confederation (SAS), Landsorganisationen (LO), and Privattjanstemannakartellen (PTK).

Baudrillard, J. (1975). *The mirror of production* (M. Poster, Trans.). St. Louis: Telos.

Beyer, J., Dunbar, R., & Meyer, A. (1988). Comment: The concept of ideology in organizational analysis. *Academy of Management Review, 13*, 488-489.

Deetz, S. (1982). Critical interpretive research in organizational communication. *Western Journal of Speech Communication, 46*, 131-149.

Deetz, S., & Kersten, A. (1983). Critical models of interpretive research. In L. Putnam & M. Pacanowsky (Eds.), *Communication and organizations: An interpretive approach* (pp. 147-172). Beverly Hills, CA: Sage.

Forester, J. (1983). Critical theory and organizational analysis. In G. Morgan (Ed.), *Beyond method: Strategies for social research* (pp. 234-246). Beverly Hills, CA: Sage.

Giddens, A. (1979). *Central problems in social theory.* Berkeley: University of California Press.

Giddens, A. (1984). *The constitution of society: Outline of the theory of structuration.* Berkeley: University of California Press.

Heydebrand, W. V. (1983). Organization and praxis. In G. Morgan (Ed.), *Beyond method: Strategies for social research* (pp. 306-320). Beverly Hills, CA: Sage.

Jehenson, R. (1984). Effectiveness, expertise, and excellence as ideological fictions: A contribution to a critical phenomenology of the formal organization. *Human Studies, 7*, 3-21.

Kersten, A. (1986, May). *Critical research and the problem of multi-level analysis: Notes on connecting micro events and macro structures.* Paper presented at the meeting of the International Communication Association, Chicago.

Kochan, T., Katz, H., & McKersie, R. (1987). *The transformation of American industrial relations.* New York: Basic Books.

Lindholm, R., & Norstedt, J. (1975). *The Volvo report* (D. Jenkins, Trans.). Stockholm: Technical Department, Swedish Employers' Confederation (SAS).

March, J., & Simon, H. (1958). *Organizations.* New York: John Wiley.

Mumby, D. K. (1988). *Communication and power in organizations: Discourse, ideology and domination.* Norwood, NJ: Ablex.

Parker, M., & Slaughter, J. (1988a). *Choosing sides: Unions and the team concept.* Boston: South End.

Parker, M., & Slaughter, J. (1988b). Management by stress. *Technology Review, 4*, 37-44.

Perrow, C. (1972). *Organizational analysis.* Belmont, CA: Wadsworth.

Rosen, M. (1985). Breakfast at Spiro's: Dramaturgy and dominance. *Journal of Management, 11*(2), 31-48.

Scott, M., & Lyman, S. (1968). Accounts. American Sociological Review, 33, 46-62.

Scott, W. (1987). The adolescence of institutional theory. *Administrative Science Quarterly, 32*, 493-511.

Selznick, P. (1957). *Leadership in administration.* New York: Harper & Row.

Steffy, B., & Grimes, A. (1986). A critical theory of organization science. *Academy of Management Review, 11*, 322-336.

Stohl, C., & Redding, C. (1987). Messages and message exchange processes. In F. Jablin, L. Putnam, K. Roberts, & L. Porter (Eds.), *Handbook of organizational communication: An interdisciplinary perspective* (pp. 451-502). Newbury Park, CA: Sage.

Therborn, G. (1980). *The ideology of power and the power of ideology.* London: Verso.

Tompkins, P., & Cheney, G. (1983). Account analysis of organizations: Decision making and identification. In L. Putnam & M. Pacanowsky (Eds.), *Communication and organizations* (pp. 123-146). Beverly Hills, CA: Sage.

Weick, K. (1979). *The social psychology of organizing* (2nd ed.). Reading, MA: Addison-Wesley.

Weiss, R., & Miller, L. (1988). Response: Ideas, interests and the social science of organizations. *Academy of Management Review, 13*, 484-494.

2 A Theater of Motives and the "Meaningful Orders of Persons and Things"

H. L. GOODALL, Jr.
University of Utah

Using the organizational detective metaphor, this study explores the influences of set pieces and properties associated with "the unique sense of place" that shape ethnographic interpretations of organizational cultures. The subject of the essay is a regional office of a Boston-based computer software firm that exhibits distinctive features of a strong culture, and the focus of the study is on how changes in cultural identity and meaning were fostered by the move to a new office building. Conclusions are drawn about the subtle and nuanced aspects of cultural display and interpretation, the writing of interpretive organizational ethnography, and the dramatic interplay of meanings associated with the firm's softball season and everyday organizational life.

T HE semiotics of organizational displays have seldom received more than casual lip service from scholars. Perhaps this is because the most obvious aspects of any culture tend to be the most overlooked. Everyday artifacts suffer similar fates; they are seldom preserved by a culture and therefore become "rare finds," years hence, for archaeologists.

Mangham and Overington (1987) suggest that the theatrical model for organizational analysis requires textual consideration of the role played by sets and properties. The point of their analysis is not to focus on a typology of organizational staging, settings, costumes, properties, and cues, but instead to show how these elements of dramatic performance "inhibit, facilitate, or function as a catalyst for actions . . . serv[ing] to predict and prescribe it" (p. 119). The purposes of this sort of dramaturgical analysis, then, are to establish the cultural bases for cues to organizational action, and to reveal how settings function as "more than physical

Correspondence and requests for reprints: H. L. Goodall, Jr., Department of Communication, University of Utah, Salt Lake City, UT 84112.

Communication Yearbook 13, pp. 69-94

adjuncts to scenes" (p. 202), to signify subtle and nuanced agents of meanings that contribute to cultural codes for communication in organizations.

Studies of organizational cultures tend to ignore settings, costumes, and properties as meaningful cultural codes. In life, however, we regularly take our interpretive cues for action from the types of structures we are entering (banks, churches, shopping malls), the costumes worn by their inhabitants (uniforms, couture, work clothes), the symbols and signs present in the environment (name tags, security badges, posters, office adornments), and the ways in which people use these props to suggest meanings that work with or against the ongoing script. Cultural studies focus either on enacted, behavioral communication (rites, rituals, jokes, gossip, stories) that is generally devoid of a feeling for the set against which these scenes are enacted or on physical artifacts that leave out the role of the set and properties in the unfolding drama. In either case, organizational scholars often leave an incomplete record of the organization's culture.

For me, the maddeningly abstract term *organizational culture* and the studies that are done in its "tradition" are perhaps best understood within the broad scope of Sahlins's (1976) reader-based definition: Cultures should be approached as meaningful orders of persons and things. The task, then, of the organizational culture analyst should be "the discovery of that meaningful ordering and the processes that sustain it" (Smircich & Stubbart, 1985, p. 65). To try to accomplish this interpretive understanding without taking into account the sets and properties is to suggest two things, both of which are problems. First, it denies the importance of certain aspects of culture despite the fact that in everyday life we use them to guide our choices and judgments (see Sennett, 1977). Second, and perhaps more important, it suggests that the sense of culture created by those meaningful orderings of behavior and artifacts does not necessarily differ from organization to organization. Clearly this claim is inappropriate to the task at hand. Cultural analyst Sonja Sackmann (1987) argues:

> The mere recording of the presence of . . . artifacts does, therefore, not give much insight into the culture if the specific meanings that are attributed to them in a particular setting are not known. What is needed is an understanding of these culture-specific meanings. This requires an understanding of the ideational aspect of culture — the underlying cognitive constructions or the cultural knowledge which exists in a particular organization and which is used to attribute meaning to things and events. (p. 1)

To display the meaningful orderings that make possible the unique cultural contexts of organizational lives should mean to examine attributions of significance to everyday scenes of organizational experience. What is named "culture" by the scholar should be what shapes or gives particular meaning to the ordinary and extraordinary experiences that emerge from episodes of communication played out against sets and with uses of properties natural to those experiences. The scholar's tasks, regardless of the study's microfocus, are to find the "meaningful ordering of persons and things" within scenes, to discover how and why meanings are attributed to them, and to convey to the reader, with a sense of verisimilitude, the results of the investigation.

DISCOVERING MEANINGFUL ORDERS
OF PERSONS AND THINGS

An organizational scholar who enters an organization for the first time suffers the fate of a newcomer entering the same organization, a fate best summed up by Louis's (1980) phrase, "surprise and sense-making" (p. 23). Out of the great delirium in which the senses are assaulted by movement without ascribable purposes, talk without clearly understood references, and a veritable bombardment of signs, symbols, and messages all vying for immediate attention, the scholar, like a theatergoer who has not yet read the play, must be willing to consort with the ambiguity and attempt, through whatever means possible, to reduce it (Weick, 1979).

When one goes to the theater one generally examines the set for initial clues. Of course, this is best done when the house lights are still up and the actors have yet to perform. For this reason I believe that one essential analysis of an organization's culture should be performed at night, after hours, or on the weekends. The objective is to have free rein over the exterior and interior of the set, an opportunity to record (with notes and diagrams or, when permissible, with video or photographs) the naturally occurring traffic of the available signs and symbols.

This is the time for doing what a theatergoer does: Look around at the set for insights into the themes, motifs, ironies, contrasts, or other evocations of meaning present in the ordering of things that, during daylight working hours, surround the players and contribute to their unique sense of place. Performing this sort of elementary but necessary analysis of sets and props has two strategic advantages. First, the analyst can document the existence and placement of objects for further study and for later evidence of evolutionary modifications or changes. This effort is important because longitudinal studies of cultures are rare, and changes in sets and properties can be as important as (because they may correspond to) changes in management, policies, or employee attitudes. Second, the analyst can learn how individuals and groups differentiate themselves, establish their own organizational or personal identities, and express their inner voices through displays of art, photographs, posters, and other memorabilia. This close examination of individual work spaces and group territories can establish premises for the orders of things (including hierarchical or status orders) that can later be connected to premises about the orders of persons obtained from observations, interviews, questionnaires, and casual talk.

Discovery of the orders of persons and things exhibited within an organization's culture requires an appreciation for interpretive possibilities that are not reflected in our literature (see Calas & Smircich, 1987). Our literature is, after all, the manufactured product of *our* academic culture, in particular a subculture devoted to interpretive cultural studies of organizations. To assume that our grammar, our perspectives, or our language is appropriate to the study of organizations is to commit an intentional fallacy under the guise of an elitist scholarship. Worse, it is to assume that *our* culture is the one against which all other cultures should be measured or understood.

Discovery of the ordering of persons and things requires two conscious decisions on the part of the scholar who will ultimately write about them. First, and most important, is the decision to record details of the set and properties (and their uses) in any account of an organization's culture. Second is the decision to write the account in a way that reveals how these signs and symbols contributed to the interpretation.

ORIENTATION TO THE CONTEXT
OF B-BCSC CULTURE

My study of the culture of a Boston-based computer software company (B-BCSC) whose regional office is located in Huntsville, Alabama, took place from May 1984 through September 1988. This was a unique and important time in the history of the company because it marked the entrance of a new corporate vice president to oversee the Human Resources (HR) Business Unit, which is the basis of all of Huntsville's operations. It was also important because during this time plans were made and carried out to move from one leased building to a new office structure specially designed for B-BCSC. Previous work on B-BCSC's culture, and the broader milieu of Huntsville, are contained elsewhere (Goodall, 1989), and references from that lengthy work are included in the present study to reflect some of the changes that took place. That study focused on the evolution of cultural rituals, stories, and legends under the influence of an "evangelical" new leader; this one focuses on the roles played by sets, costumes, and properties in the everyday forming of cultural consciousness.

In the account that follows, what I am after is rather simple: the association of choices of cars and their colors with cultural understandings, the representation of individual and group identities by displays of office art and memorabilia. Their depiction is rendered in a way that suggests the impact these taken-for-granted set pieces and properties have on my reading of the culture, which is itself a microcosm of a broader corporate culture within this geographic region. Also, by comparing the same organizational culture after a major change in location accompanied by changes in policies affecting individual and group displays, I try to show the importance of sets and properties as evolutionary signifiers, as emblems of outward, mandated change that reflect inner attitudes and sentiments. The result is admittedly a little off-putting within the context of the literature of an academic culture, because it does not fit the format, use the voice, or make use of the familiar icons of that genre. The voice of the narrator, like the voice of any author working in any genre, including academic publishing, must address the sympathies of the audience even though in this case the goal is to challenge them. But it does, I have found, represent the meaningful ordering of persons and things within the context of B-BCSC.

Geertz (1983) explains that what is going here is a "blurring of the genres," a blending of perspectives. As Pacanowsky (1984) rightly points out, interpretive scholars seem to be missing the point of Geertz's critique. The term *genre* has less to do with ways of thinking about scholarship than with how scholarship is written. For my purposes here, the theatrical genre includes appropriate considerations of sets, costumes, properties, and so forth, and the result should be a writing style that incorporates them, ripe with interpretive possibilities, within the naturally occurring contexts of a dramatic organizational story.

INDIVIDUATION AND GROUP IDENTITIES

Theatergoers appreciate the subtleties and nuances of costumes, accessories, and colors that in some cases are used to represent or embody an image or identity, and in other cases are used to suggest the absence or contrast of those effects. Rarely do we encounter descriptions of clothing, accessories, physique, movement, gesture, or manipulations of objects within office or manufacturing environments in scholarly studies (a notable exception is Miles & Leathers, 1984). It is as if we are reticent to discuss them; they represent a source of academic taboo.

This omission is particularly unfortunate for cultural studies of organizations, where, in my experience, a good deal of informal talk and most of the gossip focuses on what people wear, how they look, what kinds of cars they drive, where to go to buy objects to decorate their offices or homes, methods of weight loss/physical fitness to enhance appearance and health, what's wrong with someone's outfits or performances in them, and so forth. If the signs and symbols of nonverbal properties figure into the talk, it is hardly unreasonable to assume that they should appear, at least in a cameo role, in our literature.

My experience with B-BCSC revealed one major use of properties within the cultural context of this organization. That use was for the purpose of displaying sources of individuation and group identification, as shown in the themes and motifs of office art and posters, photographs, and so on. It is also important to point out that when the scene changed and the new building was occupied, the employees who wanted to carry over previous expressions of self and group were disappointed to learn of the new policy in a memo called "House Rules" limiting their freedom of expression. During this transition period a subculture of underground terrorists who refused to go along with the new policy found subtle ways to express their concerns, in much the same way as an earlier historical period's rebels expressed theirs (see Gregg, 1971). Clearly, individual and group egos were on the line, and these individuals were using a particular policy complaint as a rhetorical shield to protect their desires for self-expression.

CONVEYING THE CULTURE,
WITH VERISIMILITUDE, TO THE READER

A major task for the organizational cultures analyst is the writing of the final report (see Clifford & Marcus, 1986; Geertz, 1988). The writing itself is a dramatic performance (Goodall, 1989) that should be guided by an appreciation and artful use of narrative techniques such as voice, dialogue, episodes, tension, conflict, and a devotion to the craft of the word capable of reflecting a total immersion in the scene.

What I try to do in the episodes that follow is to display the organization by juxtaposing three different tales (see Van Maanen, 1988). In two representations I give you a company tour that begins in the streets leading into the building, spend a little time reflecting on the vehicles in the parking lot, and then bring you inside. However, the particular twist to this seemingly natural progression is in the attempt to build into the description the views, both individual and collective, of the employees, so that the result is sort of an *informed* show-and-tell that attempts to capture (and condense) the experiences, sentiments, and thoughts of a variety of people into a singular, occasionally naive, if seemingly omniscient, narrator. The third tale is drawn from my own participation in the organization as a member of its summer softball team, an experience that revealed itself to be a microcosm of the changes evident in the earlier evolution of the organization's culture. The three are intertwined to create a dramatic organizational story.

1

I am an organizational detective. This is a story about how I read the clues to a culture while observing and participating in it. Everything here is important.

There are some natural limitations.

I am not a video camera and I am never neutral.

I use words to capture experiences that words have no ability to capture fully, and I have readers to please.

The human frailties of this cultural investigator no doubt influence what I see, think about, and write.

Mine is a method based as much on opportunity as on motive; a desire to get out of the office and play some ball is at least as important as the desire to make a scholarly contribution. I admit to the necessity of basically hanging around, talking with the subjects of my study in much the same way as you might talk with a friend over dinner about the meaning of life.

The truth is that I just went out there and played the game, immersed myself in its metaphor, and experienced, firsthand, at least some of its drama.

2

You will want to know something about me. How else could you trust my judgment? I am the only son of a spy and a nurse, perfect environmental influences for my current work as a college professor. Secretly, I am still hoping for my break into the major leagues as a relief pitcher for the Yankees. In my youth I started writing novels and short stories, the best ones always about baseball, writing, and love; now I write articles for our professional literature about the same things, only on an analogic, interpretive level.

I'm married to a woman who is a manager at B-BCSC, and it is through her that I first began these cultural investigations. When we throw a party we invite people over who like rock and roll, sports, literature, and humor, and who still believe in the American dream.

There is a part of the American dream, however, the part they don't show you in the movies and the part you don't recognize until you are living in it. It's the part where something is gone and you think you missed it, and something else is ahead of you but it looks too much like today feels. So you open yourself up to possibilities that a year ago would have seemed absurd. This is the part of the American dream where you wake up wondering what that dream was all about, look out the window, and see that it is already mid-afternoon.

3

The spring of this story I was called up by B-BCSC's new team forming in the Industrial League. It's lower than the minors, a sort of "D" level with no bus and you have to pay for your own uniform, but it's a chance to play again so I do.

My wife has not fully bought into, but nevertheless fully repeated, some of the lies of my fabled baseball hero youth to the team's management, who in turn expected me to show up a gloved wonder capable of at least pitching them into the playoffs if not into a spot on national TV. During the first practice session out behind the new B-BCSC building, I caught a line drive in the teeth, which, while spitting blood and refusing to leave the field, I personally took as metaphorical justice being doled out by a vengeful God who at this point in my life clearly sides with my wife and is out to teach me lesson. Or it could have been a sign that what they were seeing was precisely what they were getting.

The next practice was held at an elementary school playground. This is a sign, reader, that you should not fail to read as a symbol.

4

This is a mixed league, women and men mingling together on sand diamonds, and the game is played slow-pitch. There are some interesting basic rules. The game is played on a regulation field that varies considerably in size depending on who marks off the distances between bases. Teams play for no more than 75 minutes or six complete innings, whichever occurs first or is likely to draw the fewest complaints from the coaches. To make it fair, the ballplayers are not allowed to wear any watches, and must hustle on and off the field to show good faith in their intention to move the game along or at least not to delay it.

What this means to the game is also reflected in the culture. At B-BCSC the scheduled work hours are from 8:30 to 5:00, but the unwritten rule is you work until the project is completed. Clock-watchers are not allowed to work for the Huntsville office of B-BCSC, which has a reputation for getting the job done regardless of what time it is. So it is that to get to work before 8:30 and not to leave until after 5:00 — to hustle on and off the playing field — is a sign of having the proper attitude.

There are other rules: For example, this is a "mixed" league, which means that women and men must play together. However, to field a team for regulation play means that you need only field two women for every eight men. There is an ugly assumption at work here. Furthermore, if the person batting ahead of a woman is walked by the opposing pitcher, the upcoming woman can automatically walk without ever stepping up to the plate. Usually she is encouraged to do so. Draw your own conclusions. But remember, these are league rules, not necessarily B-BCSC rules, but B-BCSC must play by them too.

Finally, this is a game of slow-pitch softball. It gives the team at bat a decided advantage, an advantage that is best realized by aiming for a steady accumulation of singles instead of long balls that more often than not turn into long fly balls easily caught by the opposing outfielders. What this rule suggests about the workplace is that rewards belong to those steady players who avoid trying to stand out too much, who know how to fit in and play the game, who are ultimately members of a team.

When the team wins, you win too. When you strike out, pop out, or fly out in a dazzling display of pumped-up glory seeking, you may stand out, but the whole team goes down with you.

5

This is a game in which attitude is very important. This is an era at the end of the twentieth century in which attitude is defined in the popular mind by its outward appearance. Contrary to the work of some cognitive psychologists, here attitude is an expression dressed out as behavior. And the behaviors that best reflect an attitude are looks, clothes, cars, actions, and colors, individually and collectively functioning as symbols to induce meanings in people through manipulation of appearances and accumulation of things.

This is an America addicted to images, craving the surface satisfaction of the desire to be consumed. This is an America where you can buy what you want as well as what you want to be. This is an America where how well you play the game is in part understood by how good you look, how well you act, and what you have consumed before, during, and after the game.

It all adds up to attitude. If Erving Goffman were still alive, perhaps he would see it as the next evolutionary move from presentation of self (see Goffman, 1959), in which saving face is the central issue, to presentation of attitude, in which the values of a culture are embodied and displayed. Something to wear; something to do; somebody to be.

6

You walk inside the new B-BCSC building and there is evidence of a B-BCSC attitude. This is, and is not, how it used to be.

In the old days and up until the move to the new building in Research Park, B-BCSC was housed in a rented structure on Sparkman Drive, across the street from the University of Alabama in Huntsville and next to Executive Plaza. In 1986 I wrote about getting to it like this:[1]

> You cross a sewer drainpipe to get there. Lately, the ditch where the sewer water runs has been the final resting place of a rusted Winn-Dixie shopping cart, an artifact no doubt stolen from the nearby Winn-Dixie Plaza, which features (in addition to the Winn-Dixie) an emergency clinic, a Buy Wise discount drugstore, a Radio Shack, a Buy Rite discount shoe store, a European Tanning Spa, a Hills' discount department store, and one of those afternoon saloons without windows, the kind of purely functional dive that might, if you walk into it, change forever your views on the nature of things. . . .
>
> Ninety people, their vehicles, their artifacts, assorted groups of customers in for training on the company's products, are crammed into a space intended for half that population. There are people and things crowded in the narrow hallways. Privacy is difficult. There is one bathroom.

Out of this environment and its people grew a powerful corporate culture, a sense of shared meanings in organizational identification and membership (Cheney, 1983). In part, it was shaped by an evangelical leader named Henry who reorganized persons and things into a new meaningful order; in part, it was influenced by the drive of individuals in the company to preserve their individuality in response to that new order; and in part, it was the development of hiring and retention practices that sought out what would later come to be known as "a B-BCSC person." Also, it was probably none of these things and something else entirely, a curious, mysterious, unnameable, magical "it" that was the traffic of meaningful symbols and attributions of significance to them during a particular time, in a particular place, shared among particular people.

In other words, it may have been a glorious accident. But as any postmodern observer knows, no matter where you go, there you are. Persons and things. Meaningful orders. Things to figure out.

7

I am bringing you into the architecture of the new B-BCSC building, although we have not yet left the old one.

We are talking about attitude, of which culture is its nature and set pieces, props, and costumes are its outward manifestations. Consider a ball team, by analogy. Its attitude is identifiable by its ways, its habits, its style of play, an aspect of which is the meanings we attribute to its artifacts, uniforms, the stadium in which the performances are carried out. Maybe it has one voice, maybe it has many. When times are good, the magical "it" of it stands out, is named, is argued about, and nothing changes on the bet that if anything changes the good times will change too. But when times are bad, changes are made and the magical "it" loses its charm.

Look at what I said about the old building in relation to an "accidental" change in costumes that became an aspect of the B-BCSC culture back in 1986:

From the parking lot you enter the building, which is one of those ordinary beige boxes with a pillared facade that suggests anything the sign on the door wants it to suggest, and you see two more significant symbols. The first is the company logo, which consists only of its name — B-BCSC — interesting because when undisguised it includes the names of the founders (as in Smith & Jones) and because one of them — let's say Smith — left the company over a year ago and for a long time everyone thought the company would become "& Jones" but it didn't, and because the founder who remained behind to run the company, a man fond of using lyrics from Dire Straits to explain company policies, a man who jogs every day and drives a silver Porsche 928, is not the kind of regular Joe you would expect to hang something as simple as his last name on a high-tech computer software company whose major product is "Z-Two." But he did.

This is also the man — let's call him Elliot Jones — who walked into the office one day in blue jeans and inspired a revolution. The blue jeans, he said, were his way of rewarding himself for a hard week of work. In corporate America, it is the simple slogans that seem to move the soul, and so it was with this statement. The idea was that B-BCSC's biweekly paydays should be special, so why not have a company policy that encourages wearing blue jeans to the office on payday?

The policy went into effect immediately, and received the sort of tentative, let-me-see-yours-before-you-see-mine kind of reception that one might expect from a radical shift of tradition. Clothes, after all, are coverings of our personalities as much as our bodies, and the sight of a moderately overweight middle-aged man who sits at a desk for a living wearing Calvins is not necessarily inspiring. Such a man might, if pressed as a senior executive in Huntsville was pressed, buy what amounted to his first-ever pair of blue jeans, not the soft, prewashed kind, but the super-stiff starched variety, and, not knowing any better, turn them up at the cuffs and snap them into place with red suspenders, giving all the world and particularly the local customers the impression of a farmer on his first Saturday at the county fair.

It was not the costume, but the calculated effects of the costume on the customers that prompted the strongest criticism. Salespeople in Alabama and Georgia objected to looking too much like where they came from, especially when talking business to someone from San Francisco or Boston. One person in the company took offense at the policy this way: "I am an adult and I don't need to be told what to wear." As the weeks passed, Elliot Jones relented a bit in deference to his sales force and modified the policy to encourage "those individuals who did not deal directly with customers" on paydays to wear blue jeans, and so on. The revolution was well under way, and its later influences on the culture could not yet be imagined.

Persons and things must be read *together*.

8

In the old building everyone contributed to the making of a culture. In the new building a culture was given to them. What is the relationship between buildings and cultures? How does a change in one lead to an alteration in the other? Territories, how we mark them and how we understand them, are the issues here (see Ardrey, 1967, 1970).

The old building was small, ugly, and cramped, but what went on inside of it was bold and new. In 1986 I described it this way:

> As you leave the receptionist's area you move through a maze of adjoining corridors, temporary walls, and meaningful symbols. The building has a "closed-in" atmosphere that is made unnerving by the generally cramped quarters, but an atmosphere that is made more bearable by the presence of interesting, colorful artifacts.
>
> . . . One significant aspect of the B-BCSC culture is nonverbally clear: There is a strong tradition of individualizing one's office area or work space. So clear is this tradition that certain motifs become apparent. The motifs include some ordinary and expected symbols: symbols of family and families with pets, symbols of academic and professional achievement, symbols of recognition and reward. These are the positive, traditional symbols that you find in American offices from sea to shining sea, symbols that suggest ordinary values, or, if looked at differently, symbols that suggest exceptional continuities.
>
> A second motif concerns symbols that are inner pathways to a mindscape of petty fears, rages, senses of humor, and bellicose warnings that coalesce into a collage of general and specific corporate psyches, and that are oddly enough correspondent to the individual positive symbols of home and learning and achievement.
>
> For example, "Shit Happens" is an emblem, a sort of badge, really, that is laced through the building next to degrees and family snapshots, a common source of strategically ambiguous identification with an anonymous but ever-present enemy. "Is this fun?" and "Are we having fun yet?" also permeate the nonverbal atmosphere, particularly at eye level. The urge for self-preservation and recognition can be seen in the variety of "me" buttons that tell their own stories. "God, I'm Good!" "Me First," "I'm wonderful in bed," "I'm getting over this," and "I'm not crazy" are some examples. . . .
>
> A third motif suggests identification with things corporate, such as "User's Conference" posters and memorabilia from company picnics, Christmas parties, and the like. One characteristic of this motif is the absence of symbols drawn from previous places of employment, despite the fact that virtually everyone at B-BCSC held at least one job somewhere else prior to joining the B-BCSC team. This characteristic is

easily understood as a show of corporate loyalty, or the nonverbal desire to make blank the past, but it is singularly at odds with other nonverbal symbols that strongly suggest a pride in past associations, schools, achievements, and times. It is also at odds with the talk exchanged between or among employees, in which stories of past companies are routine. Perhaps this absence means we guard our nonverbal communication more carefully than our verbal communication, or perhaps it is a broader reflection of a cultural value: To fit in means to make an opening in the symbols of one's life, an opening that represents a space reserved for the present, a space dominated by the visual channels of thought, where how we see or need to be seen can play a major role in demonstrating how we choose to fit in.

The new building, by stark contrast, strives to be bold and new and ends up being large, odd, open, and strangely ambiguous, and inside what goes on strains to be the same, only somehow better, and manages to be neither and so is misunderstood. In 1987 the new building was voted one of the ten ugliest by the Architectural Society of Huntsville. Inside the new building some people interpreted these results as entirely political and not at all true. Others agreed — but with whom?

When you look at the new B-BCSC structure, what do you see? I see McDonald's golden arches, or perhaps a Baptist church facade, from which jut two sides of the same ambiguous question: What? At sunrise it reflects the sunrise, when the moon is high and full it gives back a high and full moon, perhaps suggesting that it is user friendly in an adaptive, cosmic way.

Walk around the structure and you discover that the back is the same as the front, an oddly unsettling realization otherwise unknown in nature. Grass struggles for life all around it, but this has been a drought summer and you can't blame the architect for that.

Move out into the L-shaped parking lot and what do you see? Not the same cars as at the old B-BCSC. Something here has changed dramatically. Consider these paragraphs, written by me about the old U-shaped lot on Sparkman three years ago:

> You can learn to ask questions about the culture of an organization by examining the contents of its parking lot. This is particularly true if the organization in question is actively concerned with building an image, or is making a serious attempt to develop a culture. We have known for some time now that nonverbal communication predates and precedes other forms, and it is reasonable to assume that in organizations where culture is the issue, this may also be true.

> The cars you pass in the B-BCSC lot are artifacts of the interchange of traffics public and private, and they do, both singularly and collectively, suggest realities whose appearances are of primary cultural importance: Honda, Chevrolet, Buick, Toyota, another Honda, another Honda, another Buick, a Fiat, and a small Ford truck. And so on. Nothing is very much older than a 48-month note could purchase, and there are no motorcycles, bicycles, or multicolored Volkswagen microbuses.

> These are the cars and light trucks of aspiring, mostly boom-generation professionals who derive a way of knowing and being from the office that often follows them home.

In an older generation this might have been called an identity, separated into its corporate and individual components, analyzed for its dependence on the status of work or the prestige of the firm.

But for this generation identity is too large and too stable a term to describe the movement of roles we enact and functions we carry out, the intricate interplays of working and living, the changes in attitude or values that circumstances adapt us to. Ways of knowing, ways of being, ways of doing, ways of seeing all contribute to purposes more fluid than identities can catch.

Perhaps this is why a parking lot with only three red vehicles in it, and nothing vaguely exotic or even 4-wheel drive, attracts attention, appeals to the sense of mystery that any cultural investigation begins with. There is much strategic ambiguity passing for beiges and light blue and off-white on cars that are uniformly protected by optional side moldings. They rest just on either side of the B-BCSC building, straight rows of muted colors suggesting some sort of pattern.

Persons and things.

What we see at the new building is a different sort of vehicle population. There are far fewer boom-generation Hondas and Toyotas to be seen. They have been replaced by Trooper IIs and *big* black Ford 4x4s and Supercabs leading a gaggle of lesser light trucks. Of the three original red vehicles, only one remains, and that is in the hands a new owner. But now there are many red vehicles, and in general the B-BCSC lot is filled with far more aggressive color choices.

What can all of this mean for the culture of B-BCSC—Huntsville? Is the move from smaller to larger, from cramped to open, from car to truck, from muted to aggressive colors, from an active, internally defined culture to a more passive, externally prescribed one, from then to now, a correspondence to something or just a coincidence?

The difference isn't in the persons. The persons are mostly the same. In fact, less than a handful of the persons who worked here in 1986 no longer do, and there have been few new hires. The differences are evident, at this point, only in the *things*.

Persons and things. Something is being suggested here.

9

Our team has no name. We do have blue-and-white uniforms with numbers on them, however.

It was suggested by one of our coaches that should call ourselves the B-BCSCers. There was a round of polite laughter. It was suggested again, a week later. This time nothing happened.

So we have no name. This, I think, is significant. Did you ever play for a team that did not have a name? Did you ever work for a firm that didn't have a logo? A mascot? Some significant symbol? What is the meaning of this absence of common definition? This reticent stop in a flow of cultural ambiguity?

During spring training we are awkward but enthusiastic as a team. Our managers, Jim and Anthony, are stern taskmasters who run us through infield and outfield drills and batting practice, and give fair but fairly harsh criticism when our play fails to meet their standards. Every day we are reminded how tough a league this is, how strong the competition will be.

We learn a lot about each other and slowly begin to play together as a team. Positions are chosen, tried out for, changed around. Nicknames emerge. We have about twenty players, including one B-BCSC intern who was talked into joining the team after it was discovered that he had considerable athletic talent. On the day of the first regular season game an announcement goes out within the new B-BCSC building asking everyone to come out and support their team. Players wear their uniforms to work and are the envy of their colleagues. There is a lot of talk about victory, rumors about the other team.

We are defeated 38-7. I manage to give up 14 runs in the first inning, but do partially make up for it by hitting a solid home run during my first at bat, driving in 3 big ones. Our eight fans chant, "Babe!" but to no avail. We shake hands with the other team at the end of it, walk over to the assistant coach's truck, and drink a few beers while our coaches admonish us for the ugliness with which we played.

We promise to do better next time. Jack, on his own initiative, begins documenting our team's efforts and sending out memos to the HR Business Unit ("BULLSTAFF"—not a reference to the current movie hit *Bull Durham*, but an indication that most of what is displayed here is bullshit) on the company's internal network. It is an effort at communication that becomes, as the season progresses, a highly valued activity, one of those magical and spontaneous innovations that emerges from inside a culture that is—at least for now—happy with itself despite the heavy odds against its winning.

10

Come inside the new B-BCSC building. You *are* in another world. It is a glass house in which the dominant colors are maroon and gray, there are well-tended plants and a consistent sense of a submerged feeling that defines what it means to have an attitude of medium cool.

You are in a center of something, that much is certain. The floor is marbled, there are low-backed couches and loveseats and chairs around a coffee table upon which are placed recent copies of *Fortune, Newsweek*, and *Software News*. There is no Muzak. You face a large mirrored pillar that serves as the exterior housing of the elevators, but there never is an elevator sound while those who go up, go up and those who come down, come down. To the left is the receptionist's area, and her name is Mary.

Mary is an alert, attractive woman who exudes a businesslike but reserved attitude and is very fond of California. She manages a desk neatly laid out with technologies of communication — a complex telephone connecting system, inter-coms, and paging devices — and a noticeable absence of anything personal. When she isn't on duty, this space belongs to Anne, another attractive, alert woman who too exudes an attitude of medium cool.

At odds with this medium cool high tech message suggested by these meaning-ful orders of persons and things is a sign-in book usually to the left of a visitor, atop a small wall that separates you from the receptionist. In 1986, back in the old building, I found the same sign-in book but read into it a very different sense of place. Then it was a source of humor, evidence of a motif of good-hearted fun and occasional wickedness that was laced throughout the building, a book in which visitors, spouses, and delivery personnel would take pride in outdoing the previous entry. For example:

Joe Blow	11 or so	Looking for one good woman with whom to share lunch and sexual favors
Large Bear	12:01	To see smaller bear. No bear there. No honey either.
Dr. Strangelove	Zero Hour	Desperately seeking Susan

Now, there is no humor in the receptionist's book. None.

What can this mean? Is it a sign of change? Maybe. It is true that the "old" receptionist was Ellen, who now works in the phone support room. But I think there is more to it. In the old building humor was addressed to a public, a Perelmanian "universal audience," and served as a way of communicating the value of laughter to some of the meanings of work that contributed, daily, to a unique sense of place. Like graffiti, items of humorous display — whether in the receptionist's book or in the Gary Larson cartoons that were strategically placed by the coffee machine — invited meaningful contributions from others whose identities were otherwise unknown. Thus humor built a sense of community in which the act of participating was valued, and the quality of the participative performance was the stuff corporate stories and even legends were made of.

Now the humor has lost its edge, perhaps in part because it has lost its sense of public display. Cartoons for public display are "not allowed" under existing policy, and at all costs must be "professional." The receptionist's book is a place for names and dates and company affiliations, not fun. The House Rules released upon the move emphasized the professional and banished the personal. These rules are further evidence that, at B-BCSC as in America, to be a professional is to lose what is personal and passionate. It is to mask the genuine sources of your identity.

Identity is further masked by a new program called "My Secret Pal," in which "special" gifts arrive at your work space on birthdays, anniversaries, and so on from unknown company donors. How special can that be? Wouldn't you like to be able to communicate your thanks to someone who did something *special* for you? Are we having fun yet?

11

It is mid-season and we have yet to win a game.

We are down to three or four fans. As a team we are down to about twelve players who regularly show up, and that number with the addition of new female second-baseperson named Terri and a male ex-hockey star intern from the University of Alabama in Huntsville named Blim. In an effort to find the winning combination, positions continue to be reshuffled, a further sign of the desire to do well in an environment that believes in the value of rearranging the meaningful orders of persons and things. Jack's last internal memo read like this:

HOWDY Y'ALL:

WELL WE LOST AGAIN, BUT WE HAVE NOT GIVEN UP THE SHIP. LAST NIGHT'S GAME HAD SOME VERY INTERESTING PLAYS. THERE WAS A CATCH FOLLOWED BY AN INDIAN RAIN DANCE BY SLUGGER "THE SCOOP" BROWN, A DIVING SLIDE INTO THIRD FOR NO APPARENT REASON BY 00, AND A COLLISION/CATCH IN THE OUTFIELD BY HOP-ALONG AND BUCKWHEAT WHICH RESULTED IN A KIND OF FUNKY DOUBLE-PLAY. THE HIGH LITE OF THE EVENING WAS THE FINISHING OF THE MILWAUKEE'S BEST BEER. IT SHALL BE LITE FROM NOW ON. OUR GAMES ARE SO COMICAL THAT THEY DESERVE A LOOK BY ANYBODY WHO HAS A NEED TO LAUGH AND HAVE A GOOD TIME.

OUR NEXT GAME IS ON MONDAY, JUNE 13 AT 5:30 PM AT THE REDSTONE FIELD. COME ON OUT AND SUPPORT YOUR TEAM. (BY THE WAY, THE SCORE WAS 15-5).

OUCH!!!

JACK

Jack's next memo reveals another part of the unfolding story:

HOWDY Y'ALL:

IT WENT DOWN TO THE WIRE. WE WERE IN IT UNTIL THE LAST SWING OF THE GAME. BUT IN THE END THE SCORE WAS B-BCSC 11, CAS 15. GAME HIGHLITES INCLUDE A BODY BLOCK BY "GOOSE" GORDON ON 00 (THE "GOZ" MUST THINK SOFTBALL IS A CONTACT SPORT) AND A SPECTACULAR OUT MADE BY TIM "THE STITCH" LEDBEDDER WHEN HE TRIED TO CATCH AN INFIELD FLY WITH HIS NOSE (WE CAN LAUGH ABOUT IT NOW, BUT AT THE TIME IT WAS SERIOUS). WE WENT DOWN SWINGING WITH THE TYING RUN AT BAT. ALL IN ALL IT WAS A FUN TIME FOR EVERYBODY, THOUGH FOR SOME REASON OUR REFRESHMENT CONSUMPTION AFTER THE GAME WAS DOWN.

NEXT GAME: WEDNESDAY, JUN 15, 6:45 PM, CHRYSLER FIELD. BE THERE TO SUPPORT YOUR TEAM.

ALOHA

JACK

The next game is with Teledyne-Brown Engineering, on the Chrysler Field. This is also one of those Alabama midsummer evenings where the temperature hovers around 90. Along with the humidity, there is distant thunder and dry lightning that promises no rain in a summer already wet with humid drought, and everyone sweats a lot. Not a pretty sight. But we are charged with enthusiasm, want to win so badly that we outplay ourselves and our imaginations against a team that clearly expected far less from us. At game's end we win 14-13!

There is general cheering all around as the cold beer and soft drinks are handed out. Our coaches tell us that winning feels better than losing, doesn't it? and that we should remember this feeling, letting it guide us through our remaining games. This is the method-acting approach: Remember the feeling and perform it again.

What I notice is that everyone stays around to party. When we lose, this is not the case. People wander back into their own smaller worlds. They retreat to personal spaces reserved for remembering who you are when you have lost something outside of yourself while in the presence of others and there is a need to keep those borders intact.

This is how a community turns entropic, where the center does not hold. Most notable tonight is that we worked hard, played hard, and won together, and nobody wandered away. There is contrast in this scene, and a social construction of reality that hangs in the air like a single intoxicating breath: *Remember this feeling*.

There is a center here, a rush of warm emotion, laughter, victory, and camaraderie, and it is at least on this one night before the gathering of a distant storm, it is in fact *holding*. Consider Jack's next-day memo:

HOWDY SPORTS FANS:

THE THRILL OF VICTORY . . . HOW SWEET IT IS. YOUR TEAM WON LAST NIGHT, PUTTING TO BED ONCE AND FOR ALL RUMORS THAT WE WERE GOING TO GIVE BALTIMORE A RUN FOR THEIR LATEST RECORD. IT WAS AN EXCITING GAME FILLED WITH MUCH CONTROVERSY. IN FACT, WE WON AFTER HAVING FILED AN OFFICIAL PROTEST WITH THE UMPIRE. MVP FOR THE GAME WAS UNQUESTIONABLY NONE OTHER THAN BIG JIM "OH WHAT A STROKE" BANKS, WITH JIMMIE "THE ZIPPER" DEAL RUNNING A CLOSE 2ND. WINNING PITCHER WAS KATHY "#0" KELLER WITH DR. BUDDY FINISHING THEM OFF WITH SOME KILLER PITCHING. EVERYBODY DESERVES A BIG HAND, ESPECIALLY COACH SMITH AND COACH HENSON. CONGRATULATIONS ARE IN ORDER. THE FINAL SCORE WAS 14-13.

NEXT GAME: MONDAY, JUNE 20TH, 6:45 PM, TELEDYNE-BROWN FIELD AGAINST HILTON SYSTEMS. COME ON OUT TO THE BALL GAME AND CHEER YOUR TEAM ON. LET'S EXTEND THIS WINNING STREAK.

OH WHAT A FEELING

#00

And for a while, a glorious while, we won and did nothing other than continue to win.

12

There are four separate work areas in the new building.

On the first floor, behind the receptionist's area, is the Curriculum Development/Employee Services complex, which includes a large computer room, a modern weight room, and a sauna. Also on the first floor is the Customer Training Area, which includes a customer lounge consistently referred to as "the bordello" by B-BCSCers due to its soft, dim lighting and general ambience. Don't get the wrong idea—nothing like that goes on at B-BCSC.

On the second floor the work area above Curriculum Development/Employee Services is laid out for Support/Marketing/Maintenance/Administration. Also on the second floor, above the Customer Training Area, is Development/Quality Assurance/Testing.

These work areas express an "open office" concept (Klein, 1982) realized by the use of large open stages upon which sit individualized work stations known internally as "cubes" fashioned out of richly textured maroon and gray fabric panels designed to absorb sound and provide visual continuity throughout the office. This concept was first introduced in America in 1968 by Robert Propst of the Herman Miller Company, working from earlier models provided by the German-based Quickborner Team, and has in its brief history been responsible for roughly 50% of the redesign efforts of American organizations (see Klein, 1982, p. 37).

Since its inception, the open office system has attracted both praise and blame. Originally intended as an improved management technique, many workers still feel that it robs them of privacy and status, a view echoed by many employees of B-BCSC when they moved into the new building. Only senior-level managers and the corporate vice president have offices with walls, while everyone else occupies a cubicle.

The new building has six separate restrooms. The old building had one. Common sense suggested that the increase in restroom facilities within the new building would be better, but at what cost? According to Henry Peppertree (the Huntsville branch corporate VP), one cost has been a sense of shared community and communication. People simply no longer talk to each other while waiting for a pit stop, move into each other's work areas less frequently, and therefore have fewer informal exchanges than they did in the old structure.

The concern about a lack of communication is voiced by a number of other employees who attribute part of the problem to the layout of the new building. Divided into four quadrants, each with a special mission and specialized clientele, the new office impedes cross-company talk and encourages a more insular view of who one's colleagues are. Hence persons who work in Development are viewed as different sorts of individuals from those who work in Support, and, because they spend less informal time speaking with each other, there has been a deeper division in expressed attitudes toward the other's contributions. For example, there are constant references to the "support" versus the "development" side of the "house," evidence of a segregation of mental space reserved for what used to be union, a suggestion that there is a pervasive "us" versus "them" where there used to be a "we."

I am being overly polite here. This is a very touchy situation at B-BCSC, and one that fires the emotions of employees faster than anything else. But you, reader, can probably see the pattern without my help. I think anyone could. This pattern reminds us both of our initial, and pressing, questions: Does the stage affect the way in which the actors interpret the scene? Does the arrangement of set pieces, such as cubicles and props, such as decorations of workstations, influence how meanings are attributed to persons and things? Have these become rhetorical questions?

The deeper issue is one of interpretation. How, specifically, do these set pieces and props contribute to the meanings this culture holds for its participants? As I have just suggested, one way into this issue is through the use of language by B-BCSC employees, and the various embedded sensitivities that are contained in those expressions. On the inside there is a striking awareness of what persons and things mean, together.

13

There is significance and magic in numbers. Consider a team that began the season with a surplus of players that at mid-season was down to a critical level and that at season's end was worried it wouldn't have enough to field a team in the playoffs. What are the implications of this? What does it mean?

This was an up-and-down summer, a long season of trying to find the right combination to win, a time when "Oh What a Stroke" Banks continually asked the question: "Are we trying to win or are we just out here to have fun and hope to win?" It was a question that was never really answered. Frustration was evident, player turnout for practices dwindled, and there were barely enough of us to field a team for the last few games. Among the players, factions developed — things were said. The humor disappeared and with it vanished some pride.

The numbers were down and against us.

You could say that although we won three more games, that wasn't enough to inspire confidence. You could say that. You could say that the playoffs were held in early September, on the same weekend as the beginning of dove hunting season and think you've said something important. But you wouldn't have. Or you could look at the numbers as signs of something else in the broader concerns of culture, as signs of magic (or in this case its absence) within the general mystery.

Let's back up. There is more going on here than numbers alone can account for.

Late in the season there is a team party. Everyone is invited, but only a core of players and their spouses come. "Where is so-and-so?" is a question that has no necessary or sufficient answer. During the celebration awards are presented for "most improved player" (Elizabeth "Slugger Brown" Hardy-Brown), "fastest base runner" (Dr. Buddy, which, if you know me, says something other than what the words normally mean), "best swing" (Lauri Deal, who is absent), and "most valuable player" (Jimmie "The Zipper" Deal, who is also absent).

There is significance in all of these awards, both at the time they are given and later. For instance, the MVP award was an issue that found its way into the conversations of several B-BCSCers, even those who did not play on the team or ever go to a single game. The odds-on favorite was Jim "Oh What a Stroke" Banks, easily our best athlete, but who was also the subject of a controversy among some of the players because he "left" an internship at B-BCSC for a paying job at Intergraph but continued to play on our team. Some people believed he didn't get the award because he didn't work for B-BCSC. But then somebody else remembered that neither did "The Zipper"; in fact, he also worked for Intergraph. The controversy deepened when the MVP showed up late for the team awards party and didn't show up at all for any of our playoff games. "Oh What a Stroke" did, to his credit.

The "fun" awards for fastest base runner and best swing were reminiscent of a B-BCSC tradition for giving "gag" awards at public ceremonies that serve two important cultural purposes. First, they "honor" a characteristic that is designed as a corrective to a situation — the fastest base runner wasn't, the best swing was a miss. Second, the award symbolizes acceptance within the culture despite the award winner's obvious flaws. So in a way, the winning of a "fun" award is a mixed message that serves as a transcendent rite of passage. Within the broader cultural context of B-BCSC these awards have included the infamous "Pig" award to male chauvinist of the year and the "Bitch" award for top nag. It has also included, recently and within the stage setting of the new building, a thinly disguised award for "Informed Leadership" to the company's vice president, combined with a "gag" video production that showed he wasn't sure who worked here or what work was being done.

He did not respond favorably, and, although not directly intended as such, each side of the "house" now sponsors its own corporate parties and gives out its own awards. These days no gag awards are allowed to be issued at corporate-sponsored public events. Do symbols of division evident in a vocabulary ultimately lead to real divisions down on the playing field? Is this one way in which subcultures are formed?

And what about the leader, the evangelist who put something larger than himself in motion when he used his rhetorical powers to inspire, to cajole, to fire up, and to define? What happens when said leader fails to be able to see the flaws in himself, refuses to laugh at some admittedly cruel but culturally acceptable shows of affection, and decides to leave immediately after the ceremony and further separate himself from the situation that produced the need for the symbol? Something is definitely wrong. Ditto for the MVP and best swinger who didn't show up for the playoffs.

There were silences and gestures in these moments that I can't capture in words. Correspondences in evolutions. And they stole the whole show.

Persons and things.

This was a losing season. All the numbers, and some of the magic, were against us.

WHAT MEANINGFUL ORDERS OF
PERSONS AND THINGS SUGGESTED TO ME
ABOUT THE EVOLUTION OF CULTURE AT B-BCSC

This is where my voice changes. This is where I put up my glove, put on the old school tie, and begin the formal, academic analysis. In retrospect there seem to be three key ways in which the subtle, nuanced displays of organizational sets, costumes, and properties interacted with the actors to influence communication and establish some aspects of the culture of B-BCSC — Huntsville.

Theatrical Frameworks for
Cultural Depictions of Organizational Personalities

Just as every organization reveals a unique sense of culture, it may be said that every organization also displays a unique "personality." The term *personality* requires scrutiny that evokes a cultural connection. To draw on the writings of Ernest Becker, in a tradition that includes Harry Stack Sullivan, George Herbert Mead, and Karen Horney, the concept of "personality" represents a "locus of sentiments within a phenomenal field" (Becker, 1962, p. 160). It is the narrative given to what is expressed by an actor within a given context over a period of time. It is a story turned out about the reading given to a story within.

"Personality," then, lives in sentences spoken by actors who are, themselves, caught up in the scene. Like interpretations of observable behavior or physical artifacts, evaluations of "personality" reflect an engagement of a particular pattern of meaningful orderings by an analyst trained to find, and to locate meaning in, those patterns (see, for example, Lacan, 1968; Laing, 1965). By analogy, this is akin to an interpretive reading given to a multilingual organizational text from the perspective of a reader capable of responding to only one language. Viewed this way, Geertz's (1973) classic description of culture as "webs of significance spun by ourselves" applies equally well to the narratives we have created about "personality" and "culture."

As cultural narratives, patterns are meaningful orderings to which significance and meaning are attributed. Such attributions are made differently by different readers; this pattern may not change over time, but the attributions of significance and meaning often do. "Personality" within organizations is most often a story told about someone by someone else, a story that is often repeated but in the repetitions certain words, meanings, or symbols are altered or changed to reflect the character of the storyteller more so than the character of the subject of the story.

Given these conditions, what struck me in my study of B-BCSC was the presence of the word *personality* in sentences that connected judgments of persons with judgments of cultural fit. *Personality* was — and still is — a term that defines a person's relationship to the organization's culture, as in the statements "She doesn't have the right personality, she just isn't going to fit in here" and "We knew we would hire her. She's a B-BCSC person." It is as if culture and personality are integrally related, mirror images of each other, a theater of motives in which the dramatic appearance and performances of the players are pitched against an immovable set (set of values?) and whose properties are nonverbal displays of what is never clearly articulated. Cultural "fit," then, is how a player is defined within a space — a stage setting — already filled with significance and significations.

What this suggests is that our approach to studies of how newcomers "fit" into organizational cultures may be missing an important point. What we have done is to share the perspective of the newcomer, in which "surprise and sense-making" seem to wed themselves to a transcendent vision of acceptance if only the newcomer can learn how to "read" the cues, make sense of the sentences spoken by the players, and blend into the surroundings as if camouflaged.

However, what this study suggests is just the opposite. Cultural fit may not be determined by making sense out of one's environment, learning "the ropes to skip and the ropes to know" (Ritti & Funkhauser, 1977) or the other attributes of strategic organizational competence, so much as *to have already what it takes in terms of appearance, costumes, accessories, and uses of set pieces.* Cultural fit, put starkly, may have more to do with theatrical continuity than with strategic competence.

Consider, for example, some of the continuities reflected in the story I have constructed about settings, props, and costumes relevant to the culture of B-BCSC. The cars in the parking lot have changed, but collectively they reveal a common motif, and one that is subtly different from other firms in town. The influence of clothing-as-costume, both at work and when the workers are at play, suggests that to fit into the culture of B-BCSC requires attention to appearances that mark an individual as a "B-BCSCer." Decorations of office space, and particularly decorations that fit the existing pattern of stuff, are important sources of a message about who you are and how you fit in. Collectively, talk is exchanged on the basis of vehicles, clothing, artifacts, and work tasks by persons who have stories to tell, stories that fit into the existing traffic of symbols. Perhaps this is one of the reasons new hires are increasingly products of an internship experience. It is their corporate "tryout," a time to see whether or not they fit into the image B-BCSC has of itself and its employees. The idea is not merely to educate or to train them in the tasks relevant to their work, but to share space with them, take them to lunch, invite them to company functions, sell them on playing for the softball team. The summary judgment of their personality is not one of "Will they make it?" so much as "Are they the right kind of people to work here?"

Within the broader contexts of "personality" and "culture" this alternative view of cultural fit has a strong, if somewhat peculiar, appeal. If a culture is, as my oft-repeated Sahlins definition has it, "meaningful orders of persons and things," and if "personality" is, as Becker's (1962) definition expresses it, "a locus of sentiments within a phenomenal field [representing] a vocabulary of motives" (p. 22), then it is not competence or learning ability that characterizes the ability to fit into a culture, but a personality that already fits the established meaningful orders of persons and things. The judgment of cultural fit is a blend of B-BCSC personality and B-BCSC culture, a sense in which the actor and the set are interdependent. Although the art of the B-BCSC performance is far more than the sum of its set pieces and artifacts — as is any good drama from the perspective of the reader/viewer — it certainly wouldn't be, couldn't be, the same without them.

The Use of Signs and Symbols as Interpretive Bases for Character, Interests, and Flaws

If personality and culture are mirror images of each other in determinations of cultural fit, then it seems reasonable to give deeper significance to how "the locus of sentiments within a phenomenal field" and the "meaningful orders of persons and things" coalesce in and contribute to the readings given to dramatic performances. To do this at B-BCSC requires attention to how meanings are attributed to the various signs and symbols that are used to describe character, interests, and flaws.

What this suggests about our understanding of organizational cultures is subtle, but I hope persuasive. Just as ground gives meaning to figure and vice versa, so properties, costumes, and artifacts give and share in the meanings to the words and actions of the players. Scenes are played out in environments where meaningful symbols derive their powers from culturally shared understandings of character, interests, and flaws. Because I was trained in the field of rhetoric, I cannot help but read into the elements of character, interests, and flaws a modified version of an older text (see Aristotle, 1954) in which *ethos, logos,* and *pathos* further suggest that these elements of the dramatic performance of B-BCSC are best understood as *appeals.* They are inducements to know, to be, and to do (or not to do), a sort of rhetorical spell cast upon an audience with a message that can be read this way because the audience draws its vocabulary from a similarly defined field of cultural motives. Perhaps this communality is why it is better to live with the natives and go to their plays than to simply examine their artifacts in the office or generalize about the meanings of corporate behavior among colleagues if the goal is to write about a specific culture. The things to examine may be the same everywhere, but their meanings are likely to be very different according to the set they are found on. It is not the things, or the persons, but the ways in which meaningful orders of persons and things are put together that ultimately matter.

How Grammar and Vocabulary Distinguish Among
Classes of Employees, Determine Degrees of
Cultural Fit, and Induce an Observer to See
Connections Among Persons and Things and Culture

One of the questions that guided this study was, What do we talk about when we talk about an organization's culture? Another was, What do B-BCSC people talk about when they talk about their organization and the people who work there? I had hoped for answers that held a certain correspondence, and there was one. Our literature acquainted me with the vocabulary of cultural study; my study of B-BCSC's culture showed me how to make a specific grammar from that vocabulary.

When we talk about the culture of an organization, we talk about its stories, its rituals and rites, its hierarchies, its power structure and politics, and, among categories of knowledge, its artifacts. As Tyler (1987) argues, we continue our Western, Platonic tradition of creating words to measure reality, of creating definitions and categories to fit knowledge about that verbal representation into, and of creating modes of reasoning about those words, definitions, and categories that place a heavy emphasis on the *what* rather than the *how* of persons and things. Ours is a knowledge of vocabulary more often than a vocabulary of knowledge.

To get to a vocabulary of knowledge requires more than simply immersing oneself in a culture and letting something happen on the categorical assumption that this is the way it happens so when I name it this will be what it is. It is to immerse oneself in a culture, let something happen, and look for clues. There is a subtle but very important difference at work here. At one end you are happy to describe; at the other end you describe what makes you happy.

The issue is one of rhetorical appeal and a necessary dialectic between the observer and what is observed and recorded, an issue that involves the effects of symbols and performances on us that in turn have us responding to them with the vocabulary we are caught up in. Oddly enough, this response is precisely the same sort of grammatical learning that is always taking place among the actors and within the scene. It is a grammar of motives played out in a theater of motives where everything counts and nothing is ever neutral.

For these reasons it is not the *what* of cultural terminology that intrigues me about B-BCSC. It is *how*, within that theater, I was induced to respond to clues about the meaningful orders of persons and things and culture that encouraged me to be able to distinguish between and make connections to, and to believe that what I was distinguishing and connecting had similar meanings for the persons within that culture.

There is a blending of personal and professional concerns that says something unique about B-BCSC when it is read as a figure against a ground of historical and evolutionary understandings and values that also combine professional and personal concerns. Similarly, as I have tried to display, there is a consistent interplay of persons and things that somehow stands out at B-BCSC. This is a workplace rich with symbols and signs that encourage connections to be made between them and their uses and the persons who create and constitute their meanings.

One final observation on my own observations. As I pointed out earlier in this essay, I am never neutral. So it is with a sense of selectivity that I responded to the various and changing cues reported within this study. My experiences as a softball player, for example, added up to something more than they might have had I not also been involved in studying the culture of this organization. And no doubt my study of this organization's culture was influenced by my wife's position within the company, her friends' attitudes toward what persons and things represented and meant, the experiences of our university's interns at B-BCSC, and the fact that when I was there, things seemed to happen that may have happened differently, or not at all, when I wasn't there.

A culture — any culture — is like an ocean. There are many wonderful things and creatures in it that we may never understand; they change and so do we, regardless of the depth or perspective of our study. But the ocean is also made out of waves that are as regular as the cycles of the moon, and just as mysteriously musical, powerful, and enchanting. The top millimeter of the ocean is a world unto itself, and a vital one, in which the broader secrets of biological and evolutionary life itself are contained. But even their meanings must be read in a vocabulary that is separate and distant from it. So it is that within that millimeter, and watching those waves, there are clear and recurring themes. Like the great questions about culture that we pursue, these themes are always with us and not yet fully understood.

NOTE

1. This block quote and those that follow referenced to 1986 are from my field notes of that period.

REFERENCES

Ardrey, R. (1967). *The territorial imperative.* New York: Atheneum.

Ardrey, R. (1970). *The social contract.* New York: Atheneum.

Aristotle (1954). *The rhetoric and poetics* (W. R. Roberts, Trans.). New York: Modern Library.

Becker, E. (1962). *The birth and death of meaning.* New York: Free Press.

Beyer, J. M., & Trice, H. M. (1987). How an organization's rites reveal its culture. *Organizational Dynamics, 15,* 4-25.

Calas, M. B., & Smircich, L. (1987). Reading leadership as a form of cultural analysis. In J. L. Hunt, R. Baliga, C. Schriesheim, & P. Dachler (Eds.), *Emerging leadership vistas* (pp. 201-226). Lexington, MA: Lexington.

Cheney, G. (1983). On the various and changing meanings of organizational membership. *Communication Monographs, 50,* 342-362.

Clifford, J., & Marcus, G. E. (Eds.). (1986). *Writing culture: The poetics and politics of ethnography.* Berkeley: University of California Press.

Eisenberg. E. M. (1984). Ambiguity as strategy in organizational communication. *Communication Monographs, 51,* 227-242.

Geertz, C. (1973). *The interpretation of culture*. New York: Basic Books.

Geertz, C. (1983). *Local knowledge*. New York: Basic Books.

Geertz, C. (1988). *Works and lives*. Palo Alto, CA: Stanford University Press.

Goffman, E. (1959). *The presentation of self in everyday life*. Garden City, NY: Anchor.

Goodall, H. L. (1989). *Casing a promised land: The autobiography of an organizational detective as cultural ethnographer*. Carbondale: Southern Illinois University Press.

Gregg, R. B. (1971). The ego-function of the rhetoric of protest. *Philosophy & Rhetoric, 4,* 71-91.

Kantner, R. M. (1977). *Men and women of the corporation*. New York: Basic Books.

Klein, J. G. (1982). *The office book: Ideas and designs for contemporary work spaces*. New York: Facts on File.

Lacan, J. (1968). *The language of the self: The function of language in psychoanalysis*. Baltimore: Johns Hopkins University Press.

Laing, R. D. (1965). *The divided self*. Hammondsworth: Penguin.

Louis, M. L. (1980). Surprise and sense-making: What newcomers experience in entering unfamiliar organizational settings. *Administrative Science Quarterly, 23,* 225-251.

Lurie, A. (1981). *The language of clothes*. New York: Random House.

Mangham, I. L., & Overington, M. A. (1987). *Organizations as theatre: A social psychology of dramatic appearances*. New York: John Wiley.

Miles, E. M., & Leathers, D. G. (1984). The impact of aesthetic and professionally-related objects on credibility in the office setting. *Southern Speech Communication Journal, 49,* 361-379.

Morgan, G. (1986). *Images of organization*. Beverly Hills, CA: Sage.

Pacanowsky, M. E. (1984, November). *Slouching towards Chicago*. Paper presented at the annual meeting of the Speech Communication Association, Chicago.

Pacanowsky, M. E., & O'Donnell-Trujillo, N. (1983). Organizational communication as cultural performance. *Communication Monographs, 50,* 126-147.

Ritti, R. R., & Funkhauser, G. R. (1977). *The ropes to skip and the ropes to know: Studies in organizational behavior*. Columbus, OH: Grid.

Sackmann, S. (1987, July). *Beyond cultural artifacts*. Paper presented at the ICA/SCA Conference on Interpretive Approaches to the Study of Organizations, Alta, UT.

Sahlins, M. (1976). *Culture and practical reason*. Chicago: University of Chicago Press.

Sennett, R. (1977). *The fall of public man*. New York: Vintage.

Smircich, L., & Stubbart, C. I. (1985). Strategic management in an enacted world. *Academy of Management Review, 10,* 724-736.

Tyler, S. A. (1987). *The unspeakable: Discourse, dialogue, and rhetoric in the postmodern world*. Madison: University of Wisconsin Press.

Van Maanen, J. (1988). *Tales of the field: On writing ethnography*. Chicago: University of Chicago Press.

Weick, K. (1979). *The social psychology of organizing* (2nd ed.). Reading, MA: Addison-Wesley.

Rhetoric and the Display of Organizational Ethnographies

CHARLES CONRAD
Texas A&M University

PROFESSOR Goodall's essay raises at least four important issues facing scholars who are interested in developing interpretive accounts of symbolic action in formal organizations. First, his focus on "nonverbal" elements of organizations comments upon and adds to a growing literature that has examined the cultural implications of the physical trappings of various organizational ceremonies (Smircich, 1983; Walter, 1983), the ways in which nonverbal displays support the dominant metaphors of organizations (Barley, 1983), the ways in which "physical humor" contributes to the meanings employees attach to work (Boland & Hoffman, 1983), and the impact that change in physical environment has on the taken-for-granted assumptions of a culture and on patterns of communication (Wilkins, 1989). Although the essay does not provide as extensive an analysis as Rosen's (1985) classic study of the ways in which organizational power relationships are simultaneously revealed and reinforced by physical displays, it establishes a potentially productive direction for communication scholars.

Second, presenting the softball team as a representative anecdote (Burke, 1945a) of the organization's overall culture, Goodall raises important questions about how researchers should grapple with organizational actors' simultaneous involvement in multiple, overlapping cultures or subcultures (Evered & Louis, 1981; Louis, 1983). Although maintaining morale in the face of minimal fan/worker support, dealing with lack of commitment by key workers/players, and so on may be interpreted as indications of the overall culture of the organization, they also may reflect problems inherent in the maintenance of voluntary organizations (like softball teams).

Correspondence and requests for reprints: Charles Conrad, Department of Speech and Theatre, Texas A&M University, College Station, TX 77843.

Communication Yearbook 13, pp. 95-106

Third, the essay implicitly focuses attention on the very difficult task of reducing an extended cultural study to book or article length. The question is not one of whether or not textual data should be reduced, for the nature of the research process makes reduction inevitable. The question is how a researcher can create reductions that are representative of organizational actors' acts and interpretations (Burke, 1945; see also Conrad, 1984). Rhetorical critics, particularly those concerned with the rhetoric of movements or of extended persuasive campaigns, long have grappled with this issue, but it is a relatively recent concern for organizational communication scholars.

Finally, Professor Goodall explicitly raises issues about the forms of discourse through which ethnographic accounts can and/or should be displayed. Anthropologists Marcus and Cushman (1982) explain the role of mode of display in ethnographic research:

> Ethnographic description is by no means the straightforward, unproblematic task it is thought to be in the social sciences, but a complex effect, achieved through writing and dependent upon the strategic choice and construction of available detail. The presentation of interpretation and analysis is inseparably bound up with the systematic and vivid representation of a world that seems total and real to the reader. (p. 29)

In academic disciplines in which ethnographic case studies have had a lengthy history (e.g., anthropology), an extended debate has arisen about the proper use of "literary" modes of presenting social scientific data (Van Maanen, 1988, especially chap. 1). In disciplines that have more recently discovered ethnographic research (e.g., sociology and history), the debate has been less extensive, but the issues are largely the same (Clifford & Marcus, 1986; Giddens, 1979; White, 1973). In disciplines that only recently have embraced qualitative/interpretive research (e.g., organizational theory and organizational communication), there has been relatively little published analysis of the epistemic considerations underlying nontraditional modes of displaying data.[1] My goal in the remainder of this commentary is to stimulate dialogue about this important issue. I will approach the topic by adopting three "voices" — those of an advocate of narrative displays of ethnographic research, a skeptical but sympathetic social scientist, and a concerned but interested critical theorist.

A VOICE OF ADVOCACY

In *Tales of the Field*, John Van Maanen (1988) summarizes the key assumption underlying nontraditional modes of display: "An ethnography is a means of representation. Yet any claim to directly link fieldwork (and the immediacy of its experience) to the ethnography itself, unmediated or untransformed by narrative conventions, will not hold" (p. 7). When ethnographic researchers are faced with a choice between traditional and narrative modes of display, the issue is not one of achieving objectivity, because advocates of ethnographic research generally assume that positivist notions of the independence of subject and object are unjustifiable. Instead, the goal is to re-create faithfully the researcher's experiences with and in the culture examined.

Advocates of narrative forms of display claim three advantages for the approach. First, narrative forms of display can invite readers to participate (as individuals) in the culture being studied. Of course, readers' participation is not equivalent to direct involvement in the culture. However, narrative displays place less distance between reader and actor than do more traditional modes — those presenting raw data or summarizing aggregated (or other forms of abstracted) findings (Krieger, 1983; Strine & Pacanowsky, 1985). Narrative modes minimize the need to remove organizational actions from their temporal context and eliminate the distortions inherent in transforming situated actions into entries in abstract category systems. As a result, narrative forms of display allow the researcher to preserve the emotional tone of the culture and to reveal uniquenesses that differentiate one culture from others (Krieger, 1983, p. 183; Pacanowsky, 1988, p. 454). In Van Maanen's (1988) terms, "artful ethnography is evocative in addition to being factual and truthful" (p. 34).[2]

Second, narrative forms allow for the effective representation of *patterns* of action that exist within cultural data without reifying those patterns (Whyte, 1955, appendix). Finally, skillfully crafted narrative accounts can simultaneously juxtapose multiple "readings" of ethnographic texts (Strine & Pacanowsky, 1985). Although more traditional modes of display do not inevitably privilege one interpretation of "reality" over others, narrative forms provide an enhanced opportunity to weave differing interpretations together in ways that reveal the tensions that exist among them.

Van Maanen (1988) has described three approaches that sociologists in general and organizational ethnographers in particular have taken to create evocative displays of organizational texts: realist, confessional, and impressionist. These modes can be differentiated from one another along two interrelated dimensions: (a) the form of authority claimed by the narrator and (b) the form of evidence provided (see Table 1).[3] In realistic ethnography, the author severs the ethnographic text from his or her analysis of that text. Text and analysis may be separated spatially in the display, either by presenting the text first and then the analysis or by inserting interpretive comments into the text in boldface, in boxes, or in some otherwise demarcated form. The voice of the narrator is that of a "sober, civil, legal, dry, serious, dedicated, straightforward transcriber" (Van Maanen, 1988, p. 55). Textual evidence is carefully selected, edited, and presented in a way that maximally enhances the credibility of the author's interpretation: "Realist tales are not multivocal texts where an event is given meaning first in one way, then in another, and then another. . . . Little can be discovered in such texts that has not been put there by the fieldworker as a way of supporting a particular interpretation" (Van Maanen, 1988, pp. 52-53). The narrator's authority depends on her or his

TABLE 1
Van Maanen's Typology

Type of Display	Form of Authority	Mode of Presentation
Realist	narrator's experience; criterion of sufficiency	details of observations structured conceptually, rather than temporally
Confessional	personal, self-absorbed narrator/translator; criterion of verisimilitude	displays of empathy and involvement; confessions of difficulty maintaining distance
Impressionist	ambivalent/confused narrator; criterion of plausibility	dialogue through dramatic recall; fragmented structure with identifiable characters

ability to fulfill a criterion of sufficiency, that is, to provide readers with textual evidence of sufficient scope, detail, and redundancy to legitimize the single interpretation. Conversely, univocal, detailed textual data create pressures for the narrator to take on the persona of a relatively uninvolved transcriber.

In confessional tales, the narrator is a personal and self-absorbed student of the actors in a cultural scene. The narrator's voice is one of a translator. She or he explicitly discusses problems of getting "too close" to the actors to retain an independent perspective and of being "too detached" to understand. Expressions of empathy and involvement are interspersed with distantly analytical commentaries in an effort to maintain an appropriate degree of distance (Van Maanen, 1988, pp. 76-81). This narrator's authority depends on his or her ability to meet a criterion of verisimilitude; his or her problem lies in persuading readers that the texts created are "in fact authentic, natural, useful for analytical purposes, and more or less untainted by the fieldworker's touch" (p. 76).

In impressionistic tales, an ambivalent, confused, and/or perplexed narrator enters into a "conspiracy" with readers to construct a plausible interpretation of events. The form of the narrative is one of dramatic recall; its structure is fragmented, characters are given specific, detailed identities. The goal of impressionistic narration is to allow the audience to "see, hear, and feel" events as they occurred to the narrator. The narrator's authority is grounded in his or her ability to make a particular structuring of events seem plausible, with plausibility grounded in the coherence and interestingness of the text and fidelity with the readers' own reconstructed experiences. However, the authority stems from the success of the narrator's invitation to the audience to engage in a text-constructing dialogue, not in the details of the narration itself.

Van Maanen's typology suggests that a wide range of narrative options are available to ethnographers. It also suggests that narrative displays will be credible only to the degree that they fulfill three formal requirements. First, narrative forms must not obscure the impact that the researcher's own perspective has on her or his interpretations of a culture (Krieger, 1983). More important is that the recursive process through which researchers construct hypothetical explanations of actions, revise those expectations when confronted with inexplicable cultural data, and alter their frames of reference in the process ought not to be (but ordinarily is) omitted from the narrative form (Fine, 1984). Second, narrative forms of display should not suppress or obscure the multiplicity of readings possible with all cultural texts (Brown, 1977; Griswold, 1987). Although this problem may be more acute with forms of narration that "claim" omniscience for the narrator, a distinctive feature of narrative displays is the ability to present a "polyphonic authority," to invite readers to "orchestrate an open dialogic interaction" among multiple possible interpretations of ethnographic data (Strine & Pacanowsky, 1985, p. 297).

Third, authors must fulfill the differing evidentiary requirements established by different forms of narration. Modes of display differ from one another in terms of what Burke has called the "psychology" of the text. Burke (1931/1968) differentiates texts that draw their persuasive power from a "psychology of information" from those that rely on a "psychology of form" (pp. 29-44). The form of a text, he argues, creates expectations in the minds of auditors that must be fulfilled by the details of the text. The persuasive power of a text and its perceived legitimacy as a symbolic act depend on these formal expectations being, in Burke's terminology, "completed" (see Strine & Pacanowsky, 1985, p. 296). Realist tales rely on the psychology of information and persuade by arousing feelings of suspense in their readers and fulfilling those expectations through surprise (Burke, 1931/1968, p. 36). In such tales, the focus of attention is more on the hero (characters) than on the audience. Textual evidence that describes characters through their multiple, complex, and sometimes incoherent/inconsistent (i.e., human) actions adds credence to this form of display.

Impressionistic tales, in contrast, rely on the psychology of form and gain their persuasive power from their "eloquence," a covering term that for Burke means using dramatic structure and personae with a focus on the audience and its emotions. Textual details allow readers to help the narrator manage the incoherence/inconsistencies of his or her interpretations of cultural life. Confessional tales create both kinds of expectations, and thus entail a doubly difficult set of evidential demands.[4] When the narrator's voice, the details of the text (including supporting evidence), and the form of authority claimed by the text are congruent with one another, any number of forms of display may be persuasive. But each dimension of narrative form creates expectations about the other dimensions, making the "telling" of ethnographic tales a challenging undertaking indeed.

A SOCIAL SCIENTIST'S VOICE

To this point, my analysis has presumed that choosing among potential modes of ethnographic display is complicated only by intrinsic factors — the need to manage the narrator's distance from the ethnographic text, to sustain a polyphonic narrative authority, and to fulfill formal demands on textual evidence. Strine and Pacanowsky (1985) have suggested that confronting these considerations is only part of the narrative ethnographer's task:

> The form of discourse chosen is probably influenced as much by the professional audience for whom the audience writes as by the desire for accuracy in representing understanding and insight. Quite often, the professional constraints on scholarly representation become primary in determining the discursive form that ethnography will take. (p. 287)

When the audience is heterogeneous, choosing among potential modes of display becomes particularly problematic. For the organizational ethnographer, the very different concerns of two potential groups of auditors — social scientists and critical theorists — are relevant.[5]

Ethnographic researchers face an exceptionally complex rhetorical problem when they address an audience of social scientists. Their "data" are inherently subjective:

> The fieldworker's personal relationships constitute the primary data of anthropological research, but also . . . in the process of self-reflection, they [the personal relationships] are the epistemological base from which interpretations and claims . . . originate. . . . It is not a question of breaking the hermeneutic circle, but of how this circle is to be represented in a genre of writing which continues to have a priority concern with knowledge of "the other" rather than of "the self." (Marcus, 1980, p. 508)

As Whyte (1955) has suggested, a researcher-narrator's theory (which, in this case, encompasses both the narrator's assumptions about cultural analysis and the culture being observed *and* her or his experience with cultural texts) is left implicit in the structure of the story (also see Krieger, 1983, pp. 184-185). Theory must be inferred by a sensitive reader from formal and structural characteristics because it is not explicitly articulated in a description of originating assumptions.

The problem, Krieger (1983) concludes, is that

> making a world seem compelling, actual, rich, as if made of fact — may obscure the knowledge that the reality conveyed by a study, no matter how coherent or compelling, is a fiction. It is an interpretation. . . . We [readers] may not be able to see a world "out there" separate from the study's depiction. The second problem, which is the inverse of the first, is that we may also have difficulty separating such a study's interpretation from its evidence. The study's specificity may blur or even seem to

> bury the work's fictional structure, making its assumptions and organizing principles unclear. Together these twin problems . . . seem threatening to social science, since social science, at least individually, is committed to the explicit articulation of assumptions and to the separation of data from theory. Social science does not rest easy with theory that is inextricably intertwined with the forms of everyday life. (p. 180)

In short, the problem facing a researcher-narrator is simultaneously to avoid solipsism and positivism (Manning, 1979, p. 660), and to do so with an audience that is exceptionally sensitive to the possibility of a researcher imposing her or his interpretive frame on the actions of cultural actors and exceptionally concerned about the potential for obscuring deterministic readings of cultural texts in the structure of their displays of those texts.

The magnitude of this challenge is accented by a brief examination of contemporary narrative theory. Narrative ethnographies are a subset of what contemporary literary theorists call "realistic fiction." Their credibility depends on the author's ability to establish and maintain an acceptable dialogue with readers about "how to go about reality construction" (Goldknopf, 1972, p. 193). Usually narrative ethnographers choose to employ some variant of first-person narration, a choice that is appropriate because this point of view entails almost unlimited temporal flexibility: "It can contract a long time span; it can also expand the instant" (Cohn, 1978, p. 38). Consequently, first-person narration allows an organizational ethnographer to collapse a lengthy and detailed field study into a manageable and persuasive whole. When the organization being examined is involved in substantial structural and/or cultural change, first-person narration is particularly appropriate. Employees do not grasp the implications of change, nor do they accept those implications, at the same instant. Even if the researcher finds that there are stable patterns of change in employees' taken-for-granted cultural assumptions, a literal representation of each employee's shift in perspective would obscure the overall pattern. First-person narration allows the ethnographer to collapse these differences into a sensible overall description. However, this choice of point of view holds important implications for the author/narrator-reader relationship and for the actors depicted in the narration.

Symbolic acts that rely on the psychology of form are credible only if an "illusion of reality" is created and sustained. As Henry James recognized almost a century ago, the presence of a retrospective first-person narrator places an identified persona between the reader and the text, and thus undermines the illusion (Friedman, 1967, p. 113). The voice and tone of the narrator dominate the details of the text, and the potential persuasive power of textual information is reduced. For an audience whose prior expectations involve the psychology of information, the presence of the narrator makes it unlikely that their expectations will be fulfilled. In short, narratives about "real life" inherently transform "real persons" into realistic fictional characters by revealing their "hidden sides" (Cohn, 1978, pp. 4-6). The ethnographer thus becomes a fabricator (Griswold, 1987).

When the narrator also explicitly or implicitly claims omniscience by speculating about the character's thoughts and feelings (their taken-for-granted assumptions in the case of studies of organizational cultures), the authority of the text begins to depend wholly on the credibility of the omniscient narrator. But claims of omniscience in themselves threaten the narrator's credibility. Most characters slowly earn the audience's trust as autonomous, objective witnesses. But the

> I-character claims this autonomy by virtue of his egoism. . . . This strut of I is what we [the audience] resent. . . . We do not question in advance I's introspective competence. . . . But against I's advantage in reporting his inner life, we must balance his opacity to third-person investigation. (Goldknopf, 1972, pp. 27, 29)

The ethnographer/narrator thus faces a difficult dilemma. The postpositivist audience expects her or him to be introspective, to develop some degree of self-objectification. But, if the narrator offers "the processes of his mind as a primary object of attention, his mode of writing is nonrealistic" (Goldknopf, 1972, p. 187). The "technical problem which this situation creates should be clear. We know about 'I' only what he chooses to tell us, but if what he tells us seems to have a motive of self-objectification, he may aggravate our doubts as to his reliability" (p. 28). This reliability is reduced further by claims of omniscience, because only authors of fictional work have sufficient license to make these claims (Hopkins, in press, p. 12). The audience enters into the hermeneutic circle with its attention focused on displays of "self," not the actions of "others." Audience expectations are violated rather than fulfilled.

A choice of first-person retrospective narration (omniscient or not) also creates complications for the characters/actors in the text. Not only do highly visible, omniscient or partially omniscient, first-person narrators focus attention on themselves, they focus attention away from the characters in the narrative. As a result, the characters tend to be relatively undeveloped and often rather shallow (Cohn, 1978, p. 25), thereby undermining the persuasive potential inherent in the psychology of information. The credibility of the narrative account must rest on "eloquence," which makes the problems described in the previous paragraphs even more relevant.

This incongruity between formal and evidential requirements is particularly pressing when, as in Professor Goodall's narrative, the narrator maintains a distant (or dissonant) relationship with the characters and/or reveals insights into the situation or characters through *ex cathedra* statements. For example, Goodall concludes that "this is a game in which attitude is very important," and then contrasts "popular" views that attitude is a function of appearance, that others "crave surface satisfactions" (p. 76). He differentiates symbols that are "meaningful" to employees from those that are not (p. 77). Even the narrator's overall claim, that "what this [the rules and regulations of the softball game] means to the game it also reflects in the [organizational] culture," is offered from a position of omniscient insight. Again, the effect is to lead the reader "into" the hermeneutic circle at the author's position, and to deemphasize the dialogic process that makes hermeneutic perspectives most revealing.

However, these problems might be offset in two ways. First, the narrator can surrender his or her omniscience (Friedman, 1967, p. 125). The surrender can be implemented by introducing dialogue between the narrator and the characters by, for example, interviewing the characters, asking for their perceptions of the "reality" that defines the organizational culture, or by introducing secondary evidence (e.g., documents, letters, and so on) that supports multiple interpretations. Of course, this approach moves the display toward a greater reliance on the "psychology of information" and thereby risks transforming a narrative display into a more traditional form of ethnographic writing. But it does provide a cultural researcher with a means of maintaining credibility and establishing authority while retaining the advantages of narrative form.

A second solution is for the narrator to disappear entirely. One means of removing the narrator from narrative ethnography was illustrated in Krieger's *Hip Capitalism* (1979), a narrative account of organizational change in a radio station that is made up solely of statements by organizational actors arranged in a sequence and pattern that establishes a narrative form.[6] Cohn (1978) notes that narrative fiction is inherently paradoxical: It has the greatest "air of reality" in the symbol of a lone actor thinking thoughts that she or he will never communicate (p. 7). Presenting fieldwork as "truths" articulated by actors, unmediated by the ethnographer's interpretations, may be as alienating for the researcher's audience as imposing a distant, omniscient, first-person narrator. In addition, removing the narrator/ethnographer entirely ignores the very real issues of distance and "objectivity" that concern the social science audience.[7]

A CRITICAL THEORIST'S VOICE

Thompson (1984) notes that

> Ideology, insofar as it seeks to sustain relations of domination by representing them as "legitimate," tends to assume a narrative form. Stories are told which justify the exercise of power by those who possess it, situating individuals within a tissue of tales that recapitulate the past and anticipate the future. (p. 11)

The narratives articulated by organizational actors establish a context within which events are interpreted, that is, they privilege a particular symbolic reality by predisposing listeners toward certain interpretations and against others. In addition, narrative structure creates anticipations that, when fulfilled (i.e., when the form is completed), produce affective, cathartic experiences for the reader/listener. Organizational experiences are redefined and reexperienced through participation in the narrative process. The implicit rules of storytelling are unlike those of nonnarrative discourse in that there is no norm of "turn-taking" or of a dialectic of "claim and counterclaim" (Witten, 1988). The power of a story's claim to represent reality is linked to its formal characteristics, its coherence, fullness, and sense of closure (White, 1978).

Consequently, developing a critical perspective on the discourse of organizational actors begins with processes of deconstructing organizational texts, of acting "to challenge the perceptual closure that narrative often presents, . . . to show that narrative and the politics of experience are inextricably linked" (Mumby, 1988, p. 109; see also Deetz, 1984; Perrow, 1981). The goal of textual deconstruction is not to privilege a different reality, but to reveal the ideological functions of organizational discourse itself.

Narratives articulated about organizational actors share the characteristics of narratives articulated by organizational actors. They inevitably are preinterpreted because they are located within a particular social and economic power structure. They inherently privilege one interpretation because they allow the narrator to intercede in the organizational actors' story(ies) by making notations within the narration regarding elements of the action that the reader/listener cannot see or hear (Fine, 1984). Even when the narration presents multiple voices, the narrative form invites reader/listeners to transcend the multiplicity and construct a synthetic (and thus privileged) "moral" for the story (Jameson, 1981; Mumby, 1988). Goodall's explicitly polyphonic narration is filled with explicit directions about how the text should be interpreted: "Persons and things must be read *together*" (p. 79). Finally, narratives articulated about organizational actors may function to reduce the potential for dialogue through creating pressures for narrative closure. Thus narrative forms of display may serve to perpetuate a noncritical organizational theory (Benson, 1977) rather than to emancipate it. At the very least, narrative displays invite a deconstructionist response.

CONCLUDING THOUGHTS

My goal in this brief essay has been to outline some of the complexities involved in narrative displays of organizational ethnographies. I have used Professor Goodall's essay as a point of departure for these comments, but I do not intend to suggest that his effort at narrative ethnography is any more or less problematic than those of other scholars. Indeed, I hope to have indicated that attempting to display ethnographic research in nontraditional modes is an exceptionally complex activity, one that is difficult because of the nature of the task itself. Those scholars who have made the effort deserve both accolades for making that effort and a little awe for the magnitude of the task they have accepted. For, in the end, "presentational" modes of ethnographic display may be inherently problematic. To be wholly reliable and credible, narrative ethnographies must make an omniscient leap—they must portray organizational actors as lone figures thinking uncommunicated thoughts. But reliability and credibility depend on achieving a unique kind of dialogue among audience, researcher, and displayed text and on eschewing claims of omniscience.

NOTES

1. Examples of organizational ethnographies displayed in narrative form are available in Jermier (1985) and Pacanowsky (1983, 1988). A summary of the place of these displays in organizational communication research is available in Conrad (1985). Key sources for discussions of issues of ethnographic display are Clifford and Marcus (1986), sociology; White (1973), history; Brown (1977), sociology; and Van Maanen (1988), organizational theory. Typically, these sources rely heavily on four works on narrative theory: Booth's *The Rhetoric of Fiction* (1961), Burke's *The Rhetoric of Motives* (1945b), Frye's *Anatomy of Criticism* (1957), and Mitchell's *On Narrative* (1980).

2. For an excellent example, see Pacanowsky (1983).

3. This is the interpretive frame that I employ in reading Van Maanen.

4. This is paradoxical because a concern for distance leads social scientists to employ confessional modes in order to reduce demands for objectivity.

5. I have chosen not to adopt a voice of a traditional positivist, not because positivists do not impose demands on ethnographic researchers but because adapting narrative displays to meet those concerns is nearly impossible.

6. For an analysis of audience reactions to this form, see Krieger (1983, appendix).

7. It also raises a host of issues about the reliability of third-person narration of ethnographic texts; see Cohn (1978) and Marcus and Cushman (1982).

REFERENCES

Barley, S. (1983). Semiotics and the study of occupational and organizational cultures. *Administrative Science Quarterly, 28,* 393-413.

Benson, J. K. (1977). Organizations: A dialectical view. *Administrative Science Quarterly, 22,* 1-21.

Boland, R., & Hoffman, R. (1983). Humor in a machine shop. In L. Pondy, P. Frost, G. Morgan, & T. Dandridge (Eds.), *Organizational symbolism* (pp. 187-193). Greenwich, CT: JAI.

Booth, W. (1961). *The rhetoric of fiction.* Chicago: University of Chicago Press.

Brown, R. (1977). *A poetic for sociology.* Cambridge: Cambridge University Press.

Burke, K. (1945a). *A grammar of motives.* Berkeley: University of California Press.

Burke, K. (1945b). *The rhetoric of motives.* Berkeley: University of California Press.

Burke, K. (1968). *Counter-statement.* Berkeley: University of California Press. (Original work published 1931)

Clifford, J., & Marcus, G. (Eds.). (1986). *Writing culture.* Berkeley: University of California Press.

Cohn, D. (1978). *Transparent minds.* Princeton, NJ: Princeton University Press.

Conrad, C. (1984). Phases, pentads and dramatistic critical process. *Central States Speech Journal, 35,* 94-104.

Conrad, C. (1985). Chrysanthemums and swords. *Southern Journal of Speech Communication, 50,* 189-200.

Deetz, S. (1984). The politics of the oral interpretation of literature. *Literature in Performance, 4,* 60-64.

Evered, R., & Louis, M. (1981). Alternative perspectives in the organizational sciences. *Academy of Management Review, 6,* 385-395.

Fine, E. (1984). *The folklore text.* Bloomington: Indiana University Press.

Friedman, N. (1967). Point of view in fiction. In P. Stevick (Ed.), *The theory of the novel* (pp. 206-224). New York: Free Press.

Frye, N. (1957). *Anatomy of criticism.* Princeton, NJ: Princeton University Press.

Giddens, A. (1979). *Contemporary problems in social theory.* Berkeley: University of California Press.

Goldknopf, D. (1972). *The life of the novel.* Chicago: University of Chicago Press.

Griswold, W. (1987). The fabrication of meaning. *American Journal of Sociology, 5,* 1077-1117.

Gusfield, J. (1976). The literary rhetoric of science. *American Sociological Review, 41,* 16-34.

Gusfield, J., & Michalowicz, J. (1984). Secular symbolism. *Annual Review of Sociology, 10,* 417-435.

Hopkins, M. (in press). Some sites and sightings of narrative theory in the eighties. *Text and Performance Quarterly.*

Jameson, F. (1981). *The political unconscious.* Ithaca, NY: Cornell University Press.

Jermier, J. (1985). When the sleeper wakes: A short story extending themes in radical organization theory. *Journal of Management, 11,* 67-80.

Krieger, S. (1979). *Hip capitalism.* Beverly Hills, CA: Sage.

Krieger, S. (1983). *The mirror dance.* Philadelphia: Temple University Press.

Louis, M. (1983). Organizations as culture-bearing mileaux. In L. Pondy, P. Frost, G. Morgan, & T. Dandridge (Eds.), *Organizational symbolism* (pp. 39-54). Greenwich, CT: JAI.

Manning, P. (1979). Metaphors of the field. *Administrative Science Quarterly, 24,* 660-671.

Marcus, G. (1980). Rhetoric and the ethnographic genre in anthropological research. *Current Anthropology, 21,* 507-510.

Marcus, G., & Cushman, D. (1982). Ethnographies as texts. *Annual Review of Anthropology, 11,* 25-69.

Mitchell, W. (Ed.). (1980). *On narrative.* Chicago: University of Chicago Press.

Mumby, D. (1988). *Communication and power in organizations: Discourse, ideology and domination.* Norwood, NJ: Ablex.

Pacanowsky, M. (1983). A small town cop. In L. Putnam & M. Pacanowsky (Eds.), *Communication and organizations: An interpretive approach* (pp. 261-282). Beverly Hills, CA: Sage.

Pacanowsky, M. (1988). Slouching toward Chicago. *Quarterly Journal of Speech, 74,* 453-467.

Perrow, C. (1981). Deconstructing social science. *New York University Educational Quarterly, 12,* 2-9.

Rosen, M. (1985). Breakfast at Spiro's: Dramaturgy and dominance. *Journal of Management, 11*(2), 31-48.

Sanday, P. (1979). The ethnographic paradigm(s). *Administrative Science Quarterly, 24,* 527-538.

Smircich, L. (1983). Organizations as shared meanings. In L. Pondy, P. Frost, G. Morgan, & T. Dandridge (Eds.), *Organizational symbolism* (pp. 53-68). Greenwich, CT: JAI.

Strine, M. S., & Pacanowsky, M. (1985). How to read interpretive accounts of organizational life. *Southern Speech Communication Journal, 50,* 283-297.

Thompson, J. B. (1984). *Studies in the theory of ideology.* Berkeley: University of California Press.

Van Maanen, J. (1988). *Tales of the field: On writing ethnography.* Chicago: University of Chicago Press.

Walter, G. (1983). Psyche and symbol. In L. Pondy, P. Frost, G. Morgan, & T. Dandridge (Eds.), *Organizational symbolism* (pp. 257-272). Greenwich, CT: JAI.

White, H. (1973). *Metahistory.* Baltimore: Johns Hopkins University Press.

White, H. (1978). *Tropics of discourse.* Baltimore: Johns Hopkins University Press.

Whyte, W. F. (1955). *Street corner society.* Chicago: University of Chicago Press.

Wilkins, A. (1989). *Molding corporate character.* San Francisco: Jossey-Bass.

Witten, M. (1988, May). *Storytelling and obedience at the workplace.* Paper presented at the annual meeting of the International Communication Association, Chicago.

A View from Within: An Insider's Reflection on the Effect of Relocation

SANDRA SANFORD
University of Utah

I AM a writer. I do not write the sort of books or articles most of you would be interested in or familiar with. I write technical documentation for the mainframe computer company that was the focus of Goodall's article. The manuals I write are long, tedious documents full of technical jargon. The work is not why I stay with B-BCSC, it is not what gets me up in the morning or keeps me motivated during the day, neither is the money. What have kept me at B-BCSC are the people and the organization.

Mine is an insider's reflection; it is what I have worked and lived. It is meant to be viewed alongside Goodall's chapter, keeping in mind we have different perspectives. It is not being presented to challenge his perspective, but to enhance it, to modify it in some places and to clarify it in others. His tale is an impressionistic rendering, mine is a confession (Van Maanen, 1988).

In his piece, Goodall tells the tale of an organization in the midst of change. There are a number of reasons I can give for the changes B-BCSC has undergone and is undergoing—none seems textbook, none is black and white. It could have been the move to the new building and what the move represented; it could have been Henry Peppertree's influence on and manipulation of the corporate culture; or it could have been the simple evolution every company eventually must go through, which means shifting from a people and customer orientation to a budget and bottom-line orientation. It could also be a combination of all of these. What I present here are further observations, additional insights, another perspective. These can be used to form conclusions or to add to the ever-growing body of knowledge about how and why organizations work.

Correspondence and requests for reprints: Sandra Sanford, Department of Communication, University of Utah, Salt Lake City, UT 84112.

Communication Yearbook 13, pp. 107-113

FROM SPARKMAN DRIVE TO
DISCOVERY DRIVE: "I DON'T THINK
WE'RE IN KANSAS ANYMORE, TOTO"

The old building was a dump. The chair in my office was bright orange vinyl. The vinyl on the armrest had been peeled back to expose wood that had been used as a doodle pad for a number of years. Each person who sat in my chair had improved on the art work of the past sitter/doodler. The chair was voted the worst chair in the building when we moved, but it had character, something my new chair (which is just like everyone else's chair) lacks. My desk was part metal and part wood. It was missing its back two legs and had to be held up with computer paper boxes. The paper in each box was worth $30, so I had a $50 desk with $60 legs.

I now work in a small gray cube that is covered with emblems from my 2½-year stint with B-BCSC. My cube walls display the two Teamwork and Innovation (TIP) Awards I have received in the past 2 years—one for pioneering the HR direction for desktop publishing that was later shot down at the corporate level, and another for training a group of secretaries in the use of a software package.

TIP awards are hard to come by—they mean money out of someone's budget, and at B-BCSC, *budget* has become a sacred word. The first award was suggested by my boss and the second by the women I trained. I am extremely proud of these because they represent respect from the people I work with—the $150 was nice too.

Other things on display in my cell are a collection of postcards from a past intern now living in California (these remind me there is another world outside of Alabama, beyond the Mississippi, and there are dialects other than southern), a button that says "Someone has to be the bitch," given to me by a friend—it is a constant reminder of who and what I am—and the note my dad sent right before graduation that reads, "Only two more weeks, keep the GPA up." Anyone who knows my GPA knows this was meant to be a joke. The remainder of my walls hold assorted out-of-date schedules that always change and can never be kept, memos, and a little gray space.

There is something about working in a cube (or unit, as my California friend used to call them) that leads to a great deal of introspection on the meaning of life. I find myself asking around 9:00 every morning, after the excitement of beginning a new day has worn off, "Why am I here working in a cube?" and then I push it aside and write, because the answer is always the same: "I like the people, and this is a good organization to work for."

Then one day the answer changes and it catches me off guard. The organization has changed, the culture has changed, and the people have changed. To my surprise I find the answer to the question comes out something like: "I don't know."

In the old building I had an office. In the 9 months I was in the old building, I went from being the newest writer to the senior writer and had three different officemates. One was crazy and on drugs, one cried at least three times a week, and one was fairly normal, although at first painfully shy. My office was decorated by my boss with the Tom Selleck and Bruce Springstein posters she couldn't fit into her office and an ad from *Parisian's* that showed a man clad only in tight blue jeans and long hair. At first I found the posters embarrassing. I adjusted. After all, they were put there by my boss — who was I to complain?

The old building had an atmosphere of display. We displayed ourselves in a variety of ways: the way we decorated our offices, the clothes we wore, and the activities we participated in. This was a time of celebration. Henry Peppertree was our new hero and the HR product line we produced was selling its newest release blue blazes. We were all heroes; as such, we were indulged and pampered.

The new building was touted as a reward for a job well done. People began to focus on the February move date and we had clean-out and pack-up parties every Friday for two months. It was like moving from the old roach-infested apartment — the one that was all you could afford when you realized how much $18,000 a year translated into a month after rent, food, gas, a car payment, and, maybe, dinner out — to the new one you decided you had to live in after you got your first raise.

The day came when we were allowed to tour the new building. We couldn't wait for it to be our group's turn. We all piled into my car and drove down the highway, through the spiffy gray slate pillars with Cummings Research Park West in red, lighted letters, over the freshly paved road, past the landscaped, tree-lined side-walks that looped around the entire park area. We were full of ourselves.

We got out of the car in the back parking lot and walked up the sidewalk to a building that at first approach strongly reminded me of when Dorothy and friends first walked up to gates of the Emerald City. The center of the building is a glass arch that makes you feel both reverent and like you should skip at the same time. We were shown the new security system and were told we'd all have our own "card keys." This system at first was really thought to be cool, but it quickly became a pain as people lost their cards and wanted to borrow yours or when we found out we couldn't get to our computer printouts without one — which caused quite a stink.

The heavy glass doors were opened and we found ourselves standing in an area that resembled the lobby of the last Marriott I stayed in. The floor was covered in deep mauve carpet and trimmed with pink, gray, and white marble. The furniture was mauves and deep mahoganies. At the center of the lobby was a mirrored shaft that went up two floors. You could see up to the second floor, which was open and had a balcony running partially around the elevator shaft. To the left was the receptionist area. I felt oddly out of place because I had no luggage, but wanted to check in.

The tour began downstairs through the new customer education center and demo area. This area was decorated in mauve, blues, and grays. It is an area used for training customers on our software packages and in-house sales demonstrations of the system. Here it was: gray, cool, and serene. It was discovered later — after the decorator was gone and after customers started complaining — that if you had to sit in one of the classrooms after a big lunch at *Friday's*, you would fall sound asleep. These rooms are so quiet, so calm, so peace-inducing that no amount of caffeine or interest in the topic can keep you awake. This was the first major decorating goof.

The second was the customer lounge and kitchen. These rooms follow the same color scheme with one difference: Blue is the predominant color—tacky, crushed velvet, bordello blue. Which is why these two rooms have become known as the bordello—they were so dubbed by my group on our first tour and remain so known today.

The next areas we were shown were the customer education cubes, the employee kitchen, and the weight room. I wasn't impressed with the cust ed cubes— these were just the recently purchased phone-support cubes from the old building relocated here to save a bit of money (and so the emphasis on budget began). The employee kitchen was somewhat more exciting. We now had three microwaves, a frig, new vending machines (with the same old food), and ample room to sit and eat lunch for those sad few who chose to eat in the same building they spent eight hours a day in.

The tour of the weight room stirred major excitement. Here we had showers, lockers, a Jacuzzi, a steam room, and an amazing amount of exercise equipment. Most of the equipment was centered around weight training, but there were also stationary bikes, a treadmill, a scale, and jump ropes. Talk about your Silicon Valley type of setup! We all made solemn vows to begin weight training the day we moved to the new building. We were ready. This group of four women, none of whom was over 34 at the time, whose biggest form of exercise so far had been walking down the hall to the Coke machine or the restroom, was going to do weight training. And all because of this room.

We did hire a trainer for $25 an hour and we had four sessions with her, and for about two months we put on our new workout clothes and grunted and sweated and moaned. Then we quit. I never could lift more than the 20 pounds on the bar; Donna, my boss, got ill; and Mary complained her back hurt. So much for emulating those tanned, hard bodies of Silicon Valley. The weight room never does get much use.

The end of the tour downstairs was the computer room, which was just a computer room, full of mainframe equipment and painted the same dull gray as the rest of the building. It was time to go upstairs. The word *upstairs* began to take on significance. Upstairs was the place customers and visitors were not going to be allowed without visitor badges; it was where the real work was done, and it was where our new offices were.

We walked up a flight of concrete steps (carpet was added later) and opened the door into a hall that allowed only for a right or left turn. Left was to be Development; right, Support. We went left—we are part of the Development group. What we saw was a huge open cavern surrounded on three sides with windows— windows of the you-can-see-from-them-if-you-stand-up-but-not-if-you're-sitting-down variety. Inside the cavern was row after row of gray and mahogany cubes, each with its own matching mauve chair. I was told later the chairs—which are of the ergonomically designed category—cost $700.00 apiece. But the real kicker is that they are no more comfortable than my old vinyl chair. I don't like them as well either — no character.

Our group of four women, who up until this point had generated enough noise, wisecracks, and laughter to simulate a party of fifty people, fell silent. We each found our cubes. We stood there, all the excitement gone, all asking the same questions in our minds: Where will we hang the hunk posters? Where will we practice dance steps for parties? Where will we gossip without a door to close? Where will we bitch and cry when someone makes us angry? Not here, not in these cubes, not where we would be open for constant view and observation, not where we would always be overheard even at a soft whisper.

The mood had changed. We finished the rest of the tour in uncharacteristic melancholy. We were shown the senior managers' offices, which were impressive, but in our present state of mind not enough to shake the blues. We saw the conference rooms strategically located at the ends of the building. We brightened a little — at least there was someplace with a door, someplace we'd have access to that might offer solace and haven in time of disaster, when we would need to make a private phone call, or for gab sessions. We saw the library and copier rooms, the phone support and support area, and the pink and blue (how original) women's and men's restrooms.

Then we saw Henry Peppertree's suite. I was back at the Marriott — the decorator we used must have been theirs. The lobby area of his suite was carpeted in deep forest green, the furniture was all cherry, and the walls were a rich tan, not the gray of the rest of the building. His office and adjoining conference room followed the same scheme: deep, rich, and displaying the air of a man who had really made it. A theme was starting to emerge, and it made me feel uncomfortable and disturbed.

We drove back to Sparkman Drive in silence. Occasionally someone would make a crack about the bordello, or the chairs, but for the most part we were all trying to deal with the changes we knew upward mobility would bring. Even then, after one tour, it was painfully obvious that the values once highly regarded at B-BCSC — individuality, freedom, and fun — would have to be adjusted to fit the new building. Some of us knew this better than others. Some of us, myself in particular, were considering jumping ship even then, before it sprang a leak.

FROM LIGHT COMEDY TO DRAMA: MORE THAN THE STAGE HAS CHANGED

There is something about sitting in an orange vinyl chair in a rundown building that keeps you lean and hungry. The old building created an atmosphere in which everyone wanted to work hard, to make the product the best it could be, and to see the company succeed. We were a close-knit group working together toward a goal — success.

There was no transition, no in between, no time for reevaluating goals during the period we moved from the old building to the new. One day we were a group trying to make it big and the next day we had it all. The opulence of the new building made us fat and lazy. New attitudes, negative ones, began to develop. I began to hear comments like "Why should I work 70-hour weeks just to put more money in B-BCSC's pocket? What am I going to get out of it?"

Change the set and the props, and the attitude changes too. The actors change the way they read the script and the way they deliver their lines. We had rehearsed for years, opening night was a huge success, but now we find ourselves in a never-ending second-night slump. The culture, the camaraderie, the organization will never be the same.

The old building made me want to work and work hard, to be a team player and have fun playing the game. Third major decorating mistake — making the building, its furnishings, and its atmosphere portray a company that has too much money and not enough to do with it. The new building makes me feel like in some ways I've been cheated out of the in between, out of the part that comes after lean and hungry and before fat and happy. That's the part we missed, the part that could have made the transition smoother, the move more positive.

Did we really need $700 chairs? Can we really feel the difference between this chair and, say, a $400 chair? I doubt it. And what does this attitude say about the employees? Some might think we're spoiled and we can't appreciate working in such a nice place. Maybe that's true, but I think a little more thought should have gone into the psychology of the move, the effect on the people, and the effect on people's attitudes.

TWO YEARS OF CHANGE, TWO YEARS OF DISCOVERY

People are moving yet again. The 11.02 release is complete and we are gearing up for DB2 (the hottest new mainframe technology on the market). As I am writing this, my cubemate is packing up to move to the other side of the building. People have been switched around to fit new projects and the company has adopted a policy of lateral growth due to the "flattening" of the organizational structure. The old guard — 10- to 15-year B-BCSC veterans — are being slowly phased out to make room in the few middle-management positions for fresh blood.

Things have changed considerably at B-BCSC over the past two years, and we have made many discoveries. This state is evident in people's attitudes, company meetings, and the number of resumes I see coming off the laser printer every week. B-BCSC is no longer considered the best, the only place to work; it is considered now by many simply a place to work. Never before were looking for new employment, the proper format for a resume, or phone calls from headhunters standard topics of conversation. In fact, I can't remember discussions of other companies in the past unless they were references to former employers or talk about some unfortunate friend who worked for someone else and didn't have it as good as we did.

A number of years ago, when the company was still privately owned, before it became part of a large conglomerate, the owner and president came up with *The Four Basics: A B-BCSC Philosophy.* At a recent company meeting when he was asked about the move to lateral versus vertical promotions and employee growth, he asked if anyone remembered the Four Basics. No one did. This lapse was fairly remarkable, considering great expense had been incurred in having these pamphlets printed and bound in red glossy covers to be handed out to every employee. Then, not reciting them himself, he stated that he was still dedicated to these principles and especially the fourth one. The fourth principle reads, "to devote significant attention and energy to making B-BCSC the kind of company that attracts and retains the highest quality employees." Henry gave no explanation of how he planned to continue pursuing this philosophy, he gave no hint as to what the future would hold, he only stated he still believed in the words. But sometimes believing in a thing doesn't make it so.

I can't say for sure that moving from the old building to the new building caused this new attitude. If I were an industrial psychologist, maybe I could provide a detailed explanation of what was going on in the heads of people at B-BCSC over the past two years. If I were doing quantitative research I could provide the figures to support a theory as to why things have worked out the way they have. But I am simply a field worker reporting what I have lived, providing not conclusions, but another perspective on corporate change.

REFERENCE

Van Maanen, J. (1988). *Tales of the field: On writing ethnography.* Chicago: University of Chicago Press.

3 Managing Organizational Culture: Dreams and Possibilities

SONJA A. SACKMANN
MZSG and Hockschule St. Gallen

Organizational culture has gained much attention during the past decade. This chapter differentiates dreams from possibilities in the management of culture. A comparison of the term's anthropological tradition with the interests of organizational theorists and practitioners indicates the different contexts in which culture is applied. Three different conceptions of culture are discussed, including their underlying assumptions and implications for the management of culture: organizational culture as variable, as metaphor, and as dynamic construct. Culture as dynamic construct presents a synthesis of the other two: Its underlying assumptions acknowledge organizations as social systems, and it addresses the possibilities of culture-aware management. The implications of culture-aware management for the conceptualization and practice of management are discussed, followed by some final remarks.

T HE topic of organizational or corporate culture has gained much popularity in both the academic and the managerial world, in the United States and in Europe. The increasing number of publications within these different professional and continental worlds is a vivid example of the rapidly growing interest in and the perceived pertinence of the subject. Much of this interest is guided by hopes and expectations that differ for various communities. Academicians seem to see in the concept a remedy for certain organizational and theoretical problems, whereas managers see it as an ultimate form of organizational control that may help them to "master" their organizations and make them

AUTHOR'S NOTE: The ideas expressed in this chapter are in part the result of extended discussions with my "culture club" members Maggi Phillips and Dick Goodman. Special thanks to Maggi Phillips for her critical comments and suggestions on an earlier draft as well as to Professor James Anderson and the anonymous reviewer of the *Communication Yearbook* for their helpful advice. Wolfgang Zepf helped me cope with some of the technical matters involved in meeting the deadlines. Thank you all!

Correspondence and requests for reprints: Sonja A. Sackmann, MZSG and Hockschule St. Gallen, Rosenbergstrasse 38, CH-9001 St. Gallen, Switzerland.

Communication Yearbook 13, pp. 114-148

function more effectively. These different interests are accompanied by different understandings of culture and its role regarding organizations.

To what extent does the concept of culture adopted from anthropology meet these different expectations and hopes in its new field of application? Which interests do organization theorists and managers have in the topic? To what extent is culture just another fad? What is meant by the term *culture*, and what does it imply for organizational life? To what extent is culture manageable, and how? What is supported by empirical research, and what is mere speculation in regard to culture and its management? These issues will be addressed in this chapter. More specifically, different understandings of the concept of culture as applied to organizations will be discussed, and related hopes, possibilities, and limitations regarding its influence and management will be explored and evaluated. The discussion will include U.S. and European perspectives and will be based on both theoretical arguments and available empirical findings.

This chapter is organized into six sections. The section following this introduction explores and compares three different kinds of interests in the topic and related expectations: the interests of cultural anthropologists, of organization theorists, and of managers. The next section discusses the different meanings and uses of culture found in the organizational and managerial literature, their underlying assumptions and implications for a potential management of culture, and the respective problems. Conclusions about the possibilities of managing culture are drawn in the section that follows. The implications of a culture-aware management for the discipline of management and its managerial practice are then discussed, and final remarks are presented.

DIFFERENT INTERESTS IN THE
CONCEPT OF CULTURE AND RELATED EXPECTATIONS

The concept of culture is borrowed from cultural anthropology, where it has been investigated since the end of the eighteenth century. Anthropologists have therefore exerted a large influence on the concept's connotative and denotative meanings. In the process of "concept displacement" (Morey & Luthans, 1985), organization theorists and practitioners draw, however, only selectively from the body of potentially available culture concepts, without investigating the underlying assumptions made by anthropologists. This has resulted in similar definitions of culture across disciplines with differing meanings. Hence different lenses have been and are being used to explore, explain, and use the concept on theoretical, empirical, and practical grounds. To date, organizational scholars or managers have not yet addressed these contextual differences and their implications. Given the organizational focus of this chapter, only those aspects of the anthropological perspective that are relevant for a comparison across the three disciplines will be briefly discussed.

The Cultural Anthropologist's Tradition

The traditional interest of cultural anthropologists has been in increasing *understanding* or *intelligibility* of the various facets of cultural phenomena. They search for the underlying meaning behind human artifacts and behaviors of unknown or unfamiliar groups of people. They try to render the phenomenon of "culture" intelligible by discovering and interpreting observed cultural aspects. Langness (1979) explains:

> Thus the study of culture must be seen as . . . one of the keys to the understanding of man's place on earth and in the biosphere. . . . The concept of culture emerged . . . as a way of understanding human variation, and as a tool for the examination of human nature itself. (pp. 2, 11)

To accomplish the objective of increased understanding, cultural anthropologists have used historical and/or ethnographic methods to trace, observe, and take account of events. They attempt to understand human actions in the context in which they occur, from an insider's or emic perspective (Evered & Louis, 1981). For many, little importance is placed on further abstraction from their descriptive empirical data because they are not interested in establishing universal laws. As Hatch (1974) notes:

> The form of understanding that I am referring to as the interpretation of meaning may be distinguished from scientific explanation, according to which the occurrence of an event is accounted for in terms of a general covering law. . . . Scientific analysis attempts to establish the causal factors behind a phenomenon in such a way that when the necessary conditions exist, the event can always be anticipated. . . . When the anthropologist explains a phenomenon by elucidating its meaning, on the other hand, the issue of prediction does not arise. (p. 9)

Instead, cultural anthropologists traditionally point to the uniqueness of a cultural group that is displayed in detailed accounts. Several anthropologists strive to unravel this uniqueness by explicating the configurations or patterns of social life (Benedict, 1934; Kroeber, 1917). To make tribes or institutions intelligible, their "sui generis" principles must be discovered. These principles or patterns consist of a finite set of components selected from a range of possibilities.

For their fieldwork, cultural anthropologists have preferred to select small tribes or social groups to study the customs and artifacts of their members. Membership in such societies, tribes, and social groups is unconditional and long term. Individuals belong because of their birth. At a certain age, they may have to reestablish their membership consciously by going through certain rites of passage. Unless they are expelled, they remain in that society or tribe for the rest of their lives.

In addition, the societies, tribes, or small groups that are selected for detailed investigation have lived in rather secluded environments, such as tribes in Africa (Herskovits, 1924; Levine, 1954; Mair, 1934) or New Guinea (Meggit, 1965), or other peoples living on isolated islands (Mead, 1939; Radcliffe-Brown, 1922). Their environment is rather stable. Exchanges between the tribes or between tribe members and their environment are not of interest to the anthropological investigator, who prefers to take a holistic interest in the lives of members within their entire context of living.

Even though this synopsis of the traditional perspective of a cultural anthropologist does not do justice to the breadth and depth of anthropological thought, it highlights those aspects that provide a useful comparison to the thinking of organization theorists and managers. The focus of traditional anthropology on small-scale societies and the conceptualization of culture as a unique configuration or pattern of a particular tribe or society have — at least implicitly — influenced the ideas in much of the organizational and managerial literature that culture is a monolithic, consistent, and homogeneous entity. This entity consists of a finite set of components and can be applied to organizations without further adjustments or refinements.

The Organization Theorist's Perspective

The organization theorist's major interest and expectation in the concept of culture is a *revitalization of organization theory* that may ultimately lead to a *better conception* of organizations and organizational life. In the late 1970s and early 1980s, several authors expressed their discomfort with the advancements in organization theory (e.g., Morgan, 1980; Pondy & Boje, 1980; Pondy & Mitroff, 1979). Conceptualizations and research were predominantly influenced by rational, natural, and open systems thinking (Scott, 1981) and by contingency theory. These perspectives perpetuated a rather mechanical view of organizations.

The conceptualization of organizations as *rational systems* (e.g., Fayol, 1949; Simon, 1957; Taylor, 1947; Weber, 1946) emphasizes a scientific approach in managing and researching organizations. Goals are prespecified and structural arrangements are used as tools to reach these goals in the pursuit of efficiency. The scientific method is used in research to establish general principles and laws. The actual behavior of organizational participants is entirely neglected. They are considered rational rather than rationalizing individuals.

The *natural systems* approach (e.g., Mayo, 1945; Parsons, 1960; Selznick, 1948) developed as a reaction to the rational systems model. It stresses informal rather than formal structures, human relations rather than structural arrangements, organic evolution rather than mechanistic design. The *open systems* approach emphasizes the interchange of organizations with their environment, the throughput, and transformation of resources or energy. Organizations are considered cybernetic systems that have the capability for self-maintenance and renewal. This model overcomes the shortcomings of the rational and natural systems models by stressing processes within and between systems.

Contingency theory postulates that there is no best way to organize and that any ways of organizing are not equally effective (e.g., Galbraith, 1973; Lawrence &

Lorsch, 1967). It has contributed to the "scientific" study of organizations. Detailed empirical studies of various aspects were undertaken under the umbrella of contingency theory, with efforts placing emphasis on comparability, replicability, and generalizability. The objective is to uncover regularities and multiple causality (Pugh, 1981). According to Starbuck (1982), these efforts produced few meaningful results:

> Organization theorists have carried out numerous studies of so-called objective phenomena, and their aggregate finding is that almost nothing correlates strongly and consistently with anything else. (p. 3)

None of these approaches can fully account for the potential of a *human system* (Boulding, 1956; Buckley, 1967; Pondy & Mitroff, 1979). Human systems imply sociocultural aspects such as the social construction of reality (Berger & Luckmann, 1966; Weick, 1979), efforts in sense-making, and rationalization. The time has come for "bringing mind back into" organization theory (Pondy & Boje, 1980), and the concept of culture is expected to do so. The expectation is that the concept of culture can overcome the shortcomings of a mechanical view of organizations by adding a qualitatively different perspective. Within this new perspective, organizations are seen as cultural systems (Calas & Smircich, 1987; Morey & Luthans, 1985; Sackmann, 1983; Smircich, 1983) or "culture-bearing milieux" (Louis, 1983). Some authors have even suggested that the introduction of the concept of culture in organization theory may result in a paradigm shift (Calas & Smircich, 1987; Pettigrew, 1979) and lead to a new program for research (Ebers, 1985).

In general, the meaning of culture applied to organizations varies widely (Allaire & Firsirotu, 1984; Smircich, 1983). The cited authors generally consider culture predominantly as a metaphor for organizations. A cynic could argue, however, that organizational culture is whatever a particular author wants it to be.

The expectations and hopes placed on the concept of culture by organization theorists are high. Some question, however, the hopes for culture as a new paradigm (Bleicher, 1983; Ebers, 1985), and others caution against the misuse of the concept of culture applied to organizations (Calas & Smircich, 1987; Hartfelder, 1984; Seidel, 1987). To what extent can these hopes and expectations be met?

The Practitioner's Interest in Culture

The interest of managers and practitioners in culture focuses on the issues of prediction and control. Their interest goes beyond description and understanding. What they want is to have additional means and tools at their disposal to reduce the uncertainties they are faced with in organizations, to manage better and to have some kind of guarantee of an organization's survival and ultimately its financial success. Managers tend to focus on the leader as the source, shape, and control for culture, and, to managers, individuals are necessary resources and/or constraints that also need to be controlled, administered, educated, guided, instructed, paid, and so on. According to Heinen (1987), the academic field of management and business administration has to contribute to the solution of practitioners' problems if it wants to meet the expectations placed by society on the social and applied sciences. Hence a number of authors link organizational or corporate culture with the success of an organization (Baker, 1980; Peters & Waterman, 1982; Riley, 1983; Scheuplein, 1987; Tichy, 1983).[1] Or, as Denison (1984) expresses it: "The impact of corporate culture on the design and management of organizations is a constant theme in contemporary writing about American business" (p. 5). This statement applies to the European business literature as well.

The interest in culture as an additional means for managerial control arose in the United States in the early 1980s — and a couple of years later in Europe — when the U.S. economy faced increasing pressures from foreign competitors. The quality of U.S. products frequently could not compete with the quality of foreign products. Productivity lagged and markets started to become saturated. A series of events made the business environment less stable and predictable than it was 30 years ago. For instance, the increasing number of mergers and acquisitions in recent years created unprecedented turbulence and diversity within organizations. While it was possible in 1950 to predict foreign exchange rates or the price of oil, this was no longer the case in 1980. Only a few people would have predicted a dropping oil price in 1985 or the downward move of the stock market on October 19, 1987. This increased instability coincides with the growing interdependence among organizations on a national and international level. In such a turbulent business environment, in which proven practices no longer seemed to produce their usual results, managers were ready to grasp any new tool that promised help. And the newest tool was organizational culture after strategic planning had run its course.

Practitioners frequently seem to equate organizational or corporate culture with norms, the informal system, collective practices, or other tangible or directly observable aspects. Organizational culture is considered the "managerial formula for success" (Jäggi, 1985) that determines an organization's "success or failure" ("Values," 1983). Managers are promised a "culture of productivity" (Akin & Hopelain, 1986) if they understand the elements that all cultures of productivity have in common. The "right" culture may "reap a return on investment that averages nearly twice as high as those firms with less efficient cultures" (Denison, 1984, p. 6). "Sustained competitive advantage" (Barney, 1986) is expected from the "right" culture, which is also characterized as "strong" (Bleicher, 1983, p. 495; Denison, 1984, p. 5), "rich" (Deal & Kennedy, 1982, p. 14; Kieser, 1987, p. 2), "healthy, blooming" (Ulrich, 1984, p. 313), "consistent" (Hinterhuber, 1986), and "participatory" (Denison, 1984, p. 7).

These promises have resulted in expectations among practitioners who want to know how to implement, influence, or manage organizational culture so that the "right" one results, with all those positive consequences. Several answers are given, such as a "cultural audit" (Wilkins, 1983), a fit between corporate culture and corporate strategy (Deshpande & Parasuraman, 1986; Kobi & Wüthrich, 1986; Scheuplein, 1987; Schwartz & Davis, 1981; Tichy, 1983), and a formula for the

TABLE 1
The Concept of Culture in Traditional Anthropology,
Organization Theory, and Management

	Traditional Anthropology	Organization Theory	Management
Major interests and expectations	culture as pattern and construct; understanding of uniqueness	culture as metaphor; revitalization of organization theory for better understanding	culture as variable; prediction and control
Subject of interest	tribes, small-scale societies	work — organizations	work — organizations; leaders as source, shape, and control
Criteria for membership	unconditional through birth (rites of passage)	conditional exchange relationship (financial resources in exchange for skills/labor)	conditional exchange relationship (financial resources in exchange for skills/labor)
Interest in members	holistic	particularistic	particularistic; pragmatic
Duration of membership	lifelong (unless expelled)	short to intermediate	short to intermediate
Environment	stable	changing/turbulent	changing/turbulent
Exchange between subject of interest/environment	unimportant	important	important
Methodology	emic/ideographic; ethnography	alternative to positivism/scientific method/objectivism	etic/nomothetic; comparative data; implementation of practical knowledge

(better) management of culture (Baker, 1980; Davis, 1984; Siehl, 1985) as well as various recommendations on how to change corporate culture (Allen, 1985; Kobi & Wüthrich, 1986; Neuberger & Kompa, 1987; Sathe, 1983, 1985; Silverzweig & Allen, 1976; Trice & Beyer, 1985) or how to "gain control" of it (Kilmann, Saxton, & Serpa, 1985).

A Comparison of the Context of Culture
Across the Three Disciplines

Table 1 summarizes the major similarities and differences in the use of the concept of culture across organization theorists and managers in comparison with traditional anthropology as discussed above. When the concept of culture is used by anthropologists, organization theorists, or managers, they are usually not aware of their different interests, expectations, and the contextual differences in their fields of application. Hence each professional group uses culture for its own particular interest, viewing through its own particular lens and applying its own specific methods. It is therefore no wonder that organizational practitioners use culture for their managerial interests, even though *no* references are made to its management or control within the field of anthropology, from which the concept is borrowed. In addition, the common use of the same term covers the differing interests and implies, at the same time, a common understanding about the concept of culture — which does not exist in any of the fields. When different people talk about culture, they may not mean the same thing — a first obstacle in the endeavor to manage culture.

MANAGING CULTURE: A SEMANTIC PROBLEM

The above discussion shows that the contexts in which the concept of culture is applied differ. Nevertheless, organization theorists and managers both draw predominantly upon the concept's varied roots in cultural anthropology. This has led to denotative similarity but connotative confusion. A common understanding about the concept is *assumed* (Phillips, 1984), but it does not exist. *Management of culture* can therefore not be discussed without a preceding discussion of the underlying conceptions of culture.

A century of study has not led to even one definition of *culture* with which all scholars would agree, nor does a consensus exist on its most important characteristics. Kroeber and Kluckhohn (1952) list, for example, more than 250 different definitions of varying range and specificity. These definitions include components such as ideas, concepts, ideologies, values, attitudes, goals, norms, learned behaviors, symbols, rites, rituals, customs, myths, habits, and artifacts such as tools and other material representations. All these components can be found in definitions of culture within the organizational and managerial context. Smircich (1983) shows systematically how organization theorists draw from different culture concepts depending on their thematic interest.

These developed and borrowed conceptions of culture have different implications for the management of culture, but they are often unintentionally mired. Calas and Smircich (1987) lament, for example, that

the organizational culture literature, including the literature reviews, is full of competing and often incompatible views. In Burrell & Morgan's terms we have Paradigm
Wars! The organizational culture literature is made up of functionalist, interpretivist
and critical voices, all speaking at the same time. (p. 9)

In the organizational and managerial literature, basically three conceptions of
culture come to bear. One is a *material conception*, in which culture is considered
a variable — something that an organization has. The second is an *ideational
conception*, in which culture is considered a metaphor for organizations. The
organization itself is seen as a culture or "culture-bearing milieu" (Louis, 1983). A
third conception is emerging in which culture is considered a *dynamic construct*.
This conception includes both ideational aspects and manifestations that are,
however, used differently than in the culture-as-variable perspective. It is a synthesis of the other two culture concepts, overcoming some of their shortcomings.

All three conceptions are based on different assumptions and have different
consequences for a management of culture. The material conception of culture
suggests a *culture-controlling management*. Within the ideational perspective, a
management of culture does not fit into the framework and is not discussed. The
view of culture as a dynamic construct proposes a *culture-aware management*. The
three conceptions, their assumptions, and their implications for a management of
culture will be discussed in turn.

Organizational Culture as a Material Variable

The use of culture as a variable is based on three major assumptions:

(1) Culture is *one* of several organizational variables.
(2) This variable of culture consists of a finite and patterned set of components that are
    visible and manifest in artifacts as well as in collective behaviors, and, in fact,
    cultures *are* these artifacts.
(3) Culture serves several functions that contribute to the success of organizations.

Organizations have or develop, in addition to other products, the product
"culture." This culture is itself composed of subproducts such as artifacts, symbols,
and collective verbal and nonverbal behaviors (e.g., Deal & Kennedy, 1982; Dill
& Hügler, 1987; Ouchi & Wilkins, 1985; Peters & Waterman, 1982; Scheuplein,
1987). A common definition of culture within this perspective is "the way we do
things around here" (Deal & Kennedy, 1982; Peters & Waterman, 1982). A more
detailed description of culture within this perspective is given by Shrivastava
(1985, p. 103): Organizational culture can be described with a set of concrete
products through which this system (of meanings) is stabilized and perpetuated.
These products include myths, sagas, language systems, metaphors, symbols,
ceremonies, rituals, value systems, and behavior norms.

Examples of artifacts are the logo of a firm, the architecture of buildings,
existing technologies and machinery or tools, the interior design and the use of a

work setting, documents and products, the organization chart, the typical and expected clothing of employees, and existing status symbols such as company cars, reserved parking, or furniture (e.g., Neuberger & Kompa, 1987; Steele, 1979; Wolf, 1982). Verbal behaviors include language in general and speeches, jargon, humor, stories, sagas, legends, and myths in particular (Clark, 1972; Martin, 1982; Martin, Feldman, Hatch, & Sitkin, 1983; Vinton, 1983; Wilkins, 1978; Wilkins & Martin, 1979). Nonverbal behaviors include interpersonal behaviors such as the typical way individuals approach each other, gestures, and dress codes as well as existing forms and functions of rites, rituals, and ceremonies such as personal birthday wishes from the boss, congratulations for long tenure, the Friday afternoon beer bust, celebrations of company anniversaries, and the Christmas party (Berg, 1983; Trice & Beyer, 1985).

These components form together the product of culture, the major importance of which is seen in its attributed functions. It is assumed that culture serves predominantly two functions that contribute to organizational success or prevent it: (a) internal integration and (b) coordination (Dill & Hügler, 1987; Ouchi & Wilkins, 1985; Sackmann, 1983; Staerkle, 1985). The commonly held values and norms enable understanding and coordination between employees who belong to different departments and hierarchical levels. It represents the "social glue" and generates a "we feeling," thus counteracting processes of differentiation that are an unavoidable part of organizational life. In addition, culture enables coordination among organizational members. This is a prerequisite of goal-oriented work efforts to prevent goal displacement and misunderstandings due to differing interests and backgrounds of organizational members. Organizational culture offers a shared system of meanings that is the basis for communication and mutual understanding. If these two functions are not fulfilled in a satisfactory way, culture may reduce the efficiency of an organization significantly (Barney, 1986; Riley, 1983; Tichy, 1983).

Most emphasis is placed on the integration function of culture, the consistency among its subcomponents and the general consensus about acceptance of these subcomponents. As a result, cultures can be evaluated and designated "good" or "bad." A "good" culture is consistent, its components are shared among organizational members, and it makes the organization unique, thus differentiating it from other organizations. Such a culture is created primarily by an organization's leader(s) and/or founder(s), who can also influence, imprint, or change this culture (Clark, 1972; Deal & Kennedy, 1982; Peters & Waterman, 1982; Schein, 1985; Selznick, 1957; Trice & Beyer, 1985) – that is, they can control it.

If one wants to know and understand the culture of a particular organization, one must gather and study its manifestations. Several proponents of this perspective assume that the visible manifestations allow *direct* inferences about underlying norms and values. According to Beyer and Trice (1986), "Rites, rituals, myths, sagas, legends, stories, symbols, language, gestures, physical settings and artifacts are all cultural forms which are outcroppings of culture and which bring underlying, unstated understandings to the surface" (p. 6). Inferences are necessary, but since no "deep structure" is assumed within this perspective, manifestations are credited with face validity and used as immediate indicators. These assumptions have direct implications for the management of culture: Culture can be gathered, understood, controlled, and managed.

Dreams of a Culture-Controlling Management

Within the perspective of culture as one of several organizational variables, the management of culture is not problematic. Culture is manageable in terms of a culture-controlling management and follows the formulated strategy. One has only to identify the currently existing culture — that is, its components — and then change it — that is, alter its components — toward the desired culture (e.g., Bourgeois & Jemison, 1984; Kobi & Wüthrich, 1986; Pümpin, 1983; Scholz, 1988; Schwartz & Davis, 1981; Kilmann & Saxton, 1983). What is considered the desired culture depends predominantly on the anticipated strategy (Bourgeois & Jemison, 1984; Kobi & Wüthrich, 1986; Pümpin, 1983; Scholz, 1988; Schwartz & Davis, 1981). A consideration of employees' desires in formulating the new culture is less frequently proposed (Kilmann & Saxton, 1983).

The rationale behind this strategy-oriented culture change is based on considerations from contingency theory. The aim is to create the best fit between strategy and culture. Such a fit would serve two ends in a change effort: First, the implementation of the intended strategy is not jeopardized by the existing culture, and, second, the gap between the intended strategy and the existing culture is not too big. A "culture-risk analysis" (Schwartz & Davis, 1981) is used to determine the probability of successful implementation of an intended strategy in relation to the existing culture. In this approach, the intended strategy is the determining factor for the management of culture.

Deshpande and Parasuraman (1986) have proposed a less strategy-determined contingency model of "strategic culture planning." They suggest that this approach helps prevent a culture discrepancy when organizations undertake strategic changes or when they enter a new stage in their life cycles. In their model, Deshpande and Parasuraman combine the strategic marketing planning model of the Boston Consulting Group with a product and business life-cycle model and with Deal and Kennedy's (1982) typology of culture. They recommend a "tough-guy/macho culture" when a new product is launched and when the product does not yield much profit. A "bet-your-company culture" is best suited for a stage of increasing market share when the introduced product becomes a "star." A "work-hard/play-hard culture" is recommended when the product becomes a "cash-cow" and the market share is large but hardly growing. A "process culture" is indicated when the share is small in a growing market and when the product turns out to be a flop.

Such a prescriptive procedure is based on an "etic" approach (Evered & Louis, 1981), in which external experts determine the "right" culture type. Bourgeois and Jemison (1984), on the other hand, describe an "emic" process, in which organizational members first must characterize the existing culture. The subsequent environmental analysis helps to identify consistent and discrepant cultural elements. The culture analysis becomes part of the strategy assessment and the search for a realistic implementation.

In the effort to *label* an existing culture, holders of the variable conception of culture usually use typologies, profiles, or dimensions (Deal & Kennedy, 1982; Handy, 1978; Harrison, 1972; Heinen, 1987; Kobi & Wüthrich, 1986; Pümpin, 1983). For example, Heinen (1987) distinguishes sixteen ideal-type cultures dependent on the relative functionality of formal instruments for control (p. 28). The underlying rationale is, again, a contingency approach between culture type and organizational system, a rationale also supported by Dill and Hügler (1987). Deal and Kennedy's four types of culture have already been presented above. They are determined by the degree (high and low) of risk involved in a company's decision making and the speed (high and low) of feedback from the environment after a decision is made.

Kobi and Wüthrich (1986) and Pümpin (1983) propose relevant dimensions of culture that determine its special pattern and that are used to prescribe the desired culture. These authors distinguish eight basic orientations that imprint a culture. These are orientations toward (a) customers, (b) employees, (c) results, (d) innovation, (e) cost control, (f) communication, (g) the organization, and (h) technology. The eight dimensions are used to develop two culture profiles: one of the existing culture and one of the desired culture. Resulting discrepancies indicate where cultural management or change efforts are needed.

Once the existing and the desired cultures are identified and labeled, the planned and predictable change can start. Two questions arise, however: What kind of actions should be undertaken to move the existing culture toward the desired culture? Which cultural components should be changed or managed, and how? In general, *all* components of culture can be used in purposeful efforts to change culture. Which of the existing artifacts and verbal and nonverbal behaviors are specifically selected seems to depend on the interests of the particular author. Kobi and Wüthrich (1986, p. 186) give the most comprehensive, detailed, and systematic guidelines. Once the existing and the intended cultures are identified, the existing and the desired cultural patterns (in the form of profiles) are known and the discrepant orientations and their components stand out. In the next step, these discrepant dimensions need to be changed toward the intended strategy through direct and indirect means. Direct means for culture change and management are strategies and planning, structures and processes, management instruments, and actions. Indirect means are symbolic actions, leadership and communication, human resource management, and normative standards. Checklists and a series of examples illustrate concrete possibilities about how each one of the means for cultural management can be used within each one of the cultural dimensions.

A similar procedure for managing culture is proposed by Scholz (1988), who emphasizes a package of different interventions specifically selected for a particular culture change effort. The process of implementation is based on Lewin's three-phase model of unfreezing, change, and refreezing.

Neuberger and Kompa (1987) apply Türk's (1981) processes and means of social control to influencing culture. They emphasize person-oriented activities related to the human resource function such as advertisement, selection, placement, socialization, training, and development as well as person-oriented organizational development efforts. In addition, they discuss the roles of technology and structural factors for a management of culture. Regarding the actual process of change, these authors also refer to Lewin's three-phase model and Lundberg's (1985) ten-stage model of the organizational learning cycle of culture change. The ten-stage learning cycle begins with an organization or subunit culture and requires a configuration of external enabling and internal permitting conditions. If at least one precipitating pressure exists, triggering events may lead to agents' engaging in cultural visioning. A vision of a new culture guides the development of a culture change strategy. This strategy is translated into inducement, management, and stabilization of action plans that are implemented and that may result in the reformulation of the culture.

Allen (1985) assumes that normative systems and culture are the same thing, and recommends that culture be managed through a four-stage process of changing normative systems. In a first phase of analysis, top management's involvement needs to be gained or initiated, goals are set, and the culture management process is designed. Introductory workshops and a seminar with top management are conducted in the second phase. In the third phase, developmental processes are initiated at four different levels: individual, group, intergroup, and organizational. The different actions are evaluated in the fourth phase, and the program is continued and further adapted. In each of the four phases, the following nine content areas are emphasized: rewards, role modeling, information and communication systems, interpersonal relationships, management and leadership skills, organizational structures, processes, training, orientation, and the allocation of resources (p. 341).

Dill and Hügler (1987) describe a less detailed procedure for managing culture. For them, a central activity is the writing down of the desired culture. This includes the company's desired philosophy and basic guidelines, which can then be used to identify desired behaviors and sanctioning mechanisms. Within the perspective of culture as a variable, Scheuplein (1987) reduces such a management of culture further by considering the personal development of organizational members as one of the most important means for managing culture, with a focus on training.

An assessment of the impact and success of a culture-controlling management as advocated within this perspective is difficult, because few documentations or reports exist. Those that do exist are either descriptive case studies (Davis, 1984) or impressions (McKinney, 1986). The effectiveness of the different procedures and interventions is therefore still unknown. However, from theoretical and practical points of view, several problems arise in the approach of a culture-controlling management.

Problems of a Culture-Controlling Management

The underlying assumptions of this perspective lead to four major problems. First, cultural value engineering is advocated where the leaders are attributed with the power to prescribe and sanction a specific pattern of homogeneous values. Second, equating culture with one of several organizational variables implies an unproblematic "making" and controlling of culture. It remains, however, unclear which ones are the *relevant* dimensions of culture to be managed and controlled. Third, it is questionable if human behavior can be prescribed and predicted in a planned change effort. And fourth, the assumption of a stable, homogeneous, and consistent culture is rather problematic.

The focus on top management or the leaders/founders as the source of cultural values and as those responsible for infusing these values into the organization and for maintaining them has historical and practical roots. For example, Selznick (1957) states that the specific "character" of an organization results from the infusion of values by the leader. For Selznick, the most important role of the leader is the enacting and caretaking of once-infused and subsequently existing values. Such a "top-down" approach and focus on top management/leaders/founders is widespread among authors within the culture-as-a-variable perspective (e.g., Deal & Kennedy, 1982; Kobi & Wüthrich, 1986; Peters & Waterman, 1982; Van de Ven, 1983). Because all of these authors are also consultants, the access of consultants into organizations at a relatively high level may have had an influence on this perspective.

Empirical studies and theoretical discussions suggest, however, that culture may be influenced by organizational members as well (Gregory, 1983; Martin, Sitkin, & Boehm, 1983; Sackmann, 1985; Phillips, 1984). Thus the assumptions of a "good" culture being homogeneous and stable are also in question, because each organizational member is a potential source for processes of cultural differentiation. These may have positive effects in terms of innovation, diversity, and renewal, but they may also impede organizational processes if the differentiation into subcultures is too strong (Van Mannen & Barley, 1983). The changing mixture of organizational members introduces evolutionary dynamics into the cultural environment that add to its complexity and make it all but static or inert.

The approach of the culture-controlling management, or the *Macheransatz* (Neuberger & Kompa, 1987, p. 255), as advocated is rooted in a conceptualization of organizations as rational-mechanistic systems (e.g., Simon, 1957; Taylor, 1947; Weber, 1946). It is assumed that direct causal links exist between organizational members and between culture components, and that general laws can be found and applied. This assumption implies that causes and effects of cultural change efforts can be determined and predicted and, hence, controlled. Several organization scholars question such determinable cause-and-effect links in human systems. In Boulding's (1956) nine-level conceptualization of different types of systems, rational-mechanistic systems are only at the third level; open systems are at the fourth level, and social systems are located at the eighth, followed only by transcendental systems. Social systems are characterized by their self-reflexive quality, the ability to produce, absorb, and interpret symbols, and a much higher level of complexity, with multiple, reciprocal interrelations that are *probabilistic* rather than deterministic in nature. Human systems are "nontrivial machines" and function in terms of probabilities, including errors and random variation. Hence Neuberger (1984) criticizes current organizational philosophies and guiding principles as behavior codes prescribed by the top that are forced upon employees.

The incomplete transfer process of a metaphor may lead to unexpected surprises when attempts are made to implement such recommendations for a culture-controlling management. The implementation of Peters and Waterman's (1982) principles of successful companies in the National Forest Management in California has led to criticism among rangers and visitors. The values of the National Forest Management were explicated in "values clarification workshops." A new "Land and Resource Management Plan" designed according to Peters and Waterman's principles contains a series of recommendations for the management of the wilderness (McKinney, 1986, p. 18). Some people from the Forest Service would, however, rather discuss whether or not the wilderness should be "managed" at all. In their view, the new plan "takes the wildness out of wilderness." The rangers are not the only ones surprised about the newly created language — visitors have to refer to the glossary when they read the plan.

Wilkins (1986) gives a further example of the limitations of such a culture-controlling management. A fast-growing high-technology firm wanted to implement some of Deal and Kennedy's (1982) recommendations. They attempted to identify a hero among their employees whose behavior exhibited the desired values. They found such a person and declared him a hero without asking him first. When he found out, he denied the new honor because he felt that, standing in the limelight, he would be unable to continue the very behavior for which he was singled out.

The perspective of culture as a variable leads, on the one hand, to clear-cut guidelines for a culture-controlling management. However, its implementation creates a series of problems, due to the mixing of the assumptions of a metaphor adopted from a different discipline with traditional assumptions rooted in a mechanistic-rational systems view of organizations. These problems are entirely avoided in the next approach.

Organizations as Cultures

Within this perspective, culture is considered a metaphor for organizations. An organization is viewed as culture and is studied and treated as such. This perspective has roots in three interrelated assumptions:

(1) Culture applied to organizations offers a perspective that fosters the understanding of organizations.

(2) Organizations as cultures are social (collective) constructions of reality.

(3) Culture applied to organizations provides the guidelines for orientation regarding perceptions, thinking, feeling, and acting.

This perspective focuses on the *processes* that characterize organizations as cultural reality. Verbal and nonverbal behaviors such as language, stories, legends, myths, rites, rituals, and ceremonies are also discussed, but with a different rationale. Of interest are their underlying and attributed meanings, their specific interpretations within a given context (Louis, 1981, 1983; Pondy, Frost, Morgan, & Dandridge, 1983; Smircich, 1983), rather than their visible form. A typical definition of culture within this perspective is "the collective programming of the human mind" (Hofstede, 1980, p. 25) or "a set of assumptions which are commonly held by a group of organizational members" (Phillips, 1984, p. 6).

This perspective has its roots in the social construction of reality (Berger & Luckmann, 1966; Weick, 1979; Weick & Bourgon, 1986) and organization theory as advocated by Burrell and Morgan (1979), Calas and Smircich (1987), Morgan (1980), Pondy and Boje (1980), and Pondy and Mitroff (1979). Proponents of this perspective "think culturally" rather than "think of culture" (Calas & Smircich, 1987, p. 11). The cultural perspective of organizations is expected to render new insights into organizational life. Organizational members are considered active creators and enactors of their organizational world, which needs to be interpreted constantly. Culture is the *medium* in which these processes of attributing, interpreting, and negotiating meanings occur. Within this perspective, culture is not conceptualized as necessarily homogeneous or consistent. Rather, it is seen as evolving from phenomenologically based realities that are loosely connected (Lipp, 1979) and that may enhance each other, be independent of each other, or conflict with each other.

Top management and leaders play a less important role in this perspective because internal and external factors contribute to the development of specific cultural expressions. Each organizational member is a carrier and potential creator, developer, and change agent of culture that reflects enveloping influences. Gregory (1983) argues, for example, on the basis of her research of firms located in Silicon Valley, that organizations represent arbitrary boundaries around different subcultures. These subcultures can develop based on nationality, membership in professional or ethnic groups, or perceived functional domains (Sackmann, 1985). Influences of regional culture contexts on organizations have been observed by Weiss and Delbecq (1987), and influences of industry-specific contexts have been noted by Phillips (1987). Kleinberg (1986) and Hofstede (1980) have identified national influences. These influences on the potential formation of subcultures contribute to an organization's cultural reality, which does not need to be homogeneous or consistent.

Proponents of this perspective are not (yet?) interested in improving the bottom line of an organization by manipulating its culture, because culture is the *context* rather than a variable, and they do not believe that purposeful change with a predictable outcome is possible. Instead, they focus their work on a better understanding of organizations by applying a cultural interest. Such a descriptive and epistemological interest places them closer to cultural anthropologists than to the organizational proponents of culture as material. Given this interest, a management of culture is not yet discussed. To them, the level of knowledge about culture applied to organizations is not advanced far enough to warrant such a discussion. Of interest at the present time is a better understanding of the historical, evolutionary development and change of organizations as cultures, including all processes involved.

One could speculate that to these theorists the management of culture could be conceived as "culturally aware" or "culturally sensitive" management. This management would not be the exclusive task of top managers or leaders. Instead, each organizational member would have a potential impact and responsibility for influencing the organization's cultural reality. Because organizational members at all hierarchical levels act in and enact the same "medium," they constantly interpret events that occur within their organizationally relevant environment and they attribute to these events culturally relevant meanings. The cultural categories that have developed in and for that setting are applied in these attribution processes, and they are also further developed in the process. While these thoughts remain speculations within this perspective of culture, the following perspective offers suggestions in this direction.

Organizational Culture as Dynamic Construct

As a dynamic construct, culture is conceived of as something that an organization develops over time. This developing cultural reality becomes organizational reality. It is created, and this creation represents the context of organizational life, including its manifestations. Thus organizations *have* cultural aspects and they *are* cultures at the same time. It is not a mere combination, however; the perspective of culture-as-a-dynamic-construct takes it a step further and represents a synthesis. It is based on assumptions similar to the metaphor perspective, but it goes further by addressing contextual differences and by exploring possible implications for the management of culture given its assumptive base. Some of the foundations of this perspective are laid by Calas and Smircich (1987), Hofstede, (1980), Meyerson and Martin (1986), Sackmann (1985, 1989), and Schein (1985).

The major assumptions underlying this perspective are as follows:

(1) Culture within the organizational context is a multiple, dynamic construct consisting of various facets. It develops in processes of social actions and interactions.
(2) Some of the facets are visible; others are only indirectly noticeable through their influence on perception, thinking, feeling, and acting.
(3) The various facets are linked with one another in dynamic, reciprocal, and multi-causal ways that are hard to identify.

(4) Each organization has a cultural reality that is neither good nor bad. Its very existence fulfills certain functions, while others that depend on the specific cultural reality can but need not be fulfilled.

The first assumption includes both ideational and material aspects, structural and procedural ones. On the one hand, culture provides the guidelines and knowledge base for "map making and navigation" (Frake, 1977) in a specific setting as well as the value base to specify "right" (expected) and "wrong" (undesirable) behaviors within a given cultural context. These guide perceptions and thought processes in certain directions and thus *increase the probabilities* of certain actions. They are used for deciding which are "right" or expected behaviors and which are "wrong" or undesired behaviors in a specific setting.

This cultural knowledge is in part both imported into the organization by organizational members from their external realities and developed (further) in processes of solving practical problems (Sackmann, 1985; Schein, 1985). According to instrumental conditioning and social learning theory, successful solutions to a problem are more likely to be repeated than less successful solutions, and unsuccessful ones are avoided. These recipes for success and failure are gathered over time and stocked in the culture knowledge base that is passed on to new organization members, who try to interpret their new reality. This learning process occurs "naturally"; that is, individuals are rarely aware of it. They use for their orientation in the new and unfamiliar setting the visible behavior of their colleagues who have "successfully survived" in that environment, and the sanctioning behaviors as practiced (Martin, Sitkin, & Boehm, 1983; Zucker, 1977). In these subtle processes, organizational members adapt without conscious effort more and more of the cultural perspectives that are relevant for them in a given organization, department, or group. Each organizational member eventually becomes a carrier of the cultural perspectives as well as a potential source of cultural variations, mutations, and developments.

An organization may have several cultural perspectives or subcultures that may be complementary, contradictory, or independent of one another (Gregory, 1983; Louis, 1983). Depending on the most crucial long-term problems or tasks at hand, a certain cultural perspective may be most popular, dominant, or powerful, which implies for its proponents and carriers a position of strength (Hickson, Hinings, Lee, Schneck, & Pennings, 1971; Pfeffer, 1982).

When cultural knowledge is further differentiated into different kinds of cultural knowledge, a combination of overlapping and differentiating groupings may result within the same organization. In earlier work, I have differentiated four kinds of cultural knowledge: assumptional knowledge, dictionary knowledge, directional knowledge, and recipe knowledge (Sackmann, 1985). The results of this inductive study indicate that both overlapping and differentiating knowledge exist within three different locations/profit centers of the same company. Dictionary knowledge (knowledge about what exists and what is important within an organization) was found to differ from one location to another, whereas directional knowledge (knowledge about how to do things) was the same across the three locations, even though these locations operated in different industries. Assumptional knowledge — consisting of basic assumptions about identity, responsibilities, how to organize, how to conduct business, and the employees — could be found in only one of the three locations.[2] Those people who had initiated a major restructuring twelve years prior to the study were still present at that location and could recall and explain those premises.

Organizational culture as a dynamic construct also includes functional aspects that may both foster or hinder organizational processes, depending on the specific cultural perspectives that are enacted. First, cultural knowledge selects and filters information that reduces complexity. The cultural perspective serves as a lens that identifies specific information sets from the potential realm of possible information. These are then interpreted and connected according to the existing cultural categories. Different cultural perspectives may thus lead to different interpretations of the same event and eventually to different actions. Sapienza (1985) studied the decision-making process of the top management groups of two different organizations that were both faced with the same legal change. One group interpreted the event as a "box" that would limit its strategies and actions, while the other group interpreted the same event as an opportunity. Consequently, the two groups developed entirely different strategies and took different actions.

Organizational culture conceptualized as a dynamic construct may also — but need not — fulfill a motivational function. Depending on the slice of reality that is defined by a particular cultural perspective, it may create meaning for employees. The particular cultural reality may convey goals or even a vision that may generate commitment, identification, and enthusiasm for their own sake (Frankl, 1985). This form of intrinsic rather than extrinsic motivation pulls individuals toward action. Activities are undertaken because of personal commitment and desire to act, rather than because of pressure or a striving for some material rewards. However, whether or not a specific cultural reality has such a motivational function depends on the specific meanings that are conveyed or on the aspirations of the employees.

While this perspective focuses on the ideational side of culture, artifacts and collective behaviors such as rites, rituals, and ceremonies are included as well. However, these are seen as cultural manifestations that allow only limited inferences to the currently existing cultural perspectives. Because of the assumed "deep structure" and interrelated network of meanings, their visible form may be misleading and may lead to ambiguous results. For example, the visible behaviors or artifacts may be relics from the past; they may be part of a habitual but meaningless package of practiced behaviors. When asked for their specific meanings, nobody really knows. Due to incomplete processes of passing cultural knowledge to new employees, they may have become meaningless shells that exist only due to unquestioned habits (Sackmann, 1987).

Proponents of the perspective of culture as a dynamic construct are interested in both a better understanding of organizations through application of a cultural perspective and a conscious development of organizational culture. The epistemological interest of the metaphor perspective is thus combined with the pragmatic interest of the proponents of the variable perspective. On the one hand, culture is seen as a metaphor that may yield new insights into organizational life — also in regard to the management of culture. Such a management does not, however, mean the manipulation of cultural components as advocated within the variable perspective. It is not a matching of the existing culture with the prespecified desired culture, but the creation of conditions for a culturally aware management of organizations as cultural systems.

The comparison of organizations with the metaphor of culture emphasizes aspects of organizations that are different from those evoked by their comparison with "machines," "open systems," or "political systems" (Morgan, 1986; Sackmann, 1986, 1987, 1989). This constitutes the very potential of the metaphor of culture imported into the field of organizations. The special characteristics of human systems are better met than by using a culture-as-variable perspective (Buckley, 1967). Individuals are seen as "brain users" (Birkenbihl, 1988) who create and enact their organizational reality. Culture conceptualized as a dynamic construct emphasizes evolutionary processes and multiple interactions that are probabilistic rather than deterministic in nature and that lead to multiple and changing cultural realities. These are based on concrete experiences and also reflect mutations and differentiations over time. The relationships among independently thinking and acting people are more like a network than a chain of causal-deterministic events. This implies that changes in one part of the system may lead to yet unknown changes in other parts that cannot be predicted either.

The consequences for a culture-aware management are characterized by Wilkins and Patterson's (1985) "You Can't Get There from Here." In order to reach an intended reality ("there"), several prerequisites need to be accomplished first, such as a fundamental change in thinking. In the process, the point of departure ("here") changes as well. The conceptualization of organizations as cultures opens new perspectives for organizational members and thus the possibilities for a culture-aware management. The usual territory and the habitual ways of thinking are expanded or even abandoned due to a perceptual shift. This creates a base from which to reflect on and question critically the collective experiences or cultural knowledge of an organization — one of the prerequisites in the process of culture-aware management. Nystrom and Starbuck (1984) have found in their research that most organizational crises occur because managers cannot break out of their habitual ways of perceiving and acting.

A systematic collection of, critical reflection on, and questioning of the current cultural knowledge may result in a cultural map of the organization. This map contains the specific dictionary knowledge (what exists and what is important in an organization), the directional knowledge (how things are done), the recipe knowledge (strategies for improvement), and the assumptional knowledge (the assumptions reigning in the organization). Such a cultural map may indicate collective competencies and weaknesses within the organization, its "mountains" of knowledge and its "valleys" of absence of knowledge. Once these are known, they can be built upon or deliberately neglected. In the process of a culture-aware management, cultural competencies should be cherished and further developed while unintended wild growth is avoided (Sackmann, 1986; Wilkins & Patterson, 1985). However, these processes require knowledge and experience of *different* cultural settings as a basis for comparison. An awareness and critical reflection of a given cultural setting can happen only from a metaperspective — or from a different cultural perspective.

Symbolic management — that is, the creation, interpretation, negotiation, and communication of meaning — is an important part of culture-aware management (Dyllik, 1983; Neuberger & Kompa, 1987; Pfeffer, 1981). In social interactions, individuals do not have the choice of communicating or not. The only choice they have is whether or not to influence the message of their communication consciously. The spectrum of potential interpretations of events and alternatives for action are consciously reduced to a specific slice that is emphasized again and again in many different ways. All possible ways of communication can be used in this endeavor — verbal and nonverbal behaviors as well as artifacts.

Elements of symbolic management include the ways employees are greeted; the type, quality, and frequency of information exchange; the accessibility of managers; the kinds of interpersonal relationships among employees and between employees and suppliers and customers; the problems that are considered important; and the use of time and information. Important are the *specific meanings* that are attributed to these visible aspects, the frequency and intensity of their use, and the context in which they are used — not their form. *Consistency* in meaning systems can increase the chances that employees with different learning histories located in different parts of the same organization perceive and enact their organizational reality similarly despite differences in work, hierarchical levels, regions, or nations. The frequency and intensity of their use and the contexts in which they are used indicate to organizational members their importance and the priorities among different meanings.

The entire domain of human resource management presents further possibilities for a culture-aware management. Which individuals with what kind of qualifications and personal backgrounds should be attracted and hired? How are new employees introduced to the organization, to their work environment, and to their work? Which emphases are set in training and development, in the reward systems, and in promotions? The specific practices of selection, hiring, training and development, promotion and career development, and the reward systems and benefits can be used to set *framing conditions* for the cultural environment. Even though the cultural setting cannot be prespecified, deliberately chosen framing conditions can enhance the probabilities of certain ways of thinking, feeling, and behaving.

All these activities regarding human resource management serve organizational members for their orientation because they transmit specific meanings.

A culture-aware management makes conscious efforts to influence interpretations and meaning systems. It communicates in many different ways what is considered important. Over time, adaptations will be necessary based on a continuous and careful stock taking of the cultural knowledge base. Conscious efforts undertaken within the perspective of a culture-aware management are, however, no guarantee of the realization of the intentions, given the multitude of interconnected meaning systems and their dynamic nature.

Culture-aware management is not fascinated with the "right" culture in terms of "good," "strong," "rich," or "blooming." Prescriptions exist only indirectly, in recommendations to become aware of the existing cultural perspectives or knowledge, its competencies and related strengths and weaknesses. This may imply a more detailed study of the environment considered relevant, including, for example, markets, competition, customers, financial sources, and political groupings. It could also imply an expansion or change in what is considered the relevant environment. A culture-aware management evaluates actions constantly in terms of the existing meaning systems. In this process, the very meaning of what is relevant or important is also questioned. This requires, again, the ability to take a metaperspective in order to become aware of one's own cultural biases.

Examples of such culture-aware management are given by Pacanowsky (1987) and partially by Kurmann (1986) and Sackmann (1986). However, additional case studies are required if we are eventually to be able to describe the practice of a culture-aware management in more detail. This will also require the identification of fostering and hindering conditions in culture-aware management.

Some Conclusions About the Possibilities of Managing Organizational Culture

Based on the above discussion about the three different conceptualizations of culture and their implications for a management of culture, three conclusions can be drawn at this stage:

(1) A culture-controlling management as advocated by the representatives of the variable perspective is not possible given the nature of human systems and today's business environment.

(2) The proponents of the perspective of culture as a metaphor for organizations have not (yet) discussed or explored potential possibilities of some kind of management of culture. On the one hand, such an exploration does not quite fit within their point of view and interest; on the other hand, the knowledge about culture applied to organizations is not far enough advanced for them to dare such an exploration.

(3) The approach of culture-aware management as discussed within the perspective of culture as a dynamic construct seems to be the most feasible form of "managing" culture given the nature of human systems, the nature of today's business environ-

ment, and the current state of knowledge about organizations and about the concept of culture applied to organizations. However, this perspective and approach to "managing" culture needs further theoretical and empirical work to specify its conditions. It certainly has major implications for the conceptualization and practice of management.

The above discussion also indicates that culture within one perspective is not the same as culture within another perspective due to different assumptions and different interests in the topic of culture, as well as semantic differences. Consequently, the related ideas about the management of culture differ. The recommendations of the three perspectives for the management of culture are appropriate within their frameworks of assumptions if one does not question the assumptions. But only a critical analysis of these assumptions enables a comparison and a discussion about which one is most appropriate in the context of human organizations.

Table 2 summarizes the major assumptions of the three culture perspectives, their related paradigms, the functions attributed to culture, the source of culture, and its development and change, as well as the major change or management strategies. As can be seen, the management of culture is the least problematic when conceptualized from the culture-as-a-variable perspective. Culture as one of several organizational variables is manipulated, managed, changed, and controlled by top management and/or the leader(s). They use indirect and direct means to manage the existing culture toward the desired culture that is prescribed by the anticipated strategy. Such a culture is homogeneous, integrative, strong, rich, or participative — depending on the author — and leads to organizational success. Unfortunately, no empirical evidence supports these statements or dreams.

A critical analysis of the underlying assumptions questions the feasibility of such a culture-controlling management. First, human systems do not follow deterministic laws as machines do. Second, top management and leaders are not omnipotent. Even if they act in the firm belief that they control their employees like puppets, the strings in their hands may not be attached. In other words, values and other mind matters cannot be dictated, and the result of intended actions cannot be predetermined. Third, cultural manifestations do not allow direct inferences regarding underlying assumptions and cultural knowledge. And fourth, it remains unclear which ones are *the* relevant dimensions of culture that need to be managed. A cynic may wonder why the concept of culture is needed within the variable perspective. Frequently, it could be replaced by other concepts, such as organizational climate or the "value analysis" that is part of some conceptions of strategy. The potential power of the concept of culture is not used or realized within this perspective.

The perspective of culture as a metaphor uses the very potential of this concept to overcome epistemological problems of a rational-mechanistic view of organizations. The "social factist" paradigm (Ritzer, 1975) is replaced by an interpretive paradigm (Burrell & Morgan, 1979) that is more adequate for human systems. The metaphor perspective, however, also has problems. Its proponents have a tendency

TABLE 2

A Comparison of the Three Culture Perspectives and Their Implications
for a Management of Culture

	Culture as Variable	Culture as Metaphor	Culture as Dynamic Construct
Assumptions	culture = variable: composed of homogeneous components; causal-deterministic functional (important for organizational success)	culture = metaphor: heterogeneous social construction of reality; guidelines for orientation	culture = dynamic construct: only small part is visible; noncausal, multiple links between members and facets; guidelines for orientation and therefore functional
Paradigm	social factist/functional (rational-mechanistic)	interpretive	pluralistic
Functions	intraorganizational coordination and integration (necessary for organizational success)	reduction of complexity and providing meaning	reduction of complexity and providing meaning; fostering/hindering
Source for Culture	top management/leader(s)	every organizational member	every organizational member; environment
Prescriptions	the right/good culture is strong, rich, homogeneous, consistent patterned	—	—
Source for management/change	top management/leader(s)	every organizational member	every organizational member; evolutionary changes; environment
Strategies for management/change	culture-controlling management (change of culture components/ dimensions through direct and indirect means toward desired culture)	culture-avoiding management; reinterpretation of history	culture-aware management (symbolic management)

to take a position of "opposition" rather than one of "postmodern resistance" as suggested by Calas and Smircich (1987, p. 3), or developing an "unite de doctrine" as recommended by Sackmann and Phillips (1989). Possibilities of a cultural management are not yet discussed. If this should happen, this perspective could lead to feasible alternatives of a culture-caring, culture-sensitive, or even a culture-aware management as discussed in the perspective of culture as a dynamic construct.

Culture as a dynamic construct combines the pragmatic side of the variable perspective with the metaphor of organizations as cultures. The problems associated with the variable perspective are overcome since the underlying assumptions are different and closer to the metaphor perspective. Organizations are seen as evolving, dynamic, complex cultural systems with inconsistencies and paradoxes, and several cultural groupings or meaning systems. Within this perspective, the management of culture can only take the form of a culture-aware management that tries to create, interpret, negotiate, and communicate meanings in conscious efforts. The results of these efforts, however, cannot be determined in advance — they follow rules of probability rather than laws of determinism. A culture-aware management is aware of the existing meaning systems within the organization, its cultural strengths and weaknesses. These are consciously cared for or deliberately neglected. Every organizational member is a potential source of cultural variation, adding to the dynamic and pluralistic nature of culture. Unfortunately, there is hardly any empirical and inductively determined evidence about the practice of culture-aware management. However, its most important contribution is the new perspective it offers for the discipline of management and its implications for managerial practice.

IMPLICATIONS OF A CULTURE-AWARE MANAGEMENT FOR THE CONCEPTUALIZATION AND PRACTICE OF MANAGEMENT

The perspective of culture as a dynamic construct, with its recommendations for a culture-aware management, has several implications, both for the conceptualization of the discipline of management and for its practice. It promotes the idea of management as a holistic and systemic discipline whose task goes beyond the satisfactory execution of its traditional functions of control, finance, marketing, production, personnel, and so on. However, such an expanded view of management requires additional skills for its practice, such as awareness of the existing cultural contexts, cultural sensibility, and a skillful use of appropriate actions.

Implications for the Conceptualization of Management

In the tradition of "scientific management" and its rationally based followers, efforts in the field of management were geared toward identifying and isolating causal factors with the intention of controlling them. The underlying model of organizations was a machine analogy. The theoretical responses to scientific management, such as natural systems theory, contingency theory, and even open systems theory, have perpetuated the scientific approach to management, which can be more appropriately characterized by the term *business administration*. In these models, aspects of organizations are emphasized that need to be controlled.

However, the discipline of management consists of much more than isolating certain aspects and controlling them. It is more than a technique for obtaining goals. A fundamental requirement for a viable conceptualization of management is the appropriate inclusion of one of its major resources: people. Individuals and groups of people working together to accomplish results are the major building blocks of organizations. By "appropriate inclusion" I mean a recognition of the peculiarities and special faculties of human beings, such as learning, thinking, awareness, and self-consciousness; the capacity to reflect in time, space, and history; the ability to produce, absorb, and interpret symbols; and the capacity to choose and enact different kinds of roles. The models of organizations as rational, natural, or open systems cannot fully account for these human faculties (e.g., Pondy & Boje, 1980; Pondy & Mitroff, 1979). Management conceptualized as business administration does not offer enough for an appropriate management of complex and dynamic human systems.

The introduction of the concept of culture as a metaphor for organizations provides a basis for the management rather than the business administration of human systems. The conceptualization of organizations as cultural systems acknowledges the potentials of organizational members as human beings who actively construct their reality, who are skilled in symbolizing, who rationalize, who learn, and who act on the basis of preferences, values, and emotions. The outcomes of their actions are therefore not always consistent, rational, or logical in the eyes of other persons.

The conceptualization of organizations as cultural systems and the correlate of culture-aware management offer the theoretical and practical basis of such an expanded, systemic, and holistic rather than compartmentalized approach to management. An appropriate conceptualization is, however, not enough. For culture-aware management to come alive, special skills are required in support of the practice.

Implications for the
Practice of Culture-Aware Management

One prerequisite of practicing culture-aware management is an awareness of existing cultural contexts. Reaching such an awareness is not an easy task, because culture is taken for granted, implicit, and pervasive. It is the air that every organizational member breathes. It constitutes the medium in which one lives within an organization. How can one become aware of something that is invisible yet everywhere and interrelated with everything? Wherever one starts to assess it, one taps only aspects of it, which are interrelated with many others. And there are no gauged or calibrated instruments available for its measurement because it is a social phenomenon constantly in motion. The few questionnaires that have been developed within the perspective of culture-as-a-variable only scratch some of its surface and do so from one specific, and hence biased, perspective (e.g., Cameron, 1984; Gordon, 1985; Kilmann & Saxton, 1983; Pümpin, 1983).

To complicate matters further, culture is not only part of one's own breath, it is also part of one's habits. Culture is acquired in subtle processes of social learning (Sackmann, 1983; Schein, 1985) and its everyday use becomes unreflected habit. The cultural perspective becomes ingrained and is unconsciously applied, as are the component actions involved in walking or driving a car. These learning processes happen fast. Martin, Feldman, Hatch, and Sitkin (1983) found that new employees know the organization-specific jargon already after one week.

The only way to become aware of implicit, pervasive, and taken-for-granted cultural contexts is through questioning and in-depth probing. This may be accomplished in individual interviews by an outsider or in a group setting as suggested by Mitroff, Emshoff, and Kilmann (1979) and Kilmann (1983). The proposed assumptional analysis is a first step in surfacing underlying cultural assumptions and perspectives. Becoming aware of the existing cultural contexts requires an outsider who is not "trapped" or "seduced" by the cultural knowledge. The outsider, with his or her different cultural biases, acts as a catalyst and sounding board. He or she enables comparisons that are necessary for an understanding of the meaning of the cultural knowledge. The difficult part for a culture-aware management is to stay aware of the existing cultural environment over time and to resist the seduction of the comfortably familiar. A constant questioning of the obvious in a dialectical fashion may help in this endeavor.

However, awareness of the existing cultural contexts is not enough for managerial practice, because it renders only a *static* picture of the status quo. What is needed as well is the ability to recognize changes in the cultural contexts, that is, its *dynamic* side.

Culture in today's organizations of the Western world is most likely pluralistic. This pluralistic nature adds a dynamic to organizational life that poses the problem of how to stay aware in practicing such a management. Cultural sensitivity implies an expanded consciousness and recognition of choice, a spirit of inquiry in interpersonal relations (Blumberg, 1977), and an awareness of the dynamics within a social system. It implies the ability to notice even small differences, the reading and understanding of changes in cultural contexts. In addition, cultural sensitivity helps the manager to notice when he or she has crossed a cultural boundary, indicating that a change in behavior may be required. Cultural sensitivity thus enables a person in his or her interactions with others to take their point of view, to see the world from their perspective. It is the basis for effective communication in dealing sequentially or simultaneously with members of different cultural groupings that may all be part of an organization.

Cultural subgroupings may exist in regard to functions (Burns, 1985; Handy, 1978; Harrison, 1972), perceived functional domains (Sackmann, 1985), tenure and hierarchy (Martin, Sitkin, & Boehm, 1983), ethnicity and occupation (Gregory, 1983), industries (Grinyer & Spender, 1979; Phillips, 1987), or nations (Hofstede, 1980; Everett, Stening, & Longton, 1982). They may exist separately or they may overlap or be superimposed or nested (Louis, 1983). Subcultures may simply coexist, enhance each other (Sackmann, 1985), or conflict with each other (Martin & Siehl, 1983), and membership is not necessarily restricted to one particular subculture (Sackmann, 1985).

The complexity introduced by the pluralistic nature of culture places great demands on the cultural reading skills of managers and their ability to adapt to the changing cultural contexts. However, these are prerequisites of effective discussions, negotiations, and decision-making processes when people from different cultural groups are involved. Cultural sensibility enables the differences in perspectives to surface and allows the group to focus on problem solving rather than blaming. A culturally sensitive person is aware of the cultural peculiarities and differences within an organization and can deal with them effectively, but he or she also needs knowledge about actions that can be taken in the framework of culture-aware management.

SOME FINAL REMARKS

Culture applied to organizations is both a new and an old concept. Its organizational roots can be traced back to Barnard (1938), Selznick (1957), and literature in the field of organizational development (e.g., Bennis, 1969; Burke, 1982). Its rediscovery in the late 1970s and early 1980s had a rather pragmatic nature. Given the changes in business conditions, the traditional practices did not lead to their usual results.

Culture-aware management and its theoretical correlates offer new perspectives for the discipline of management and its practice. The traditional focus on compartmentalized functions is replaced by a systemic view that acknowledges organizations as human systems rather than equating them with machines. Specialized functional skills are expanded by additional skills such as cultural awareness, cultural sensitivity, and actions taken within the framework of culture-aware management. The practice of such an expanded management will not be easy, because rationality is replaced by rationalizing, cause and effect by probabilities and scenarios, objective reality by socially constructed reality. The choice of perspective, and its related implications for managerial practice, remains with the organization theorist and manager—but it is a choice that should be made consciously.

NOTES

1. No clear distinctions exist in the literature between the terms *organizational culture* and *corporate culture*. In my view, *corporate culture* is a term that applies only to for-profit organizations; *organizational culture* includes not-for-profit organizations as well. No other distinctions will be made in this chapter.

2. This location was the corporate headquarters of the company. Since it was designed and perceived as a service division rendering services to the rest of the company, it is treated as a division.

REFERENCES

Akin, G., & Hopelain, D. (1986). Finding the culture of productivity. *Organizational Dynamics, 15*, 19-32.

Albert, U., & Silverman, M. (1984). Making management philosophy a cultural reality: Part 1. Get started. *Personnel, 61*(1), 12-21.

Allaire, Y., & Firsirotu, M. E. (1984). Theories of organizational culture. *Organization Studies, 5*, 193-226.

Allen, R. F. (1985). Four phases for bringing about cultural change. In R. H. Kilmann, M. J. Saxton, & R. Serpa (Eds.), *Gaining control of the corporate culture* (pp. 332-350). San Francisco: Jossey-Bass.

Baker, E. L. (1980, July). Managing organizational culture. *Management Review*, pp. 8-13.

Barnard, C. I. (1938). *The functions of the executive.* Cambridge, MA: Harvard University Press.

Barney, J. B. (1986). Organizational culture: Can it be a sustained source of competitive advantage? *Academy of Management Review, 11*(3), 656-665.

Benedict, R. (1934). *Patterns of culture.* New York: Houghton Mifflin.

Bennis, W. W. (1969). *Organization development: Its nature, origins, and perspectives.* Reading, MA: Addison-Wesley.

Berg, P. O. (1983, March). *Symbolic management of organizational cultures.* Paper presented at the Organizational Folklore Conference, Santa Monica, CA.

Berger, P. L., & Luckmann, T. L. (1966). *The social construction of reality.* Garden City, NY: Anchor.

Beyer, J. M., & Trice, H. M. (1984). Studying organizational cultures through rites and ceremonies. *Academy of Management Review, 9*, 653-669.

Beyer, J. M., & Trice, H. M. (1986). How an organization's rites reveal its culture. *Organizational Dynamics, 15*, 5-24.

Birkenbihl, V. (1988). *Stroh im Kopf* [Straw in the head]. Landsberg: MVG-Verlag.

Bleicher, K. (1983). Organisationskulturen und Führungsphilosophien im Wettbewerb [Organizational cultures and philosophies of leadership in competition with each other]. *Zeitschrift für betriebswirtschaftliche Forschung, 35*, 135-146.

Bleicher, K. (1984). Unternehmungspolitik und Unternehmungskultur: Auf dem Wege zu einer Kulturpolitik der Unternehmung [Corporate policy and corporate culture: On the way to a culture policy]. *Zeitschrift für Organisation, 53*, 494-500.

Blumberg, A. (1977). Laboratory education and sensitivity training. In R. T. Golembiewski & A. Blumberg (Eds.), *Sensitivity training and the laboratory approach* (3rd ed., pp. 14-24). Itasca, IL: Peacock.

Boas, F. (1940). The limitations of the comparative method of anthropology. In F. Boas, *Race, language and culture* (pp. 271-304). New York: Macmillan.

Boulding, K. E. (1956). General systems theory: The skeleton of science. *Management Science, 2*, 197-208.

Bourgeois, L. J., & Jemison, D. B. (1984). Die Analyse der Unternehmenscultur [The analysis of corporate culture]. *GDI-Impuls, 1*, 55-62.

Buckley, W. (1967). *Sociology and modern systems theory*. Englewood Cliffs, NJ: Prentice-Hall.

Buffa, E. (1984). *Meeting the competitive challenge*. New York: Dow Jones-Irwin.

Buono, A. F., Bodwitch, J. L., & Lewis, J. W., III (1985). When cultures collide: The anatomy of a merger. *Human Relations, 38*(5), 477-500.

Burke, W. W. (1982). *Organization development: Principles and practices*. Glenview, IL: Scott, Foresman.

Burns, R.O.L. (1985). *Innovation: The management connection*. London: Heath.

Burrell, F., & Morgan, F. (1979). *Sociological paradigms and organizational analysis*. London: Heinemann Educational Books.

Calas, M. B., & Smircich, L. (1987, June). *Postculture: Is the organizational culture literature dominant but dead?* Paper presented at the Third International Conference on Organizational Symbolism and Corporate Culture, Milan.

Cameron, K. S. (1984). *Cultural congruence, strength and type: Relationships to effectiveness*. Unpublished manuscript, National Center for Higher Educational Management Systems, Boulder, CO.

Card, D. (1985, January 1). The computer-aided wave will continue in 1985. *Electronic Bus*, p. 164.

Clark, B. R. (1972). The organizational saga in higher education. *Administrative Science Quarterly, 17*, 178-184.

Clarkson, J. (1984). *Beyond portfolios: A special commentary published by the Rosaton Consulting Group*. Winnipeg: University of Manitoba Press.

Collier, D. A. (1983). The service sector revolution: The automation of services. *Long Range Planning, 26*(6), 10-20.

Davis, S. M. (1984). *Managing corporate cultures*. Cambridge, MA: Ballinger.

Deal, T. E., & Kennedy, A. A. (1982). *Corporate cultures: The rites and rituals of corporate life*. Reading, MA: Addison-Wesley.

Denison, D. R. (1984). Bringing corporate culture to the bottom line. *Organizational Dynamics, 12*, 5-22.

Deshpande, R., & Parasuraman, A. (1986). Linking corporate culture to strategic planning. *Business Horizons, 3*, 28-37.

Dill, P., & Hügler, G. (1987). Unternehmenskultur und Führung betriebswirtschaftlicher Organisationen: Ansatzpunkte für ein kulturbewußtes Management [Corporate culture and management of corporations: Points of discussion for a culture-aware management]. In E. Heinen (Ed.), *Unternehmenskultur* [Corporate culture] (pp. 141-210). München: Oldenbourg.

Dyllik, T. (1983). Management als Sinnvermittlung [Management as the transmission of meaning]. *GDI-Impuls, 3*, 3-12.

Ebers, M. (1985). *Organisationskultur: Ein neues Forschungsprogramm?* [Organizational culture: A new program for research?]. Wiesbaden: Gabler.

Evered, R., & Louis, M. R. (1981). Alternative perspectives in the organizational sciences: "Inquiries from the inside" and "Inquiries from the outside." *Academy of Management Review, 3*(3), 385-389.

Everett, J. E., Stening, B. W., & Longton, P. A. (1982). Some evidence for an international managerial culture. *Journal of Management Studies, 19*(2), 153-162.

Fayol, H. (1949). *General and industrial management*. London: Pitman.

Frake, C. O. (1977). Plying frames can be dangerous: Reflections on methodology in cognitive anthropology. *Quarterly Newsletter of the Institute for Comparative Human Development, 3*, 1-7.

Frankl, V. E. (1985). *Der Mensch vor der Frage nach dem Sinn* [The human being confronting the question of meaning]. München: Piper.

Frost, P. J., Moore, L. F., Louis, M. R., Lundberg, C. G., & Martin, J. (Eds.). (1985). *Organizational culture*. Beverly Hills, CA: Sage.

Galbraith, J. (1973). *Designing complex organizations*. Reading, MA: Addison-Wesley.

Garfinkel, H. (1967). *Studies in ethnomethodology*. Englewood Cliffs, NJ: Prentice-Hall.

Gordon, G. G. (1985). The relationship of corporate culture to industry sector and corporate performance. In R. Kilmann, M. J. Saxton, & R. Serpa (Eds.), *Gaining control of the corporate culture* (pp. 103-125). San Francisco: Jossey-Bass.

Gregory, K. L. (1983). Native-view paradigms: Multiple cultures and culture conflicts in organizations. *Administrative Science Quarterly, 28,* 359-376.

Grinyer, P. H., & Spender, J. C. (1979). Recipes, crises, and adaptation in mature businesses. *International Studies of Management and Organization, 9*(3), 113-133.

Handy, C. B. (1978). Zur Entwicklung der Organisationskultur durch Management Development Methoden [Developing organizational culture through methods of management development]. *Zeitschrift für Organisation, 7,* 404-410.

Harrison, R. (1972, May/June). Understanding your organizational character. *Harvard Business Review,* pp. 119-128.

Hartfelder, D. (1984). Man wollte doch den "harten Führungsstil" abbauen? . . . [Wasn't it intended to reduce the "hard style of leadership"? . . .]. *Management-Zeitschrift, 54*(10), 459-461.

Hatch, E. (1974). *Theories of man and culture.* New York: Columbia University Press.

Heinen, E. (1987). *Unternehmenskult* [Corporate culture as subject of management]. München: Oldenbourg.

Herskovits, M. J. (1924). A preliminary consideration of the culture areas of Africa. *American Anthropologist, 26,* 50-63.

Hickson, D. J., Hinings, C. R., Lee, C. A., Schneck, R. E., & Pennings J. M. (1971). A "strategic contingencies" theory of intra-organizational power. *Administrative Science Quarterly, 16,* 216-229.

Hinterhuber, H. H. (1986). Strategie, Innovation und Unternehmenskultur [Strategy, innovation and organizational culture]. *Blick durch die Wirtschaft, 20*(10).

Hofstede, G. (1980). *Culture's consequences: International differences in work-related values.* Beverly Hills, CA: Sage.

Howell, R. (1980). Plan to integrate your acquisition. *Harvard Business Review, 49*(6), 66-76.

Jäggi, D. (1985, November). *Corporate Identity als unternehmerische Erfolgsformel* [Corporate identity as formula for corporate success]. Paper presented at the Second WEMAR-Tagung.

Kieser, A. (1987). *Von der Morgenansprache zum gemeinsamen HP-Frühstück: Zur Funktion von Werten, Mythen, Ritualen und Symbolen* [From the morning speech to the common breakfast at HP: The functions of values, myths, rituals and symbols]. Working paper, Institut für Allgemeine Betriebswirtschaftslehre und Organisation, University of Mannheim.

Kilmann, R. H. (1983). A dialectical approach to formulating and testing social science theories: Assumptional analysis. *Human Relations, 36*(1), 1-22.

Kilmann, R. H., & Saxton, M. J. (1983). *The culture gap survey.* Pittsburgh: Organizational Design Consultants.

Kilmann, R. H., Saxton, M. J., & Serpa, R. (Eds.). (1985). *Gaining control of the corporate culture.* San Francisco: Jossey-Bass.

Kleinberg, J. (1986). *Concepts of work among Japanese and American managers.* Working paper 2-86, Organization and Strategic Studies, Graduate School of Management, University of California, Los Angeles.

Kluckhohn, F. R., & Strodtbeck, F. L. (1961). *Variations in value orientations.* New York: Row, Peterson.

Kobi, J.-M., & Wüthrich, H. A. (1986). *Unternehmenskultur verstehen, erfassen und gestalten* [Understanding, measuring and managing corporate culture]. Landsberg: Verlag der Industrie.

Kroeber, A. L. (1917). The superorganic. *American Anthropologist, 19,* 163-213.

Kroeber, A. L., & Kluckhohn, C. K. (1952). Culture: A critical review of concepts and definitions. *Harvard University Peabody Museum of Archaeology and Ethnology Papers, 47.*

Kurmann, B. (1986). *Firmenkultur am Beispiel der Sarna* [Sarna as an example for corporate culture]. Bern: Paul Haupt.

Langness, L. L. (1979). *The study of culture.* San Francisco: Chandler & Sharp.

Lawrence, P. R., & Lorsch, J. (1967). Differentiation and integration in complex organizations. *Administrative Science Quarterly, 12*, 1-47.

Leiter, K. (1980). *A primer on ethnomethodology*. New York: Oxford University Press.

Levine, R. A. (1954). *Culture, behavior and personality*. Chicago: Aldine.

Lipp, W. (1979). Kulturtypen, kulturelle Symbole, Handlungswelt: Zur Plurivalenz von Kultur [Culture types, culture symbols, world of action: The pluralism of culture], *Kölner Zeitschrift für Soziologie und Sozialpsychologie, 31*, 450-484.

Louis, M. R. (1981). A cultural perspective on organizations: The need for and the consequences of viewing organizations as culture-bearing milieux. *Human Systems Management, 2*, 246-258.

Louis, M. R. (1983). Organizations as culture-bearing milieux. In L. R. Pondy, P. Frost, G. Morgan, & T. Dandridge (Eds.), *Organizational symbolism* (pp. 39-54). Greenwich, CT: JAI.

Lundberg, C. C. (1985). On the feasibility of cultural intervention in organizations. In P. J. Frost, L. F. Moore, M. R. Louis, C. G. Lundberg, & J. Martin (Eds.), *Organizational culture* (pp. 169-186). Beverly Hills, CA: Sage.

Mair, L. (1934). *An African people in the twentieth century*. London: Routledge.

Marks, M. L., & Mirvis, P. H. (1985). Merger syndrome: Stress and uncertainty. *Mergers and Acquisitions, 20*(2), 50-55.

Martin, J. (1982). Stories and scripts in organizational settings. In A. Hastorf & A. Isen (Eds.), *Cognitive social psychology* (pp. 255-305). New York: Elsevier.

Martin, J., Feldman, M. S., Hatch, J. J., & Sitkin, S. B. (1983). The uniqueness paradox in organizational stories. *Administrative Science Quarterly, 28*(3), 438-453.

Martin, J., & Siehl, C. (1983). Organizational culture and counter culture: An uneasy symbiosis. *Organizational Dynamics, 12*(2), 52-64.

Martin, J., Sitkin, S., & Boehm, M. (1983). *Wild-eyed guys and old salts: The emergence and disappearance of organizational subcultures*. Working paper, Graduate School of Business, Stanford University.

Mayo, E. (1945). *The social problems of an industrial civilization*. Cambridge, MA: Harvard University, Graduate School of Business Administration.

McKinney, J. (1986, October). Brave new forest. *Los Angeles Times Magazine*, pp. 13-19.

Mead, M. (1939). *From the South Seas: Studies of adolescence and sex in primitive societies*. New York: Morrow.

Meggit, M. (1965). *The lineage system of the Mea Enga of New Guinea*. Edinburgh: Oliver & Boyd.

Meyerson, D., & Martin, J. (1986, May). *Questioning the assumptions of value engineering: Alternative views of the cultural change process* (Research Paper No. 885). Stanford, CA: Stanford University, Graduate School of Business.

Mitroff, I. I., Emshoff, J., & Kilmann, R. H. (1979). Assumptional analysis: A methodology for strategic problem solving. *Management Science, 25*, 583-593.

Morey, N. C., & Luthans, F. (1985). Refining the displacement of culture and the use of scenes and themes in organizational studies. *Academy of Management Review, 10*(2), 219-229.

Morgan, G. (1980). Paradigms, metaphors, and puzzle solving in organization theory. *Administrative Science Quarterly, 25*, 605-622.

Morgan, G. (1986). *Images of organization*. Beverly Hills, CA: Sage.

Naisbitt, J. (1982). *Megatrends: Ten new directions transforming our lives*. New York: Warner.

Neuberger, O. (1984). *Führung: Ideologie, Struktur, Verhalten* [Leadership: Ideology, structure, behavior]. Stuttgart: Enke.

Neuberger, O., & Kompa, A. (1987). *Wir, die Firma* [We, the firm]. Weinheim: Beltz.

Nystrom, P. C., & Starbuck, W. H. (1984). To avoid organizational crises, unlearn. *Organizational Dynamics, 12*(4), 53-65.

Olson, L. (1983, March). Training for a transformed labor market. *Training and Development Journal*, pp. 46-53.

Ouchi, W. G., & Wilkins, A. L. (1985). Organizational culture. *Annual Review of Sociology, 11*, 457-483.

Pacanowsky, M. (1987). Communication in the empowering organization. In J. A. Anderson (Ed.), *Communication yearbook 11* (pp. 356-379). Newbury Park, CA: Sage.

Parsons, T. (1960). *Structure and process in modern societies*. Glencoe, IL: Free Press.

Peters, T. J., & Waterman, R. H. (1982). *In search of excellence*. Reading, MA: Addison-Wesley.

Pettigrew, A. M. (1979). On studying organizational cultures. *Administrative Science Quarterly, 24*, 570-581.

Pfeffer, J. (1981). Management as symbolic action: The creation and maintenance of organizational paradigms. In L. L. Cummings & B. M. Staw (Eds.), *Research in organizational behavior* (pp. 1-52). Greenwich, CT: JAI.

Pfeffer, J. (1982). *Organizations and organization theory*. Reading, MA: Addison-Wesley.

Phillips, M. E. (1984). *A conception of culture in organizational settings*. Working paper 8-84, Graduate School of Management, University of California, Los Angeles.

Phillips, M. E. (1987, August). *Cultural influences at the industrial level of analysis*. Paper presented at the annual meeting of the Academy of Management, New Orleans.

Pondy, L. R., & Boje, D. M. (1980). Bringing mind back in. In W. M. Evan (Ed.), *Frontiers in organization and management* (pp. 83-101). New York: John Wiley.

Pondy, L. R., Frost, P. J., Morgan, G., & Dandridge, T. C. (Eds.). (1983). *Organizational symbolism*. Greenwich, CT: JAI.

Pondy, L. R., & Mitroff, I. (1979). Beyond open systems models of organizations. In B. M. Staw (Ed.), *Research in organizational behavior* (pp. 3-39). Greenwich, CT: JAI.

Pugh, D. S. (1981). Rejoinder to Starbuck. In A. H. Van de Ven & W. F. Joyce (Eds.), *Perspectives on organization design and behavior* (pp. 199-203). New York: John Wiley.

Pümpin, C. (1983, May 3). *Unternehmenskultur, Unternehmensstrategie und Unternehmenserfolg* [Corporate culture, corporate strategy and corporate success]. Paper presented at the ATAG conference, Die Bedeutung der Unternehmenskultur für den künftigen Erfolg Ihres Unternehmens [The Meaning of Corporate Culture for the Future Success of Your Company], Zurich, West Germany.

Radcliffe-Brown, A. R. (1922). *The Andaman islanders*. Glencoe, IL: Free Press.

Riley, P. (1983). A structurationist account of political cultures. *Administrative Science Quarterly, 28*, 414-437.

Ritzer, G. (1975). Sociology: A multiple paradigm science. *American Sociologist, 10*, 156-167.

Sackmann, S. A. (1983). Organisationskultur: die unsichtbare Einflussgrösse [Organizational culture: The invisible influence]. *Gruppendynamik, 4*, 393-406.

Sackmann, S. A. (1985). *Cultural knowledge in organizations: The link between strategy and organizational processes*. Unpublished doctoral dissertation, Graduate School of Management, University of California, Los Angeles

Sackmann, S. A. (1986, June). *Managing the transformation process with new metaphors for cultural change and "engineering."* Paper presented at the Standing Conference on Organizational Symbolism, "Cultural Engineering: The Evidence For and Against," Montreal.

Sackmann, S. A. (1987, June). *Beyond corporate artifacts: Uncovering culture in organizations*. Paper presented at the Standing Conference on Organizational Symbolism, Milan.

Sackmann, S. A. (1989). 'Kulturmanagement': Lässt sich Unternehmenskultur 'machen'? [Managing culture: Is corporate culture manageable?]. In K. Sandner (Ed.), *Politische Prozesse in Organisationen* [Political processes in organizations] (pp. 157-183). Berlin: Springer Verlag.

Sackmann, S. A. (in press). The role of metaphors in organization transformation. *Human Relations*.

Sackmann, S. A., & Phillips, M. E. (1989, June). *Grasping the leadership role in culture research: More than a symbolic task for SCOS*. Manuscript prepared for the Fourth International SCOS Conference on Organizational Symbolism and Corporate Culture.

Sapienza, A. M. (1985). Believing is seeing: How organizational culture influences the decisions top managers make. In R. H. Kilmann, M. J. Saxton, & R. Serpa (Eds.), *Gaining control of the corporate culture* (pp. 66-83). San Francisco: Jossey-Bass.

Sathe, V. (1983). Some action implications of corporate culture. *Organizational Dynamics, 11*, 5-23.

Sathe, V. (1985). How to decipher and change corporate culture. In R. H. Kilmann, M. J. Saxton, & R.
  Serpa (Eds.), *Gaining control of the corporate culture* (pp. 230-261). San Francisco: Jossey-Bass.
Schein, E. H. (1985). *Organizational culture and leadership.* San Francisco: Jossey-Bass.
Scheuplein, H. (1987). Unternehmenskultur und persönliche Weiterent-wicklung: Von der Ist-Kulture
  zur Soll-Kultur [Corporate culture and personal development]. *Zeitschrift für Organisation, 36,*
  301-304.
Scholz, C. (1988). Management der Unternehmenskultur [The management of corporate culture].
  Harvard Manager, 1, 81-91.
Schwartz, H., & Davis, S. (1981). Matching corporate culture and business strategy. *Organizational
  Dynamics, 10*(1), 30-48.
Scott, W. R. (1981). *Organizations: Rational, natural and open systems.* Englewood Cliffs, NJ:
  Prentice-Hall.
Seidel, E. (1987). Unternehmenskultur: Warnung vor der Selbstzerstörung eines Konzepts [Corporate
  culture: Warning of the self-destruction of a concept]. *Zeitschrift für Organisation, 52,* 295-300.
Selznick, P. (1948). Foundations of the theory of organizations. *American Sociological Review, 13,*
  25-35.
Selznick, P. (1957). *Leadership in administration: A sociological interpretation.* Evanston, IL: Row,
  Peterson.
Shrivastava, P. (1985). Integrating strategy formulation with organizational culture. *Journal of Business
  Strategy, 6,* 103-111.
Siehl, C. (1985). After the founder: An opportunity to manage culture. In P. J. Frost, L. F. Moore, J. R.
  Louis, C. C. Lundberg, & J. Martin (Eds.), *Organizational culture* (pp. 125-140). Beverly Hills, CA:
  Sage.
Silverzweig, S., & Allen, R. F. (1976). Changing the corporate culture. *Sloan Management Review,
  17*(3), 33-50.
Simon, H. A. (1957). *Administrative behavior* (2nd ed.). New York: Macmillan.
Smircich, L. (1983). Concepts of culture and organizational analysis. *Administrative Science Quarterly,
  28,* 339-358.
Staerkle, R. (1985). Wechselwirkungen zwischen Organisationskultur und Organisationsstruktur [Inter-
  dependencies between organizational culture and organizational structure]. In G.J.B. Probst &
  H. Siegwart (Eds.), *Integriertes Management: Bausteine eines systemorientierten Managements*
  [Integrated management: Building blocks of a system's oriented management] (pp. 529-553). Bern,
  Stuttgart: Haupt.
Starbuck, W. H. (1982). Congealing oil: Inventing ideologies to justify acting ideologies out. *Journal
  of Management Studies, 19*(1), 3-27.
Steele, F. I. (1979). *Physical settings and organizational development.* Reading, MA: Addison Wesley.
Taylor, F. W. (1947). *Scientific management.* New York: Harper & Brothers.
Tichy, N. (1983). *Managing strategic change: Technical, political, and cultural dynamics.* New York:
  John Wiley.
Trice, H. M., & Beyer, J. M. (1985). Using six organizational rites to change culture. In R. H. Kilmann,
  M. J. Saxton, & R. Serpa (Eds.), *Gaining control of the corporate culture* (pp. 370-399). San
  Francisco: Jossey-Bass.
Türk, K. (1981). *Personalführung und soziale Kontrolle* [Personnel management and social control].
  Stuttgart: Enke.
Ulrich, P. (1984). Systemsteuerung und Kulturentwicklung [Systems steering and culture develop-
  ment]. *Die Unternehmung, 38,* 303-325.
Values: The hard-to-change values that spell success or failure. (1983, October 25). *Business Week,*
  pp. 148-159.
Van de Ven, A. H. (1983). *Creating and sustaining a corporate culture in fast changing organizations.*
  Paper presented at the Executive Seminar on Corporate Excellence, University of Santa Clara, CA.

Van Maanen, J., & Barley, S. R. (1983). Culture organizations: Fragments of a theory. In L. R. Pondy, P. J. Frost, G. Morgan, & T. C. Dandridge (Eds.), *Organizational symbolism* (pp. 31-53). Greenwich, CT: JAI.

Vinton, K. (1983, March). *Humor in the work-place: It's more than telling jokes.* Paper presented at the annual meeting of the Western Academy of Management, Santa Barbara, CA.

Walter, G. A. (1986). *Value conflict and induced change in mergers and acquisitions.* Working paper, Graduate School of Management, University of California, Los Angeles.

Weber, M. (1946). *From Max Weber: Essays in sociology* (H. H. Gerth & C. W. Mills, Eds.). New York: Oxford University Press.

Weick, K. E. (1979). *The social psychology of organizing* (2nd ed.). Reading, MA: Addison-Wesley.

Weick, K. E., & Bourgon, M. (1986). Organizations as cognitive maps. In J. P. Sims, Jr., & D. A. Gioia (Eds.), *The thinking organization* (pp. 102-135). San Francisco: Jossey-Bass.

Weiss, J., & Delbecq, A. (1987). High-technology cultures and management. *Group and Organization Studies, 12,* 39-54.

Wilkins, A. (1978). *Organizational stories as an expression of management philosophy: Implications for social control in organizations.* Unpublished doctoral dissertation, Graduate School of Business, Stanford University.

Wilkins, A. (1983). The culture audit. *Organizational Dynamics, 11,* 24-38.

Wilkins, A. (Chair). (1986, March). [Symposium held at the annual meeting of the Western Academy of Management, Reno, NV].

Wilkins, A., & Martin, J. (1979). *Organizational legends.* Working paper, Graduate Schools of Business, Brigham Young University and Stanford University.

Wilkins, A. L., & Patterson, K. J. (1985). You can't get there from here: What will make culture-change projects fail. In R. H. Kilmann, M. J. Saxton, & R. Serpa (Eds.), *Gaining control of the corporate culture* (pp. 262-291). San Francisco: Jossey-Bass.

Wolf, W. B. (1978). *Management and consulting: An introduction to James O. McKinsey.* Ithaca, NY: Cornell University.

Wolf, W. B. (1982). *Organizational diagnosis.* Seminar given at the Graduate School of Management, University of California, Los Angeles.

Zucker, L. (1977). The role of institutionalization in cultural persistence. *American Sociological Review, 45*(5), 726-743.

Trade-Offs in Managing
Organizational Culture

CONNIE J.G. GERSICK
University of California, Los Angeles

ONE implication of Sonja Sackmann's chapter is that commentators ought to identify the contexts from which they write. My background is in organizational theory and behavior, and my expertise is in group development and change. I therefore have the advantage of being vested in none of the viewpoints Sackmann describes, and the disadvantage of being unable to evaluate closely the accuracy of her literature review. Accordingly, I would like simply to point out some questions and issues I believe the chapter raises.

My own training has stressed the value of appreciating trade-offs in organizations. By virtue of its suitability for accomplishing some purposes well, any given course of action will neglect others. The challenge, then, is not to design a flawless organization — which is impossible — but to discover what is best for which purposes and to deal with the inevitable costs that will follow. Sackmann's chapter seems to exhibit two related dilemmas in its search for the single best approach toward managing organizational culture: the trade-offs between complexity and simplicity, and those between observation and control.

COMPLEXITY VERSUS SIMPLICITY

In her chapter, Sackmann argues that culture is extremely complex. She describes it as an always-changing, multifaceted, unpredictable phenomenon, as pervasive and invisible to its members as the air. One of the serious flaws of the culture-as-variable point of view, she argues, is its simplistic reduction of culture to a set of features that can be identified and planfully manipulated. Arguably, some of the trade-offs of simplifying appear in her own descriptions of the four

Correspondence and requests for reprints: Connie J.G. Gersick, Organization and Strategic Studies, Graduate School of Management, University of California, Los Angeles, CA 90024.

Communication Yearbook 13, pp. 149-155

academic approaches to culture. At least three of these approaches — cultural anthropology, culture-as-variable, and culture-as-metaphor — are presented as homogeneous monoliths of scholarship with, for the most part, fairly static, narrowly bounded agendas.

As Sackmann points out, simplification inevitably omits and distorts parts of reality; one risks leaving out so much that one falsifies what one wants to describe, forgoes significant portions of what it has to offer, and draws incorrect conclusions about how to work with it.

At the same time, however, simplification has its benefits. To the extent that her characterizations of competing viewpoints are accurate, Sackmann's concise summaries allow her to accomplish purposes that might otherwise drown in detail. She can point out essential differences among the fields and discuss major implications of each. Her portrayals are sharp enough to be provocative and readily grasped. Simplification is risky, but when it can be done well, it facilitates action and provides usable conceptual tools that highly complex, fully detailed descriptions alone cannot.

It seems that the same trade-offs apply toward approaches to organizational culture. Since Sackmann makes the case for complexity, I will mostly take the role of devil's advocate. Is organizational culture invariably as complicated, dynamic, and unpredictable as she suggests? Are we well served by the argument that cultures must always be apprehended in as much complexity as she advocates?

The first part of my question arises from my skepticism that organizational culture is, in fact, as impossible to capture as Sackmann suggests. One contributor to the inscrutability of organizational culture, in her view, is that it is impossible to predict how an organizational culture may change, since any member may potentially alter it. On one hand, this provocative claim should be a good warning not to underestimate the task of identifying organizational leaders. As Melville Dalton's (1959) classic exposé of actual versus official power structures in real organizations shows, those who wield influence may be found in unexpected places. One cannot assume that "obvious" indicators such as organizational charts are accurate directories of leadership in organizational cultures.

However, pushing Sackmann's point to its extreme, one might infer that all individuals in a culture can be both sufficiently connected with others and sufficiently influential to instigate nontrivial change. This characterization seems to be at odds with everyday experience, as well as with the literatures on social stratification and deviance. Those sources suggest that social systems divide into subgroups, that there are usually hierarchies of influence both within the subgroups and of some subgroups over others, and that members create norms and enforce sanctions against deviance to keep their norms stable. I question the impossibility of identifying those members of an organizational culture or subculture who would be more and less likely to change it, although clearly such an undertaking would require hard work and an open mind.

In Sackmann's view, two other sources of difficulty in capturing organizational culture are its continual dynamism and irreducible complexity. In contrast to the idea that culture is always in flux, Barnard (1945), March and Simon (1958), and others have proposed that much of daily life in organizations is so routine and automatic that it ordinarily does *not* change. This position is based on the assumption that human rationality is bounded. Only by acting as if our choices were limited at any given moment are we able to proceed without being paralyzed by the need for decisions. There are many parts of their organizational work that people seldom even consider doing differently.

The work of Daniel Levinson (1978) on adult development, my own work on groups (Gersick, 1988), and the work of several scholars on organizations (e.g., Miller & Friesen, 1984; Tushman & Romanelli, 1985) suggest, furthermore, that much of the day-to-day variety that does exist in human systems is constrained and shaped by an internally consistent order. The order derives from a set of basic choices that the individual, group, or organization has made — whether consciously or not — about how it will behave. Levinson calls this set of choices a life structure, I call it a framework, and Miller and Friesen call it a configuration. These authors would probably agree that the particular set of choices any individual, group, or organization makes is unique, and therefore it requires painstaking study to characterize any one human system. Nonetheless, this work, all of which is based on qualitative, empirical field research, argues not only that such structures can be found, but that without them, human systems are "up in the air," unable to function comfortably and well for sustained periods of time. Indeed, if a site under observation did *not* appear to embody any coherence or stable structure at all (even a shared view of itself as a hotbed of change), it would seem important to question whether it should be considered an organizational culture at all.

The work of Ruth Benedict extends this argument, applies it to the realm of culture, and brings me to my second question about the trade-off cost of approaching organizational culture as irreducibly complex. Toward the close of World War II, the U.S. government commissioned Benedict (1946) to study Japanese culture, because, as she explained it, "we had to understand their behavior in order to cope with it" (p. 1). Faced with the bewildering panorama of exotic customs and contradictions that Japan represented to Americans at that time, Benedict would surely have failed if she had tried solely to produce a description of Japanese culture in all its complexity. Her accomplishment, it seems to me, was to identify several stable, key assumptions or beliefs that she felt underlay, stimulated, and explained myriad more specific facets of Japanese life. These insights offered some comprehensible guidelines to understanding the Japanese culture, and to understanding it from a more empathic point of view. Without this analytical work, a catalog of cultural details would have been overwhelming at best. Given the necessity to act, Americans would most likely have relied on their own stereotypes to make sense out of the complexity.

Sackmann does us a service by insisting on a healthy respect for cultural complexity, and by warning that to oversimplify culture in pursuit of organizational "fixes" is to court disaster. I would like to suggest, however, that it is equally important to be able, ultimately, to draw a manageable number of "simplified" abstractions about key premises underlying an organizational culture and/or its primary subcultures. Otherwise, the details may add up to nothing more than a thick book of etiquette that can only be memorized, forgotten, or misinterpreted. In the end, to leave the complexity of organizational culture as unreduced description — regardless of how much careful work went into the data collection — may be as much an easy out for a social scientist as the oversimplification Sackmann decries.

OBSERVATION VERSUS CONTROL

My comments above are based on a premise that I believe to be implicit in Sackmann's chapter, that the study of organizational culture is most valuable when it has the ultimate potential to improve organizational management in some way — that is, when it can be applied. This analysis brings me to the second basic tension in the chapter, the question of whether organizational culture can only be observed, or whether it can be actively controlled. Sackmann opposes, as extremes, one view that culture can be straightforwardly manipulated with another view that predictable culture change is impossible. She then suggests a view of "culture as dynamic construct" as a realistic middle ground. I would first like to raise some questions about Sackmann's approach, and then to suggest that the three approaches may be less a display of two extremes with a reasonable middle than they are three approaches appropriate for different purposes.

My questions begin with a sense that Sackmann has sent some different messages about how far she believes culture can be managed. These might be characterized in increasing degrees of control, as follows:

(1) Individuals cannot control culture, but should simply be aware that it matters at all times.
(2) Individuals should infuse everything they do with culture consciousness, because in order to communicate the signals they actually want others to receive, they must know how their meanings will be filtered through various cultural lenses.
(3) Individuals can influence an organization's culture through selective reinforcement, by rewarding the aspects they want and allowing unwanted aspects to wither.

As Sackmann points out, it is extremely difficult to distance oneself from "the air one breathes" enough to be aware of it in the first place. An individual would have to be intensely vigilant to remain sensitive to organizational culture as she describes it — a dynamic, diverse set of characteristics expressed in virtually every aspect of an organization. If culture sensitivity is important, then it is equally important to ask how anyone could sustain this kind of observational energy in addition to his or her normal work load, especially if convinced of the message that no gains in predictable control would result.

A stronger message is that individuals should — and can — know organizational culture thoroughly in order to *adapt* to it. This approach also raises questions. As above, the first difficulties would arise in merely staying abreast of an organization's culture(s). But second, if an organization is truly as complex a mix as Sackmann suggests, how can managers adjust to differing subgroups yet remain believably consistent? How can managers address members of different groups simultaneously in cases where the same action would be interpreted variably according to the cultural lenses of each segment of the audience? The implication of this section of Sackmann's argument may well be that the more managers appreciate the power of culture to condition individuals' perceptions of reality, the more they should seek to enforce cultural homogeneity.

The third of Sackmann's messages seems to be that individuals *can* shape organizational culture through continuous work — on every front, and in seemingly small ways — to reward or ignore selected behaviors. Interestingly, this approach (called "operant conditioning" in behavioral psychology) resembles one advocated by Tom Peters (1978), who argues that executives can change their organizations through subtle, pervasive actions taken on everyday matters. In some ways, this message shows agreement with the proponents of the "culture as variable" view. Even with the caveat that the direction may be approximately, not precisely, what one had in mind, it would be pointless to advocate this kind of organizational shaping without some confidence that organizational culture can be nudged in predictable directions.

Indeed, though Sackmann points out some critical ideological differences among views of organizational culture as "variable," "dynamic," and "metaphor," I would like to suggest that it is premature to treat these primarily as competing approaches from which one should be chosen as best. They may instead be appropriate for different purposes and situations.

There is a new, growing body of empirical work that suggests organizations change through patterns of punctuated equilibrium: long periods of basic stability punctuated by briefer periods of radical alteration (Greiner, 1972; Miller & Friesen, 1984; Tushman & Romanelli, 1985). Larry Greiner (1972) refers to this pattern as evolution and revolution. During evolutionary periods, the system retains its basic underlying structure (see my discussion of work by Levinson, Gersick, and Tushman & Romanelli, above) but exhibits fluctuations, incremental changes, and refinements in character. Examples would include extensions to existing product lines and efforts to execute a given strategy more effectively.

At such times — which predominate for most organizations — the approach that Sackmann advocates seems appropriate. She seems to suggest working on the manifestations of underlying structure, not on the underlying structure itself. Rather than trying to install something completely new into a system, selective reinforcement involves a subtle shaping of behaviors that already exist. It is an approach suited to incremental change.

However, the emerging evidence suggests that incremental approaches are unlikely to propel organizations into genuinely radical change. As Miller and Friesen (1984) explain it, organizations are configurations of parts that are ordinarily too strongly interdependent to be pulled out of shape by events occurring in only one area or at the surface. There are too many forces throughout the organization that, just by operating normally, will bring inconsistencies into line. If basic cultural assumptions remain in place, then, it seems that changes generated on the surface will either be reinterpreted as new manifestations of old assumptions or remain rote behaviors that may make little sense to those performing them. Radical transformation seems to require direct changes in the underlying structure. Empirically, this has been found to involve the dismantling of the old structure, followed by a period of uncertainty and the establishment of a new structure, all within a relatively short period of time (Dyer, 1987; Tushman, Newman, & Romanelli, 1986). An example would be the restructuring of AT&T, involving new markets, new products, new organizational design, and new strategies, as well as changes in the organization's culture.

Many aspects of an organization aside from its culture would require attention during that kind of change. Furthermore, the predictability of efforts to plan such change — much more difficult and risky than incremental adjustments — would be far from perfect. Nevertheless, to the extent that the "variable" approach involves identifying the basic assumptions of an organization's culture and working on them directly (e.g., Sathe, 1985), it would seem most appropriate.

In contrast with these two approaches, both fairly applied, the third approach to culture as metaphor might be viewed as basic research. As Sackmann portrays them, its proponents seem interested in describing what exists rather than in changing it. Such an endeavor appears to be closer to the traditional discipline of cultural anthropology. The work of cultural anthropologists has been collected over the years in the Human Relations Area Files, a vast, rich resource that documents the variety of human cultures and offers scholars from all over the world a data bank to which they may put their own research questions. The work of culture-as-metaphor proponents might eventually offer scholars a similar kind of resource for organizational culture.

CONCLUSION

In closing, I would like to note one last trade-off that seems neglected, though it hovers just below the surface of Sackmann's chapter. It deals with the implications of organizational culture research and publication for the work force. On one hand, the more we can provide managers with a sophisticated appreciation for the extent and impact of cultural differences, the more potential there will be for them to understand organization members accurately, communicate clearly, and treat people in fair, productive ways. On the other hand, as managers realize the complexity involved and the perceptiveness required, they may well want to try to make their organizations culturally homogeneous.

In her chapter, Sackmann advocates applying culture-sensitive management particularly in personnel areas — selection, training, and promotion. She does not discuss who should be setting policies, with what degree of participation, how, or to what specific ends. It seems particularly important to deal with these questions thoughtfully and responsibly, in order to avoid the kind of easy answers that could exclude anyone who appears to be culturally different from the majority, and thus "too difficult."

Finally, I feel that Sackmann's lively chapter is an excellent stimulus for further thought about the management of organizational culture. It offers one way to map out a variety of approaches toward the field, and it raises many challenging questions.

REFERENCES

Barnard, C. I. (1945). Foreword. In H. A. Simon (Ed.), *Administrative behavior.* New York: Free Press.

Benedict, R. (1946). *The chrysanthemum and the sword: Patterns of Japanese culture.* New York: Meridian.

Dalton, M. (1959). *Men who manage.* New York: John Wiley.

Dyer, W. G. (1987). *Cultural transformations in organizations.* Paper presented at the annual meeting of the Academy of Management, New Orleans.

Gersick, C.J.G. (1988). Time and transition in work teams: Toward a new model of group development. *Academy of Management Journal, 31,* 9-41.

Greiner, L. E. (1972, July/August). Evolution and revolution as organizations grow. *Harvard Business Review,* pp. 37-46.

Levinson, D. J. (1978). *The seasons of a man's life.* New York: Alfred A. Knopf.

March, J., & Simon, H. (1958). *Organizations.* New York: John Wiley.

Miller, D., & Friesen, P. (1984). *Organizations: A quantum view.* Englewood Cliffs, NJ: Prentice-Hall.

Peters, T. J. (1978, Autumn). Symbols, patterns, and settings: An optimistic case for getting things done. *Organizational Dynamics.*

Sathe, V. (1985). How to decipher and change organizational culture. In R. H. Kilmann and Associates (Eds.), *Managing corporate cultures.* San Francisco: Jossey-Bass.

Tushman, M., Newman, W., & Romanelli, E. (1986). Convergence and upheaval. Managing the unsteady pace of organizational evolution. *California Management Review, 29*(1), 29-44.

Tushman, M., & Romanelli, E. (1985). Organizational evolution: A metamorphosis model of convergence and reorientation. In L. Cummings & B. Staw (Eds.), *Research in organizational behavior* (Vol. 7, pp. 171-222). Greenwich, CT: JAI.

More Thought Provoking
Than a New Paradigm

LARRY E. GREINER
University of Southern California

S ACKMANN'S chapter presents me with a dilemma; while I agree with many of its basic tenets, I find myself distracted by its polemical tone. Nevertheless, the chapter is sufficiently provocative and frequently on target with its criticism that it should serve as a useful focus for future debate and constructive action.

My own background is more in the field of organizational change than of organizational culture. This bias probably makes me more susceptible to the culture-as-variable camp; however, I find myself less amenable to its simplicities (as portrayed by Sackmann) and more receptive to her advocacy of the "dynamic construct" school of organization culture. I have seen too many change efforts founder on the rocks of a resistant culture to know that it cannot simply be tweaked on or off at the whim of charismatic leaders or brilliant consultants. Still I suspect that Sackmann's concept is intended less as a new paradigm than as an unstated challenge to push on with vitally needed field research.

Let me highlight some major points of agreement, while inserting my occasional discomforts with Sackmann's arguments.

PHENOMENOLOGY/EXISTENTIAL BIAS

Sackmann's theoretical roots clearly lie in existential psychology, and she extends this position to conceptualizing about organization culture. The notion of "shared meaning" probes more deeply at the personal level than do externally

Correspondence and requests for reprints: Larry E. Greiner, Department of Management and Organization MC-1421, School of Business, University of Southern California, Los Angeles, CA 90089-1421.

Communication Yearbook 13, pp. 156-161

defined "social control" concepts more common to sociological and anthropological concepts of culture. We clearly need to know more about how a collectivity of people perceives and feels about their institutional surroundings, and how they share these inner thoughts and feelings to affect each others' behavior.

At the same time, Sackmann leaves us in a bit of metaphorical limbo—what is meant by "deep structure" in organizations? Is it shared meaning at a conscious cognitive level, such as implied by her original concepts of assumptional, dictionary, directional, and recipe knowledge derived from a field study? Or is it some deeper related pattern of enduring and unconscious (though somehow shared between people) emotional attachments to cognitions of past and present organizational symbols and practices? Do these artifacts and practices persist, even when plainly dysfunctional for organization performance, because of their "nonrational" emotional basis? Does Sackmann's social/existential approach have serious theoretical limits, as do social control theories of culture, for unraveling the deeper "whys" behind culturally rooted behavior? Must one (including Sackmann), for example, turn to psychoanalytic concepts to understand the emotional power of myths, rituals, heroes, and taboos (Kets de Vries & Miller, 1984)?

MULTIPLICITY OF SUBCULTURES

The simplistic notion of the "variable" school that all organizations have (or should have) only one homogeneous culture consisting of a few salient values is strongly criticized by Sackmann, and I agree. Academics know that each of the various schools within a modern university takes on a culture of its own, just as do separate manufacturing plants within a large industrial organization. My own consulting once identified a distinct "top management" culture in a company that maintained a club of White, male, Protestant, Ivy League, and politically liberal members who espoused equal opportunity for all employees but never admitted a Black, woman, or Jew to their club at the top. Thus Sackmann's recommendation that senior management should become more aware of and sensitive to the internal diversity of organization culture within an organization seems eminently sensible.

At the same time, we also know that the total organization often takes on certain shared meanings that cross subunit boundaries and bind them together. Unfortunately, this notion is not adequately acknowledged or explored by Sackmann. In addition, could it be that organizations with single products or stable technologies or limited geographical ranges or long-tenured management are more likely to develop a homogeneous set of commonly shared meanings? And are there certain "core" shared meanings that may even make possible more diverse cultures in organizations? These are important research questions that need the attention of Sackmann and others.

SOCIAL CREATION OF ORGANIZATIONS

For Sackmann, organization culture is everything about organizational life, superseding and underlying such supposedly "objective" realities as formal structure, business strategy, and information systems. In contrast, many researchers in the management field have come to treat these phenomena as "independent" and "rationally conceived" variables that "cause" behavior. Sackmann, on the other hand, would regard this positivistic logic as failing to recognize that such structures and systems are created and re-created by people.

She clearly has a point, but must we accept her contention that there is such a pervasive, direct, and continuously interactive connection with organization culture? I doubt it, if we assume that formal structures are created by a minority of people with relatively greater power and that institutional inertia can take on a life of its own that frequently extends beyond the careers of its creators. For these reasons, many scholars (not just uninformed consultants) would contend that organizational culture has rightly acquired its "variable" status. Nevertheless, too much research has been done on the behavioral effects of structures at the expense of examining the creation process behind organizational forms and their subsequent evolution. Moreover, are there other "realities" of organizations, such as technology and products, that need to be considered for how and why they are created by people, as well as for their evolving cultural meaning to new generations of organization members? A knotty empirical question concerns the extent to which organization culture encompasses and is affected by these "other" phenomena of modern organizations.

CHANGE PROCESS

Sackmann strongly attacks the culture-as-variable school for its unidimensional and manipulative approach to cultural change. No doubt the subjects of her criticism would argue that they operate from a greater level of sophistication, and would cite dramatic results achieved through their efforts. However, I find myself more in Sackmann's camp, given the lack of systematic evaluation research, the faddism of cultural consulting, and strong empirical evidence showing that new CEOs have little impact on organization performance (Friedman & Singh, 1986). How else is one to explain the historical failure of American steel and auto companies to modernize themselves? Their organization cultures produced insider leaders who, year after year, perpetuated status quo practices despite threatening environmental signals. Today we find consultants of the culture-as-variable school advocating cultural change toward idealized models that the client organization is to be trained into — an approach that Sackmann correctly criticizes for ignoring the existing culture.

Without falling into cultural determinism, Sackmann argues that organization cultures can and do change, but only through a gradual process in which leaders act out of greater "awareness" of their existing organization cultures. Sackmann adheres to her pedagogical roots by recommending that increased cultural awareness occurs through the reeducation of organization leaders. Further, she confines the resulting new behaviors of these sensitized leaders to enlightened human resource practices and symbolic actions that resonate with the deep structure of organizations, and thereby change its form. This influence process is quite different from one we have recently reported on successful strategic change, which is time phased and involves intense political action within the top team around substantive decisions (e.g., formulation of business strategy and structural reorganization; Greiner & Bhambri, 1989). In the field study giving rise to these findings, the negative hold of the culture on a financially troubled company was broken by gaining the commitment of the top team to a new strategy, redesigning the formal structure, shifting many managers to new positions, and only later engaging in reeducation efforts at lower levels.

At the same time, and in support of Sackmann, we know that businesses that "stick to their knitting" while growing through acquisitions of *closely related* businesses are more likely to perform better than diversified conglomerates (Rumelt, 1974). This finding suggests that existing cultural attributes can and should be capitalized upon in the growth-planning process. However, the leveraged buyout era may give little time for this incremental process to germinate, since entire organizations can disappear overnight through decisions made by a few outsiders. Private sector organizations are not only cultural phenomena but legal entities with owners who frequently lack socialization or attachment to an organization's culture. The point of this argument is that knowledge about the function and importance of organizational culture in the change process is limited and changing itself because of new external contingencies. Although Sackmann pleads for greater internal cultural understanding and gradualism, the realities of today's environmental turbulence may not afford that luxury.

DEPTH MEASUREMENT

Given Sackmann's existential orientation, it is not surprising that she prescribes in-depth interviews conducted by outsiders for learning about organizational culture. This move is in contrast to the likely approach of the sociologist, who observes and infers social norms from behavioral regularities, or the organization theorist, who uses standardized surveys to ascertain quantifiable comparisons of organization climate. Each of these approaches has some distinct advantages and serious limits. The advantage of Sackmann's interviewing method is that it probes for the internalized and underlying meanings and feelings behind social behavior patterns. This method corrects for a serious limitation of observations and surveys, which seldom reveal *why* groups of people behave in predictable ways. Such "deeper" data can in turn be used for determining how seriously attached people are to certain ritualistic behavior patterns, for therapeutically raising the awareness level for previously unquestioned behaviors, and for determining how proposed changes in behavior may be accepted or rejected by a targeted subculture. Unfortunately, the interviewing method is time-consuming, costly, and of questionable scientific validity. Systematic observations and numerical surveys are more likely to overcome these limitations, but they need to be supplemented by in-depth interviews to inform remotely derived inferences as well as to rein in insensitive and unrealistic recommendations made by commercial consultants.

FUTURE DIRECTIONS

There are likely more issues to raise from Sackmann's chapter, and that is its main benefit — it makes you stop and think, evaluate your theoretical position, and even get angry. I particularly disliked the manner in which Sackmann lumped just about every existing school of organization thinking (e.g., open systems, natural systems, contingency theory) into the culture-as-variable camp. I have always believed that these points of view (espoused by my "heroes" from bygone days) came into being as ways to understand organizations better, not simply to provide action-taking rationales for managers and consultants. But Sackmann is perhaps right for the wrong reasons; younger scholars may not recognize that years of translation have caused yesterday's breakthrough theories to become rationalized and trivialized into tools for solutions rather than concepts for insight. Sackmann does not acknowledge these injustices, and in so doing she engages a bit too much in righteous advocacy for her singular point of view.

Nevertheless, Sackmann is to be commended for squarely confronting the most difficult problem facing organization theory today — that of attempting to integrate micro aspects of the individual psyche with macro organization functioning. Too many of us have chosen one side or the other as a way of serving our narrow disciplinary interests, and, as a result, we have failed to capture and portray a richer picture of organization life.

Sackmann fortunately sticks her neck out, and her forefront kind of theorizing is understandably going to be rough, incomplete, and open to criticism. Where we need to go next, I believe, is toward a greater level of specificity and concreteness in cultural theory, research methodology, data analysis, and action taking by practitioners. Sackmann's chapter gives rise to hints of questions that should puzzle and stimulate us all: Is pursuing the concept of organizational culture a fruitful bridge between the individual and the organization? Is "shared meaning" the critical linking concept, and what does this concept really mean at cognitive, emotional, and behavioral levels? Must we make the concept of culture more dynamic and longitudinal in its conceptualization for a fuller understanding of organization change? How are environmental factors to be accounted for as they impinge on and interact with organizational culture? How can we improve upon and better integrate the crude measurement techniques now available? Is the lack of cultural awareness on the part of organization leaders critical to explaining why so many of them stumble? How can this myopia be overcome and translated into skillful action? And what does greater leadership sensitivity to organization culture imply for its interaction with so-called independent variables of organization structure, systems design, and strategic planning?

These questions will be answered through confronting and groping with the applied problems of field research in an ongoing program of study in actual organizations.

REFERENCES

Friedman, S. D., & Singh, H. (1986). *Why he left: An explanation for the succession effect.* Paper presented at the annual meeting of the Academy of Management, Chicago.

Greiner, L. E., & Bhambri, A. (1989, Summer). New CEO intervention and dynamics of deliberate strategic change. *Strategic Management Journal.*

Kets de Vries, M., & Miller, D. (1984). *The neurotic organization.* San Francisco: Jossey-Bass.

Rumelt, R. P. (1974). *Strategy, structure, and economic performance.* Boston: Harvard University, Graduate School of Business Administration, Division of Research.

4 Defining Stories in Organizations: Characteristics and Functions

MARY HELEN BROWN
Auburn University

Stories are an important and influential aspect of an organization's discourse. This essay explores the characteristics and functions of stories in the organizational setting. In this examination, definitional criteria are established for the identification of organizational stories as a conversational unit. Stories must exhibit (a) a ring of truth, (b) relevance for the membership, (c) a story grammar, and (d) a sense of temporality. In addition, stories in organizations perform a variety of functions that work toward shaping organizational reality for members. These functions include (a) uncertainty reduction, (b) management of meaning, and (c) bonding and identification. Sample stories drawn from a county jail are used throughout the chapter to illustrate the points being established. In addition, two major areas for research examining organizational stories are outlined: (a) story circumstances and (b) story applications.

T HIS chapter is grounded in the assumption that stories are a dominant narrative form of an organization's discourse. This perspective is not without precedent. White (1981) notes that narratives, as expressed by stories, serve as a universal metacode to transmit reality. White argues that placing information in story form gives the events of everyday life richness, coherence, and closure. Indeed, Bateson (1979) contends that all individuals think in story form and that this common thought pattern provides connectedness and relevance for the events of life.

The work of Fisher (1984, 1985a, 1985b) amplifies these ideas. Fisher examines the notion of narrative as a paradigm for human communication. In this view, individuals are storytellers who form and evaluate stories in real life as well as in literature. Moreover, Fisher notes that institutions continually supply the grist

Correspondence and requests for reprints: Mary Helen Brown, 6030 Haley Center, Department of Speech Communication, Auburn University, Auburn, AL 36849-5211.

Communication Yearbook 13, pp. 162-190

for story lines (Fisher, 1985b). And Mumby (1987) uses the narrative paradigm to examine how stories relate to the politics of an organization.

In an examination of organizational culture, Weick and Browning (1986) comment that "stories are not a symptom of culture, culture is a symptom of storytelling" (p. 251). If this perspective is combined with the idea that "a culture is not something an organization has; a culture is something an organization is" (Pacanowsky & O'Donnell-Trujillo, 1983), then it may be argued that a good part of organizing is storytelling.

IDENTIFYING STORIES IN ORGANIZATIONS

Stories are a vital part of organizations. As Martin (1982) argues, all members hear and tell stories. However, the identification of these stories has not always been clear or consistent. In this regard, this chapter (a) develops definitional criteria to identify organizational stories and (b) outlines certain functions stories play in organizations. More specifically, the criteria for classifying discourse as an organizational story are as follows: First, organizational stories display a sense of temporality. Second, the conversational unit exhibits a story grammar, including a preface, recounting, and closing sequence. Third, a story in an organization rings true to the membership. Fourth, the story has relevance to the membership.

In addition, three story functions are discussed here. First, stories function to reduce uncertainty by providing information about organizational activities. Second, stories manage meaning by framing organizational activities in terms of organizational values. Third, organizational stories act to bond members together by presenting points of shared identity.

The analysis presented draws from the literature of a variety of areas, including, but not limited to, management, communication theory, discourse analysis, sociology, applied psychology, and folklore. This essay attempts to examine stories in organizations by exploring their characteristics and functions. This effort in many ways is based on Rowland's (1987) argument that narrative studies should focus on the talk that actually forms a story. The sections that follow characterize organizational stories in terms of their format and content as related by and to members and look at stories in terms of the work that these narratives perform for the organization and its membership. The combination of form, content, and function constitutes the essence of an organizational story.

EXEMPLAR STORIES

Throughout this chapter, several stories will be used as examples for the points being described. Although the sample stories used here are not the major focus of this essay, some discussion of the context that surrounds them seems in order. These stories are from a research project conducted in a county jail in a medium-sized southwestern city. The primary purpose of this facility is detention rather than rehabilitation or punishment. For the most part, inmates serve time waiting for their transfer to a state mental institution or prison or for their release. The primary activity of the corrections officers is monitoring the inmates' behavior.

The jail depicted in these stories is a grimy, roach-infested facility located on the fifth and sixth floors of the county's courthouse. The fifth floor primarily houses administrative offices, while the sixth floor consists of the cell areas. Access to the jail is restricted. An individual must first pass a checkpoint and identification area on the first floor in order to enter the one elevator that serves the jail. The elevator is controlled by keyed access and essentially "skips" the second, third, and fourth floors. Individuals encounter an additional checkpoint and identification area when exiting the elevator on the sixth floor. The jail is divided into two major sections—male and female. These areas are separated by a kind of "neutral ground" consisting of the elevator, a watch post/control room, and hallway. The neutral ground is bracketed by two heavy metallic mesh cell doors. To enter or exit either of the major cell areas, one must be recognized and cleared by a corrections officer.

Each of the major cell areas is divided into a variety of subsections or "tanks," including isolation, disciplinary, aggressive, and passive areas. On the whole, the jail, which has a recommended capacity of 275 inmates, suffers from overcrowding. Inmates sleep on the floor regularly and the recommended inmate to corrections officer ratio of 45:1 is consistently exceeded.

Both male and female officers work on the male side of the jail; however, only female officers work on the female side except during emergency situations. Administrators report that officers are so allocated primarily to avoid problems with or accusations of harassment. The officers' workday at the jail is divided into three shifts: 7:00 a.m.-3:00 p.m., 3:00-11:00 p.m., and 11:00 p.m.-7:00 a.m.

A research team of graduate students trained in qualitative methods entered the county jail primarily to investigate corrections officers' morale.[1] In carrying out this investigation, members of the research team conducted observations of and unstructured interviews with several of the corrections officers. In this way, information gained from interactions with the corrections officers was enriched through observation of the officers' daily activities. Topics of interest included but were not limited to the following: job stress; reasons for turnover; communication with inmates, fellow corrections officers, and superiors; job satisfaction; and training.

Members of the research team prepared extensive field notes based on their experiences with the officers in the county jail. The field notes of all members of the research team were pooled to form a data base for investigations into life in the county jail. The corrections officers' stories presented here were drawn from this data pool.

Stories are used here to clarify and amplify points presented throughout the essay. These stories serve primarily as examples of story characteristics and functions rather than as a representation of the jail (although more commentary on the values of the jail is presented in line with the discussion). This use of stories as explanatory examples rests in Weick's (1979) notion of "ten o'clock research." As Weick notes: "It remains true that any explanation dreamed up by anyone will be true for some other person at some time at some place. All explanations, no matter how bizarre, are likely to be valid part of the time" (p. 39). Admittedly, the discussion that follows consists of some speculation; however, the process of speculation "brings feelings and intuitions into conscious awareness, a process that leads the speculator more deeply into the phenomenon about which he is speculating" (Weick, 1979, p. 40).

CHARACTERIZING ORGANIZATIONAL STORIES

The chapter now turns to the establishment of definitional criteria for the identification of organizational stories as a conversational unit. In this regard, stories must have (a) a sense of temporality, (b) a story grammar, (c) relevance for the membership, and (d) a ring of truth. The first two issues focus on the telling of the story; the second two deal with the interpretation of the story.

A Sense of Temporality

Organizational stories reflect a sense of temporality. This sense of temporality distinguishes a story as a sequence of events from a list of events (Scholes, 1981; Stewart, 1982). Storytelling can be considered to be a verbal form of time travel (Beach & Japp, 1983). The past is thrust into the present through stories. Further, by bringing the past to the present, a new "reality" for the past is created (Sacks, 1978). In this way, the past is being re-created and defined as it is being recounted in the present (Brown, 1983).

Storytelling acts as a transformation, a phenomenon that exists when a primary activity is changed into a framed, or secondary, activity (Goffman, 1974). In storytelling, certain features of the primary event, situation, or circumstance remain constant while other features undergo a "slippage" or alteration (Hofstadter, 1979). Appropriate events are told, while other events are not related (Scholes, 1981). In other words, the secondary activity, the storytelling, is not identical to the primary activity, the actual event. The event itself is not redone, but certain elements remain the same; for example, the individuals or characters involved in both the primary and secondary activities may remain constant, while the presentation of the order of events may change.

White (1981) notes that the stories individuals tell do not necessarily mirror the reality of an event. White claims that humans use temporal sequencing to reflect a narrative form of reality. Chatman (1981) argues that in this way a double time structuring is created. This structure consists of two types of time sequences:

historic time, which consists of the actual, clock-time ordering of events, and discourse time, which consists of the presentation of those events in temporal story form. As Mink (1981) points out, the events of the world do not, by definition, happen in story form. However, individuals use stories to give voice to a reordered view of reality that is at once more appealing and understandable to individuals than the actual events may have been.

Story A: "I've Been Hit"

Question: What sort of thing might cause you to quit your job?

Answer: I've been hit — last November when I'd been here three months. We don't want males and females together visiting. And one day I was taking a woman out and there was a male there. They'd known each other and had been dating. The male spotted her and yelled at her to come over and she refused to come. He said something like, "I'm gonna kick your ass," and she said something like, "You'll have to come get me," and he was after her. I was just coming out and saw this happening and didn't know what was happening. It seemed like several minutes, but it couldn't have been more than a few seconds. My mind was just a-clicking. As she was running, she grabbed me and swung me around and he hit me on the lip. I went to the local hospital and then went home early. My head was pounding. When I got home, I thought, was it worth it? I hadn't ever had a man hit me before and here this man had, and he wasn't even *my man.* I finally decided that it was an accident. He was after someone else. If he'd been after my ass, it would have been different.

In Story A, the corrections officer specifically mentions a type of temporal slippage. The officer states: "It seemed like several minutes but it couldn't have been more than a few seconds." She restructures the confusing events into a story form that "makes sense." In addition, the officer shows how reality may be reordered in stories. She notes: "I was just coming out and saw this happening and I didn't know what was happening." Nevertheless, the officer is able through reflection to relate a coherent story based upon a series of events of which she was initially unaware. In this way, she illustrates the slippery nature of time, reality, and storytelling.

On a more obvious level, the time involved in experiencing the historic event and the discourse time involved in narrating the story are dramatically different. In Story A, the circumstances involved in the attack, the trip to the hospital, and the period of reflection at home are encapsulated in an organizational story that takes less than two minutes to relate.

Organizational members use stories to manipulate time to reorder reality. A set of events that may have seemed chaotic, unpredictable, or haphazard at the time of occurrence is given sequencing that adds to its meaning. Thus organizational stories simultaneously help create a new version of past events and define the present situation.

Story Grammars

The identification of stories from ongoing, turn-by-turn conversation is made by attending to the characteristic structure or grammar that stories manifest (Jefferson, 1978; McLaughlin, 1984; McLaughlin, Cody, Kane, & Robey, 1981). This conversational structure, while not specific to stories found in organizations, makes it possible to identify stories from the stream of discourse found in organizations. In its most basic form, a story is a multiutterance, descriptive form of talk that presents a sequence of events that has occurred in the past (Goodwin, 1984; Sacks, 1972; Tannen, 1984). Stories generally consist of a preface sequence, a recounting sequence, and a closing sequence appearing in predictable "slots" (Sacks, 1972).

Preface sequence. The preface sequence acts as a point of transition between a story and the talk that immediately precedes it (Jefferson, 1978). This sequence provides audience members with an orientation to the significance of the story itself (Ryave, 1978).

Story A displays a form of prefacing. As an interactional activity (Pacanowsky & O'Donnell-Trujillo, 1983), the prefacing is shared by both participants in the conversation. The conversation preceding the story deals with turnover in the facility and leads to the question: "What sort of thing might cause you to quit your job?" That question is a request for comment. The corrections officer uses the statement "I've been hit" to indicate the significance and orientation of the recounting sequence that follows.

Recounting sequence. In general, the recounting sequence requires more than one utterance (McLaughlin, 1984) and presents the sequence of events that has occurred in the past events (Kermode, 1981). Here, the narrator provides the setting for the story, the course of action that occurred, and the outcomes resulting from that course of action (McLaughlin, 1984). Goodwin (1984) also points out that background information may be embedded parenthetically within a story.

Once again, Story A acts as an exemplar. The officer sets the story by presenting the time ("last November"), the place (that facility), and her particular circumstances ("I'd been there three months"). Next, the officer takes the story through the following plot: moving the prisoner, the confrontation between the male prisoner and female prisoner, the point at which the officer was struck, and the results of the incident. During the course of the story, the officer provides relevant parenthetical background information, for example: "We don't want males and females together" and "They'd known each other and had been dating."

Closing sequence. As the recounting ends, the story moves into the closing sequence. The closing sequence acts as a transition point between the story and the conversation that follows (Goodwin, 1984). In the closing, the teller provides some indication that the story has been completed (McLaughlin, 1984) and/or conveys the relevance of the story (Sacks, 1974).

In Story A, the closing appears as a type of retrospective rationalization. The officer is at home, the incident is over, and she must decide on a future course of action. In reflecting upon the incident, the officer determines that the event constitutes "an accident" and even includes some humor ("I hadn't ever had a man hit me before and here this man had, and he wasn't even *my man*"). She concludes the story by implying that an intentional attack would result in her resignation. In this manner, the officer not only resolves the story, but brings the story back to the original question as well.

Significance of the story grammar. The ability to construct a well-structured story is important in enhancing its impact on organizational members. Moch and Fields (1985) note that a speaker's competence in storytelling may bolster or impede a listener's ability to interpret the meaning or significance of that particular message. Along these lines, Agar (1980) claims that a story that is competently formed leads to greater comprehension and recall among listeners than a less well-developed story.

These notions relate closely to Fisher's narrative paradigm and the concept of narrative probability. Fisher (1984, 1985a, 1985b) argues that individuals naturally judge the narrative probability of any story, its formal characteristics, as they determine the story's relevance and merit. As such, the coherence of a story, the extent to which it "hangs together," helps determine whether or not that story will be accepted (Fisher, 1985a). In an organization, a story that is not accepted loses its power (Weick & Browning, 1986). Thus the corrections officer's ability to structure a story in a clear and coherent fashion adds impact to her thoughts concerning a possible reason to leave her job.

Relevance for the Membership

The relevance of a story is determined by the audience. That is, while the storyteller holds responsibility for framing the story in an appropriate way, the listener ultimately judges its relevance. An effective way to determine if a story indeed has relevance and applicability to the organizational membership is to employ the notions of Bormann (1983, 1985). In his discussion of symbolic convergence theory, Bormann claims that humans tell stories as a social activity. These stories work to fulfill the psychological needs of a group or organization by accounting for their experiences and shared realities. The persistence and dissemination of a story or story theme reflect its relevance. A story or story theme on a "popular" topic that is told, understood, and appreciated by the body of the membership therefore may be considered relevant. Although the factors that contribute to a story's relevance are largely unexplored, one factor may be a focus on members and/or on issues that are of significance to the membership (Martin, Feldman, Hatch, & Sitkin, 1983; Martin & Siehl, 1983).

Many times, the storyteller him- or herself acts as the hero of a story. Sacks (1978) points out that this orientation does not result from particularly heroic actions, but rather that the teller presents the story from his or her own perspective.

Story A exemplifies the storyteller-as-hero perspective. The officer does not lay claim to any type of heroism. To the contrary, she reveals a certain degree of helplessness and confusion — "I was just coming out and saw this happening and didn't know what was happening." However, the story does present the incident from her perspective.

Pacanowsky and O'Donnell-Trujillo (1983) emphasize the role of members as relevant figures by noting that members figure into stories in three ways. First, members tell *personal stories* about themselves in order to enhance or clarify their organizational identities. Second, members relate stories about other members in *collegial stories*. Collegial stories are seen to present what really happens in an organization. Third, members present organizationally sanctioned viewpoints in *corporate stories.* Story A is a type of personal story. The following stories represent a collegial story and a corporate story.

Story B: "War Zone"

> The most frightening experience was when a group of inmates had taken fluorescent bulbs and broken them in half and put them in sheets to use like swords. Then they took their mattresses and made barricades and some of the inmates even grabbed pipes from the jail. It was like a war zone. It turned out that the whole thing was over the leader of that particular cell group not being able to make a phone call that he was promised. The lieutenant who was on duty waited for the next shift to come on and took two details of corrections officers to the cell area, hoping that the show of force would help the problem. When the lieutenant found out what was at the root of the problem, he walked right in the cell and took the arm of the leader and told him they were going to the telephone. That ended the problem.

The narrator presents the lieutenant as a hero to his colleagues. Rather than attempting to restore order immediately, the lieutenant waits for an appropriate set of circumstances in which to quell the chaos. The lieutenant displays "cool" leadership by going to the heart of the matter and resolving the conflict informally.

Story C: "Jim Ed"

> We had one man, a trustee, an older man, who was picked up DWI. It was his second time so he had to do time [at the state corrections facility]. We kept him here as long as we could — probably slowed down the paperwork — we all liked him. Well, the other morning he told me he was going. I said, "Jim Ed, don't tell me you're going." He was serious. I told the other officers, "Jim Ed pulled chain this morning." You get attached. We all felt bad, but that's how it goes.

Story C seemingly begins as a collegial story. The story reveals a relationship between the corrections officers and a prisoner who is well liked. The story points out that corrections officers are able to exert some control over the system by delaying the inmate's departure by stalling the necessary paperwork. However, the system eventually prevails and the inmate "pulls chain" to the state prison. The story also highlights the danger of violating an implicit organizational sanction; that is, officers are not "supposed to" become attached to inmates.

Thus organizational stories deal with members and their shared concerns. This criterion separates organizational stories from extraneous stories that just happen to occur within the walls of an organization. For example, a worker may relate a "my vacation at the beach" story. If that story presents a straightforward account of the events that took place during the visit, then it is not an organizational story even if the story is told on the job. If, on the other hand, the story deals with the reproduction of "vacation" as an organizational concept, problems with obtaining vacation time, or other organizationally relevant elements, then an organizational story exists. As such, examinations of stories in organizations should distinguish between organizational stories and stories that fall beyond organizational interests.

A Ring of Truth

Stories in organizations should ring true to members. To "ring true" means a story makes sense in the organizational context. Again, as in the case of relevance, the determination of sensibleness rests with the listeners. (Evidence suggests that individuals rarely question whether a particular story is absolutely true or false; for example, see Bennett, 1978; Sathe, 1983.) Even the most vehement critic of an organization generally accepts the truthfulness of a story while continuing to be skeptical of the action or policy that spurred the storytelling (Martin & Powers, 1983b).

Wilkins (1984) suggests that stories may be judged to ring true because they provide concrete evidence for abstract ideas. Stories communicate information about facts in relatively brief form (Lucaites & Condit, 1985). As Weick and Browning (1986) note, brevity contributes to persuasiveness, and managers who tell stories are more persuasive than managers who do not utilize this form.

In a study along these lines, Martin and Powers (1983a) examined a group of M.B.A. students in an attempt to determine the truth-in-context qualities of different types of evidence: (a) a story, (b) statistics, (c) statistics and a story, and (d) a direct policy statement (accompanied by a story, story with statistics, or statistics). They found that the story generally had a stronger impact than the story coupled with the statistics, while the story coupled with statistics had greater impact than did statistics alone. Further, subjects found policy statements to be more truthful when the statements appeared with a story that provided support or confirmation.

On the other hand, Martin and Powers note that the credibility of stories is not limitless. For example, subjects perceive stories that contradict or disconfirm a policy statement to have less credibility than statistics or the combination of story and statistics that disconfirm the statement. Martin and Powers claim that in this case stories are seen as exceptions to the norm rather than as exemplars of the norm. As such, if a story is to ring true, it should fit with listeners' perceptions of life in the organization.

Martin and Powers's findings confirm Fisher's (1984, 1985a, 1985b) notion of narrative fidelity. The narrative fidelity of a story rests in its truth qualities. The strength of these qualities results from the extent to which the story fits with the history, knowledge, background, and experience of audience members (Weick & Browning, 1986). Thus the members who interpret the story ultimately hold the power to determine if it rings true.

In summary, stories in organizations may be identified by four characteristics. First, organizational stories manifest a sense of temporality as past events are brought to the present. Second, organizational stories exhibit a specific story grammar consisting of a preface sequence, a recounting sequence, and a closing sequence. Third, organizational stories have relevance to the membership. Fourth, organizational stories ring true to the membership of an organization. The first two of these characteristics rest primarily with tellers, while the second two rest with interpreters.

These criteria are essential to establishing that an organizational story exists. That is, these criteria are useful for identifying and defining stories within organizations. Once those tasks are accomplished, the particular function(s) or purpose(s) of an organizational story may be investigated.

FUNCTIONS OF STORIES IN ORGANIZATIONS

Stories in organizations serve a variety of functions. In this perspective, stories move beyond reflecting organizational reality to working toward shaping organizational reality. Stories are more than organizational artifacts; they are organizing agents. After all, a story is more than the relation of a sequence of events (Scholes, 1981). Rather, a story relates events to someone for some reason. As such, stories are constructed around functions and are tied in some way to the particular teller, setting, and occasion (Smith, 1981).

In this regard, stories do more for organizational members than act as escape routes from the mundane. Georges (1987) observes that traditional analyses of stories emphasize the notion of stories as diversions by pointing out that stories work to entertain and amuse listeners. However, stories in organizations go beyond simple entertainment (Weick & Browning, 1986); they operate instead to inform, influence, reassure, and so on (Georges, 1981). As such, stories may perform multiple functions (Martin et al., 1983). For example, Browning, Korinek, and Cooper (1979), in examining the negotiation of organizational culture of the military, note that an organizational story can (a) encourage members to work hard in order to get ahead in the system, (b) explain "how things get done" within a particular organization, and (c) present the uncertainty arising from the events occurring in the lives of organizational members.

The outline of story functions presented here should in no way be thought to constitute an exhaustive list. Rather, the functions outlined below are presented because they echo throughout the literature. For purposes of this discussion, three primary functions of organizational stories are considered: the uncertainty reduction function, the management of meaning function, and the bonding/identification function. This approach reflects Sullivan's (1988) examination of the roles language plays in organizational motivation. In his analysis of language action, Sullivan notes that language used in organizations works to reduce uncertainty, make meaning, and bond members together.

Organizational Stories and Uncertainty Reduction

Uncertainty exists within organizations. Many aspects of organizational life involve procedures and relationships that are largely unwritten and loosely coupled, but that are nonetheless influential (Weick, 1976, 1979). The uncertainty evolving from loosely coupled elements may be more appropriately addressed through informal means, such as storytelling, than through more formal sources, such as the employee handbook. Stories help organizational members "fill in the blanks" of their institutional lives. In other words, stories provide information that reduces the uncertainty members experience from day to day.

For example, in the county jail, a great deal of uncertainty exists that is not addressed effectively by the organization through formal means. During a conversation about the county's officer training programs, one officer pointed out: "The majority of the things they teach you in those classes aren't related to what we do. What they don't do, and I wish they would, is teach officers how to handle situations. Like, how do you handle an inmate who's calling you names? How do you handle somebody who's beating to death everybody you put in the cell with them? They focused on things like transactional analysis and psychology theory. I mean when you've got an inmate who is threatening you, possibly throwing hot water on you, are you gonna stand there and say, 'You're talking like a child, let's relate on an adult level?' It's just not gonna work." [2]

Here the officer refers to the uncertainty resulting from the uselessness of employing recommended methods of dealing with conflicts in the case of an actual organizational crisis. The officer notes that formally approved practices are of little value in the life world of the jail. Moreover, the officer presents a hypothetical situation ("an inmate . . . possibly throwing hot water on you") to showcase the uncertainty. This case graphically highlights the inappropriateness of using the organization's formal procedures in a crisis situation.

Some of the uncertainty the officer expresses is addressed by a story told by another, more experienced officer:

Story D: "Hot Water"

The other night a guy kept shouting, "I want to move to isolation." But we didn't have an empty cell. Two days later he's shouting from a cell with four others, "I want to move out." Then . . . "I have a message for you," and he throws a cup of water at me. I'm soaked right down my front. I guess he expected me to run because I'm a female or to be shaken up. I stood right there. He said he'd throw hot water next time. That's when I left and got the lieutenant. I'm not a fool.

Here the narrator encounters the very situation proposed by the first officer — an inmate throwing hot water. The narrator implies that formal methods are ill suited to the situation. When faced with the possibility of attack, the officer points out, "I'm not a fool," and goes for backup rather than utilizing the "transactional analysis and psychology theory" recommended by the organization. In answer to the first officer's questions about an appropriate, realistic response to threats, the narrator recommends seeking assistance from others who perhaps have more authority as an alternative to working one on one with an inmate.

Hawes (1974) notes that stories such as Story D are useful tools for sense-making. He suggests that events and experiences are organized in a sensible and understandable fashion through story use. In Hawes's framework, a story starts from a set of circumstances, outlines critical issues evolving from these circumstances, and then reaches some form of resolution.

Story D follows Hawes's framework by first presenting the background information about the incident. A number of critical elements arise from this set of background circumstances, including the following: (a) Inmates have power, (b) inmates interact with officers in unpredictable and sometimes dangerous ways, and (c) "cool" responses by officers are appropriate. The officer resolves the story by noting that in cases of potential danger "cool" should be coupled with or replaced by common sense. The commonsense approach outlined in this story seems more applicable and appropriate to life in the jail than the formal procedures presented in training classes.

Stories, Uncertainty Reduction, and Organizational Socialization

In a discussion of the role of stories in the creation of organizational cultures, Wilkins (1984) observes that excellent organizations differ from less successful organizations by virtue of the presence of a set of concrete examples of organizational action expressed in stories passed on by the membership. These stories help members learn about culture by providing definition for the more abstract aspects of how a particular organization operates. Stories act as "an important way to map social territory" (Wilkins, 1984, p. 44).

According to Wilkins, stories provide information about how individuals should perform in certain situations; they are also concrete enough to exemplify abstract concepts or uncertain situations so that organizational members can more readily comprehend the activities that go on around them. Moreover, Kelly (1985) argues that stories work as a kind of survival mechanism for organizational members. Stories assist in survival by providing lessons regarding appropriate coping strategies for members who face the complexities of life in a particular organization.

In reducing uncertainty, stories act as a type of aligning activity for members of an organization. Aligning acts are used when problematic situations occur. Problematic situations arise when people do not know what is happening to them (Stokes & Hewitt, 1976). When a situation becomes problematic, participants attempt to get the situation aligned on some recognizable course. Goffman (1971) proposes that individuals cope with problematic situations by recalling some familiar form of communication and placing it into the situation at hand. Fine (1984) contends that individuals who encounter a new or problematic situation turn to stories to provide guidelines for behavior.

In reducing uncertainty, then, stories help organization members understand the complex circumstances surrounding them by organizing information and connecting facts (Weick & Browning, 1986). From this vantage point, stories function as structures to aid comprehension. These structures operate efficiently because they require only a small number of facts to facilitate sense-making (Martin, 1982). Thus stories act effectively as a mode of information transmission that reduces the uncertainty swirling within the cultural environment of an organization (Turner, 1986).

Along these lines, Buono, Bowditch, and Lewis (1985) present a cultural analysis of the merger of two banks. As they point out, mergers tend to result in a great deal of uncertainty for all parties involved. The researchers observe that the stories members tell about each of their initial organizations and about the merger process itself provide effective guidelines regarding the course of action that should be followed in the newly organized institution. Further, Buono et al. echo the notions of Wilkins (1984) by arguing that clear, concrete stories are a powerful tool for directing organizational activities.

The concrete nature of stories as examples provides an uncertainty reduction function critical for the survival of members, especially new members, within an organization. New members acquire the norms and behaviors associated with their positions as they are socialized into an organization. Typically, this acquisition process occurs in stages, as former outsiders are transformed from raw recruits into fully functioning organizational members (Feldman, 1976; Jablin, 1985). New members must interact with experienced members in order to survive successfully in the organization (Brown, 1982).

Uncertainty for new members exists in two areas: role-related learning and cultural learning. Role-related learning deals with the concrete, "how-to-do-it" facets of the organization. Cultural learning focuses on the abstract, "personality" elements of the organization (Louis, 1980). As noted, stories are one way to transmit informal, cultural elements. Indeed, Louis (1980) notes that stories are an effective means through which experienced members may explain or illustrate cultural elements. Stories provide uncertainty reducing information that describes the organization from an experienced point of view (Dandridge, Mitroff, & Joyce, 1980). Further, because stories are concrete, natural, and appealing, they may constitute a type of memorable socializing message (Stohl, 1986).

An earlier study of mine reveals that as members proceed through the socialization process their stories change (Brown, 1985). During early stages of socialization, members recount stories primarily as sequences of events. These stories reduce uncertainty by describing events as they occur. New members, then, use these descriptive, informative stories to outline "what is going on" in the organization.

In sum, stories provide concrete, memorable exemplars of abstract concepts, fill in the blanks of organizational existence by providing useful information, and are particularly important for new members. Meaning management, the function of stories discussed in the next section, frames this information in terms of organizational values and expectations.

Organizational Stories and the Management of Meaning

Wilkins (1983a) notes that members do not directly express their assumptions about the meaning of organizational activities. Rather, they imply meanings through stories and other cultural artifacts. Smircich (1983), in examining the notion of organizational culture as a root metaphor, observes that stories produce and transform the meanings that define the essential nature of an organization. These meanings undergird the basic values members hold concerning an organization and the legitimacy of its activities (Jones, 1983).

Through stories, then, organizational members are capable of conveying the messages that present the basic values and meanings housed within an organization (Deal & Kennedy, 1983). A story brings value statements issued by the organization to life in the minds of its members. Moreover, stories, even though concrete in nature, are flexible in possible interpretations. Stories do not act as inflexible rules, therefore; rather, they may be applied as expressions of meaning for a variety of circumstances.

Dandridge et al. (1980) observe that members use stories to bring coherence to the organizational system. Stories bring reason, order, differentiation, integration, and so on to organizational activities. Through these actions, stories create a coherent system of meaning that houses the values of the organization and its members (Myrsiadis, 1987). Further, as members become more familiar with an organization, they are better able to express organizational values through stories (Brown, 1985).

Along these lines, members use stories as symbolic structures to recount the significance of activities in terms of organizational values, goals, traditions, expectations, and so on (Feldman, 1986; Meyer & Rowan, 1977; Mitroff & Kilmann, 1976). Stories reveal organizational perceptions and act as an effective vehicle for a culture's values (Trevino, 1987). By functioning to manage meaning, stories illustrate acceptable coherent patterns of behavior in line with organizational values (Dandridge et al., 1980). That is, stories provide a symbolic interpretation of events by framing those events in terms of the organization's expectations (Bennett & Edelman, 1985; Pettigrew, 1979).

Stories also manage meaning by providing retroactive explanations that rationalize past events in terms of organizational values (Martin et al., 1983). Wilkins (1984) observes that stories generate commitment to values by interpreting events for individuals who become members after the occurrence of the event. Bennett (1978) also notes that stories serve as a way of relaying interpretations of key events to individuals who were not only not present for the event but who also do not understand how the event fits within the culture of the organization.

Shrivastava and Schneider (1984) argue that in this way stories implicitly articulate organizational frames of reference. These frames of reference communicate to members the expectations and values of the organization and present to members acceptable patterns of behavior. Shrivastava, Mitroff, and Alvesson (1987) extend this notion by suggesting that organizational frames of reference constitute the basis of organizational belief systems. Stories thus provide expressions of such "logic frameworks" that provide meaning for members of an organization (Harrison, 1987).

For example, the officer in Story A expresses some of the tension between personal considerations and organizational values that arise from the incident in which she was struck. Initially, the officer states that she considered quitting her job. However, through the story, the officer implies that "these things happen" and are a part of the circumstances underlying this job. Thus this story manages meaning by framing the incident as a sort of occupational accident rather than a personal attack. This reframing indicates that some sacrifice of personal safety is expected of and perhaps valued by this organization's members.

Stories of this nature exhibit some sense of organizational coherence and control. For example, Mumby (1987) argues that stories express the meanings that can be associated with particular organizational events. Stories re-create and maintain the power structures set in place by the organization. For instance, in Story C, the narrator notes that members finally act in accordance with organizational values and send Jim Ed to the state correctional facility. However, the narrator never considers a variety of other possible activities that the organization would not accept — changing Jim Ed's conviction to a lesser offense; substituting another, more troublesome inmate for Jim Ed; or releasing Jim Ed. In this way, the story tacitly defines organizational options. Kelly (1985) notes that stories such as these communicate "cultural givens" that indicate what the organization expects of its members. Stories define the realities of organizational members through the use of appropriate assumptions of meaning.

Further, stories effectively manage meaning because of their power as a strategy in argument. Managers, for example, use stories as persuasive, powerful arguments that support and justify certain types of behavior (Rowland, 1987). Along these lines, a study on managerial communication as cultural performance reveals that certain hospital administrators combine storytelling and argumentation to present an image of rational behavior (Trujillo, 1985). Moreover, Weick and Browning

(1986) suggest that a manager who argues logically with stories is more effective in conveying meaning than a manager who does not use stories in structuring arguments. As Dandridge (1985) notes, influence may be achieved by using symbolic forms such as stories with imagination and creativity. Thus stories help managers control perceptions and present coherent accounts about acceptable organizational values and meaning.

Some studies of organizational culture specifically examine the notion of meaning management as control. Stories, from this point of view, exist as a sort of prescription for behavior (Kelly, 1985). For example, Wilkins (1983b) argues that stories operate as a sort of third-order control that shapes and gives coherence to the assumptions and values that direct organizational members.

In addition, Ray (1986) claims that managers are capable of controlling workers through manipulation of cultural elements such as stories. Ray presents the following formula for managing worker behavior: (a) Managers use cultural elements such as stories to create a coherent system of values; (b) the coherent system of values leads workers to experience a greater identification with the organization and its values; (c) increased productivity results from strengthened values.

Contradictory stories and multiple levels of meaning. The preceding paragraphs suggest that stories function to manage meaning for organizational members by expressing coherent values of the system. At this point, the discussion may appear to imply that this management of meaning rests in the upper echelons of the organization. However, stories do not function solely for managers. Storytelling is widespread throughout the membership of an organization and is relatively immune to corporate rank. That is, stories reveal the values and beliefs of members at the lowest levels of the organization as easily as they reveal the values and beliefs of the executives in the boardroom. As Shrivastava et al. (1987) suggest, competing, at times contradictory, frames of reference and their stories help ensure the survival of an organization. As such, in the jail, administrators have stories, officers have stories, and inmates have stories.

Once again, Story C is useful in illustrating a concept. This story points out the possible existence of a subculture within the jail. Members at the uppermost levels of the organization would no doubt point to the speedy and efficient completion of procedures as a concept valued by the membership of the organization. However, the officer who tells the story reveals that certain members of the organization manipulated the system because they "like" Jim Ed and apparently value this relationship more than they value following standard procedures. As noted, the system prevails, but not before corrections officers create and recount Jim Ed's story. In addition, the possibility exists that the inmates have their own Jim Ed story.

Morgan (1986), in an examination of the organizational culture of Hewlett Packard, observes that story use is broadly spread throughout the membership of the organization. He argues that while a company's formal leaders have an advantage in presenting the values of the organization because of their ability to reward or punish members, members at all levels of the organization have the power to express cultural values. This shared power results in the existence of a set of multiple, often contradictory, story sets housed within an organization.

In fact, Riley (1983) warns investigators not to anticipate finding *a* culture within an organization. Rather, she calls for investigations into the existence of organizational subcultures. This notion may be extended to include the existence of countercultures. Reimann and Wiener (1988) note that a counterculture exists when managers promote one set of organizational values while members at lower levels of the organization communicate a contradictory value set.

Along these lines, Glaser, Zamanov, and Hacker (1987) examine the themes and patterns around which cultural entities, such as stories, emerge. Basically, the differences in organizational themes mirror the differences in the values expressed by managers and workers. For example, managers may indicate that important information is easily accessible, while workers at lower levels may feel that important information is unavailable. Glaser et al. (1987) observe that thematic differences such as the one noted in the preceding paragraph point to the existence of multicultures rather than to the existence of one overriding megaculture. From this vantage point, stories act as a means of expressing the alternative values associated with multiple cultures or countercultures.

To summarize, stories function to manage meaning in an organization by implicitly or, at times, explicitly presenting the values associated with organizational activities. Stories such as these act as a powerful way to argue for the appropriateness of organizational values. Members at all levels of an organization tell stories for this reason. Unified, coherent stories reveal strongly shared value systems. Stories expressing contradictions in value systems reveal the existence of subcultures or even multiple cultures. The next section of this chapter discusses a third function of stories, bonding and identification.

Organizational Stories
and Bonding and Identification

A story may function as a point of bonding and identification for the members of an organization by depicting a particular organization and its members as special or unique. As individuals share stories, they develop a kind of kinship through the messages transmitted (LeGuin, 1981). Trujillo (1985) notes that cultural performances such as "bitching together" act to create and maintain interpersonal bonding and sociability among the membership of an organization.

Ingersoll and Adams (1986) argue that each and every organization generates its own set of stories. Ulrich (1984) suggests that such story sets are offered as proof of the unique quality of an organization as a whole. In addition, as new members become acquainted with the organization through the socialization process, they tell stories that reveal identification and bonding with the organization and its membership (Brown, 1985). As such, the bonding/identification function creates a type of "us versus them" or "insider versus outsider" mind-set for organizational members. As Harrison (1987) observes, members perceive that "their" stories have meaning for insiders that remain mysterious for outsiders. In this way, stories reinforce the development of identity by providing points of association among insiders and points of dissociation from outsiders.

The following story illustrates the manner in which stories function as a point of identification for members.

Story E: "Break Out"

> When I was at [the state correctional facility], something would happen and she [the officer's wife] just wouldn't understand when I would have to stay late. The first time I was there I was working the twelve to eight shift. We lived eighteen miles from there, so it takes about fifteen minutes to drive. We didn't have a phone and our neighbors didn't have a phone. There's no way to call and we had a break one time. We had to stay until he was found. And I came home and the door was locked. Like if you don't come home on time, then don't come at all.

This story graphically presents the tension the officer experiences between his organizational life and his home life. Further, the officer suggests that outsiders, including members of his own family, are incapable of understanding life in the organization. In noting that outsiders "just wouldn't understand," the officer implies a point of identification with other members of the law enforcement profession.

A number of studies in folklore concentrate on the ways in which stories act as bonding and identification agents. For example, Santino (1983) examines stories as expressions of the occupational identity of Pullman porters. Through stories, narrators relate the contradictory experiences that are associated with their jobs. As the stories are exchanged, the porters point out similarities and differences in experience—"I too experienced that sort of thing" and "I handled it slightly different" (p. 393). Santino claims that by presenting these similarities and differences, the porters use stories to negotiate a "communal discourse" as a point of identification.

Another study by Santino (1988) focuses on a set of ghost stories told by the employees of an airline. In this case, the ghost stories qualify as organizational stories because the narratives meet the criteria noted above, including the notion that the stories ring true to the members (Santino, 1988). These stories generally focus on the ghost of a former colleague who returns to warn co-workers of some form of danger or an impending accident. Santino observes that the storytelling involves several members of the organization who share the tales with other members. These stories receive enthusiastic and positive support from fellow members of the organization, who seriously consider the stories to be adequate, plausible explanations of events. According to Santino, these stories are seen as "sacred" to that occupation and are not willingly shared with outsiders who might not fully appreciate their significance. Thus the power of these stories as agents of bonding and identification is enhanced by their insulated position in the organizational community.

IMPLICATIONS FOR STORY STUDIES

A variety of related research possibilities are suggested by these story characteristics and functions. I will focus on two as points of departure for explorations into stories in organizations: story circumstances and story applications.

The Circumstances Surrounding a Story's Telling

Examinations of the circumstances surrounding the telling of an organizational story might be directed to (a) the tellers of stories, (b) the settings in which stories are told, and (c) the audience's response to the telling of stories.

Storytellers. A variety of storyteller studies are possible here. For one, the number of stories a member tells could be examined. Individuals who tell a variety of stories are likely to be more informed about organizational operations and more involved in the relational aspects of the organization than are others. As such, these members are apt to be highly visible in the organizational context. This visibility increases their access to the informational fodder necessary for the creation of organizational stories.

However, the number of stories told may eventually begin to yield diminished returns. A person who continually tells self-promoting, often lengthy stories on any subject under discussion may in fact be a detriment to the organization. That member may not be valued but, rather, at best, tolerated. Further, his or her stories may begin to speak more to the teller than to the organization.

On a deeper level, the effect of a teller's credibility on stories should be observed. In examining television news stories, Drew and Reeves (1980) point out that believability and likability are important in determining how well a story will be accepted by audience members. A similar effect should occur with stories and storytellers in organizations. Here, perception of the believability of a source is more important than the number of stories told by that person.

Further, credible storytellers within an organization should be at the heart of story networks or pockets of storytelling. These pockets are marked by highly consistent, firmly entrenched story lines that are shared by several members. Conversely, the member with low credibility is likely to be a story isolate, who may tell a variety of stories, but whose stories are not adopted by other members. In addition, this narrator's stories are likely to be considered to be irrelevant, time-consuming, and a detriment to effective communication.

Further, the "talent" or competence of a storyteller is a topic for exploration. Smith (1981) notes that not all stories are good stories and lays much of the responsibility for a good story with the teller. Moreover, Moch and Fields (1985) argue that the skills of a storyteller determine whether or not the story communicates meaning effectively. A member who relates clear, relevant stories with some flair is more likely to be valued than a member who tells rambling, marginally relevant stories.

This viewpoint relates well to notions of communication competence that suggest that competent communicators effectively and appropriately convey messages to receivers (Wellmon, 1988). The talent of a particular storyteller should affect the performative quality of the story as well as the future use of the story. A competent storyteller should, therefore, have more organizational influence than a member who exhibits less talent. However, a full understanding of the skills and abilities characteristic of a good storyteller remains to be achieved.

Story settings. Examinations of a story's setting focus on the context of a story — that is, where and when a story is told becomes important. On a basic level, studies could identify the places in and times during which stories are likely to be told in an organization.

More focused examinations are also possible. For example, Santino (1988) observes that most occupational ghost stories are told during "down time" for members. Participants in the storytelling, in this case, are seen to have free time at their disposal. Storytelling fills this time by providing information that reinforces identification with organizational values. Storytelling during down time seems to be a common occurrence within organizations. Corrections officers in the county jail report meeting informally to "talk things out," while Trujillo (1985) observes that managers "bitch together." Examinations of these informal settings should result in rich information concerning the frequency and nature of organizational storytelling.

However, stories are not told in informal settings alone. For example, an examination of stories told in group decision-making efforts should also prove fruitful. An investigation of this nature deals with the use of stories as a process variable in decision making. If stories are used as evidence in support of assertions being made, then stories may be a critical variable in swaying the course of a group's interaction. In other words, stories that are offered as proof that a certain course of action will fail or succeed may greatly affect the outcomes of a group's discussion. Possible examinations could investigate the frequency of stories told during the discussion, the conversational paths that lead to stories, and ways in which story use affects the tenor of the decision-making process.

The settings in which organizational leaders use stories could also be examined. A study could focus on the use of stories during annual reports to the membership or to the stockholders. The study might focus on determining the frequency of stories, the functions of stories, and the effect of stories.

Further, stories told by leaders in a variety of settings could be compared. Story use by leaders speaking to organizational members could be compared with stories told to organizational outsiders. A similar sort of comparison could be conducted as leaders adapt messages to different organizational groups, for instance, stories told to line workers versus stories told to staff members.

Studies of this nature should not be limited to leaders at the top of the organization. Similar studies all along the hierarchy should be conducted. Likely settings for such examinations are unit managers' instructional meetings, union gatherings, and so on. The stories told by informal leaders should also be examined. Although the settings for these stories are likely less clear-cut than the settings for formally designated leaders, the stories told by informal leaders are influential in establishing subcultures and countercultures, and they deserve examination.

Story results. A third type of story circumstance consists of the effects resulting from the telling of a story. Studies might explore the ways in which members act with regard to stories. Three potential options might be considered: (a) The story could be dropped, (b) the story could continue to be told, but elicit no other behavioral response, or (c) the story could result in a particular behavioral response from the membership. The first option likely results from some fundamental flaw in the story—for example, it does not ring true, or it does not have relevance for the membership. Identifying the weaknesses of stories that do not survive should inform us further with regard to critical story characteristics.

Moreover, a study could be directed toward determining which characteristics of an organizational story lead members to take action rather than simply repeating or spreading the story. For example, suppose members attest to the validity and applicability of a story suggesting that change is needed within an organization. Members spread this narrative throughout the organization. However, these same members take no specific action, other than telling the story, to initiate or facilitate the change promoted by their story.

This lack of overt action calls into question the effectiveness of the story. The story might be considered a success because it is believed by and spread by the membership; on the other hand, it might be considered a failure because it leads to no concrete action by the membership. Studies investigating this particular phenomenon should provide a deeper understanding of the role and importance of stories in organizations.

A variation of Katz and Kahn's (1978) notion of role-sending might also prove to be a useful focus for investigation. Briefly, Katz and Kahn argue that a role that is communicated to a member is not necessarily the role that the member receives. In other words, the role-sent is not always the role-received. Examinations of organizational stories could utilize a similar notion to examine whether or not the stories members tell are the same as the stories members receive.

A variety of research possibilities emerge from this perspective. A study could explore whether or not a story remains constant between sender and receiver in terms of content and function. In terms of content, studies of comprehension could reveal if stories communicate more memorable messages than other forms of messages. In terms of function, studies could explore whether or not sources and receivers sense the same purpose for a narrative.

More in-depth examinations could identify the factors that influence differences in the story sent as compared to the story received. Some such factors might include, but are not limited to, the power differentials among members, personality characteristics, interpersonal relationships, the specificity of the message, message topic, and the credibility of the storyteller.

On another level, the evolution of the story as it passes from member to member might be examined. If the story sent differs from the story received as it passes from member to member, then a particular story is likely to have a history of alterations. Moreover, several forms of the same root story are likely to exist as different groups mold the narrative to represent their own view of organizational reality. Investigations of the various branches of an organizational story's narrative tree should provide valuable insights into the nature of subcultures and countercultures within an organization.

Applications of Organizational Stories

Investigations into applications of stories in organizations explore the ways in which stories might be used by various organizations. Three potential uses are described in this section: the use of stories (a) in training, (b) in portraying organizations by the mass media, and (c) in consulting.

Stories and training. As noted above, stories are capable of communicating information in a memorable and attractive form, and are compelling as a form of evidence in presenting arguments. Stories also act as effective points of identification and bonding for members. These three functions should be extremely useful in training members about the ins and outs of organizational operations.

Organizational trainers should be able to apply stories derived from the discourse of the organization being examined as a strategy in training new members. Stories could supplement the "transactional analysis and psychology theory" the corrections officer found so lacking with real-world examples from organizational experience. By exposing new members to stories drawn from the organization's history, experienced organization members help present a more comprehensive, well-rounded view of the organizational culture than may be available from other sources of information. Moreover, new members may find this form of information more familiar, memorable, and meaningful than other training formats.

In addition, providing information in story form may increase the accuracy and completeness of new members' knowledge about the organization. The likelihood of discrepancies occurring between organizational training and organizational reality could be reduced. This reduction of discrepancies should help facilitate new members' adaptation to the organization.

The differences between newcomers who have been exposed to an organization's stories and those who have not should also be analyzed. The awareness of these stories should play a role in the transition from newcomer to experienced organizational member. As such, knowledge of stories and their implications should help the newcomer better assess and understand the workplace by incorporating the information gained from the stories into his or her organizational knowledge bank.

An effective way to check these assumptions would be to monitor the progress of groups of trainees or individual trainees who have been told stories during training compared with groups or individuals who have not been told stories during training. Similar types of explorations could be conducted in connection with training other than that presented to new members. Such situations might include training in new organizational technology, training in cases of corporate mergers, or training in regard to policy changes.

Organizational stories and the media. Organizational life is a popular source of stories for mass media presentations. From *Duffy's Tavern* to *Desk Set* to *WKRP in Cincinnati* to *Wall Street* to *L.A. Law,* organizations provide backdrops for a number of popular productions. The manner in which members of the mass media use story elements to portray organizations is of interest to researchers (see, for example, Deming, 1985). However, additional areas exist for possible research regarding relationships among organizations, stories, and the mass media.

One such area for investigation rests in members' perceptions of the reality of organizational story lines presented by the mass media. In a study along related lines, Pacanowsky and Anderson (1982) note that police officers use portrayals of "media cops" as points of reference for comparisons with the reality they actually experience. These authors observe that police officers generally dissociate themselves from their media counterparts; this dissociation then acts as a point of identification for the officers.

A similar type of study might examine the ways in which members assess the reality of media story lines. Interviews with members should reveal if the story lines portrayed by the media ring true with the actual story lines of the organization. Further, studies might focus on whether or not members find portrayals with realistic story lines to be more or less appealing than portrayals with fabricated story lines. Members may enjoy the more realistic story lines for reasons of identification; on the other hand, members may enjoy less realistic story lines for reasons of escapism or dissociation.

A second area for study rests in the ways in which media story lines affect organizational socialization. At least part of the socialization process, anticipatory socialization, occurs prior to organizational entry. Anticipatory socialization consists of the factors that influence a person's expectations regarding his or her future life in an organization. Realistic expectations that are congruent with organizational activities ease adjustment. Logically, the story lines presented by the media constitute a part of organizational socialization. For example, a regular viewer of a television program such as *St. Elsewhere* is likely to have an entirely different perspective on life as a hospital employee than a viewer of a program such as *General Hospital.* These story expectations may then differ from or be congruent to the actual stories a new member hears or tells on the job. The amount of congruence between expected story lines and actual story lines should affect a person's overall adjustment to an organization.

Stories and consulting. The use of stories may also be of value to consultants. If, in fact, storytelling reflects members' true understanding of the organizational system, stories should act as a viable source of information for the consultant. In making use of organization stories, the consultant may conduct at least two story-gathering interventions.

The consultant might initially gather stories from the focal organization regarding whatever aspect of organizational life is of particular interest—for example, job satisfaction or effectiveness of supervision. Stories on these issues could then be analyzed and possible solutions could be developed and implemented based on the analysis.

A second story-gathering intervention may be conducted after a reasonable period of time for purposes of comparison. If stories gathered during the second intervention indicate that problems have abated after the initial intervention, the consultant has evidence that the solutions employed are effective. On the other hand, if stories reveal no change or a negative change in perceptions regarding the problem, the consultant possesses evidence that suggests that further effort is warranted. Additional interventions might be conducted as needed.

In this way, organizational stories provide a means to discern the organization and changes within it. These stories give the consultant the capability of viewing before-and-after pictures of organizational operations. The practicality of this approach should be assessed.

SUMMARY

Stories are a vital part of the communication processes of an organization. In fact, as noted above, understanding an organization's stories may be critical to understanding the organization itself. This essay, in an attempt to define the nature of organizational stories, began with two stated purposes: (a) to outline the characteristics that mark the presence of organizational stories, and (b) to describe the functions of stories as told to and by organizational members.

This analysis suggests that stories in organizations display distinct characteristics that separate them from other common forms of communication. First, stories ring true for the members; that is, members consider stories to be accurate portrayals and interpretations of events within the organization. Second, stories have relevance for the membership. Stories are told by members about members; these stories are thought to be pertinent to organizational functions. Third, a story grammar—consisting of a preface sequence, a recounting sequence, and a closing sequence—is present in these units. Fourth, stories exhibit a sense of temporality. Historic, clock time is distinguished from narrative time as organizational events are packaged temporally into story form.

In addition to displaying these characteristics, stories perform three major functions in organizations. First, stories reduce uncertainty for members. Stories provide information that helps members clarify the loosely coupled aspects of their organization and cope with both its formal and its informal operating procedures. Uncertainty reduction of this nature is especially important for new members of the organization.

Second, stories function to manage meaning for members by framing events coherently in terms of appropriate organizational values and expectations. This framing results in a form of control of organizational activities by implicitly defining the parameters of behavior. Members at the upper levels of the organization have some advantage in managing meaning through stories because these individuals have the resources available to support their positions. Nevertheless, the power of story use is widely available throughout an organization, and all members may tell stories that manage meaning. As such, the presence of stories with coherent meanings throughout the membership of an organization indicates that a unified culture is present. On the other hand, the presence of stories with contradictory meanings for different groups reveals that subcultures or even countercultures are housed within the organization.

Third, stories function as points of bonding and identification for the members of an organization. Stories of this nature point out the reasons an organization and its members are special or unique. Stories work in this way to differentiate members from outsiders and to increase the commitment of members toward each other, their organization, and their occupation.

NOTES

1. The investigators were trained in qualitative research methods as described by Glaser and Strauss (1967) and Browning (1978).

2. The threat of throwing hot water is more serious than might be apparent. According to the officers, inmates mix extremely hot water with sugar, which raises the temperature and causes the mixture to cling to the skin. This concoction reportedly results in painful burns.

REFERENCES

Agar, M. (1980). Stories, background knowledge, and themes: Problems in the analysis of life history narrative. *American Ethnologist, 7,* 223-239.

Bateson, G. (1979). *Mind and nature: A necessary unity.* New York: Bantam.

Beach, W. A., & Japp, P. (1983). Storifying as time-traveling: The knowledgeable use of temporally structured discourse. In R. Bostrom (Ed.), *Communication yearbook 7* (pp. 867-888). Beverly Hills, CA: Sage.

Bennett, W. L. (1978). Storytelling in criminal trials: A model of social judgment. *Quarterly Journal of Speech, 64,* 1-22.

Bennett, W. L., & Edelman, M. (1985). Toward a new political narrative. *Journal of Communication, 35,* 156-171.

Bormann, E. G. (1983). Symbolic convergence: Organization communication and culture. In L. L. Putnam & M. E. Pacanowsky (Eds.), *Communication and organization: An interpretive approach* (pp. 99-122). Beverly Hills, CA: Sage.

Bormann, E. G. (1985). Symbolic convergence theory: A communication formulation. *Journal of Communication, 35,* 128-138.

Brown, M. H. (1982, November). *Did you hear about the time . . . ? The uses of stories in organizational socialization*. Paper presented at the annual meeting of the Speech Communication Association Convention, Louisville, KY.

Brown, M. H. (1983, May). *Reminiscing: A verbal form of time travel*. Paper presented at the annual meeting of the International Communication Association, Dallas.

Brown, M. H. (1985). That reminds me of a story: Speech action in organizational socialization. *Western Journal of Speech Communication, 49,* 27-42.

Browning, L. D. (1978). A grounded organizational communication theory derived from qualitative data. *Communication Monographs, 45,* 93-109.

Browning, L. D., Korinek, J. T., & Cooper, M. (1979, May). *Downplaying formal rules negotiating a military cultural system*. Paper presented at the annual meeting of the International Communication Association, Philadelphia.

Buono, A. F., Bowditch, J. L., & Lewis, J. W. (1985). When cultures collide: The anatomy of a merger. *Human Relations, 38,* 477-500.

Chatman, S. (1981). What novels can do that films can't (and vice versa). In W.J.T. Mitchell (Ed.), *On narrative* (pp. 117-136). Chicago: University of Chicago Press.

Dandridge, T. C. (1985). The life stages of a symbol: When symbols work and when they can't. In P. J. Frost, L. F. Moore, M. R. Louis, C. C. Lundberg, & J. Martin (Eds.), *Organizational culture* (pp. 141-153). Beverly Hills, CA: Sage.

Dandridge, T. C., Mitroff, I. I., & Joyce, W. F. (1980). Organizational symbolism: A topic to expand organizational analysis. *Academy of Management Review, 5,* 77-82.

Deal, T. E., & Kennedy, A. A. (1983). Culture: A new look through old lenses. *Journal of Applied Behavioral Science, 19,* 498-505.

Deming, C. J. (1985). *Hill Street Blues* as narrative. *Critical Studies in Mass Communication, 2,* 1-22.

Drew, D., & Reeves, B. (1980). Learning from a television news story. *Communication Research, 7,* 121-135.

Feldman, D. C. (1976). A contingency theory of socialization. *Administrative Science Quarterly, 21,* 433-452.

Feldman, S. P. (1986). Management in context: An essay on the relevance of culture to the understanding of management change. *Journal of Management, 23,* 587-607.

Fine, G. A. (1984). Negotiated orders and organizational cultures. *Annual Review of Sociology, 10,* 239-262.

Fisher, W. R. (1984). Narration as human communication paradigm: The case of public moral argument. *Communication Monographs, 51,* 1-22.

Fisher, W. R. (1985a). The narrative paradigm: An elaboration. *Communication Monographs, 52,* 347-367.

Fisher, W. R. (1985b). The narrative paradigm: In the beginning. *Journal of Communication, 35,* 74-89.

Georges, R. A. (1987). Timeliness and appropriateness in personal experience narrating. *Western Folklore, 46,* 115-120.

Glaser, B. G., & Strauss, A. L. (1967). *The discovery of grounded theory: Strategies for qualitative research*. Chicago: Aldine.

Glaser, S. R., Zamanov, S., & Hacker, K. (1987). Measuring and interpreting organizational culture. *Management Communication Quarterly, 1,* 173-198.

Goffman, E. (1971). *Relations in public*. New York: Harper & Row.

Goffman, E. (1974). *Frame analysis: An essay on the organization of experience*. New York: Harper & Row.

Goodwin, C. (1984). Notes on story structure and the organization of participation. In J. M. Atkinson & J. Heritage (Eds.), *Studies of social action: Studies in conversation analysis* (pp. 225-246). Cambridge: Cambridge University Press.

Harrison, T. M. (1987). Frameworks for the study of writing in organizational contexts. *Written Communication, 4,* 3-23.

Hawes, L. C. (1974). Social collectives as communication: Perspective on organizational behavior. *Quarterly Journal of Speech, 60*, 497-502.

Hofstadter, D. R. (1979). *Godel, Escher, Bach: An eternal golden braid.* New York: Vintage.

Ingersoll, V. H., & Adams, G. B. (1986). Beyond organizational boundaries. *Administration & Society, 18*, 360-371.

Jablin, F. M. (1985). An exploratory study of vocational organizational communication socialization. *Southern Speech Communication Journal, 50*, 261-282.

Jefferson, G. (1978). Sequential aspects of storytelling in conversation. In J. Schenkein (Ed.), *Studies in the organization of conversational interaction* (pp. 219-248). New York: Academic Press.

Jones, G. (1983). Transaction costs, property rights, and organizational culture. *Administration Science Quarterly, 28*, 454-467.

Katz, D., & Kahn, R. L. (1978). *The social psychology of organization.* New York: John Wiley.

Kelly, J. W. (1985). Storytelling in high tech organizations: A medium for sharing culture. *Journal of Applied Communication Research, 13*, 45-58.

Kermode, R. (1981). Secrets and narrative sequence. In W.J.T. Mitchell (Ed.), *On narrative* (pp. 79-97). Chicago: University of Chicago Press.

LeGuin, U. K. (1981). It was a dark and stormy night, or, why are we huddling around the campfire? In W.J.T. Mitchell (Ed.), *On narrative.* Chicago: University of Chicago Press.

Louis, M. R. (1980). Surprise and sense-making: What newcomers experience in entering unfamiliar organizational settings. *Administrative Science Quarterly, 25*, 226-251.

Lucaites, J. L., & Condit, C. M. (1985). Re-constructing narrative theory: A functional perspective. *Journal of Communication, 35*, 90-108.

Martin, J. (1982). Stories and scripts in organizational settings. In H. A. Hasdorf & A. M. Isen (Eds.), *Cognitive social psychology* (pp. 255-305). New York: Elsevier-North Holland.

Martin J., Feldman, M. S., Hatch, M. J., & Sitkin, S. B. (1983). The uniqueness function in organizational stories. *Administrative Science Quarterly, 28*, 438-453.

Martin J., & Powers, M. (1983a). Organizational stories: More vivid and persuasive than quantitative data. In B. M. Staw (Ed.), *Psychological foundations of organizational behavior* (pp. 161-168). Glenview, IL: Scott, Foresman.

Martin, J., & Powers, M. E. (1983b). Truth or corporate propaganda: The value of a good war story. In L. R. Pondy, P. J. Frost, G. Morgan, & T. C. Dandridge (Eds.), *Organizational symbolism* (pp. 81-92). Greenwich, CT: JAI.

Martin, J., & Siehl, C. (1983). Organizational culture and counterculture: An uneasy symbiosis. *Organizational Dynamics, 12*, 52-64.

McLaughlin, M. L. (1984). *Conversation: How talk is organized.* Beverly Hills, CA: Sage.

McLaughlin, M. L., Cody, M. J., Kane, M. L., & Robey, C. S. (1981). Sex differences in story receipt and story sequencing behaviors in dyadic conversations. *Human Communication Research, 7*, 99-116.

Meyer, J. W., & Rowan, B. (1977). Institutionalized organizations: Formal structure as myth and ceremony. *American Journal of Sociology, 83*, 340-363.

Mink, L. O. (1981). Everyman his or her own annalist. In W.J.T. Mitchell (Ed.), *On narrative,* (pp. 233-239). Chicago: University of Chicago Press.

Mitroff, I. I., & Kilmann, R. H. (1976). On organization stories: An approach to the design and analysis of organizations through myths and stories. In R. H. Kilmann, L. R. Pondy, & D. P. Slevin (Eds.), *The management of organization design* (pp. 189-207). New York: North-Holland.

Moch, M. K., & Fields, W. C. (1985). Developing a content analysis for interpreting language use in organizations. In S. B. Bacharach & S. M. Mitchell (Eds.), *Research in the sociology of organizations* (pp. 81-126). Greenwich, CT: JAI.

Morgan, G. (1986). *Images of organization.* Beverly Hills, CA: Sage.

Mumby, D. K. (1987). The political function of narrative in organizations. *Communication Monographs, 54*, 113-127.

Myrsiadis, L. S. (1987). Corporate stories as cultural communications in the organizational setting. *Management of Communication Quarterly, 1*, 84-120.

Pacanowsky, M. E., & Anderson, J. A. (1982). Cop talk and media use. *Journal of Broadcasting, 26*, 741-755.

Pacanowsky, M. E., & O'Donnell-Trujillo, N. (1983). Organizational communication as cultural performance. *Communication Monographs, 50*, 126-147.

Pettigrew, A. M. (1979). On studying organizational cultures. *Administrative Science Quarterly, 24*, 570-581.

Ray, C. A. (1986). Corporate culture: The last frontier of control. *Journal of Management Studies, 23*, 287-297.

Reimann, B. C., & Wiener, Y. (1988). Corporate culture: Avoiding the elitist trap. *Business Horizons, 31*, 36-44.

Riley, P. (1983). A structuralist account of political culture. *Administrative Science Quarterly, 28*, 414-437.

Rowland, R. C. (1987). Narrative: Mode of discourse or paradigm? *Communication Monographs, 54*, 264-275.

Ryave, A. L. (1978). On the achievement of a series of stories. In J. Schenkein (Ed.), *Studies in the organization of conversational interaction* (pp. 113-132). New York: Academic.

Sacks, H. (1972). On the analyzability of stories by children. In J. J. Gumperz & D. Hymes (Eds.), *Sociolinguistics: The ethnography of communication* (pp. 325-345). New York: Holt, Rinehart & Winston.

Sacks, H. (1974). An analysis of the course of a joke's telling in conversation. In R. Bauman & J. Scherzer (Eds.), *Explorations in the ethnography of speaking* (pp. 337-353). London: Cambridge University Press.

Sacks, H. (1978). Some technical considerations of a dirty joke. In J. Schenkein (Ed.), *Studies in the organization of conversational interaction* (pp. 249-269). New York: Academic.

Santino, J. (1983). Miles of smiles, years of struggles: The negotiation of black occupational identity through personal experience narratives. *Journal of American Folklore, 96*, 393-412.

Santino, J. (1988). Occupational ghostlore: Social context and the expression of belief. *Journal of American Folklore, 101*, 207-218.

Sathe, V. (1983). Implications of corporate culture: A manager's guide to action. *Organizational Dynamics, 12*, 5-23.

Scholes, R. (1981). Language, narrative, and anti-narrative. In W.J.T. Mitchell (Ed.), *On narrative* (pp. 200-208). Chicago: University of Chicago Press.

Shrivastava, P., Mitroff, I. I., & Alvesson, M. (1987). Nonrationality in organizational actions. *International Studies of Management and Organization, 17*, 90-109.

Shrivastava, P., & Schneider, S. (1984). Organizational frames of reference. *Human Relations, 37*, 795-809.

Smircich, L. (1983). Concepts of culture and organizational analysis. *Administrative Science Quarterly, 28*, 339-358.

Smith, B. H. (1981). Narrative versions, narrative theories. In W.J.T. Mitchell (Ed.), *On narrative* (pp. 209-232). Chicago: University of Chicago Press.

Stewart, S. (1982). The epistemology of the horror story. *Journal of American Folklore, 95*, 32-50.

Stohl, C. (1986). The role of memorable messages in the process of organizational socialization. *Communication Quarterly, 34*, 231-249.

Stokes, R., & Hewitt, J. P. (1976). Aligning actions. *American Sociological Review, 41*, 838-849.

Sullivan, J. J. (1988). Three roles of language in motivation theory. *Academy of Management Review, 13*, 104-115.

Tannen, D. (1984). *Conversational style: Analyzing talk among friends.* Norwood, NJ: Ablex.

Trevino, L. K. (1987). Media symbolism, media richness, and media choice in organizations. *Communication Research, 14*, 553-557.

Trujillo, N. (1985). Organizational communication as cultural performance. *Southern Speech Communication Journal, 50*, 201-224.

Turner, B. A. (1986). Sociological aspects of organizational symbolism. *Organization Studies, 7*, 101-116.

Ulrich, W. L. (1984). HRM and culture: History, ritual, and myth. *Human Resource Management, 23*, 117-128.

Weick, K. E. (1976). Educational organizations as loosely coupled systems. *Administrative Science Quarterly, 21*, 1-19.

Weick, K. E. (1979). *The social psychology of organizing*. Reading, MA: Addison-Wesley.

Weick, K. E., & Browning, L. D. (1986). Argument and narration in organizational communication. *Journal of Management, 12*, 243-259.

Wellmon, T. A. (1988). Conceptualizing organizational communication competence: A rules-based perspective. *Management Communication Quarterly, 1*, 515-534.

White, H. (1981). The value of narrativity in the representation of reality. In W.J.T. Mitchell (Ed.), *On narrative* (pp. 1-23). Chicago: University of Chicago Press.

Wilkins, A. L. (1983a). The culture audit: A tool for understanding organizations. *Organizational Dynamics, 12*, 24-38.

Wilkins, A. L. (1983b). Organizational stories as symbols to control the organization. In L. R. Pondy, P. J. Frost, G. Morgan, & T. C. Dandridge (Eds.), *Organizational symbolism* (pp. 81-92). Greenwich, CT: JAI.

Wilkins, A. L. (1984). The creation of cultures: The role of stories and human resource systems. *Human Resource Management, 23*, 41-60.

Stories as Repositories of Organizational Intelligence: Implications for Organizational Development

GARY L. KREPS
Northern Illinois University

P ROFESSOR Brown provides a cogent overview of the structure and functions of organizational stories, making a strong case for the importance of stories and storytelling in organizational life. My major frustration with her chapter, however, is its failure to capture fully the pragmatic value of stories for organizational development. This essay expands upon Professor Brown's functional analysis of stories by examining the information retention and dissemination functions of stories in organizational life.

Stories are cultural storehouses for organizational intelligence (a very useful commodity). As repositories of organizational intelligence, stories can provide communication researchers/consultants with extremely rich data for directing organizational development. This essay will describe strategies for and examples of how stories can be used in organizational development efforts.

THE INFORMATION VALUE
OF ORGANIZATIONAL STORIES

Stories are communication mechanisms used to preserve and share important information. Salient information is embedded in the stories organization members tell. That is why the case study method (which relates organizational stories to students) is such a powerful pedagogical tool in organizational communication

Correspondence and requests for reprints: Gary L. Kreps, Department of Communication Studies, Northern Illinois University, De Kalb, IL 60115.

Communication Yearbook 13, pp. 191-202

education (Kreps & Lederman, 1985). The engaging drama of story plots and storytelling performances provides punctuation and emphasis to the relevant information communicated through storytelling.

Each of the story functions identified by Professor Brown is accomplished through the ability to store and disseminate relevant information in stories. Stories reduce uncertainty by providing organization members with pertinent information, enhancing their abilities to understand and to make predictions about organizational phenomena. Stories manage meanings by providing members with common explanations for collective sense-making. Stories also facilitate member bonding and identification by providing members with shared organizational information, giving them common symbolic frames of reference.

Stories serve powerful interpretive functions in organizational life, illustrating cultural themes operating within organizations and influencing member activities and interpretations of reality (Weick & Browning, 1986; Wilkins, 1984). Every organization has unique cultural themes, made up of interpretations about organizational history and the combination of members that constitute the organization. Stories represent these unique cultural themes of organizationwide cultures and the many subcultures that develop in organizational life to organization members and environmental representatives.

The primary ingredients of culture are the collective interpretations members create about organizational activities and outcomes (Kreps, 1986). Stories illustrate these collective interpretations, describing interpretive frameworks that inform members about the meanings cultures prescribe for organizational phenomena (such as how members, products, equipment, property, and rules should be interpreted). Interpretive frameworks direct members' actions and interpretations, influence members' attitudes and values, and teach members to use specialized linguistic codes and engage in culturally approved social and professional rituals. Interpretive frameworks also reinforce organizational history, philosophies, informal norms, and logics, and present visions of organizations' futures, as well as identify potential organizational heroes and villains.

Stories are important cultural dissemination media, using formal and informal channels of communication to develop and maintain organizational cultures. Stories are communicated informally (through the grapevine) and formally (through advertising, newsletters, annual reports, pamphlets, group meetings, and public presentations) to provide members with information about organizational identity. In fact, organizational identity has been described by Bormann (1988) as a story, the organizational saga, including "the shared group fantasies, the rhetorical visions, and the narratives of achievements, events, and the future dreams of the entire organization" (pp. 396-397).

Stories are used to socialize new members into cultures (Brown, 1985; Pacanowsky & O'Donnell-Trujillo, 1982). Current members initiate new members formally through job instruction/orientation by telling stories about how they accomplish organizational activities. New members are socialized informally through dramatic "war" stories and "success" stories about how organizational activities have failed or succeeded in the past. Such communication socializes new members into cultures by providing them with key vignettes about cultural history, values, and expectations (Kreps, 1983a; Louis, 1980).

As an organization's identity emerges, members interpret its past and present, making sense of organizational phenomena, creating and passing on stories about organizational activities. Funny stories, serving as "inside jokes," are used to illustrate cultural themes vividly. For example, jokes that exalt the host organization while vilifying competitor organizations serve to increase member pride in the organization, as well as enhance member solidarity in competing against "enemy" organizations. Such stories provide a thematic base for the development of collective visions about the future development of the organization. Stories provide culturally derived explanations about what the organization is, what it does, how it goes about accomplishing its goals, where it has been, where it is going, and what role members play in these activities, and thus are essential elements in the development of an organizational identity (Bormann, 1983; Kreps, 1983a).

STORIES AND ORGANIZATIONAL INTELLIGENCE

Stories act as instrumental, equivocality-reducing mechanisms for organization members, providing a sense of order for interpreting unique organizational situations. Stories reduce the complexity of organizational life by providing members with information about the organization and their role within it. Weick (1979) describes the organizing process as adaptation to equivocality. Members demonstrate organization by establishing structure, predictability, and coordination. Stories provide members with information that helps them interpret and respond to equivocal situations, facilitating organized behavior. "Human beings act toward things on the basis of the meanings that the things have for them," and the meanings created develop through "the social interaction one has with one's fellows" (Blumer, 1969, p. 2).

Stories present members with culturally approved explanations of organizational phenomena, providing them with shared perceptions of reality and a common sense of social order, facilitating their abilities to coordinate, collaborate, and organize. Stories, therefore, serve as cultural storehouses for organizational intelligence, providing members with insights about how to react to the difficult situations they encounter. Organizational intelligence develops from experience; through preservation of key information about organizational adaptation (Kreps, 1986). Every time members cope with a unique situation they learn something new about how to organize. Rather than responding to every situation as though it were totally unique, in effect "reinventing the wheel," members can utilize information from past experiences stored in organizational intelligence (Johnson, 1977; Wilensky, 1977). Stories about organizational triumphs and failures give members insight into how problems have been dealt with in the past, providing information about how they can effectively respond to present and future situations (Kreps, 1983b).

STORIES AND ORGANIZATIONAL DEVELOPMENT

Organizational development (OD) is a renewal and change effort that is planned, organizationwide, and managed from the top to increase organization effectiveness through planned interventions in organizational processes and/or structures (Beckhard, 1969). OD efforts involve systematic diagnosis of the organization, development of a strategic plan for change, and the mobilization of resources to carry out the effort. The data generated by interpretive analysis of organizational stories can provide the organization development specialist with key diagnostic information about organizational difficulties, as well as suggest strategies for organizational intervention (Kreps, 1989).

Organizational communication research, especially interpretive research, has great potential for generating data that can provide organization members with reflexive feedback about their organization that they can use to identify pressing organizational problems and facilitate development of problem-solving interventions. The interpretive researcher can probe members' and environmental representatives' interpretations of organizational life by conducting open-ended, in-depth interviews, observing communicative behaviors and rituals in organizations, and analyzing key communication texts and artifacts to evoke organizational stories. Relevant issues confronting the organization are often embedded in these stories, which, when presented to the organization, can help members recognize and resolve current and potential organizational problems (Kreps, 1983a, 1989; Schein, 1969, 1987).

IMPLICATIONS FOR
ORGANIZATIONAL DEVELOPMENT

Leaders need feedback about environmental constraints on organizational activities to direct enlightened change (Nadler, 1977). Feedback about organizational performance increases organizational reflexivity (the ability of members to see the current state of the organization clearly) and guides successful organizational development (Kreps, 1986). The stories members and representatives of the relevant environment tell about the organization provide feedback to organizational decision makers, helping them understand the current condition of their organizations from the points of view of members, as well as from the perspectives of environmental representatives (Bormann, 1983; Kreps, 1986, 1989; Mitroff & Kilmann, 1975; Wilkins, 1984).

Feedback increases organizational reflexivity, helping organization leaders assess the adequacy of organizing processes, detect the need for innovating activities, and direct the development and implementation of intervention strategies for promoting ongoing organizational development (Kreps, 1989). Increased reflexivity enables members to recognize important performance gaps (discrepancies between organizational expectations and actual performance) (Rogers & Agarwala-Rogers, 1976). Organizations regularly experience performance gaps when organizational goals are not fully accomplished. The further the organization is at any point in time from the accomplishment of established goals, the wider the performance gap.

Story analysis can be used to gather information from members and relevant others about the nature and seriousness of performance gaps, serving as a feedback method that can provide OD specialists with key information about organizational facilities (Mitroff & Kilmann, 1975). Identification of important performance gaps is a key step in OD efforts, helping the OD specialist diagnose organizational problems and design adaptive intervention strategies to help the organization meet current and future goals effectively.

To illustrate the power of stories as data for directing OD efforts, brief descriptions of two applied communication research projects that used story analysis to direct organizational interventions are offered below. The first study analyzed members' stories about their experiences in a large electronics industry manufacturing corporation, RCA, to investigate organizational culture and enhance employee socialization (Kreps, 1983a). The second study analyzed relevant environmental representatives' stories about their experiences with a health care treatment organization to evaluate organizational performance and enhance marketing efforts (Kreps, 1988).

Study 1: Analysis of Stories by Organization Members

This study was conducted with RCA VideoDisc Operations in Indianapolis (Kreps, 1983b). This division of RCA had experienced tremendous growth as it began gearing up to introduce the RCA VideoDisc system to the commercial electronics market. In fact, the number of employees working at the division expanded over a period of months from approximately 300 to more than 900. Traditional means of orienting new employees to the organization, its goals, operation, and culture were found to be insufficient to handle the increased volume of new employees. As a result, many new employees were confused about their roles in the organization and the nature of the product they were working on, as well as the history and philosophy of the company.

A descriptive study of the significant symbols that made up the culture of the organization was conducted. Interpretive data were gathered through in-depth interviews with members at all levels and areas of the organization (several interviews were videotaped and were used in an organizational intervention), as well as through analysis of documents and direct observations of organizational behavior. In the interviews, organization members were asked to discuss their experiences with the organization. The stories the members told provided the research team with extremely revealing information about both the nature of the problems facing the organization and the strategies by which they had been able to overcome the problems.

The stories not only provided rich data about the organization, they were also used as primary components of the OD intervention that was implemented. The data gathered from the interpretive research were translated into a meaningful script about RCA organizational culture, which was further developed into a videotape orientation tool designed to educate new members about the culture of RCA. Several videotaped stories members told about their experiences at RCA were incorporated into the orientation program to help new members better understand the RCA culture and learn of the organizational strategies other employees used to overcome organizational constraints.

Six of the stories that were told by members and used in the orientation videotape are presented below to illustrate the reflexive cultural information they provided to organization members. In these stories, two major recurring cultural themes developed. The first theme concerns a major problem facing members, the demanding, fast-paced, complex information environment at RCA. The second theme expressed in these stories describes a cultural logic used to overcome the first problem, the expression of respect, shared competence, teamwork, and cooperative problem solving among organization members.

The first theme is demonstrated in Story 1A by the description of a typical "panic situation," in Story 1B by the technically "demanding" environment, in Story 1C by description of "the fights between production and engineering," in Story 1D by the amount of new information learned, in Story 1E by the need to find new ways to do things, and in Story 1F by the "challenge" of getting the best materials to the production line. The second theme is demonstrated in Story 1A by the employee's willingness to put in extra time to help solve problems, in Story 1B by the peer group's level of competence and the ability to use mathematics to persuade others, in Story 1C by the cooperation between departments to solve problems, in Story 1D by the helpfulness of employees in sharing their expertise, in Story 1E by the willingness of others to listen to suggestions, and in Story 1F by the "team effort to solve problems."

Story 1A, as Told by an Engineering Specialist

The thing I like most about it is my boss always says we work better in a panic situation and I really believe that. You know, when you get a phone call in the middle of the afternoon and he says: Man, we have problems here. And you end up staying there until nine o'clock at night. But when you go home at night you've put everything to bed and everything's in good shape, it's just a tremendous feeling. It's one that a lot of people have a hard time understanding. But it's — it couldn't be more exciting.

Story 1B, as Told by a Manager of Systems Engineering

In terms of growing as an engineer that's pretty straightforward. It's been much more demanding technically. The peer group in general is more demanding than anyplace I've been. So you sharpen up. You learn to deal with abstract things. You learn to deal with mathematics in a way that you communicate with it. Where it used to be the kind of thing where you could go off in the corner and play with your mathematics and see what was going on a little bit, but you didn't dare use it as a persuasive tool. In general, that also means that you, if the whole group is that way, you definitely have to sharpen up the way you look at things because they'll catch you if you goof up. Not that everybody's laying in wait. The interaction is at that level and its pretty real.

Story 1C, as Told by a Quality Control Analyst

My main job is to analyze the defect that the quality control technicians find, and I also act as a liaison between engineering and manufacturing. Quality always seems to be in the middle of all the fights between production and engineering and how things should be done and when they should be done. I also evaluate the processes that go on in manufacturing, trying to find out where problems arise, why they're happening, and relate that information back to the design engineering department. And hopefully between the two of us and manufacturing, we can find a way to get rid of the defects.

Story 1D, as Told by a Product Assurance Technician

What I've learned in the past year has been phenomenal. It's amazing, you know, and it's all on the job. You know, its just asking questions. Why does this happen? What do they do to correct it? Where does this come from? It's all just asking questions. Everybody is very helpful.

Story 1E, as Told by a Security Guard

It seems that if you have an idea or you think there is some way something can be done a little better they'll listen to you. It's not as if you're just there to put in your eight hours and get out the door.

Story 1F, as Told by a Materials Supervisor

Our product is really a unique product. Um — it provides a challenge in the fact that the materials that we use for it, and that's where I come in quite a bit, coordinating with our purchasing department. They're real precision materials, and as a result we have some problems getting good quality materials sometimes to run our assembly lines with. And it really takes a lot of effort on a lot of people's part to provide our floor with good products so we can produce a good product. It's really a team effort, quality control, PMI, which is the Purchase Material Inspection group, and our purchasing organization as well as the engineers. We all have our hands in trying to give our manufacturing department the best product we can.

Analysis

In the orientation videotape, all of these six stories were presented to new members to help them recognize the complex and challenging nature of life at RCA, as well as to help them identify the important role that cooperation among members performed in the organization. The vignettes presented in the videotape provided new members with reflexive feedback about the nature of organizational life and identified key bits of organizational intelligence to facilitate effective socialization into the company. The stories did not carry the entire burden of organizational socialization, since descriptions of RCA history, heroes, products, and processes were also presented in the videotape to help socialize new employees. However, the stories provided vivid and compelling data for accomplishing the OD goals of this study.

Study 2:
Analysis of Stories by Environmental Representatives

A market research OD study was conducted to gather information about public perceptions and attitudes toward a residential adolescent substance abuse rehabilitation program in a large midwestern city, as well as to identify strategies for increasing public acceptance and support for the program (Kreps, 1988). Three relevant groups of parents participated in this study: (a) parents with children who had already *completed* treatment at the program; (b) parents with children who were *currently* in treatment at the program; and (c) representative parents with children within the *potential* age range and geographic region served by the program. Focus group discussions were held with each of these groups of parents to identify their key experiences, ideas, and concerns about the specific programs and services of the rehabilitation program, as well as their more general perceptions about adolescent substance abuse and sources of information about treatment and support.

In the focus groups, parents were encouraged to discuss their ideas and experiences concerning adolescent substance abuse and treatment. Each focus group discussion was audiotaped to preserve group member comments. The tapes were transcribed and content analyzed to identify primary themes concerning parents' specific impressions of and experiences with the program, as well as their general experiences and ideas about adolescent substance abuse and treatment. Parents often told stories about their experiences. These stories generated rich and revealing data. The stories were used to identify specific strengths and weaknesses within the program, as well as to direct future marketing, education, and public relations efforts.

Four of the stories related by the parents, two from the completed treatment group and one each from the current treatment and potential treatment groups, are presented below to illustrate the reflexive information the stories provided to the client organization. In these stories, the completed and current groups had positive reactions to the program, while the potential group was more neutral toward the organization and apprehensive about interpreting the behaviors of their children. Stories 2A, 2B, and 2C, from the completed and current groups, identified strengths in the organization's staff and programs. The warmth of staff communication was an extremely important theme. For example, in Story 2A the emphasis on the staff's expression of eye contact and their genuine smiles, in Story 2B the description of the staff's upbeat attitude, and in Story 2C the depiction of how the staff helped change parents' attitudes about the program all support a positive theme about the value of staff communication. In Story 2D, from the potential treatment group, the parent is concerned about identifying substance abuse warning signals. The parent's indecision about interpreting the child's behavior is evident in the story.

Story 2A, as Told by a
Parent from Completed Treatment Group

I wanted to make sure I said that the eye contact, the first impression you get of this place, when you feel like you're going to die, even thinking about it is reminding me of it. Patty is wonderful. She puts you at ease immediately. They take the guilt completely off your shoulders. Everyone always looks at you and you can see that their smiles are genuine. They're not just smiles you use at work sometimes when you really don't feel like smiling. They're sincere. They're real people and they like kids. They like working with them and helping with them, and they have the patience of Job. They dealt with my child easier than I could, and I love him. I was really impressed with that. It's almost unbelievable how dedicated these people are. And I know probably what they're making. And I know what kind of education they have to have. And I know the hours they must spend, and yet they never raise their voices. They never made those kids feel like they were stupid or act condescending, ever.

Story 2B, as Told by a
Parent from Completed Treatment Group

I think it's very constructive and positive for the kids. I think they develop a very happy situation for the kids and they're trying to uplift them instead of beating them down. When they come here, counselors and everybody have a very upbeat attitude. The counseling tries to lift these kids up, get their morale up, and that's what they need. I know our son responded to that. They could make him laugh a little bit, where we couldn't at home. So, I think this is a good place. It really is.

Story 2C, as Told by a
Parent from Current Treatment Group

I've been very, very pleasantly surprised with everything we've learned. I was somewhat apprehensive coming here. I wondered, in my case, I guess because I didn't have to come here, does my child really belong here, am I putting them in a — you know — am I throwing him to the wolves? Within a week I didn't feel that way at all, because I came to understand the family counseling aspect of it that isn't very well perceived in the community.

Story 2D, as Told by a
Parent from Potential Treatment Group

> I might mention one situation myself. My son is just finishing up sixth grade and I'd
> say between fifth and sixth grade I started seeing some changes in his behavior. But,
> what I said was, and I think it's probably true, that it's a stage, ya know. It's like a
> change because sometimes it's hard to differentiate if it might be a problem or if
> they're just kind of changing because of their age or ya know. I was aware there was
> a change and even knowing exactly and you don't want to think the worst. But, you're
> aware of some of the behavior changes. And right away, I just kind of talked with
> other parents. And oh, they'll go through with what they'll go through that so I just
> said okay it's a stage. I wasn't really liking it in terms of the behavior and the attitude
> problem and that kind of thing.

Analysis

The interpretive data from this study provided a wealth of information about
public attitudes toward the program and adolescent substance abuse treatment. The
stories helped identify suggestions for increasing public acceptance and support
for the program. Support for the program was high among parents who had worked
with the program, but more neutral among parents with no program experience,
indicating a need to reach these parents in marketing efforts. Vignettes from the
completed and current groups were used in developing advertising messages to
reach this target audience, providing them with organizational intelligence from
parents who had experience with the program. Parents were found to be very
concerned about adolescent substance abuse and clearly indicated a need for more
information about risks, symptoms, and services. Based upon these data the
organization developed strategies to disseminate information to meet the needs
identified by parents in the study.

CONCLUSION

Stories provide collective structure and predictability to organizational life by
linking members together in a common cultural reality. Stories enable members to
interpret phenomena in the framework of organizational history and join them in
a common frame of reference. Stories, as repositories for organizational intelligence, are important equivocality-reducing communication mechanisms that
foster enlightened member behavior in organizations.

Organizational stories and storytelling should be recognized as important communication media for disseminating cultural information. Storytelling is generally
an enjoyable form of interaction that enables members to get to know one another
and develop cooperative relationships. Storytelling can also be used to help
members learn about their organization by providing them with personalized
information about organizational history. Stories educate members about how they

can use organizational intelligence to accomplish individual and collective goals. Knowledge of organizational intelligence helps to guide members' future organizational activities.

The information value of stories as repositories for and disseminators of organizational intelligence implies that organizations can utilize stories to promote organizational development. Interpretive organizational communication research can be used to evoke, preserve, and analyze stories. By applying story analysis to informing organizational intervention and change, the researcher/consultant can use organizational intelligence to guide ongoing organizational development.

REFERENCES

Beckhard, R. (1969). *Organization development: Strategies and models.* Reading, MA: Addison-Wesley.

Blumer, H. (1969). *Symbolic interaction: Perspective and method.* Englewood Cliffs, NJ: Prentice-Hall.

Bormann, E. G. (1983). Symbolic convergence: Organizational communication and culture. In L. Putnam & M. Pacanowsky (Eds.), *Communication and organizations: The interpretive approach* (pp. 99-122). Beverly Hills, CA: Sage.

Bormann, E. G. (1988). "Empowering" as a heuristic concept in organizational communication. In J. A. Anderson (Ed.), *Communication yearbook 11* (pp. 391-404). Newbury Park, CA: Sage.

Brown, M. H. (1985). That reminds me of a story: Speech action in organizational socialization. *Western Journal of Speech Communication, 49,* 27-42.

Johnson, B. M. (1977). *Communication: The process of organizing.* Boston: Allyn & Bacon.

Kreps, G. L. (1980). A field experimental test and revaluation of Weick's model of organizing. In D. Nimmo (Ed.), *Communication yearbook 4* (pp. 389-398). New Brunswick, NJ: Transaction.

Kreps, G. L. (1983a). The use of interpretive research to develop a socialization program at RCA. In L. Putnam & M. Pacanowsky (Eds.), *Communication and organizations: An interpretive approach* (pp. 243-256). Beverly Hills, CA: Sage.

Kreps, G. L. (1983b, August). *Organizational communication and organizational culture: A Weickian perspective.* Paper presented at the annual meeting of the Academy of Management, Dallas.

Kreps, G. L. (1986). *Organizational communication.* White Plains, NY: Longman.

Kreps, G. L. (1988). *Adolescent substance abuse rehabilitation program market research program.* Rockford, IL: DKW.

Kreps, G. L. (1989, May). *A therapeutic model of organizational communication consultation.* Paper presented at the annual meeting of the International Communication Association, San Francisco.

Kreps, G. L., & Lederman, L. C. (1985). Using the case study method in organizational communication education: Developing students' insight, knowledge, and creativity through experience-based learning and systematic debriefing. *Communication Education, 34,* 358-364.

Louis, M. R. (1980). Surprise and sense making: What newcomers experience when entering unfamiliar organizational settings. *Administrative Science Quarterly, 23,* 225-251.

Mitroff, I., & Kilmann, R. (1975). Stories managers tell: A new tool for organizational problems solving. *Management Review, 64,* 19-20.

Nadler, D. R. (1977). *Feedback and organizational development: Using data-based methods.* Reading, MA: Addison-Wesley.

Pacanowsky, M., & O'Donnell-Trujillo, N. (1982). Communication and organizational cultures. *Western Journal of Speech Communication, 41,* 115-130.

Rogers, E., & Agarwala-Rogers, R. (1976). *Communication in organizations.* New York: Free Press.

Schein, E. H. (1969). *Process consultation: Its role in organization development.* Reading, MA: Addison-Wesley.

Schein, E. H. (1987). *The clinical perspective in fieldwork.* Newbury Park, CA: Sage.

Weick, K. E. (1979). *The social psychology of organizing* (2nd ed.). Reading, MA: Addison-Wesley.

Weick, K. E., & Browning, L. D. (1986). Argument and narration in organizational communication. *Journal of Management, 12,* 243-259.

Wilensky, H. (1977). *Organizational intelligence.* New York: Basic Books.

Wilkins, A. L. (1984). The creation of cultures: The role of stories and human resource systems. *Human Resource Management, 23,* 41-60.

Symbolic Emancipation in the Organization: A Case of Shifting Power

JILL J. McMILLAN
Wake Forest University

P ROFESSOR Brown's profile of what constitutes organizational stories gives rise to an interesting question: Why have organizational scholars so recently discovered organizational stories and, more generally, organizational symbols? Surely we cannot be so partisan or myopic as to believe that our generation of organizational members invented organizational symbols. What is fundamentally different about organizations today — or our perceptions of them — that suddenly inflates the significance of organizational stories? Specifically, how is it possible that Brown's topic, which 10 years ago was a nonissue, commands a lead position in a prestigious publication of our discipline today? I see this question as an important one because it reveals a shift in our perceptions of contemporary organizations that is critical to the understanding and assessment not only of organizational stories but of all organizational symbols.

I will argue that this work has been occasioned by a symbolic emancipation in human organizations, fueled by a broad and ever-growing reconceptualization of organizational power. Because this freeing up of organizational symbols has been extensive, I will not attempt to track the widespread effects of this emancipation across the entire organizational terrain. I hope simply to demonstrate how the evolution of one concept — "organizational rhetoric" — reflects the symbolic freedom that has become contagious in contemporary organizations. I will first describe the unique connection between rhetoric and power in the organization, then demonstrate how contemporary functions of rhetoric within the organization reveal a reconceptualization of power there, and, finally, suggest how a focus on

Correspondence and requests for reprints: Jill J. McMillan, Box 7347, Reynolda Station, Wake Forest University, Winston-Salem, NC 27109.

Communication Yearbook 13, pp. 203-214

organizational power might instruct our analysis of organizational stories and other symbols. When my argument is completed, I hope that it will be apparent that the recent "discovery" of organizational symbols of all types is no accident, but the evolution of understanding about who has power in the organization, how they get it, and how they keep it.

THE UNIQUE RELATIONSHIP BETWEEN
POWER AND RHETORIC IN THE ORGANIZATION

Charles Redding (1987) has observed that "when we begin to study influence [power], we inevitably encounter . . . rhetoric" (p. 17). I will take the position that in organizations, rhetoric *is* power (Foucault, 1980; Tompkins, 1989; Tucker & Wilson, 1980), but it is power that is tightly circumscribed by the unique context of organizational structure and practice.[1] Given the inherent "humanness" of rhetoric, one may be tempted to assume that rhetorical activity most likely proceeds in human organizations much as it does in other interpersonal interactions. But such is not necessarily the case. Take, for example, Bitzer's rhetorical situation, which Conrad (1985) argues is applicable to organizations. When Bitzer (1972) describes the rhetorical situation, there is a symmetry implied between the two interacting agents. Clearly the speaker has power. He or she is able to "make words" in support of a position, and, given some skill and a little luck, others likely will listen and respond. The use of rhetoric indicates that there is power residing in the receiver as well; the receiver's power lies in his or her potential to assess a message and to act on it (Blau, 1964; Habermas, 1975; Rus, 1980). If I can force you to do a thing on the mere authority of my position or my good name or my capacity to reward or to punish you, then why would I bother to try to persuade you? The answer is, of course, that I will go to the trouble to persuade you because I may need your understanding, goodwill, and commitment, as well as your compliance. Otherwise, coercion or force would accomplish my purpose much more quickly and easily. In short, "who says power says counter power" (Rus, cited in Hickson, Astley, Butler, & Wilson, 1981).

It is, then, this reciprocal power that calls forth persuasion. Symmetry, however, is never absolute. We come to each interpersonal interaction with different measures of skill, status, and savvy, and in dialogue, the balance shifts back and forth (Hocker & Wilmot, 1985). The critical difference in the rhetorical situation within organizations is that this power imbalance is inherent in the hierarchy (Coleman, 1974; Edelman, 1977). Now the rhetorical game changes for the two rhetorical agents. Everyone may not "speak to" organizational events and concerns; perhaps only those legitimized by organizational position or status are allowed to do so. Even within horizontal ranks or in voluntary organizations, there are levels of seniority and expertise that unofficially "qualify" organizational speakers (Conrad, 1985; Mumby, 1987).

Just as the source of the message may be constrained by the asymmetrical hierarchy, so may be the receiver (Frost, 1987). Many organizational members may be excluded from rhetorical situations because they are perceived by message senders as lacking the "right" to information, or the expertise to handle it, or the discretionary powers to act upon it (Edelman, 1977). Low status organizational members especially are perceived as unfit recipients for persuasive messages; when the passage of information is necessary, simply telling underlings what to do — giving them orders — is more cost-efficient and less time-consuming. Rhetorical roles, then, that are practically taken for granted in normal interpersonal interaction may not be so freely assumed in organizational contexts (Tompkins, 1989). Furthermore, the assumption of these roles is mediated by perceptions of power.

Rhetoric, then, signifies power in the organization, identifies it, defines it, tracks it. By locating those organizational members who are legitimized to use rhetoric, the issues around which their messages turn, and those to whom the rhetoric is addressed, it is possible to locate within the organization the places where power resides. This link between power and rhetoric is not new, but because we have narrowly interpreted organizational power, as Tompkins (1984) argues, we have also underestimated how rhetoric works in the organization.

CONTEMPORARY FUNCTIONS
OF ORGANIZATIONAL RHETORIC

Historically, rhetoric (persuasion) has fared poorly in organizational contexts because "orders" were the more efficient and cost-beneficial form of communication. Numerous sociological and cultural factors, such as the humanist era, the labor movement, and the Japanese challenge, have changed the face of contemporary organizations — and their sounds as well. There is more rhetorical activity in more arenas of organizational life than ever before. This circumstance is true, I believe, because there is also more widespread power. And where there is power, people cannot be ordered; they must be persuaded.

Clearly, organizational persuasion does not flow freely and evenly in contemporary organizations. Management has the same decided advantage that it has always had — easy access to organizational symbols and the authority and visibility to make them stick (Frost, 1987). However, new rhetorical demands for superiors and opportunities for subordinates are changing the face of the modern organization.

Management as a Rhetorical Arena

Phillip Tompkins (1984) has made the interesting and provocative observation that the widespread ineffectiveness of downward communication in the organization may be a failure of persuasion rather than one of misunderstanding. In this statement, Tompkins speaks to a new kind of managerial responsibility and, I think, to a greater decentralization of organizational power. Specifically, Tompkins is referring to the responsibility of contemporary management to "talk membership into" organizational commitment rather than to demand it. The traditional manager who was formerly regarded as "cop, referee, devil's advocate, . . . naysayer, . . . etc." is now expected to be a "cheerleader, enthusiast, nurturer of champions, hero finder, wanderer, coach, facilitator, builder" (Peters & Austin, 1985, p. 265).

Previously, managers were thought to be people who "did things"; in other words, they were defined and evaluated by their actions. Today, managers *interact* (Pacanowsky & O'Donnell-Trujillo, 1983), and one of their most important inter- active functions is managing the organizational symbols at their disposal (Pfeffer, 1981; Smith & Peterson, 1988; Weick, 1980). Smircich and Morgan (1982) insist that "the key challenge for a leader is to manage meaning in such a way that individuals orient themselves to the achievement of desirable ends. . . . To fail in this obligation is to fail in one's organizational role" (pp. 260, 262).

Pondy (1978) describes leadership as a language game in which the leader's power and ability to "put into words what the group is about" is tantamount to social fact: "The real power of Martin Luther King was not only that he had a dream, but that he could describe it, that it became public and therefore accessible to millions of people" (pp. 94-95). Besides instilling members with the company's "dream," managerial symbols can accomplish such mundane tasks as "mobiliza tion and motivation of support, . . . cooling off or placating opposition . . . , and focusing and organizing activity" (Pfeffer, 1981, p. 37).

Besides the importance of these managerial "wordsmiths" becoming "manag- ers of eloquence" (Weick, 1980, p. 18), Pfeffer (1981) and Smith and Peterson (1988) describe this symbolic management as an important power source. Because leaders have primary access to the organization's symbol pool and the prerogative to structure symbols into a "dominant organizational reality," they enjoy a tremen- dous advantage over other organizational members (Conrad, 1985; Gray, Bouson, & Donnellon, 1985) in establishing the ground rules for organizational life. In her chapter, Brown observes that these "organizationally sanctioned viewpoints" (p. 169) show up consistently in the stories of the members for which they were intended.

However, this symbolic edge of management is not absolute. Gramsci (cited in King, 1987) insists that the voices that prevail are not necessarily the loudest, the most authoritative, or even the most powerful; they are those that offer versions of reality that are useful in allowing ordinary people to make sense of their lives and to act in the world (March & Olsen, 1979; see also Weick, 1976). So the symbolic advantage of management is clearly held in check by the subtle, implicit power of the audience whom managers must persuade and on whose allegiance they must depend. Managers have been "talking" to members for years; only recently have we acknowledged that managers' talk must be persuasive, and not coercive.

The Rhetorical Activity of the Work Force

There is evidence that the recipients of managerial messages are also becoming more rhetorically active.

Individual rhetorical activity. Historically, we have heard little about the rhetorical machinations of the average organizational member because, like others, we have taken a "managerial perspective" (Deetz, 1985). Not only were we more interested in managerial symbols, the business and professional speaking courses that were our primary interface with organizations were aimed at training the "rhetorical elite"—those who were destined to manage others rather than to be managed.[2]

Today, however, new perceptions of organizational power have broadened the ownership and the use of rhetorical skills. Conrad (1985) argues, for example, that average members are empowered when they are able to "articulate" their expertise successfully—to talk well about what they do, to ask for and obtain scarce resources, to manage and maintain effective interpersonal relationships through rhetorical skill and know-how.

Members have also learned to use verbal influence in ways that are not organizationally sanctioned. For example, we know that individuals will withhold and/or distort information passed upward in the organization in order to balance an inequitable power arrangement or to facilitate personal goals (Krivonos, 1982; Mechanic, 1962; O'Reilly & Roberts, 1974; Read, 1962). Jim Ed, in Brown's Story C, would have "pulled chain" earlier had it not been for the slow paperwork of some determined subordinates (p. 169).

Another verbal activity of organizational members that has been widely explored of late is the phenomenon of whistle-blowing—the public exposure of a company by an individual member who believes that organization to be involved in "corrupt, illegal, fraudulent, or harmful activity" (Nader, Petkas, & Blackwell, 1972, p. vii). While whistle-blowing is clearly an ethical issue, it is also inherently a rhetorical one. The troubled employee must articulate the wrongdoing that he or she perceives in order for a case of whistle-blowing to exist, and this risky verbal behavior has been steadily growing (e.g., NASA and Morton Thiokol). At great professional and personal costs, individuals are opting to speak out against such questionable organizational practices as racism, sexism, unsafe products, and environmental pollution (Parmerlee, Near, & Jensen, 1982).

One might argue that whistle-blowing has emerged because organizations are more corrupt today or because the press is more tenacious and more interested in corporate sensationalism. Another possible explanation, however, is that the average organizational member is more rhetorically courageous and adept than ever before. It could be that once power and symbolization were freed up in the organization, the articulation of important organizational issues, which once was the sole priority of managers and official spokespersons, became fair game for all.

While it is true that whistle-blowers often pay for their rhetorical stance with lost promotions and/or jobs, the fact remains that the number of whistle-blowing incidents continues to rise. Apparently, organizational members at all levels are becoming aware of their potential as rhetorical agents of action and change, and are opting to exercise that right despite serious sanctions.

Collective rhetorical activity. If the rhetorical gyrations of an individual member carry as much potential impact to the organization as has been suggested, then how much more potent is this rhetorical force when it becomes contagious? There is widespread evidence that organizational members are extending this newfound rhetorical freedom to the groups to which they belong by participating in group decision making, forming coalitions, and structuring their own symbolic subcultures, which may or may not align with those of the organization (Frost, 1987).

One such form of group symbolizing is participative decision making (e.g., quality circles). This decentralized mechanism represents a significant departure for management, which traditionally made and announced decisions. Now the experience and knowledge of members at all levels of the organization is tapped into the official decision-making apparatus of the organization. While the use of quality circles has been criticized by some as a pseudoparticipative event (Pfeffer, 1981), there are also widespread examples of employee empowerment. In the best cases, the collective discourse of the group has the potential to translate into significant organizational policy and practice. Besides being afforded "voice" in organizational concerns (Hirschman, 1970), employees are further empowered as they develop personal commitments to the organizational decisions of which they are a part (Salancik, 1977).

Other forms of collective rhetorical action are not so readily sanctioned or controlled by the organization. For example, individuals form linkages with others from their interpersonal contacts and networks of friends and acquaintances, and these relationships serve as "power currencies" that can be used against competing positions or ideologies (Hocker & Wilmot, 1985, p. 74). Mechanic (1962) suggests, for instance, that a secretary may use informal contacts to provide services for higher-ranking members, thereby increasing his or her worth and future bargaining potential.

Another somewhat amorphous, yet potentially powerful, example of rhetorical activity by the group emerges in the symbolic production of subcultures. While management attempts to instill the *dominant* organizational culture, there appears to be rhetorical activity going on at other levels of the organization as well, as members seek to construct and to "sell" those accounts of organizational life and activity that best represent their interests and well-being. Brown and McMillan (1985), Conrad (1985), and March and Olsen (1979) see this widespread symbolizing as somewhat of a defense mechanism against the chaotic and confusing stimuli that regularly bombard members. In the face of inadequate or perplexing information, members may simply "make up" explanations that are personally comfortable and satisfying. Brown's Story D, "Hot Water," demonstrates an organizational narrative that functioned to "make sense of" an event and to reduce uncertainty for a frustrated officer (pp.172-173). Gregory (1983) suggests that these "alternative" accounts, or "deviant" premises (Tompkins & Cheney, 1985), may even take the form of countermyths.

Therefore, Riley (1983) puts it well when she characterizes organizations as complex systems of cultures and subcultures, in which the cultures are created and fueled by the symbolic collaboration of the groups who live and abide by them. Hall (1985) describes how discourse creates these cultures and why culture-building represents widespread rhetorical emancipation:

> Ideologies do not operate through single ideas; they operate, in discursive chains, in clusters, in semantic fields, in discursive formations. . . . So a variety of ideological systems or logics are available in any social formation. The notion of *the* dominant ideology and the subordinated ideology is an inadequate way of representing the complex interplay of different ideological discourses and formations in any developed society. (p. 104)

Bormann's (1983) work on fantasy chaining and the creation of rhetorical visions explains the process of collaborative group symbolizing; Story B, "War Zone," in Brown's work demonstrates such an organizational saga (p. 169).

With the rhetorically spawned and fueled machinations of the organizational subcultures (or multicultures), we have, in a sense, come full circle. Power, which once was held and dispersed by a few upper-level elites, now resides in numerous and untold places throughout the organization, and, in effect, the rhetorical model has been transformed. While the organizational hierarchy still does not allow absolute symmetry, the contemporary rhetorical roles of both management and members attest to a shifting balance that favors the ordinary Joe.[3]

If managers are talking more persuasively, and members are talking more and with more effect, we can assume, I believe, a vastly improved status in the rhetorical lot of the member as both source and receiver of organizational messages. How is this symbolic emancipation affecting the stories that emanate from all levels of the organization?

THE RHETORICAL PERFORMANCE OF ORGANIZATIONAL STORIES

Some would say that organizational stories can only perform rhetorically — that all communication in fact does so. Brown does not address this dilemma in her treatise, but I think that she well might. If I have a complaint with Brown's presentation of organizational stories (or perhaps with current research about them), it is that there is too much emphasis on what they *are* and not enough on what they *do*. Furthermore, I believe that this somewhat anemic perception of organizational narratives creates methodological problems in studying them. Perhaps a more accurate and helpful way to view organizational stories — at all levels of the organization — is as tools of power, busily, proactively working to influence the people and the environment in which they are spawned.[4] If we juxtapose my discussion of organizational power and Brown's exposition of organizational stories, some important insights emerge:

(1) People are not telling stories just to pass the time; these organizational narratives are performing important rhetorical functions that may vary greatly along political dimensions.

For example, Brown determines that the functions of organizational stories are to reduce uncertainty, to manage meaning, and to create bonding and identification. A closer look at each of these functions reveals a complex political interaction that is fraught with special interests, mixed motives, and hidden agendas. Take uncertainty reduction, for example. Management must of course reduce uncertainty in order to present an image of itself as rational and in control (Weick, 1979). Furthermore, any good manager knows that members work better if they are calm and reassured. Ordinary members, on the other hand, have to reduce uncertainty just to cope — to hold down the inevitable panic that arises from the absurd and anomalous events that characterize most of their organizational lives (Frost, 1987; March & Olsen, 1979).

Managing meaning is also a symbolic sparring match. Management must present a particular linguistic interpretation of organizational reality that reinforces the goals and aspirations of corporate decision makers. The "company line" must be articulated often and well, and must embed the "master premises" (Tompkins & Cheney, 1985) that control decisions and behavior. Members, however, must find ways to understand and to symbolize their "multiple realities" (Weick, 1976), which are not excessively alien to the dominant reality that the organization is espousing. Sometimes these verbal constructions at the lower levels of the organization appear to dismantle the official company line deliberately.

Finally, the process of bonding and identification is also shot through with power maneuvers by various organizational constituencies. Management encourages bonding and identification because it is efficient and pragmatic to do so; the organization whose membership lacks cohesion and unity does not fare well in the marketplace. It is to management's advantage, then, to construct accounts of organizational life that build allegiance to organizational goals (Smircich & Morgan, 1982). Members will also be taught what is expected of them through the recounting of the adventures of past and present organizational actors (Bormann, 1983).

The membership at large, on the other hand, bonds and identifies for entirely different reasons and from a drastically different power position. Individual members unite to prevent being alone in this sometimes threatening and alien organizational environment. They seek comfort, solace, and camaraderie in the stories that they tell, but most of all they seek power (Brown & McMillan, 1985). In an organizational world where there is an overabundance of one-down positions, two is always better than one, and if I can somehow combine my limited power with yours, we will improve our chances in any sort of an organizational showdown. Bonding and identification, then, for those at the bottom of the organization, are the stuff of which coalitions are made.

(2) A rhetorical perspective that features power and persuasion might facilitate the analysis and the understanding of organizational stories.

Brown suggests that we need to reexamine our research possibilities with regard to organizational narratives. In the past, research about stories appears to have bogged down in such questions as these: Are they mythical? Are they true? Are they consistent? Are they believable? Consistent with the thesis of this treatise, I would like to suggest a different set of questions to ask of organizational stories: What are they "doing"? How are they exhibiting influence and power? Whom are they attempting to persuade and why? How might the story differ if it were told at other levels of the organization? In short, I submit that research in this fascinating area would be enhanced by a perspective that views all organizational members as symbolically powerful and all organizational accounts as potentially persuasive. Furthermore, a rhetorical frame could accommodate well Brown's admonition to study the tellers, settings, results, and applications of organizational stories.

By now I trust that the facetious question posed at the beginning of this essay has been successfully answered. Modern-day organizations have no corner on the market of organizational storytelling; surely, organizational members of all places and times have swapped tales just as readily and as enthusiastically as do their contemporary counterparts. What is significant, however, is that organizational scholars and practitioners have finally taken notice, and that their interest is not confined to official company legends, but rather extends to the sagas of the total membership (Frost, 1987). I would argue that the enhanced status of stories in organizations indicates improved status of the storytellers. We now regard all organizational accounts as important cultural data and their creators as significant symbolizers in their own right.

If symbolic emancipation is, in truth, emerging in contemporary organizations, then *all* members are moving to possess the right to construct accounts that seek to influence the people and the events of their world. It behooves story analysts, then, to assess organizational accounts from the rhetorical context in which they reside by asking such questions as: What is the organizational status of this storyteller — position, seniority, communicative competence, technical expertise? What is the nature of the storyteller's organizational world that would call forth this narrative — does he or she exhibit job satisfaction? Commitment? Alienation from some authority figure? Does some organizational exigence threaten the storyteller's personal security and happiness? And finally, who is the audience — either primary or secondary — for whom this story is intended? What is the nature of the listeners' power and influence? What sort of organizational advantage might be gained now or in the future from the recounting of this story? How would this account change if it moved up and down the hierarchy?

Besides offering an excellent organizing principle for random organizational accounts, the rhetorical perspective provides a method for understanding organizations holistically and longitudinally. Scholars have long lamented the inadequacies of ad hoc organizational research that addresses one segment of organizational life at a time and fails to integrate that understanding with the varied and complex dimensions of the system as a whole as it operates over time. It appears that an excellent way to avoid these obvious limitations might be to accumulate stories at all levels of the organization over time, to assess their intrinsic rhetorical functions for their intended audiences in a particular time and place, and then to juxtapose the various accounts and to assess their wider rhetorical import for the organization. Furthermore, "listening" to these narratives adjust and change over time could provide a rich and insightful record of organizational growth or demise.

NOTES

1. When I refer to "rhetoric" in the organization, I am referring to those purposeful attempts to persuade or to influence (Aristotle, 1932; Burke, 1969; Mintzberg, 1983; Porter, Allen, & Angle, 1981), as opposed to those messages that simply convey information or express feelings. Like Conrad (1985), I am not sure that I believe in those distinctions, but they are useful in this treatise because they align with traditional arguments that seek to distinguish communication and rhetoric, and allow us to focus more clearly on the permutations of symbolic emancipation. Most important, to limit our consideration to influence attempts alone enables us to apprehend more readily the figure of power from the complex symbolic ground that surrounds it.

2. Sproule (1988) affirms that the tendency of the "old rhetoric" was to move society by "focusing on the sociopolitical elite."

3. Consistent with the argument of this treatise, Sproule (1988) also argues that the "institutional flavor" of contemporary rhetoric is gradually reversing the direction of social influence from the *few* to the *many*. Sproule's assertion is simply the rhetorical counterpart of an argument that has been made by many other organizational writers. See, for example, Naisbitt (1982), who insists that a trend of decentralization in America is transforming politics, business, and culture.

4. Frost (1987) identifies stories as particularly potent vehicles for the playing of organizational power games. See his discussion for suggestions about applying game criteria to the analysis of organizational narratives.

REFERENCES

Aristotle. (1932). *The rhetoric* (L. Cooper, Trans.). New York: Appleton-Century-Crofts.
Bitzer, L. (1972). The rhetorical situation. In D. Ehninger (Ed.), *Contemporary rhetoric* (pp. 39-49). Glenview, IL: Scott, Foresman.
Blau, P. M. (1964). *Exchange and power in social life.* New York: John Wiley.
Bormann, E. (1983). Symbolic convergence: Organizational communication and culture. In L. L. Putnam & M. E. Pacanowsky (Eds.), *Communication and organization: An interpretive approach* (pp. 92-122). Beverly Hills, CA: Sage.
Brown, M. H., & McMillan, J. J. (1985, April). *Organizational myths developed by superiors and subordinates: Relationships and differences.* Paper presented at the annual meeting of the Southern Speech Communication Association, Winston-Salem, NC.

Burke, K. (1969). *A rhetoric of motives.* Berkeley: University of California Press.

Cheney, G. (1983). The rhetoric of identification and the study of organizational communication. *Quarterly Journal of Speech, 89*, 143-158.

Coleman, J. S. (1974). *Power and the structure of society.* New York: W. W. Norton.

Conrad, C. (1985). *Strategic organizational communication: Cultures, situations, and adaptations.* New York. Holt, Rinehart & Winston.

Deetz, S. (1985). Ethical considerations in cultural research in organizations. In P. J. Frost, L. F. Moore, M. R. Louis, C. C. Lundberg, & J. Martin (Eds.), *Organizational culture* (pp. 253-270). Beverly Hills, CA: Sage.

Deal, T. E., & Kennedy, A. A. (1982). *Corporate cultures: The rites and rituals of corporate life.* Reading, MA: Addison-Wesley.

Edelman, M. (1977). *Political language: Words that succeed and policies that fail.* New York: Academic Press.

Frost, P. J. (1987). Power, politics, and influence. In F. M. Jablin, L. L. Putnam, K. H. Roberts, & L. W. Porter (Eds.), *Handbook of organizational communication* (pp. 503-549). Newbury Park, CA: Sage.

Foucault, M. (1980). *Power and knowledge: Selected interviews and other writings 1927-1977* (C. Gordon, Trans.). New York: Pantheon.

Gray, B., Bouson, M., & Donnellon, A. (1985). Organizations as constructions and destructions of meaning. *Journal of Management, 11*, 83-98.

Gregory, K. R. (1983). Native view paradigms: Multiple cultures and culture conflicts in organizations. *Administrative Science Quarterly, 28*, 359-376.

Habermas, J. (1975). *Legitimation crisis* (T. A. McCarthy, Trans.). Boston: Beacon.

Hall, S. (1985). Signification, representation, ideology: Althusser and the post-structuralist debates. *Critical Studies in Mass Communication, 2*, 91-114.

Hickson, D., Astley, N., Butler, K., & Wilson, D. (1981). Organization as power. In L. L. Cummings & B. H. Staw (Eds.), *Research in organizational behavior* (Vol. 3, pp. 151-196). Greenwich, CT: JAI.

Hirokawa, R. Y. (1981). Improving intra-organizational communication: A lesson from Japanese management. *Communication Quarterly, 30*, 35-40.

Hirschman, A. O. (1970). *Exit, voice, and loyalty: Responses to decline in firms, organizations, and states.* Cambridge, MA: Harvard University Press.

Hocker, J. L., & Wilmot, W. W. (1985). *Interpersonal conflict* (2nd ed.). Dubuque, IA: William C Brown.

King, A. (1987). *Communication and power.* Prospect Heights, IL: Waveland.

Krivonos, P. D. (1982). Distortion of subordinate to superior communication in organizational settings. *Central States Speech Journal, 33*, 345-352.

March, J. G., & Olsen, J. P. (1979). *Ambiguity and choice in the organization.* Bergen, Norway: Universitetsforlaget.

Mathews, M. C. (1988). *Strategic intervention in organizations.* Newbury Park, CA: Sage.

Mechanic, D. (1962). Sources of power of lower participants in complex organizations. *Administrative Science Quarterly, 7*, 349-364.

Mintzberg, H. (1983). *Power in and around the organization.* Englewood Cliffs, NJ: Prentice-Hall.

Mumby, D. (1987). The political function of narrative in organization. *Communication Monographs, 54*, 113-127.

Nader, R., Petkas, P., & Blackwell, K. (1972). *Whistleblowing: The report on the Conference of Professional Responsibility.* New York: Grossman.

Naisbitt, J. (1982). *Megatrends.* New York: Warner.

O'Reilly, C. A., & Roberts, K. A. (1974). Information filtration in organizations: Three experiments. *Organizational Behavior and Human Performance, 11*, 253-265.

Pacanowsky, M. E., & O'Donnell-Trujillo, N. (1983). Organizational communication as cultural performance. *Communication Monographs, 50*, 126-147.

Parmerlee, M. A., Near, J., & Jensen, T. C. (1982). Correlates of whistleblowers' perceptions of organizational retaliations. *Administrative Science Quarterly, 27*, 17-34.

Peters, T. J., & Austin, N. (1985). *A passion for excellence*. New York: Random House.

Peters, T. J., & Waterman, R. H. (1982). *In search of excellence*. New York: Warner.

Pfeffer, J. (1981). Management as symbolic action: The creation and maintenance of organizational paradigms. In L. L. Cummings & B. H. Staw (Eds.), *Research in organizational behavior* (Vol. 3, pp. 1-52). Greenwich, CT: JAI.

Pondy, L. R. (1978). Leadership is a language game. In M. W. McCall, Jr., & M. M. Lombardo (Eds.), *Leadership: Where else can we go?* (pp. 87-99). Durham, NC: Duke University Press.

Porter, L., Allen, R. N., & Angle, H. L. (1981). The politics of upward influence in organizations. In L. L. Cummings & B. H. Staw (Eds.), *Research in organizational behavior* (Vol. 3, pp. 109-150). Greenwich, CT: JAI.

Read, W. H. (1962). Upward communication in industrial hierarchies. *Human Relations, 15*, 3-15.

Redding, C. (1987, May). *Communication implications of Mintzberg's "Power in and Around the Organization."* Paper presented at the International Communication Association Seminar on Communication and Power in the Organization, Montreal, Canada.

Riley, P. (1983). A structuralist account of political culture. *Administrative Science Quarterly, 28*, 414-437.

Rus, V. (1980). Positive and negative power: Thoughts on the dialectic of power. *Organization Studies, 1*(1).

Salancik, G. R. (1977). Commitment and control of organizational behaviors and belief. In B. M. Staw & G. R. Salancik (Eds.), *New directions in organizational behavior* (pp. 1-55). Chicago: St. Clair.

Seelye, H. N., & Sween, J. A. (1982). Quality circles in U.S. industry: Survey results. *Quality Circles Journal, 5*, 26-29.

Smircich, L., & Morgan, G. (1982). Leadership: The management of meaning. *Journal of Applied Behavioral Science, 18*, 257-273.

Smith, P. B., & Peterson, M. F. (1988). *Leadership, organizations, and culture.* Newbury Park, CA: Sage.

Sproule, J. M. (1988). The new managerial rhetoric and the old criticism. *Quarterly Journal of Speech, 74*, 401-415.

Stohl, C., & Jennings, K. (1988). Volunteerism and voice in quality circles. *Western Journal of Speech Communication, 52*, 238-251.

Tompkins, P. K. (1984). The functions of human communication in organization. In C. C. Arnold & J. W. Bowers (Eds.), *Handbook of rhetoric and communication theory* (pp. 659-719). Boston: Allyn & Bacon.

Tompkins, P. K. (1989). Organizational communication: The central tradition. *Spectra, 25*, 2-3.

Tompkins, P. K., & Cheney, G. (1985). Communication and unobtrusive control in contemporary organizations. In R. McPhee & P. K. Tompkins (Eds.), *Organizational communication: Traditional themes and new directions* (pp. 179-210). Beverly Hills, CA: Sage.

Tucker, C. O., & Wilson, G. L. (1980). Confrontation rhetoric in institutional settings. *Central States Speech Journal, 31*, 42-52.

Weick, K. (1976). Educational organizations as loosely coupled systems. *Administrative Science Quarterly, 21*, 1-19.

Weick, K. (1979). *The social psychology of organizing* (2nd ed.). Reading, MA: Addison-Wesley.

Weick, K. (1980). The management of eloquence. *Executive, 6*, 18-21.

SECTION 2

INTERPERSONAL CONVERSATIONS, ARGUMENTS, EMBARRASSMENTS, AND NEGOTIATIONS

5 Orienting to the Phenomenon

WAYNE A. BEACH
San Diego State University

A central concern of this chapter is to articulate relationships among researchers' and interactants' methods for orienting to naturally occurring social activities. Basic questions are raised as central to the future course of research on social interaction. Following an overview of research commitments of conversation analysis, a discussion of "coding" is offered as a practical achievement enacted by all researchers as they orient to interaction. A transcribed segment of courtroom interaction is offered so as to examine, in turn-by-turn detail, the nature of participants' achieved orientations to a civil hearing. It is argued that by examining actual sequences of interaction as displays of social order, priority is given to the talk itself. This position is in contrast to accounting for the detailed work of speakers and hearers by invoking "macroconcepts" such as power, status, identity, institution, or related forces in any way "external" to the interaction.

W HENEVER social interaction becomes the locus of communication inquiry, certain basic questions emerge regarding interactants' and researchers' methods for displaying, detecting, and thus orienting to phenomena constituting social order. The following questions are central both to the present essay and to the future course of research on communication:

- Have we located a phenomenon yet?
- Would we recognize a phenomenon of interest if we *observed* one communicatively "at work" — as speakers and hearers orient to the occasions in which they are interactionally engaged?
- What evidence could be provided that is available for critical inspection to all researchers interested in the discovery and justification of that phenomenon?
- How would we know that a phenomenon is convincingly and uniquely of one type rather than another?
- To what extent is the object of study a phenomenon-in-the-world or an artifact of the research enterprise?

Correspondence and requests for reprints: Wayne A. Beach, Department of Speech Communication, San Diego State University, San Diego, CA 92182.

Communication Yearbook 13, pp. 216-244

These and related queries apply equally well to all modes of inquiry focusing upon the organizing features of social interaction. With increasing regularity, however, such questions are being raised by researchers attempting to understand the constituent features of everyday conversation. Throughout Zimmerman's (1988) overview of the "conversation analytic (CA) perspective" in *Communication Yearbook 11*, for example, attention is drawn to how speakers and hearers noticeably achieve interaction in the first instance, by and for themselves (see Jefferson, 1973; Schegloff, 1986). Consideration is also given to how researchers go about the business of observing, analyzing, and providing evidence for the existence of an interactional "phenomenon."

Guided by the questions posed above, this essay examines issues and recurring problems associated with "orienting to the phenomenon" from five interrelated perspectives. First, an overview is provided of CA's basic commitment to the study of naturally occurring interaction. Consideration is given to the location and recognition of social phenomena, wherein "phenomena" consist of conversational activities existing (in the first instance) independently of the research enterprise. Second, a reflexive consideration of "coding," as a set of activities enacted by all interactional researchers, is offered. When coding tasks are viewed as achieved orientations to social order, it becomes possible to render them as problematic. Doing so addresses how the routine nature of coding tasks leads to their typically being overlooked as methodical glosses of phenomena routinely oriented to by speakers and hearers. Third, a transcribed segment of a videotaped interaction is provided as an opportunity to examine empirically how speakers and hearers orient to phenomena that make up a social occasion. The turn-by-turn analysis of this segment begins to locate how particular phenomena are shaped and fashioned within the environment of a three-party speech exchange system, informing and thereby directing both the analyst and readers in the search for patterns and recurring social structures. Fourth, it is argued that social phenomena exist in and through interactional sequences. Invoking macroconcepts "external" to the talk itself (e.g., power, status, identity) serves only to gloss the detailed and achieved character of routine social occasions. Finally, this chapter concludes with an overview of specific methodological and thus theoretical issues implicit within the positions developed above. Particular attention is given to the degree and type of correspondence between researchers' and interactants' methods for displaying and detecting social phenomena.

LOCATING AND RECOGNIZING PHENOMENA

A basic tenet of CA is the recognition that social order, evident in and through the detailed and contingent activities of societal members, exists *independently* of social scientific inquiry. Irrespective of the possibility of being examined and in some way analytically dissected for purposes of research, everyday interactants simply go about their business performing routine and often mundane tasks.

Whether these tasks are occasioned during family dinners, service encounters, corporate meetings, prayer support groups, or any other type of interactional involvement, the indisputable fact is that they are ordinarily achieved in the course of daily life in the process of "doing being" (Sacks, 1984b) a friend, a parent, a customer, a boss, a prayer partner, a lawyer, a doctor, and so on. How these tasks get done is a direct function of the ways in which persons' identities get worked out turn by turn, moment by moment, in and through the methods employed to accomplish the routine character of everyday living. In the eventual course or evolution of a conversational involvement (see Goffman, 1981), the practical consequences of interactions (e.g., their outcomes) evidence little more or less than how participants display and detect one another's orientations to the occasion at hand. Exactly what gets achieved is undeniably the upshot of how speakers and hearers fashion, shape, and make available to one another their understandings of the local environment of which they are an integral part.

For conversation analysts, the unparalleled goal is to seek understanding of the independent and natural existence of social order. The reliance upon carefully produced transcripts of audio and video recordings, allowing for repeated hearings, viewings, and inspections of archived but nonetheless "actual and determinate" (Schegloff, 1986) sequences of interaction, reflects a basic commitment to employing research methods fashioned after the phenomenon being examined. While neither recordings nor transcriptions are conversations in and of themselves (Zimmerman, 1988), they nevertheless preserve and embody the integrity and distinctiveness of many conversational activities. Such activities are drawn from natural settings, examined *on their own merits* as interesting phenomena—for example, openings and closings in telephone conversations (Schegloff, 1968; Schegloff & Sacks, 1973), compliments (Pomerantz, 1978b), teases (Drew, 1987), laughter (Jefferson, 1979, 1985a), audience responses to public speaking (Atkinson, 1984a, 1984b, 1985)—and made available to readers (in the form of transcribed instances of interaction) for their critical inspection. Evidence for claims regarding the routine ways in which interactions get done is, within the constraints of publication outlets, offered to the public rather than remaining within the relative privacy of a researcher's workplace. Shared analyses of actual conversational instances (with priority given to repeated listenings of recordings, aided by carefully produced transcriptions) are invited, simply because the detailed nature of ordinary talk is best *seen* by readers in unison with descriptions and explanations of some phenomenon. In short, working *with* recorded and transcribed data (as heard and seen) is qualitatively different than merely writing and/or talking *about* the intricate ways in which participants organize conversation. As Zimmerman (1988) notes:

> As procedures *in use*, they [participants] reflexively fashion and engage the detailed opportunities and constraints of actual circumstances of talk and thus serve as a resource for permitting speakers-hearers to *achieve* that order for one another, and hence, for the analyst. (p. 409; emphasis added)

It becomes obvious that when some phenomenon is purported to exist within interaction, it is much more difficult to show exactly what a given set of methods and/or techniques (or series of "action sequences"; see Heritage, 1984, 1985; Pomerantz, 1978a, 1978b, 1984) are *occupied* with. For example, what an utterance is achieving in its placement and construction, how a series of utterances are overlapped or latched together to accomplish particular activity types, the ways in which coparticipants display and thereby build understanding into interaction vocally and nonvocally, and/or the methods for both creating and repairing routine problems as conversation unfolds. Consequently, there appears to be a growing realization by researchers working with conversational materials of the time and detail required to describe and explain instances and sequences thoroughly. One analytic priority of such research efforts is to produce insightful (and inherently defensible) accounts of the routine tasks of social life. The attainment of such a priority entails orienting as best possible to the same kinds of phenomena produced, in the first instance, by and for interactants as they routinely orient to, and therein organize, occasions made up of their participative efforts.

Ironic as it may seem, however, most communication researchers are not trained to look *directly* at interaction itself. Only rarely is interaction examined *on its own merits* as an achievement — as ordinary and collaboratively produced sequences of action, used and relied upon by speakers and hearers to get the work of social life done. Thus many researchers are retooling to accommodate the detailed organization of naturally occurring talk while at the same time training students not to dismiss prematurely some phenomenon as insignificant or disorderly (see Heritage, 1984, p. 241; Zimmerman, 1988). In this sense, seemingly "small" and what may at first appear to be relatively unimportant phenomena (e.g., pauses, overlaps, turn constructions, laughter, gazes, gestures) turn out to be dense achievements (e.g., Goodwin, 1981). Microinteractional achievements constitute the organization of both "larger" units of social order (e.g., power, identity, sex, culture; see Schegloff, 1987a) and less encompassing but no less important social encounters, such as telephone calls, family picnics, courtroom interrogation and testimony (see Atkinson & Drew, 1979), and medical diagnostic interviews (Frankel, 1984, in press). Thus providing convincing accounts of the detailed nature of conversational organization is, at the very least, a formidable task — one in which issues regarding the location and recognition of some phenomenon must constantly be examined rather than discounted as trivial or untimely.

Such issues have been repeatedly and directly addressed within sociology (e.g., see Atkinson & Heritage, 1984; Button, Drew, & Heritage, 1986; Button & Lee, 1987; Heritage, 1984; Psathas, 1979; Schenkein, 1978; Sudnow, 1972; Zimmerman & West, 1980), and have been raised in a preliminary fashion by speech communication researchers representing a diverse set of concerns with language, interaction, and features of everyday conversation (e.g., see Beach, 1982, 1989; Craig & Tracy, 1983; Ellis & Donahue, 1986). Yet it is important to recognize that nearly two decades ago Harvey Sacks (1984a) articulated the need for treating "interactions as products of a machinery," the goal being to "see how finely the details of actual, naturally occurring conversation can be subjected to analysis that will yield the technology of conversation" (pp. 26-27). Similarly, Schegloff's (1986) concerns with the study of conversation have long been rooted in

> what appears to be the primordial site of sociality—direct interactions with others. Wherever else we might locate [the] society—the economy, the polity, the law, the organized systems for the reproduction of the population and the membership of the society, etc.—the organization of persons dealing with one another in interaction is the vehicle through which those institutions get their work done. On these and other grounds, interaction and talk-in-interaction merit recognition as a strategic locus of the social. It is at the elucidation of this fundamental aspect of social life that inquiries such as this are aimed. (p. 112)

TOWARD A REFLEXIVITY OF CODING

All research on interaction is grounded in some form of coding, at least in the simplistic and somewhat generic sense that coding is a set of activities necessarily transforming the first-order world of doing (and displaying the experience of being involved in) interaction into various kinds of evidence and claims regarding interaction as a topic of inquiry. The nature and degree of these transformations vary considerably, depending upon questions raised, basic commitments to research methods employed, and what count as "data" in the process of providing answers to certain questions.

Viewed in this manner, methods may be understood as arguments generating from sequences of events (see Jackson, 1986; Jacobs, 1986) commonly referred to by researchers as observations, measurements, transcriptions, procedures, steps, and the like. These sequences of events may or may not be linear in their evolution. Yet in each and every case, certain categories, labels, and/or classifications must be invoked in order to render some claimed phenomenon as existing, thus providing for the very possibility of the phenomenon to be describable and retrievable for purposes of analysis. Moreover, researchers must somehow compare and contrast instances of observed and/or measured phenomena with one another, so as to identify similarities and differences among the instances being examined. Finally, continued observations and/or measurements require ongoing categorizing—coding or placing of instances in various groups. As types of instances evolve into constructed sets of categories or "groupings," the routine work of coding involves discernment among (and the creation of new) categories for organizing and making sense of social order.

As briefly sketched above, "coding" is not a sequence of activities that one group of researchers does and another does not. Rather, coding is inevitable in the achievement of scientific inquiry; it is how sense is made in and through the discernment and imposition of order on the social world via the location, categorization, and identification of types of instances. Moreover, determining how a corpus of instances constitute a given phenomenon is also a form or phase of coding, simply because attention is rendered to similarities and differences between instances with respect to criterion attributes of that being observed. The important issue when examining coding, therefore, is not who engages in coding and who does not. Rather, the focus should be upon how coding gets accomplished (e.g., the methods enacted or "schemes" employed) and the ways in which coding — as an inevitable set of abstracting, transforming moves — accounts for the original (first-order) set of interactional achievements. Put simply, the focus should be upon how coding represents underlying patterns of the social world. Because the enactment of coding routines determines, in an ultimate sense, those empirical findings we subsequently put forth as knowledge claims, there exists a need to examine reflexively our procedures for revealing how the social world gets organized and worked out — by and for the members themselves.

Such reflexivity presupposes a shift from coding as a taken-for-granted resource to a problematic set of achievements in need of critical inspection. It is only through reflexive examinations of research achievements that relationships can be made evident between the social world and researchers' accounts of interaction.

Coding as Achievement

As an achievement, coding may be viewed synonymously with how researchers come to locate phenomena and make sense of interaction by imposing scientific order upon the social world (and its working features). Coding is the general process of translating *raw data* into *symbolic data* (see Ford, 1975, pp. 383-395), and it is constituted by a set of moves through which gathered data are observed and made sense of, that is, ordered so as to be used and relied upon in the explanation of patterns constituting some phenomenon. These coding moves constitute the accounting practices of the researcher; they reflect the situated production of analyst's practical methods for shaping data into analyzable, reportable, and thus readable forms. Coding accomplishments are frequently unarticulated, and thus taken for granted, as useful resources for understanding how findings and results got produced by the "research machinery" (see Ford, 1975; Garfinkel, 1967; Sacks, 1984a).

The intermittent formulation of coding methods, as meaningful data, reflects a heuristic concern for constant refinements of observational techniques. Studying how coding gets done (and even reported as an activity) is not particularly useful as an end in and of itself. Rather, reflexive examination allows for the possibility of questioning underlying presuppositions of empirical outcomes as displayed connections between theory and method. A reflexivity of coding can also reveal gaps and overlaps between conceptual intrigue and empirically justified "reality."

While it is not "news" to suggest that an essential reflexivity exists between knowledge claims and modes of observation (e.g., Delia & Grossberg, 1977; Fisher, 1978; Kaplan, 1964; Phillipson, 1973; Polanyi, 1962), it is a somewhat different claim to suggest (as discussed in a subsequent section) that coding methods inevitably function to gloss (and perhaps even misrepresent) the phenomena accounted for with empirical findings. The key issue, however, is the nature and degree of glossing that occurs, and the implications such glossing holds for understanding how interaction gets organized.

A useful point of departure for understanding coding is Garfinkel's (1967) classic examination of coding achievements (chap. 1). Throughout daily "commonsense situations of choice" (p. 19), Garfinkel and his associates were curious about how staff members accomplished their daily routines within the UCLA outpatient clinic. In asking the question "By what criteria are its applicants selected for treatment?" they decided to investigate clinic records "because clinic folders contain records that clinic personnel provide of their own activities" (p. 18). They employed two graduate students to examine 1,582 folders and transfer relevant information to coding sheets, and subsequently ran conventional reliability tests to assess coders' level of agreement. These tests were run because it is typically assumed that level of coder agreement at some point in the research process presumes "agreement on the end results" (p. 20). Their concerns with reliability coefficients, however, went beyond their routine employment as a resource for substantiating agreement of coders. The research focused upon not only the actual practices through which "reliability" was obtained, but also how it became possible for coders to "follow coding instructions." Rather than considering coders to be "right or wrong" in their answers (i.e., codes), the researchers assumed that "whatever they did could be counted correct procedure in *some* coding 'game.' " The question was, what were these "games" (p. 20)?

It was discovered that in the process of attempting to follow coding rules, coders relied more heavily upon their practical knowledge of the organizational activities of the clinic to make decisions about clinic folders than they did upon the a priori instructions. Coders engaged in several "ad hocing" procedures that better allowed them "to grasp the relevance of the instructions to the particular and actual situations they were intended to analyze" (p. 21). In attempting to "fit" and classify the contents of the folders, ad hoc considerations attained priority over the coding rules themselves. Only by ad hocing could the coders work with the a priori category scheme, suggesting that instructions are essentially incomplete and inherently "indexical" guidelines for research procedures. Garfinkel and his colleagues concluded that ad hocing procedures were inevitable simply because *that's what happens* when coders rely upon their native competence as part of the research "arrangement":

> Coding instructions ought to be read instead as consisting of a grammar of rhetoric; they furnish a "social science" way of talking so as to persuade consensus and action within the practical circumstances of the clinic's daily organized activities. (p. 24)

Garfinkel's study of coding practices has much to say about the relationship between reliability coefficients and validity claims. It raises as problematic the basic difficulties involved in training coders to follow instructions or rules, and thus casts doubt on exactly what "interrater reliability coefficients" imply when employed as an argument for "getting at the phenomenon." Coders must agree on more complex issues such as: What counts as an instance of the phenomenon being observed? How might instances be coded into categories that, in varying degrees, are glosses of the detailed work of speakers and hearers? How should problematic decisions be resolved as ambiguity arises throughout the coding procedure?

Of equal if not greater importance, however, are basic questions regarding the creation of categories imposing artificial order onto interaction. To the extent categories do not emerge from or represent underlying achievements of interactants, they remain macroconcepts invoked as an explanatory resource for getting at the phenomenon. Similarly, coding instructions may themselves prove ambiguous in light of categories employed.

An extended example may be useful here. In an examination of coders trained to employ the REL/COM manual and category system as a means of studying "relational control" (see Beach, 1980, 1981), an analysis of training session recordings and coder diaries revealed specific, local solutions to problems in the routine accomplishment of coding. First, problems were frequent in following the "transactional coding rule" whereby each act should be coded as it relates to the previous act. Exactly what counted as an "act" became problematic, as did the coding of acts adjacent to a prior act yet not appearing to be designed as a receipt of a speaker's turn-at-talk. Second, coding "transactionally" was further complicated by the fact that coders were instructed to determine "the definition of the relationships among communicators, that is, how the communicator interprets her/his relationship with other." Here coders had difficulty understanding how they were to impute "interpretations" from transcripts or recordings. Third, exactly what counted as a "unit of analysis" (i.e., "an uninterrupted verbal utterance; an act; independent of length") was difficult to operationalize: What counted as an "interruption" (compared, for example, to an "overlap")? (See Drummond, 1989.) How carefully were "interruptions" displayed in the transcripts and "hearable" in recordings? What kinds of conclusions should be drawn about "relational control" upon the occurrence of an "interruption"? Fourth, the "moves versus turns" rule was particularly troublesome, since coders were instructed to assign one of five codes (dominance, structuring, equivalence, deference, or submissiveness) to each and every act. As might be expected, however, coders frequently determined that certain acts contained multiple "control" functions. Thus: Which portion of an act had more impact on the control dimension of an utterance in sequence? One utterance studied during a training session included what coders believed to be six different "functions": an insult, an expression of opinion, a humorous statement, a disagreement, a question, and an "I don't know." Coders were perplexed, yet they gradually reached a consensus that, in this and other cases, they would individually attempt to "average" the contents of each utterance and in so doing make a categorical judgment best reflecting the "tone" of the act. Though none of the coders felt satisfied with the outcome, the training manual did not provide a sufficient alternative; they had to improvise.

While other problems did emerge throughout coding (e.g., questions were raised about working alone and in pairs, determining how often to assess reliability among coders, and the extent to which working with transcripts and recordings was an "equivalent" task), perhaps the most revealing and recurring finding was coders' unanimous agreement that the five categories of relational control did not reflect or capture the subtleties of conversational control in everyday interaction. This task was described as "fitting a square peg into an undersized round hole" and as "taking an axe to a spider web."

In summary, all coding tasks involve routine problems in need of continuing resolution. How coding is achieved has much to say about the degree of correspondence between theories and findings. And in a sense, the reflexive stance of not taking coding for granted refines understanding of how research methods abstract and transform the detailed workings of interactants as they orient to phenomena.

Coding and Transcribing

In the prior discussion of how conversation analysts attempt to locate and recognize phenomena, it was noted how the use of transcriptions of naturally occurring interactions, drawn from and employed in unison with audio and video recordings throughout analysis, are carefully produced so as to mirror the unfolding details of conversational activities. These transcriptions are fashioned after the interactions being examined have taken place, and care is taken to produce an adequate record of events that actually (rather than "presumably," "hypothetically," or "could have") occurred. Arguing for the theoretical relevance of transcriptions, Ochs (1979) notes:

> A pervasive sentiment among those who draw from [speech] performance data is that the data they utilize are more accurate than intuition data: Their data constitute the real world — what *is* as opposed to what *ought* to be. (p. 43)

While transcriptions are themselves subject to constant refinement and adjudication, so as to more precisely capture and reflect recorded talk in text, the key issue is what they are designed to "attend to." Jefferson (1985a) summarizes this point in her examination of laughter by observing:

> Transcription is one way we try to "get our hands on" actual occurrences in order to study social order in fine detail. The crucial point is that we are, in whatever ways we go about it, trying to proceed by detailed observation of actual events . . . that the detailed study of small phenomena can be useful and informative, that the results may be orderly, that without "close looking at the world" one might not know such phenomena exist, and that the absence of a range of phenomena from the data base upon which theories about the social world are built can be consequential. (pp. 26-27)

As detailed attention is given to the production of transcripts of naturally occurring interactions, the more readily available phenomena become to the analyst. Whether the analyst is conducting an unmotivated search through a transcript or seeking multiple instances of particular types of phenomena (e.g., overlaps, pauses, laughter tokens, repairs, presequences, question-answer pairs), analysis is constrained by (a) the quality of the recordings and transcripts available, (b) how phenomena are described as achieved in character, and (c) relationships among descriptions offered and the organization of actual recorded events.

WORKING THROUGH A TRANSCRIBED SEGMENT

It may be useful at this point to examine, in some detail, the following segment of interaction. This examination provides readers with the opportunity to inspect (and thereby gain a sense of) how this extended instance unfolds — the nature of the occasion being organized, participants' orientations to and creation of the task at hand, how phenomena such as identities, power, and status get worked out in and through the talk itself — and thus to ground prior discussions of CA and coding in an actual instance of interaction.

The segment below is drawn from a growing corpus of videotaped courtroom interactions. In a rather unmotivated fashion, my attention was drawn to this segment as it appeared both interesting and deserving of further inquiry. An analysis of this extended segment begins to locate what interactants are "up to" in achieving a courtroom hearing, and is not exhaustive in its location and recognition of a "phenomenon" — at least not in the sense that a series of instances of some phenomenon are displayed and examined for recurring features. Rather, as will become apparent, working through this segment evidences the kinds of data and issues routinely addressed in CA research in the process of searching for patterns of social interaction. (See Schegloff, 1987b.)It also reveals the necessity of constantly cycling back to the transcriptions (and recordings, when available) to check and refine observations made, and ultimately of substantiating any conclusions drawn representing empirical claims. (Transcription symbols are described in the Appendix to this chapter; speaker designations are as follows: J = judge; D = defendant; and PL = plaintiff lawyer.)

```
(1)     ELAC:T5:CU v. ADAMS — 121-180

121 J:   So the claim of exemption: u:::h
122      further proceedings can go off calendar
123       subj ect to the receipt (0.8) by: thee:=
               [    ]
               [    ]
124 D:   Sir    ((raises hand, leans forward in chair))
125 J:   = uh (1.4) > you're still gonna be invo:lved <
```

126   so it's (.) gonna go to yo u
                                    [
                                    [
127 PL: > Ya (.) your honor um <
128   (0.4) my question:'u:h since we have no answer
129   from the marshall i:s uh whether the (1.4)
130   thousand dollars was uh (0.3) plus was being held
131   °in the° bank account
132   (0.8)
133 J: I ↑ dunno
          [   ]
          [   ]
134 D: It's be- It's being he:ld (I   dun no-)
                                  [   ]
                                  [   ]
135 PL: Well why don't we
136   release all monies all over: (0.8) for a thou   sand=
                                  [   ]
                                  [   ]
                            ((D shakes head))
137   = dollars °your honor°
138   (2.6)
139 J: Response?
140   (0.8)
141 D: I- I feel that it shudn't.
142   (1.6)
143 D: (eh) be- b- > for the simple reason that they
144   din't- < (1.8) i- it's very confusing an (0.3)
145   what ↑I want to know your honor is (0.8)
146   why wasn't I s:erved with a supeenee ta (.)
147   appear in court that's (all I) that's wha -   confuses me
                                              [   ]
                                              [   ]
148 J: Not- not   into
149   that.
          [   ]
          [   ]
150 D: Okay aright sir =
151 J: =You'(ve)-=
152 D: = °aright° =
153 J: =won the claim of exemption
                          [   ]
                          [   ]
154 D: o k a y   3okay=
155 J: =you've got the claim reduced by::. (   )
                                          [   ]
                                          [   ]
156 D: And

```
157        I'm  will    ing to live by-
                  [       ]
                  [       ]
158  J:           (wey)
159  D:    I'm willing to go   by  my  agreement
                        [                      ]
                        [                      ]
160  J:                       Please don't interr      u(pt)=
161  D:    = °Okay° (.) well I'm sor ry
                             [
                             [
162  J:                             By: uh > several
163        hundred < dollars.
164             (1.2)
165  J:    U(m) (1.2) and u:h (1.0) I need to know why:
166        (0.2) you still need the two installments as
167        long as there's a thou:sand are you=
168  D:    =Because th at(s)
                      [       ]
                      [       ]
169  J:               Are  you     s t a r :     ving because=
                              [                ]
                              [                ]
170  D:                            the only rea-
171  J:    =of the second (.) five hundred that's
172             (0.8)
173  D:    Ye:s (.) your honor I (am)
174             (1.2)
175  J:    (Then the) moneys uh held by the mar:shall are
176        to be: released to thee uh (0.6) defenda:nt?
177        except the five hundred (0.8) to be (.)
178        released (2.6) to the (uh) plaintiff Creditors
179        Unlimited
180        ((Judge continues))
```

Even a preliminary inspection of the segment above reveals evidence that the occasion being organized is some kind of court proceeding. For example, J appears to be addressed as "sir" by D (lines 124, 150) and as "your honor" by both PL and D (lines 127, 137, 145, 173), and there are references to "marshall" (line 129), "defendant" (line 176), and "plaintiff" (line 178). The mere use of these address terms in unison with certain invoked identities, however, does not substantiate how J, D, or PL orient to phenomena emerging within this segment of an informal hearing.

Before turning to an analysis of the interactional environment of this hearing, however, it might be useful to inform readers that this proceeding began the civil 10:00 a.m. call involving the collection of a debt by Creditor's Unlimited from

Mark Adams (names have been changed). It was the second of two hearings concerning a proposed settlement (e.g., balance due, installment payment, and dates) convened by J to discuss a motion filed by D. This segment is approximately 90 seconds in length, occurring 2 minutes and 30 seconds into a proceeding lasting 6 minutes and 50 seconds.

Closing and Opening

We begin by noticing that J, as turn occupant, appears to initiate a closing of the "official" business of the motion (i.e., "the cl<u>ai</u>m of exemption:") in lines 121-123. That this turn-at-talk is in fact an attempt to close down the hearing and thus take it "<u>off</u> calendar" (line 122) also seems to be recognized by D and PL.

First, D's "Sir" in line 124 is an unsolicited (i.e., self-selected) utterance, inserted in close proximity to a possible turn completion by J (projected by "calendar," line 122), yet overlapping with "subject" — a "syntactically coherent next utterance component" (Jefferson & Schegloff, 1975, p. 3). D's "Sir" was positioned in such a way as to indicate sufficient and carefully attended recognition that J had reached a "transition place" — the closing down of a motion being only one transition-relevant example. And by not elaborating, D orients to J's continuation in a manner preserving the "one party talks at a time" assumption of conversational turn-taking (see Sacks, Schegloff, & Jefferson, 1974).

Second, following J's (lines 125-126) " > you're still gonna be inv<u>o</u>:lved < so it's (.) gonna go to yo u," PL achieves overlap onset ("<u>Ya</u>," line 127) in a minimal and transitory fashion by starting up within the final sound and thus word produced by J (see Jefferson, 1983). PL's overlapped utterance does exhibit an immediate response to J's query, yet it also displays his recognition that J is, for all practical purposes, nearing completion of closing down the motion. In this sense there is more at work here in PL's 127-131. PL's response to J's query appears rushed, as evidenced by the quickened delivery "Y<u>a</u> (.) your honor um < " (line 127), as though he is orienting less to J's query than to the opportunity for asking J a question about the "thousand dollars" owed to his client. While more could be said about the manner in which PL constructs his question to J in 128-131, the point remains that as J attempted to take the proceeding "off calendar," PL raised a question meriting possible further consideration by J.

In summary, D's "Sir" is slotted in close proximity to the business being initially closed down by J in lines 121-122. Such proximity provides a first possible opportunity for raising a new and/or related topic or issue by D, or possibly clarifying and/or questioning previously transacted business. There is additional evidence indicating the usage of such a slot, namely, PL's response to J's prior turn and extension with his own question (lines 127-131). In short, it may be at just this point in the hearing that J becomes informed of additional business yet to be taken care of, at least part of which is directly related to the motion at hand (e.g., payments).

Having briefly worked through this initial sequence, certain questions should now appear particularly relevant: What phenomena were J, D, and PL orienting to in lines 121-131? How were they achieving this orientation? And what consequences might these achievements hold for analysts attempting to understand courtroom interaction? If one reinspects lines 121-131, as below, it should become increasingly clear that the routine work of courts has something to do with taking care of business (e.g., getting cases in and moving them along).

```
121  J:    So the claim of exemption: u:::h
122        further proceedings can go off calender
123          subj ect to the receipt (0.8) by: thee:=
             [    ]
             [    ]
124  D:    Sir    ((raises hand, leans forward in chair))
125  J.    = uh (1.4) > you're still gonna be invo:lved <
126        so it's (.) gonna go to yo  u
                                      [
                                      [
127  PL:                       > Ya (.) your honor um <
128        (0.4) my question:'u:h since we have no answer
129        from the marshall i:s uh  whether the  (1.4)
130        thousand dollars was uh (0.3) plus was being held
131        °in the° bank account
```

Yet, at the same time, both defendants and lawyers may have agendas they would like to have considered that are (at least for them) also important "business." One problem consists of when and how these issues/questions/agendas might be raised and subsequently treated in some fashion by the court (i.e., J). For example, J did not yield the floor by acknowledging D's "Sir" in line 121, D did not continue without receiving J's deferral, and it was only after J asked PL a question that PL gained access to the floor and subsequently asked his own question. Though any conclusions to be drawn thus far must emerge from a short segment of interaction, the following observations might be made: (a) As current speaker, J takes extended turns-at-talk and does not yield the floor until his current turn is completed. Constructing and completing extended turns is thus one integral part of "doing being a judge." (b) Access to the floor is heavily influenced by J's willingness to provide the opportunity for others to speak. Perhaps it is the case that in the ways and to the extent provided by J, the floor may be (and typically is) taken up by coparticipants of the hearing. If this is the case, defendants and lawyers must attend closely to the opportunities provided by judges. Whether such opportunities are self-selected recognitions of possible utterance completions (as in D's "Sir"), and/or elaborations/extensions of a response requested by the judge and thus granting floor access (as with PL's question to J), it is clear that phenomena such as "overlaps" are not random, loosely occasioned utterances within courtroom or other interactional settings. Rather, they are artful techniques displaying precise orientations to the occasion at hand.

Initiating the "Complaint"

Exactly what D's "Sir" in line 121 projected, however, cannot be determined until and unless one moves forward to the portion of the segment beginning with line 135:

```
135 PL:                         Well why don't we
136        release all monies all over:   (0.8) for a thou    sand=
                                  [                    ]
                                  [                    ]
                                ((D shakes head))
137        = dollars °your honor°
138            (2.6)
139 J:     Response?
140            (0.8)
141 D:     I- I feel that it shudn't.
142            (1.6)
143 D:     (eh) be- b- > for the simple reason that they
144        din't- < (1.8) i- it's very confusing an (0.3)
145        what ↑ I want to know your honor is (0.8)
146        why wasn't I s:erved with a supeenee ta (.)
147        appear in court that's (all I) that's wha -  confuses me
                                  [                ]
                                  [                ]
148 J:                                  Not- not     into
149        that.
```

Here PL's question to J is subsequently marked by a noticeable pause in line 138, after which J elects not to answer PL's question by opting instead to request D's response (line 139). Following a short pause (line 140), D constructs a multifaceted turn (lines 141-147) in which several different yet related activities are achieved. He begins by disagreeing with PL's prior suggestion and quickly moves on to what may appear to be a partial justification (see Atkinson & Drew, 1979, chap. 5) for disagreeing—the providing of an account of the position he is constructing. This justification remains incomplete, or so D states in line 144, because "i- it's very confusing."

However, a closer inspection of the structural organization of lines 141-144 might yield a competing explanation regarding whether a justification was, in fact, being provided by D—and if not an explanation, it might offer an alternative course of action rationally tied to D's subsequent utterance in lines 145-147. The alternative is to treat lines 141-144 as leading up to what appears to be one type of "complaint" in lines 146-147, "why wasn't I s:erved with a supeenee ta appear in court." D produces several false starts and self-repairs—"I- I"; "(eh) be- b-"; "i-it's" (see Schegloff, Jefferson, & Sacks, 1977) — fails to complete "for the simple reason that they didn't" (lines 143-144) by immediately stating his own confusion, and finally explicitly informs J that all he really wants to know is information regarding why he was not served with a subpoena. Viewed in this light, D used his first direct and granted access to the floor in a manner leading up to the formulation of an apparent "complaint" that did not emerge following his "Sir" in line 124. In so stating his concerns and constructing the turn in this manner, D gives priority to responding directly to PL's suggestion (to "release all the monies over:," line 136) by stating "I- I feel that it shudn't. (1.6) (eh) be- b-" (line 143).

Such priority given to floor access by D is only one indicator of the importance of using turns as valued opportunities for expressing feelings, setting agendas, and thereby interjecting more "personal" concerns within the handling of "official" business in a routine court hearing. In this instance, the significance of D's 141-147 is rooted in the timing and placement of his turn-at-talk, as well as the artful construction of a turn including (in part) an answer to PL's question, a preface to an account, and a possible complaint.

The phrase *possible complaint* is employed here to call attention to the fact that little has been said about an issue central to the analysis of D's turn: Exactly what makes D's "why wasn't I s:erved with a supeenee ta appear in court" (lines 146-147) *hearable* as a "complaint"? To begin answering such a question one might focus upon features of D's constructed turn. At least (but not exclusively) three features of lines 146-147 appear to indicate such a hearing. First, D's "why wasn't" might be heard as one form of accusation attributing possible blame to the failure of the court to act appropriately and on his behalf (as a defendant with legal rights). The "why wasn't" (as one type of negative formulation) can be usefully contrasted with a construction such as "Was I served . . . ," for example, in which the latter could have functioned as a simple request for information. Yet another possibility could have been an instance such as "Would you please tell me if there was a problem in serving me with a complaint?" a more polite request leaving open the possibility that the court was not necessarily at fault in serving the defendant. Second, the mode of delivery apparent in lines 146-147 of D's turn begins to suggest that D was troubled by the possibility of not having been served a subpoena. The words "s:erved," "supeenee," "appear," and "court?" were delivered with vocal emphasis by D. Note especially his prolongation of the first portion of "s:erved." Finally, attention might be drawn to D's "what ↑ I want to know . . . ," most important, the stress on "I" as an indicator of D's concern in gaining knowledge about the subpoena process.

Dismissing the Initial "Complaint"

While the constituent features of D's turn construction may well be crucial to understanding the delivery and hearability of a portion of D's lines 141-147 as "offering up a complaint," the work produced by D in 141-147 does not necessarily predetermine and thus guarantee J's receipt and treatment of D's expressed concerns. Of equal if not greater importance in assessing how D's 146-147 might be hearable as a complaint, however, is to examine how J oriented as next speaker to D's prior turn. Though D would likely have preferred that his turn be responded to with positive appraisal by J, such is not the case in lines 148-149. Here J overlaps his turn onto D's prior with the dismissal "Not- not into that." Two brief observations merit attention here. First, that the overlap occurred in this instance should not be surprising, since it is quite possible that J had ample time to notice how and what D was up to in his 141-147 construction. Whatever else D's turn might have been an instance of, as noted previously, it was more than a direct and detailed response to PL's suggestion in lines 135-137. Second, built into J's rather abrupt response is an assessment that what D was doing was somehow untimely and/or inappropriate (see Pomerantz, 1984).

Orienting to the "Complaint's" Dismissal

Yet something more may be at work here, namely, J informing/reminding D that he has gotten what might be roughly formulated as a "good deal" up to this point in the hearing. To substantiate this observation, once again it is useful to move to subsequent actions taken by J and D in order to achieve an even better grasp of each participant's orientation to the local environment of the sequence. Notice what J added onto his dismissal in the form of an explanation of his position:

```
148 J:                              Not- not into
149        that.
           [      ]
           [      ]
150 D:     Okay aright sir =
151 J:     =You'(ve)-=
152 D:     = °aright° =
153 J:     =won the claim of    exemption
                         [            ]
                         [            ]
154 D:                       o k a y      okay=
155 J:     =you've got the claim reduced by::. (     )
                                       [    ]
                                       [    ]
156 D:                                     And
157        I'm    will ing to live by-
              [     ]
              [     ]
158 J:     (wey)
159 D:     I'm willing to go    by   my   agreement
                        [                      ]
                        [                      ]
160 J:                       Please don't interr      u(pt)=
```

```
161  D:   = °Okay° (.) well I'm sor ry
                              [
                              [
162  J:                          By: uh > several
163        hundred < dollars.
```

In lines 151, 153, 155, and 162-163, J informs/reminds D that he has won the claim of exemption *and* had the claim reduced by several hundred dollars. Of course J is neither required nor judicially mandated to provide such an explanation, but he did so nonetheless. Perhaps J oriented to his own dismissal of D's 141-147 as overly abrupt, and thus quickly moved to soften its potential impact on D. (Early on in the hearing, prior to the segment under discussion, J acknowledged that D had been ignored and uninformed in this case, and thus had every right to be confused as to the details of the proceedings. In addition, D was without legal counsel, and at times J attempted to "fill in" details as the hearing unfolded.) Both the tonal qualities of J's voice and his request, "Please don't interr u(pt)" in line 160 would further indicate an orientation whereby J was attempting to assist D's under-standings of court proceedings.

Overlapped with J's dismissal of D's 141-147 and subsequent explanation are several compliant utterances from D (lines 150, 152, 154, 156-157, 159, 161). D's first "Okay aright sir = aright" (lines 150, 152) displays immediate deference to the force of J's dismissal. Yet shortly after the overlapped compliance continues in line 154, D not only overlaps once again but appears a bit overly eager in lines 151-157 and 159 to comply with the unfolding situation (see also his softened compliance and possible apology in line 161). In and through these few turns-at-talk, D displays his recognition of J's attempts to inform/remind him of his already having won the "claim of exemption." Yet there is some irony in this recognition, given that this short flurry of activity was itself initiated with D's 141-147 — not with an effort to offer any kind of appreciation to J for his understanding and favorable ruling on the motion.

Packed into lines 141-163 there is a rather intricate balance struck between the possibility of complaining and dismissing, on one hand, and explaining/requesting and compliance on the other. It is as though the adjacency of D's complaint and J's dismissal hinge, for the moment at least, on a quick flurry of mutual challenge and even rejection. Yet immediately thereafter, J and D appear to collaborate in supporting one another — even to the point where J accommodates D with a request rather than a command in line 160, followed by D's compliance and possible apology in line 161. In each of these action types, both J and D orient symmetri-cally and instantaneously to the other's displayed orientations.

The negotiated character of this sequence evidences how it is that such different orientations eventuate in a collaboratively produced structure. It is also an instance of a legally constrained encounter, evident in and through a set of methods allowing each participant the opportunity to achieve preferred outcomes. However, in D's case, opportunity was shown not to be synonymous with the satisfaction of having his concerns addressed — at least up to this point in the hearing.

Back to the Motion

A final comment on this interactional segment. Should the reader have lost track of the original business at hand addressed prior to D's multifaceted turn (lines 141-147), namely, PL's question suggesting that the entire thousand dollars be released to the creditor, it should become clear in lines 165-180 that the lack of resolution of this issue has not gone unnoticed by J. Here it is apparent that the unspecified reason underlying D's disagreement in line 141 had to do with his needing five hundred dollars for living expenses, a realization displayed in J's question (lines 169, 171) and finally confirmed by D in line 173. This possibility might imply that D's priorities rest less with receiving living expenses than with attaining some kind of restitution regarding his not having been served with a subpoena.

The analysis offered herein is only partial in the sense that the hearing continues, with D once again raising concerns about not having been served with a subpoena to appear in court. He does so in a location following an attempted closing down of "business" by J, yet in such a manner and slot that J receipts D's prior turn by taking the time and effort to provide a set of legal responses. Additional, interesting contrasts emerge within the second handling of D's concerns, and there is much to say about J's eventual dismissal of D from court. Exactly how D takes certain liberties not tolerated by J, however, requires another discussion of achievements — one intended to illustrate how it is that forms of legal interaction exist, in the first instance to participants themselves, as they display and thus orient to the moment-by-moment problems routinely addressed in courts.

OCCASIONING IDENTITIES IN THE TALK

To say that defendants have rights in a hearing is to identify the possibility that a claim may be made or an exception taken about due legal process. How this work gets done offers insight into the interdependence of "official" and "personal" agendas, not to mention the displayed competencies involved in opening, closing, and adapting to numerous courses of action. But to describe the ways in which phenomena such as "complaints" emerge and are oriented to as court business is achieved is to explain the local environment within which power and status are occasioned *in* the talk as speakers and hearers employ diverse methods for accomplishing an informal hearing. The articulation and unpacking of these methods allows for the possibility of understanding the turn-by-turn organization of an occasion, and thus the interactional machinery produced by and for the participants themselves. By turning directly to actual instances of interaction as displays of social order, rather than attempting to account for the detailed work of participants by invoking macroconcepts such as power, status, identity, or related forces "external" to the talk (e.g., institution, age, gender, ethnicity, socioeconomic position), priority is given to the talk itself.

In short, attention is given to the sequentially relevant features constituting these more encompassing concepts and theories, and in so doing research inquiries begin from the "bottom up" rather than from the "top down." The preceding section of this chapter displays the work of speakers and hearers routinely engaged in interaction as they attend to the moment-by-moment evolution of a conversational involvement, and accordingly such is the research priority of those examining the sequential character of social occasions.

One alternative is to impose, a priori, a series of macroconcepts and theories "onto" the interaction as a template (made up of selected categories, terms, and so on) intended to carve out understandings of the detailed workings of speakers and hearers. One result of such an orientation is the recurring difficulty of describing some phenomenon, and attributing to that phenomenon specific features and components, without providing actual instances as evidence of the claims made for others' inspection and consideration. In light of these concerns, it is not uncommon to finish reading an article in which a "phenomenon" is proposed that suggests interesting and possibly even compelling implications regarding social interaction, and yet still have questions about the extent to which the phenomenon being queried exists within social order "in the first instance" (see Schegloff, 1984), compared to having been born as a useful tool (or possibly even an artifact) of the research enterprise. Specifically, readers may query: What would an instance of such a phenomenon look like? From where and under what circumstances did this phenomenon emerge? What is the detailed nature of the phenomenon as it is oriented to and noticeably worked out by speakers and hearers in normal, everyday settings? These questions are most certainly applicable to an issue such as agenda-setting in courts and/or in more casual conversations. The brief data analysis offered in the preceding section only begins to raise issues surrounding the sequential character of phenomena such as complaining and responding to complaints (dismissals being only one possible response type).

An examination of van Dijk's (1987, 1989) "sociocognitive" perspective on "power and discourse," for example, provides an expansive overview of how people may exercise power "over" others in interaction across a variety of settings. Attention is also given to specific features and definitions of power. One example is: "If A limits B's cognitive or social action control, A may be said to have power over B" (van Dijk, 1987, p. 5). How might we orient to "limits" and "over" as interactional achievements?

Turning to a review of research on courtroom interaction, van Dijk (1987) offers summaries of such findings as restrictions on turn allocation and speech acts, obligations to answer questions when requested (and in specific manners), questions functioning as informative and accusatory, lack of topic control by defendants and witnesses, and how "style" may influence ongoing talk (e.g., powerless styles are noticeable by such features as "the frequent use of intensifiers, hedges, hesitation forms, and questioning intonation"; p. 451). While these summarized findings may begin to articulate a framework for understanding the constraints on talk in courts, they should not be mistaken for empirical generalizations replacing (or, in many cases, adequately formulating) the detailed orientations displayed by court participants (e.g., see Atkinson & Drew, 1979; Maynard, 1984). A close examination of segment 1, for example, reveals that informal hearings — though equally binding and "official" as an occasion — are composed of interactions exhibiting less restricted turn allocations than "formal" examination formats (i.e., direct, cross, redirect, and rebuttal), fewer and different restrictions on answering questions, a more diverse use of questions than either "informative" or "accusatory," and more active contributions by the judge and defendant in controlling "topic."

In fact, the latter instance of "topic" provides a pointed example of distinct differences between the "macro" approach taken by van Dijk (1987) and the microanalytic examination of talk sequences evidenced in CA research. When examined as an interactional achievement, "topic" remains as an extremely difficult "concept" to get a handle on — to articulate (and provide evidence for) in its organized manifestations and conversational variations (e.g., see Button & Casey, 1984; Maynard, 1980; Maynard & Zimmerman, 1984). As treated by van Dijk, however, "topic control" (and related components of courtroom interactions, such as "sequencing" and "speech acts") is assumed to be working in particular ways and thereby influencing particular court outcomes, even though such components are in each and every case glossed as interactional achievements.

To describe and explain the complex orientations of court participants, it is at times useful to summarize research findings as a means of formulating the empirical nature of participants' solutions to routine matters and problems. Yet when the argument is offered that "power" is the key issue in accounting for the precise nature of "institutional discourse," questions must be raised about what *counts* as power in particular interactional environments. This is especially the case when, as apparent in van Dijk's overview, researchers' methods for gaining access to interactional phenomena remain unarticulated. Without careful consideration of the manner in which empirical results are generated — or even raising the more basic question of what count as "data" and the ways and extent to which such data are made available to readers for their critical inspection — the tendency is to disregard social order in its naturalistic state by invoking "macro" explanatory concepts offering minimal information about how interaction gets done.

A final example may prove beneficial here. After critiquing the work in Atkinson and Drew's (1979) *Order in Court* for paying little attention "to the social and legal power structures that become manifest in such interactions" (p. 44), van Dijk (1987) provides the following argument:

> It may certainly be granted that we may first need insight into the properties of courtroom talk, before we are able to pinpoint conversational specifics as expressions of power or social structure. On the other hand, it may be argued that many properties

of conversational organization in court, such as strategies of face-keeping and impression management, or persuasive defense and directive accusation, as well as of turn allocation and speech act control in the first place, can of course not be understood without a presupposed knowledge of their functions and goals in the courtroom and the legal process. In other words, instead of methodical ignorance of the properties of the social context, we argue for an interplay between conversation analysis and social analysis, in ways that continue and refine the analysis of strategic verbal interaction proposed by scholars such as Goffman (e.g., in Goffman, 1967).
(p. 44)

Several questions might be raised in response to this position: Exactly how might such concepts as "face work and impression management" or "strategy" influence courtroom contexts if they are not, in the first instance, displayed and oriented to by speakers and hearers as methodical achievements? Of what practical benefit is locating "properties of the social context" *outside* of the interaction itself? How is it possible to identify "social and legal power structures that become manifest in the interactions" without turning initially and directly to sequencing of the talk by and for participants? These and related questions rest on the assumption that even though analysts inevitably trade on their "presupposed knowledge" while examining interactional data (see Turner, 1970), so doing does not satisfy the requirements for providing evidence of the claims made and positions taken. A simple example may suffice here: If speaker designations were removed from a carefully produced transcript of courtroom interaction, analysts should be able to provide evidence of the "context" in and through the methods employed to achieve orientations to the problems at hand. And if "power" eventually emerged as a relevant category for describing ways in which sequences get organized, it would most certainly be invoked only as a global reference accounting for the constituent features/methods constituting speakers' and hearers' achievements.

METHODOLOGICAL ISSUES

One methodological issue of interest stems from an earlier discussion of the inherent independence of social order, since by definition naturally occurring interactions exist apart from being isolated as a topic of research and irrespective of the possibility of being discovered and dissected for purposes of social science. When research commitments rest with the recovery and reconstruction of the social world, as best possible "on its own merits," attempts are made to seek evidence for claims regarding *how* interaction is the vehicle for accomplishing the world of everyday life. By gathering and examining in detail transcribed versions of audio and video recordings of everyday talk and providing available evidence of transcribed instances for readers' critical inspection, conversation analysts attempt to minimize the diverse ways in which research orchestrations, as methodical achievements, produce data and findings *only* as a result of the methods employed in the investigation process. This claim is not to say that CA results can be separated from the research practices relied upon to "capture" interaction. Rather, the point here is that priority is given to speakers' and hearers' displayed methods for organizing everyday settings, as phenomena routinely existing *even if* they were not gathered for subsequent scientific analysis.

Any consideration of the correspondence between a researcher's and an interactant's methods necessarily leads to the question: To what extent do all research orientations inevitably transform, reflect analogies of, and in varying degrees distort the sense and structure of interaction that is produced by and for speakers and hearers? Though this question is considerably easier to raise than to answer, it does draw attention to further issues: If researchers are not looking directly at interactional achievements in natural settings, what counts as data? From what resources is evidence drawn for purposes of substantiating claims? And in what ways might the circumstances and methical solutions to everyday interactions vary from natural to contrived concepts, settings, and simulations?

There is a responsibility shared by speakers, hearers, and communication researchers alike: to enact methods for displaying and detecting social order. Ingrained within interaction and the researching of interaction are certain basic constraints inherent to the achievement of the task at hand, namely, showing how talk unfolds in and through the identification and use of key practices for accomplishing such tasks. The patterns constituting these tasks ultimately reflect both the sense and the structure of social order.

As noted, both routine social encounters and research investigations are methodical achievements, understandable as managed attempts to enact certain procedures in the process of structuring and making sense of ordinary talk (and demonstrating the working machinery through which sense gets made). Understanding the complex relationships between collaborative productions of interaction and social scientific formulations of how interaction gets done (an inherently reflexive enterprise) is of central importance to ethnomethodological work in general (e.g., see Garfinkel, 1967; Sacks, 1984a).

Having provided a brief glimpse of selected commitments and research practices of CA, it may be useful at this juncture to examine how such commitments differ from alternative empirical and theoretical approaches. Given the focus on stable and locally occasioned (i.e., detailed, contingent, turn-organized, moment-by-moment) features of naturally occurring interactions, Zimmerman (1988) has noted how the general approach of CA seems to reflect

> a methodological posture seemingly at odds with the procedures generally favored in social science at large . . . [and an] apparent disregard of mainstream topics and methodologies not only in its initiating discipline of sociology, but also of communication. (p. 407)

The priorities and commitments unique to CA reflect an obvious dispreference for certain empirical orientations to social order, especially methods reflecting an insensitivity to the natural contingencies of interaction. Concerns rest with research methods that unreasonably alter, and thus distort, the detailed work "produced and oriented to by participants as orderly and informative, and relied upon as a basis for further inference and action" (Zimmerman, 1988, p. 408). Questions are raised regarding the extent to which research methods fail to capture, display, and allow for the possibility of accounting for how speakers and hearers actually create phenomena they collaboratively produce, in and through the "rules, techniques, procedures, methods, maxims . . . that can be used to generate the orderly features we find in the conversations we examine" (Sacks, 1984b, p. 413). Put simply: To what extent (and in what precise ways) are social phenomena artificially constructed and/or lost as a function of researchers' methods for observing interaction?

Though Jefferson's (1985b) concerns rest exclusively with how "glossing" procedures in conversations get done — as "a formulation which, on its occurrence, is quite adequate, but which turns out to be incomplete, ambiguous, even misleading" (p. 462) — we might herein borrow a few of her observations to formulate the problem of research methods in yet another way: "Most roughly, a gloss can be a generalization and/or somewhat inaccurate and/or incomplete and/or a masking or covering-up of what really happened" (p. 436). Since no report or "telling about" some event can totally escape glossing in some manner, at least in the sense that it is impossible to break each and every datum and circumstance "down into its bedrock details" (p. 436), the key issue is how glossing occurs and the consequences projected by its occurrence. The implications for understanding research methods, although diverse, hinge on what may appear upon first glance to be a rather straightforward matter: how research reports do justice to the phenomenon under investigation. Determining (as well as possible) what *counts* as "justice," and the implications of how researchers get their work done, is what Garfinkel (1967) has aptly formulated as the "problematic crux of the matter" (p. 10).

As Heritage (1984) observes, researchers' methods tend to promote a "process of idealization":

> The contemporary methodology of conversation analysis has maintained Sacks's pioneering focus on the details of actual interactions and his effort to forestall the process of idealization. Its insistence on the use of data collected from naturally occurring occasions of everyday interaction is paralleled by a corresponding avoidance of a range of other research methodologies as unsatisfactory sources of data. . . . These techniques have been avoided because each of them involves processes in which the specific details of naturally situated interactional conduct are irretrievably lost and are replaced by idealizations about how interaction works. (p. 236)

To extend Heritage's argument, when interaction is explicitly treated as data (i.e., a phenomenon in and of itself), it is typically coded into abstract and idealized categories, the results of which produce findings bearing vague and thus problematic relationships to the organizing and sequential features of the interaction observed. In this sense, coding schemes are limited in their descriptive and even explanatory potential while functioning to gloss, in an idealistic and/or artificial fashion, the detailed organization of participants' displayed orientations to actual occasions of talk. A key issue here is the overall "goodness of fit" (i.e., the nature and type of correspondence) among members' methods for accomplishing tasks, researchers' categories for "capturing" and representing these methods, and exactly what kinds of explanations alternative analyses can and cannot provide about how interaction gets done (see Jacobs, 1988; Wieder, 1988). Not only are selected concepts/categories (e.g., "power") incapable of capturing speakers' and hearers' methods for achieving tasks, but (as noted previously) rarely is coding itself examined as an inherently indexical (i.e., essentially incomplete and thus problematic) set of practical achievements.

CONCLUSION

A central concern of this chapter has been to articulate the need for assessing ways in which interactants and researchers orient to phenomena. Such an assessment has much to do with priorities and methods in the production and analysis of social order, both "in the first instance" as speakers and hearers organize occasions and in a reconstructed (scientific) sense as attempts are made to explicate those organizing features of everyday (naturally occurring) interaction. In the latter sense, moving directly to the analysis of carefully produced transcriptions generated from audio and video recordings of social occasions reflects a commitment to locating social order within actual talk sequences.

Though only a single episode of courtroom interaction has been offered and examined to evidence the kinds of analytic tools available when working through a sequence of talk (see Schegloff, 1987b), it should be noted that this appears not to be an isolated instance. These data were drawn from a larger, ongoing project, one in which a corpus of videotaped hearings reveals recurring and collaborative orientations by speakers and hearers. Within those moments when judges attempt to close down the business of the court, for example, such closings provide openings for defendants and lawyers to achieve their agendas. Several methods employed to get such moments worked out have been identified and described in earlier portions of this chapter, but the analytic tasks are to make sense of a growing set of fragments revealing such orientations and, in so doing, to locate the phenomena and account for the shape of its organization.

Collections and analyses of numerous fragments of naturally occurring interactions are central to conversation analysis, and are becoming increasingly relevant to researchers whose priorities rest with interaction as an achievement. An ongoing task is to locate and recognize other phenomena and justify their empirical nature. Problems requiring resolution involve how to treat empirically the ways in which interactants orient to whatever phenomena emerge during the course of routine talk (see Sacks, 1963). The elucidation of these methods reveals how communication is finely organized and fashioned after interactants' orientations to social occasions.

APPENDIX

The transcription notation system employed for data segments is an adaptation of Gail Jefferson's work (see Atkinson & Heritage, 1984, pp. ix-xvi; Beach, 1989, pp. 89-90). The symbols may be described as follows:

:	colon:	extended or stretched sound, syllable, or word
_	underlining:	vocalic emphasis
(.)	micropause:	brief pause of less than (0.2)
(1.2)	timed pause:	intervals occurring within and between same or different speaker's utterance
(( ))	double parentheses:	scenic details
( )	single parentheses:	transcriptionist doubt
.	period:	falling vocal pitch
?	question mark:	rising vocal pitch
↑ ↓	arrows:	marked rising and falling shifts in intonation
° °	degree symbols:	a passage of talk noticcably softer than surrounding talk
=	equal signs:	latching of contiguous utterances, with no interval or overlap
[ ]		
[ ]	stacked brackets:	speech overlap
[[	double brackets:	simultaneous speech orientations to prior turn
!	exclamation point:	animated speech tone
-	hyphen:	halting, abrupt cutoff of sound or word
> <	greater/less than signs:	portion of an utterance delivered at a pace noticeably quicker than surrounding talk

REFERENCES

Atkinson, J. M. (1984a). *Our master's voices: The language and body language of politics*. London: Methuen.

Atkinson, J. M. (1984b). Public speaking and audience responses: Some techniques for inviting applause. In J. M. Atkinson & J. Heritage (Eds.), *Structures of social action: Studies in conversation analysis* (pp. 370-409). Cambridge: Cambridge University Press.

Atkinson, J. M. (1985). Refusing invited applause: Preliminary observations from a case study of charismatic oratory. In T. van Dijk (Ed.), *Handbook of discourse analysis: Vol. 3. Discourse and dialogue* (pp. 161-181) London: Academic Press.

Atkinson, J. M., & Drew, P. (1979). *Order in court: The organization of verbal interaction in judicial settings*. London: Methuen.

Atkinson, J. M., & Heritage, J. (Eds.). (1984). *Structures of social action: Studies in conversation analysis*. Cambridge: Cambridge University Press.

Beach, W. A. (1980). *Reflexivity and the analysis of conversational coding.* Paper presented at the annual meeting of the American Educational Research Association, Boston.

Beach, W. A. (1981). *Perspectives on the analysis of conversational sequencing in group systems.* Unpublished doctoral dissertation, University of Utah, Salt Lake City.

Beach, W. A. (1982). Everyday interaction and its practical accomplishment: Progressive developments in ethnomethodological research. *Quarterly Journal of Speech, 68,* 314-327.

Beach, W. A. (Ed.). (1989). Sequential organization of conversational activities [Special issue]. *Western Journal of Speech Communication, 53*(2).

Button, G., & Casey, N. (1984). Generating topic: The use of topic initial elicitors. In J. M. Atkinson & J. Heritage (Eds.), *Structures of social action: Studies in conversation analysis* (pp. 167-190). Cambridge: Cambridge University Press.

Button, G., & Casey, N. (1985). Topic nomination and pursuit. *Human Studies, 8,* 3-55.

Button, G., Drew, P., & Heritage, J. (Eds.). (1986). Interaction and language use [Special Issue]. *Human Studies, 9*(2-3).

Button, G., & Lee, J.R.E. (Eds.). (1987). *Talk and social organisation.* Clevedon, England: Multilingual Matters.

Craig, B., & Tracy, K. (Eds.). (1983). *Conversational coherence: Studies in form and strategy.* Beverly Hills, CA: Sage.

Delia, J., & Grossberg, L. (1977). Interpretation and evidence. *Western Journal of Speech Communication, 41,* 32-42.

Drew, P. (1987). Po-faced receipts of teases. *Linguistics, 25*(1), 219-253.

Drummond, K. (1989). A backward glance at interruptions [Special issue]. *Western Journal of Speech Communication, 53*(2).

Ellis, D. G., & Donahue, W. A. (Eds.). (1986). *Contemporary issues in language and discourse processes.* Hillsdale, NJ: Lawrence Erlbaum.

Fisher, B. A. (1978). *Perspectives on human communication.* New York: Macmillan.

Ford, J. (1975). *Paradigms and fairytales: An introduction to the science of meanings* (Vol. 2). London: Routledge & Kegan Paul.

Frankel, R. (1984). From sentence to sequence: Understanding the medical encounter through micro-interactional analysis. *Discourse Processes, 7,* 135-170.

Frankel, R. (in press). Talking in interviews: A dispreference for patient initiated questions in patient-physician encounters. In G. Psathas (Ed.), *Interaction competence.* Lanfram, MD: University Press of America.

Garfinkel, H. (1967). *Studies in ethnomethodology.* Englewood Cliffs, NJ: Prentice-Hall.

Goffman, E. (1967). *Interaction ritual: Essays on face-to-face behavior.* Garden City, NY: Doubleday.

Goffman, E. (1981). *Forms of talk.* Oxford: Basil Blackwell.

Goodwin, C. (1981). *Conversational organization: Interaction between speakers and hearers.* New York: Academic Press.

Goodwin, C., & Goodwin, M. H. (in press). In A. Grimshaw (Ed.), *Conflict talk.* Cambridge: Cambridge University Press.

Goodwin, M. H. (1982). Process of dispute management among urban black children. *American Ethnologist, 9,* 799-819.

Heritage, J. (1984). *Garfinkel and ethnomethodology.* Cambridge: Polity.

Heritage, J. (1985). Recent developments in conversation analysis. *Sociolinguistics Newsletter, 15,* 1-18.

Hopper, R. (in press). Hold the phone. In D. Boden & D. Zimmerman (Eds.), *Talk and social structure.* Cambridge: Polity.

Jackson, S. (1986). Building a case for claims about discourse structure. In D. G. Ellis & W. A. Donahue (Eds.), *Contemporary issues in language and discourse processes* (pp. 129-148). Hillsdale, NJ: Lawrence Erlbaum.

Jacobs, S. (1986). How to make an argument from example in discourse analysis. In D. G. Ellis & W. A. Donahue (Eds.), *Contemporary issues in language and discourse processes* (pp. 149-168). Hillsdale, NJ: Lawrence Erlbaum.

Jacobs, S. (1988). Evidence and inference in conversation analysis. In J. A. Anderson (Ed.), *Communication yearbook 11* (pp. 433-443). Newbury Park, CA: Sage.

Jefferson, G. (1973). A case of precision timing in ordinary conversation: Overlapped tag-positioned address terms in closing sequences. *Semiotica, 9*, 47-96.

Jefferson, G. (1979). A technique for inviting laughter and its subsequent acceptance/declination. In G. Psathas (Ed.), *Everyday language: Studies in ethnomethodology* (pp. 79-96). New York: Irvington.

Jefferson, G. (1983). *Notes on some orderlinesses of overlap onset.* Tilburg, Netherlands: Tilburg Papers in Language and Literature.

Jefferson, G. (1985a). An exercise in the transcription and analysis of laughter. In T. van Dijk (Ed.), *Handbook of discourse analysis: Vol 3. Discourse and dialogue* (pp. 25-34). London: Academic Press.

Jefferson, G. (1985b). The interactional unpackaging of a gloss. *Language in Society, 14*, 435-466.

Jefferson, G., & Schegloff, E. (1975). *Sketch: Some orderly aspects of overlap in natural conversation.* (Available from American Anthropological Association)

Kaplan, A. (1964). *The conduct of inquiry.* New York: Thomas Y. Crowell.

Mandelbaum, J. (1987). Couples sharing stories. *Communication Quarterly, 35*, 144-170.

Maynard, D. W. (1980). Placement of topic changes in conversation. *Semiotica, 30*, 263-290.

Maynard, D. W. (1984). *Inside plea-bargaining: The language of negotiation.* New York: Plenum.

Maynard, D. W. (Ed.). (1987). Language and social interaction [Special issue]. *Social Psychology Quarterly, 30*(2).

Maynard, D. W., & Zimmerman, D. H. (1984). Topical talk, ritual, and the social organization of relationships. *Social Psychology Quarterly, 47*, 301-316.

Ochs, E. (1979). Transcription as theory. In E. Ochs & B. Schieffelin (Eds.), *Developmental pragmatics* (pp. 43-72). New York: Academic Press.

Phillipson, M. (1973). Theory, methodology, and conceptualization. In P. Filmer, M. Phillipson, D. Silverman, & D. Walsh (Eds.), *New directions in sociological theory* (pp. 77-116). London: MIT Press.

Polanyi, M. (1962). *Personal knowledge.* Chicago: University of Chicago Press.

Pomerantz, A. M. (1978a). Attributions of responsibility: Blamings. *Sociology, 12*, 115-121.

Pomerantz, A. M. (1978b). Compliment responses: Notes on the cooperation of multiple constraints. In J. N. Schenkein (Ed.), *Studies in the organization of conversation interaction* (pp. 79-112) New York: Academic Press.

Pomerantz, A. M. (1984). Agreeing and disagreeing with assessments: Some features of preferred and dispreferred turn shapes. In J. M. Atkinson & J. Heritage (Eds.), *Structures of social action: Studies in conversation analysis* (pp. 57-101). Cambridge: Cambridge University Press.

Psathas, G. (Ed.). (1979). *Everyday language: Studies in ethnomethodology.* New York: Irvington.

Sacks, H. (1963). Sociological description. *Berkeley Journal of Sociology, 8*, 1-16.

Sacks, H. (1984a). Notes on methodology. In J. M. Atkinson & J. Heritage (Eds.), *Structures of social action: Studies in conversation analysis* (pp. 21-27). Cambridge: Cambridge University Press.

Sacks, H. (1984b). On doing being ordinary. In J. M. Atkinson & J. Heritage (Eds.), *Structures of social action: Studies in conversation analysis* (pp. 413-429). Cambridge: Cambridge University Press.

Sacks, H., Schegloff, E., & Jefferson, G. (1974). A simplest systematics for the organization of turn-taking for conversation. *Language, 50*, 696-735.

Schegloff, E. A. (1968). Sequencing in conversational openings. *American Anthropologist, 70*, 1075-1095.

Schegloff, E. A. (1984). On some questions and ambiguities in conversation. In J. M. Atkinson & J. Heritage (Eds.), *Structures of social action: Studies in conversation analysis.* Cambridge: Cambridge University Press.

Schegloff, E. A. (1986). The routine as achievement. *Human Studies, 9*, 111-151.

Schegloff, E. A. (1987a). Between macro and micro: Contexts and other connections. In J. Alexander, B. Giesen, R. Münch, & N. Smelser (Eds.), *The micro-macro link*. Berkeley: University of California Press.

Schegloff, E. A. (1987b). Analyzing single episodes of interaction. *Social Psychology Quarterly, 30*(2).

Schegloff, E. A., Jefferson, G., & Sacks, H. (1977). The preference for self-correction in the organization of repair in conversation. *Language, 53*, 361-382.

Schegloff, E. A., & Sacks, H. (1973). Opening up closings. *Semiotica, 7*, 289-327.

Schenkein, J. N. (Ed.). (1978). *Studies in the organization of conversational interaction*. New York: Academic Press.

Sudnow, D. (1972). *Studies in social interaction*. New York: Free Press.

Turner, R. (1970). Words, utterances, and activities. In J. Douglas (Ed.), *Understanding everyday life* (pp. 169-187). London: Routledge & Kegan Paul.

van Dijk, T. A. (1987). *Discourse and power*. Unpublished manuscript, University of Amsterdam.

van Dijk, T. A. (1989). Structures of discourse and structures of power. In J. A. Anderson (Ed.), *Communication yearbook 12* (pp. 18-59). Newbury Park, CA: Sage.

Wieder, D. L. (1988). From resource to topic: Some aims of conversation analysis. In J. A. Anderson (Ed.), *Communication yearbook 11* (pp. 444-454). Newbury Park, CA: Sage.

Zimmerman, D. H. (1988). On conversation: The conversation analytic perspective. In J. A. Anderson (Ed.), *Communication yearbook 11* (pp. 406-432). Newbury Park, CA: Sage.

Zimmerman, D. H., & West, C. (Eds.). (1980). Language and social interaction [Special issue]. *Sociological Inquiry, 50*(4).

Describing Speech Phenomena

ROBERT HOPPER

University of Texas, Austin

W HAT are the phenomena of speaking? Beach's essay argues that we must
base a science of speech in descriptions of message phenomena that
occur in naturally occurring interaction. Researchers must describe how
speakers orient to these phenomena. Beach also argues that researchers' coding
processes include reflexive procedural dimensions as well as representational
dimensions. The present remarks extend consideration of these themes.

Beach urges researchers to orient to phenomena; however, his essay provides
only a prelude to analytical descriptions of conversation phenomena in courtroom
discourse. Beach provides some commentary on theory and method, some critique
of discourse analytic coding in studies of courtroom discourse, and some discussion of a transcribed segment of a courtroom hearing. The present response extends
and supplements this work by touching on two issues: (a) How do researchers
construct empirical descriptions of speech phenomena? (b) How do researchers
accomplish descriptive "coding"?

BEING EMPIRICAL

Discourse scientists share a preoccupation with "being empirical," that is, with
offering observations that (a) are in accord with factual events, (b) are available to
sense perceptions, and (c) are vulnerable to replication. Empirical descriptions
must survive tests, or trials, against factual evidence. Research methods in discourse analysis may be characterized in terms of researchers' procedures for being
empirical.

Various discourse analysts approach being empirical in various ways. Some
analysts cast measures within experimental designs, for instance. Conversation analysis, one school of discourse analysis, offers a unique approach to these

Correspondence and requests for reprints: Robert Hopper, Speech Communication Department, University of Texas, Austin, TX 78712.

Communication Yearbook 13, pp. 245-254

issues. (For remarks on that orientation, see Hopper, Koch, & Mandelbaum, 1986; Livingston, 1987; Sacks, 1984. For contrasts between conversation analytic empiricism and social psychological empiricism, see essays in Roger & Bull, 1989. For summaries of the findings of conversation analysts, see Atkinson & Heritage, 1984; Heritage, 1984, chap. 8; Levinson, 1983, chap. 6.)

Conversation analysis combines detail-centered empiricism with a conservative and rigorous approach to theory (Levinson, 1983, p. 286). The conversation analyst describes phenomena to which participants in conversation are orienting, and grounds descriptions in evidence from tape recordings.

Beach summarizes conversation analytic orientations to phenomena. Having pointed the reader toward these issues, he turns (in the third part of his essay) to describing a segment from a court hearing. He displays a transcription of the segment, and offers some observations about what he characterizes as a "complaint" by the defendant. Beach does not introduce a definitive empirical set of observations about the notion of "complaint," but rather allows readers to "peak over his shoulder" as he notes details in the segment.

Much of the daily work in conversation analysis consists of listening repeatedly to recorded segments, such as the one from which Beach reports a transcription. The transcription itself is produced during such repeated listening, and researchers record observations such as those in Beach's essay. These are not advanced as analyses of phenomena, but as notes of observations from listening exercises. To a conversation analyst such routine repeated-listening exercises are somewhat like the daily exercises of a gymnast or a dancer; published analyses of phenomena are more like public performances. Analyses of phenomena render scientific activity into public contexts of justification. Beach takes note of some observations from the context of discovery—a candid glance at products of his daily bench work. As such, these observations have value as documents on important practices that conversation analysts label "unmotivated listening," or listening repeatedly to recordings of speech events without allowing oneself to be driven by particular theoretical considerations. But these observations are not empirical descriptions of phenomena.

Beach characterizes one turn-at-talk by a defendant as a "complaint." To support this characterization Beach notes ways in which the "complaining" turn includes various verbal markings: stress, pause, restart, and hesitation. Most of the observations focus on the "complaining" turn itself. There is less attention to sequential issues, although Beach mentions sequence in this treatment and throughout the essay. Consider this portion of Beach's segment:

```
146      why wasn't I s:erved with a supeenee ta (.)
147      appear in court that's (all I) that's wha -  confuses   me
                                              [        ]
                                              [        ]
148 J:                                         Not- not    into
149      that.
```

Beach's argument that D is "complaining" turns on prosodic and temporal characteristics of D's turn. Stronger evidence seems to occur in J's next turn. However one characterizes D's turn (only the last part of which is shown here), one can observe that J's next turn, offered in overlap of D, displays strong sequential relevance to D's turn. Use of the pronoun "that" indexes J's speech as sequentially cohesive with D's turn, or as a response to it. The semantics of "not into that" (at least in California) implies a denial of assent to something D suggests be taken up — the subject of whether D was served with a subpoena.

Is D "complaining"? I cannot answer that based either on this segment or on conversation analytic literatures. However, conversation literatures do offer descriptions of various kinds of "assessments," including "compliments" (Pomerantz, 1978, 1984). Pomerantz describes these "assessing" actions less in terms of the assessing turns themselves than in terms of the sequential relevance of next turns following assessments. Perhaps descriptions of complaints will also find a useful focus in immediate-next turns. It is (for many kinds of speech actions) at next turn that speakers show interpretation of immediately previous turns. This provides the analyst with numerous resources:

> But while understandings of other turn's talk are displayed to co-participants, they are available as well to professional analysts, who are thereby afforded a proof criterion (and a search procedure) for the analysis of what a turn's talk is occupied with. (Sacks, Schegloff, & Jefferson, 1974, p. 729)

Conversation analytic descriptions mine details of turns for indications of speakers' interpretations of previous turns. That is one way to move from observations collected during listening exercises and to point toward descriptions of phenomena.

These responses to Beach's observations instantiate the sort of dialogue that enlivens conversation listening sessions. It is intended more as supplement toward description of phenomena than as refutation. And this present critique also *has not* yet described a phenomenon. The point of this discussion is that Beach does not purport to advance the description of a conversational phenomenon in his notes on the court hearing, but he does advance the literature on method by disclosing some of the flavor of analysts' day-to-day exercises.

In sum, Beach's critique (Where are the phenomena and how shall we know them?) is well stated, yet it is not remedied by his own treatment. This critique *is*, however, amply remedied in conversation analytic literatures — *and in very few others*. The larger point is that conversation analytic descriptions display phenomena of speaking and that this is quite rare in other schools of discourse analysis.

Some examples of analytic descriptions of phenomena appear in Sacks et al. (1974), Schegloff (1986, 1987), Pomerantz (1978, 1984), Goodwin (1980), Jefferson (1979, 1980), and Hopper (in press). These examples are listed here because they show phenomena in similar essay formats. Each of these essays advances a set of data segments to exemplify proposed phenomena. Conversation analysts use exemplars much as linguists do, with an added restriction to exemplars that actually have occurred (Hopper, 1989). Each of the above-listed essays show how descriptions account for details of each instance.

These essays are not the only format acceptable to conversation analysts, but this format is in frequent use, and it is described here to illustrate some features of conversation analytic specification of phenomena. One such set of data fragments is introduced below and then applied to Beach's courtroom instance to show readers one path toward specification of phenomena in that segment.

One phenomenon relevant to Beach's courtroom segment is labeled "recycled turn beginnings" (Schegloff, 1987). These are repeats near the beginning of turns, in which material spoken at or near the start of the turn essentially gets redone, or recycled. Schegloff (1987) presents three instances to exemplify recycled turn beginnings:

[1]

A: I didn't know what days you had   ⌈classes or anything
B: ⌊Yeah an I didn't know
     I didn't know when you were home . . . (pp. 80-81)

[2]

A: He's been in the hospital for a few days, right?
     Takes a   ⌈bout a week to grow a culture   ⌉
B: ⌊I don't think they grow a   ⌋
     I don't think they grow a culture to do a biopsy. (p. 75)

[3]

A: Why dontchu ⌈(I mean   )   ⌉
B: ⌊You know I wo-   ⌋
     I wonder if Donna went back to school . . . (p. 80)

In each of these instances, the second speaker (speaker B) begins a turn in overlap with continuing speech by speaker A. This is a routine sort of problem in turn-taking, and speakers have routine ways of dealing with such a problem. Among these ways are to recycle turn beginnings. These recyclings can be placed such that

> the recycle begins at precisely the point at which the "new" turn emerges "into the clear"; that is, as the overlap ends by the "old" turn coming *to* its "natural" or projected completion or by being stopped or withdrawn *before* its projected completion. (p. 74)

In instances 1, 2, and 3, the recycled beginning appears as the last line of the displayed fragment. One can observe how these recyclings are redoings of material from the second speaker's turns that had begun in overlap. Why do these recycled turn beginnings occur in these settings? One explanation is that if you begin a turn when your conversation partner is speaking, there is some risk that you may not be heard. One way to deal with this risk is to repeat precisely those portions of your turn beginning that might have been inaudible during overlap.

Recycled turn beginnings seem to have multiple uses (see Goodwin, 1980, for a description of their role in seeking a listener's attention). One use described by Schegloff (1987) is in conjunction with occurrences of speech overlap. This use is illustrated in instance 3 above. Speaker A seems to be forwarding a proposal: "Why dontchu, I mean . . . ." Speaker B's turn beginning truncates, or interrupts, speaker A's projected turn space. Further, speaker B seems to attend to when A stops speaking, for it is precisely at the moment that A stops speaking that B begins to recycle the turn beginning. The recycled turn beginning in instance 3 displays speaker B's perception that an interruption has been successfully completed. In sum, instance 3 illustrates the occurrence of a recycled turn beginning just at the point that an interrupting party has forced a previous speaker from the floor.

Schegloff's observations about recycled turn beginnings have some relevance to Beach's court instance, shown again here in part:

```
146     why wasn't I s:erved with a supeenee ta (.)
147     appear in court that's (all I) that's wha -  confuses    me
                                              [          ]
                                              [          ]
148 J:                                 Not- not    into
149     that.
```

In this instance, the judge recycles a turn beginning and, by means of deploying this speech phenomenon, interrupts what likely would have been some further speaking by the defendant. Perhaps these arguments can be made relevant to the sequential characterization of this fragment that was offered earlier in the present essay. Not only does J respond in a relevant way and a negative way in this segment, but J's use of recycled turn beginning also indicates orientation to his having interrupted D. These features combine to indicate that J is taking a confrontive tack against the action in D's turn.

An additional point about speech and power can perhaps be developed from the description of the environment of this recycled turn beginning. Participants in institutionally constrained discourse (such as courtroom hearings) rely upon ordinary conversational phenomena to do various kinds of work, and to accomplish such states as "being powerful." Van Dijk (1989) might argue that the judge shows institutional "power" by interrupting during this segment. Perhaps that claim is interesting to pursue, but it does not treat one central empirical issue: If the judge is "being powerful" on this occasion, how is the judge accomplishing this action? The description of recycled turn beginning in this instance shows one speech phenomenon put to work here — a phenomenon that works in ordinary conversation as well as in the courtroom. In fact, this technique works in the courtroom because it works in everyday talk. With this description we may begin to consider *how* this judge, on this occasion, goes about accomplishing "being powerful." People who do power rarely invent entirely new ways of doing so. Rather, they adapt rather universal speech phenomena to these uses.

One could proceed to outline how collections of instances of phenomena function within any of the essays cited above. In the pages remaining here, however, I will address an issue less treated in extant literatures: the issue of researchers' practices for "coding." Since Beach's major inspiration for this discussion is Garfinkel's (1967/1987) work, I begin there.

RESPECIFYING CODING

Garfinkel's (1967/1987) discussions of "coding" in *Studies in Ethnomethodology* take two directions: coding by scientists and coding by participants in conversation. On the one hand, scientists perform "coding" tasks. Researchers may perform coding by writing descriptions of certain contents of a mental patient's written case record, or by reading a transcription of speech and categorizing each turn-at-talk — giving it, for instance, a label from theories of dominance or from speech act theories. Alternatively, researchers might accomplish coding by transcribing speech according to the international phonetic alphabet, or using Jefferson's conversation analysis transcription system. All discourse analysts perform codings. In the present essay scientists' codings are labeled C_s.

Garfinkel's (1967/1987) discussion also describes coding activities of conversation participants, or C_p. Participants in conversation display C_p each time they speak. Codings$_p$ are displayed in the features of speech itself, "on the fly," implicitly, in ways that do not stop the business of talking to show these interpretations. This is how turns-at-talk display interpretations of previous turns. For instance, when a person says "hi" right after another person says "hi," the second "hi" displays coding of the first "hi" by means of offering an appropriately timed next utterance that shows indexical relevance to the preceding turn. The two utterances taken together constitute an exchange of greetings.

One difference between many C_p and C_s efforts is that the latter may attempt representational explicitness of articulation. By contrast, C_p orient to accomplishment of tasks. Participants in conversation orient to constraints against tiresome explicitness. Garfinkel (1967/1987) terms these constraints "let it pass." It is not that speakers follow immutable "let it pass" rules, but rather that speakers "let it pass" in various ad hoc ways. Participants in conversation orient to getting the tasks of communication done while calling minimal attention to the ways in which the tasks get accomplished.

However, the apparent contrast between scientific and everyday coding begins to dissolve upon closer examination. For instance, researchers whose task is to "code" the contents of patient records were found to employ not only explicit and content-centered rules in their coding manuals, but also a number of (usually) implicit seat-of-the-pants procedural constraints. Garfinkel calls these coder procedures "ad hocing" to display their based-in-the-current-situation, make-it-up-as-you-go-along manner of occurrence. "Let it pass" is Garfinkel's (1967/1987) label for one genre of ad hocing (pp. 21-22).

Beach approaches these issues in his description of difficulties he and cocoders$_s$ encountered in using a coding scheme to divide interaction into discrete "acts" and to assign one of five category values to each "interact." Beach discovered that "acts" could not always be separated from one another, since utterances routinely accomplish many things at the same time. Further, the imputing of dominance relations to interact moments seemed variably informative for various instances of coding. Beach concurs with Garfinkel in observing that coders$_s$ faced with these difficulties employ a variety of ad hoc procedures — situated decision criteria that do not appear in coding manuals, and perhaps could not be exhaustively summarized in any coding manual of any length.

Garfinkel (1967/1987) argues this point by reporting an assignment in which students were asked to describe a conversation in which they participated

> by writing on the left side of a sheet what the parties actually said, and on the right side what they and their partners understood they were talking about. . . .
>
> Students filled out the left side of the sheet quickly and easily, but found the right side incomparably more difficult. . . . As I progressively imposed accuracy, clarity, and distinctiveness, the task became increasingly laborious. Finally . . . they gave up with the complaint that the task was impossible. (pp. 25-26)

This example illustrates that complete coding of everyday lived experience may be in principle impossible. It is important not to misconstrue Garfinkel's argument as naive skepticism or as rejection of particular coding manuals. Rather, as Beach notes in passing, "ad hocing procedures were inevitable" (p. 222).

Garfinkel (1967/1987) belabors this point by arguing not against particular coding manuals, but rather against attempts of scientists to reduce coding to representational categorization, thus ignoring the fact that coding is generated as much by situated ad hoc considerations as by any fixed coding scheme. He notes that "attempts to rid the practices of a science of these nuisances lends to each science its distinctive character" (p. 6) and its preoccupation with methodological issues. But there is no remedy for situated indexical ad hocing (p. 6). Coding is, in principle, indexical and ad hoc. Coders$_s$ who attempt to expunge ad hocing from their coding manuals are actually excluding from their science the very phenomena they ought to be studying.

> To treat instructions as though ad hoc features in their use were a nuisance, or to treat their presence as grounds for complaint about the incompleteness of instructions, is very much like complaining that if the walls of a building were only gotten out of the

way one could see better what was keeping the roof up. Our studies showed that *ad hoc* considerations are essential features of coding procedures. (Garfinkel, 1967/1987, p. 22)

In science, as in life, situated ad hoc accomplishment is the essential work of coding. To exclude such matters from science because they cannot be formulated as complete coding rules is to consign most of the real phenomena of communication to the status of error variance.

Garfinkel's remedy is to propose (and to begin) description of ad hoc procedures of reasoning. This description must be based in details of single instances in which displays of this reasoning occur, because ad hoc procedures of reasoning are in principle *situated* — or adapted to the unique properties of each local occasion.

Garfinkel proposes to describe ad hoc procedures employed in coding along with describing representation; second, he proposes *to treat all coding as tentative, incomplete, and open to continual reexplication.* Actually, Garfinkel appears to argue (as does Husserl, 1934/1970) that C_s are instances of C_p. Scientific description, in this view, is embedded in everyday life, and must be understood to be floating in the "natural attitude."

In contrast to this view, some scientists believe that their perspective, or a perspective grounded in an accredited theory, privileges C_s over C_p. Husserl (1934/1970) describes Galileo as a proponent of the view that everyday lived experience happens within the natural universe. The goal of science, in this view, is to describe the natural universe. The goal of human studies, then, is to describe human communication as a set of natural events.

Initially, the Galilean position seems appealing. Is it not the case that all phenomena, including speaking, occur within the spatiotemporal bounds of the physical cosmos? In what circumstances, then, is complete description of such phenomena impossible? An answer from phenomenology-ethnomethodology is as follows: Description of experience must be as precise and complete as experienced phenomena. Whatever one might argue about all phenomena, the phenomena of human speaking are in principle partial, incomplete, situated, and occasioned by local circumstances. Scientists, like Garfinkel's students who described their own conversations, can expect only frustration and failure if they aim to explicate for any instance of speaking all matters communicated and taken for granted by participants.

These issues may help readers appreciate some characteristics of conversation analytic research reports. The presentation of transcribed instances gives readers open-textured access to evidence for claims. By means of presentation of transcriptions, analysts attempt to provide readers

with the opportunity to inspect the analyst's descriptions of what appears to be going on with reference to exactly the same material as that to which the analyst's descriptions refer. Any attempts by the analyst to explicate members' methods ... [are] *open for inspection and scrutiny by others.* (Atkinson & Drew, 1979, p. 26)

In sum, conversation analytic notions of coding indicate ongoing processes never to be taken as complete, yet in which empirical descriptions may be advanced. Readers may test these claims against verifiable details preserved in transcriptions, recordings, and materials. No description is considered finished for all time. Analysts may at any point take up previously described instances and add new facets to these descriptions. These processes, taken as a group, treat researchers' codings as continually open to reexplication. Coding, like poetry, is never finished. Still, at some point, analysts forward claims on the nature of phenomena, and support these claims with arrays of data.

CONCLUSION

Conversation analysts have achieved successful descriptions of communicative phenomena not by assuming a privileged observational position, but by relying upon empirical displays of participants' orientations as these are displayed in naturally occurring speech events. One outcome of this empirical care is that conversation analysts frequently describe small phenomena. This reflects both the size of many spoken phenomena and the present stage of inquiry. Many conversation analytic descriptions show how speakers systematically deploy numerous concrete particular features such as uses of recycled turn beginnings at the resolution of interruptions (Schegloff, 1987), or uses of pauses and noncontent speech (e.g., um, well) to preface disagreements (Pomerantz, 1984; Sacks, 1987).

Most schools of social psychology and discourse analysis attempt, at the outset of any inquiry, to specify an adequate theory of information processing or a transcendent set of presuppositions, operational definitions, and hypotheses. From a conversation analytic view, the attempt to describe a wider domain is not worth sacrifices of descriptive underspecification. Conversation analysts are suspicious of premature theory formulation based upon underspecified descriptions of phenomena.

The procedures and practices of conversation analysts may be puzzling to readers encountering them for the first time, or to those without experience in repeated listening to tape recordings. But these procedures are of critical importance to developing descriptions of communication phenomena, and therefore are basic to the development of a science of speech. Beach's essay puts us on that path. The present response extends and illuminates the journey. There are plenty of problems with the present treatments. Conversation analysts, like all empirical scientists, make mistakes. But the work remains cumulative in its offering of descriptions of speech phenomena. Conversation analysts are orienting to phenomena of speaking.

REFERENCES

Atkinson, J. M., & Drew, P. (1979). *Order in court: The organization of verbal interaction in judicial settings*. London: Methuen.

Atkinson, J. M., & Heritage, J. (Eds.). (1984). *Structures of social action: Studies in conversation analysis*. Cambridge: Cambridge University Press.

Garfinkel, H. (1987). *Studies in ethnomethodology*. Cambridge: Polity. (Original work published 1967)

Goodwin, C. (1980). Restarts, pauses, and the achievement of a state of mutual gaze at turn-beginning. *Sociological Inquiry, 50*, 277-302.

Heritage, J. (1984). *Garfinkel and ethnomethodology*. Cambridge: Polity.

Hopper, R. (1988). Speech, for instance: The exemplar in studies of conversation. *Journal of Language and Social Psychology, 7*, 47-63.

Hopper, R. (1989). Conversation analysis and social psychology as descriptions of interpersonal communication. In D. Roger & P. Bull (Eds.), *Conversation*. Clevedon, England: Multilingual Matters.

Hopper, R. (in press). Hold the phone. In D. Boden & D. Zimmerman (Eds.), *Talk and social structure*. Cambridge: Polity.

Hopper, R., Koch, S., & Mandelbaum, J. (1986). Conversation analysis methods. In D. G. Ellis & W. A. Donahue (Eds.), *Contemporary issues in language and discourse processes* (pp. 169-186). Hillsdale, NJ: Lawrence Erlbaum.

Husserl, E. (1970). *The crisis of European sciences and transcendental phenomenology* (D. Carr, Trans.). Evanston, IL: Northwestern University Press. (Original work published 1934)

Jefferson, G. (1979). A technique for inviting laughter and its subsequent acceptance/declination. In G. Psathas (Ed.), *Everyday language: Studies in ethnomethodology* (pp. 79-96). New York: Irvington.

Jefferson, G. (1980). On trouble-premonitory response to inquiry. *Sociological Inquiry, 50*, 153-185.

Levinson, S. (1983). *Pragmatics*. Cambridge: Cambridge University Press.

Livingston, E. (1987). *Making sense of ethnomethodology*. London: Routledge & Kegan Paul.

Pomerantz, A. (1984). Agreeing and disagreeing with assessments: Some features of preferred/dispreferred turn shapes. In J. M. Atkinson & J. Heritage (Eds.), *Structures of social action: Studies in conversation analysis* (pp. 57-101). Cambridge: Cambridge University Press.

Pomerantz, A. (1978). Compliment responses: Notes on the corporation of multiple constraints. In J. Schenkein (Ed.), *Studies in the organization of conversational interaction* (pp. 79-112). New York: Academic Press.

Roger, D., & Bull, P. (Eds.). (1989). *Conversation*. Clevedon, England: Multilingual Matters.

Sacks, H. (1984). Notes on methodology. In J. M. Atkinson & J. Heritage (Eds.), *Structures of social action: Studies in conversation analysis* (pp. 21-27). Cambridge: Cambridge University Press.

Sacks, H. (1987). On the preferences for agreement and contiguity in sequences in conversation. In G. Button & J.R.E. Lee (Eds.), *Talk and social organisation* (pp. 54-69). Clevedon, England: Multilingual Matters.

Sacks, H., Schegloff, E. A., & Jefferson, G. (1974). A simplest systematics for the organization of turn-taking for conversation, *Language, 50*, 696-735.

Schegloff, E. A. (1986). The routine as achievement. *Human Studies, 9*, 111-152.

Schegloff, E. A. (1987). Recycled turn beginnings: A precise repair mechanism in conversation's turn-taking organisation. In G. Button & J.R.E. Lee (Eds.), *Talk and social organisation* (pp. 70-85). Clevedon, England: Multilingual Matters.

van Dijk, T. A. (1989). Structures of discourse and structures of power. In J. A. Anderson (Ed.), *Communication yearbook 12* (pp. 18-59). Newbury Park, CA: Sage.

Communication Phenomena as Solutions to Interactional Problems

JENNY MANDELBAUM

Rutgers University

I N his chapter, Beach takes up issues surrounding what could constitute a "phenomenon" for communication studies. He poses a number of questions for himself and for research on interaction concerning the nature of communication phenomena. In this response to Beach, I take up the issue of what we, as communication researchers, could mean by a communication "phenomenon." Beach's assumption is that a phenomenon located in *interaction*, oriented to by speakers and hearers, is to be counted as a phenomenon for communication studies. His chapter treats issues pertaining to what a phenomenon might consist of, and how one might go about locating one, proposing conversation analysis (CA) as a suitable method for locating and developing a phenomenon. He then provides some observations about a fragment of courtroom interaction. As Beach proposes, just what a "communication phenomenon" might consist of is a difficult problem. His discussion raises the question of what we mean by a phenomenon: For scholars in speech communication, what counts as a phenomenon worthy of note and study? Further, how might we best go about producing an account of a phenomenon?

In a sense, that we should need to ask this question is curious. For if communication phenomena are "real" — that is, existing in the real world — surely they should be available to the naked eye or ear, or amenable to the research tool. If we are having problems identifying phenomena, could it be that we are somehow ap-

AUTHOR'S NOTE: Some of the general themes presented in this commentary have benefited from ongoing discussions with Anita Pomerantz.

Correspondence and requests for reprints: Jenny Mandelbaum, Communication Department, 4 Huntington Street, Rutgers University, New Brunswick, NJ 08903.

Communication Yearbook 13, pp. 255-267

proaching communication in a way that does not assist us in seeing or hearing the stuff of which it is made? Like the goldfish to whom water is imperceptible, is our medium (or *Lebenswelt*) transparent to us? Much of the research currently published in leading communication journals attends to factors that affect communication and how communication affects psychological and social factors, in contrast with a focus upon the structures and characteristics of communication itself. The multiplicity of definitions of communication (Dance, 1970) suggests the problematic nature of what is to constitute "communication" for the field.

Beach's chapter proposes that a possible solution to these problems lies in examining ordinary interaction. In this commentary I examine this solution, suggesting ways in which the features of talk in interaction can be seen as intrinsically communication phenomena, and taking a next turn in the dialogue Beach begins about how conversation presents us with communication phenomena, and how we might go about developing accounts of them that are cumulative with communication theory and research. I begin by proposing a way in which features of interaction may be treated as communication phenomena. I then distinguish between different "orders" of phenomena available for inspection, both in Beach's observations about his data and in published conversation analytic research. Next, by reexamining parts of the data fragment Beach presents in his chapter, I suggest how we might begin to identify a phenomenon in ordinary conversation, and how observations about that phenomenon might be developed subsequent to its initial discovery.

THE STATUS OF CONVERSATIONAL PHENOMENA
AS COMMUNICATION PHENOMENA

"Talk in interaction" seems to be a natural candidate for the location of raw communication phenomena, for interaction may be seen as "the primordial site of sociality" — that is, as the locus of, and means through which, much of our communicative activity gets done (Schegloff, 1987a). How do we communicate? We communicate through talk and through the body behaviors accompanying that talk. If this interactional activity is indeed foundational to concerted social action, then perhaps scrutiny of it might yield communication phenomena that are "real" not just for researchers, but for communicators also. If we examine interaction up close and in detail, we may be able to "capture alive" some communication phenomena.

Implicit in this view is the assumption that interaction is indeed structured and orderly; that we have routine, normal, ordinary, regular ways of interacting that can be located and inspected in any piece of talk one might examine. As Sacks (1984) points out, we may choose to "take it that there is order at all points" (p. 22). This is a claim that can be tested quite simply by inspecting interaction. The opportunity to do this is made available by video- and audiotape recorders. A theoretical explanation may be added to the empirical claim, however, for we can describe interaction as posing specific structural problems for interactants to which there are routine, structured solutions. This is exemplified by the routine ways we have of ending conversations (Schegloff & Sacks, 1973). At the possible end of any given turn at talk, it is normally relevant for a next speaker to start a turn. Ending a conversation involves suspending the relevance of next speaker's turn upon the completion of prior speaker's. Interactants therefore face the specifiable problem of suspending the relevance of next speaker's turn when prior speaker's turn is possibly complete. Examination of the endings of conversations reveals that communicators deploy routine solutions to this problem. These solutions have been observed and described (Schegloff & Sacks, 1973). Thus we can propose that some phenomena of interaction may consist of routine structures for the accomplishment of various activities in conversation, in the format of regular solutions to recurrent, structural problems. (It is important to note that communicators are not *limited* to these solutions, but exceptions to these solutions usually show orientation to the "routine" way of doing things, as is illustrated in the instance discussed below.)

The proposal that features of conversation may be treated as communication phenomena needs further refinement. Communication does not consist simply of the structural features of the architecture of interaction; it is also made up of the activities for which those structural features may be the vehicles. The availability to the researcher of both the structures of interaction and the activities carried out by way of these structures is illustrated in Beach's treatment of the fragment of conversation he presents. Further discussion of his treatment of these different phenomena of interaction suggests that they present us with different "orders" of phenomenon. In the following pages these two different "orders" of phenomenon are explained, and their implications for finding and explicating communication phenomena are explored.

TWO "ORDERS" OF COMMUNICATION PHENOMENON

In his account of "working through a transcribed segment," Beach offers a sketch of how a conversation analyst might begin to examine the details of a recording. He shows first that a transcription of many of the details of the talk may be made. While the transcription is not sufficient for analysis without the tape-recorded details of talk, it provides analysts with a thorough "guide" to the interaction. Next, preliminary observations are made. Note that in this catalog of observations, Beach picks up and lists "noticeables." Many of these are instances of structural phenomena described in prior research (e.g., details of turn-taking, such as the placement of turns, gaps, overlaps, and the like, as described by Sacks, Schegloff, & Jefferson, 1974). Beach notes that CA may involve coding operations. This is instantiated in observations of this kind. These comments have a "there's one of those" flavor — as when a nature guide points out in the wild some life-form previously described on the pages of a book. Other observations are attempts to describe what it is that coparticipants are "doing" through the way in which their talk is produced (e.g., showing themselves to be judge or defendant, complaining, or closing something down).

These two different "orders" of observation suggest two different ways of discovering communication phenomena and, indeed, two different kinds of communication phenomenon. One mode of discovery of communication phenomena is to find in a particular piece of interaction an object that has been described in previous research. This suggests the existence of "generic" phenomena of interaction that may be found in any (or possibly every?) piece of conversation. In this way, a tape-recorded segment of interaction becomes a kind of mine from which "further instances" of a particular phenomenon may be excavated.

In contrast, one may approach a piece of talk with the questions, What is being done here? and How is it being done? That is, the activity or activities carried out in the talk may be what the researcher attempts to uncover. So initially a researcher may go for the structural features of a piece of talk (one order of phenomenon), or, alternatively or simultaneously, for the activity being carried out in and through those features of the talk (another order of phenomenon).

The second approach to some extent relies on the first, for in saying what is getting done, and how, we may frequently find that the structures described in prior research provide the vehicles for the activity in question. However, presumably all of the generic features of conversation have not yet been uncovered.

The above discussion outlines the two "orders" of communication phenomenon available for inspection in conversation. First, there are generic features of interaction; the routine, structured solutions to generic structural problems of talking together. These may be referred to as practices *of* conversation (Schegloff, 1983). Descriptions of some of these practices are available in existing research. For instance, *turn-taking* has been described by Sacks et al. (1974). Connected, interdependent *sequences* of turns have been described by Schegloff and Sacks (1973) and by Schegloff (1972, 1984); *repair organization*, the structure through which troubles in talk may be resolved, has been described by Schegloff, Jefferson, and Sacks (1977).

Second, these features, and others, may be "deployed" in such ways as to accomplish particular activities. Practices *in* conversation may include the activities carried out by way of practices *of* conversation, or in other ways. These include such actions as complimenting (Pomerantz, 1978b), blaming (Pomerantz, 1978a), inviting (Drew, 1984), and teasing (Drew, 1987). Thus practices *of* conversation constitute the architectural features of talk in interaction, while practices *in* conversation are the rich human dramas acted out in and through these and other structures of talk in interaction.

Beach discusses orienting to the phenomenon. If our goal is to find communication phenomena to which *participants*, as well as researchers, are oriented — that is, those that are not simply created by the research process — we must examine what it is about the kinds of phenomena described above that enables us to see them as objects to which participants, rather than simply researchers, orient. This is best considered by examining particular examples. I begin by taking up some of the observations Beach makes about the data fragment he presents. I point out two possible approaches to beginning to examine a piece of conversation for communication phenomena, starting with observations about practices *of* conversation, or, alternatively, with practices *in* conversation. I suggest the consequences of these different approaches, and begin to show how initial observations may be developed in beginning to provide a thorough account of a communication phenomenon, oriented to by participants, demonstrably occurring in conversation, and formulated as "solutions" to routine interactional "problems."

HOW MIGHT WE BEGIN TO
IDENTIFY A COMMUNICATION PHENOMENON?

Distinguishing between practices *of* conversation and practices *in* conversation enables us also to distinguish between two different approaches to data. For instance, one may start by observing the occurrence of particular practices *of* conversation, and then build an account of what is getting done through them — what they are vehicles for. Alternatively, starting with practices *in* conversation, one may begin by observing that an activity of a certain kind is being accomplished in the talk under consideration — that is, noting *what* is getting done — and proceed by describing *how* various features of conversation are deployed to accomplish that activity. Both of these approaches are available in Beach's treatment of the fragment of courtroom interaction. I consider his treatment of each in turn, and suggest how they may be extended to include *recipients'* orientations. In addition, I show how describing these practices as solutions to interactional problems enables us to formulate them as *communication* phenomena.

Practices of Conversation

As discussed above, the activity of interaction presents participants with specifiable "problems" to which they may have routine solutions. These solutions include such matters as how a conversation is to be begun (Schegloff, 1968) or ended (Schegloff & Sacks, 1973); who should talk next, and when — the problem of turn-taking (Sacks et al., 1974); how series of turns may be shown to hang together — the organization of talk into sequences (Schegloff & Sacks, 1973); and how troubles or disturbances in talking may be resolved — the organization of conversational repair (Schegloff et al., 1977). Since these are fundamental problems that participants must resolve for interaction to take place, their occurrence is likely to be observable at some point in most conversations. Therefore one way to "cut into" the data is to note some feature of one of these practices *of* conversation, and then proceed by explicating the problem for which it may be a solution (Schegloff, 1987b). For instance, one could note the occurrence of overlap in line 124 of the interaction described by Beach (p. 225).

Simply noting the occurrence of overlap in these turns ("Sir" in line 124 overlapping with "subject" in line 123, and the overlap with the very end of "you" in line 126) achieves only a preliminary coding of this fragment of conversation for the presence of the conversational practice of overlap. However, it does provide a starting place for an account of what is going on in the conversation. The preliminary observation of the *occurrence* of overlap could be developed by drawing on existing findings about overlap in conversation. For instance, it has been noted that overlaps are frequently placed at points where they show their speaker's awareness of the *possible* end of prior speaker's turn. That is, by the placing their turns at points where prior speaker's turn is possibly almost complete, and a turn by next speaker is possibly almost relevant, overlappers *maintain* an orientation to the turn-taking rule that speakers speak one at a time, without gaps or overlaps. Rather than being interruptive (and hence "rude"), these overlapping turns suggest that a recipient may constantly monitor an ongoing turn for a possible point of completion, at which point the next turn might rightfully begin. In starting up in overlap, then, a possible next speaker shows an orientation to that point as a possible point of completion of the prior speaker's turn (Jefferson, in press). Jefferson shows how a turn may have "a strong sense of finality about it" (p. 3). In such a case, recipient's orientation to this "strong sense of finality" may be shown when he or she starts up, while prior speaker's turn in fact continues. In this way, both participants show a "lawful" orientation to the usual organization for turn-taking in which one party talks at a time.

Such a case of overlap is displayed in lines 122 and 123 of Beach's data fragment (p. 225). In line 122, D may be hearing J's turn as about to be completed with the words "*off* calendar." The stress on "*off*" could be heard by recipients as preterminal stress — the syllable preceding the last part of a turn is often stressed just prior to the completion of the turn. However, it is not only the *turn* that is possibly hearable as complete at this point. In the proposal that "further proceedings can go *off* calendar," recipients may also hear that the judge could be about to propose closing down the proceedings involving this case. Note that it is at *precisely* this point — immediately upon the completion of "calendar," the possibly hearable end of the turn, and the proposal — that D's "Sir" is produced. D's "problem" at this point, then, to which his "Sir" may be a "solution," could be formulated as follows: Given the hearable possibility that J's turn is approaching a possible end, and that this possible end of J's turn coincides with the possible end of a proposal to close down the current proceedings, how might D begin a turn? In starting up precisely at this point, D resolves the problem by beginning a turn at a possibly hearable completion point in J's turn.

In beginning an account of the occurrence of this overlap, however, it is not enough to describe just the behavior of the overlapper. The production of overlap is a *collaborative* effort; it is one of those activities that cannot be done alone. For overlap to occur, J must continue at the same time that D talks. While the occurrence of D's turn is hearable to J, J's turn nonetheless continues. That is, J does not yield the floor to D. Rather, he continues talking (lines 123-124; see p. 225). Overlap provides the "overlapped" party—the one whose turn was under way when another speaker began to talk—with the options of relinquishing the overlapped turn or continuing it. In the situation presented above, since D's "Sir" and J's "subject" begin simultaneously, it is possible that, on beginning to continue his turn, J was not initially aware of D's turn. However, as can be observed throughout conversation, participants orient to each other's talk on a micro-momentary basis. It would be possible for J to relinquish his turn at any point in the progress of "subj," or thereafter. That is, he has the option of showing orientation to D's turn by responding to it in some way. This response could involve dropping out, thereby providing D with the possibility of continuing to talk. Alternatively, orientation to the overlapping turn could be shown by J responding to it by treating "Sir" as a summons, eliciting a response from him (see Schegloff, 1968, regarding the operation of summonses). However, the overlap is effectively *not* oriented to here. Instead, J's turn continues. In this setting, then, where the continuation of his turn is overlapped by another speaker, J's problem may be formulated in turn-taking organizational terms as, What should be done in the face of overlapping talk by a coparticipant? Available solutions to the problem include relinquishing his turn, or continuing to talk with the possibility of continued overlap.

The above account of D's overlapping of a turn by J shows that simply noting precise placement of an overlap—a practice *of* conversation—on the face of it does not constitute so much an analysis as an observation. In order to build a case for this overlap as a conversational *phenomenon*, then, a first step is to specify the "work" that the producer of the overlap could be doing by placing his turn at this particular point: In doing this, the account becomes a story of *interaction*, for it involves describing where the overlap is placed in relation to what is going on in the prior turn with which it overlaps. In building the account in interactional terms, D's turn is described as a solution to the problem of when and how to begin a turn. (Note that, as is mentioned in passing above, the turn could also be formulated quite differently—as a summons, as well as an overlap. This could provide for another account of it.) J's continuation in overlap with D's turn, and after it is complete, may then be described as his solution to the problem of simultaneous talk—to hold onto his turn.

The account provided above relies on the assumption that the placement of recipient's turn is orderly, and not random; that D's "Sir" is not placed immediately after the possibly hearable end of J's turn simply by chance. Rather, it suggests a precise organization of interaction, in which coparticipants show orientation to each other's ongoing behavior. By including coparticipants' orientations in this way, *interactants'* orientation to (and creation of) the orderliness of communication phenomena is demonstrated and explicated.

Through an insistence on the *interactional* production of conversational practices (such as overlap), where coparticipants show specific and strong orientation to precise details of each other's behavior, an account may begin to be built of where overlaps occur. As Jefferson (in press) has shown, the account can be built so as to provide a description of the *orderliness* of the organization of overlap in conversation, so that it may be regarded as an orderly phenomenon, produced precisely (and sometimes even strategically) by participants. This contrasts with the view of it as a violation of ordinary turn-taking — a kind of rude conversational aberration. This brief description of one occurrence of overlap in conversation suggests that by positing conversational behavior as a solution to a conversational problem — where to place a turn in the course of an ongoing stream of talk by another, for D, and how to hold on to a turn and bring it to completion, for J — we may begin to build an account of a miniature piece of conversational activity as a communication *phenomenon*, one that accomplishes specifiable actions and is governed by describable structural features of talking.

Starting an analysis by choosing a recognizable practice *of* conversation, already described in published research, may be contrasted with beginning with an observation about what is *going on* in the fragment in question — that is, describing the practices *in* conversation. This contrast is illustrated in the account below of what may be getting done in the fragment just discussed.

Practices in Conversation

Beach's commentary on the data fragment points out two different ways in which particular activities are achieved through the way in which conversation is used. First, he suggests that participants are "doing" a courtroom hearing, and shores up that claim by noting some features of the conversation at hand (p. 229). Next he claims that the activity under way at the beginning of the transcription he presents is the "closing down" of the "official" business of the motion (p. 228). He treats both of these as activities achieved through particular kinds of conversational practice. Both are treated as practices *in* conversation by basing preliminary evidence for claims about them in some features of the recorded talk. I briefly discuss how each of these candidate phenomena is described by Beach, and suggest ways of extending his analysis in beginning to develop an account of a phenomenon. My discussion shows how describing the activity as providing solutions to interactional problems enables us to begin to build an account of a conversational phenomenon as a recognizable phenomenon for communication studies. In discussing both "type 1" practices *in* conversation and "type 2" practices *in* conversation, I indicate the importance of locating the candidate phenomenon in interactional context.

Type 1 practices in conversation. In the first approach he takes to practices *in* conversation, Beach supports his claim that the data at hand are from a court proceeding by noting that participants address each other in particular ways. He cites the address terms "Sir," "Your honor," "marshall," "defendant," and "plaintiff" to warrant this claim (p. 227). Beach notes that these observations are the product of "a preliminary inspection." There are various ways in which they may be extended.

First, clearly not all of these address terms are peculiar to court hearings. Therefore, one might want to go on and specify what it is about the use of these terms that makes them understandable to participants here as peculiar to the courtroom. Also, if these features of the talk are to count as warranting the characterization of the setting as "courtroom interaction," what it is about these address terms that specifically invokes that characterization for participants could be spelled out. Putting the problem in this way suggests the importance of including in an account both how items in talk are treated by participants and where they are placed with respect to ongoing talk. That is, an account of the location in interaction and treatment of the address terms may help to show how they are used by interactants as part of the constitution of the scene as a courtroom. By locating the terms in the interaction in this way, that participants are "doing a courtroom hearing" is shown to be the case *for them*.

Often we are led to characterize a conversation on the basis of the environment in which it occurs—"medical" interaction, "classroom" interaction, "interview" interaction, and so on. Of course, however, it is possible for people in the physical setting of a hospital or school or job interview to engage in nonmedical, non-classroom, or noninterview interaction. Similarly, it is possible for a casual conversational exchange to "feel like" a medical, classroom, or interview interaction (Schegloff, 1987a). This suggests that it is not just the setting but also the behavior that occurs *in* that setting that constitute it as one or the other. While on the one hand it therefore becomes important to warrant claims about the character of the interaction in observable features of that interaction, it is also important to be wary of co-opting features of conversation as warrants for a priori claims about what makes (for example) a court hearing into a court hearing (Schegloff, 1987a).

For there is a certain amount of circularity involved in attending to a piece of conversational interaction that took place in a courtroom as "courtroom" interaction—if we "know" that to be the case, we may be led to treat any possibly relevant features of the interaction in the setting as providing evidence for what we already "know." We may be tempted to treat the *setting* as constituting the action, rather than vice versa, and simply look to the interaction to confirm the belief that the setting creates action of a particular kind. That is, we may tend to treat action found in that setting as "courtroom interaction" simply *because* it is found to take place in a courtroom. This involves the researcher in a kind of coding operation in which features of the interaction are judged for the extent to which they can be assimilated to the canon of "courtroom interaction." In other words, data are approached with a particular "category" that is to be filled out and exemplified with details from the talk.

Despite these possible problems, noting such features of talk as the address terms that are used is a valuable starting point for building an account of how participants "produce" the courtroom setting. However, the above discussion suggests that we should also examine the way in which the noted features occur—that is, their interactional environment, the local details of the talk, and the ways in which they provide a particular solution to a specifiable problem.

The rather global category of "courtroom interaction," formulated as a practice *in* conversation — that is, an *activity* achieved through the way in which interaction is done — may be contrasted with local episodes of activity, such as "closing down official business," which are also achieved through the way in which specifiable features of conversation are deployed. As the following discussion indicates, however, in dealing with this somewhat different order of detail, similar concerns must be taken into account. An account of the conversational details of the candidate phenomenon, "closing down the official business of the motion," also involves locating the activity in its sequential environment.

Type 2 practices in conversation. Where Beach notes that J "appears to initiate closing of the 'official' business of the motion (i.e., 'the claim of exemption') in lines 121-123" and offers observations in support of this claim, he takes a second approach to practices *in* conversation. Here he makes claims about the activity being achieved through various particulars of the fragment of talk discussed above (p. 228). Beach notes features of *recipients'* turns in lines 124 and 127-130 that suggest *their* orientation to J's turn as "closing down." For instance, he notes the overlap in line 124 (discussed above) as showing D's orientation to J's having (possibly) reached a place where speaker transition may be relevant (p. 228). He also notes that overlap in line 127. He claims that "PL's overlapped utterance does exhibit an immediate response to J's query, yet it also displays his recognition that J is, for all practical purposes, nearing completion of closing down the motion." This orientation is displayed, Beach suggests, in PL's asking a question about "additional business yet to be taken care of" in lines 127-131. While these observations provide some evidence for an orientation on the part of recipients to the possible end of J's *turn*, and the possible relevance of their taking a turn, more evidence is needed to support the claim that J is hearably bringing to a close the motion at hand. Viewing the occurrence in this way highlights the importance of placing the turns in question in their sequential environment.

The process of explicating the sequential environment of the occurrence is begun by Beach in his description of how recipients' turns may show some orientation to the possible "closing." This account can be filled out by discussing what it is recipients might be orienting to. That is, the researcher may pose the question, What is it that makes J's turn orientable to as possibly initiating a closing down of this case? As the following discussion suggests, in order to show how J's turn may be heard as possibly closing down the motion, it is necessary to build an account of the conversational environment of the activity—that is, the turns that precede it, as well as those that follow it—making it hearable as performing the activity of "closing down." Once this has been achieved, the question of the structural problem to which J's turn is a solution may be raised, and the activity of "closing a motion" may be formulated as an orientable to practice in conversation.

First, in locating J's utterance in lines 121-126, it is necessary to examine the talk that immediately precedes it. The beginning of J's turn in line 121, "So," indicates that this turn is to be taken as "consequent" to something prior to it. Examining the preceding few lines enables the researcher to see what lines 121 126 are part of *for participants.* Just before the additional lines presented, discussion about D's payment of installments is under way. Note that J's turn in line 121 is specifically built as subsequent to a question and answer that precede it (in lines not included in Beach's discussion).

Briefly, note that in line 165 J directs a question to D. D answers the question in line 168. This response appears to resolve the issue of the installment. (Much more could be said about *how* each of these actions is achieved.) Given the apparent resolution of the issue of the installment, it could be hearable that the matters of the case are complete, and discussion of it may relevantly be suspended. J's "problem" at this point, then, is how to suspend discussion of the case. The solution to this problem begins to be displayed (thereby displaying the "problem" itself) in J's turn in lines 121-122, where, with "So," he first displays that what he is about to say is to be taken as consequent to the prior exchange, and then begins to propose that "further proceedings can go *off* calendar." As was described above with respect to the overlap in line 123, D apparently makes a bid for a turn. As Beach notes, this may suggest D's orientation to the possibility that J may be initiating the closing down of the proceedings, making this a relevant place for "any other business" (p. 228). Recipient's problem here, then, is how to get the floor for the consideration of "any other business." To close down any kind of interactional event, the cooperation of all parties to the event is needed (Schegloff & Sacks, 1973), for an interaction is not "closed" if one party to it continues to take turns. In disattending D's turn here, J may provide for the continued possibility of closing down the proceeding, rather than taking up whatever D may be about to initiate.

In specifically addressing his turn in lines 125-126 to PL, however, J provides for PL to be incorporated into the proceedings at this point (see lines 125-131, p. 225-226). This brief account suggests that, in the face of the recognizable activity of possible closing down — the proposal that the case go "off calendar" immediately after a key problem, the payment of installments, has been resolved — the "problems" of the other parties to the case, D and PL, include how to resolve any other case-relevant issues that may be pending for them.

The above account of both type 1 and type 2 practices *in* conversation poses candidate phenomena as solutions to problems. This format for examining phenomena of conversation places the objects under consideration firmly in *interaction*. In each case, the question of the sequential location of the objects is used to fill out an account of the possible phenomenon. In this way the phenomena of conversation are shown to be intrinsically *interactional* in character, both in their construction and in the activity they come to perform.

CONCLUSIONS

The above account of possible approaches to communication phenomena in conversation suggests that they may be viewed as practices *of* conversation and practices *in* conversation. From the starting point of noticing a practice *of* conversation, it is possible to come up with an account of what that instance of conversational practice is being used to do in that particular environment. This is done by drawing on the particulars of the conversational environment in which the object occurs. In providing the account presented above, I simply chose an object about which I felt I might have something to say. The object I chose was a feature of conversational practice that has been described by Jefferson (in press). I applied her explanation of the phenomenon of overlap in attempting to provide an account of this particular instance of overlap. My starting point, then, was simply to "cut into" the data, using preexisting research as a tool. A possible problem with this approach is that, in simply "picking features off the transcript," the researcher runs the risk of "missing the action." That is, by starting with a feature that is initially simply of note to the researcher, we may disattend what is of prime concern to the *communicators* — the activities conveyed by way of the interaction. In this way, this approach faces a danger similar to that of coding operations: We may end up throwing the baby out with the bathwater, missing the real *action.*

In contrast, starting with practices *in* conversation involved noting some activity that was being achieved in the talk in question. Details of the talk were then taken to provide support for the claim being made about the activity in question. It was noted that it may be possible to avoid imposing researchers' categories on data if the sequential location of the talk under examination is described in building a case for the problems to which the phenomenon in question is a solution. This emphasizes for communication researchers the importance of noting the ways in which communicators "work up" or "work through" communication phenomena, creating them interactionally in the course of ongoing conversation. It stresses a focus on *participants'* orientations, as they are displayed in and through their talk. It is in this way that the close analysis of the details of ordinary conversation may provide us with access to naturally occurring, oriented-to communication phenomena.

REFERENCES

Dance, F. (1970). The "concept" of communication. *Journal of Communication, 20*, 201-210.

Drew, P. (1984). Speakers' reportings in invitation sequences. In J. M. Atkinson & J. Heritage (Eds.), *Structures of social action: Studies in conversation analysis.* Cambridge: Cambridge University Press.

Drew, P. (1987). Po-faced receipts of teases. *Linguistics, 25*(1), 219-253.

Jefferson, G. (in press). Notes on some orderlinesses of overlap onset. In G. Jefferson, *Two explorations of the organisation of overlapping talk in conversation.* Tilburg, Netherlands: Tilburg Papers in Language and Literature.

Pomerantz, A. M. (1978a). Attributions of responsibility: Blamings. *Sociology, 12*, 115-121.

Pomerantz, A. M. (1978b). Compliment responses: Notes on the cooperation of multiple constraints. In J. N. Schenkein (Ed.), *Studies in the organization of conversation interaction* (pp. 79-112) New York: Academic Press.

Sacks, H. (1984). Notes on methodology. In J. M. Atkinson & J. Heritage (Eds.), *Structures of social action: Studies in conversation analysis* (pp. 21-27). Cambridge: Cambridge University Press.

Sacks, H., Schegloff, E., & Jefferson, G. (1974). A simplest systematics for the organization of turn-taking for conversation. *Language, 50*, 696-735.

Schegloff, E. A. (1968). Sequencing in conversational openings. *American Anthropologist, 70*, 1075-1095.

Schegloff, E. A. (1972). Notes on a conversational practice: Formulating place. In D. Sudnow (Ed.), *Studies in social interaction*. New York: Free Press.

Schegloff, E. A. (1983, Fall). [Class lectures]. University of California, Los Angeles, Department of Sociology.

Schegloff, E. A. (1984). On some questions and ambiguities in conversation. In J. M. Atkinson & J. Heritage (Eds.), *Structures of social action: Studies in conversation analysis*. Cambridge: Cambridge University Press.

Schegloff, E. A. (1987a). Between macro and micro: Contexts and other connections. In J. Alexander, B. Giesen, R. Münch, & N. Smelser (Eds.), *The macro-micro link*. Berkeley: University of California Press.

Schegloff, E. A. (1987b, October 30). [Data workshop]. University of Texas at Austin.

Schegloff, E. A., Jefferson, G., & Sacks, H. (1977). The preference for self-correction in the organization of repair in conversation. *Language, 53*, 361-382.

Schegloff, E. A., & Sacks, H. (1973). Opening up closings. *Semiotica, 7*, 289-237.

6 Perspectives on Group Argument: A Critical Review of Persuasive Arguments Theory and an Alternative Structurational View

RENEE A. MEYERS
University of Oklahoma

DAVID R. SEIBOLD
University of Illinois, Urbana-Champaign

This chapter summarizes a program of research undertaken to examine a prominent cognitive-informational theory of group argument — persuasive arguments theory (PAT). An examination of PAT seems especially germane for communication researchers, for PAT predicts particular group outcomes without direct analysis of interaction. Four tasks are undertaken in this chapter. First, key assumptions of two metatheoretical approaches to argument — the cognitive-informational (CI) and the social-interactional (SI) perspectives — are surveyed. Second, PAT is identified as a particularly prominent CI approach to group argument, and its theoretical underpinnings are detailed. Third, a critique of PAT is offered that identifies three conceptual difficulties: (a) an assumption of correspondence between individual cognition and group discussion, (b) a focus on noninteractional predictor factors, and (c) a methodological commitment to research conducted at the individual level of analysis. Finally, an alternative approach to group argument — structuration — is presented as a perspective capable of integrating the CI and SI approaches within a single framework that accords interaction a central role.

J ACKSON (1983) recently argued that past interpersonal argument research can be parceled into two broad categories. The first grouping views argument as a social, emergent phenomenon in which argument is conceived as a "social institution or rule system which is not reducible to

Correspondence and requests for reprints: Renee A. Meyers, 331 Kaufman Hall, Department of Communication, University of Oklahoma, Norman, OK 73019.

Communication Yearbook 13, pp. 268-302

properties of individual users of the system" (p. 631). The second conceives of argument as an individual-level, fixed phenomenon where "structure and patterning at the social level are seen as derivative from the characteristics of individuals" (p. 632). Jackson continues:

> The difference between these two groups of analyses is not so much *what* each chooses to study as *how* each looks at the phenomena chosen for study. Confronted with "the same" set of phenomena to explain, the individual-level analyst and social-level analyst choose quite different points of entry. (p. 632)

We have distinguished these two categories of argument research as the cognitive-informational (CI) and social-interactional (SI) perspectives on argument (Meyers & Seibold, 1987). The cognitive-informational approach focuses primarily upon the arguer, and views both the process of arguing and the resultant arguments as relatively fixed and stable. Within the social-interactional view, researchers implicitly or explicitly treat argument as a jointly produced, socially governed, interactive activity. Their focus is primarily upon the social unit, and the process of arguing and resultant arguments are seen as emergent, creative, and transformational.

Although social-interactional research on argument is evident in communication (see research by Jackson & Jacobs, 1980, 1981; Jacobs & Jackson, 1981, 1982), most research on interpersonal and group argument in our field has embraced a cognitive-informational view (Burleson, 1979, 1980a, 1980b, 1981, 1982; Hample, 1980, 1981, 1985; Willard, 1976, 1978, 1979, 1981). Yet Jackson (1983) cautions that the latter view is adequate only if both the cognitive and interactional are accounted for within the same theory: "Communication, by its nature, involves individuals trying to coordinate their individual beliefs and behaviors with others', so that it must involve both individual-level and social-level processes" (p. 631).

OVERVIEW

Jackson's warning serves as a touchstone for a program of research we have undertaken to examine more thoroughly a prominent cognitive-informational theory of *group* argument — persuasive arguments theory (PAT). We think an examination of PAT is especially germane for communication researchers, for PAT predicts particular group outcomes without direct recourse to interaction. Although PAT proponents acknowledge that group discussion may be an efficient medium for information exchange, they contend it is only one of several possible channels for accomplishing that task; examination of group discussion content does not figure into their analyses of group outcomes. From a PAT view, the primary purpose of group discussion is to display or disclose members' prediscussion autodetermined (cognitive) arguments. Hence the PAT perspective offers a testable and potentially falsifiable position that challenges communication researchers to assess empirically presumptive beliefs about the centrality of communication in the prediction and production of group outcomes. As Hewes (1986) has recently warned, unless we proceed by challenging our own assumptions, "we face the very real possibility of erecting our theoretical foundations on sand" (p. 33).

This chapter summarizes our work on PAT to date and suggests avenues for continued research in this domain. Four tasks are undertaken here. First, we survey the key assumptions of both the cognitive-informational and social-interactional approaches to argument and draw upon this distinction to explicate one representative theory of interpersonal argument within each domain. Second, we identify persuasive arguments theory as a particularly prominent cognitive-informational approach to group argument and detail its assumptions and theoretical commitments. Third, we offer a critique of PAT that identifies three conceptual difficulties with the CI-based PAT perspective: (a) an assumption of correspondence between individual cognition and group discussion, (b) a focus on noninteractional predictor factors, and (c) a methodological commitment to research conducted at the individual level of analysis. Finally, we present an alternative approach to group argument that integrates the CI and SI approaches within a framework that accords interaction a central role.

COGNITIVE-INFORMATIONAL
PERSPECTIVE ON ARGUMENT

The cognitive-informational approach to argument assumes that (a) *individual arguers* are the focus of study, (b) *arguing* occurs within the individual as he or she responds to and integrates information from the immediate environment, and (c) *arguments* are stable products/responses that result from individual information processing. CI researchers typically view arguing as a process of self-influence occurring within individuals (Hample, 1980, 1984). Much of the information people need to produce arguments is available in memory, and individuals need only recall it to construct a relevant cognitive response. If such information is not immediately available, individuals can reconsider the problem or interact with others. These activities are equally capable of providing the new information needed to stimulate the cognitive system into argument production or opinion change (Burnstein, 1982; Burnstein & Sentis, 1981). Any change in individual attitude, belief, or opinion that occurs following public discussion is viewed primarily as a product of individualistic information processing. Interaction may evoke or stimulate cognitive processing (e.g., self-argumentation), thereby indirectly affecting argument generation and opinion change, but interaction is not considered a direct cause of influence or opinion change (Petty & Ostrom, 1981; Trommsdorff, 1982). Benoit (1985) explains this view:

> The basic tenet of this perspective on persuasion is that receivers actively participate in influence attempts, producing cognitions [thoughts] in response to the stimulus

provided by the persuasive communication. These thoughts are arguments which either support or refute the speaker's position. . . . [This] "cognitive response" is a mediating variable between persuasive communication and attitude change. (p. 593)

Although many CI proponents acknowledge the importance of social factors to the study of argument (Hewes & Planalp, 1987), their central concern is with understanding the cognitive processes undergirding individuals' interpretation and production of messages. Investigations specifying how cognitive processes translate to social capacities, how cognition and behavior relate, or how cognitive abilities mediate social competencies are rare (Planalp & Hewes, 1982). Typically the assumptions undergirding the CI perspective guide research toward individual-level analyses and psychologically based explanations. This approach to understanding argument is apparent in several current perspectives on interpersonal argument (Burleson, 1979, 1980a, 1980b, 1981, 1982, 1983; Hample, 1980, 1981, 1985; and to a lesser extent Willard, 1976, 1978, 1979, 1981). One of the more prominent of these perspectives is Hample's work.

Hample's Cognitive View

Relying upon previous cognitive models as exemplars (Fishbein, 1967; McGuire, 1960; Wyer, 1974a, 1974b, 1975), Hample (1977) has advanced a model to predict how individuals process evidence to produce beliefs and belief change. Hample (1980) describes the cognitive process of arguing and opinion change as follows:

A stimulus impinges on a cognitive system (possibly because the system sought it), and the system then processes, interacts with, and integrates its interpretation of the environment (that is to say, it *argues*), so that the system is changed in some respect. (p. 152; emphasis added)

Hample (1981) contends that argument is "something that happens within a person, not within a message" (p. 148). Arguing is the cognitive processing of information, stimulated by messages but not contained in them. For Hample (1985), "the only *necessary* role of messages to play in a cognitive theory is to perform as a stimulus for the receiver's (cognitively generated) argument" (p. 3). He supports a restricted research emphasis on messages, believing that messages alone are insufficient explanations of argument. Hample (1985) asserts that public argument mirrors private invention and is therefore best understood by reference to cognition. In a recent explanation of the cognitive-informational perspective, Hample (1988) details this stance: "Public utterances grow from private sources, and are controlled by them. . . . And the pragmatics of argument—the human effects of discourse—are mediated by cognition" (p. 14). Hample and Dallinger have also begun to investigate individuals' cognitive editing standards (Dallinger & Hample, 1986; Hample, 1984; Hample & Dallinger, 1985a, 1985b, 1986, 1987), especially how individuals determine which arguments to suppress and which to make public.

They have recently proposed that researchers "examine the generative cognitive processes which support the production of conversations, essays, or speeches — the artifacts of cognitive argument" (Hample & Dallinger, 1987, p. 232).

Although most CI perspectives on argument acknowledge a social component of argument (Willard, 1976, 1978, 1979, 1981; even Hample, 1988, notes a limited role for the social element), CI researchers are interested first and foremost in the individual and cognitive bases of argument. A summary of the key concepts undergirding these theories, and the CI perspective on argument in general, is provided below (for more elaboration, see Meyers, 1987/1988; Meyers & Seibold, 1987):

(1) Individuals are the primary sources of arguing and argument.
(2) Arguing is best explained as an individual cognitive-informational process.
    (a) Arguing is a self-reasoning process stimulated by information from the immediate environment.
    (b) Arguing is a process of self-influence.
(3) Arguments are individuals' cognitive responses, stable indicators of prior cognitive information processing.

Interestingly enough, within the communication discipline, CI approaches to argument are decidedly more numerous than studies that take a more social, message-centered view. While that may appear contradictory, three factors may explain the scarcity of interactional views of argument in communication. First, the definition of argument as an interactional activity was only recently articulated (O'Keefe, 1977). Communication scholars have traditionally viewed argument as something a person makes, a product of individual reasoning, and have only recently begun exploring argument as interactional. Work on the analysis of children's arguments (Benoit, 1981; O'Keefe & Benoit, 1982), on naturally occurring instances of argument (Jackson & Jacobs, 1980, 1981; Jacobs & Jackson, 1981, 1982), on the generic characteristics of argument in everyday discourse (Trapp, 1982, 1983), on serial argument in interpersonal relationships (Trapp & Hoff, 1985), on strategies of interactants to initiate and terminate argument sequences (Benoit, Borzi, & Drew, 1984), and on argument in groups (Alderton, 1981; Alderton & Frey, 1983; Frey & Alderton, 1983) reflects more socially based approaches.

Second, the preoccupation with cognitive explanations of argument corresponds with research trends in other areas of communication, especially interpersonal communication (Hewes & Planalp, 1987; Planalp & Hewes, 1982). Elements of cognitive explanation appear in research on nonverbal communication (Cegala, Alexander, & Sokuvitz, 1979), communication under uncertainty (Berger, 1987), conflict resolution (Sillars, 1980b), information exchange in social interaction (Kellermann, 1987), persuasion and compliance-gaining (Cappella & Folger, 1980; Dillard, Omdahl, & Segrin, 1988; Greene, Smith, & Lindsey, 1988; Smith, 1982, 1984), message adaptation (Sillars, 1980a), schematic interpretations of communication (Berger, 1985; O'Keefe & Delia, 1982; Planalp, 1985, 1986; Taylor & Crocker, 1981; see also reviews by Berger & Roloff, 1982; Hewes & Planalp, 1982; Roloff & Berger, 1982), and discourse analysis (Brown & Yule, 1983; Hewes, 1979; Planalp & Tracy, 1980), among other interpersonal research areas.

Finally, studying argument as interactive is complex. Investigation of interpersonal or group interaction involves hours of videotaping, observing, transcribing, and coding data. Actual interaction data are often less easily obtained, controlled, and analyzed than cognitive data. Such drawbacks have deterred social psychological researchers (Dion, Baron, & Miller, 1978), including group researchers (Davis, 1986; Steiner, 1983); perhaps they have deterred communication scholars as well.

While we agree with others that the study of the individual and attendant cognitive processes is vital to a complete understanding of communication (Hewes & Planalp, 1987), we also believe that research, such as PAT, that focuses exclusively upon individual psychological factors to explain interaction may reflect an overly simplistic and incomplete picture of *group* communication processes. In the next section, we describe an alternative research view, the social-interactional approach to argument, delineate its key assumptions, and detail a representative program of research within this perspective.

SOCIAL-INTERACTIONAL APPROACH TO ARGUMENT

In contrast to the CI perspective, the social-interactional approach to argument emphasizes collectivities and institutions rather than individuals, and casts social phenomena as emergent in interaction rather than as stable individual properties (Jackson, 1983; Meyers & Seibold, 1987; Poole, Seibold, & McPhee, 1985). In this view (a) the *group* is the primary focus of study, (b) *arguing* is an interactive activity occurring between two or more individuals, and (c) *arguments* are the communicative messages produced in argumentative discourse. Arguing is viewed as a social activity; a rule-governed, collaborative, public process generated by, and existing in, interaction. Arguments are the messages generated in negotiated dissensual discourse. SI researchers locate the force of argument in public discourse, not in individuals. Their investigations are rooted in communication texts, and psychological factors are never examined prior to message production or viewed as primary explanatory elements.

Jackson and Jacobs's Discourse Analytic Approach

The most fully articulated social-interactional perspective on argument in communication is Jackson and Jacobs's discourse analytic approach (Jackson & Jacobs, 1980, 1981; Jacobs & Jackson, 1981, 1982). Jacobs and Jackson (1982) characterize their perspective on argument as "an alternative to seeing argument as 'something which happens within a person' and arguing as 'the way beliefs are processed within an individual's cognitive system' " (p. 215). They add: "Not only does the identification of argument with reasoning overlook the appearance of argument in concrete acts and interactions; it ignores the institutional structuring of individual cognitions" (p. 215).

Jackson and Jacobs (1981) indicate that "conversational argument and influence are collaborative activities; influence is not something that a speaker does to an addressee, nor is a line of argument developed from the plan of a single speaker" (p. 79). Their work is guided by three metatheoretical assumptions: (a) Argument is a type of language game; (b) argument is significant communication; and (c) argument is organized by a social orientation. Although they grant that "patterns of argumentative discourse certainly require interpretation and reasoning by natural language users, and the cognitive resources that enable them to engage in argument is a fascinating subject" (p. 215), they contend that the system of rules that guides argumentative discourse transcends individual reasoning faculties; it exists publicly and independently and can be described without recourse to cognitive processes. The key concepts of their approach, and of the SI perspective in general, are as follows:

(1) Social units (dyads, groups) are primary sources of arguing and argument.
(2) Arguing is best explained as a process of mutual interactive influence.
(3) Arguments are collaboratively produced public messages, emergent in interaction.

SUMMARY AND COMPARISON
OF CI AND SI PERSPECTIVES

The cognitive-informational and social-interactional perspectives can perhaps best be summarized by noting important differences between them. Three specific contrasts seem especially germane for purposes of this chapter: (a) differences in how argument is conceived, (b) divergence on the role of interaction in the argument process, and (c) varying commitments to level of analysis.

Conception of Argument

A CI explanation conceives of argument as the observable results of individual cognitive reasoning processes. These cognitive arguments are directly transported into the public domain. Hence group discussion has its roots in, and can be traced back to, individual member cognition. An SI explanation, on the other hand, views arguments as emergent in interaction. They include reason-based messages produced by participants seeking agreement in discordant interaction. Arguments exist only as they are generated in interaction and transcend individual reasoning faculties.

Role of Interaction

To a strict CI proponent, interaction is a stimulus for cognitive argument production, or a medium for displaying individuals' cognitive reasoning outputs. In this view, interaction is not central, or even always necessary. In contrast, an SI proponent locates argument in interaction. Group discussion is not a stimulus or display channel; it is itself the object of study. From a social-interactional view, the analysis of interaction is central to the investigation of argument.

Level of Analysis

The CI approach to argument conducts research at the individual level of analysis. Interpersonal and group argument are investigated as processes that occur within individuals. Arguing ensues when an environmental stimulus impinges on the cognitive system and generates production of relevant responses or arguments. The SI approach, conversely, assumes that the collectivity is the focus of study. Groups are not merely coacting individuals; they constitute a separate system that is more than the sum of its parts (Warriner, 1956). Arguing is a social activity that occurs *between* individuals.

These points of contrast serve as a basis for the critique we offer next of a particularly prominent CI perspective on group argument — persuasive arguments theory. First, we explicate the historical development of PAT by detailing its emergence within the group polarization research tradition. Second, we more fully describe the PAT position on group argument by identifying its assumptions and research procedures. Then, utilizing the alternative SI approach as a framework for critique, we identify three conceptual difficulties with the PAT/CI perspective on argument: (a) the PAT assumption of correspondence between individual cognitions and group arguments, (b) PAT's exclusive focus upon noninteractional factors to predict discussion processes, and (c) research that is conducted at the individual level of analysis. We propose that if communication researchers are to determine fully the utility (or lack thereof) of PAT for communication research, examination of these issues is a necessary first step.

PERSUASIVE ARGUMENTS THEORY

Persuasive arguments theory has its origins in research on group polarization/choice shift. Polarization/choice shift research investigates the tendency for some group deliberations to result in outcomes more extreme than members' prediscussion choices (Stoner, 1961). Historically, researchers investigated polarization and choice shifts for *pragmatic* reasons (Pruitt, 1971a). The discovery that groups often make riskier decisions than individuals challenged conventional assumptions about group conservatism (Stoner, 1961; Wallach, Kogan, & Bem,

1962) and contradicted prevailing beliefs that group decisions were moderate relative to individual inclinations (Cartwright, 1973). Davis and Hinsz (1982) suggest that the political climate of the late 1960s fueled beliefs that groups (especially student groups) display more extreme attitudes following free discussion than they possess prior to interaction. Speculations that groups harbor inherent biases toward risk and willingly choose improbable goals over prudent decisions became common. In time, concerns emerged regarding utilization of groups in decision situations that affect large numbers of constituents (e.g., juries, strategic military decisions, government policy decisions, international decision bodies, town councils). From a pragmatic standpoint, then, understanding risky shift had extensive and important consequences.

Investigators in the next decade discovered that shifts were unrelated to *risk* per se, but were a general outcome of group decision-making discussion (Doise, 1969; Moscovici & Zavalloni, 1969; Myers & Bishop, 1970). Not only did some groups produce *cautious* shifts (Baron, Baron, & Roper, 1974; Stoner, 1968), but risk-neutral and risk-irrelevant items also evoked prominent shifts (Davis, Kerr, Sussman, & Rissman, 1974). Abandoning their preoccupation with *risk* as a central concept, researchers moved toward understanding causes of changes in decision choices among group members. Many sought answers through examination of antecedent and mediating factors. Investigations conducted in several nations studied the effects on group shifts of consensus achievement (Teger & Pruitt, 1967; Wallach & Kogan, 1965; Wallach, Kogan, & Burt, 1965), communication patterns (Cline & Cline, 1979, 1980), experimenter instruction (Clark & Willems, 1969), relevance of the decision task to the subjects (Burnstein, 1969; Laughlin & Earley, 1982; Madsen, 1978), group size (Myers & Arenson, 1972; Vidmar & Burdeny, 1971), ambiguity of the task (Boster & Hale, 1983; Boster, Hale, Mongeau, & Hale, 1985; Hale, 1984; Hale & Boster, 1988), and task type (Moscovici & Zavalloni, 1969; Myers, 1975), among other factors. As research findings accumulated, other investigators began pondering ways to integrate results. Researchers' attention turned toward *theoretical* issues of prediction and explanation.

Due to contradictory and inconclusive findings, and results revealing that some theories were capable of explaining only *risky* shifts, the number of explanations proposing *necessary* conditions for choice shift has been greatly reduced (Belovicz & Finch, 1971; Dion et al., 1978; Myers & Lamm, 1976; Pruitt, 1971b). Among theories that have lost favor are (a) diffusion of responsibility theory (Bem, Wallach, & Kogan, 1965; Kogan & Wallach, 1967; Wallach & Kogan, 1965; Wallach, Kogan, & Bem, 1964; Wallach et al., 1965), which holds that groups allow individuals to "share" responsibility for negative consequences, thus lessening perceptions of adversity associated with risky choices; (b) familiarization theory (Bateson, 1966; Flanders & Thistlethwaite, 1967), which suggests that group participation increases members' familiarity with the decision task and reduces their uncertainty about taking risks; and (c) leadership theory (Collins & Guetzkow, 1964; Marquis, 1962), which contends that leaders, as higher risk takers, persuade the group to choose risky alternatives. But other theoretical approaches that offer broader, more comprehensive explanations are still popular, for example, social decision scheme theory and social comparison theory (see Seibold & Meyers, 1986, for a review of these perspectives). Currently the most prominent theory in the area of decision shifts is persuasive arguments theory.

PAT Assumptions and Theoretical Commitments

Persuasive arguments theory is a noninteractional theory of group decision making that predicts polarization/choice shift from the cognitive arguments members generate while making private decision choices prior to group discussion. While endemic to social psychology (Burnstein & Sentis, 1981; Burnstein & Vinokur, 1973, 1975, 1977; Burnstein, Vinokur, & Pichevin, 1974; Burnstein, Vinokur, & Trope, 1973; Hinsz & Davis, 1984; Laughlin & Earley, 1982; Madsen, 1978; Vinokur & Burnstein, 1974, 1978a, 1978b; Vinokur, Trope, & Burnstein, 1975), it also has been the subject of investigations in communication (Alderton, 1981, 1982; Alderton & Frey, 1983; Boster, Fryrear, Mongeau, & Hunter, 1982; Boster & Mayer, 1984; Boster, Mayer, Hunter, & Hale, 1980; Frey & Alderton, 1983; Hale, 1984; Hale & Boster, 1987, 1988; Kellermann & Jarboe, 1987; Mayer, 1985). Following an extensive review of the polarization/choice shift literature, Myers and Lamm (1976) conclude that evidence for a PAT explanation of group polarization is compelling. Vinokur and Burnstein (1974), originators of PAT, have claimed the theory is both sufficient and necessary for explaining group shifts.

Persuasive arguments theory attributes members' observed response shifts to cognitive learning processes that obtain following exposure to information presented in group discussion (Burnstein, 1982; Burnstein & Vinokur, 1973, 1975; 1977; Burnstein et al., 1973; Vinokur & Burnstein, 1974; Vinokur et al., 1975). Predictions are made from the prior-to-discussion arguments members generate after making private decision choices. Argument "novelty" and "persuasiveness" are proposed as causal factors. Proponents of the theory suggest that if all members have thought of the same arguments prior to discussion (i.e., all arguments are nonnovel and consequently less persuasive), no shift will occur following interaction. On the other hand, if each member of the group proposes novel, highly persuasive arguments, then polarization and choice shift will occur in the direction of the alternative eliciting the most novel and persuasive arguments.

Burnstein (1982) provides the following PAT analysis of discussion effects. Consider a group of three members who must choose between alternatives J and K. Imagine that members together possess six pro-J arguments (a, b, c, d, e, f) and three pro-K arguments (l, m, n). Depending upon how the arguments are processed by members, one of several outcomes is predicted to occur. If all three persons contemplate the same arguments (i.e., their prior considerations are identical), no shift will occur following discussion. Alternately, if arguments a, b, and m come to mind for one member, arguments c, d, and m for a second member, and arguments e, f, and m for the third member (i.e., each individual has different pro-J arguments but the same pro-K arguments), marked shifts toward J will occur following discussion. Similarly, if one member considers arguments a, b, and l, a second member recalls arguments a, b, and m, and a third member possesses arguments a, b, and n (i.e., all members consider the same pro-J arguments but different pro-K arguments), a shift toward K will obtain following discussion.

Vinokur and Burnstein (1974) assert that individuals' thoughts mediate opinion change and final group polarization/choice shift. When members are exposed to novel arguments in group discussion, they are stimulated to rethink and reconsider their own arguments in light of this new information. As members become convinced of the merits of the novel arguments, they alter opinions in the direction of the alternative that elicits them (Burnstein et al., 1974). Burnstein and Vinokur (1975) explain: "Discussion leads each individual to *reweigh* his old reasons for selecting a particular course *and* to consider *new* reasons others have introduced, which process is often followed by a revision in choice" (p. 423).

Despite general support for the theory in early investigations (Bishop & Myers, 1974; Vinokur & Burnstein, 1974), recent evidence has been more mixed regarding the theory's predictive ability (Boster & Hale, 1983; Hale, 1984; Hale & Boster, 1987, 1988; Hinsz, 1981; Hinsz & Davis, 1984; Laughlin & Earley, 1982; Madsen, 1978; Mayer, 1985; Meyers, in press; Meyers & Seibold, 1988; Stasser, Kerr, & Davis, 1980). Among other things, these studies have questioned the sufficiency of the PAT explanation, the validity of the PAT predictive model, the adequacy of PAT to predict shifts at the group level of analysis, and the ability of the model to predict magnitudes of shifts accurately — questions that would be anticipated from an SI perspective. The SI approach to argument motivates the critique of PAT we offer next. It directly contrasts with the PAT approach, which views arguing as an individual reasoning process, and instead focuses upon interaction as central to the generation and explanation of argument. It undergirds and frames three issues we identify as problematic in the PAT position: (a) the PAT correspondence assumption, (b) PAT's use of noninteractive predictor factors, and (c) PAT's commitment to individual-level research.

CRITIQUE OF PERSUASIVE ARGUMENTS THEORY

PAT assumes that any social community has a standard set of socially derived and culturally specific arguments for any decision option. Although vague in this regard, persuasive arguments theorists suggest that this standard set constitutes all available arguments that exist for a decision alternative in a given social community, and that each individual possesses some or all of these arguments, acknowledging the limitation of ignorance or frailty of thought (Burnstein, 1982).

Belief in this standard set of arguments undergirds the PAT assumption that cognitively generated arguments will correspond to, or be isomorphic with, discussion-generated arguments. Cognitive arguments are therefore substitutable for discussion arguments in predictions of group shifts. In a study designed to test the comparability of cognitive and discussion arguments, Vinokur et al. (1975) conclude:

> The two distributions of arguments (private or discussion) were very similar, suggesting that discussion does not elicit new kinds of arguments (e g , those concerning the value of riskiness or caution *per se*) which have not been considered by subjects privately before the discussion. (p. 146)

In a previous investigation conducted within our program of research on PAT, we examined and tested the PAT correspondence assumption by comparing members' cognitively generated arguments with their subsequent discussion-generated arguments (Meyers, in press). Findings revealed that cognitive and discussion arguments are *not* correspondent either in number or in content. Significant differences were found between the number of cognitive and discussion arguments generated across all groups and within many individual groups. Similarly, the content of cognitive- and discussion-generated arguments differed significantly in several groups. Although we recognize that the design of this research (modeled after PAT procedures), in which the same subjects generated both cognitive and discussion arguments, does not unequivocally eliminate rival hypotheses (e.g., increased motivation, social facilitation, greater familiarity with the task in discussion, and additional time to think of arguments), it does suggest initial support for the moderating influence of interaction in argument generation. More fundamentally, these results suggest that cognitive and discussion arguments are not correspondent; how much of that effect is attributable to the impact of interaction still remains to be clarified.

PAT Focus on Noninteractional Predictor Factors

A mainstay of PAT is the presumption that "discussion is not crucial for producing shifts in individual choice. It is merely one common and effective medium for the exchange of important information regarding the solution of a choice dilemma" (Vinokur & Burnstein, 1974, p. 314). Although communication researchers may decry the limited role accorded to group discussion, Vinokur and Burnstein are not alone in their assessment that discussion is nonessential for producing shifts. Investigations have shown that *passive* receipt of decision arguments or information *outside* an interactive discussion context can produce shifts (Bishop & Myers, 1974; Clark & Willems, 1969; Madaras & Bem, 1968; St. Jean & Percival, 1974; Teger & Pruitt, 1967), as can merely listening to a group discussion (Bell & Jamieson, 1970; Kogan & Wallach, 1967; Lamm, 1967).

However, results of these studies also qualify PAT claims: Although choice shifts may obtain in these contexts, their *magnitude* is consistently smaller than shifts produced following group discussion. For example, Bishop and Myers (1974) compared a condition in which groups actively discussed decision items with an argument exchange condition in which members shared information by reading each others' written arguments. Results showed shifts in the argument exchange condition to be small and not statistically significant when compared with shifts in the discussion condition. Similarly, Kogan and Wallach (1967) compared interacting groups' decisions with decisions made by groups who merely listened to discussions. While both conditions produced individual shifts, the shifts following actual discussion were much stronger. After reviewing 160 group polarization research items, Myers and Lamm (1976) conclude that members' *passive receipt* of arguments, or awareness of arguments, is not enough to generate individuals' decision polarization following group discussion. Unwilling to endorse discussion as *the* central element, they argue that interaction provides a forum for the arousal of individual rehearsal and active learning processes. Through verbal confrontation of their own and others' beliefs, individuals consider others' arguments, reassess their own arguments, and revise their opinions accordingly. Finally, most recently, Hale and Boster (1988) found that shifts were typically stronger in discussion conditions than in conditions where individuals were not allowed to discuss their decision choices.

Other writers concerned with the polarization/choice shift research domain have more willingly endorsed communication as a central research variable. Cartwright (1971) has chastised polarization/choice shift researchers, stating that "since it has been firmly established that group discussion is essential for the occurrence of shifts it is remarkable how little attention has been paid to its content and to the function it serves" (p. 370). Dion et al. (1978) also criticize researchers for ignoring direct experimental analysis of actual group decision making. They criticize researchers who merely interpret polarization/choice shift as mediated by different social psychological processes and then *assume* those processes actually occur in discussion to affect group shift outcomes. Finally, Moscovici and Lecuyer (1972) move beyond advocating mere observation of group discussion; they argue that "a real theory of the decision-making process in groups has to be a theory of interaction between the member of these groups" (p. 243).

Despite such repeated calls for direct examination of group interaction, communication researchers have been slow to respond. Consequently, social psychological theories that ignore group interaction (such as PAT) have gained prominence and acceptance in the polarization/choice shift research domain. As indicated earlier, explanations grounded in psychological and situational predictor variables pose a serious challenge to communication researchers. If they constitute both sufficient and necessary accounts, why study communication? Communication researchers recently have begun to address this challenge. Most pertinent for purposes of this chapter is recent research by Poole and his colleagues (McPhee & Poole, 1980; McPhee, Poole, & Seibold, 1981; Poole, 1980; Poole, McPhee, & Seibold, 1982; Poole, Seibold, & McPhee, 1985, 1986; Seibold, Poole, & McPhee, 1980).

In a set of two studies, Poole and his colleagues tested a noninteractional model of group decision making against a congruent interactional model. The initial investigation involved creating an interactional model of group decision making that could be rigorously compared to the noninteractional model of interest. McPhee et al. (1981) utilized Hoffman's (1979) valence model, which posits that final group outcomes will be a result of those options that accumulate the highest group valence. Although the valence model was ostensibly sound, McPhee et al. (1981) contend that its predictive mechanism—overall group valence—was not inherently interaction based and was too general a view of the group discussion process. They argue that final group outcomes are a result of members' influencing and persuading one another in discussion that is best captured by examining the *distribution* of members' comments rather than by the mere *number* of total comments (as Hoffman assumed). They propose an alternative model, the distribution of valence (DV) model, which assumes that *individual* comments count, that a positive reaction by one member is not a positive response by all, and that influence is reflected in members' *distribution* of valenced comments. In comparative tests of the two models' predictive abilities, the DV model yielded a greater number of accurate predictions. Moreover, the valence distribution model accounted for 71.4% of the variance, compared to 63.4% for Hoffman's valence model. McPhee et al. (1981) conclude that the relationship of total valence to final group choices was spurious, and that the *distribution* of valence among group members is more important in predicting and explaining final group choices.

In the second study, Poole et al. (1982) tested the predictive power of the interactional valence distribution model against a noninteractional model of group decision making, Davis's (1973) social decision scheme (SDS) model. Similar to a PAT approach to research, SDS researchers view the distribution of member preferences combined with group decision schemes as elegant and parsimonious summaries of group negotiation and accommodation, and the study of group interaction is virtually ignored. As Stasser et al. (1980) argue, "The distribution of preferences that exist within a group succinctly summarizes the social foundation of both informational and normative influence that may occur during group discussion" (p. 441).

A test of the noninteraction-based SDS model and the interaction-based DV model revealed the valence distribution model to be a better predictor of group outcomes. The results supported the hypothesis that the effect of decision schemes on group outcomes is mediated by interaction processes. Poole et al. (1982) conclude that "the general thrust of this research substantiates the assumptions that interaction *per se* is a crucial factor in group decision making. Although input conditions may also have an impact on decision outcomes, they are mediated by interaction processes" (p. 17).

While more rigorous and supportive tests are needed to establish the moderating and transformative effects of group interaction on members' decision choices (see the baseline approach recommended by Hewes 1986, 1988), both the "passive receipt" studies and the two studies by Poole and colleagues cast serious doubt on the sufficiency of noninteractional processes for explaining choice shifts, as assumed by PAT. When these results are taken together with Jarboe's (1988) findings that models that incorporate both "individual conditions" (input factors) *and* the effects of communication accounted for significantly more variance in group outcome measures than input-only or process-only models, it seems clear that explanations of individual and group decision change processes must acknowledge and account for the interpenetration of cognitive and interactional causes of choice shift.

Individual Level of Analysis

Although PAT is considered a theory of *group* argument, all PAT investigations are conducted at the individual level of analysis: Comparisons are made between the *average of individuals'* pre- and postdiscussion decision preferences (Burnstein & Vinokur, 1973, 1975, 1977; Burnstein et al., 1973; Vinokur & Burnstein, 1974, 1978a, 1978b; Vinokur et al., 1975). But research findings indicate that although PAT is able to predict quite accurately at an aggregate individual level of analysis (where all members' arguments are entered into a single model across all groups), it fares less well when predicting at the group level of analysis. In a study that replicated Vinokur and Burnstein's (1974) initial investigation, Bishop and Myers (1974) found that PAT was an incomplete explanation of *group*-level shifts. They conclude:

> The present study reveals only limited support for an informational influence explanation of group-induced response shifts. At a molar level [aggregate individual level], the informational resources available on an item seem to correspond closely with the mean shift observed on that item. . . . However, at a more molecular level [group level], the shift index [*s*] failed to successfully predict variation between groups within particular items. (p. 101)

Our recent research findings have supported those results (Meyers & Seibold, 1988). PAT inadequately predicted the variation that existed between groups in argumentative discourse. While we recognize that this is not an inherent flaw of theories or models that claim to predict for *aggregates of individuals* only, it appears to run contrary to PAT proponents' claim that PAT is a theory of group argument and group shifts. Because from a PAT perspective, groups are merely interacting aggregates, convened only for purposes of obtaining a dependent variable for the predictive model, characteristics such as membership, interrelated dependencies, interaction, mutual influence, and conflict that distinguish most SI definitions of groups are considered unimportant.

Summary

PAT's focus on the individual, emphasis on noninteractional predictor factors, and assumption that cognitive arguments represent discussion messages are not without merit. Like Hewes and Planalp (1987), we believe that an understanding of individuals' cognitive capacities and knowledge is necessary for building adequate theories of communication. But theories, especially theories of group processes, that focus exclusively on individual cognitive capacities seem to us to ignore important elements of the group decision-making context. In the next section, we propose an alternative approach for viewing group argument that we have found to be capable of wedding both cognitive and social foci within a single framework, and in which communication is a central force. The advance of structuration theory for the study of group decision making was formally proposed in communication by Poole et al. (1985) and applied to the study of group argument by Seibold and colleagues (Canary, Ratledge, & Seibold, 1982; Seibold, Canary, & Tanita-Ratledge, 1983; Seibold, McPhee, Poole, Tanita, & Canary, 1981; Seibold & Meyers, 1986). After a brief overview of the structurational perspective on argument, we propose a preliminary framework for combining individual cognitive factors and social interactional factors within a single theory of group argument.

STRUCTURATIONAL PERSPECTIVE ON GROUP ARGUMENT

Poole et al. (1985) recently introduced a theoretical perspective for studying group decision making derived from Giddens's (1974, 1976, 1979, 1984) theory of structuration. The sociological foundation of Giddens's structurational perspective offers an appropriate frame for studying group decision making and argument processes, given that groups evidence many features of higher-order social institutions. Decision making and argument can be viewed as social subprocesses within the larger macroscopic institutions of government and bureaucratic organizations (Poole et al., 1982, p. 19). More important, the structurational approach depicts interaction as a central force: Social practices are produced and reproduced in interaction. In the next section, we review the central elements of Giddens's (1984) theory of structuration. Then we utilize these elements as a frame for detailing a structurational conception of argument that subsumes both the SI and CI explanations within a single perspective.

Central Elements of Structurational Perspective

In his writings, Giddens focuses upon social actors' day-to-day activities as a basis for understanding the reproduction of institutionalized practices. Central to the study of social action as structurated practice are the concepts of system, structure, and duality of structure. *Structure* is conceived as recursively organized sets of rules and resources, and social *systems* are reproduced relations among actors in which structure is implicated. The *duality of structure* exists in its production and reproduction as accomplished by active subjects in social interaction. In this sense, structure is both medium and outcome of the practices it recursively organizes (Giddens, 1984, p. 25), and the study of individuals' interaction is key to understanding the structuration of social practices.

Giddens (1984) argues that the production and reproduction of structure are accomplished by *active, knowledgeable agents* who reflexively monitor and rationalize their actions. He conceives of actors as possessing a "practical consciousness" that consists of knowing the rules and tactics whereby daily social life is constituted (p. 90), as well as a "discursive consciousness" that allows actors to report their intentions and reasons for acting. He explains that "if there is any continuity to social life at all, most actors must be right most of the time; that is to say, they know what they are doing, and they successfully communicate their knowledge to others" (p. 90).

Knowledgeable actors' intentional actions, however, often produce *unintentional consequences* that serve as *unacknowledged conditions* for future acts. The production of this cycle in regularized activities reproduces institutionalized practices (Giddens, 1984, p. 14). Giddens argues that investigation of this cycle is central to a structurational analysis.

Giddens (1984) is additionally concerned with the *modalities* of structure that allow linkages between the knowledgeable capacities of actors and institutional structural features (signification, domination, and legitimation) in the context of interaction (p. 28). In order to mobilize the structural dimensions of signification (rules of language and semantics), domination (rules and resources of authority), and legitimation (rules of appropriateness and morality), actors draw upon the modalities of structure rather than upon the structure itself. These modalities of structure include interpretive schemes, facilities, and norms, respectively. In short, institutional structures (signification, domination, legitimation) are transformed through modalities (interpretive schemes, facilities, norms) into actions (communication, power, sanctions).

Finally, while the notion of production and reproduction of structure suggests a seemingly simple, cyclic process, Giddens (1984) asserts that its complexity derives from the *interpenetration* of structures. Interpenetration occurs when a structure either contradicts (undermines production of) or mediates (invokes production of) another structure. Both contradiction and mediation of structure are integral to understanding the production and reproduction of social practices (see Poole et al., 1985, for additional detail).

Although this overview of Giddens's theory of structuration is necessarily brief, it highlights the central concepts and guiding assumptions that undergird this perspective. On the simplest level, understanding the structurational process requires examination of members' *social practices*, the day-to-day activities that produce and reproduce structure. Previously we have defined group argument as one such social practice that interpenetrates other structures in the production of group decisions. Our application of Giddens's theory to group argument is discussed next.

Argument as Social Practice

We have recently advanced a conception of argument grounded in the structurational perspective (Seibold & Meyers, 1986). Argument is conceived as a *social practice* produced and reproduced in interaction. Argument is at once both *system* (regularized, observable patterns of interactive argument) and *structure* (the unobserved rules and resources undergirding argumentative interaction). Argument systems are evident in members' discursive claiming and reason-giving concerning facts, values, or policies. As structures, arguments are the rules and resources individuals draw upon to create this form of disputatious interaction. The *duality of structure* is in the production and reproduction of argument in interaction. Arguments are produced in use, but reproduced through use; they are both medium and outcome of interaction.

Arguments are produced and reproduced by knowledgeable actors. As argument unfolds in interaction, members' "practical consciousness" allows them to understand how the game of argument is played and to participate as competent, knowledgeable players. Members' "discursive consciousness" allows actors to report why they think one argument is more rational or logical than another, or why they set forth a given proposal. Together these knowledge structures allow group members to accomplish the practice of argument in a seemingly routine and recognizable manner.

The production and reproduction of argument in groups is conditioned by *unacknowledged conditions* and *unintended consequences*. Unacknowledged conditions serve to both enhance and constrain argumentative activity. For example, unacknowledged historical precedents may enhance argument by establishing rational, efficient, and organized communicative formats, while simultaneously restricting the types of arguments accepted for discussion. Unintended consequences that constitute the unexpected results of an intended action also condition the group's argument. A group leader who insists on free and unrestrained argument with the intention of creating an open and cohesive atmosphere may unwittingly create a chaotic discussion characterized by conflict, personal attack, and destructive relational behavior. The unintended consequence of this behavior undermines not only the future of the leader but also, simultaneously, the quality of the group's argument.

Group argument invokes all three modalities of structure — interpretive schemes, norms, and facilities. Introduction of an argument in group discussion draws upon group members' *interpretive schemes* to identify attempts at reasoning and proposal advancement, reflects and reproduces *norms* about legitimate and appropriate arguments, and allows members to draw upon knowledge and skill *facilities* to challenge others' positions. Modalities are the means by which argument institutions (rules of arguing, canons of logic, cultural values and premises) are transformed in interaction.

Finally, two forms of interpenetration of structure are distinguishable in argument practices. *Mediation* occurs when the production and reproduction of one structure reproduce another. For example, the production of arguments acceptable to powerful members in the group may reproduce a practice wherein only arguments like these are legitimated thereafter, thus reproducing existing power structures. *Contradiction* implies that the production or reproduction of one structure is undermined by a second structure. For instance, while members' arguments may enhance the quality of the group's decisions, disagreement and conflict associated with those arguments may simultaneously erode decision-making quality and efficiency. Members are caught between the need to achieve a high-quality decision and the desire to maintain a healthy relational climate.

In sum, a structurational conception of argument as social practice delineates a complex and intricate picture. It transcends PAT's conception of argument as members' cognitive responses *and* moves beyond the social-interactional view of argument as merely collaboratively produced messages. More specifically, a structurational view of argument is not interested in cognitive responses as singular predictive mechanisms, but instead as potential knowledge structures that inform, enhance, or constrain argumentative interaction. It seeks to understand how individuals use these resources to produce argument and, subsequently, how these resources are reproduced in those practices. In addition, unlike the social-interactional perspective, a structurational account does not view interactional properties of argument as sole and singular predictors of group outcomes. Argumentative messages are governed by historical precedents, informed by individuals' knowledge and use of rule structures, and shaped by unacknowledged conditions and unintended consequences. In short, messages cannot be studied in isolation but must be considered in both present and historical context, and as the achievement of actors.

From a structurational perspective, both the PAT and SI accounts alone are incomplete explanations of argument. To study argument as a social practice, elements from both perspectives must be explained, not as isolated subprocesses, but within a seamless account of group argument. In the next section, we outline a preliminary description of how that task might be accomplished. Although our ruminations are still incomplete, they are intended to lay a foundation for an increasingly complex and intricate structurational explanation of argument.

Structuration as an Integrative Framework

From a structurational perspective, argument is constituted in the group's interaction via the production of rules and resources. In the dual sense of structure, members' arguments are produced in interaction and reproduced by it. In short, neither the CI view that argument is rooted in individuals' cognitive systems nor the SI view that argument is produced solely in groups' interactive activity is a satisfactory account of this more complex process of group argument.

We believe that the SI view of argument is best subsumed in the structurational perspective as argument-as-system — the observable patterns of messages and discourse. Specifically, group argument is the production of *interactive messages* by *social arguers* in group *discussion*. These messages are patterned, rule governed, and collaboratively produced. Argument can be viewed as "streams of interrelated activities produced and reproduced in interaction" (Meyers, 1987/ 1988, p. 353). Past research within the structurational research program has begun to elucidate what these patterns of arguments look like. Seibold and colleagues reported that group argument evidences at least two unique patterns: (a) formalistic, claim-advancing acts, and (b) sequences of argument/response pairs characterized by disagreement repair and preference for agreement (Canary, Brossman, & Seibold, 1987; Canary et al., 1982; Meyers, 1987/1988; Seibold et al., 1981, 1983; Seibold & Meyers, 1986).

More recently, we have postulated that the system of group argument is characterized by at least three features (see Meyers, 1987/1988; also see Meyers & Seibold, in press). Preliminary qualitative analyses and coding of 45 group decision-making interactions reveal, first, that argument is constituted by *disagreement*. Arguables are advanced as potentially disagreeable utterances that evoke disputes that unfold over a series of interactions. Second, argument in these groups evidenced a process of increasingly overt *reason-giving* and *reason-defending*. Our preliminary research indicates that the groups' argument was aimed at examining, testing, and establishing the veridicality of members' reasons offered for a decision proposal. Third, our analyses demonstrate that group argument is typically characterized by *convergence-producing* activity. Although constituted in disputatious discourse, argument functions to move the group toward consensus. So while the *form* of argument is inherently based on disagreement, the ultimate *function* of argument is to forge agreement. In that sense, the stream of discourse manifesting argument centers on agreement production while at the same time reproducing a "disagreement" structure. This basic contradiction appears to be endemic to groups that must produce a final single outcome.

Our initial and preliminary work on argument-as-system begins to address how the SI view of argument might be subsumed within a structurational account. It offers glimpses of how argument is patterned in members' interaction, and provides the groundwork for detailing how argument surfaces, unfolds, and is sustained in group decision-making interaction. Less clear, however, is how the CI view fits into a structurational perspective on argument. The next section addresses that integration.

The CI view and structuration. Although it is clear that a structurational and CI view work from very different theoretical assumptions, the CI view is subsumable within a structurational framework on two fronts. First, both the CI view and structuration acknowledge that the practice of argument is constituted by knowledgeable agents. Second, both perspectives grant the collectively based nature of argument rules and resources. Consequently, the CI view of argument seems best integrated into a structurational perspective at the level of argument-as-structure — the rules and resources individuals use to produce, render meaningful, and maintain argument in the interactive context. Individuals' interpretive schemes regarding appropriate rules and resources allow them to understand and successfully accomplish the social practice of argument. This notion, in particular, is consistent with the PAT assumption that communities of individuals possess *standard* sets of arguments (i.e., resources) for given decision problems.

While a CI perspective accepts these standard sets of arguments as sole producers and predictors of argument processes, a structurational view treats them as a single element in a complex realm of interrelated factors. In the next section, we speculate on additional types of rules and resources members might use to produce and sustain argument, and suggest research strategies for determining whether or not such resources are viable components of the argument process. Two types of argument resources seem important to a structurational view of argument: (a) *collective* rules and resources shared by individuals in a given community or group, and (b) *individual* rules and resources voiced and sustained by group members in the group interaction.

Collectively shared rules and resources. It seems probable that individuals bring to the group argument situation collectively shared rules and resources regarding argument in general. One set of rules may include knowledge about how argument should proceed on a *conceptual* level. For example, individuals may share the view that argument is a logical, rational, issue-oriented activity in which one person wins and the other loses. Televised political debates, media coverage of debates on the floor of Congress, experience on debate teams in high school or college, and television news programs such as *Firing Line* and *Meet the Press* all inform a collectively shared understanding of what argument is and how it is accomplished. These collective conceptual orientations allow members to function coherently without overt verbalization of the underlying rules.

For that reason, validation of the existence of these conceptual frames is difficult. Access might be attained by asking individuals to write down their conceptions of argument, how they would define argument, what argument looks like, examples of arguments they remember, lists of adjectives they would use to describe argument, differences between argument and other discourse activities — conversations, conflict, discussion, among other possibilities. Similarly, individuals could be asked to view videotapes of argumentative interactions and to "talk aloud" during the viewing, describing what they see (Ericsson & Simon, 1984), how they interpret it, and reactions to the event in general. Employing multiple measures across many subjects may begin to illuminate general theories that individuals share regarding the practice of argument.

Complementing these research strategies must be a thorough examination of argumentative discourse itself. For example, group members in our group discussion data disregarded various arguments because they were "illogical" or "irrelevant." If such ideas are discovered to be common across groups, they may be indicative of deeper, underlying social/ideological commitments regarding how argument functions in discourse. If such statements evidence greater force than others in discussion (e.g., the group abandons the line of argument it was pursuing or the member of the group who voiced the argument is visibly embarrassed or withdraws the argument), a case might be made for a shared collective conception of argument as logical and rational, as well as what kinds of statements define the categories "logical" and "rational." Written and verbal protocol analysis (Vessey, 1988) and intensive analysis of group discussion transcripts should offer some insight into how individuals use collectively shared conceptions to produce an organized system of argument.

In addition to collectively shared conceptual interpretations, members may also share collective rules about how argument is to be accomplished *interactively*. Examination of the decision transcripts indicates that argument may be governed by conversational rules that differ from those found in friendlier conversations. For example, turn-taking appeared less sequential, with interruptions more readily tolerated than in general conversation. In addition, members were more likely to repeat themselves, reiterating the same argument several times in a short period, a communicative behavior rarely tolerated in other forms of discourse. Finally, members issued more blatant denials of others' ideas and opinions and used more emotional language. Knowledge of the rules of argumentative interaction and of how they differ from rules in other conversational activities allows individuals to appear competent and informed.

Researchers might begin to study these collectively shared rules regarding argumentative interaction by asking individuals to write down or voice how they think argumentative interactions differ from ordinary conversations and how their behavior changes (or remains the same) when they participate in an argument as opposed to a friendly conversation. Additionally, participants might be asked to recount *verbally* a recent argument or to comment upon an argument as they watch it on videotape. These research strategies might lend insight into the rules and norms individuals expect and follow in argumentative interaction. Simultaneously, these written and verbal protocols could be complemented by analyses of interactive discourse (utilizing discourse or conversational analysis techniques) to identify the use of various collective rules. Specifically, analysis of interruptions and how they function in argument (especially if compared to interruptions in other types of communicative activities) might indicate how individuals' collectively shared rules regarding *argument interaction* differ from those utilized in other forms of discourse.

Finally, members may share collective sets of *standard arguments* for particular decision problems. If PAT is correct on this count, then evidence of a standard set of arguments should be apparent in members' lists of cognitive arguments as well as their interactive argument activity. A first step might be to analyze the commonalities in members' lists of cognitive arguments for given decision tasks. Second, closer investigation of discussion arguments common across groups might indicate additional shared argument resources. Especially important might be the examination of members' amplification and justification of arguments to determine the types of collectively shared warrants and generalized arguments members use across groups and perhaps even across decision tasks.

Individual rules and resources. Besides collective types of rules and resources, members may also bring to the argument situation various individual resources. Different sets of rules or resources corresponding to various institutional practices may be introduced in group discussion by separate members of the group. While we locate these individual rules or resources in members' memory traces, implicit theories, or cognitive systems, unlike PAT proponents, we contend that they have a basis in socially or culturally derived knowledge structures. We speculate that these individual rules and resources are of at least two types: (a) individual interpretations of the task (Poole & Doelger, 1986), and (b) individual interpretations of how argument should proceed.

Poole and Doelger (1986) posit that group members enter group discussion either sharing a common interpretation of the task or possessing widely divergent interpretations. As group discussion unfolds, interaction displays individuals' common or variant task interpretations. As these authors explain, "Individual task representations are members' implicit theories about the decision; each member may hold a different representation. Each member's task representation guides his or her conduct in the discussion" (p. 52). We speculate that differing individual interpretations form the core of the group's argument activity, and are observable in the various arguments that members produce in discussion. When one member (or a coalition of members) presents an interpretation of the problem/task and that interpretation clashes with another group member's (or coalition of members') interpretation, argument ensues. The group seeks to work through these different interpretations in public interaction so that, in the end, a single collective interpretation is accomplished. If, or when, such an outcome is achieved, the group's argumentative activity ceases.

It seems probable that included in these individual interpretations are the "novel" arguments that undergird the PAT explanation of persuasion. An interesting challenge for future structurational research will be to discover how these individual interpretations enhance or constrain the practice of group argument. One possible explanation might be that novel arguments produce change in group interaction, while collective arguments maintain stability. For example, novel arguments might be examined for their impact in group discussion to change group opinion, redirect the group's discussion and thinking, or to help stimulate novel argument production by other group members. Additionally, novel arguments might be examined across *decision tasks* discussed by the same group. Examination of whether novel arguments presented in the initial discussion also reoccur in subsequent discussions might lend insight into how these arguments produce change in the group's analytical and argumentative procedures. In a structurational sense, the production of this novel argument may have important consequences for changes in the group's criteria for judging acceptable arguments in subsequent discussions.

In addition to individual interpretations and arguments, members may bring with them individual interpretations about how argument is to proceed in interaction. Family traditions may undergird the rules members utilize to accomplish argument. If reared in an atmosphere where heated, emotional, no-holds-barred arguments are accepted and deemed appropriate behavior, an individual might view name-calling, assertiveness, and perhaps even physical aggression as acceptable behavior in group argument as well. On the other hand, a group member reared in a family where argument rarely occurred might have difficulty understanding and rendering meaningful emotion-laden, hostile, aggressive argumentative discourse. Furthermore, members' experiences in groups like the one in which they find themselves enmeshed in argument may inform their expectations and practices concerning how argument will proceed in future groups.

Research might begin to investigate individuals' representations of how argument should be accomplished through the use of written or verbal protocols (similar to those indicated earlier) and examination of specific members' interaction across group situations. Common interactive behaviors may provide clues to the types of individual representations members bring to the argument situation. Such research might be especially enlightening for interpreting argument interactions in settings where members of varied backgrounds and assumptions must work together to produce consensual outcomes, such as organizational decision-making situations.

Finally, a structurational analysis must indicate not only how members' collective and individual rules and resources are produced in interaction, but also how their reproduction serves to position the individual in the interactive context. From a structurational view, the actor is not a stable nexus, but is produced and reproduced in group interaction (Poole et al., 1986). In interaction, members emerge as experts, devil's advocates, or jokesters, among other roles. The group's interaction reinforces and channels individuals toward certain positions and designated commitments.

In short, from a structurational view, the study of individual cognitive arguments (as defined by PAT) apart from the interactive context in which they function is incomplete. Similarly, the investigation of members' interactive arguments without studying their bases in collectively shared resources paints only half a picture. Study of the production and reproduction of both these elements is imperative. We believe that such an analysis is capable of offering a richer and more complete explanation of the group argument process. It not only describes how the observable system of argument unfolds in interaction, but also offers a framework for investigating *why* the system unfolds as it does. It is capable of detailing group members' actions as well as tying those actions to broader cultural and social institutions. It can account for how argument is produced in interaction and how it is reproduced. Finally, it is able to account for both the actor and the institution, for both stability and change, within a single coherent theory of argument as a social practice.

Example. While a complete illustration of a structurational analysis cannot be accomplished here, the example below indicates the additional insights a structurational analysis might render beyond those provided by the SI or CI perspective alone. The excerpt offered next is taken from our transcripts in which group members discussed a polarization item concerning whether an individual should attend graduate school at a prestigious university that offered no guarantee of graduating or a less prestigious university from which graduation was virtually guaranteed. This example is used to illustrate the increased understanding that accrues when argument-as-structure (individuals' use of rules and resources) is examined in conjunction with argument-as-system.

Tom: When you're talking, think of what they mean when they say the University of Illinois School of Engineering has prestige. They mean its the best damn education you can get.

Terry: Just think of all the guys in Engineering who got here and are getting, getting C's and D's. They're still getting jobs.

Kathy: No they don't.

Terry: I know a lot of them who do.

Kathy: I know a lot of them who don't.

Terry: I know a lot of them who do.

Kathy: No, if you're in Engineering, your grade point is everything. If you have a 4.0 or above, you got, you got the good jobs. You get $30,000 a year. I know people who get $30,000 all over the place. My boyfriend, my boyfriend only had a 3.6. Couldn't get a, you know, he got one. Now he's making $25,000, but it's a small company. The small companies take you. Those big companies, like IBM, like um . . .

Analysis of this dialogue from an argument-as-system view reveals that this group's interaction is characterized by constant questioning and testing of each others' propositions. Assumptions and assertions are challenged, members refuse to accept premises and propositions at face value, and constant disagreement permeates the discussion. Members offer reasons, explanations, and justifications. They force the argument into more complex lines of reason-establishing and reason-testing. Although space precludes a complete analysis of argument-as-system, such an undertaking should provide an exhaustive description of what is occurring at the surface level of argument and an explication of how interaction functions to produce the observable patterns – the social practice of argument.

When an analysis of argument-as-structure is added, the more complex nature of structurated argument is revealed. Members not only *question and test* others' assumptions, they use collectively shared rules and resources to interpret, understand, and inform their questioning and testing. This discussion, and the questioning and testing procedures, is perceived as relevant to the task because participants share knowledge about the social institutions of universities and organizations, and the link between these two types of institutions in the job market, as well as mutual interpretations that the process of arguing calls for testing and questioning of others' opinions. These collectively shared resources are tacitly invoked by the actors who (rightfully) assume them to be mutual knowledge among group members. All participants share knowledge about university grading systems, how grades affect job possibilities, how jobs are evaluated according to pay received, the differing status of various organizations in this country, the significance of obtaining a degree from a prestigious institution, and so on. Individuals make use of their knowledge of these factors to argue their opinions and to question the proposals of others successfully. Equally important to this analysis might be elements that the group chooses not to discuss. For example, members do not argue about the meaning of a C or D grade, what constitutes a grade point, or what IBM stands for. The fact that certain ideas are never discussed may indicate cultural beliefs so thoroughly shared that they do not require public appraisal.

Similarly, individuals invoke *individual*, novel arguments as available resources. Kathy's argument regarding her boyfriend represents her interpretation of this problem situation. How other group members respond to it and whether it functions as an agent of change could be investigated by observing members' comments later in discussion, by examining whether or not other members reiterate it or refer to it later in the transcript, and by determining whether or not other members extend or elaborate upon Kathy's example. In addition, this excerpt illustrates how members' interactions begin to produce and reproduce their positions in the group system. Kathy's example has potential to position her as an "expert," and/or Terry's contention (if proven wrong) may position her as uninformed. Members make use of shared resources and rules to render what they do intelligible. In the process of invoking these institutional orders, they also reproduce them. Social institutions such as grading systems, job requirements, and organizational status hierarchies are reproduced as legitimate social orders in the group's interaction. Analysis of these underlying rules and resources, how they are produced to create meaningful discourse and, subsequently, how they are reproduced in that discourse provides the foundation for a rich and illustrative view of group argument.

While this illustration merely scratches the surface of how a structurational analysis must proceed, it offers glimpses of how the CI and SI perspectives complement each other to produce a richer and more complex view of group argument but within a single framework. Only in the study of both argument-as-system and argument-as-structure can the duality of structure (i.e., structuration) be fully articulated.

CONCLUSION

Our focus in this chapter has been on theoretical explanations for the cognitive and social processes in polarization/choice shift groups, groups in which there are significant changes between members' prediscussion decision choices and either their collective postdiscussion decision (choice shift) or the average of their individual preferences following discussion (polarization). We have paid particular attention to persuasive arguments theory, which predicts postdiscussion polarization/choice shift outcomes from members' cognitive arguments in personal decision making *prior* to group discussion. The theory should be of special interest to group researchers in the communication discipline for two reasons: (a) Proponents of the perspective have supplied evidence that is generally supportive of PAT predictions — an important finding in an area in which other prominent theories have fallen by the wayside; (b) communication is relegated to a "carrier" role in this input-output perspective — a challenge to fundamental assumptions in our field about the transformative role of communication processes in the production of group outcomes.

The thrust of this chapter has been to offer a critical assessment of PAT, and, as with other cognitive-informational perspectives on argument in our field that we have discussed here and elsewhere (Meyers & Seibold, 1987), PAT has been found wanting in three respects. First, while PAT assumes that members' cognitive arguments are isomorphic with, and therefore substitutable for, arguments generated in discussion, empirical evidence from studies we recently reported revealed significant differences in number and content of arguments between members' cognitive and discussion arguments. Second, PAT proponents posit that members' group discussion is not essential for producing shifts. Yet, (a) research pitting noninteractional models of decision making — similar in character to PAT — against interactional forms of the same models showed input effects on group outcomes to be substantially mediated by interaction processes, and (b) research inside our field and by social psychologists has demonstrated that although choice shift can occur merely from group members' passive receipt of information outside of group discussion contexts, the magnitudes of shifts are strongest following group discussion. In short, there is strong reason to doubt PAT researchers' contentions concerning the sufficiency of noninteractional psychological processes for explaining choice shift. Third, although proponents cast PAT as a theory of *group* argument and *group* shifts, all analyses reported are conducted on individuals' arguments and decision preferences averaged across groups. Once again, the work of researchers outside our field and our own investigations indicate that PAT does not fare nearly as well when comparisons are made at the group level.

While it is essential to incorporate cognitive factors in explanations of communication-related phenomena such as group decision making, these difficulties with PAT underscore the limitations of accounts rooted solely in cognitive dynamics. Analyses of group decisions, no less than explanations of other social practices, must explain the *interplay* of cognitive and interactional forces affecting these outcomes.

In the last part of this chapter we drew upon the theory of structuration to erect a conceptual framework in which individual and social foci are wedded and in which communication is central. Our previous work has begun to reveal how argument is patterned in members' interaction, how argument is manifested in decision-making discussion. This effort extends that work by identifying a number of ways in which individual rules and resources may be drawn upon to produce and sustain argument, and by outlining research strategies for studying the ways in which these resources interpenetrate group argument practices. Although our worked example provides some of the richness afforded by a structurational analysis of micro-level dynamics in one decision-making group, the real test of this utility will rest in systematic qualitative and quantitative pursuit of the interconnections among micro- and macro-level processes as we attempt to build a structurational theory explaining how cognition and social interaction mediate each other in decision-making groups.

REFERENCES

Alderton, S. (1981). A processual analysis of argumentation in polarizing groups. In G. Ziegelmuller & J. Rhodes (Eds.), *Dimensions of argument: Proceedings of the second summer conference on argumentation* (pp. 693-703). Annandale, VA: Speech Communication Association.

Alderton, S. M. (1982). Locus of control-based argumentation as a predictor of group polarization. *Communication Quarterly, 30*, 381-387.

Alderton, S. M., & Frey, L. R. (1983). Effects of reactions to arguments on group outcome: The case of group polarization. *Central States Speech Journal, 34*, 88-95.

Baron, P. H., Baron, R. S., & Roper, G. (1974). External validity and the risky shift: Empirical limits and theoretical implications. *Journal of Personality and Social Psychology, 30*, 95-103.

Bateson, N. (1966). Familiarization, group discussion, and risk-taking. *Journal of Experimental Social Psychology, 2*, 119-129.

Bell, P. R., & Jamieson, B. D. (1970). Publicity of initial decisions and the risky shift phenomenon. *Journal of Experimental Social Psychology, 6*, 329-345.

Belovicz, M. W., & Finch, F. E. (1971). A critical analysis of the risky shift phenomenon. *Organizational Behavior and Human Performance, 6*, 150-168.

Bem, D. J., Wallach, M. A., & Kogan, N. (1965). Group decision making under risky or aversive consequences. *Journal of Personality and Social Psychology, 1*, 453-460.

Benoit, P. J. (1981). The use of argument by preschool children: The emergent production of rules for winning arguments. In G. Ziegelmuller & J. Rhodes (Eds.), *Dimensions of argument: Proceedings of the second summer conference on argumentation* (pp. 624-642). Annandale, VA: Speech Communication Association.

Benoit, P. J., Borzi, M., & Drew, S. (1984, April). *Prompting and closing arguments: Strategies used by social actors to initiate and terminate argument strategies.* Paper presented at the annual meeting of the Central States Speech Association, Chicago.

Benoit, W. L. (1985). The role of argumentation in source credibility. In J. R. Cox, M. O. Sillars, & G. B. Walker (Eds.), *Argument and social practice: Proceedings of the fourth SCA/AFA conference on argumentation* (pp. 592-603). Annandale, VA: Speech Communication Association.

Berger, C. (1985). Social power and interpersonal communication. In M. L. Knapp & G. R. Miller (Eds.), *Handbook of interpersonal communication* (pp. 439-499). Beverly Hills, CA: Sage.

Berger, C. R. (1987). Communicating under uncertainly. In M. E. Roloff & G. R. Miller (Eds.), *Interpersonal processes: New directions in communication research* (pp. 39-62). Newbury Park, CA: Sage.

Berger, C. R., & Roloff, M. E. (1982). Thinking about friends and lovers: Social cognition and relational trajectories. In M. E. Roloff & C. R. Berger (Eds.), *Social cognition and communication* (pp. 151-192). Beverly Hills, CA: Sage.

Bishop, G. D., & Myers, D. G. (1974). Informational influence in group discussion. *Organizational Behavior and Human Performance, 12*, 92-104.

Boster, F. J., Fryrear, J. E., Mongeau, P. A., & Hunter, J. E. (1982). An unequal speaking linear discrepancy model: Implications for the polarity shift. In M. Burgoon (Ed.), *Communication yearbook 6* (pp. 395-418). Beverly Hills, CA: Sage.

Boster, F. J., & Hale, J. L. (1983, May). *Social comparison and the polarity shift.* Paper presented at the annual meeting of the International Communication Association, Dallas.

Boster, F. J., Hale, J. L., Mongeau, P. A., & Hale, J. (1985, May). *The validity of choice dilemma response scales.* Paper presented at the annual meeting of the International Communication Association, Honolulu.

Boster, F. J., & Mayer, M. E. (1984, May). *Differential argument quality mediates the impact of a social comparison process of the choice shift.* Paper presented at the annual meeting of the International Communication Association, San Francisco.

Boster, F. J., Mayer, M. E., Hunter, J. E., & Hale, J. L. (1980). Expanding the persuasive arguments explanation of the polarity shift: A linear discrepancy model. In D. Nimmo (Ed.), *Communication yearbook 4* (pp. 165-176). New Brunswick, NJ: Transaction.

Brown, G., & Yule, G. (1983). *Discourse analysis.* Cambridge: Cambridge University Press.

Burleson, B. R. (1979). On the analysis and criticism of arguments: Some theoretical and methodological considerations. *Journal of the American Forensic Association, 16,* 112-127.

Burleson, B. R. (1980a, November). *Argument and constructivism: The cognitive-developmental component.* Paper presented at the annual meeting of the Speech Communication Association, New York.

Burleson, B. R. (1980b). The development of interpersonal reasoning: An analysis of message strategy justifications. *Journal of the American Forensic Association, 17,* 102-110.

Burleson, B. R. (1981). A cognitive-developmental perspective on social reasoning processes. *Western Journal of Speech Communication, 45,* 133-147.

Burleson, B. R. (1982, April). *Foundations for the study of argument: Assumptions and contributions of the cognitive-developmental perspective.* Paper presented at the annual meeting of the Central States Speech Association, Milwaukee.

Burleson, B. R. (1983). Interactional antecedents of social reasoning development: Interpreting the effects of parent discipline on children. In D. Zarefsky, M. O. Sillars, & J. Rhodes (Eds.), *Argument in transition: Proceedings of the third summer conference on argumentation* (pp. 597-610). Annandale, VA: Speech Communication Association.

Burnstein, E. (1969). An analysis of group decisions involving risk ("the risky shift"). *Human Relations, 22,* 381-395.

Burnstein, E. (1982). Persuasion as argument processing. In H. Brandstatter, J. H. Davis, & G. Stocker-Kreichgauer (Eds.), *Group decision making* (pp. 103-124). New York: Academic Press.

Burnstein, E., & Sentis, K. (1981). Attitude polarization in groups. In R. E. Petty, R. M. Ostrom, & T. C. Brock (Eds.), *Cognitive responses in persuasion* (pp. 197-216). Hillsdale, NJ: Lawrence Erlbaum.

Burnstein, E., & Vinokur, A. (1973). Testing two classes of theories about group induced shift in individual choice. *Journal of Experimental Social Psychology, 9,* 123-137.

Burnstein, E., & Vinokur, A. (1975). What a person thinks upon learning he has chosen differently from others: Nice evidence for the persuasive arguments explanation of choice shifts. *Journal of Experimental Psychology, 11,* 412-426.

Burnstein, E., & Vinokur, A. (1977). Persuasive argumentation and social comparison as determinants of attitude polarization. *Journal of Experimental Social Psychology, 13,* 315-332.

Burnstein, E., Vinokur, A., & Pichevin, M. F. (1974). What do differences between own, admired, and attributed choices have to do with group induced shifts in choice? *Journal of Experimental Social Psychology, 10,* 428-443.

Burnstein, E., Vinokur, A., & Trope, Y. (1973). Interpersonal comparison versus persuasive argumentation: A more direct test of alternative explanations for group induced shifts in individual choice. *Journal of Experimental Social Psychology, 9,* 236-245.

Canary, D. J., Brossman, B. G., & Seibold, D. R. (1987). Argument structures in decision-making groups. *Southern Speech Communication Journal, 53,* 18-57.

Canary, D. J., Ratledge, N. T., & Seibold, D. R. (1982, November). *Argument and group decision-making: Development of a coding scheme.* Paper presented at the annual meeting of the Speech Communication Association, Louisville, KY.

Cappella, J. N., & Folger, J. P. (1980). An information processing explanation of attitude-behavior inconsistency. In D. P. Cushman & R. McPhee (Eds.), *The message-attitude-behavior relationship* (pp. 149-193). New York: Academic Press.

Cartwright, D. (1971). Risk taking by individuals and groups: An assessment of research employing choice dilemmas. *Journal of Personality and Social Psychology, 20,* 361-378.

Cartwright, D. (1973). Determinants of scientific progress: The case of the risky shift. *American Psychologist, 28,* 222-231.

Cegala, D. J., Alexander, A. F., & Sokuvitz, S. (1979). An investigation of eye gaze and its relation to selected verbal behavior. *Human Communication Research, 5,* 99-108.

Clark, R. D., & Willems, E. P. (1969). Where is the risky shift? Dependence on instructions. *Journal of Personality and Social Psychology, 13,* 215-221.

Cline, T. R., & Cline, R. J. (1979). Risky and cautious decision shifts in small groups. *Southern Speech Communication Journal, 44,* 252-263.

Cline, T. R., & Cline, R. J. (1980). A structural analysis of risky-shift and cautious shift discussions: The diffusion-of-responsibility theory. *Communication Quarterly, 28,* 26-36.

Collins, B. E., & Guetzkow, H (1964). *A social psychology of group processes for decision-making.* New York: John Wiley.

Dallinger, J. M., & Hample, D. (1986, April). *Argumentativeness and cognitive editing of arguments.* Paper presented at the annual meeting of the Central States Speech Association, Cincinnati.

Davis, J. H. (1973). Group decisions and social interaction: A theory of social decision schemes. *Psychological Review, 80,* 97-125.

Davis, J. H. (1986). Foreword. In R. Y. Hirokawa & M. S. Poole (Eds.), *Communication and group decision-making* (pp. 7-12). Beverly Hills, CA: Sage.

Davis, J. H., & Hinsz, V. B. (1982). Current research problems in group performance and group dynamics. In H. Brandstatter, J. H. Davis, & G. Stocker-Kreichgauer (Eds.), *Group decision making* (pp. 1-20). New York: Academic Press.

Davis, J. H., Kerr, N. L., Sussman, M., & Rissman, A. K. (1974). Social decision schemes under risk. *Journal of Personality and Social Psychology, 30,* 248-271.

Dillard, J. P., Omdahl, B. L., & Segrin, C. (1988, May). *Attributions and expectations about interpersonal influence attempts.* Paper presented at the annual meeting of the International Communication Association, New Orleans.

Dion, K., Baron, R., & Miller, N. (1978). Why do groups make riskier decisions than individuals? In L. Berkowitz (Ed.), *Group processes* (pp. 227-299). New York: Academic Press.

Doise, W. (1969). Intergroup relations and polarization of individual and collective judgments. *Journal of Personality and Social Psychology, 12,* 136-143.

Ericsson, K. A., & Simon, H. A. (1984). *Protocol analysis: Verbal reports as data.* Cambridge: MIT Press.

Fishbein, M. (1967). *Readings in attitude theory and measurement.* New York: John Wiley.

Flanders, J. P., & Thistlethwaite, D. L. (1967). Effects of familiarization and group discussion upon risk-taking. *Journal of Personality and Social Psychology, 5,* 91-97.

Frey, L. R., & Alderton, S. M. (1983, August). *A content analytic scheme for the study of argumentation in decision-making groups.* Paper presented at the Third Summer Conference on Argumentation, Alta, UT.

Giddens A. (1974). *The class structure of the advanced societies.* New York: Harper & Row.

Giddens, A. (1976). *New rules of sociological method.* New York: Basic Books.

Giddens, A. (1979). *Central problems in social theory.* Berkeley: University of California Press.

Giddens, A. (1984). *The constitution of society: Outline of the theory of structuration.* Berkeley: University of California Press.

Greene, J. O., Smith, S. W., & Lindsey, A. E. (1988, May). *Of things unseen: Searching for cognitive representations of compliance-gaining acts.* Paper presented at the annual meeting of the International Communication Association, New Orleans.

Hale, J. L. (1984, May). *The effect of ambiguity on polarity shift processes.* Paper presented at the annual meeting of the International Communication Association, San Francisco.

Hale, J. L., & Boster, F. J. (1987, May). *A test of persuasive arguments, social comparison, and dual process models of choice shifts.* Paper presented at the annual meeting of the International Communication Association, Montreal.

Hale, J. L., & Boster, F. J. (1988, May). *Ambiguity as a moderator of decision-making processes.* Paper presented at the annual meeting of the International Communication Association, New Orleans.

Hample, D. (1977). Testing a model of value argument and evidence. *Communication Monographs, 44,* 106-120.

Hample, D. (1980). A cognitive view of argument. *Journal of the American Forensic Association, 17,* 151-158.

Hample, D. (1981). The cognitive context of argument. *Western Journal of Speech Communication, 45,* 148-158.

Hample, D. (1984, April). *Roads not taken, arguments not made.* Paper presented at the annual meeting of the Central States Speech Association, Chicago.

Hample, D. (1985). A third perspective on argument. *Philosophy and Rhetoric, 18,* 1-22.

Hample, D. (1988). Argument: Public and private, social and cognitive. *Journal of the American Forensic Association, 25,* 13-19.

Hample, D., & Dallinger, J. M. (1985a, November). *Cognitive editing of argument strategies.* Paper presented at the annual meeting of the Speech Communication Association, Denver.

Hample, D., & Dallinger, J. M. (1985b). Unused compliance gaining strategies. In J. R. Cox, M. O. Sillars, & G. B. Walker (Eds.), *Argument and social practice: Proceedings of the fourth SCA/AFA conference on argumentation* (pp. 675-691). Annandale, VA: Speech Communication Association.

Hample, D., & Dallinger, J. M. (1986). *Individual differences in cognitive editing standards.* Unpublished manuscript, Western Illinois University.

Hample, D., & Dallinger, J. M. (1987). The judgment phase of invention. In F. H. van Eemeren, R. Grootendorst, J. A. Blair, & C. A. Willard (Eds.), *Argumentation: Perspectives and approaches — proceedings of the conference on argumentation 1986* (pp. 225-235). Dordrecht, Netherlands: Foris.

Hewes, D. E. (1979, November). *Discourse can't "behave": Structure, structure, where is the structure?* Paper presented at the annual meeting of the Speech Communication Association, San Antonio, TX.

Hewes, D. E. (1986). A socio-egocentric approach to small group communication. In R. Y. Hirokawa & M. S. Poole (Eds.), *Communication and group decision-making* (pp. 265-291). Beverly Hills, CA: Sage.

Hewes, D. E. (1988, May). *Small group research: Are we asking the right questions and are we answering them well?* Paper presented at the annual meeting of the International Communication Association, New Orleans.

Hewes, D. E., & Planalp, S. (1982). There is nothing as useful as a good theory . . . : The influence of social knowledge on interpersonal communication. In M. E. Roloff & C. R. Berger (Eds.), *Social cognition and communication* (pp. 107-150). Beverly Hills, CA: Sage.

Hewes, D. E., & Planalp, S. (1987). The individual's place in communication science. In C. R. Berger & S. H. Chaffee (Eds.), *Handbook of communication science* (pp. 146-183). Newbury Park, CA: Sage.

Hinsz, V. B. (1981). *Persuasive arguments, group polarization and choice shifts.* Unpublished master's thesis, University of Illinois, Urbana-Champaign.

Hinsz, V. B., & Davis, J. H. (1984). Persuasive arguments theory, group polarization, and choice shifts. *Personality and Social Psychology Bulletin, 10,* 260-268.

Hoffman, L. R. (1979). *The group problem-solving process: Studies of a valence model.* New York: Praeger.

Jackson, S. (1983). The arguer in interpersonal argument: Pros and cons of individual-level analysis. In D. Zarefsky, M. O. Sillars, & J. Rhodes (Eds.), *Argument in transition: Proceedings of the third summer conference on argumentation* (pp. 631-637). Annandale, VA: Speech Communication Association.

Jackson, S., & Jacobs, S. (1980). Structure of conversational argument: Pragmatic cases for the enthymeme. *Quarterly Journal of Speech, 66*, 251-265.

Jackson, S., & Jacobs, S. (1981). The collaborative production of proposals in conversational argument and persuasion: A study of disagreement regulation. *Journal of the American Forensic Association, 18*, 77-90.

Jacobs, S., & Jackson, S. (1981). Argument as a natural category: The routine grounds for arguing in conversation. *Western Journal of Speech Communication, 45*, 111-117.

Jacobs, S., & Jackson, S. (1982). Conversational argument: A discourse analytic approach. In J. R. Cox & C. A. Willard (Eds.), *Advances in argumentation theory and research* (pp. 205-237). Carbondale: Southern Illinois University Press.

Jarboe, S. (1988). A comparison of input-output, process-output, and input-process-output models of small group problem-solving effectiveness. *Communication Monographs, 55*, 121-142.

Kellermann, K. (1987). Information exchange in social interaction. In M. E. Roloff & G. R. Miller (Eds.), *Interpersonal processes: New directions in communication research* (pp. 188-219). Newbury Park, CA: Sage.

Kellermann, K., & Jarboe, S. (1987). Conservatism in judgment: Is the risky shift-ee really risky, really? In M. L. McLaughlin (Ed.), *Communication yearbook 10* (pp. 259-282). Newbury Park, CA: Sage.

Kogan, N., & Wallach, M. A. (1967). Risky-shift phenomenon in small decision-making groups: A test of the information-exchange hypothesis. *Journal of Experimental Social Psychology, 3*, 75-84.

Lamm, H. (1967). Will an observer advise higher risk taking after hearing a discussion of the decision problem? *Journal of Personality and Social Psychology, 6*, 467-471.

Laughlin, P. R., & Earley, P. C. (1982). Social combination model, persuasive arguments theory, social comparison theory, and choice shift. *Journal of Personality and Social Psychology, 42*, 273-280.

Madaras, G. R., & Bem, D. J. (1968). Risk and conservatism in group decision-making. *Journal of Experimental Social Psychology, 4*, 350-365.

Madsen, D. B. (1978). Issue importance and group choice shifts: A persuasive arguments approach. *Journal of Personality and Social Psychology, 36*, 1118-1127.

Marquis, D. G. (1962). Individual responsibility and group decisions involving risk. *Industrial Management, 3*, 8-23.

Mayer, M. E. (1985). Explaining choice shift: An effects coded model. *Communication Monographs, 52*, 92-101.

McGuire, W. J. (1960). A syllogistic analysis of cognitive relationships. In M. J. Rosenberg, (Eds.), *Attitude organization and change* (pp. 65-111). New Haven, CT: Yale University Press.

McPhee, R. D., & Poole, M. S. (1980, November). *The theory of structuration as a metatheory for communication research*. Paper presented at the annual meeting of the Speech Communication Association, New York.

McPhee, R. D., Poole, M. S., & Seibold, D. R. (1981). The valence model unveiled: A critique and reformulation. In M. Burgoon (Ed.), *Communication yearbook 5* (pp. 259-277). New Brunswick, NJ: Transaction.

Meyers, R. A. (1988). Argument and group decision-making: An interactional test of persuasive arguments theory and an alternative structurational perspective (Doctoral dissertation, University of Illinois, Urbana-Champaign, 1987). *Dissertation Abstracts International, 49*, 12A.

Meyers, R. A. (in press). Persuasive arguments theory: A test of assumptions. *Human Communication Research*.

Meyers, R. A., & Seibold, D. R. (1987). Interactional and non-interactional perspectives on interpersonal argument: Implications for the study of group decision-making. In F. H. van Eemeren, R. Grootendorst, J. A. Blair, & C. A. Willard (Eds.), *Argumentation: Perspectives and approaches — proceedings of the conference on argumentation 1986* (pp. 205-214). Dordrecht, Netherlands: Foris.

Meyers, R. A., & Seibold, D. R. (1988, May). *Testing persuasive argument theory's predictor model: Alternative interactional accounts of group argument and influence.* Paper presented at the annual meeting of the International Communication Association, New Orleans.

Meyers, R. A., & Seibold, D. R. (in press). Persuasive arguments and group influence: Research evidence and strategic implications. In M. J. Cody & M. L. McLaughlin (Eds.), *Psychology of tactical communication.* Clevedon, England: Multilingual Matters.

Moscovici, S., & Lecuyer, R. (1972). Studies in group decision I: Social space, patterns of communication and group consensus. *European Journal of Social Psychology, 2,* 221-244.

Moscovici, S., & Zavalloni, M. (1969). The group as a polarizer of attitudes. *Journal of Personality and Social Psychology, 12,* 125-135.

Myers, D. G. (1975). Discussion-induced attitude polarization. *Human Relations, 28,* 699-714.

Myers, D. G., & Arenson, S. J. (1972). Enhancement of dominant risky tendencies in group discussion. *Psychological Reports, 30,* 615-623.

Myers, D. G., & Bishop, G. D. (1970). Discussion effects on racial attitudes. *Science, 169,* 778-779.

Myers, D. G., & Lamm, A. (1976). The group polarization phenomenon. *Psychological Bulletin, 83,* 602-627.

O'Keefe, B. J., & Benoit, P. J. (1982). Children's arguments. In J. R. Cox & C. A. Willard (Eds.), *Advances in argumentation theory and research* (pp. 154-183). Carbondale: Southern Illinois University Press.

O'Keefe, B. J., & Delia, J. G. (1982). Impression formation and message production. In M. E. Roloff & C. R. Berger (Eds.), *Social cognition and communication* (pp. 33-72). Beverly Hills, CA: Sage.

O'Keefe, D. J. (1977). Two ... epts of argument. *Journal of the American Forensic Association, 13,* 121-128.

Petty, R. E., & Ostrom, T. M. (1981). Historical foundations of the cognitive response approach to attitudes and persuasion. In R. E. Petty, T. M. Ostrom, & T. C. Brock (Eds.), *Cognitive responses in persuasion* (pp. 5-29). Hillsdale, NJ: Lawrence Erlbaum.

Planalp, S. (1985). Relational schemata: A test of alternative forms of relational knowledge as guides to communication. *Human Communication Research, 12,* 3-29.

Planalp, S. (1986). Scripts, story grammars, and causal schemas. In D. G. Ellis & W. A. Donohue (Eds.), *Contemporary issues in language and discourse processes.* Hillsdale, NJ: Lawrence Erlbaum.

Planalp, S., & Hewes, D. E. (1982). A cognitive approach to communication theory: Cogito ergo dico? In M. Burgoon (Ed.), *Communication yearbook 5* (pp. 49-77). New Brunswick, NJ: Transaction.

Planalp, S., & Tracy, K. (1980). Not to change the topic but . . . : A cognitive approach to the management of conversation. In D. Nimmo (Ed.), *Communication yearbook 4* (pp. 237-258). New Brunswick, NJ: Transaction.

Poole, M. S. (1980, November). *Structuration and the problem of reification.* Paper presented at the annual meeting of the Speech Communication Association, New York.

Poole, M. S., & Doelger, J. A. (1986). Developmental processes in group decision-making. In R. Y. Hirokawa & M. S. Poole (Eds.), *Communication and group decision-making* (pp. 35-62). Beverly Hills, CA: Sage.

Poole, M. S., McPhee, R. D., & Seibold, D. R. (1982). A comparison of normative and interactional explanations of group decision-making: Social decision schemes versus valence distributions. *Communication Monographs, 49,* 1-19.

Poole, M. S., Seibold, D. R. & McPhee, R. D. (1985). Group decision-making as a structurational process. *Quarterly Journal of Speech, 71,* 74-102.

Poole, M. S., Seibold, D. R., & McPhee, R. D. (1986). Group decision-making and theory development: A structurational approach. In R. Hirokawa & M. S. Poole (Eds.), *Communication and group decision-making* (pp. 237-264). Beverly Hills, CA: Sage.

Pruitt, D. G. (1971a). Choice shifts in group discussion: An introductory review. *Journal of Personality and Social Psychology, 20,* 339-360.

Pruitt, D. G. (1971b). Conclusions: Toward an understanding of choice shifts in group discussion. *Journal of Personality and Social Psychology, 20,* 495-510.

Roloff, M. E., & Berger, C. R. (1982). Social cognition and communication: An introduction. In M. E. Roloff & C. R. Berger (Eds.), *Social cognition and communication* (pp. 9-32). Beverly Hills, CA: Sage.

St. Jean, R., & Percival, E. (1974). The role of argumentation and comparison processes in choice shifts: Another assessment. *Canadian Journal of Behavioural Science, 6,* 297-308.

Seibold, D. R., Canary, D. J., & Tanita-Ratledge, N. (1980, November). *Argument and group decision making: Interim report on a structurational research program.* Paper presented at the annual meeting of the Speech Communication Association, Washington, DC.

Seibold, D. R., McPhee, R. D., Poole, M. S., Tanita, N. E., & Canary, D. J. (1981). Argument, group influence, and decision outcomes. In G. Ziegelmuller & J. Rhodes (Eds.), *Dimensions of argument: Proceedings of the second summer conference on argumentation* (pp. 663-692). Annandale, VA: Speech Communication Association.

Seibold, D. R., & Meyers, R. A. (1986). Communication and influence in group decision-making. In R. Y. Hirokawa & M. S. Poole (Eds.), *Communication and group decision-making* (pp. 133-156). Beverly Hills, CA: Sage.

Seibold, D. R., Poole, M. S., & McPhee, R. D. (1980, April). *New directions in small group research.* Paper presented at the annual meeting of the Central States Speech Association, Chicago.

Sillars, A. L. (1980a). Attributions and communication in roommate conflict. *Communication Monographs, 47,* 180-200.

Sillars, A. L. (1980b). The sequential and distributional structure of conflict interactions as a function of attributions concerning the locus of responsibility and stability of conflicts. In D. Nimmo (Ed.), *Communication yearbook 4* (pp. 217-237). New Brunswick, NJ: Transaction.

Smith, M. J. (1982). Cognitive schemata and persuasive communication: Toward a contingency rules theory. In M. Burgoon (Ed.), *Communication yearbook 6* (pp. 330-362). Beverly Hills, CA: Sage.

Smith, M. J. (1984). Contingency rules theory, context, and compliance behaviors. *Human Communication Research, 10,* 489-512.

Stasser, G., Kerr, N. L., & Davis, J. H. (1980). Influence processes in decision-making groups: A modeling approach. In P. B. Paulus (Ed.), *Psychology of group influence* (pp. 431-477). Hillsdale, NJ: Lawrence Erlbaum.

Steiner, I. D. (1983). Whatever happened to the touted revival of the group? In H. H. Blumberg, A. P. Hare, V. Kent, & M. Davies (Eds.), *Small groups and social interaction* (Vol. 2, pp. 539-547). Chichester: John Wiley.

Stoner, J.A.F. (1961). *A comparison of individual and group decisions involving risk.* Unpublished master's thesis, Massachusetts Institute of Technology.

Stoner, J.A.F. (1968). Risky and cautious shifts in group decisions: The influence of widely held values. *Journal of Experimental Social Psychology, 4,* 442-459.

Taylor, S. E., & Crocker, J. (1981). Schematic bases of social information processing. In E. T. Higgins, P. Herman, & M. P. Zanna (Eds.), *Social cognition: The Ontario Symposium* (Vol. 1, pp. 89-134). Hillsdale, NJ: Lawrence Erlbaum.

Teger, A. I., & Pruitt, D. G. (1967). Components of group risk taking. *Journal of Experimental Social Psychology, 3,* 189-205.

Trapp, R. (1982, November). *Some generic characteristics of argument.* Paper presented at the annual meeting of the Speech Communication Association, Louisville, KY.

Trapp, R. (1983). Generic characteristics of argumentation in everyday discourse. In D. Zarefsky, M. O. Sillars, & J. Rhodes (Eds.), *Argument in transition: Proceedings of the third summer conference on argumentation* (pp. 516-530). Annandale, VA: Speech Communication Association.

Trapp, R., & Hoff, N. (1985). A model of serial argument in interpersonal relationships. *Journal of the American Forensic Association, 22,* 1-11.

Trommsdorff, G. (1982). Group influences on judgments concerning the future. In M. Irle & L. B. Katz (Eds.), *Studies in decision making* (pp. 145-166). Berlin: Walter de Gruyter.

Vessey, I. (1988, August). *Introduction to concurrent verbal protocol analysis.* Paper presented at the annual meeting of the Academy of Management, Anaheim, CA.

Vidmar, N., & Burdeny, T. C. (1971). Effects of group size and item type on the "risky shift" effect. *Canadian Journal of Behavioural Science, 3,* 393-407.

Vinokur, A. (1971). Review and theoretical analysis of the effects of group processes upon individual and group decisions involving risk. *Psychological Bulletin, 76,* 231-250.

Vinokur, A., & Burnstein, E. (1974). Effects of partially shared persuasive arguments on group induced shifts: A group problem-solving approach. *Journal of Personality and Social Psychology, 29,* 305-315.

Vinokur, A., & Burnstein, E. (1978a). Depolarization of attitudes in groups. *Journal of Personality and Social Psychology, 36,* 872-885.

Vinokur, A., & Burnstein, E. (1978b). Novel argumentation and attitude change: The case of polarization following group discussion. *European Journal of Social Psychology, 8,* 335-348.

Vinokur, A., Trope, Y., & Burnstein, E. (1975). A decision-making analysis of persuasive argumentation and the choice-shift effect. *Journal of Experimental Social Psychology, 11,* 127-148.

Wallach, M. A., & Kogan, N. (1965). The roles of information, discussion, and consensus in group risk taking. *Journal of Experimental Social Psychology, 1,* 1-19.

Wallach, M. A., Kogan, N., & Bem, D. J. (1962). Group influence on individual risk taking. *Journal of Abnormal and Social Psychology, 65,* 75-86.

Wallach, M. A., Kogan, N., & Bem, D. J. (1964). Diffusion of responsibility and level of risk taking in groups. *Journal of Abnormal and Social Psychology, 68,* 263-274.

Wallach, M. A., Kogan, N., & Burt, R. B. (1965). Can group members recognize the effects of group discussion upon risk taking? *Journal of Experimental Social Psychology, 1,* 379-395.

Warriner, C. H. (1956). Groups are real: A reaffirmation. *American Sociological Review, 21,* 549-554.

Willard, C. A. (1976). On the utility of descriptive diagrams for the analysis and criticism of arguments. *Communication Monographs, 43,* 308-319.

Willard, C. A. (1978, November). *Epistemological functions of argument studies: A constructivist/interactionist view.* Paper presented at the annual meeting of the Speech Communication Association, Minneapolis, MN.

Willard, C. A. (1979). The epistemic functions of argument: Reasoning and decision-making from a constructivist/interactionist point of view. *Journal of the American Forensic Association, 15,* 169-191.

Willard, C. A. (1981). The status of the non-discursiveness thesis. *Journal of the American Forensic Association, 17,* 190-214.

Wyer, R. S. (1974a). *Cognitive organization and change: An information-processing approach.* Hillsdale, NJ: Lawrence Erlbaum.

Wyer, R. S. (1974b). Some implications of the "Socratic effect" for alternative models of cognitive consistency. *Journal of Personality, 42,* 399-419.

Wyer, R. S. (1975). The role of probabilistic and syllogistic reasoning in cognitive organization and social inference. In M. Kaplan & S. Schwartz (Eds.), *Human judgment and decision processes* (pp. 229-269). New York: Academic Press.

Group Argument, Social Pressure, and the Making of Group Decisions

FRANKLIN J. BOSTER
Michigan State University

R ENEWED interest in choice shift through group argument is due largely to a theoretical controversy, persuasive arguments theory (PAT) and social comparison theory (SCT) being the competing explanations. Central to PAT is the axiom that the choice shift results from informational influences, particularly the persuasive arguments that are advanced during group discussion, whereas SCT posits that normative influence, or group pressure, exerts the most important causal impact on group decisions. In the chapter that is the focus of this comment, Meyers and Seibold do not address the issue of normative influence, leaving us with the assertion that "currently the most prominent theory in the area of decision shifts is persuasive arguments theory" (p. XXX). But the authors' goal is to develop a grand theory of group decision making, and in so doing they commit a sin of omission by dismissing an important component in the process. There is strength in numbers as well as in arguments, and any complete explanation of the choice shift in particular, and group decision making in general, must account for both.

In the remarks that follow I first discuss the relative roles of argument and social pressure in modifying attitudes and shaping group decisions. Next, the utility of the concept of argument for predicting group decisions is considered. Finally, the process by which arguments combine to affect attitudes and decisions, when they do, is addressed.

Correspondence and requests for reprints: Franklin J. Boster, Department of Communication, Michigan State University, East Lansing, MI 48824.

Communication Yearbook 13, pp. 303-312

INFORMATIONAL AND NORMATIVE INFLUENCE

The distinction between informational and normative influence was, to my knowledge, first made by Deutsch and Gerard (1955), although Festinger's (1950) work certainly suggested it. Furthermore, this distinction has been expanded substantially as scholars have observed other processes of social influence (e.g., French & Raven, 1968; Kelman, 1961), although the nature of choice shift experiments is such that processes such as identification and legitimate power are unlikely to influence these group decisions.

According to Deutsch and Gerard (1955), "An *informational social influence* may be defined as an influence to accept information obtained from another as *evidence* about reality" (p. 630). An argument certainly has the potential to influence group members in this way, but, as we know from a long history of persuasion research conducted in the passive communication context, arguments, even sound ones, do not always affect persons' attitudes or behavior. So, for example, even strong and numerous arguments lack suasive force when involvement is low (Chaiken, 1980; Petty, Cacioppo, & Goldman, 1981; Stiff, 1986).

According to Deutsch and Gerard (1955), *normative social influence* refers to "an influence to conform with the positive expectations of another" (p. 629). Subsequent elucidation of this concept indicates that it includes those instances in which one conforms, but without any corresponding change in attitude. In Festinger's (1950) terms, there is public conformity without private acceptance, or, as Kelman (1961) prefers it, there is compliance.

Group pressure has the potential to affect group members in this way, as can be seen from several classic experiments (Asch, 1956; Sherif, 1935), although there are conditions under which, and persons for whom, group pressure is relatively ineffectual. For example, Moscovici's research program emphasizes how group members taking a minority position are able not only to resist group pressure, but also to influence the majority (e.g., Moscovici & Faucheux, 1972), and Tanford and Penrod's (1984) review of the minority influence research literature concludes that minorities can affect majorities when the group is small, the minority is greater than one, and the minority is consistent in asserting its position. Furthermore, Crutchfield (1955) demonstrates that the influence of group pressure decreases as the ambiguity of the stimulus decreases, and that it is less effective when group members are low in authoritarianism, high in ego strength, and high in intellectual competence.

Deutsch and Gerard (1955) conclude that both processes affect group judgments and decisions, a conclusion endorsed by those who have reviewed the choice shift literature (Isenberg, 1986; Myers & Lamm, 1976). The difficulty, however, is in sorting out their effects. Suppose that I observe a group member advance an argument during discussion, and I also observe a subsequent change in the positions taken by the other group members. PAT theorists would claim these observations to be consistent with their theory, but SCT theorists could argue that these data were consistent with their thinking as well, concluding that it was the *mere statement of opinion, or conclusion, not the argument, that changed the other group members.* Or, to take another commonly cited pro-PAT datum, the larger choice shifts produced by group discussion could be explained by SCT theorists as being due to increased group pressure resulting from the greater amount of time available to state and restate opinions.

Alternatively, suppose that I observe group members advance opinions without reasons to back them, and I also observe subsequent change in the positions of other group members. SCT theorists would claim these observations as consistent with their theory, but PAT theorists could argue that these data were consistent with PAT as well, concluding that *the opinion statements included implicit arguments and that it was these implicit arguments, rather than the group pressure, that changed the group members.*

While I am reluctant to accept the soundness of such conclusions completely, the confound of opinion statements and arguments, be they explicit or implicit, makes it difficult to observe the content of group interaction and to separate informational and normative influence. As a result, some have tried to separate the effects experimentally. One method of approaching this task has been the previously mentioned tactic of having group members state their opinions either without discussion (mere exposure treatment) or with discussion (group discussion treatment).

An alternative method involves varying both item content and group composition (Boster, Fryrear, Mongeau, & Hunter, 1982). Given that there is a larger pool of pro-risky (or cautious) arguments associated with a choice dilemma (CD) item that commonly produces a risky shift, a difference in the magnitude of the shift in discussions of a risky item can imply informational influence effects when group composition is controlled. And group composition can be controlled by assigning varying numbers of pro-risky and pro-cautious group members, these assignments made on the basis of pretest judgments. So, for instance, if a group composed of two pro-caution persons and one pro-risk person is discussing a CD item that yields a consistent risky shift, then a risky shift from that group implies the presence of informational influence, while a cautious shift implies the presence of normative influence.

Although it does not incorporate group discussion, another alternative is to expose persons to tapes of group discussions. These tapes can be created so that both arguments and group composition are controlled. So, for example, Michael Mayer and I pretested the persuasiveness of arguments and exposed persons to a tape of a group discussion in which both the group majority (pro-risk, pro-caution) and argument quality (strong, weak) were crossed (Boster & Mayer, 1984). In this design, argument effect indicates the presence of informational influence, and a majority effect indicates the presence of normative influence.

Given the importance of both informational and normative influence processes, experiments such as these allow one to probe the ways in which these processes combine to produce the choice shift. And there are several ways in which they could combine. One possibility is that both types of influence exert a direct effect on the magnitude of the choice shift, and their respective contributions are additive. Borrowing analysis of variance terminology, if the choice shift is the dependent variable and normative and informational influence are represented by two experimental factors, then there is a main effect for both factors but no interaction effect. Data consistent with this hypothesis have been reported (Boster et al., 1982).

But these results do not imply that there are no additional factors that moderate the impacts of informational and normative influence, or, in analysis of variance terminology, three-way interactions. Isenberg (1986) suggests that, "given the support for both PAT and SCT as mediating processes, it behooves investigators to develop theories that account for the interaction between SCT and PAT and that address the factors that moderate the emergence of one or the other form of influence" (p. 1149). And, indeed, such moderator variables have been uncovered. Laughlin and Earley (1982) found that informational influence was stronger than normative influence when CD items were intellective, but found the opposite relationship when CD items were judgmental. Boster, Hale, Mongeau, and Hale (1985) have reported strong informational influence when CD response scales were unambiguous, but stronger normative influence when CD response scales were ambiguous. Isenberg (1986) posits several additional potential moderators, such as ego involvement, source characteristics, and message characteristics, but these hypotheses remain untested.

The possibility also exists that if informational and normative influences are allowed to vary naturally, rather than being controlled experimentally, they would be linked causally. In one of our experiments such serial causal relations (in path-analytic terms, a causal string) were obtained (Boster & Mayer, 1984). We found that normative influence had a direct effect on informational influence, which, in turn, had a direct impact on the choice shift. Specifically, group composition had an impact on the ways in which persons perceived arguments; majority arguments were perceived as more compelling than minority arguments (even when they were the same arguments!), and, as the perceived persuasiveness of the arguments increased, the corresponding shifts increased proportionally.

These data explain why the effect of normative influence is smaller than the effect of informational influence: The normative influence effect is mediated by the informational influence effect. Therefore, as the mathematics of causal analysis indicates, the correlation between majority and the choice shift must be the product of the majority-perceived argument quality correlation and the perceived argument quality-choice shift correlation. The product of two fractions being a smaller fraction, this operation results in a majority-choice shift correlation that is small relative to the perceived argument quality-choice shift effect.

I hasten to add that I am not fully satisfied with this model. A relatively unambiguous response scale and a relatively intellective CD item were employed in the experiment, and varying these parameters may produce different effect size estimates, or perhaps alter the structure of the model. Such hypotheses invite further experimentation, but to my knowledge none has been published to date.

The conclusion that I draw from this literature is that the choice shift cannot be understood without consideration being given to normative influence. In fact, given the Boster and Mayer data, it is reasonable to conclude that a complete understanding of informational influence cannot be reached without attention to normative influence.

GROUP ARGUMENT

Meyers and Seibold do deal in detail with informational influence, however, and they do so adroitly. In their recent work, the authors point out what they see as a flaw in PAT, that it disregards the distinction between social and cognitive argument. While I do not particularly like the labels — it is difficult for me to see how any argument can be other than social — the central point developed from this distinction is an important one. I agree that reasons for accepting or rejecting a position unknown prior to group discussion can occur to group members during group discussion and that arguments based on these reasons may then be generated during discussion.

This proposition is, however, a difficult one to test. One problem lies in being able to specify the set of arguments of which persons are aware prior to discussion. A failure to list an argument that arises during a subsequent discussion may be more a function of faulty memory, lack of attention or effort, or some combination of these factors than of the social nature of argument.

But, methodological questions aside, granting the fact that such arguments *can* occur is not the same as saying that they *do* occur or occur to the same extent in all circumstances or for all persons. As Meyers and Seibold have noted in the past, the reasons for action, and the arguments based upon these reasons, that come to mind during discussion are similar to ideas generated in a brainstorming experiment. In some experiments, brainstorming groups have generated more ideas than nominal groups (Meadow & Parnes, 1959), but null or opposite results have been obtained in other experiments (e.g., Dunnette, Campbell, & Jaastad, 1963; Taylor, Berry, & Block, 1958).

These data suggest the existence of variables that moderate the relationship between group participation and idea generation, and, in fact, there are some data consistent with this claim. For example, Jablin, Seibold, and Sorenson (1977) report that high communication apprehensives (CAs) generated more ideas in brainstorming than nominal groups, but that type of group participation had no effect on idea generation for low CAs. It is not unlikely that the generation of arguments during group discussion will produce similar results, although the specific moderator variables may be different, and the pursuit of this line of inquiry promises to be fruitful.

To fulfill this promise, however, some conceptual refinement is required. Specifically, it is not perfectly clear what Meyers and Seibold mean by *argument*, although I suppose that they conceive of it as reason-giving behavior. Conceiving of argument in this way entails some subsequent difficulties, although it may be the most useful conceptualization.

Alternatively, one could, I suppose, employ a definition commonly invoked by logicians:

> An argument may be defined as any group of propositions of which one is claimed to follow from the others, which are regarded as supplying evidence for the truth of that one. (Copi, 1967, p. 3)

Unfortunately, this definition is of little help in evaluating discourse. Persons do not often speak in clearly identifiable conclusions that follow from a set of carefully documented premises, and so the validity of the former cannot be derived from *Modus Ponens, Modus Tollens,* or DeMorgan's theorems. Additionally, even if persons spoke this way during group discussion, the length of discussions, the rapidity with which they proceed, and the limitations of human information processing would prevent group members from constructing the elaborate formal proofs and the careful consideration of the truth of the premises necessary to evaluate the soundness of the arguments.

Many messages transmitted during discussion can be characterized by stated conclusions and some associated reason(s), but most often there are several unstated premises, or enthymemes, needed to complete the argument. The vagueness and ambiguity generated by these missing premises compels group members to elaborate on messages in order to make sense of them, which persons appear to do extensively under certain conditions (e.g., Petty & Cacioppo, 1981).

Also, persons' elaborations are known to vary as a function of a number of factors. For example, Asch (1948) showed that when provided with the same ambiguous statement, one attributed to Karl Marx and the other to John Adams, his subjects responded more favorably to the message attributed to Adams. Furthermore, he demonstrated that this effect was due to the difference in the *meaning of the message*, not the prestige of the source. That is, persons perceived the message to have a different, and more acceptable, meaning when attributed to Adams than when attributed to Marx.

In the Boster and Mayer (1984) experiment it was not a matter of the speaker determining the meaning of the message, but rather of the *number of speakers* determining the meaning of the message. Arguments were judged to be more compelling when presented by three persons than when presented by one person (see also Harkins & Petty, 1981a, 1981b).

Therefore, both the characteristics of the speaker and the number of speakers, and likely a host of other factors, have an impact upon the meaning that group members ascribe to any reason-giving discourse. But, despite these relatively systematic effects, there is no assurance that all group members will perceive a message, or elaborate on it, in the same way.

To take an example from experimental public address research, the mean correlation between messages varying in the quantity of fear-arousing stimuli and participants' perceptions of the amount of fear in the message was only .36 (Boster & Mongeau, 1984). Thus in fear appeal experiments there are quite a number of participants for whom the low fear message is frightening, and there are also quite a few for whom the high fear message is not frightening. Similarly, in group discussion person A's message may be perceived as compelling by person B, but as logically unsound by person C.

A reasonable causal model of the impact of such a piece of reason-giving discourse is that the message has a direct effect on each group member's perceptions of and elaboration on the message. This cognitive work then exerts a direct effect on each group member's attitude. During group discussion, however, there is no control over the messages emitted by the group members, and this lack of experimental control creates serious difficulties for researchers trying to trace these causal chains. For example, to stop the discussion after each message and ask questions concerning the speaker's intention, the perceptions of the other group members, and the extent to which attitudes were affected would certainly cripple several features of both the internal and the external validity of the experiment. To have persons who were involved in the discussion review transcripts or tapes after the discussion and then provide these data may inform us more about their ability to construct accounts or introspect accurately than about their cognitive states during the discussion. To employ raters to provide these data requires that they have the ability to report what the group members were thinking, a formidable task to say the least.

So, defining an argument as involving reason-giving behavior will, I believe, be less than useful for the purpose of understanding the way in which argument affects group decisions, and extensive analysis of discourse will not provide a spate of useful insights in this domain of inquiry. Rather, I suspect that the concept of "argument" is best employed as a latent variable. Theories of group decision making that posit different ways in which arguments affect group decisions can then be developed and pitted against one another. This assertion bring me to my final point.

SPECIFYING ARGUMENT EFFECTS DURING DISCUSSION

One axiom of theory construction is that it is desirable to state a theory as clearly and precisely as possible. This axiom might be better conceived as a theorem, however, since it is derivable from more basic propositions. One proposition necessary to the derivation is that in order to be useful, a scientific theory must be capable of being falsified; a second is that the more clearly and precisely a theory is stated, the easier it is to know whether data suggest that one reject it or not.

For example, my colleagues and I have developed a model of the choice shift experiment (Boster et al., 1982; Boster, Mayer, Hunter, & Hale, 1980). This model emanates from French's (1956) linear discrepancy theory, a precursor to

Anderson's (1971) information integration theory. This model is stated in the language of difference equations, and yields precise predictions concerning the choice shift, individual postdiscussion attitudes, and the variance of postdiscussion attitudes. Moreover, it has exhibited, by the standards of our discipline, remarkable fit to empirical outcomes, correlations between predicted and obtained outcomes exceeding .80 slightly. It is also, in my opinion (I cannot speak for my coauthors), incorrect.

Without deriving the predicted results, the essence of the model is that persons develop some opinions after reading a CD item, and when they begin to discuss it, the arguments they advance reflect their opinions *at the time they speak*. When one group member advances an argument, the other members compare this new information with their previous opinions and become more favorable toward the position advocated in the message. So member A, let us say, speaks first, advocating her or his prediscussion opinion. This message modifies the opinions of the remaining members, their new opinions being closer to A's than before. Person B then speaks, and the process is repeated. Discussion continues until consensus is reached, this point being predicted to be the mean of the group's prediscussion opinions when members speak with equal frequency, a weighted mean when this assumption is dropped.

I believe the model to be wrong because my observations of scores of CD discussions, as well as other kinds of group discussions, contradict several features of the model. For example, the model has no parameter for argument strength, and there are, even in CD discussions, some arguments that are more persuasive than others. According to the model, change toward each argument is a constant, but we know that some persons are more easily persuaded than others. There is no parameter in the model for compromise, but I have observed it in many discussions. There is no parameter for normative influence, either.

It is interesting to note that these factors cannot be too substantial, because if they were, the model would be in error to a considerable extent, and it is not that far off. In fact, were I to be an advocate of the model, I would point out that error of measurement in the CD items would be sufficient to account for all of the observed error in predicting experimental outcomes. Nevertheless, I believe the model to be an oversimplification of the process, a belief that I held while developing it. Our purpose was to provide a plausible, clear, and precise account of what occurs in a choice shift experiment. To do so, we had to make simplifying assumptions. Model error then allows one to go back, relax certain assumptions, and revise the model, assuming it is close to describing the process accurately in the first place and that one can think of ways to relax the assumptions.

In fact, it is generally a preferable state of affairs when the model does go awry. When the data are consistent with the model, one has learned nothing that was unknown prior to the experiment. Inconsistencies force new theorizing, and, one hopes, increasingly better models. At any rate, such is the spirit of mathematical modeling.

The Meyers and Seibold account does not provide the kind of clarity found in our model, or, for that matter, in several other models of group decision making. From their discussion it is not obvious how to predict the magnitude and direction of choice shifts. Furthermore, it is also not obvious how one would construct experiments that could, in principle, falsify their ideas. Finally, it is not clear how one could pit their theory against other theories of the choice shift in a critical experiment.

CONCLUSION

In their chapter, Meyers and Seibold make a number of contributions to the group decision-making literature. To list a few: Their careful critique of PAT is excellent, and serves as an example of the kind of important insights communication scholars provide by virtue of their attention to messages; by pointing out that arguments can arise as a result of interaction, they open up (I hope) numerous research avenues; their distinction between arguments in messages and arguments in persons is important for tracking the causal impact of persuasive messages. The reader will undoubtedly note many other contributions.

On the other hand, their theory of group decision making remains incomplete, because it does not provide a detailed treatment of normative influence. It also lacks the formal clarity necessary to be an optimally useful account of the phenomenon. And the difficulties in identifying specific arguments and their effects suggest to me that detailed examination of discourse will not be a particularly fruitful method of generating information about group decision making.

REFERENCES

Anderson, N. H. (1971). Integration theory and attitude change. *Psychological Review, 78,* 171-206.
Asch, S. E. (1948). The doctrine of suggestion, prestige, and imitation in social psychology. *Psychological Review, 55,* 250-277.
Asch, S. E. (1956). Studies of independence and conformity: A minority of one against a unanimous majority. *Psychological Monograph, 70*(9, Whole No. 416), 1-70.
Boster, F. J., Fryrear, J. E., Mongeau, P. A., & Hunter, J. E. (1982). An unequal speaking linear discrepancy model: Implications for the polarity shift. In M. Burgoon (Ed.), *Communication yearbook 6* (pp. 395-418). Beverly Hills, CA: Sage.
Boster, F. J., Hale, J. L., Mongeau, P. A., & Hale, J. (1985, May). *The validity of choice dilemma response scales.* Paper presented at the annual meeting of the International Communication Association, Honolulu.
Boster, F. J., & Mayer, M. E. (1984). Choice shifts: Argument qualities or social comparisons. In R. N. Bostrom (Ed.), *Communication yearbook 8* (pp. 393-410). Beverly Hills, CA: Sage.
Boster, F. J., Mayer, M. E., Hunter, J. E., & Hale, J. L. (1980). Expanding the persuasive arguments explanation of the polarity shift: A linear discrepancy model. In D. Nimmo (Ed.), *Communication yearbook 4* (pp. 165-176). New Brunswick, NJ: Transaction.

Boster, F. J., & Mongeau, P. A. (1984). Fear-arousing persuasive messages. In R. N. Bostrom (Ed.), *Communication yearbook 8* (pp. 330-375). Beverly Hills, CA: Sage.

Chaiken, S. (1980). Heuristic versus systematic cue processing and the use of source versus message cues in persuasion. *Journal of Personality and Social Psychology, 39,* 752-766.

Copi, I. M. (1967). *Symbolic logic.* New York: Macmillan.

Crutchfield, R. S. (1955). Conformity and character. *American Psychologist, 10,* 191-198.

Deutsch, M., & Gerard, H. G. (1955). A study of normative and informational social influence upon individual judgment. *Journal of Abnormal and Social Psychology, 51,* 629-636.

Dunnette, M. D., Campbell, J., & Jaastad, K. (1963). The effect of group participation on brainstorming effectiveness for two industrial samples. *Journal of Applied Psychology, 46,* 30-37.

Festinger, L. (1950). Informal social communication. *Psychological Review, 57,* 271-282.

French, J.R.P., Jr. (1956). A formal theory of social power. *Psychological Review, 63,* 181-194.

French, J.R.P., Jr., & Raven, B. (1968). The bases of social power. In D. Cartwright & A. Zander (Eds.), *Group dynamics* (pp. 259-269). New York: Harper & Row.

Harkins, S. G., & Petty, R. E. (1981a). Effects of source magnification of cognitive effort on attitudes: An information-processing view. *Journal of Personality and Social Psychology, 40,* 401-413.

Harkins, S. G., & Petty, R. E. (1981b). The multiple source effect in persuasion: The effects of distraction. *Personality and Social Psychology Bulletin, 7,* 627-633.

Isenberg, D. J. (1986). Group polarization: A critical review and meta-analysis. *Journal of Personality and Social Psychology, 50,* 1141-1151.

Jablin, F. M., Seibold, D. R., & Sorenson, R. L. (1977). Potential inhibitory effects of group participation on brainstorming performance. *Central States Speech Journal, 28,* 113-121.

Kelman, H. C. (1961). Processes of opinion change. *Public Opinion Quarterly, 25,* 57-78.

Laughlin, P. R., & Earley, P. C. (1982). Social combination models, persuasive arguments theory, social comparison theory, and choice shift. *Journal of Personality and Social Psychology, 42,* 273-380.

McGuire, W. J. (1985). Attitudes and attitude change. In G. Lindzey & E. Aronson (Eds.), *The handbook of social psychology* (Vol. 2, pp. 233-346). New York: Random House.

Meadow, A., & Parnes, S. (1959). Evaluation of training in creative problem-solving. *Journal of Applied Psychology, 43,* 189-194.

Moscovici, S., & Faucheux, C. (1972). Social influence, conforming bias, and the study of active minorities. In L. Berkowitz (Ed.), *Advances in experimental social psychology* (Vol. 6, pp. 149-202). New York: Academic Press.

Myers, D. G., & Lamm, H. (1976). The group polarization phenomenon. *Psychological Bulletin, 83,* 602-627.

Petty, R. E., & Cacioppo, J. T. (1981). *Attitudes and persuasion: Classic and contemporary approaches.* Dubuque, IA: William C Brown.

Petty, R. E., Cacioppo, J. T., & Goldman, R. (1981). Personal involvement as a determinant of argument-based persuasion. *Journal of Personality and Social Psychology, 41,* 847-855.

Sherif, M. (1935). A study of some social factors in perception. *Archives of Psychology, 187,* 5-60.

Stiff, J. B. (1986). Cognitive processing of persuasive message cues: A meta-analytic review of the effects of supporting information on attitudes. *Communication Monographs, 53,* 75-89.

Tanford, S., & Penrod, S. (1984). Social influence model: A formal integration of research on majority and minority influence processes. *Psychological Bulletin, 95,* 189-225.

Taylor, D. W., Berry, P. C., & Block, C. H. (1958). Does group participation when using brainstorming facilitate or inhibit creative thinking? *Administrative Science Quarterly, 3,* 23-47.

Exploiting the
Predictive Potential
of Structuration Theory

DENNIS S. GOURAN
Pennsylvania State University

I N their examination of perspectives on "group argument," Meyers and Seibold address the question of whether or not communication makes a difference in the decisional outcomes groups achieve. In so doing, they enter the voluminous body of scholarship spawned by Stoner's (1961) discovery that groups do not necessarily exercise the sort of conservative influence on members commonly attributed to them. The fact that group decisions in Stoner's pioneering study were different from, and frequently more risky than, those one would expect on the basis of prediscussion individual choices led almost immediately to a number of competing explanations for this initially puzzling occurrence. Of those, one of the longest surviving and most influential accounts has been the so-called persuasive arguments theory (Vinokur & Burnstein, 1974). The particular perspective offered by persuasive arguments theory (PAT) is a major object of Meyers and Seibold's attention.

The very label "persuasive arguments theory" would seem to imply a critical role for communication in situations in which groups' decisions are at variance with their members' initial preferences. Yet, as Meyers and Seibold note, persuasive arguments theorists ascribe a limited, almost inconsequential role function to communication in accounting for the phenomenon of interest. That function consists of exposing individual members to arguments favoring particular decision options that are not among those they themselves possess or are in the process of generating. The increase in the collective stock of arguments not already in the

Correspondence and requests for reprints: Dennis S. Gouran, College of Liberal Arts, Department of Speech Communication, 234 Sparks Building, Pennsylvania State University, University Park, PA 16802.

Communication Yearbook 13, pp. 313-322

individual members' repertoires, then, according to these theorists, is the factor to which a group's final choice, if it represents shift, is attributable.

If communication functions primarily in the ways persuasive arguments theorists suggest, in principle, there should be little difference in the average of members' individual choices following discussion and the group's selection of a particular decision option. In research utilizing both types of indices, however, this type of congruence has not always been evident. Meyers and Seibold develop this point as well as summarize research establishing that individually held arguments are not necessarily the ones that surface in group discussion and that interactional factors, when coupled with noninteractional factors, bear a stronger relationship to decisional outcomes than do noninteractional factors alone. The authors bolster their position on the importance of communication further by citing several authorities and researchers (for example, Cartwright, 1971; Dion, Baron, & Miller, 1978; Jarboe, 1988; Moscovici & Lecuyer, 1972) who see more obvious connections between interaction and group decisions than most proponents of PAT.

Given the inadequacies they identify in the PAT perspective, Meyers and Seibold present the outlines of an alternative perspective grounded in notions articulated by Giddens (1984) in his theory of structuration. Although Giddens's work is concerned with societal development and change, Meyers and Seibold and others (most notably, Poole, 1981, 1983a, 1983b) believe that these notions extend to social entities like groups because they "evidence many features of higher-order social institutions" (p. 283).

Although Meyers and Seibold have constructed a strong case for believing that communication contributes to outcomes in substantially more critical respects than persuasive arguments theorists are willing to acknowledge, their essay is not without some problems. First, the critique of persuasive arguments theory overlooks some important issues. Second, and perhaps more critical, the perspective developed leaves questions about its own adequacy for dealing with the phenomena to which it purportedly applies. In raising these matters, I am not implying that the essay is of questionable merit. On the contrary, it represents an excellent piece of scholarship and an instance of informed thought that should serve interested scholars well for some time to come. The deficiencies are worthy of note, however, and discussion of them may contribute to further refinements in the authors' thinking as well as in the perspective itself.

CRITIQUE OF PERSUASIVE ARGUMENTS THEORY

Meyers and Seibold's critique of PAT reveals a number of its inadequacies for fully explaining the specific phenomena to which it historically has been applied. As a body of principles having general theoretical value beyond the limited context of choice dilemma problems, it probably has even greater deficiencies. Although I have no disagreements with Meyers and Seibold's assessment of PAT, their criticisms do not appear to go far enough, especially if they seek to establish a more vital role for communication in group decision making than persuasive arguments theorists are prone to credit it with having. One such area is the task situation protocol used in PAT research. There are several aspects of the type of task situation used that make it inherently unlikely that one will find communication's functioning as the critical force in shaping the choices groups make. Three such aspects come to mind: the relevance of the tasks for those performing them, the meaningfulness of the choices made, and the limited need for persuasive influence the tasks pose.

Choice dilemma problems have been a staple of research on choice shift, polarization, and, in earlier history, the "risky shift." These problems afford a certain methodological convenience to researchers. Choices are made from among a set of probabilities that relate to the likelihood of a given outcome's occurrence in an uncertain but attractive situation compared to a certain but not particularly attractive alternative. The associated probabilities allow for precise calculation of shift for both individuals and groups.

In choice dilemma problems, any value other than a 1.00 expectation that the desired outcome will occur entails some degree of risk. The problems, however, refer to hypothetical persons, not those making the probability selections. Since the situation is not risk inherent for those recommending given probability levels, making a bad decision would be inconsequential. One can, therefore, afford to be liberal in selecting the probability value one believes constitutes an appropriate level of risk some other person should be willing to take in choosing between a less attractive but certain situation and a more attractive but uncertain one.

In addition, because the level of ego involvement on the part of the person or persons selecting probability levels is not likely to be very great, in the language of Sherif, Sherif, and Nebergall (1965), the individual's "latitude of rejection" presumably would be small and his or her "latitude of acceptance" and "noncommitment" comparatively large. This circumstance would, of course, facilitate assimilation of other positions — be they more or less risky. Under such conditions, eliciting shifts would not require much in the way of persuasive influence. The simple exposure to arguments unfamiliar to the parties involved, in many instances, might be sufficient to stimulate change. Such a possibility is consistent with Zajonc's (1968) hypothesis that mere exposure is a sufficient condition for attitude change. Strictly speaking, the probability values selected in choice dilemma problems are not measures of attitudes, but they are undoubtedly reflections of them. Hence the same principle would appear to be at work.

Stoner (1961) did not originally think of the items included in his choice dilemma questionnaire as individually posing situations that are risk inherent for those who discuss them. Rather, he conceived of them as collectively constituting a measure of propensity to take risks. Difficulties arose when this measure was shown not to be an especially good predictor of shift to risk and inclinations toward risk were demonstrated to be problem specific. Scholars, however, have continued to employ the items constituting the choice dilemma questionnaire to assess choice shift and the tendencies toward polarization exhibited by many groups. They have done so without reference to the fact that the problems presented are typically not consequential to those who discuss them, and therefore do not require much in the way of argument to convince others of the desirability of selecting some probability value other than the ones they initially prefer.

A second feature of choice dilemma problems that unfortunately contributes to the credibility of assumptions of persuasive arguments theorists about the relative nonimportance of communication in group decision making has to do with both the gradations in the probability values from which groups and individuals considering these problems must choose and the meaningfulness of the changes they are used to assess. These values are commonly separated by intervals of .10. An individual who selects a probability of .80 that the desired outcome associated with a given problem will occur, for instance, is presumed as less risk prone than one who requires a probability of, say, only .70 or .60. Whether individuals understand the differences among the values given or think about probabilities in such precise terms is questionable.

In a recently published article, mathematician John Allen Paulos (1989) discusses the problem of "innumeracy" in the American populace, including presumably well-educated people, and indicates that, in general, we do not have a very good grasp of the concept of probability. As an example, he cites the case in which an individual concluded that a .50 chance of rain for each of two consecutive days establishes a virtual certainty that it will rain on one of the two days (p. 16). Nisbett and Ross (1980) have further reminded us that individuals often identify the least probable of two or more events as the most probable. Finally, Kellermann and Jarboe (1987) have produced evidence that questions whether shifts toward risk actually represent riskiness. In light of such revelations, one has reason to question the assumption that shifts of the kind observed in studies utilizing choice dilemma problems actually reflect an understanding on the part of those exhibiting them of the differences in the probabilities involved. In addition, if individuals judge probabilities in more general terms—for instance, likely and unlikely—than the finer discriminations a ten-interval scale allows, then shifts such as the one mentioned (from .80 to .70 or .60) may be meaningless to those reporting them and obviously would not require a very convincing line of argument, or even much in the way of interaction, to bring about. It is hardly surprising, then, that researchers find evidence of shift but little corresponding evidence of communication's being the responsible agent.

Still another aspect of the task situation to which PAT has been applied that favors discovery of communication's having a limited role as a factor in choice shift, polarization, or similar phenomena involving changes in judgment or position is the fact that the options are externally generated and preset. Rarely, if ever, would an individual or group have to make a decision in accordance with the dictates of a choice dilemma problem. Even if it were realistic and common to participants' experience, however, the type of situation in which these problems are discussed represents, at best, a limited domain—one that restricts decision makers to the set of options given. If one must work within a set of alternatives someone else has generated, then, as persuasive arguments theorists suggest, making a choice may often, in fact, consist of little more than identifying the arguments that can be made in support of each and selecting the one for which the largest number of different arguments appears to exist. This process seems especially likely in cases involving decisions that are not consequential for those who must make them. Despite the fact that decision makers are asked to make choices from a set of given alternatives, perhaps as often, they are in a position of having to generate decision options themselves. Under these circumstances, interactional factors conceivably would have a good deal more to do with the choices made than would be true under conditions in which choosing is the only necessity.

Consider the case of a group asked to discuss a choice dilemma problem like that in Meyers and Seibold, but without the selection of a probability value as the objective. Suppose instead that the task were put to the group in the following manner: "Given Mr. R's dilemma, please identify the circumstances under which he should choose university X." In such a case, alternatives would be a product of members' thought and creative efforts. With different recommendations being generated and compared, it seems likely both that participants would attempt to influence one another and that the achievement of agreement would be affected by how successfully argument functions. Inasmuch as the alternatives decision-making groups consider so frequently are created or arise in the course of interaction rather than prior to it, PAT insufficiently applies to the range of choice situations into which interactional factors enter and significantly focuses on one in which communication, by virtue of the particular requirements of the task, need not play a very substantial role.

By overlooking specific characteristics of the type of task and task environment with which persuasive arguments theorists have been concerned, Meyers and Seibold miss a good opportunity to strengthen the case for the point of view they espouse. A good deal of their essay addresses the question of whether persuasive arguments theory satisfactorily explains choice shift and polarization as assessed in studies employing choice dilemma problems. While this is a legitimate issue to raise, as the previous examination of the context in which these phenomena have been observed suggests, the more critical questions may be whether PAT can adequately account for the variance in decisional outcomes in any other kind of task environment and whether the role of communication in such environments can be reduced to making clear what the arguments in support of given decision options are. The answers to these questions, of course, must await the results of empirical tests and inquiry.

THE STRUCTURATIONAL PERSPECTIVE

Meyers and Seibold present a very clear discussion of the general elements in the theory of structuration that relate to decision making in groups and give particular attention to argument as the crucial communicative activity that leads to collective choices. From the structurational perspective, decisions evolve in the course of a group's interaction, with arguments and the activities they represent playing vital roles in this evolution. Arguments, according to the authors (citing Meyers, 1987/1988), are "streams of interrelated activities produced and reproduced in interaction" (p. 353). These "streams of activity," moreover, have three essential features: disagreement, reason-giving and -defending, and convergence production. The overt behavior (social practices) of groups is a product of underlying resources (knowledge, broadly conceived) and rules that define or otherwise determine appropriate and permissible conduct and ways of thinking.

Rules and resources may be unique to the individual or collectively shared. They may also have to do with both the substance of matters under discussion and how arguments are to be conducted. In either case, they constitute the generative mechanism by which statements relating to the reasons for supporting or opposing given alternatives and the peculiar manner in which they are expressed become manifest. The social practices of which arguments are composed, in turn, affect individual and collective rules and resources. Thus arguments are produced and reproduced through interaction in a cyclical, almost spiral-like fashion until such time as sufficient agreement is achieved for a particular alternative, or until it becomes apparent that consensus cannot be reached.

The general description of how groups reach decisions provided by Meyers and Seibold seems intuitively sensible. Absent from the description, however, is a sufficient discussion of either the rules and resources or social practices that make some choices likely and others unlikely. If this issue is not resolved, then the principal value of the structurational perspective may be reduced to providing post hoc explanations of specific instances of decision-making activity. Perhaps the authors have no greater ambition for the theory than that at this stage, but if its predictive potential could somehow be established, the utility of the theory would be considerably greater. The remaining portion of this commentary deals with this matter.

Rules and resources, as Meyers and Seibold acknowledge, are difficult to assess because they are not always explicit in interaction and are continuously in the process of evolving. Consequently, trying to identify the social practices that incline and disincline the members of decision-making groups toward particular decision options represents the more realistic starting point. An excellent lead about those social practices related to the likelihood of a given choice is provided in the research by Hoffman (1979), McPhee, Poole, and Seibold (1981), and Poole, McPhee, and Seibold (1982) testing predictive models of choice that Meyers and Seibold cite. Both Hoffman's valence model and the adaptation referred to as the "distribution of valence" model in Poole et al. relate the probability of endorsing a given decision option or proposal to the net proportion of favorable comments made in its support. Unfortunately, Meyers and Seibold draw on these findings only to question the supposition of persuasive arguments theorists that interactional factors have little direct impact on the decisions groups make. At least on the surface, the data from these studies would appear to provide a better basis for demonstrating the predictive utility of the perspective the authors advocate than their description suggests.

Perhaps the reason that Meyers and Seibold failed to discuss the implications of research testing the valence and distribution of valence models in their development of the structurational perspective is that the research in question did not focus on argument as such. In these studies, valence was conceived as the attractiveness of decision proposals and was assessed by the number of positive and negative comments made by group members about them. Arguments, of course, can be positive or negative, but not all comments that are positive and negative constitute arguments, especially as Meyers and Seibold conceive of the phenomenon. Since they are particularly concerned with the role of argument in decision making, the previously cited research may not have appeared that germane.

With some slight modifications and a little reconceptualization, one could utilize the notions implicit in the valence and distribution of valence models for making predictions about the argument/choice relationship in decision-making discussions. This move would require separating arguments from favorable and unfavorable comments in general and identifying appropriate units of analysis. Reasons for supporting or opposing decision proposals would be one such unit. If arguments are constituted in the reasons members of groups generate and offer for supporting or opposing given decision proposals, and if those arguments are of equal weight, then it would seem to follow that *the probability of a group's endorsing any given decision proposal is a function of the difference in the number of reasons offered in its support and the number of reasons offered for opposing it.* Differences that are both positive and large would suggest a greater probability of endorsement than differences of low magnitude or that are negative in sign.

Given Poole et al.'s reservations about "total valence" as a predictor of choice, a second and more refined proposition implicit in their work with the distribution of valence model, again with arguments of equal weight, is that *the greater the proportion of group members who offer more supporting than opposing arguments, the greater the likelihood of the group's endorsing that proposal.* This proposition reflects a recognition of the fact that the overall difference between the number of reasons offered in support of a decision proposal and the number offered in opposition could be both positive and large but not lead to endorsement because the difference is a result of a minority's having engaged in more discussion than other group members.

As noted, the first two propositions assume reasons of equal weight. If the theory of structuration is correct, however, there may be many instances in which the weight of the reasons offered in support of or in opposition to particular decision proposals is uneven. Such unevenness might not manifest itself until late in a discussion. Hence there exists the possibility of situations in which a decision proposal having a low probability of endorsement or acceptance on the basis of the first and second propositions, in fact, becomes a group's choice. Conversely, proposals having a high probability of selection might be rejected. These possibilities could occur under circumstances in which some reasons for endorsing or opposing a decision proposal are "better" or more compelling than others. If the better or more compelling reasons do not surface early in a group's interaction, the members conceivably will have offered a good many other reasons for supporting or opposing a given decision proposal. Once the more compelling reason is offered, however, it would have greater weight in determining the group's choice. If this type of reason ran counter to the tenor of the others, then it is understandable how an outcome other than the one expected from the overall distribution of reasons offered in support of or opposition to the various alternatives would accrue.

It is difficult to specify all of the factors that may contribute to some reasons for supporting or opposing particular decision proposals being "better" or more compelling than others. In principle, however, any factor (for example, in a rational world, the inclusion of expert opinion, the degree to which a reason is elaborated, factual grounding) that can be legitimately taken as an index of the strength of an argument would lead to the same expectation. There is some evidence, moreover, suggesting that those who back their arguments with relevant information are more influential than others in creating agreements and securing adoption of proposals they support (see, for example, Bradley, Hamon, & Harris, 1976; Gouran, 1969; Hill, 1976). The proposition suggested by these considerations, then, is that *the better substantiated the reasons offered in support of a given decision proposal relative to the reasons for opposing it are by relevant factual information and sources that are credible to the members, the greater the likelihood of a group's endorsing that proposal.*

Potentially as important to the endorsement of a given decision proposal as the development of reasons discussion participants offer in support of or in opposition to it are the responses these reasons elicit. If responses are generally positive, they are likely to increase the probability of a group's acting in accordance with the position expressed in the related argument even if the reasons that accompany it are not especially well founded. Comments that reinforce the reasons offered in support of a particular decision proposal, by implication, also constitute support for the proposal. More formally, then, one can posit that *the greater the average ratio of favorable to unfavorable reactions to reasons offered in support of a given decision proposal, the greater the likelihood of a group's endorsing that proposal.* In addition to the indirect support provided in the previously mentioned research by Hoffman (1979), McPhee et al. (1981), and Poole et al. (1982), other studies (for example, Gouran, 1983, 1984; Janis, 1982) dealing with both laboratory and historical groups suggests that the reinforcing tendencies exhibited in response to statements supportive of given alternatives may function at a psychological level in much the same way as evidence. As a result, group members exposed to one another's positive comments are more likely to endorse a decision proposal because of the appearance of its being well founded that favorable reactions and expressions of agreement create.

The four propositions I have developed are by no means exhaustive, nor do I offer them as ones that necessarily should have been included in Meyers and Seibold's treatment of the subject their essay addresses. Rather, they serve as illustrations of the predictive potential the more general assumptions and related features of the structurational perspective possess and as elements that could be included in more refined hypothetical formulations of theories that focus on the communication/argument/choice relationship in decision-making groups. I offer them, then, as "friendly amendments" to a motion expressing strong approval of what already has proved to be a fruitful and even more promising approach to scholarly study of how groups make decisions.

REFERENCES

Bradley, P. H., Hamon, C. M., & Harris, A. M. (1976). Dissent in small groups. *Journal of Communication, 26*, 155-159.

Cartwright, C. (1971). Risk taking by individuals and groups: An assessment of research employing choice dilemmas. *Journal of Personality and Social Psychology, 20*, 361-378.

Dion, K., Baron, R., & Miller, N. (1978). Why do groups make riskier decisions than individuals? In L. Berkowitz (Ed.), *Group processes* (pp. 227-229). New York: Academic Press.

Giddens, A. (1984). *The constitution of society: Outline of the theory of structuration.* Berkeley: University of California Press.

Gouran, D. S. (1969). Variables related to consensus in group discussions of questions of policy. *Speech Monographs, 36*, 387-391.

Gouran, D. S. (1983). Communicative influences on inferential judgments in decision-making groups: A descriptive analysis. In D. Zarefsky, M. O. Sillars, & J. Rhodes (Eds.), *Argument in transition: Proceedings of the third summer conference on argumentation* (pp. 667-684). Annandale, VA: Speech Communication Association.

Gouran, D. S. (1984). Communicative influences related to the Watergate coverup: The failure of collective judgment. *Central States Speech Journal, 35*, 260-268.

Hill, T. A. (1976). An experimental study of the relationship between opinionated leadership and small group consensus. *Communication Monographs, 43*, 246-257.

Hoffman, L. R. (1979). *The group problem-solving process: Studies of a valence model.* New York: Praeger.

Janis, I. L. (1982). *Groupthink* (2nd ed.). Boston: Houghton Mifflin.

Jarboe, S. (1988). A comparison of input-output, process-output, and input-process-output models of small group problem-solving effectiveness. *Communication Monographs, 55*, 121-142.

Kellermann, K., & Jarboe, S. (1987). Conservatism in judgment: Is the risky shift-ee really risky, really? In M. L. McLaughlin (Ed.), *Communication yearbook 10* (pp. 259-282). Newbury Park, CA: Sage.

McPhee, R. D., Poole, M. S., & Seibold, D. R. (1981). The valence model unveiled: A critique and reformulation. In M. Burgoon (Ed.), *Communication yearbook 5* (pp. 259-277). New Brunswick, NJ: Transaction.

Meyers, R. A. (1988). Argument and group decision-making: An interactional test of persuasive arguments theory and an alternative structurational perspective (Doctoral dissertation, University of Illinois, Urbana-Champaign, 1987). *Dissertation Abstracts International, 49*, 12A.

Moscovici, S., & Lecuyer, R. (1972). Studies of group decision I: Social space, patterns of communication and group consensus. *European Journal of Social Psychology, 2*, 221-244.

Nisbett, R. E., & Ross, L. (1980). *Human inference: Strategies and shortcomings of social judgment.* Englewood Cliffs, NJ: Prentice-Hall.

Paulos, J. A. (1989, January 1). The odds are you're innumerate. *New York Times Book Review*, pp. 1, 16-17.

Poole, M. S. (1981). Decision development in small groups I: A comparison of two models. *Communication Monographs, 48*, 1-24.

Poole, M. S. (1983a). Decision development in small groups II: A study of multiple sequences in decision-making. *Communication Monographs, 50*, 206-232.

Poole, M. S. (1983b). Decision development in small groups III: A multiple sequence model of group decision-making. *Communication Monographs, 50*, 321-341.

Poole, M. S., McPhee, R. D., & Seibold, D. R. (1982). A comparison of normative and interactional explanations of group decision-making: Social decision schemes versus valence distributions. *Communication Monographs, 49*, 1-19.

Sherif, C. W., Sherif M., & Nebergall, R. E. (1965). *Attitude and attitude change: The social judgment-involvement approach.* Philadelphia: W. B. Saunders.

Stoner, J. A. F. (1961). *A comparison of individual and group decisions involving risk.* Unpublished master's thesis, Massachusetts Institute of Technology.

Vinokur, A., & Burnstein, E. (1974). Effects of partially shared persuasive arguments on group induced shifts: A group problem-solving approach. *Journal of Personality and Social Psychology, 29*, 305-315.

Zajonc, R. B. (1968). Attitudinal effects of mere exposure. *Journal of Personality and Social Psychology* (Monograph Supplement, Part 2), 1-27.

7 Remedial Processes in Embarrassing Predicaments

WILLIAM R. CUPACH
SANDRA METTS
Illinois State University

Embarrassing predicaments are a routine part of social interaction arising from the display of untoward or inappropriate behavior. Such events create feelings of chagrin, engender negative attributions about the embarrassed person, and disrupt social interaction. Consequently, both embarrassed actors and observers employ remedial face work in response to embarrassing predicaments in order to repair damaged identities, maintain face, and restore interactional equilibrium. This chapter summarizes the relevant literature in four areas related to embarrassment: (a) the nature of embarrassing predicaments, (b) remedial strategies employed by embarrassed actors, (c) responses of observers to an embarrassing predicament, and (d) factors influencing the use and effectiveness of remedial strategies. While prior research has offered some useful knowledge about general remedial processes, it fails to capture some of the unique and subtle aspects of coping with embarrassment. To promote greater understanding of the inherent complexities of remedial processes, we propose a preliminary taxonomy of embarrassing predicaments and suggest avenues for future research.

> Man is the only animal who blushes, or needs to.
>
> Mark Twain

Embarrassing failure events — blunders, faux pas, gaffes, boners, improprieties, miscues — are a routine part of social interaction. These predicaments are likely to arise when untoward or inappropriate behavior is displayed in front of real or imagined audiences, casting "aspersions on the lineage, character, conduct, skills, or motives of an actor" (Schlenker, 1980, p. 125). When an actor perceives that such an event projects an undesired image to others present, an aversive state of arousal ensues, and "there is usually a resulting feeling of deficiency or *abashment*, as if one had failed to comport oneself properly" (Miller, 1986, p. 296). This state of uncomfortable arousal is termed *embarrassment*.

In addition to creating discomfiture for the embarrassed person and discrediting that person's identity, embarrassment typically disrupts the social routine. As

Correspondence and requests for reprints: William R. Cupach, Department of Communication, Stevenson 114, Illinois State University, Normal, IL 61761-6901.

Communication Yearbook 13, pp. 323-352

Goffman (1967) has remarked, "Face-to-face interaction in *any* culture seems to require just those capacities that flustering seems guaranteed to destroy" (p. 101). Consequently, competent social actors attempt to maintain face, regain social approval, repair the projected identity, and restore interactional equilibrium by employing various impression-management strategies. The ability to repair a failure event successfully through face work is considered an important social skill (Goffman, 1967; Schlenker, 1980) and a reflection of communication competence (Bandera & Cupach, 1986; Spitzberg & Cupach, 1989).

Although scholarship concerned with characteristics of and remedial processes in social predicaments enjoys a long and systematic history, scholarship focused on embarrassment as a special class of predicaments is much more derivative and fragmented. Indeed, advances in our understanding of embarrassing predicaments tend to be obscured by the confusing array of typologies of embarrassing events and the lingering assumption that remedial practices in social predicaments are sufficient to explain remedial practices in embarrassing predicaments. The recent proliferation of studies on embarrassment in the communication field (e.g., Bandera & Cupach, 1986; Cupach, Metts, & Hazleton, 1986; Metts & Cupach, 1989; Petronio, 1984; Petronio, Olson, & Dollar, 1988; Sharkey & Stafford, 1988, 1989) signals the need for reflection and integration. The purpose of the present essay, therefore, is twofold: to summarize and integrate existing research, and to provide directions toward which future research should be directed.

We will examine the literature in four general areas related to embarrassment: (a) the nature of embarrassing predicaments, (b) remedial strategies employed by embarrassed actors, (c) responses of others to an embarrassing predicament, and (d) the use and effectiveness of remedial strategies. We will then offer an alternative taxonomy of embarrassing situations.

CONCEPTUALIZATION OF
EMBARRASSING PREDICAMENTS

In order for a predicament to create embarrassment, several conditions must exist (e.g., Edelmann, 1985, 1987; Semin & Manstead, 1981, 1982). First, some trigger event (usually a behavior or action) occurs that violates a taken-for-granted rule or is incongruent with a person's desired social image. This trigger event may be precipitated by the embarrassed person or by actions of others that create the predicament for the embarrassed person. Second, the embarrassed person is cognizant of the incongruence and the negative attributions it may entail, either through personal awareness or through the reactions of others. Third, although the trigger event may include a behavior that was intentionally performed, the disruption of social order, the inconvenience to others, or the negative attributions it may entail are generally perceived to be unintentional. Finally, the embarrassed person believes that the event is witnessed by others or believes that it will at some future date be known to others.

As this profile indicates, then, embarrassing predicaments are social constructs. Other social actors play an important role in the occurrence of embarrassing predicaments and the manner in which they unfold. We therefore address two specific aspects of embarrassing predicaments in this section. First, we summarize scholarship that attempts to identify categories or types of embarrassing situations. Second, we investigate the interactional consequences of embarrassing predicaments and the role of others who become participants in the predicament.

Typologies of Embarrassing Events

Several researchers have concerned themselves with identifying the types of circumstances that typically create an embarrassing predicament (Buss, 1980; Gross & Stone, 1964; Modigliani, 1968; Sattler, 1965; Weinberg, 1968). According to Edelmann (1987), most of this research has "attempted to classify embarrassing events into categories on the basis of actions or situations as causes of embarrassment" (p. 47). The early research by Gross and Stone (1964), for example, focused on three broad circumstances that cause embarrassment: loss of social identity (inability to perform one's role), loss of personal poise (inability to control one's body and nearby props), and loss of confidence in the expectations for interaction. Buss (1980), summarizing and extending previous work by Sattler (1965), identifies five more specific types of events that commonly cause embarrassment: (a) impropriety (e.g., improper dress, dirty talk), (b) lack of competence (e.g., a failure of social graces), (c) conspicuousness (e.g., being singled out for attention by others), (d) breach of privacy (e.g., invasion of personal space or undesired leakage of emotion), and (e) overpraise (e.g., receiving more acclaim than is deserved). Sharkey and Stafford (1988) have inductively derived six types of embarrassing situations embedded in respondents' recollected accounts: (a) revealing privacy (e.g., body exposure, verbally exposing private affairs), (b) forgetfulness or lack of knowledge/skill, (c) positive or negative criticism (e.g., teasing, flattery), (d) awkward acts (e.g., clumsiness, improper expression of emotion), (e) verbal blunders (e.g., using a wrong name, dirty talk), and (f) image/appropriateness (e.g., concern for personal appearance or possessions).

While these typologies of embarrassing situations share certain similarities, they are not directly comparable. Moreover, categories within the Buss (1980) and Sharkey and Stafford (1988) typologies do not appear to be equivalent and mutually exclusive. For example, in the Buss system, it would seem that "overpraise" is one specific manifestation of "conspicuousness." Similarly, in the Sharkey and Stafford system, it would appear that using a wrong name is as much an example of "forgetfulness" as it is of "verbal blunder." In short, typologies based on inductive sorting of specific instances of embarrassing situations may be inherently problematic if the categories that constitute the typology are not derived from orthogonal underlying dimensions.

One attempt to derive types of embarrassing situations from underlying dimensions is offered by Weinberg (1968), who conceptualizes fundamental "forms of embarrassment" by crossing two dimensions intrinsic to social actors' interpretation of a disrupted routine: the intended or unintended nature of the offending act, and the correct or incorrect definition of the situation. These two dimensions can be used to differentiate four forms of embarrassment: (a) faux pas (intentional behavior that is defined post facto as inappropriate to the situation), (b) accidents (unintended acts occurring in correctly defined situations), (c) mistakes (unintended acts occurring in incorrectly defined situations), and (d) duties (intended acts occurring in correctly defined situations but causing embarrassment because of one's internal audience).

Because Weinberg's categories emerge from the crossing of orthogonal dimensions, they have the advantage of being equivalent and mutually exclusive. However, the four categories thus derived are not in actuality exhaustive of all situations that might create embarrassment. In particular, they do not allow for instances in which embarrassment is caused by others or results from behavior that is incongruent with an individual's personal identity, despite its being intentionally performed in a correctly interpreted context. Later we present a tentative alternative taxonomy of embarrassing predicaments that attempts to ameliorate these problems.

Participation of Others
During an Embarrassing Predicament

Structurally, the roles of social interactants are interdependent. When an individual becomes embarrassed, other persons who witness the embarrassment are often drawn into the predicament. Because identities are negotiated in interaction, face work initiated by the embarrassed person requires the willing cooperation of others. Further, because embarrassment has the potential to disrupt smooth interaction, others have a vested interest in initiating remedial face work, even in situations where the offending party seems not to have "sufficient sense of shame or appreciation of the circumstances to blush on his own account" (Goffman, 1967, pp. 99-100). Indeed, merely observing an actor's predicament can create *empathic* embarrassment for the observer. Miller (1987) argues that "we may know embarrassment so well and dread its abashment so much that simply knowing embarrassing circumstances may cause us chagrin, even when our social identities are not threatened" (p. 1062; also see Buss, 1980).

It should be noted that because predicaments are socially determined, the person who causes the embarrassment, the person who feels the embarrassment, and the person for whom the embarrassment is felt are not necessarily the same individual. Suppose Gary spills coffee on Denise. Gary may feel embarrassed for himself. By the same token, Denise may feel embarrassed for herself, even though Gary actually created the predicament. Furthermore, Denise may feel embarrassed for Gary, whether or not Gary experiences chagrin for his own loss of poise. Given the complexity of embarrassing predicaments, remediation is a process that involves observers as well as embarrassed actors.

COPING WITH EMBARRASSMENT:
REMEDIAL FACE WORK

Because embarrassment is aversive to the individual and disruptive to social interaction, actors are motivated to avoid embarrassment where possible, and to repair the predicament when embarrassment does occur. Goffman (1967) has illustrated that actors engage in a host of protective practices designed to avoid or prevent threats to face. Such practices might include avoiding situations where face threat is likely, avoiding dangerous topics in conversation, and ignoring faux pas whenever possible.[1] Empirical research demonstrates that individuals will even forfeit tangible rewards in order to avoid performing an embarrassing act, particularly when an audience is perceived as being evaluative of the individual's behavior (Brown, 1970).

When a predicament cannot be avoided and embarrassment does occur, efforts to reduce felt embarrassment and restore social order are necessary (Modigliani, 1971). The term *face work* is used by Goffman (1967) to describe "the actions taken by a person to make whatever he is doing consistent with face" and to minimize the pejorative implications that might be drawn from being "out of face" (p. 12). Face work is also applied to those actions taken by others to restore an embarrassed person's face and realign social structure. Thus face work may be considered an essential social skill used to manage both one's own public performance and the public performance of other social actors. Face work employed in predicaments has been variously labeled "remedial tactics" (Schlenker, 1980), "excuses" (Snyder, 1985), "impression-management strategies" (Tedeschi & Riess, 1981), and "motive talk" (Semin & Manstead, 1983). We will refer to the use of face work here generically as *remedial strategies*.[2]

Typologies of remedial strategies derive principally from the literature on face work (e.g., Goffman, 1967, 1971; Modigliani, 1971) and on predicaments or failure events (e.g., Blumstein et al., 1974; Cody & McLaughlin 1985; Schlenker, 1980; Schonbach, 1980; Scott & Lyman, 1968; Tedeschi & Riess, 1981). Although face work may be necessitated by events other than embarrassment, and predicaments may lead to responses other than embarrassment, traditional research in these areas provides a framework within which remedial strategies for embarrassment can be situated. Thus we begin this section with a summary of the remedial strategies identified in the literature on social predicaments. We then offer qualifications of these typologies based on the results of a series of studies exploring remedial strategies used by *embarrassed persons* specifically. We will also comment on the sequencing of remedial strategies used by embarrassed persons.

Remedial Strategies
Used by Those Caught in Predicaments

Strategies used by persons caught in predicaments as a generic event are typically divided into four classes of acts: apologies, accounts, avoidance, and humor. Apologies are statements through which offenders accept responsibility for an untoward or inappropriate act and acknowledge that the act was blameworthy (Goffman, 1971; Schlenker, 1980; Tedeschi & Riess, 1981). Other authors have labeled apologetic acts "concessions" (Schonbach, 1980) and "requests for atonement" (Petronio, 1984). The complexity of an apology may range from simple ("Pardon me" or "I'm sorry") to elaborate, including expressions of remorse, offers of restitution, self-castigation, and attempts to obtain forgiveness (Darby & Schlenker, 1982; Schlenker & Darby, 1981).

The distinguishing features of apologies are that (a) they express guilt over having violated cultural or social rules, (b) they express remorse over having caused harm to a victim, and (c) they express embarrassment over the discrepancy between the individual's public behavior and his or her "true" identity (Tedeschi & Riess, 1981). In essence, apologies indicate to others present that the offender is competent enough to know that an infraction has occurred, and that he or she is responsible and, most important, repentant. Thus the need to instruct the offender in proper comportment or to sanction the offense is thwarted. Although a challenge of ignorance or ineptitude may be issued after an apology, it is much less likely and potentially casts the challenger in the unflattering light of being "heartless" (Goffman, 1967) and unforgiving.

Accounts are a second class of remedial strategies used by social actors caught in predicaments and are often given in response to a challenge or reproach from an offended party (Cody & McLaughlin, 1985). Scott and Lyman (1968) define accounts as statements "made by a social actor to explain unanticipated or untoward behavior" (p. 46). Accounts may be of two types: excuses and justifications. According to Scott and Lyman, excuses express denial of responsibility for an untoward act without denying its severity (e.g., "It was an accident" or "I was distracted"), whereas justifications express responsibility for an untoward act but deny the pejorative nature of the event or its consequences (e.g., "No harm done" or "I got what I deserved"). Other scholars, most notably Schonbach (1980), Tedeschi and Riess (1981), and Semin and Manstead (1983), have elaborated Scott and Lyman's original typologies of excuses and justifications.

A third category of acts associated with predicaments is less overt, but still provides ways for offenders to cope with their circumstances. We refer to this class of acts as *avoidance strategies* because they provide the offender with a mechanism for avoiding addressing both the degree of personal responsibility and the degree of severity of the event. One manifestation of avoidance is reflected in Goffman's (1956) notion of preventive face work, whereby awkward situations are prevented before they happen by careful monitoring of participants, context, and conversational topics, or are simply ignored if they arise unexpectedly. The face-threatening nature of an impending act can be somewhat mitigated by the use of disclaimers (Hewitt & Stokes, 1975), anticipatory excuses (Snyder, Higgens, & Stuckey, 1983), and forms of polite discourse (Brown & Levinson, 1978).

If, however, preventive face work fails, or if the infraction is so great that it cannot be ignored, the offending person may be called upon to rectify the situation. According to Goffman (1967), the issuance of a "challenge" signals the need for corrective face work and commences a remedial interchange. The offending person is obligated to provide an "offering" in response to a challenge. An offering typically redefines the event (justification) or the creator of the event (excuse). However, the offending person may refuse to provide an offering, either through silence (McLaughlin, Cody, & Rosenstein, 1983) or through some form of evasive message called refusals (Schonbach, 1980) or meta-accounts (Scott & Lyman, 1968; Tedeschi & Riess, 1981). This explicit refusal to remediate when challenged to do so is the second manifestation of avoidance.

In some instances actors are likely to gloss over the face-threatening event and avert the need to deal with it verbally, in the hope that it will be quickly forgotten. So as not to draw additional undue attention to an incident, an individual can change the topic (Goffman, 1967), be silent (McLaughlin, Cody, & O'Hair, 1983), or physically retreat from the encounter (Cupach et al., 1986). These strategies, like the preventive face work mentioned previously, are evasive face work. Unlike apologies or accounts, they fail to express guilt or remorse, fail to redress the face needs of others, and fail to restore disrupted interaction. They do not, however, entail the additional threat to negative face (i.e., the desire to be unimpeded and free of restraint) that is associated with apologies and other self-deprecating messages (Brown & Levinson, 1978). Evasive tactics allow the transgressor to assert, and sometimes to maintain, a position irrelevant to or beyond reproach.

A fourth general category of acts that are used in coping with predicaments is loosely identified as humor (Edelmann, 1987; Emerson, 1970; Fink & Walker, 1977; Goffman, 1971). Humor seems to acknowledge implicitly that an infraction has occurred and that the perpetrator is responsible without providing an explanation for it. In discussing laughter and joke work as two forms of humor, Edelmann (1985) notes that "both can be used to reduce tension inherent in the situation, while a joke can have the added advantage of turning a potential loss of social approval into a gain in social approval" (p. 209). Obviously, humor is not always appropriate for coping with predicaments, particularly when the offense is severe and the harm to others great. However, a well-formed joke, especially one reflecting on the unintentional incompetence of the transgressor, can express remorse, guilt, and embarrassment as an apology would without unduly lowering the individual's status vis-à-vis others who are present.

As mentioned previously, these four types of coping strategies—apologies, accounts, avoidance, and humor—provide the framework within which strategies for coping with embarrassment can be situated. Because these strategies are applied to all predicaments or failure events, and because their descriptions are theoretically rather than empirically motivated, they need to be adapted to the more specific situations causing embarrassment.

Remedial Strategies Used by Embarrassed Persons

In an effort to determine the extent to which theoretically derived strategies are actually used by embarrassed persons, and the extent to which theoretical divisions are adequate for capturing the range of actual messages, we conducted a series of studies focused on strategy use and perceived effectiveness. In the first study, respondents were asked to provide examples of strategies they would use in response to two researcher-generated embarrassing scenarios (Cupach et al., 1986). One scenario, representing a loss of poise, involved spilling gravy on oneself at a dinner party. The other scenario represented a presentation of an improper identity when the person attempts to pay for groceries and realizes that he or she forgot to bring money. In the second study, respondents were asked to describe the remedial strategies they actually had used in their own recollected embarrassing situations (Metts & Cupach, 1989). The findings reported in this section are based upon these two investigations.

First, in terms of frequency of reported use, we found that despite the significant attention they have garnered in the literature, accounts (excuses and justifications) were used infrequently. Justifications, particularly, seemed to be an unfavored option, appearing among the least often reported strategies for both the researcher-generated scenarios and the recollected events. Edelmann (1987) also reports evidence that accounts constitute infrequent responses to embarrassment. It appears that in the case of embarrassing predicaments, people are not very likely to deny their responsibility (since the event has been witnessed by others present) and are even less likely to try to minimize the severity of the event, either because most embarrassing events are not critically severe or because they incur more "harm" for the offender than for others present. In addition, we offer an explanation based on the unique quality of embarrassing predicaments to arouse an emotion that discomfits and possibly disorients the transgressor. This arousal may do two things: (a) It may temporarily preclude the ability of a person to construct a reasonable account, and (b) it may motivate a person to seek relief from the discomfiture, a relief that is not provided by the offering of an account to others.

By contrast, avoidance and humor were reported comparatively more frequently than were accounts, perhaps because they in some way attenuate the unpleasant arousal felt by the embarrassed person without also requiring the cognitive effort necessary to produce an acceptable account. Interestingly, for recollected events, respondents reported that avoidance was the most frequently used strategy (23% of strategies reported). Avoidance was followed by humor (15% of strategies reported), and simple apologies ranked last among the four major strategy types (11% of strategies reported).

In terms of adequacy, we found the four-part classification system derived from the scholarly literature to be insufficient. Respondents reported four additional strategies not easily accommodated by existing typologies or explicitly mentioned in the scholarly literature on apology, accounts, avoidance, and humor. The first such strategy was labeled "remediation" because it represents the overt and immediate effort of an embarrassed person to correct the cause of the predicament (e.g., cleaning up the spilled coffee, picking oneself up quickly after a fall on the ice). Although previous descriptions of apologies include references to "offers" of remediation and "promises" of restitution, these are verbal messages rather than actualized behaviors. Remediation accounted for 17% of all strategies reported for recollected embarrassing situations and was second only to avoidance in frequency of reported use.

A second strategy that is also associated with traditional definitions of apologies was labeled "description." Descriptions are simple, nonevaluative statements of the nature of the embarrassing event (e.g., "I have left my checkbook at home and can't pay you" or "I forgot that today was your birthday"). At one level, descriptions are like apologies in that they do acknowledge that some infraction has occurred. However, unlike apologies, they contain no indication of regret for the occurrence. In fact, descriptions share with avoidance strategies the inability to remediate the face needs of others or to restore the social order. Unlike the avoidance strategies of refusals and meta-accounts, however, descriptions are given independent of a reproach or challenge. Description accounted for only 3% of the total strategies reported for recollected embarrassing situations, although in the researcher-generated embarrassing scenario involving improper identity, description was very common (33% of the strategies reported).

A third strategy that emerged from the open-ended responses is a variant of the avoidance category. "Escape" is a particular form of avoidance involving a physical retreat from the awkward situation (e.g., running into the house after being caught necking in the driveway, or leaving a party after realizing that one is inappropriately attired). As is the case with avoidance, the infraction is not acknowledged, the face needs of others are not met, and the social order is not restored (except as performed by others in the embarrassed person's absence). However, when an embarrassed person uses avoidance (e.g., continuing with a public performance after a blunder as though nothing had happened), at least some modicum of poise is maintained in the presence of others. Ironically, avoidance, with its characteristic mustering of restraint and control, is typically reported in those incidents where an embarrassed person does not perceive that escape is a viable option (e.g., at a basketball game, during a dance recital, or in a speech class). Escape accounted for 11% of all strategies reported for recollected embarrassing situations and 24% of strategies listed for the researcher-generated scenarios.

The fourth category of acts used to cope with embarrassment was labeled "aggression." When using aggression, the embarrassed person turns his or her frustration into a physical or verbal attack on another person present, presumably the cause of the event that resulted in the embarrassment (e.g., after being forced into the hall from the locker room wearing only a towel, the embarrassed person attacks the boys responsible). Obviously, this strategy is akin to Goffman's (1967) notion of aggressive face work, although for Goffman, aggressiveness is contrasted with cooperation as a style of accomplishing corrective face work, rather than as a

TABLE 1
A Comparison of Traditional Categories of Remedial Strategies
with Categories Derived from Respondent Descriptions of
Recollected Embarrassing Situations

Traditional Classification	Extended Classification
Apology	Simple apology
	Remediation
	Description
Accounts	Accounts
excuse	excuse
justification	justification
Avoidance	Avoidance
	Escape
Humor	Humor
Aggressive facework	Aggression

class of strategies. Unlike all of the other strategies that might be used to cope with embarrassment, aggression actually intensifies the face loss of others and further complicates the already-disrupted social order. As might be expected, aggression accounted for only 4% of all strategies reported for recollected embarrassing situations and was not reported at all for the researcher-generated scenarios. Sharkey and Stafford (1989) similarly classify 3% of responses reported by embarrassed actors in their study as "hostility."

Table 1 provides a summary list of the strategies that were derived from the studies reported here. It also indicates the association between these strategies and those found in the traditional social predicaments literature.

Sequencing of Remedial Strategies
by Embarrassed Persons

In addition to finding existing typologies inadequate, our research indicates that remedial action is emergent and processual. In both the researcher-generated scenarios and the recollected descriptions of embarrassing situations, respondents reported multiple sequenced strategies. The regularity in these sequences suggests that individual strategies are not necessarily equivalent in terms of remedial utility and that sequences of strategies may function, in a sense, as a metastrategy.

Extricating oneself from an embarrassing predicament can be somewhat complicated. Given that predicaments are interactively managed, some remedial strategies are likely to be augmented or embellished by additional strategies. An initial remedial strategy may not be met with immediate acceptance by others, thus motivating the embarrassed person to try alternative strategies. Moreover, predicaments vary in the degree to which they disrupt social order and implicate the face needs of others. Spilling wine on oneself is easier to remediate than spilling wine on one's dinner guest. Although accounts alone and simple apologies alone are relatively ineffective in aggravating predicaments (i.e., situations that are face-threatening or inconveniencing to others), there is evidence to suggest that sequencing an apology with an account may be more effective. In his investigation of apologies, Fraser (1981) found that where others were significantly inconvenienced or injured, accounts tended to be appended to apologies. Likewise, Knapp, Stafford, and Daly (1986) found that regrettable messages that incurred strong consequences produced explanations as well as apologies.

Our own research indicates that embarrassed persons frequently sequence several strategies when extricating themselves from a predicament.[3] The data taken from the recollected embarrassing situations indicate that 35% of all respondents reported combinations of two, three, or four strategies (Metts & Cupach, 1989). Sharkey and Stafford (1989) similarly report that 33.4% of the embarrassed persons in their sample reported multiple responses.

Of all remedial strategies, the simple apology is most likely to initiate a remedial sequence. In fact, the simple apology very seldom terminates a remedial sequence and virtually never appears as an isolated strategy. Although the simple apology can be followed by any other strategy except aggression, three sequences are most common: (a) apology-remediation, (b) apology-description-remediation, and (c) apology-escape-remediation. If an embarrassed person uses escape to retreat from a situation only temporarily, he or she is highly likely to apologize and remediate immediately upon return. Humor is much like the simple apology in that it is frequently used as a sequence-initiating strategy. It is somewhat more likely, however, to be used occasionally as an isolated strategy, particularly when embarrassment arises from accidental loss of poise. When humor initiates a sequence, the most typical next strategies are a simple apology, an excuse, or escape (often followed by remediation).

In contrast to the simple apology and humor, remediation and avoidance (continuing in role performance as though nothing had happened) are frequently used in isolation or as sequence-terminating strategies, generally following a simple apology and/or humor. Interestingly, when remediation and avoidance appear in the same sequence, they are equally likely to precede each other. In other words, an embarrassed person might apologize (or do joke work) and then, while acting with some degree of poise, repair the situation. An embarrassed person might also apologize (or do joke work), repair the situation, and then continue interacting as though the disruption had not occurred. Either way, the embarrassed person signals an intent to resume social order without further attention to the untoward event.

The only strategy that does not lend itself to sequencing is aggression. Because aggression is a hostile response against others who have caused a person's embarrassment, it is not logical to expect apologetic, self-deprecating, or remediating responses to accompany it. Indeed, if such responses appear in the embarrassing predicament, they are more likely to be offered by those who have perpetrated the embarrassment.

The discovery of remedial sequences underscores the interactive nature of coping with predicaments. Although the evidence is preliminary, it suggests that actors may employ routines of remedial action as well as selecting single strategies from their repertoire. Research relying on checklists of strategies may fail to capture these patterns and the variations that arise in particular contexts.

We turn our attention now to a consideration of the responses of others to an embarrassing predicament. First, we summarize the strategies other persons might employ to accomplish the same goals outlined for the embarrassed person: reducing felt embarrassment (primarily for the embarrassed person, although others may also suffer negative arousal), addressing face needs, and restoring social order. This discussion is based on the findings presented in Metts and Cupach (1989). Next, we will briefly comment on the sequencing of remedial strategies by observers. We will also summarize the responses of others, inadvertent or intentional, that are perceived by embarrassed actors to exacerbate the severity and/or duration of their embarrassment.

RESPONSES OF OTHERS
TO AN EMBARRASSING PREDICAMENT

Although observers use some of the same remedial strategies as embarrassed persons, we find that these strategies do not provide an entirely adequate representation of the responses attributed to observers in respondents' accounts of their embarrassing experiences. Humor is employed by observers with moderate frequency (accounting for 16% of all strategies reported in recollected embarrassing situations). Likewise, accounts appear to be employed moderately by observers (16% of all strategies reported in recollected embarrassing situations). Reformulating the responsibility of the transgressor and reformulating the severity of the event appear to be somewhat common reactions of those who witness an embarrassing incident, possibly because they experience less intense discomfiture than the embarrassed person. Apologies and aggression, on the other hand, are not used by observers (except in cases of embedded episodes, where the observer's own embarrassing behavior has set off a chain reaction of subsequent embarrassing predicaments).

Instead, we find that observers use remediation, variations of avoidance, and two unique strategies: support and empathy. In descriptions of recollected embarrassing situations, respondents reported that remediation constituted 5% of all remedial strategies. Although this number seems small, it represents primarily only those instances in which remediation was necessary, but the embarrassed person was unwilling or unable to provide it. From this perspective, then, remediation must be considered a viable option for both embarrassed person and observer.

Variations of avoidance include "civil inattention" and "diversion." Civil inattention (taken from Goffman) is a passive strategy comparable to the avoidance

TABLE 2
A Comparison of Remedial Strategies Used by
Embarrassed Persons and Observers

Embarrassed Persons' Strategies	Observers' Strategies
Apology	Apology
Remediation	Remediation
Accounts	Accounts
excuse	excuse
justification	justification
Avoidance	Avoidance
escape	civil inattention
	diversion
Humor	Humor
Aggression	
	Support
	Empathy

strategy used by the embarrassed person by which participants simply act as though no infraction has occurred (e.g., ignoring an unintentional obscene phrase or accidental tripping). Diversion is a more proactive strategy in which observers overtly (but subtly) change the topic or activity that has prompted the embarrassment without directly responding to the embarrassment itself. In descriptions of recollected embarrassing situations, respondents attributed 12% of all observer strategies to these forms of avoidance.

By far the most frequently used strategy by observers appears to be "support." Support includes all verbal and nonverbal messages that assure the embarrassed person of continued positive regard despite the transgression (e.g., a warm smile, a pat on the arm, or a "Don't worry about it"). Support alone accounted for 32% of all strategies attributed to an observer's effort to reduce the embarrassed person's predicament. In some respects, support is the obverse of a challenge, indicating that both the offender and the offense are exempted from the need for reformulation. Empathy includes all messages that assure the embarrassed person that his or her predicament or behavior is not unique and that it happens to other people (e.g., "I know how you feel; I did the same thing in my history class" or "I've done the same thing and worse"). Empathy is in effect the obverse of an apology, in that it disindividuates the embarrassed person and says that he or she need not castigate him- or herself for incompetence. It may also constitute a graceful way of accepting an apology presented or implied by the embarrassed person. Empathy accounted for 19% of all strategies attributed to an observer in descriptions of recollected embarrassing situations. A comparison of the remedial strategies used by embarrassed persons with the strategies used by others is presented in Table 2.

Sequencing of Remedial Strategies Used by Others

Analysis of recollected embarrassing situations indicated that observers, like embarrassed persons, employ sequences of strategies. Respondents reported that, of those occasions when an observer helped them through an embarrassing situation, 32% involved more than one strategy (Metts & Cupach, 1989). Similar findings are reported by Sharkey and Stafford (1988).

Although all strategies used by other persons lend themselves to sequencing, two sequences were most common: support followed by empathy (e.g., "Don't worry about it; I fall up the stairs all the time"), and civil inattention followed by support. Overall, respondents' descriptions indicate that support and empathy were involved in all but three of the sequences reported; of those three, two involved remediation followed by humor, and one involved an excuse followed by remediation.[4]

Responses of Others That Increase Embarrassment

Although we generally assume that rational social actors avoid threats to other persons' role performances (Goffman, 1967), there are occasions when intentional and unintentional affronts do occur. Gross and Stone (1964), for example, identify three possible motivations for intentional orchestration of an embarrassing predicament: to teach children tactful and poised responses to predicaments, to negatively sanction an actor who is enacting an illegitimate role, and to exert power. Petronio et al. (1988) found that relational partners are sometimes the cause of each other's embarrassment. Attributions of cause for intentional embarrassment in this situation include attempts to control the relationship or to impress others at the partner's expense and use of embarrassment as an intentional norm violation or as a way to retaliate. Attributions for unintentional embarrassment include accidental embarrassment and attempts to be humorous.

Perhaps more common, however, than creating an embarrassing predicament is failing to help an embarrassed person restore face during the unfolding of an embarrassing predicament. An observer might unintentionally exacerbate another person's embarrassment by not knowing what to do (and hence doing nothing) or by attempting a corrective strategy (such as humor) that backfires. An observer may also feel justified in disregarding or even intensifying face loss if the offending person displays remedial strategies that do not seem commensurate with the severity of the predicament. Two structural features determine the severity of a predicament: the undesirability of the event and the actor's apparent responsibility for the event (Buttny, 1987; Schlenker, 1980; Snyder, 1985). The greater the undesirability of an event and the greater the actor's ascribed responsibility for that event, the more threatening the predicament is for the actor's image. As predicaments become more severe, actors are more inclined to mitigate negative repercussions by employing appropriate remedial strategies. Paradoxically, as predicaments become more severe and more aggravating to observers, they are less willing to assist embarrassed actors to regain face, and are more likely to intensify face threat by calling for an account.

In order to understand the role of observers in embarrassing predicaments more fully, we asked respondents reporting on situations in which they were embarrassed what other participants did (intentionally or unintentionally) that increased their embarrassment (Metts, Cupach, & Hazleton, 1987). Of those reporting on an embarrassing predicament, 43% indicated that their embarrassment was exacerbated by others who were present at the time of the event. These behaviors were of four general types: failure to recognize the event, humor, calling attention to the event, and sanctioning the embarrassed person.

A small percentage of cases of intensified embarrassment (5%) involved instances where observers failed to exhibit any reaction whatsoever to the embarrassed person or the predicament. This situation is occasionally distressing to the embarrassed actor, as it poses an enigma. The actor is unsure whether the lack of overt response is a sign of support, as it usually is when recognized as civil inattention, or a sign of dissatisfaction or lack of support. In a seminaturalistic study of the effect of embarrassment on dyadic interaction, Edelmann and Hampson (1981) found a number of reciprocated nonverbal behaviors. They infer from their data that "it may be necessary for the resumption of smooth interaction for both pair members to be embarrassed" (p. 177). Just as appearing embarrassed can assist the embarrassed actor's repair of the predicament, so too, perhaps, can the appearance of embarrassment on the part of others help to restore the social order. We suspect that actors possess a repertoire of subtle behaviors that can be used to signal to an embarrassed person that the predicament is recognized, but that it does not merit comment. In the absence of any detectable cues, however, the perception that others are ascribing negative attributions to the embarrassed actor increases.

Just as not responding to a predicament is ambiguous and can be interpreted by the embarrassed actor either positively or negatively, such is also the case with humor. Although laughter is somewhat less vague than a failure to recognize a predicament, it is somewhat more negative as a sanction. Clearly, humor used both by embarrassed persons and by others constitutes one of the most effective means of recovery from a predicament. There is often a fine line between "laughing with" someone and "laughing at" someone, however. We suspect that the perceived difference between the former and the latter is a matter of vocal and linguistic style (e.g., does the humor sound sarcastic?) and perhaps the timing of the response. Humor constituted 38% of all responses by other persons that increased the embarrassed person's discomfiture.

Calling attention to a predicament or sanctioning the embarrassed person are moves akin to a reproach. During a failure event the offended party may reproach the offending party, that is, request that a repair be offered. Reproaches probably occur less frequently in situations of embarrassment than in other types of predicaments, but when they do occur, they are likely to intensify the embarrassment of the challenged actor. McLaughlin, Cody, and O'Hair (1983) found five strategies that can be used by a reproacher: (a) projected concession (e.g., "Aren't you sorry you did it?"), (b) projected excuse (e.g., "Didn't you see the stop sign?"), (c) projected justification (e.g., "Did you have something more important to do?"), (d) projected refusal (e.g., "Don't try to pretend you didn't see me"), and (e) silence. Although any type of reproach is to some extent face-threatening and is likely to exacerbate the anxiety of the embarrassed person, mitigating moves (i.e., projected concessions and excuses) are generally more polite, deferential, and face-preserving, while aggravating moves (i.e., silence and projected refusals) tend to be more impolite, challenging, and face-threatening.

In 36% of the cases where embarrassment was intensified, someone called attention to the predicament (Metts et al., 1987). While such behavior does not express strong sanction, it does function like a mitigating reproach. Pointing out a person's error or impropriety is a face-threatening act, and therefore can further erode the already disintegrating interaction.

Sanctions in the form of overtly negative appraisals of the embarrassed person's behavior made up 21% of the responses that magnified embarrassment. These behaviors included nonverbal expressions of displeasure or disapproval as well as verbal criticisms or corrections. These responses further disrupt social interaction by exacerbating the loss of face for the embarrassed person. They also serve to place the embarrassed person in a defensive posture, in much the same manner as an aggravating reproach does.

Although exacerbation of embarrassment occurs with moderate frequency, it is much more common for others to assist the embarrassed actor in coping with the predicament. Given knowledge about the array of strategies exhibited by individuals in embarrassing predicaments, it is logical to examine factors that influence the likelihood that particular remedial strategies will be selected.

SELECTION OF REMEDIAL STRATEGIES

Although empirical research on this issue is relatively sparse, two studies demonstrate that the nature of the event creating embarrassment exerts influence on the selection of remedial responses. Sharkey and Stafford (1989) instructed respondents to describe three embarrassing incidents — one in which they were "highly" embarrassed, one in which they were "moderately" embarrassed, and one in which they were "slightly" embarrassed. Although strategy differences were not found across the three levels of intensity, type of embarrassment predicted the use of remedial strategies. They found that embarrassed persons tended to respond to violations of privacy with remediation, while others present tended to escape the situation or display objective symptoms (e.g., laughing, blushing). Forgetfulness was associated with the use of apologies and accounts by embarrassed actors and the display of hostility by others. In response to an awkward act, embarrassed persons provided accounts, while others exhibited remediation (i.e., provided encouragement or support) or displayed objective symptoms. When criticism was the cause of embarrassment, the embarrassed person responded with hostility, whereas the others escaped or exhibited avoidance (such as by changing the topic). When embarrassment was due to image/appropriateness, embarrassed persons tended to avoid or provide an account or apology. Similarly, other persons engaged in avoidance, such as by pretending nothing happened.

Based on Weinberg's (1968) work, we have analyzed respondents' open-ended descriptions of recollected embarrassing predicaments (see Metts & Cupach, 1989). While descriptions were easily coded into the first three of Weinberg's categories (i.e., faux pas, accident, mistake), the fourth category of duties was not supported. Instead, a category labeled *recipient* emerged. This consisted of predicaments arising for the embarrassed person because of the behavior of others (such as being ridiculed, or having privacy invaded).

We also asked respondents how they dealt with their recollected embarrassing predicaments. The data indicate that remedial strategies vary as a function of the type of situation creating the embarrassment. Specifically, excuses are more likely to be used in mistake situations than in other situations, but are less likely to be used in recipient situations where someone else caused the embarrassment; justification is more likely in response to a faux pas situation than in other situations; humor and remediation are more likely following an accident situation than other situations; and aggression is used exclusively in recipient situations (Metts & Cupach, 1989).

Although extant research is limited, it is clear that the type of situation causing the embarrassment influences remedial behavior. In addition, other factors are likely to influence the selection and implementation of remedial strategies by embarrassed actors and others. Presumably, the use of strategies is prefigured by their projected effectiveness, given the nature of the predicament eliciting the embarrassment.

Because the responses by actors to an embarrassing predicament are intended to fulfill multiple functions, the efficacy of remedial strategies can be judged in several ways. In general, remedial strategies are designed to mitigate the negative repercussions of the predicament. One of the most obvious functions of a remedial strategy, therefore, is to reduce felt embarrassment. Additionally, remedial strategies are intended to redress the face loss of others, and to minimize negative attributions about the offending actor. These functions are perhaps all tied to the supraordinate goal of restoring equilibrium to the interaction.

Ironically, although reducing felt embarrassment, redressing the face loss of others, and minimizing negative attributions about the offending actor are all goals toward which remedial strategies are directed, these goals are not likely to be achieved equally. Specifically, an embarrassed actor can more easily redirect negative attributions (for example, with a self-deprecating apology) than redress the face loss of others. And an embarrassed actor can more easily redress the face loss of others (for example, by remediating the harm or inconvenience that has incapacitated role performance) than reduce his or her own felt embarrassment.

More important, an embarrassed person can do virtually nothing to accomplish a reduction in his or her own felt embarrassment other than to endure it and wait for it to pass. This somewhat pessimistic conclusion is based on our study of recollected embarrassing predicaments (Metts et al., 1987).

We found that remedial strategies were only moderately effective at best in reducing respondent's felt embarrassment (Metts et al., 1987). Only humor, remediation, and excuse were rated at or above the neutral midpoint on the effectiveness scale. Respondents who reported using humor perceived that they were more effective in reducing their own embarrassment than people who did not use humor. Other strategies were generally only mildly effective. Moreover, respondents who reported using escape perceived that they were significantly less effective in reducing their embarrassment compared to those who did not use escape. It thus appears that remedial strategies offered by those creating their own embarrassment function primarily to redress the face needs of others and to repair the disrupted social order. These strategies are not seen by embarrassed actors as especially powerful techniques for reducing their level of felt embarrassment. Humor, in the form of spontaneous laughter, may be the exception when it provides a physiological release of tension (see Edelmann, 1987).

These findings contrast sharply with the findings related to the effectiveness of other persons' strategies in reducing the offender's embarrassment. Except for excuse, which was perceived to be ineffective, *all* other strategies were perceived to be at least moderately effective in reducing the offender's embarrassment. Remediation was judged to be most effective in reducing embarrassment, followed by empathy, justification, diversion, support, civil inattention, and humor.

Thus it appears that embarrassed persons are able to direct remedial strategies more effectively toward the causes of their anxiety (the potential for negative attribution and others' face loss) than toward the anxiety itself. Observers, on the other hand, who can offer assurances that negative attributions were not made and that face loss has been restored, can direct remedial strategies effectively toward all aspects of the predicament.[5]

SUMMARY OF PREVIOUS RESEARCH

The remedial process following embarrassment is complex. At the risk of oversimplification, we offer three basic principles that characterize effective remedial behavior. First, *following embarrassment, the maintenance of poise is desirable.* This does not mean that there should be no display of emotion. In fact, *appearing* embarrassed probably helps the individual overcome the predicament by acknowledging that the failure event has occurred (Edelmann, 1982; Semin & Manstead, 1982). By the same token, getting too flustered or physically escaping from the situation may damage the interaction irreparably. Competent social actors are adept at getting on with social interaction after quickly recovering from a predicament.

The second key principle in effective remedial behavior is that *mitigating the negative attributions ascribed by others is essential to restoring one's own face.* This explains why we often apologize or excuse ourselves even when we do not feel that a predicament is our fault. Face restoration is inherently a cooperative process, particularly in predicaments that are embarrassing. Remedial face work thus seems to work best when an orientation toward others is maintained. This principle is reflected in the fact that individuals can remediate their own embarrassment only minimally. Instead, the support of others present during a predicament is instrumental in helping an individual overcome anxiety stemming from embarrassment. At the same time, such support from others is likely to be forthcoming only to the extent that the face loss of those others has been redressed by the offending actor.

The third principle of remediation is that *as an embarrassing incident becomes increasingly offensive to others, the embarrassed actor is obligated to redress the face of others in order to mitigate negative attributions.* The remedial response following embarrassment must therefore be commensurate with the nature and severity of the event giving rise to the predicament. Awkwardness, clumsiness, or ineptitude may be personally distressing, but they are usually not particularly offensive to others. Given the supraordinate goal of restoring interactive equilibrium, and given the primacy of preserving the face of others, too elaborate a response to awkwardness or ineptitude will be inappropriate. An elaborate account for ineptitude will probably only draw undue attention to the incident. Unnecessarily dwelling on an event that has not yet adversely affected others to a great extent probably also begins to threaten the negative face (i.e., desire for autonomy; see Brown & Levinson, 1978) of others. Thus avoidance is frequently used in response to awkwardness or ineptitude, and remediation (restitution) is effective when possible. Predicaments arising from social or relational impropriety, however, may require more explicit penitence on the part of the offender. Such situations represent infractions of taken-for-granted rules of proper conduct and may evoke perceptions of rudeness, impoliteness, or tactlessness. The more others are offended, the less effective a justifying response will be. Also, it will be more difficult to obtain the help of others when they have been severely offended. More elaborated responses on the part of the offender are necessary to satisfy others and to gain their cooperation in restoring normalcy to the interaction.

FUTURE DIRECTIONS: TOWARD A TAXONOMY

Initial efforts to understand the use and effectiveness of remedial behavior have been promising. However, research has been circumscribed, in part, by somewhat simplistic schemes for categorizing embarrassing events. More precise and sophisticated schemes are needed to capture the important nuances of remediation. As Edelmann (1987) observes:

> What is required is a classification system taking into account both the nature of the rule-breaking episode and the actor's and observer's interpretation of this event. Orthogonal dimensions of rules known-rules not known; intentional action-accidental action; actor responsible-observer responsible; could provide a useful starting point. (p. 53)

In an effort to advance the conceptualization of situations giving rise to embarrassment, we propose a preliminary taxonomy of embarrassing predicaments. It reflects the spirit of Edelmann's call for a dimensional approach, but recognizes that not all dimensions are equally relevant or salient in any particular situation. For example, situations in which the actor is responsible for his or her own embarrassment are characterized by dimensions that are irrelevant in situations where observers are responsible for an actor's embarrassment. Likewise, judgments as to whether a rule is known or not known are irrelevant in situations where no rule is violated, such as tripping, falling, or dropping packages.

We propose, therefore, a hierarchical sorting technique for embarrassing situations. At the highest level, a decision is made as to whether the incident is caused by an action of the actor or of the observer. Different paths are then taken for each of these two general classes of events. In the following pages we elaborate the details of this taxonomy and illustrate specific types of predicaments with examples drawn from respondents' written descriptions (Metts & Cupach, 1989).

Actor Responsible

If an actor is responsible for his or her own embarrassment, he or she has necessarily performed some act or behavior that is incongruent with or inappropriate to one of three levels of competence: the idealized social actor, the accomplished role performer, or the idealized self-image.

As an *idealized social actor*, a person envisions his or her behavior to be congruent with normative expectations. One type of normative expectation carries the force of a social rule, a "followable prescription that indicates what behavior is obligated, preferred, or prohibited in certain contexts" (Shimanoff, 1980, p. 57). When a social rule is violated, the transgressor is subject to possible sanctions from the social network. Thus one class of acts likely to cause embarrassment is "rule violations." These acts may then be distinguished according to whether the rule is known or not known. If the rule is known, then the act occurred because of forgetfulness/inattentiveness or because of misinterpretation of the scope conditions in which the rule is operative. If the rule is not known, then the act occurred because of ignorance. The following are examples of forgetfulness and misinterpretation, respectively:

I was supposed to meet a friend for lunch. This date had been set for some time. I had classes that morning — in fact an exam. I started home and it dawned on me — I think this is the day I was supposed to meet Pam, but I wasn't sure and it was written on my calendar at home, 20 miles away. So, I drove to where we were to meet, arriving late but she was there waiting for me. I was embarrassed because I was forgetful and felt a little out of control of things at the moment.

My boyfriend and I were at another couple's house for dinner. We were all a little tipsy — talking and laughing. During the course of conversation I used a word (can't remember what) that no one else understood. Don, the male partner of the couple, made a snide comment about my "superintellectualism." I thought he was just kidding and responded with what I thought was a joking response about his "illiteracy." I suddenly realized that he really didn't understand the word and that everyone was uncomfortable with the exchange.

A second type of normative expectation is what might be called "public comportment," expectations that social actors conduct themselves with a certain degree of dignity and poise. They do not typically wear their clothes unbuttoned, cry excessively, or fall down while dancing. The question as to whether these expectations are known or not known is irrelevant. Rather, the question of domain in which control is lost allows us to distinguish three types of embarrassment due to failure of "public comportment": physical control, emotional control, and environmental control (including clothing and props). These three types of control are reflected in the following examples:

When I was attending a good friend's wedding, I was walking down the aisle for communion when I started to slip around by one of the pews. I luckily caught my balance in time and didn't fall down, but I did do some sliding on the floor, right in front of the whole church. I was very embarrassed because of the humiliation of almost falling on my face in front of a crowd.

The most embarrassing moment that I have faced in my lifetime was when I was studying abroad in 1982 and the time had come to return to the states. My heart was crushed, and at a farewell party my emotions ran wild. In front of my classmates, and my girlfriend, the tears began to flow. I knew that it was all right for guys to show emotions, but I was still very embarrassed.

At my boyfriend's sister's wedding, I was dancing with his great uncle and the dress I was wearing, which buttoned up all the way in the front, came unbuttoned from the neck to the waist. It was embarrassing because there were so many people around, and they were strangers. Also, I don't usually expose myself to people, let alone people who I don't know and who I am trying to make a good impression on.

A second broad class of embarrassing situations are those in which a person has failed to display competence as an *accomplished role performer.* Embarrassment arises from an incongruence between displayed behavior and the expectations that attend a particular role being performed. The important question here is whether the incongruent behavior is related to abilities/skills one has presumably acquired or to responsibilities/obligations one has presumably agreed to meet. In the former instance might fall such failures as missing a free throw during a basketball game or missing steps during a ballet recital. For example:

> The most embarrassing thing that has happened to me was when I was in high school Swing Choir. Our group was performing a grand finale song, and in this we did the Charleston. I was front and center and during the song I did a step out of sequence. The whole group was laughing, and I didn't think we would make it through the rest of the song. I was embarrassed because I don't like to make mistakes when I sing or dance.

Failure to display behavior consistent with role-relevant responsibilities or obligations includes such predicaments as parents forgetting to pick up their children from day care, secretaries forgetting to post important letters, and students failing to perform expected role behaviors such as taking exams. For example:

> I had stayed up until 7 a.m. to study for a final. I fell asleep for three hours and missed the exam. I was very embarrassed when I went to talk to my teacher because I did something that was irresponsible and stupid.

A third broad class of embarrassing situations involves behavior that is incongruent with one's identity as a particular person, not simply one's competence as a social actor or as a role performer. In a sense, the embarrassed person has displayed public behavior that is not in accordance with the values, attitudes, and conduct that he or she would like others to believe are characteristics of his or her *idealized self-image.* Two more specific instances of this type of embarrassment can be distinguished depending upon whether the public behavior has created a false image or has threatened an established image. Creating a false image is exemplified by the following:

> The incident in which I was embarrassed happened in a bar. I was with a few friends. We all agreed that we had met a girl who was sitting across the bar on a previous occasion. I went and asked her name and it was not the same person. I was embarrassed because of the simple fact that I was wrong and she thought it was a pickup line. However, I had not consumed enough alcohol for this to be true.

Threatening an established image is illustrated in the following example:

> I was necking in a car with my boyfriend in front of my house. I was 16 and things were getting carried away so to speak. All of a sudden the car door opened and I fell out only to look up and see my mother staring down at me with a very serious look on her face. Clearly, she was not pleased. I was embarrassed because I had my mother

TABLE 3

Classification of Embarrassing Predicaments Where Actor Is Responsible

Act is incongruent with

Idealized social self
(1)   rule violation
        rule known
          forgetfulness
          misinterpretation
        rule not known
          ignorance
(2)   comportment
        physical
        emotional
        environmental

Accomplished role performer
(1)   abilities/skills
(2)   responsibilities/obligations

Idealized self-image
(1)   create false image
(2)   threaten established image

and entire family believing I was an angel and would never park with a boy. And here she caught me red-handed.

Table 3 summarizes the types of embarrassing predicaments brought about by the embarrassed actor's own behavior.

Observer Responsible

On occasion, the triggering event that produces embarrassment is not an act performed by the embarrassed person but an act performed by some other person. In these instances, the embarrassed person is "thrust" into a predicament rather than originating a predicament. Two general classes of observer-responsible predicaments can be distinguished based upon how directly the embarrassed person is implicated in the event. Direct involvement occurs when the embarrassed person is targeted explicitly as the recipient of the embarrassing act. Indirect involvement occurs when the embarrassed person is a passive observer to an embarrassing event or is implicated in an embarrassing event while absent.

There are two general modes of *direct* embarrassment caused by other persons: individualization and causing to look unpoised. In both instances, the embarrassed person is caused to be the center of attention. However, in the former, attention is drawn to a person through actions that somehow distinguish the embarrassed person from others, while in the latter, attention is drawn to a person through actions that make a person look awkward or unpoised in front of others. *Individualization* may involve one of three forms of attention: recognition/praise, criticism/correction, and teasing. These forms of attention are illustrated in the following examples:

> When I was in high school I hung around with a bunch of kids who didn't take grades too seriously. At the graduation assembly, the principal announced the scholarship winners. I had won a scholarship and had to go to the stage and accept a certificate. I was embarrassed by all the attention.

> My first year at college I took a nutrition class. One day in class I was talking to the girl next to me and the instructor took offense to this and made a public spectacle of me in front of the whole class. The rest of the class broke out laughing, something I didn't find the least bit amusing.

> I was sitting with my three roommates after my girlfriend had left after visiting for the weekend. Then my roommate who usually shares a room with me (except when my girlfriend comes down, when he sleeps on the couch) started asking if anybody heard "weird noises." When all of us replied "no," he began describing these noises so that we all knew he was describing me and my girlfriend. My roommates just laughed but I was embarrassed.

Causing to look unpoised typically occurs when a person is the recipient of someone else's clumsiness, as when tripped or bumped accidentally:

> I was significantly embarrassed when I was cocktail waitressing and a man suddenly turned around and knocked the drinks I was carrying off my tray (some splashed upon another customer). Everyone in the immediate bar area (it was very crowded) turned to look. It looked at first as if I just spilt my tray, and that was very embarrassing.

However, a person may also, on occasion, be made to look unpoised or awkward by the intentional behavior of others. For example:

> I was playing games in an arcade at the mall in my town. Someone from the movie theater where I worked at the time came over and pulled my shorts down to my knees.

Indirect involvement in embarrassing events may arise in one of three ways: association, empathic embarrassment, and privacy violation. Embarrassment through *association* occurs when the embarrassed person feels embarrassment because he or she is associated with someone who is enacting untoward behavior and assumes that negative attributions will be generalized to him or her from those actions. For instance:

> One incident I can think of when I was embarrassed was when a group and I were all standing around talking. One of my friends had been drinking, and he started yelling

TABLE 4
TABLE 4
Classification of Embarrassing Predicaments Where Observer Is Responsible

Involvement of embarrassed person is

Direct
(1) individualize
     recognition/praise
     criticism/correction
     teasing
(2) cause to look unpoised

Indirect
(1) association
(2) empathic
(3) privacy violation

obscenities at people (girls) going by in cars. I was embarrassed to be with my friend. He had too much to drink and was making a fool of himself in front of a lot of people.

Empathic embarrassment occurs when a person observes someone else's embarrassment and feels embarrassment "for" that person:

Last week I went home and also took my boyfriend home. Before going home, I went inside with him to chat with his parents, whom I don't know very well. And right away they started to yell at him about a letter from the university telling them about something he got in trouble for. I was not so much embarrassed for me, but for him. His parents were yelling at him with me there.

Embarrassment arising from *privacy violation* occurs when a person learns through indirect means that personal information has been revealed to other persons without his or her knowledge or presence. This type of embarrassment is unique in that it may be felt initially when the violation is revealed and also on subsequent occasions when interacting with the parties who have acquired the private information. The following example represents privacy violation:

When I went to my girlfriend's home, she told her sister some private things about me. I was not present at the time she told her, but I'm still embarrassed when I see her sister. It's embarrassing because someone who shouldn't know (I'm not personal or close enough to) some personal things about me does.

Table 4 summarizes types of embarrassment caused by observers.

The taxonomy presented here is an initial step toward formalizing a comprehensive and reliable method for classifying types of embarrassing predicaments. We think it merits elaboration and refinement through additional research. However, we encourage investigators to avoid reifying this or any other taxonomy. Theoretically derived categories may indeed capture the range of possible circumstances inducing embarrassment; however, whether any particular experience should be counted as, for example, misinterpretation or ignorance, correction or teasing, may well depend upon the interpretation of the actor, not that of the investigator. Thus grounded theory approaches that incorporate actors' feedback to researchers during the coding process should be used to augment traditional content-analytic approaches.

FUTURE DIRECTIONS:
REMEDIAL STRATEGIES AND BEYOND

Prior research on predicaments and accounting sequences has been useful in describing remedial processes generally, but it fails to capture some of the unique and subtle aspects of coping with embarrassment. The taxonomies of remedial strategies used by embarrassed persons and observers that we have presented here were derived from repeated analyses of respondents' descriptions of embarrassing predicaments. However, our confidence that they exhaust the domain of possible strategies available to social actors depends upon their adequacy for other researchers working with data sets drawn from a variety of populations. Likewise, the behaviors that observers exhibit that exacerbate embarrassment for the embarrassed person have received only preliminary investigation and merit more careful attention. Continued descriptive analyses of the domain of behaviors that occur in embarrassing predicaments is essential.

Future research should continue to explore the complexities of remedial processes. Managing embarrassing predicaments entails a variety of strategies, nonverbal as well as verbal, by multiple parties, and in sequences and combinations. Sharkey and Stafford (1989) have presented preliminary evidence of the interdependence of the responses of parties to an embarrassing predicament. They found, for example, that when embarrassed persons responded with remediation or accounts, others responded with remediation; when embarrassed persons responded with concealment of their embarrassment, others responded with concealment as well. Although gathering interactive data is problematic when studying social phenomena such as embarrassment, it is an important next step in learning how strategies are sequenced by multiple parties in a predicament.

The fact that social actors sequence remedial strategies within embarrassing episodes suggests that they may also orchestrate individual and collaborative "long-term" strategies in their relationships. For example, idiosyncratic issues or topics are considered taboo in interpersonal relationships, in part because they may provoke embarrassment for one or both partners (see Baxter & Wilmot, 1985). Once recognized, such topics are simply avoided. Social actors may also anticipate potentially embarrassing but unavoidable behaviors and attempt to reframe these so that recurrence evokes little or no embarrassment. As an example, assume that Todd is frequently clumsy and accident prone. With new friends, he may apologize for his ineptitude and even use self-deprecating humor. Over time, however, he may also attempt to manipulate the attributions for his clumsiness by reinforcing the claim, "I'm just a klutz." Providing a dispositional attribution may seem counterintuitive as a short-term strategy, but it accomplishes the long-term goal of manipulating attributions about inevitably recurring and identity-damaging behavior. The effect of reinforcing the dispositional attribution for the untoward behavior is to lower the expectations for performance over time, thereby lessening negative attributions about Todd and consequently mitigating his embarrassment. In effect, Todd's clumsiness becomes the norm, and it is only minimally face-threatening among friends who know what to expect. Thus we suspect that identities threatened by embarrassing predicaments are managed relationally over time, as well as episodically. Although this issue is only speculative at this point, we believe it deserves formal investigation in future research.

Another goal for future research is to discern how strategy clusters by the embarrassed person and others interact with features of context to result in effective remediation. One such feature is the nature of the relationship between parties to a predicament. We believe that familiarity, for example, represents one aspect of the social relationship that affects the nature of a remedial response. Because familiar relationships are more important to actors, and because there is an expectation of a continuation of the relationship, actors will feel more obligated to remedy an embarrassing predicament *if* it involves a familiar and liked other. In general, one is more concerned with avoiding or mitigating an embarrassing event witnessed by friends, by strangers with whom the actor anticipates interacting again in the future (Brown & Garland, 1971), or by anonymous others whose evaluation is important (e.g., a political candidate). If, however, a relationship is unimportant and/or the actor does not expect future interaction with the other person, then there is less need to maintain and repair face.

Although familiarity seems to magnify the obligation to remedy an event that offends, at the same time, the form of an account or an apology may be personalized or idiosyncratic. Because of less formality and greater perceived understanding, an offering typically need not be elaborated to the extent necessary with a relatively unfamiliar other (e.g., Fraser, 1981). There is some evidence that low intimacy and low familiarity between a reproacher and an accounter tend to lead to the offering of an excuse, while high intimacy leads to the presentation of a justification (Cody & McLaughlin, 1985; McLaughlin, Cody, & O'Hair, 1983). This suggests that offenders may feel more responsible for their actions when called to account by a familiar other than when called to account by a stranger. More important, a developed relationship can withstand more aggravating forms of communication as persons have less need to worry about engendering negative attributions in partners. A justification is probably not perceived to be as aggravating when presented to a familiar other because it is not as face-threatening.

Of course, this connection between familiarity and remedial action is qualified by the relative infrequency of embarrassing events in intimate relationships (Sharkey & Stafford, 1988) and by the fact that what constitutes an embarrassing predicament is likely to be different for close versus distant others. Faux pas, for example, are less likely to occur and are less likely to be embarrassing in intimate relationships (see Harris, 1984; Knapp et al., 1986). Likewise, acts of losing poise that are humiliating in the early stages of a relationship (e.g., flatulence) may become merely humorous or annoying in intimate stages. On the other hand, calling someone by the wrong name in an initial encounter may be only mildly embarrassing and aggravating, whereas calling one's spouse by the wrong name while having sex has severe repercussions. Thus predicaments vary according to the nature of the relationship between the parties.

Finally, we close with a call not only for more research, but for more creative research on embarrassing predicaments. To date, most research has employed traditional methods such as analyses of recollected embarrassing events. Whether these descriptions adequately represent the nuances of contextual variables and remedial behaviors is an important consideration. Unobtrusive observation of predicaments in progress, accompanied by detailed and immediate interviews of both embarrassed persons and observers, may yield new insights into the forms and functions of remedial processes. Such research should ultimately reveal how social actors competently manipulate situated social identities.

NOTES

1. We will focus specifically on the remedial practices that occur *after* an embarrassing event. For information on practices designed to prevent or avoid face threats, see the work by Hewitt and Stokes (1975) on disclaimers and Brown and Levinson (1978) on politeness phenomena.

2. We prefer to use the term *strategy* to describe general types of behavior (such as apologies or excuses) and the term *tactic* to refer to specific instantiations of a strategy (such as "I'm sorry" or "It's not my fault").

3. These conclusions are based on the findings reported in Cupach et al. (1986) and a reanalysis of the data reported in Metts and Cupach (1989).

4. These findings are based on a reanalysis of the data reported in Metts and Cupach (1989).

5. Remedial strategies used by others were not found to vary significantly as a function of situation. However, a small sample may have impaired statistical power.

REFERENCES

Bandera, B. R., & Cupach, W. R. (1986, May). *Perceived competence of face saving strategies in embarrassing situations.* Paper presented at the annual meeting of the International Communication Association, Chicago.

Baxter, L. A., & Wilmot, W. W. (1985). Taboo topics in close relationships. *Journal of Social and Personal Relationships, 2,* 253-269.

Blumstein, P. W., Carssow, K. G., Hall, J., Hawkins, B., Hoffman, R., Ishem, E., Maurer, C. P., Spens, D., Taylor, J., & Zimmerman, D. L. (1974). The honoring of accounts. *American Sociological Review, 39,* 551-566.

Brown, B. R. (1970). Face-saving following experimentally induced embarrassment. *Journal of Experimental Social Psychology, 6*, 255-271.

Brown, B. R., & Garland, H. (1971). The effects of incompetency, audience acquaintanceship, and anticipated evaluative feedback on face-saving behavior. *Journal of Experimental Social Psychology, 7*, 490-502.

Brown, P., & Levinson, S. (1978). Universals in language usage: Politeness phenomena. In E. Goody (Ed.), *Questions and politeness: Strategies in social interaction* (pp. 56-289). Cambridge: Cambridge University Press.

Buss, A. H. (1980). *Self-consciousness and social anxiety*. San Francisco: W. H. Freeman.

Buttny, R. (1985). Accounts as a reconstruction of an event's context. *Communication Monographs, 52*, 57-77.

Buttny, R. (1987). Sequence and practical reasoning in accounts episodes. *Communication Quarterly, 35*, 67-83.

Cody, M. J., & McLaughlin, M. L. (1985). Models for the sequential construction of accounting episodes: Situational and interactional constraints on message selection and evaluation. In R. L. Street & J. N. Cappella (Eds.), *Sequence and pattern in communicative behavior* (pp. 50-69). Baltimore: Edward Arnold.

Cupach, W. R., Metts, S., & Hazleton, V. (1986). Coping with embarrassing predicaments: Remedial strategies and their perceived utility. *Journal of Language and Social Psychology, 5*, 181-200.

Darby, B. W., & Schlenker, B. R. (1982). Children's reactions to apologies. *Journal of Personality and Social Psychology, 43*, 742-753.

Edelmann, R. J. (1982). The effect of embarrassed reactions upon others. *Australian Journal of Psychology, 34*, 359-367.

Edelmann, R. J. (1985). Social embarrassment: An analysis of the process. *Journal of Social and Personal Relationships, 2*, 195-213.

Edelmann, R. J. (1987). *The psychology of embarrassment*. Chichester: John Wiley.

Edelmann, R. J., & Hampson, S. E. (1981). Embarrassment in dyadic interaction. *Social Behavior and Personality, 9*, 171-177.

Emerson, J. P. (1970). Behavior in private places: Sustaining definitions of reality in gynecological examinations. In H. P. Dreitzel (Ed.), *Recent sociology: No. 2. Patterns of communicative behavior* (pp. 74-97). New York: Macmillan.

Fink, E. L., & Walker, B. A. (1977). Humorous responses to embarrassment. *Psychological Reports, 40*, 475-485.

Fraser, B. (1981). On apologizing. In F. Coulmas (Ed.), *Conversational routine: Explorations in standardized communication situations and prepatterned speech* (pp. 259-271). New York: Mouton.

Goffman, E. (1956). Embarrassment and social organization. *American Journal of Sociology, 62*, 264-271.

Goffman, E. (1967). *Interaction ritual: Essays on face-to-face behavior*. New York: Pantheon.

Goffman, E. (1971). *Relations in public*. New York: Basic Books.

Gross, E., & Stone, G. P. (1964). Embarrassment and the analysis of role requirements. *American Journal of Sociology, 70*, 1-15.

Harris, T. E. (1984). The "faux pas" in interpersonal communication. In S. Thomas (Ed.), *Communication theory and interpersonal interaction* (pp. 53-61). Norwood, NJ: Ablex.

Hewitt, J., & Stokes, R. (1975). Disclaimers. *American Sociological Review, 40*, 1-11.

Knapp, M. L., Stafford, L., & Daly, J. A. (1986). Regrettable messages: Things people wish they hadn't said. *Journal of Communication, 36*, 40-58.

McLaughlin, M. L., Cody, M. J., & O'Hair, H. D. (1983). The management of failure events: Some contextual determinants of accounting behavior. *Human Communication Research, 9*, 208-224.

McLaughlin, M. L., Cody, M. J., & Rosenstein, N. E. (1983). Account sequences in conversations between strangers. *Communication Monographs, 50*, 102-125.

Metts, S., & Cupach, W. R. (1989). Situational influence on the use of remedial strategies in embarrassing predicaments. *Communication Monographs, 56*, 151-162

Metts, S., Cupach, W. R., & Hazleton, V. (1987, February). *Coping with social dis-ease: Remedial strategies and embarrassment.* Paper presented at the annual meeting of the Western Speech Communication Association, Salt Lake City.

Miller, R. S. (1986). Embarrassment: Causes and consequences. In W. H. Jones, J. M. Cheek, & S. R. Briggs (Eds.), *Shyness: Perspectives on research and treatment* (pp. 295-311). New York: Plenum.

Miller, R. S. (1987). Empathic embarrassment: Situational and personal determinants of reactions to the embarrassment of another. *Journal of Personality and Social Psychology, 53*, 1061-1069.

Modigliani, A. (1968). Embarrassment and embarrassability. *Sociometry, 31*, 313-326.

Modigliani, A. (1971). Embarrassment, facework, and eye contact: Testing a theory of embarrassment. *Journal of Personality and Social Psychology, 17*, 15-24.

Petronio, S. (1984). Communication strategies to reduce embarrassment: Differences between men and women. *Western Journal of Speech Communication, 48*, 28-38.

Petronio, S., Olson, C., & Dollar, N. (1988). Relational embarrassment: Impact on relational quality and communication satisfaction. In D. O'Hair & B. R. Patterson (Eds.), *Advances in interpersonal communication research: Proceedings of the Western Speech Communication Association convention, Interpersonal Communication Interest Group* (pp. 195-206). Las Cruces: New Mexico State University, Communication Resources Center.

Sattler, J. M. (1965). A theoretical, developmental, and clinical investigation of embarrassment. *Genetic Psychology Monographs, 71*, 19-59.

Schlenker, B. R. (1980). *Impression management: The self-concept, social identity, and interpersonal relations.* Monterey, CA: Brooks/Cole.

Schlenker, B. R., & Darby, B. W. (1981). The use of apologies in social predicaments. *Social Psychology Quarterly, 44*, 271-278.

Schonbach, P. (1980). A category system for account phases. *European Journal of Social Psychology, 10*, 195-200.

Scott, M. B., & Lyman, S. M. (1968). Accounts. *American Sociological Review, 33*, 46-62.

Semin, G. R., & Manstead, A.S.R. (1981). The beholder beheld: A study of social emotionality. *European Journal of Social Psychology, 11*, 253-265.

Semin, G. R., & Manstead, A.S.R. (1982). The social implications of embarrassment displays and restitution behaviour. *European Journal of Social Psychology, 12*, 367-377.

Semin, G. R., & Manstead, A.S.R. (1983). *The accountability of conduct: A social psychological analysis.* London: Academic Press.

Sharkey, W. F., & Stafford, L. (1988, November). *I've never been so embarrassed: Degree of embarrassment and its effect upon communicative responses.* Paper presented at the annual meeting of the Speech Communication Association, New Orleans.

Sharkey, W. F., & Stafford, L. (1989, May). *So, how embarrassing was it? . . . Whadja do?: The relationship between the situation, the degree of perceived embarrassment and responses to embarrassment.* Paper presented at the annual meeting of the International Communication Association, San Francisco.

Shimanoff, S. B. (1980). *Communication rules: Theory and research.* Beverly Hills, CA: Sage.

Snyder, C. R. (1985). The excuse: An amazing grace? In B. R. Schlenker (Ed.), *The self and social life* (pp. 235-260). New York: McGraw-Hill.

Snyder, C. R., Higgens, R. L., & Stuckey, R. J. (1983). *Excuses: Masquerades in search of grace.* New York: John Wiley.

Spitzberg, B. H., & Cupach, W. R. (1989). *Handbook of interpersonal competence research.* New York: Springer-Verlag.

Tedeschi, J., & Riess, M. (1981). Verbal strategies in impression management. In C. Antaki (Ed.), *The psychology of ordinary explanations of social behavior* (pp. 271-309). New York: Academic Press.

Weinberg, M. S. (1968). Embarrassment: Its variable and invariable aspects. *Social Forces, 46*, 382-388.

Coping with Embarrassment and Chronic Blushing

ROBERT J. EDELMANN
University of Surrey

I N order to evaluate the issues raised by Cupach and Metts, I begin this commentary by presenting a working model of embarrassment. The remedial processes discussed by Cupach and Metts are then discussed in relation to this model.

The general thesis offered by Cupach and Metts derives from Goffman's (1967, 1971) writings on self-presentation and face work. Indeed, there have been a number of attempts to conceptualize the process underlying embarrassment derived from Goffman's work (Edelmann, 1985, 1987b, in press; Modigliani, 1968, 1971; Semin & Manstead, 1981, 1982; Silver, Sabatini, & Parrott, 1987). Within this framework, embarrassment has three central components: First, embarrassment occurs only in real or imagined social interactions; second, it is the result of an undesired and unintentional social predicament that has occurred or that the person fears may occur; third, the person anticipates or perceives a discrepancy between his or her current self-presentation and his or her standard for self-presentation (Edelmann, 1987b, in press).

The second of these component parts suggests that the experience of embarrassment is generated by a clearly defined antecedent event, that is, a faux pas, gaffe, or impropriety. In fact, it is difficult to find any exceptions to this view, a view that is also offered by Cupach and Metts. For example, the starting point for Modigliani's model is the assumption that an incident has occurred that is the immediate cause of embarrassment; for Semin and Manstead, the starting point is a public violation of a taken-for-granted social rule that is part of the actor's repertoire. It is undoubtedly the case that embarrassment is frequently evoked by

Correspondence and requests for reprints: Robert J. Edelmann, Department of Psychology, University of Surrey, Guildford, Surrey GU2 5XH, United Kingdom.

Communication Yearbook 13, pp. 353-364

a clearly defined event that results in the actor's presented image creating an undesired impression.

It is also clear, however, that some actors experience embarrassment even in the absence of a clearly defined antecedent event (Edelmann, 1987a, 1987b, 1989). First, it is possible to elicit embarrassment by informing the actor that he or she looks embarrassed even if this is not the case and/or the situation is not defined as embarrassing. Second, it is possible to become embarrassed as a result of blushing, even in a situation that is not deemed by others present or by the actor to be intrinsically embarrassing. There are individuals for whom it appears that internal and expressive cues, notably blushing, are sufficient to provoke extreme embarrassment (Edelmann, 1987a, 1989; Timms, 1980). Any conceptualization of embarrassment must therefore be able to explain the multiplicity of the phenomenon.

TOWARD A
CONCEPTUALIZATION OF EMBARRASSMENT

It is widely acknowledged that embarrassment is characterized by a well-defined behavioral display. Eye contact is reduced, body movement and speech disturbances increase (Edelmann & Hampson, 1979, 1981), and facial flushing occurs; in fact, blushing has been described as the hallmark of embarrassment. It does appear, however, that it is possible to experience embarrassment without blushing and to blush without being embarrassed. Nonetheless, in certain instances blushing seems to precede the experience of embarrassment — the latter emotion is then experienced in the absence of any clearly defined external antecedent event. It seems, therefore, that stimuli that can evoke feelings of embarrassment can be either external (a faux pas, impropriety, social transgression, or the like) or internal (bodily and facial cues).

The notion that feedback from one's facial and expressive behaviors gives rise to the experience of the emotion has had a long and checkered history, and a wealth of contradictory evidence has been produced. The issues have been reviewed and commented upon elsewhere (Buck, 1980; Edelmann, 1987b; Laird, 1984). Inevitably, in light of the controversial nature of the topic, there are those who support (or who claim that the evidence supports) some version of the facial feedback hypothesis and those who are less convinced by the available evidence. While it is difficult to assert that facial expression *is* the emotion, it seems clear that expressive behavior can add to or accentuate emotional experience. As Tomkins (1981) comments: "I have come to regard the skin in general and the skin of the face in particular as of the greatest importance in producing the feeling of affect" (p. 386).

It seems plausible to assume, then, that skin blood-flow changes associated with blushing play a part in influencing the intensity of reported embarrassment. Of central importance in this process is likely to be the part played by cognitive factors in evaluating the bodily and situational cues available, and perhaps creating embarrassment from these factors. Theories emphasizing the importance of cognitive or inferential decisions in building up emotional experience stress the importance of three central elements: the existence of some perceptible internal state that differs from one's baseline; the focusing of sufficient attention on the internal state to result in awareness of its existence; and the use of some knowledge structure to interpret the state. In interpreting feelings of embarrassment, autonomic arousal and cognitive interpretation undoubtedly play an important part.

One assumption that is often noted in the literature is that we have a relatively fixed amount of attention to allocate to our object of focus (whether ourselves or the environment) (Duval & Wicklund, 1972; Scheier, Carver, & Matthews, 1983). Assuming that a person has only a limited amount of attention to allocate to a particular stimulus, increasing the salience or input from one source of information will of necessity decrease the salience or input from other sources. Thus as attention inward to the self increases, attention outward to others in the environment will decrease.

One possibility is that our attention is shifting between ourselves and environmental cues on a continual but nonrandom basis (Hull & Levy, 1979; Scheier et al., 1983). Thus, if a social accident has occurred, attention may initially be directed toward an appraisal of the event itself. This shift may be followed quickly by an inward focus of attention directed specifically at those aspects of the self that are presumed to be associated with embarrassment (blushing, trembling, averted gaze, stammering). Subsequently attention may again be directed toward the environment, but, on this occasion, guided by a search for the evaluation or reaction of others. Subjective appraisal may partially alternate with environmental appraisal and partially occur in parallel. The fact that the process can be repeated may also serve to increase the subjective experience of embarrassment. Chronic blushers may be predisposed to attend to bodily cues, so that for these individuals the sequence of appraisals is initiated internally rather than externally.

A further component of embarrassment that forms the central theme of Cupach and Metts's chapter is the use of impression-management strategies that can be evoked by the actor to deal with his or her predicament. As they note, these are attempts to correct, minimize, explain away, or excuse the behavior (either externally or internally elicited) that has given rise to embarrassment. They also offer tentative suggestions concerning the interlinking of the antecedent event, degree of felt embarrassment, and use of particular strategies. It may further be the case that coping with a discernible external eliciting stimuli is easier than coping with an internal event. The tendency to overconcentrate on internal cues may be mediated by individual difference factors that may be more difficult to modify. Further, because the actor believes that the observer is noticing the actor's extreme blushing, he or she may try to hide or decrease it, whereas an external event (which is clearly noticed) can be coped with by verbal or nonverbal comment (e.g., laughter).

The experience of embarrassment thus necessitates the actor making appraisals of (a) the social event (i.e., the social setting, expected behaviors, expectations of others, the rules of conduct), (b) the behavioral and physiological consequences of that event (i.e., the behaviors associated with negative consequences of failure to follow the rules of conduct), and (c) the behaviors associated with subsequent attempts to rectify the situation once a negative event has occurred. The label "embarrassment" can then be assigned as a result of the subjective experience of the actor and/or based upon an evaluation of the event that precipitated the experience and/or based upon an evaluation of the behavioral display that results from this event. The interactions among coping attempts, the initial nonverbal display, and the internal or external evoking event clearly need to be taken into account. These issues will be dealt with in relation to both the foregoing model and the discussion by Cupach and Metts.

STRATEGIES FOR COPING WITH EMBARRASSMENT

Cupach and Metts provide a useful summary of remedial strategies identified in the literature, examine how these can be applied to embarrassing predicaments, and offer a typology of remedial strategies used by embarrassed persons and observers of the embarrassing predicament. As they note, existing typologies are applied to all social predicaments and not specifically to situations causing embarrassment and are theoretically rather than empirically motivated. The data provided by Cupach and Metts and the resulting classification of strategies for coping with embarrassment attempt to fill in some of the gaps. My colleagues and I have collected similar data on coping with embarrassment across cultures and coping with chronic blushing that will be used for comparison with and extension of the data obtained by Cupach and Metts.

CROSS-CULTURAL ASPECTS
OF COPING WITH EMBARRASSMENT

The initial impetus for examining embarrassment across cultures was derived from Ekman's (1972, 1977) neurocultural model of emotional expression. While antecedent events may differ across cultures, Ekman assumes the existence of at least six fundamental emotions with innate expression. He also argues that it is possible to modify these innate expressions by learning "display rules." Attempts at controlling or regulating embarrassment (i.e., display rules and associated remedial strategies) are much more likely to be culture specific, as they depend upon the individual's perception of the expressive behavior that is to be controlled or regulated and the rules of performance that are determined by cultural norms.

Data concerning cross-cultural aspects of embarrassment have been collected by questionnaire from more than 1,000 subjects in seven countries. Full details of the studies have been presented elsewhere (Edelmann et al., 1987, Edelmann &

TABLE 1
Verbal Responses as Attempts to Deal with Embarrassment

	Greece	Italy	Japan	Portugal	Spain	United Kingdom	West Germany
Not specified	57	65	63	59.2	37	35	43
Would not respond verbally	16	11	2	6.7	29	27	21
Excuse	2	3	7	3.3	5	8	3
Comment on own feelings	2	2	8	4.2	6	8	8
Exclamation	2	3	5	8.3	3	6	1
Apology	3	2	8	3.3	2	6	7
Apology + excuse	1	—	—	1.7	1	4	1
Apology + justification	—	—	—	—	—	—	2
Justification	13	8	6	1.7	14	3	10
Joking	4	6	1	1.7	3	3	4

NOTE: Figures represent percentages coded in categories for each nation.

Iwawaki, 1987; Edelmann & Neto, 1989); only a summary of relevant details will be presented here. All subjects had lived since childhood in the countries concerned — namely, Greece, Italy, Japan, Portugal, Spain, the United Kingdom, and West Germany — and were native speakers of the language in question.

The questionnaire was an adapted and extended version of a questionnaire used in a study on the antecedents and components of emotion (joy, anger, fear, and sadness) by Scherer, Summerfield, and Wallbott (1983). Equivalent forms of the questionnaire were developed in Greek, Italian, Japanese, Spanish, Portuguese, English, and German. The questionnaire itself was divided into sections dealing with the circumstances surrounding the event, the reaction associated with embarrassment, and coping attempts. Specific aspects of coping attempts will be discussed here. Questions of relevance to the present discussion asked for (a) verbal coping strategies and (b) observers' verbal reactions.

Verbal Coping Strategies

Verbal coping strategies were coded into eight categories derived from theoretical analyses by Austin (1970), Scott and Lyman (1968), Tedeschi and Riess (1981), Schlenker (1980, 1982), and Semin and Manstead (1983). Table 1 gives the frequencies with which a particular verbal reaction was recorded. The most striking feature of the results is that two-thirds to three-quarters of the subjects in each nation either specified that they would not respond verbally or failed to indicate that they would make a verbal response. For those who did indicate that they would make a verbal response, there was no particular response that was used with any great regularity. Subjects were also asked to rate variables associated with their embarrassment, including perceived intensity and duration. There was no discernible association between these variables and the use of a specific verbal coping response.

Comparison of these results with those referred to by Cupach and Metts requires a certain degree of caution. The remedial strategies referred to by Cupach and Metts and described in their recent paper (Cupach, Metts, & Hazleton, 1986) deal with behavioral actions (running into the house, cleaning up the spilled coffee) as well as verbal remediation attempts. Over half the remedial strategies to which they refer are behavioral actions classified as remediation, avoidance, and escape, with little more than one-third involving verbal reactions. As Cupach and Metts point out, escape does not necessarily save face for the actor, and one would similarly have to question the extent to which remediation and avoidance achieve such an objective. The remaining categories used by Cupach and Metts show close correspondence to those developed by my colleagues and me and seem to provide a useful framework for examining reactions to embarrassment.

There does, however, seem to be a general lack of verbal comment associated with attempts to regain composure following an embarrassing event; there are several possible explanations for this. First, in our own study, it is possible that subjects did in fact offer a verbal response but were unable to recall it during completion of the questionnaire. This circumstance may have been because a verbal response is less salient than a particular behavioral reaction (subjects were asked to record nonverbal behaviors but not specific remediation behaviors as referred to by Cupach and Metts). Alternatively, recall of verbal responses may be disrupted by the embarrassing nature of the event that generated them. Certainly embarrassment leads to a disruption of speech (Edelmann & Hampson, 1979), and subjects may initially be unable to respond. Second, subjects may be genuinely left speechless or at a loss for words by their embarrassment. Third, verbal coping may not be the most effective way of dealing with embarrassment. The actor concerned has to decide rapidly whether to ignore the event (hoping the observer does the same), acknowledge it (and hence focus the observer's attention on it), or attempt to deal competently and effectively with the incident in order to reestablish his or her damaged image. Given that composure has already been disrupted by the nature of the embarrassing event, many actors may choose some form of behavioral remediation (which may serve to distance them physically and psychologically from others present) or may otherwise attempt to avoid addressing the event. This remediation may well explain the lack of verbal comment in our own studies and the frequent use of avoidance and behavioral remediation noted by Cupach and Metts.

As Cupach and Metts note, further research is clearly required to tap a number of issues such as the interrelationships among the initial provoking event, variables associated with the embarrassment experienced (such as perceived intensity), and the coping strategy used. The likely use of behavioral versus verbal remediation also requires analysis in relation to these variables. Studying the observers' evaluation of the actors' coping attempts could also shed further light on appropriateness of remedial actions across situations.

TABLE 2
Observer's Verbal Response to Actor's Embarrassment

	Greece	Italy	Japan	Portugal	Spain	United Kingdom	West Germany
Not specified	39	38	45	37.5	29	37	43
Nothing	22	16	7	25.8	26	17	19
Joking	2	6	—	0.8	5	9	3
Empathic	15	9	6	9.2	10	19	20
Exclamation	3	2	9	7.5	1	5	1
Comment on actor's embarrassment/stupidity	7	6	28	1.7	7	5	6
Apology (i.e., if the observer is the cause of the embarrassment)	2	4	2	1.7	3	2	1
Starting/continuing conversation	7	10	—	13.3	15	6	6
Pretending nothing has happened	3	9	3	2.5	4	—	1

NOTE: Figures represent percentages coded in categories for each nation.

Observers' Verbal Reactions

As part of our cross-cultural comparison, respondents were asked to recall observers' *verbal responses*. These were coded into seven categories that partially reflect the coding system used for the actors' verbal coping attempts, with some of the previous categories combined and with additional categories covering empathic response, starting/continuing conversation, and pretending nothing has happened. Table 2 gives the frequencies with which a particular verbal reaction was recorded. Over half the subjects in each of the seven samples either specified that the observer did not respond verbally or failed to indicate a verbal response for the observer. For those who did indicate an observer's verbal response, an empathic reaction was mentioned most frequently in Greece, the United Kingdom, and West Germany (for these countries, the use of an empathic response corresponds closely to the figure obtained by Cupach and Metts); a comment on the actor's embarrassment/stupidity was mentioned most frequently in Japan (referred to by over a quarter of the sample); and starting/continuing the conversation was mentioned most frequently in Spain.

As with the actors' verbal responses, comparison of these results with the results presented by Cupach and Metts requires a certain amount of caution. Many of the observer reactions refer to behavioral actions (a pat on the arm, ignoring an accidental trip), and thus the actual percentage of verbal comments is difficult to ascertain. It is clear, however, that there is a considerable degree of overlap between the categories used by Cupach and Metts and those developed independently by my colleagues and me. Some categories are identical between the studies (empathy, joking/humor), while others show close correspondence (civil inattention corresponds to pretending nothing has happened, diversion corresponds to starting/continuing a conversation). It is interesting to note that while Cupach and Metts refer to strategies that draw attention to actors' embarrassment, they subsume these strategies within their other categories; we have kept this as a separate category (comment on actor's embarrassment/stupidity). Of the seven countries we studied, the Japanese sample stood out in that one-third of the observers' verbal responses were classified as comments on the actor's embarrassment or stupidity. It is interesting to note that the perceived duration of embarrassment experienced for the Japanese sample was greater than in the other six samples we studied. As Cupach and Metts note, sanctions in the form of overtly negative appraisals of the embarrassed person's behavior preclude the possibility of restoring social equilibrium and hence are likely to be responsible for exacerbating the embarrassment experienced. That observers' reactions may serve to exacerbate embarrassment in Japan may account for the stereotypical notion that embarrassment is particularly disturbing in Far Eastern nations (Argyle, 1969).

The classification system proposed by Cupach and Metts thus corresponds closely to our own and provides a useful starting point for examining observers' reactions to embarrassment. As with verbal coping attempts, it would seem that verbal reactions from observers may not necessarily be the most appropriate reaction, and behavioral remediation may be the preferred option. Further research is clearly required to evaluate the interrelationship between variables associated with embarrassment and observers' likely reactions.

My comments have so far been restricted to remediation associated with embarrassment caused by external eliciting circumstances. A further set of data that can be used for comparison with the findings of Cupach and Metts concerns data derived from chronic blushers. Embarrassment in such instances is frequently generated by internal cues.

COPING WITH CHRONIC BLUSHING

Data concerning self-reported coping attempts were generated from a sample of self-defined chronic blushers (Edelmann, 1987a). The initial sample pool consisted of 500 people who had written requesting a fact sheet titled "Blushing: What It Is and What to Do About It" that was advertised with an article published in a well-known U.K. women's magazine. Returned to each person with the fact sheet was a request for factual information concerning chronic blushing. Of the initial 500 subjects, 100 returned sufficiently detailed information to allow for data to be generated. Given both the method of recruiting subjects and the low response rate from the initial sample, it may well be that the final sample is not representative of either the general population or the population of chronic blushers. The sample is large enough, however, to provide some preliminary descriptive data.

Each subject was asked to answer ten questions, two of which are relevant to the present analysis; these specifically asked subjects about the method used for making a blush go away (i.e., coping with a current blush) and general methods for coping with the problems of blushing.

Coping with a current blush seems to present extreme difficulty: 62% of respondents stated that they were unable to cope and did not have an available strategy. A total of 17% chose behavioral avoidance (e.g., leaving the room), 10% chose cognitive strategies (e.g., distraction), and 9% used physiological strategies (e.g., relaxation), with the remaining 2% using some combination of strategies. Verbal coping strategies were not referred to by any of the respondents.

Coping with blushing in general also seems to present extreme difficulties: 22% were totally unable to cope and 44% resorted to either tranquilizers or makeup. A total of 3% reported always using behavioral avoidance, 23% used cognitive strategies (including hypnosis), and 13% employed physiological strategies. Again, verbal remediation attempts were not referred to as a coping strategy.

The way in which embarrassment is generated by blushing and the hope that observers will not notice was emphasized by respondents. One respondent commented:

> When I blush I think of what the other people must be thinking. Things like she has gone bright red or she is blushing or she must be really embarrassed or even why is she blushing?

The use of verbal remedial strategies is thus substantially less likely for internally generated embarrassment than for events-associated embarrassment. Avoidance and escape are the two most likely remedial strategies to be used for internally generated embarrassment. Whether this is due simply to the differing manner in which embarrassment is generated or whether there is a fundamental difference in the degree of felt embarrassment resulting from personally induced embarrassment that exceeds the degree experienced after situationally induced embarrassment remains to be seen. One might suppose, however, that personally induced embarrassment, by its enduring nature, would result in greater intensity of felt embarrassment. This supposition would tie in with Cupach and Metts's suggestion that in highly embarrassing situations, embarrassed actors are more likely to respond with escape.

OVERVIEW

It is clear from the foregoing analysis that the present position has a number of features in common with that presented by Cupach and Metts. Both regard Goffman's theorizing as central and emphasize the complex nature of remedial processes following embarrassment. There is also overlap between the categorization of remedial strategies used by embarrassed persons and observers suggested by Cupach and Metts and that derived from our own studies. It is, however, worth highlighting three important points of departure.

The first relates to the conceptualization of embarrassment presented at the outset of this commentary. While Cupach and Metts, together with many other writers (including myself), emphasize external eliciting circumstances, it is clear that embarrassment can be experienced in the absence of any clearly defined external eliciting stimuli.

The second departure concerns the need to differentiate verbal and behavioral remediation. It may well be the case that as degree of felt embarrassment increases, the likelihood of verbal remediation decreases while the likelihood of behavioral remediation increases.

The third difference concerns the need to differentiate between externally and internally induced embarrassment in relation to remedial strategies. It seems that coping with internally induced embarrassment presents extreme difficulties, and behavioral avoidance and escape seem to predominate as remedial strategies.

Finally, it is important to reiterate the point made by Cupach and Metts concerning future research needs. It is clearly important to examine the inter-relationships among the initial provoking event (both external and internal), variables associated with embarrassment experienced (such as perceived intensity), and the coping strategy used. The associations among these variables and likely use of behavioral versus verbal strategies and between strategy use and perceived effectiveness require investigation. The part played by the observer also requires careful scrutiny. As I have commented elsewhere, embarrassment is a common and highly uncomfortable form of social anxiety that can have a disruptive effect upon social interaction (Edelmann, 1985). Chronic blushing can also disrupt the social lives of those concerned. Unraveling the complex interrelationships among eliciting stimuli, experienced embarrassment, and coping attempts will provide theoretical insight and practical solutions.

REFERENCES

Argyle, M. (1969). *Social interaction*. London: Methuen.

Austin, J. L. (1970). *Philosophical papers* (2nd ed.). New York: Oxford University Press

Buck, R. W. (1980). Nonverbal behavior and the theory of emotion: The facial feedback hypothesis. *Journal of Personality and Social Psychology, 38*, 811-824.

Cupach, W. R., Metts, S., & Hazleton, V. (1986). Coping with embarrassing predicaments: Remedial strategies and their perceived utility. *Journal of Language and Social Psychology, 5*, 181-200.

Duval, S., & Wicklund, R. A. (1972). *A theory of objective self-awareness.* New York: Academic Press.

Edelmann, R. J. (1985). Social embarrassment: An analysis of the process. *Journal of Social and Personal Relationships, 2*, 195-213.

Edelmann, R. J. (1987a, December). *Chronic blushing: A model and some preliminary descriptive data.* Paper presented at the annual meeting of the British Psychological Society, London.

Edelmann, R. J. (1987b). *The psychology of embarrassment.* Chichester: John Wiley.

Edelmann, R. J. (1989). *Chronic blushing, self-consciousness and social anxiety.* Manuscript submitted for publication.

Edelmann, R. J. (in press). Embarrassment and blushing: A component process model, some initial descriptive and cross cultural data. In R. Crozier (Ed.), *Shyness and embarrassment: Perspectives from social psychology.* Cambridge: Cambridge University Press.

Edelmann, R. J., Asendorpf, J., Contarello, A., Georgas, J., Villanueva, C., & Zammuner, V. (1987). Self-reported verbal and non-verbal strategies for coping with embarrassment in five European cultures. *Social Science Information, 26,* 869-883.

Edelmann, R. J., & Hampson, S. E. (1979). Changes in non-verbal behaviour during embarrassment. *British Journal of Social and Clinical Psychology, 18,* 385-390.

Edelmann, R. J., & Hampson, S. E. (1981). Embarrassment in dyadic interaction. *Social Behavior and Personality, 9,* 171-177.

Edelmann, R. J., & Iwawaki, S. (1987). Self-reported expression and consequences of embarrassment in the United Kingdom and Japan. *Psychologia, 30,* 205-216.

Edelmann, R. J., & Neto, F. (1989). *Self-reported expression and consequences of embarrassment in Portugal and the U.K.* Manuscript submitted for publication.

Ekman, P. (1972). Similarities and differences between cultures in expressive movements. In J. R. Cole (Ed.), *Nebraska Symposium on Motivation* (pp. 207-283). Lincoln: University of Nebraska Press.

Ekman, P. (1977). Biological and cultural contributions to body and facial movement. In J. Blacking (Ed.), *The anthropology of the body* (pp. 39-84). London: Academic Press.

Goffman, E. (1956). Embarrassment and social organization. *American Journal of Sociology, 62,* 264-271.

Goffman, E. (1967). *Interaction ritual: Essays on face-to-face behavior.* New York: Pantheon.

Goffman, E. (1971). *Relations in public.* New York: Basic Books.

Hull, J. G., & Levy, A. S. (1979). The organizational functions of the self: An alternative to the Duval and Wicklund model of self-awareness. *Journal of Personality and Social Psychology, 37,* 756-768.

Laird, J. D. (1984). The role of facial response in the experience of emotion: A reply to Tourangeau and Ellsworth, and others. *Journal of Personality and Social Psychology, 47,* 909-917.

Modigliani, A. (1968). Embarrassment and embarrassability. *Sociometry, 31,* 313-326.

Modigliani, A. (1971). Embarrassment, facework, and eye contact: Testing a theory of embarrassment. *Journal of Personality and Social Psychology, 17,* 15-24.

Scheier, M. F., Carver, C. S., & Matthews, K. A. (1983). Attentional factors in the perception of bodily states. In J. T. Cacioppo & R. E. Petty (Eds.), *Social psychophysiology: A sourcebook* (pp. 510-542). New York: Guilford.

Scherer, K. R., Summerfield, A., & Wallbott, H. G. (1983). Cross-cultural research on antecedents and components of emotion: A progress report. *Social Science Information, 22,* 355-385.

Schlenker, B. R. (1980). *Impression management: The self concept, social identity and interpersonal relations.* Monterey, CA: Brooks/Cole.

Schlenker, B. R. (1982). Translating actions into attitudes: An identity analytic approach to the explanation of social conduct. In L. Berkowitz (Ed.), *Advances in experimental social psychology* (Vol. 15, pp. 193-247). New York: Academic Press.

Scott, M. B., & Lyman, S. B. (1968). Accounts. *American Sociological Review, 33,* 46-62.

Semin, G. R., & Manstead, A.S.R. (1981). The beholder beheld: A study of social emotionality. *European Journal of Social Psychology, 11,* 253-265.

Semin, G. R., & Manstead, A.S.R. (1982). The social implications of embarrassment displays and restitution behaviour. *European Journal of Social Psychology, 12,* 367-377.

Semin, G. R., & Manstead, A.S.R. (1983). *The accountability of conduct: A social psychological analysis.* London: Academic Press.

Silver, M., Sabatini, J., & Parrott, W. G. (1987). Embarrassment: A dramaturgical account. *Journal for the Theory of Social Behaviour, 17,* 47-61.

Tedeschi, J. T., & Riess, M. (1981). Verbal strategies in impression management. In C. Antaki (Ed.), *The psychology of ordinary explanations of social behavior* (pp. 271-309). New York: Academic Press.

Timms, M.W.H. (1980). Treatment of chronic blushing by paradoxical intention. *Behavioural Psychotherapy, 8*, 59-61.

Tomkins, S. S. (1981). Affect theory. In P. Ekman (Ed.), *Emotion in the human face* (2nd ed., pp. 353-395). Cambridge: Cambridge University Press.

The Use of a Communication Boundary Perspective to Contextualize Embarrassment Research

SANDRA PETRONIO
Arizona State University

W ITHIN the past few years, Cupach and Metts have made a major contribution to a research literature on embarrassment, a literature that was very limited only a short time ago. Their present discussion identifies a multitude of ways to conceptualize the embarrassing predicament, draws some conclusions that offer a preliminary synthesis of situations resulting in embarrassment, presents several empirical generalizations developed from their own program of research in remedial face work, and integrates the findings of other scholars. However, while their discussion is thorough, one underlying question remains. How does studying embarrassment contribute, in a larger sense, to our understanding of communication? The work by Cupach and Metts implicitly addresses this issue, but the focus of this commentary is to show explicitly the importance of studying embarrassment as a way to understand the phenomenon of communication. My goal is to contextualize the research that Cupach and Metts present by introducing a framework that suggests new directions and questions for investigating embarrassment as a critical communication issue.

THE LOGIC

In researching embarrassment, Cupach and Metts focus on a behavioral outcome that is observable but is not situated within a larger theoretical context. In

Correspondence and requests for reprints: Sandra Petronio, Department of Communication, Arizona State University, Tempe, AZ 85287-1205.

Communication Yearbook 13, pp. 365-373

order to construct a useful framework, I begin with one basic assumption made by Cupach and Metts and use that premise to propose a theoretical orientation from which to study embarrassment. Most of Cupach and Metts's research is contingent upon the notion that embarrassment results from a failed public performance. There are three issues implied in this assumption.

First, the maintenance of a public presentational face is critical to those engaging in communicative interactions. Given the importance of face, people probably erect a protective boundary when communicating to guard against potential vulnerability resulting in feelings of embarrassment.

Second, a failure event not only implies that there is a need to protect oneself but suggests the importance of criteria to judge appropriate communicative action proactively. One way people protect themselves from potential feelings of discomfiture in public is to use an agreed-upon system of expectations in which rules for guiding appropriate communicative interaction patterns are implemented. These rules provide the basis for expectations of communication with others and help to protect individuals proactively from possible embarrassment. A failed public performance, however, signals a breakdown in the protective system as well as an understanding of the rule structure for that situation, and leads to the observed behavioral outcome of embarrassment.

Third, because people feel a public discomfiture when there is a breakdown, the resulting embarrassment instigates the need to repair the loss of face. To do so, the individual must use remedial measures to reconstruct retroactively the protective boundaries used to manage face in interactions.

Thus, out of this analysis, there are three issues that form the basis of a thesis explaining embarrassment as a communication phenomenon: (a) the use of communication boundaries as a protective mechanism for public face, (b) embarrassing predicaments as violations of expectations, and (c) reconstruction of the communication boundary after violations of expectations result in loss of public face.

COMMUNICATION BOUNDARY PERSPECTIVE:
A THESIS EXPLAINING EMBARRASSMENT

In order for individuals to function in public with minimal face loss when communicatively interacting, they must construct communication boundaries that are used to regulate the ebb and flow of both verbal and nonverbal message exchange. The concept of boundaries has been applied to interactions by a number of scholars (e.g., Altman, 1975; Boss, 1984; Goffman, 1963, 1974; McCall & Simmons, 1966; Minuchin, 1974; Simmel, 1950). The theme found among all of these scholars' work is the assumption that individuals wish to control their public presentation when communicating. Individuals erect invisible boundaries to protect themselves from incoming information and likewise attempt to manage the dissemination of information to others. To protect themselves from face loss while interacting, individuals assess the collective communication rules and determine appropriate ways of communicating with others. The implementation of communicative rules makes it possible for individuals to regulate the communication boundary and to judge how to interact in a way that minimizes face loss. The communication boundary is thereby managed, in part, by employing expectations perceived as appropriate for a given social situation.

These expectations may range from general cultural rules — such as those found in rituals, rites, or norms for etiquette — to relational expectations, social situational expectations, and personal expectations for the communication exchange. Individuals implement the appropriate rules according to their own assessment of the situation following the expectations they have interpreted from the larger collective norm. The goal is protection of face during interaction in public. Sometimes, however, there is a breakdown in the communication system, resulting in embarrassment and failure to achieve that goal.

Embarrassment may be thought of as an observable outcome of a communication breakdown that results from breaching implicit communicative interaction rules. The communication boundary has been compromised and the regulatory system fails to protect the self from vulnerability in a public setting. Embarrassment is the behavioral indicator that signals a breakdown in the boundary protection system and identifies the violation of a collectively held communication rule. Thus in studying embarrassment, researchers are able to pinpoint a behavioral outcome that clearly represents consensually validated assumptions about the way communication exchanges "ought" to work but have not worked in that situation. By inference, the researcher is able to trace backward from the observable reaction of embarrassment as an indicator to a communication breakdown in the progression of an interaction sequence and more readily identify a normative rule that "should" have functioned but did not. The researcher also is able to assess the way a boundary system is reconstructed to repair loss of face.

Given this basic thesis, the research program presented in Cupach and Metts's essay provides support for this framework. The remainder of this discussion attempts to integrate the research of Cupach and Metts into a communication boundary perspective.

PREDICAMENTS AS VIOLATIONS OF EXPECTATIONS

Cupach and Metts suggest that many of the predicament typologies are "not directly comparable" (p. 325). The apparent incompatibility of the situations identified thus far may have more to do with the lack of a theoretical framework than the actual incongruity of these categories. The current categories typically define the predicament in terms of something that is missing or lost from the interaction (i.e., loss of social identity, loss of poise). However, there may be a commonality among the predicaments representing what has apparently not functioned in the interaction. Hence it seems that all predicaments may result from some type of violation of expectations. Cupach and Metts imply in their typology that breaking a rule leads to embarrassing predicaments. Most of the categories they propose have to do with violating social rules or personal rules for public behavior.

Assuming that expectations are not being met in a given predicament, perhaps a better way to conceptualize embarrassing situations is in terms of a communication boundary approach, where embarrassment results from violations of expectations that are used to regulate interaction. Thus, stated more generally, there might be at least three conditions under which embarrassment occurs: (a) when individuals unintentionally violate the expectations because they either misread or misinterpreted the rules; (b) when other individuals draw attention to breaches in collectively held interpretations of the rules, whether or not the embarrassed person is acting intentionally or unintentionally; and (c) when individuals empathically experience embarrassment for others who have violated expectations. As implied, any of these conditions may occur with many types of expectation violations.

The expectations for interaction may be thought of as a hierarchical system that includes cultural, social situational, relational, and personal expectations. These levels seem to be implied in the typology Cupach and Metts propose. However, making them explicit within the framework of a boundary perspective gives the categories a context. Thus when these expectations are violated and there is breakdown in the regulatory system maintaining the communication boundary, the outcome is embarrassment for the person or persons involved in breaching the rules for interaction. For example, cultural expectations represent rules that collectivities use to maintain social order on a large scale. Rituals, rites, cultural rules for etiquette, language usage, and the communication of values all reflect the "personality" (Hart, 1957) of the collectivity. When individuals communicate with others, they implement these rules as a way to regulate a boundary for face maintenance. When a cultural expectation is violated, this results in a communication breakdown contributing to embarrassment for one or all participants. Cultural expectations tend to be the most all-encompassing in this hierarchy; however, there are times when the social situation calls for less general and more specific types of behaviors idiosyncratic to a circumstance or environment.

Social situational expectations for communicative interaction include rules for dinnertime talk, telephone and elevator behavior, bar conversations, church interactions, and the like. Within social situations, appropriate behavior is determined by the rules that are agreed upon and sometimes negotiated by the group of interactants. When there is a communication breakdown in the boundary system, the rules for appropriate behavior have been violated, and embarrassment results.

Relational expectations also are concerned with the use of appropriate communicative interaction in a public setting to save face and maintain communication boundaries. There are many ways to define relationships among people. For this category, relational role expectations represent the basis for rules guiding interaction. The role relationships are presumed to range on an intimacy continuum from nonintimate roles (such as customer-clerk relationships) to intimate roles (such as marital couples). The extent to which appropriate interaction rules are negotiated or more general societal rules apply depends upon the degree of intimacy. Also, Cupach and Metts point out that predicaments vary "according to the nature of the relationships between parties" (p. 349). This may occur because of the variations in expectations that develop as the relationship moves from a nonintimate to an intimate level. Increases in familiarity contribute to the need for renegotiating expectations used to guide interaction within a given relationship. The need for renegotiation of the expectations may be indicated by resultant embarrassment, which shows that the communication boundary is in need of repair to protect the public face of the individuals in the relationship.

The last type of expectations represent those reflecting personal rules for interaction. We all have certain expectations for ourselves when we interact with others. For example, we may hope our performance is competent, that we have a certain degree of confidence, that we exhibit personal poise while communicating with others, and that we maintain a presentational self that is respected by others. When we breach our own expectations we may feel conspicuous, and others' attention may be focused on us at a time when we wish to be anonymous. Personal expectations represent communication rules that we ideally hope to fulfill when interacting with others. Embarrassment often results when those expectations are not realized, producing a need to reconstruct our communication boundary to redeem face for the current interaction and to gather information for future interactions.

As this discussion has proposed, within a communication boundary framework, the basis for embarrassing predicaments is a violation of several types of expectations, ranging from a macro level to a micro level. The majority of categories Cupach and Metts report from previous research do not necessarily "cause" embarrassment, but may better reflect the way the regulatory system malfunctions in attempting to maintain a communication boundary to protect face in interaction.

For instance, mistakes, accidents, improprieties, loss of control, faux pas, loss of confidence, awkward acts, verbal blunders, and conspicuousness all represent ways in which expectations may be violated in communication interactions. The boundary-controlling communicative interaction is regulated by assumptions for appropriate actions in public between individuals. The categories identified by Cupach and Metts represent examples of how the boundaries are compromised, but they do not show why. The "why" has to do with expectations that have been breached; the "how" is through a breakdown in the regulatory system marked by malfunctions such as faux pas and verbal blunders.

Hence the embarrassing predicament has two levels of analysis: (a) the expectations that have been violated and (b) the mechanisms that fail to regulate or control the communication boundary adequately for face protection. To understand the reasons for embarrassment accurately, we must study both of these levels in relationship to each other. Perhaps the loss of confidence is more a result of boundary breakdowns for violations of personal expectations than social situational expectations. Or conspicuousness is more a result of boundary breakdowns for violations of social situational expectations than cultural expectations. However, it may be that failure of any of these boundary mechanisms contributes to the violation of expectations on all levels. Research is necessary to test these assumptions and verify the validity of these suggestions.

As breakdowns in the regulatory system controlling the communication boundary occur and individuals experience feelings of embarrassment, there is a need to reconstruct the boundary retroactively and restore public face. *Reconstruction* refers to repairing the communication boundary to regain face. In reconstructing, individuals must use strategies to redress the situation and salvage violated rules or to invent new rules by which to communication in that circumstance.

RECONSTRUCTION:
EMBARRASSMENT AS A CHANGE MECHANISM

Evidence that individuals show discomfiture when their public performance is disrupted speaks to the expectations actors have and to the implicit rules they follow for communication interactions. The reconstruction of the communication event often functions as a catalyst for change and illustrates the need for social rules to provide actors with dependable ways to function in social situations.

The reconstruction process involves two interrelated levels. First, after embarrassment has occurred, individuals need to restructure their communication boundaries. Second, a disruption in the system has made obvious that the interpretations of social interaction rules by which the individual was functioning did not apply in that circumstance. Thus a change in interpretation is necessary and/or a reason for the event must be posited to reclaim face.

On the first level, the boundary surrounding the individual in the communicative interaction is used as a protective device. When the boundary has been penetrated by exposure from others or inappropriately opened by the self, repair work must be done to restore the boundary screening process. Boundary reconstruction to restore or protect public face is either proactive or reactive in nature, and often involves restoration by self and others participating in the event; the strategies used to restore the boundary concern attributions of responsibility for the embarrassing event.

With the proactive strategies, the self uses these tactics to avert embarrassment when he or she anticipates a possible breach in expectations because the rules seem unclear. These strategies include disclaimers, topic changes, and avoiding the situation altogether. The individual is taking responsibility for the situation by acting to avoid the threat to face when communicatively interacting. The communication boundary is not compromised and the individual's public face is protected.

Proactive strategies may also be enacted by others. The categories presented by Cupach and Metts of inattention, silence, and diversion represent proactive strategies that others might use to prevent embarrassment for the person. These strategies help avert embarrassment because others quickly understand that the person has breached a rule or expectation, and they shift attention away from the person or ignore the action to avoid embarrassment. These proactive strategies represent the other taking responsibility for protecting the face of the person.

Reactive boundary repair strategies are also used by the embarrassed self and others experiencing the event. Most of these tactics focus on attributions of responsibility and are conducted in a public setting, with the exception of escape. Escape is the one strategy that does not involve the embarrassed person's attempt to restore face in front of other people. Instead, individuals who use escape flee the situation and privately work on boundary restoration.

Conversely, strategies such as apologies are publicly conducted and attribute competence to self, take responsibility for the action leading to embarrassment, and appear to show repentance for violations of expectations. Accounts are attributions that deny responsibility for breaches in rules leading to embarrassment (excuses) or acceptance of responsibility (justification) for violating expectations.

The use of humor implicitly attributes responsibility to self or other. Humor (sometimes misunderstood) is a subtle tool with which to alleviate the embarrassing moment. If the embarrassed person feels the other caused this discomfiture, he or she may tease or joke about the events that led to the embarrassment in order to repair face. By so doing, the individual sends the implicit message that the other is the responsible party and "should" contribute to boundary reconstruction. Or an embarrassed person may make fun of his or her own inadequacies and misunderstandings that resulted in embarrassment, thereby suggesting that he or she is responsible for his or her own discomfiture.

Others also use reactive strategies to help embarrassed persons overcome their feelings of discomfiture. As Cupach and Metts suggest, others involved in the embarrassing predicament may use support and empathy. These strategies share in the responsibility of the event by helping to restore public face. They are used to assure the embarrassed person that the violations of expectations did not cause long-term negative effects on how others view him or her, or that the person was not alone in having misunderstood the rules for interaction in that circumstance.

Cupach and Metts point out several issues regarding these proactive and reactive strategies regarding the role of others. First, embarrassed persons often challenge the others participating in the event to provide remedial action to restore the communication boundary and repair their public face. Second, when others fail to take coresponsibility or predominant responsibility for boundary reconstruction, embarrassment increases for the person. There are times when the embarrassed person aggressively forces others to take responsibility for the event leading to embarrassment or to issue a reproach. This need for others to participate in boundary restoration emphasizes the public nature of this type of communication experience. When there is a collective move by others to repair the public face of another, this action may carry more weight and be more effective in alleviating discomfiture for the embarrassed person.

Whether self and other use a proactive or reactive remedial strategy to restore communication boundaries protecting face, as Cupach and Metts point out, these strategies are not used in isolation but frequently are implemented in a sequence. The type of sequencing may be influenced by the kind of rule violation. Cupach and Metts suggest that "predicaments vary in the degree to which they disrupt social order and implicate the face needs of others" (p. 332). Thus when the predicaments resulting from violations of expectations greatly disrupt the social interaction, a specific series of strategies might be used to restore the boundary and repair the embarrassed person's public face. These sequences may be different from those used with predicaments that disrupt interaction only slightly.

As reconstruction of the communication boundary is enacted to restore face, the disruption of the system resulting from violations of expectations also indicates a need to reassess the interpretations of interaction rules. For example, as Cupach and Metts point out from the research by Baxter and Wilmot (1985), if topics are considered taboo by one person but are brought up by another, this violation of expectation resulting in embarrassment may instigate queries into the appropriateness of talking about this topic within the context of the relationship. The embarrassment often signals the need to reassess whether a new rule should be instituted so that interaction between these people may function more smoothly.

The example Cupach and Metts use to illustrate the notion of "long-term" strategies also illustrates the point that underlying rules become obvious and change or become redefined because of embarrassment. They suggest that if a person is clumsy, he or she may experience embarrassment when encountering new people, but over time, in an ongoing relationship, the clumsiness may become the norm. Thus expectations may change as a ramification of initial embarrassment and subsequent boundary reconstruction to redefine what was once a stimulus for discomfiture to routine behavior.

The last issue discussed in this essay is derived from the ideas on rules change and focuses on the use of embarrassment as a means of socialization concerning expectations for communication. Initiating embarrassment may be implemented as a method of teaching rules to children as well as to adults in significant relationships. Parents may tease or joke with a child concerning issues about which they wish to teach a lesson. Such embarrassment tends to be mild in comparison to embarrassment in other predicaments, but the message is noteworthy. Causing embarrassment in these circumstances may be less face-threatening because the relationship is more likely to be supportive and confirming. Close friends and significant others may also use teasing and joking that results in embarrassment as a way to indicate expectations that have been breached. While the supportive environment of a relationship may remove some of the potential vulnerability, using embarrassment as a way to institute change in the rule structure is risky at best (Petronio, Olson, & Dollar, 1989). The success of this move is contingent upon the strength of the relationship.

CONCLUSION

I was once asked (in a reviewer's letter) what significance the study of embarrassment has for our understanding of communication. By framing the research that Cupach and Metts present in terms of a communication boundary perspective, it is my hope that the salience of investigating embarrassment as a communication phenomenon is more explicitly understood.

REFERENCES

Altman, I. (1975). *The environment and social behavior: Privacy, personal space, territory and crowding.* Monterey, CA: Brooks/Cole.

Baxter, L., & Wilmot, W. (1985). Taboo topics in close relationships. *Journal of Social and Personal Relationships, 2,* 253-269.

Boss, P. (1984). Family boundary ambiguity: A new variable in family stress theory. *Family Process, 23,* 535-546.

Goffman, E. (1963). *Behavior in public places.* New York: Free Press.

Goffman, E. (1974). *Frame analysis.* New York: Harper & Row.

Hart, C. (1957). Cultural anthropology and sociology. In H. Becker & A. Boskoff (Eds.), *Modern sociological theory in continuity and change* (pp. 528-549). New York: Dryden.

McCall, G., & Simmons, J. (1966). *Identities and interactions: An examination of human associations in everyday life.* New York: Free Press.

Minuchin, S. (1974). *Families and family therapy.* Cambridge, MA: Harvard University Press.

Petronio, S., Olson, C., & Dollar, N. (1989). Privacy issues in relational embarrassment: Impact on relational quality and communication satisfaction. *Communication Research Reports, 6*(1), 21-27.

Simmel, G. (1950). *The sociology of Georg Simmel.* New York: Free Press.

8   Interaction Goals
in Negotiation

STEVEN R. WILSON
Michigan State University

LINDA L. PUTNAM
Purdue University

Negotiation is a strategic process, carried out through maneuvers designed to accomplish goals. Most negotiation theorists, however, treat goals as global, predetermined, and static task-oriented objectives. This chapter focuses on the role of interaction goals in negotiation. Bargainers' interaction goals are organized within a scheme that varies in two respects: type (instrumental, relational, and identity) and level of abstraction (global, regional, local). Following the discussion of goal types, the chapter explores the dynamic and conflictual nature of negotiators' interaction goals, and then suggests that goal analyses could shed insight into how bargaining contexts influence strategies and outcomes, and how negotiators develop expertise. A goals focus emphasizes that negotiators act purposefully but with "bounded rationality," constantly manage conflicting objectives, and enact bargaining behaviors that are guided by interaction goals but often reframe those goals.

N
EGOTIATION is a fundamental activity within interdependent relationships. Although we typically think of it in relation to such formal events as the settlement of labor contracts, international disputes, and legal tangles, engaging in give-and-take to reach mutually agreeable solutions also characterizes an array of interpersonal and group activities. Husbands and wives negotiate free time, child-care responsibilities, and household chores; managers engage in budget negotiations; and consumers and merchants haggle over the prices of goods and services. Negotiation, then, clearly is a prevalent form of social interaction.

Negotiation traditionally has been described as a strategic process, carried out through maneuvers designed to accomplish goals (Schelling, 1960). Parties engage in bargaining to accomplish one or more instrumental goals, such as changing or

Correspondence and requests for reprints: Steven R. Wilson, Department of Communication, Michigan State University, East Lansing, MI 48824.

Communication Yearbook 13, pp. 374-406

maintaining status quo policies or finding mutually agreeable solutions to joint problems. According to one contemporary theory, bargaining "is a process of developing tactical action from motives and intentions. . . . Bargaining is goal-directed behavior" (Bacharach & Lawler, 1981, p. 41).

In fact, negotiation can be defined as a process whereby two or more parties who hold or believe they hold incompatible goals engage in a give-and-take interaction to reach a mutually acceptable solution (Putnam & Jones, 1982b). Both parties then must cooperate to attain a settlement and both have the potential to block or interfere with the other party's goal attainment. This interdependence between parties makes the situation simultaneously cooperative and competitive — contributing to the mixed-motive nature of negotiations. That is, they "must cooperate to reach individual goals while they simultaneously compete with one another for [perceived] divergent interests" (Putnam, 1989, p. 176). In a proto-typical bargaining situation, both parties give provisional offers, engage in un-restricted communication, and strive for a mutually acceptable agreement within a range of possible settlements (Pruitt, 1981). Specific types of negotiation tasks, however, may not exemplify all the characteristics of this prototype. These charac-teristics distinguish bargaining from related types of social interaction. Negotiators typically want more from the process than simply getting their opponents to do something they would not ordinarily do. Hence bargaining incorporates com-pliance-gaining tactics, but it melds these strategies with problem-solving and conflict-management activities. Because it is characterized by mixed motives, bargaining also differs from controversies, disagreements, and differences of opinion. In sum, negotiation is a form of social interaction and problem solving characterized by the pursuit of perceived incompatible goals.

Although many negotiation theorists agree that bargainers pursue goals through interaction, most use the term *goal* in a highly restrictive sense. "Goal-setting" is described as a process of defining issues and setting target points that occurs prior to the initiation of bargaining interaction (e.g., Lewicki & Litterer, 1985). During this process, negotiators form objectives for the entire negotiation or even multiple negotiations (Kochan & Katz, 1988). Recent studies on the effects of goal difficul-ty have assigned bargainers minimum monetary targets for final settlement prior to interaction (Huber & Neale, 1986; Neale & Bazerman, 1985a). Similarly, earlier gaming studies investigated the effects of initially assigning bargainers either cooperative or competitive goals for the entire negotiation (Greenwood, 1974; Smith, 1969; Wilson, 1971). In sum, many negotiation theorists, implicitly or explicitly, treat goals as global, predetermined, and static, task-oriented objectives.

Communication scholars currently adhere to a broader sense of goal. Goal-set-ting at times occurs prior to interaction, but initial objectives often are modified and new objectives emerge during interaction (Berger, 1987; Burke, 1986; Putnam, 1984). Bargainers decompose instrumental goals for entire negotiations into smaller social-influence and information-exchange objectives, which vary in salience across time (Donohue, Diez, & Stahle, 1983; Keogh, 1987; Putnam & Jones, 1982b; Walker, 1985). As interaction unfolds, relational and identity goals also become salient to negotiators (Clark & Delia, 1979; Donohue et al., 1983). Although negotiation theorists recognize the importance of bargaining relationships (e.g., Bacharach & Lawler, 1981) and identities (e.g., Brown, 1977), they do not emphasize that bargainers pursue multiple goals (O'Keefe & Delia, 1982; O'Keefe & Shepherd, 1987; Tracy, 1984).

Our contention is that focusing on interaction goals, in the expanded sense, would give insight into a variety of phenomena falling under the general rubric of communication and negotiation. A goals focus would emphasize the purposeful nature of bargaining interaction while recognizing that negotiators operate at varying levels of conscious awareness (Craig, 1986) within the limits of "bounded rationality" (Bazerman & Carroll, 1987; Thompson & Hastie, 1987). Accordingly, this chapter examines the role of interaction goals in negotiation. After clarifying our view of goals, we discuss types of interaction goals in negotiation, explore why negotiators pursue dynamic and conflicting goals, and suggest four directions for future research.

CONCEPTION OF INTERACTION GOALS

Goals are people's cognitive representations of states of affairs that they desire to bring about or maintain (Hobbs & Evans, 1980; von Cranach, Kalbermatten, Indermuhle, & Gugler, 1982). Desired end states become *interaction goals* when communication and coordination with others are necessary to achieve those states (Clark & Delia, 1979). For example, a consumer who wishes to purchase an automobile at less than the sticker price must evoke a desired response from the dealer, just as a labor negotiator who desires to present an assertive self-image must negotiate particular definitions of the bargaining situation. Since negotiation occurs between interdependent parties who cannot impose their desires on the other side, many bargaining objectives become interaction goals.

Not all of the objectives that bargainers pursue, however, are interaction goals. For example, during the negotiation bargainers may want to form an impression of a new opponent or to remember dialogue for later caucus meetings (Srull & Wyer, 1986). They also will try to make sense of the opponents' actions by making inferences about their plans and intent (Bazerman & Carroll, 1987; Thompson & Hastie, 1987). After the negotiation, bargainers may look back on sessions, searching for objectives that clarify how they reached agreement or impasse (Weick, 1979). These examples illustrate "interpretive" or "information-processing" rather than interaction goals, since they do not necessitate communication and coordination.[1]

Although pursued through communication, interaction goals are part of the cognitive rather than the behavioral domain. As will become evident, a complex and indeterminate relationship exists between interaction goals and conversational forms and sequences (Craig, 1986). Negotiators' messages provide clues about their interaction goals, but these objectives are distinct phenomena, separate from the discursive forms, patterns, or practices that they invoke.

In addition to interaction goals, negotiators also pursue discourse goals, or states of affairs making communication possible. Discourse objectives include producing relevant turns, introducing and changing topics, and meeting syntactic constraints (Greene, 1984; Tracy, 1984). Interaction and discourse goals do not operate independently; for example, the interaction goal of concealing decision preferences may limit the conversational topics that a negotiator is willing to discuss. In most instances, however, interaction goals place only loose constraints on how people accomplish discourse objectives (Greene, 1984; van Dijk & Kintsch, 1983). This chapter, then, focuses primarily on the pursuit of interaction goals within negotiation.

Interaction Goals and Planning

Once bargainers form interaction goals, they rely in part on preexisting knowledge about means or procedures to accomplish their objectives. Bargainers draw on plans that represent their prior knowledge about necessary conditions and potential obstacles for reaching goals (Miller, Gallanter, & Pribram, 1960; Schank & Abelson, 1977). Within labor negotiations, for example, altering an opponent's utility estimates of alternative proposals might constitute one necessary condition within a plan for maximizing one's own gain on agenda items (Bacharach & Lawler, 1981; Walker, 1985). After repeated encounters within the same context, negotiators may develop scripts, or cognitive structures representing a stereotyped sequence of events (see Abelson, 1981; Bazerman & Carroll, 1987; Kellermann, 1984; Schank & Abelson, 1977). Certain aspects of labor negotiations, such as making excessive demands and attacking the opponent as an opening offer (Douglas, 1962; Keogh, 1987) or matching repetitive cycles of attack-attack or attack-defend (Donohue, 1981; Putnam & Jones, 1982a), take on this scripted quality.

Although bargainers develop plans and scripts prior to negotiation, much of their reasoning about means for avoiding obstacles and for attaining goals occurs during ongoing interaction (see Berger, 1987; Bruce & Newman, 1978; Burke, 1986). Negotiation creates an extremely complex planning environment, since bargainers must (a) coordinate goals with an opponent and their own constituents, both of whom frequently thwart initial plans, (b) manage conflicts between their own goals, and (c) develop plans related to multiple issues and proposals that may not be defined clearly, or even conceived of, prior to the negotiation. Thus any description of planning during negotiation must recognize that bargainers both retrieve and invent means for accomplishing goals.

As evidence that people's goals and plans often are not well developed prior to interaction, Hayes-Roth and Hayes-Roth (1979) contrast predetermined and opportunistic approaches to planning. The *predetermined approach* views planning as an orderly, top-down process. People initially develop abstract goals and strategies for entire events, break those into a limited number of chronological steps, and finally formulate the precise details for carrying out each step. Since they attend to each step of the planning process, people's detailed goals and tactics follow logically from their abstract plans. In accordance with this approach, feedback acquired from executing details is not used to modify plans.

The *opportunistic approach*, in contrast, views planning as a combination of top-down and bottom-up processes. Abstract strategies may constrain options for detailed goals and tactics, but feedback can reframe abstract plans when obstacles are encountered, or when the opponent's responses reveal previously unforeseen strategies. People move their attention across levels of abstraction as they perceive opportunities for plan development; thus some development of plans occurs at low levels of conscious awareness. Detailed planning is initiated before abstract plans are completed, and plans and scripts guiding action at various levels may not be logically integrated.

According to Hayes-Roth and Hayes-Roth (1979), the opportunistic approach reflects how people actually plan in complex environments such as negotiation. Throughout this chapter we apply an opportunistic model to explain qualities of goals in negotiation.

Proactive Versus Retrospective Goals

Even though plans are developed and refined during interaction, goals influence negotiation behavior. By definition, the term *interaction goal* is used in a proactive rather than a retrospective sense; that is, the concept assumes that negotiation behavior is goal directed rather than (or in addition to) goal interpreted.

Several experimental findings illustrate that people's interaction goals affect their communicative behavior. Specifically, negotiators who are assigned difficult monetary goals differ from those assigned easily attainable goals in the amount of time spent negotiating settlements, the profitability of settlements, and the types of goals set for future sessions (Huber & Neale, 1986; Neale & Bazerman, 1985a). In addition, research on compliance-gaining reveals that subjects who are explicitly instructed to pursue multiple goals produce qualitatively different messages (Kline, 1984) and engage in more planning during ongoing interaction (Greene & Lindzey, 1989) than do subjects told only to gain compliance. Moreover, Tracy (1984) reports that manipulating the relative priority of multiple goals influences the use of topical introductions and extensions during interactions. Numerous correlational studies also show that personality, social-cognitive, and situational variables that affect people's messages also influence their interaction goals (see Wilson, 1987).

Despite these findings, some scholars argue that people invent goals only after interaction to interpret or to account for their actions (see Donohue et al., 1983; Hawes & Smith, 1973; Weick, 1979). For example, Donohue et al. (1983) invoke the concept of convention or rule rather than goal to explain how negotiators make communicative choices: "Convention dictates that routine communicative forms are produced, and the evidence indicating that forms occur routinely is overwhelming" (p. 275). However, "strategic" models of coherence stand in opposition to this view by purporting that forms become conventional because they are useful means for accomplishing goals (see Craig, 1986). For example, Brown and Levinson (1978) offer extensive cross-cultural evidence that many politeness conventions aid people in managing multiple, conflicting goals. In sum, unless one argues that negotiation behavior is random or environmentally determined, it is difficult to explain discourse forms and patterns without reference to interaction goals.[2]

Bargainers' interaction goals influence their behavior in two respects (Bruce & Newman, 1978). Interaction goals function as "achievement" objectives — states of affairs not currently in existence that bargainers strive to bring about. Labor negotiators attempt to win salary raises; merchants desire to reduce overstocked inventory. Interaction goals also function as "maintenance" objectives — states of affairs currently in existence that bargainers strive to retain. For example, participants attempt to avoid losing face or to maintain an equitable power relationship when these states are threatened (Brown, 1977; Pruitt & Smith, 1981). Maintenance goals may serve as criteria for editing plans aimed at achievement goals (Bruce & Newman, 1978; Hample & Dallinger, 1987). We do *not* assume that goals are static, logically consistent, or pursued with conscious awareness. We do assume that negotiators "act purposefully, even in what they perceive as a fast-moving and fluid situation" (Walton & McKersie, 1965, p. 9).

In sum, bargaining behaviors are guided by interaction goals, but behaviors also may alter or reframe goals. Bargainers may attempt to accomplish numerous interaction goals during negotiation.

DIMENSIONS OF INTERACTION GOALS

Our discussion of interaction goals in negotiation is based on a scheme that varies in two respects: type and abstraction. Negotiators attempt to achieve various types of goals, including instrumental, relational, and identity objectives (Clark & Delia, 1979). Within each type, goals vary in degree of abstraction, or in the length of interaction segments to which they have relevance (Carver & Scheier, 1982; Greene, 1984; Kellermann, 1987; Miller et al., 1960).

We cast goals and plans at three levels of abstraction. *Global* goals pertain to entire negotiations.[3] Prior to bargaining, each party usually establishes target and resistance points for final settlement of agenda items (Gulliver, 1979; Lewicki & Litterer, 1985). The following excerpts, taken from a prenegotiation caucus meeting between representatives of a teachers' association and their professional negotiator, illustrate this level (TR = teacher representative, TN = teachers' negotiator, SR = school board representative, SN = school board's negotiator):

TR: We need to make sure middle and high school chairs and coordinators are paid equally. If [the school district] pays for two of them equally, [they] should do it for all of them. Let's make all of them the same.

TN: The average [raise of salary] is now about 6%, some 5.5%. [Another school district] got 5% plus binding arbitration. We should be reluctant to look at anything below 6%.

Agenda items emerge when parties form incompatible goals (Pruitt, 1981). Consequently, labor negotiators usually form global objectives involving salary, insurance, retirement, performance evaluation, grievance procedures, and control over which issues are negotiable (e.g., Putnam, Wilson, Waltman, & Turner, 1986). In buyer-seller negotiations, global objectives typically center on product price and quality, warranty, service reputations and responsibilities, finance rates, and delivery schedules (e.g., Neale & Bazerman, 1985a). Even though global goals change, the revised global objectives are framed for the remainder of the negotiation.

To pursue these objectives, bargainers develop global "strategies," or abstract lines of behavior designed to accomplish goals (Putnam & Jones, 1982b). Global strategies include making reciprocal concessions, showing firmness on ends but flexibility on means, or sequencing demands with varying degrees of acceptability (Cialdini, 1988; Esser & Kormorita, 1974; Fisher & Ury, 1981). The following excerpt from the same caucus meeting illustrates a sequencing strategy:

TN: When we set the money, let's hit them with reduction in force procedure coupled with binding arbitration, or if we cut out binding arbitration, let's go with reduction in force and due process or due process and binding arbitration. How does that sound?

Bargainers also plan at more *regional* levels, formulating goals and plans not only for the entire negotiation, but for single sessions or encounters. The following illustration of regional planning occurred in the same initial caucus meeting:

TN: Let's talk about our strategy tonight. I don't know if [SN] and I will go out in the hall first or later. I think there's a good chance we won't settle tonight. They know they have one more chance.

Bargainers pursue other initial regional goals that are formed and pursued with less awareness. For example, establishing an assertive image appears to be a salient goal early in the negotiation (Douglas, 1957, 1962; Keogh, 1987; Putnam, 1984).

Throughout the negotiation, parties utilize breaks to formulate regional goals and plans for upcoming sessions. The following excerpt occurred in a mid-negotiation caucus meeting of school board representatives:

SN: Should we indicate willingness to move [on dues deduction]? I'll start with a 3rd pay period for dues deduction. Need to probe here—a possible item for movement.

Regional goals can function as intermediate steps within global plans; however, they also may contradict a party's global goals.

Finally, negotiators plan at even more *local* levels, formulating goals and tactics pertinent to small discourse segments. Bargaining tactics, the concrete actions that instantiate behavioral strategies, include speech act types (e.g., threats or promises) and forms (e.g., directives varying in illocutionary force) (see Donohue & Diez, 1985; Donohue et al., 1983; Putnam & Jones, 1982a). Local goals are objectives related to individual acts (Kellermann, 1987). These goals can emerge as intermediate steps in plans for regional and global goals. A consumer's global goal of purchasing a product at the lowest possible price, for example, could generate a local goal of refuting a seller's argument that the product was in short supply. Similarly, a negotiator's global goal of maintaining face could generate a local goal of separating him- or herself from a naive proposal.

Bargainers' local goals, however, may be more responsive to perceptions of the opponent's current actions and intentions than to long-range plans (see Craig, 1986, pp. 263-264). For instance, a merchant might form a local-level information-giving objective when a consumer asks for clarification of a technical term used in the merchant's previous turn, even if the merchant's global plan is to withhold information about the product. Local goals are influenced by the negotiator's global concerns, the opponent's prior moves, and interactional constraints.

A number of instrumental, relational, and identity goals all can be identified at each of these three levels of abstraction.

Instrumental Goals

Instrumental goals are objectives that require the opponent to remove a specific obstacle blocking completion of a task (Clark & Delia, 1979, p. 200). In bargaining, both sides' global instrumental goals emerge from their (a) interdependent relationship and (b) specific bargaining roles.

Interdependence and instrumental goals. As noted at the beginning of this chapter, interdependence between bargaining parties creates a need to coordinate the competitive aim of maximizing self-gain and the cooperative one of working with the other person to reach an acceptable settlement. Walton and McKersie (1965) capture these mixed motives in treating negotiation as the merger of two key subprocesses, distributive and integrative bargaining. The numerous objectives that stem from these subprocesses are separated in our discussion to illustrate differences in global instrumental goals defining the two subprocesses. Distributive and integrative negotiations, then, as presented in this section, represent distinct types of bargaining behavior. However, in a later section we will argue that these subprocesses are interdependent and function as dilemmas that each negotiator faces in selecting and making sense of communication strategies and tactics.

In distributive bargaining, both parties emphasize the individualistic goal of maximizing their own share of a fixed-sum payoff (Lewicki & Litterer, 1985;

Walton & McKersie, 1965). Agenda items are conceptualized in zero-sum fashion: Goal attainment by one party precludes the other party from attaining his or her goals. The global goal of maximizing self-payoffs has implications for persuasion and information exchange.

Parties engaged in distributive bargaining must persuade their opponents to forgo their proposals or make concessions (Gulliver, 1979). Thus both parties have a number of regional and local influence goals, including the following: to affect the other party's belief about what is possible in the settlement; to change the opponent's utility estimates concerning possible outcomes, proposals, and counterproposals; to promote one's own objectives as desirable, necessary, or inevitable; to present self-supporting information while limiting the other party's ability to do the same; to keep the other party from becoming firmly committed to a position; to change the other party's resistance points, to convince the opponent that his or her goals are unattainable; and to manipulate a final settlement as close as possible to the other party's resistance point (Donohue et al., 1983; Lewicki & Litterer, 1985; Walton & McKersie, 1965).

A second set of regional and local goals involves information exchange. Negotiators do not enter into bargaining with complete information about their opponents; they thus need to gain information about opponents' preferences, goals, expectations, demands, strengths, and weaknesses (Gulliver, 1979). Negotiators also reveal information through their own bargaining messages.

Information exchange within distributive bargaining is a strategic process tied to social influence (Rubin & Brown, 1975, p. 260). Since information about one's position can be used by the opponent, the bargainer attempts to discover the opponent's target and resistance points without revealing his or her own (Rieke & Sillars, 1975). This objective can be broken down into several more specific goals: to control topics of discussion, to ask the opponent questions without answering questions, and to express preferences in equivocal terms (Donohue et al., 1983).

In integrative bargaining, each party accents the global goal of increasing the total available payoffs (Lewicki & Litterer, 1985; Walton & McKersie, 1965). Agenda items are conceptualized in variable-sum fashion: Problem solving can generate creative solutions that allow both parties to achieve most or all of their goals. This global objective has implications for regional and local influence goals, including persuading the opponent or one's constituents that goals important to self have implications for both parties, that excessive aspirations should be modified, and that the "best" decision criteria or policy proposals should be adopted (Lewicki & Litterer, 1985; Walker, 1985).

Integrative bargaining also affects regional and local information-exchange objectives. Walton and McKersie (1965) assert that an open and accurate exchange of information is critical for integrative bargaining. This approach consequently gives rise to a number of specific information goals, including the following: to create a free flow of information; to communicate problems and exchange information at different levels of management and union organizations; to understand the other's true needs and preferences; to emphasize commonalities and minimize differences; to identify and define essential problems; to generate a variety of creative, plausible alternative solutions; to report changing evaluations of potential solutions accurately; and to keep decisions tentative until alternatives are generated, issues are defined, and packages are determined (Lewicki & Litterer, 1985; Walton & McKersie, 1965).

Bargaining roles and instrumental goals. Instrumental goals also arise from the specific roles occupied by negotiators. Schank and Abelson (1977, p. 119) describe roles as one type of "theme" or a "package of goals that tend to occur together because of some property of one or more actors." Within organizational negotiations, labor and management representatives pursue somewhat different interaction goals (see Donohue, Diez, & Hamilton, 1984; Fossum, 1979; Haire, 1955; Kochan & Katz, 1988; Morley & Stephenson, 1977; Putnam & Jones, 1982a; Putnam et al., 1986; Walton & McKersie, 1965). In general, the labor role takes the offensive, with the negotiator pursuing such global goals as changing status quo policies, improving wages and working conditions, and participating in organizational decision making. Regional and local goals associated with this role include demonstration of the significance of harms within the present system, protection and separation of proposals from the management domain, and aggressiveness in probing and advancing ideas.

The contrasting management role theme emphasizes the global goals of defending status quo policies and decision rights. Specific instrumental goals are to defend the present system against accusations of problems or inefficiency, to prevent changes in current policies, especially in the philosophy underlying those policies, and to prevent currently nonnegotiable items from being added to the contract.

Bargaining roles also influence the goals pursued within buyer-seller negotiations (Cialdini, 1988; Neale & Bazerman, 1985a). Global buyer goals include purchasing quality merchandise and paying competitive prices. More concrete goals may include the following: to acquire data about product features, repair records, warranty, and financing; to assess the number of other potential buyers; and to convince the seller that concessions on price or features are necessary to compete with alternative sellers. Merchants have the global goals of maintaining optimal inventory and selling products at profitable prices. Regional and local goals include convincing the potential buyer that the product is in demand and that it compares favorably with those manufactured by competitors, acquiring information about the buyer's level of knowledge and finances, encouraging inclusion of accessories in the final agreement, and arranging feasible delivery and maintenance schedules.

In summary, interdependence and bargaining roles shape both parties' instrumental goals. We have presented an extensive, but by no means exhaustive, list of potential instrumental goals.

Relational Goals

In addition to instrumental goals, a second type of interaction goal involves the establishment and maintenance of relationships with others (Clark & Delia, 1979). Relational goals may operate concomitantly with instrumental goals or may become intermediate states when negotiators center on their relationship as a means for reaching instrumental goals. The negotiation literature highlights two relational goals that surface frequently during bargaining interaction — power and trust.

Power. Bargaining power is often regarded as the key to integrating relationships with contexts, processes, and outcomes (Bacharach & Lawler, 1981). Although often treated as an individual attribute or system of resources that bargainers bring to the situation (Bonoma, 1976; Leusch, 1976; Spector, 1977), power is more than a potential to influence the opponent or an outcome measured after the negotiations. Rather, power is a manifestation of changing dependency between negotiators that is exerted through the strategies and tactics that shape the direction of negotiations and the emergence of alternatives for a settlement (Bacharach & Lawler, 1981; Folger & Poole, 1984; Lax & Sebenius, 1986).

Both parties bring to the negotiation such resources as expertise, information, formal sanctions, authority, skills, likability, and personality traits. Hence power is always present in negotiations in the form of legitimacy, expertise, and control of the ongoing relationship between the parties. Negotiation power, a particular form of relational power, centers on the dynamics of the bargaining interaction and on the control of options for a potential settlement (Lax & Sebenius, 1986). Negotiation power surfaces in the moves and countermoves of participants as bargainers monitor and try to control the balance of power and level of dependency between them. The need to maintain a balance of power in negotiations is manifested in two global goals: to gain power and to protect oneself from becoming powerless. These global goals are interactional, as each bargaining move constrains the other party's response and tests the limits of power (Bacharach & Lawler, 1981; Lax & Sebenius, 1986).

Overt attempts to gain power are especially evident at the regional and local levels of interaction. At the regional level, bargainers often begin their deliberations by engaging in a power ritual. According to Douglas (1957, 1962), the first phase of bargaining interaction is characterized by exaggerated demands, long, dogmatic pronouncements, "muscle flexing," and jockeying for a one-up tactical position (also see Cialdini, 1988; Trice & Beyer, 1984). These overt and hostile "power plays" can extend over the entire negotiation when bargainers do not share a relational history, and especially when one or both parties hold adversarial positions toward the process (Derber, Chalmers, & Edelman, 1965).

Regional power goals also emerge at other stages of the bargaining. When both parties are getting close to tacit agreement, one or both members may threaten to break off deliberations or to reaffirm past commitments, and thereby reassure constituents that negotiations have been tough (Douglas, 1962; Trice & Beyer, 1984). In addition, after a long period of exploratory problem solving, bargainers may use threats and attacking arguments to guard against possible exploitation by reminding the opponent of their strengths (Bacharach & Lawler, 1981; Lax & Sebenius, 1986).

When a bargainer feels his or her power is slipping, the maintenance goals of restoring the balance of power may become salient. For example, if a dealer and a customer cannot agree on the terms for the sale of a car, the customer might concede on the price but insist on an extended warranty as compensation for losing control. In this instance, maintenance goals are enacted in the final stages of bargaining to replenish the power lost in making the last concession. Reviewing gains and losses at the end of bargaining is another means of offsetting the power imbalance that stems from making the final concession, as the following example illustrates:

> SR1: Yea, we sit here and say every year it's the same story. They won't budge and we have to give.
> SN: You've always got to lose to win. If you lose some money and gain morale it is worth it.
> SR2: Well, what have they given up — academic freedom, binding arbitration, 4 days personal leave, 5 days leave for Association president, due process, RIF — they've given up a lot.
> SR3: Yea, we bought off language with money.
> SN: Do we have a settlement?

At the local level, power goals are evident in the choice, form, and sequencing of tactics. Persuasive arguments, threats, demands, and positional commitment statements often signal attempts to gain power (Putnam & Jones, 1982b). Repressing or monopolizing information and appealing to coalitions may signal efforts at maintaining the power balance between bargainers (Putnam & Jones, 1982a). Power also is asserted through variation in the form of directives. Attempts to assert power are signaled by direct imperatives, need statements (e.g., "We need more data on the number of teachers who have five or more preparations"), and questions that lead the opponent, embody a value judgment, or confront the other party with "why" and "how" issues (Brown & Levinson, 1978; Donohue & Diez, 1985; Donohue et al., 1983; Ervin-Tripp, 1976).

Finally, sequencing of tactics also serves to maintain the power balance between bargainers. For example, Bednar and Currington (1983) report observing a form of competitive symmetry in which both parties struggle for relational power through reciprocating control bids rather than by deferring to the opponent or by using equivalence messages. In addition, Donohue and Diez (1983) report that power symmetry is facilitated through a chain sequence pattern that consists of a question followed by a short, abrupt response that monitors information flow and then by additional questioning. The questioner controls the obligation to respond, while the respondent controls the information flow. In sum, the goals of gaining and maintaining power are reflected at local levels in numerous tactical variations.

Trust. Relational goals also center on the degree of trust between bargainers. At the global level, trust is viewed as the confidence, assurance, or credibility placed in the opponent's behavior. In structuring bargaining attitudes, trust is associated with moving a relationship toward cooperation, friendliness, and respect (Walton & McKersie, 1965). Trust grows as negotiators discover common associations, similar dislikes, and similar language that deemphasize differences between the sides (Walton & McKersie, 1965).

A minimal level of trust between the bargainers is essential for bringing issues to the table and for establishing a shared understanding of the negotiation process. Denying completely the legitimacy of the other party undermines the entire process and often leads to bargaining in bad faith. Moreover, trust is essential for integrative bargaining, for identifying high-priority issues, and for administering contracts and grievances (Pruitt & Smith, 1981; Walton & McKersie, 1965).

The mixed-motive nature of bargaining, however, makes trust problematic. Negotiators must take calculated risks to make concessions, but too many disclosures signal weakness and leave the bargainer open to exploitation. Rubin (1983) refers to this tension as a "quintessential illustration of interdependence" that pulls negotiation in extreme directions and requires a bargainer to walk a tightrope between trust and distrust, risk of exploitation and risk of escalation, and honesty and misrepresentation. This dilemma is particularly problematic for disclosure because of the positive relationship between open exchange of information and joint gain. Trust and openness aid in uncovering common interests between disputants and in generating alternatives for reaching a mutually satisfactory settlement (Fisher & Ury, 1981; Pruitt & Smith, 1981). Hence trust develops gradually, through bargainers' disclosing information incrementally, maintaining consistency between actions and words, making commitments and threats believable, separating issues and demands, and unearthing a common fate or a common enemy (Putnam & Jones, 1982a; Walton & McKersie, 1965).

This gradual building of trust suggests regional goals that operate at different times during the negotiation. Specifically, during the early stages of negotiation, feigned fights test the consistency, believability, and integrity of opponents (Peters, 1955). In the middle stages of bargaining, negotiators might reveal key information on needs, interests, or priorities as a basis for solidifying trust and working toward a mutually acceptable goal. Once the sides reach an acceptable degree of trust, one party might reveal resistance on an issue (Walton & McKersie, 1965). Local goals are manifested through exploratory problem solving, sharing key information, revealing priorities, and giving other-supporting arguments (Schlenker, Helm, & Tedeschi, 1973; Tedeschi, Hiester, & Gahagan, 1969). Developing trust also stems from the use of long pauses or time lapses in saying no to an opponent's offer, nonverbal expressions that show an opponent's position is taken seriously, and expressions of positive sentiment or familiarity between the bargainers.

Trust is also influenced by the relationship between a bargainer and his or her constituents. If constituents distrust their negotiator, they are more likely to monitor his or her behavior and hold him or her accountable for the settlement (Carnevale, Pruitt, & Seilheimer, 1981). Bargainers, in turn, may see their opponents as cooperative and trustworthy, but, to execute their representative role, they behave "tougher" with the opponent by giving small concessions, using more pressure tactics (efforts to persuade the other party to concede), and reaching lower joint outcomes (Carnevale, Pruitt, & Britton, 1979; Frey & Adams, 1972). Hence the building of trust between negotiators is directly related to developing and maintaining trust between bargainers and their constituents.

Global goals of developing a trusting relationship with constituents include increasing flexibility and distance between negotiators and constituents, strengthening goal congruence, and raising or lowering constituent aspirations (Adams, 1976; Organ, 1971; Turner, 1988). Developing and maintaining trust with constituents may occur through regional goals that operate at different times during the negotiations. Early in the bargaining or in prenegotiation meetings, the negotiator may aim to persuade team members that a particular proposal is not workable or will not be acceptable to the other side. Within the middle phase of bargaining, the negotiator's goal may be to revise his or her constituents' initial expectations through appeals to expert, referent, or legitimate power (Walton & McKersie, 1965). Near the end of the bargaining, when a settlement is imminent, bargainers may aim to rectify discrepancies between actual outcomes and their constituents' expectations.

In effect, bargainers often hold objectives of maintaining a balance of power and building a trusting relationship with their opponents and their constituents. These relational goals may operate interchangeably or simultaneously, may be subordinate to instrumental goals or become central aims in their own right, or may be reframed by interaction goals at the regional and local levels.

Identity Goals

Bargaining involves not only substantive policies and relational control but also identities and images. The desire to create and sustain positive identities in the eyes of significant others has been described as the goal of maintaining face (Goffman, 1967). Face goals exert a strong influence on all types of bargaining, from international to interpersonal negotiations (Rubin & Brown, 1975). Bargainers attempt to manage the interaction to project a desired self-image and to aid the opponent in doing likewise (Clark & Delia, 1979). In addition to face-maintenance and face-support goals, bargainers sometimes desire to attack the opponent's face.

Face-maintenance goals. During negotiation, bargainers enact various role identities, which include information from social roles but also involve idiosyncratic ideas about effective role performance (McCall & Simmons, 1978). Every negotiator "has a certain image of himself which he would like to preserve. . . . the manager's self image may emphasize trustworthiness, while an important aspect of the self concept of the union official may be his status" (Walton & McKersie, 1965, p. 258). Bargainers attempt to shift attention from actions that could be construed as inconsistent with desired identities, thereby maintaining face.

The global goal of maintaining face can give rise to regional or local objectives at specific points in the negotiation, such as distancing oneself from arguments that might be viewed as naive or foolish, fulfilling constituents' expectations when making demands or defending positions, preempting or rationalizing perceived inconsistencies between proposals, concealing disagreement among constituents from the opponent, and avoiding the appearance of weakness when making concessions (Brown, 1977; Pruitt & Smith, 1981). These goals become more salient when negotiators are highly accountable to and receive feedback from constituents, and when they possess certain personality characteristics (Brown, 1977; Carnevale et al., 1979; Roloff & Campion, 1987).

Bargainers often adopt distributive goals when face concerns move from background to central issues (Folger & Poole, 1984; Pruitt & Smith, 1981):

> In some instances, protecting against loss of face becomes so central an issue that it "swamps" the importance of the tangible issues at stake and generates intense conflicts that can impede progress toward agreement and increase substantially the costs of conflict resolution. (Brown, 1977, p. 275)

Bargainers have been willing to suffer strikes (Walton & McKersie, 1965, p. 85) and sacrifice monetary rewards (Brown, 1968) to save face.

Face-support goals. Bargainers also have concerns about opponents' role identities. Negotiators may offer face support to their opponents; that is, they may have the goal of helping the other party fulfill role obligations and protect role identities. Motives for forming face-support goals include allowing the opponent to make concession without loss of bargaining reputation, preventing or defusing escalating rounds of face attacks, helping the opposition negotiator moderate his or her constituents' excessive demands, receiving reciprocal role-support in future situations, and fulfilling relational expectations (Brown & Levinson, 1978; Folger & Poole, 1984; Goffman, 1967; Walton & McKersie, 1965).

Face-attack goals. Bargainers at times adopt attacking goals; that is, they purposefully portray the opponent as weak, incompetent, or untrustworthy. In fact, interdependence creates motives both to support *and* to attack the other party's face (Craig, Tracy, & Spisak, 1986; Folger & Poole, 1984). Bargainers may adopt face-attack goals when they perceive their opponent is (a) attacking, (b) resisting a warranted persuasive appeal, especially in the presence of constituents, (c) violating an organizational or relational obligation, or (d) failing to make reciprocal concessions or to bargain in good faith (Brown, 1968, 1977; Craig et al., 1986; Folger & Poole, 1984; Goffman, 1967; Putnam & Jones, 1982a, 1982b).

In summary, bargainers pursue instrumental, relational, and identity objectives, individually or in combination. Some interaction goals in each category are global objectives for entire negotiations; others are local objectives relevant to small segments of discourse. Yet, to understand the roles that goals play in bargaining, researchers need to be cognizant of the qualities of goals within the negotiation process. Two qualities — the dynamic and conflicting natures of goals — emerge as salient for our discussion of bargaining interaction.

THE DYNAMIC NATURE OF INTERACTION GOALS

Even though negotiators enter the bargaining process with an initial set of objectives, these goals frequently are modified, dropped, or replaced by new objectives. Gulliver (1979) introduces the concept of preference set, "an ordered evaluation of the issues and outcomes" (p. 88), to describe emergent and dynamic goals. As Gulliver observes, "[While] a party usually enters negotiations with some goals in mind . . . the party refines and adjusts his preference set, and he continues to do this until the end of the negotiation" (p. 89). Goals change in priority, substance, and relevance at all three levels of abstraction across instrumental, relational, and identity objectives.

Preference sets are emergent and dynamic for four reasons. First, negotiators often enter the process with vague and ill-defined goals. Initial goals may be vague because negotiators have limited information about concrete policy alternatives, are uncertain how the other side will react to proposals, represent constituents who have yet to reach consensus on their preference set, or have difficulty comparing diverse agenda items on the same utility scale (Gulliver, 1979; Walton & McKersie, 1965).

Second, dynamic goals reflect the *opportunistic* manner in which bargainers plan to accomplish goals. Global goals and strategies at times are altered by feedback from regional and local levels (Hayes-Roth & Hayes-Roth, 1979). Planning at global levels is adjusted when an opponent is perceived as blocking preconditions for reaching goals (Berger, 1987; Schank & Abelson, 1977). For example, lawyers in a plea-bargaining situation might lose trust as a result of numerous power plays at regional and local levels. Subsequently, they might change their global goal of settling a case outside of court to one of pursuing an advantageous settlement from a jury. Also, feedback from lower levels also can reveal alternatives to current global goals. For instance, if a negotiator makes a concession and the opponent unexpectedly reciprocates, the negotiator might place increased importance on problem-solving and face-support goals, and consider reciprocal concessions as a strategy for accomplishing those goals.

A third reason preference sets are dynamic is that bargainers constantly attempt to influence each other's positions. Bargainers present arguments as tactics aimed "at recasting the opponent's definition of the bargaining situation" (Bacharach & Lawler, 1981, p. 157). Arguments become the primary means of changing perceptions of the advantages of one's own proposals, the nonfeasibility and undesirability of the opponent's counterproposals, the importance or value of both sides' demands, and the cost of nonagreement for both sides (Bacharach & Lawler, 1981; Keogh, 1987; Rieke & Sillars, 1975; Walker, 1985; Walton & McKersie, 1965).

For example, an academic department chair who is facing uncontrolled enrollment pressures might propose to the dean that the department receive three new faculty lines. The dean, operating under tight budget constraints, might respond by saying that no lines are available. As the department head provides reasons for his proposal — pointing out the harm of overloading staff, the mobility of faculty in the field, and the costs connected with lowering the quality of education — the dean might alter her goal from protecting resources to increasing faculty lines without creating budget problems.

A fourth reason preference sets are dynamic is that they involve the process of interactive argument. Bargaining is conducted not only through arguments that involve the giving of reasons and claims aimed at influencing the opponent's proposals, but also through patterns of reason-giving and disagreement that are jointly produced and less susceptible to either negotiator's control (Benoit, 1983; Burleson, 1981; O'Keefe, 1977). The argumentation processes of disagreeing about claims can reshape issues and redefine perceived relationships between proposals and goals.

Issues, and underlying goals, can change in several respects: Single issues may be split into multiple ones, new proposals may emerge and reframe issues, new issues may evolve from arguments over original agenda items, initial items may be dropped, and multiple issues originally conceived as independent items may be packaged into large wholes (Bacharach & Lawler, 1981; Gulliver, 1979; Putnam, 1984; Putnam et al., 1986). For instance, parents may argue with their children about the children's adhering to a bedtime. This issue may splinter into discussions of routines enacted before going to bed, wake-up time, fears about going to sleep, bedtime snacks, and winding down before bedtime. Arguments for and against going to bed on time might lead to redefining the issue as wind-down time and time to enact bedtime routines. Splintering and recasting issues allows bargainers to explore alternatives outside their initial proposals and original goals.

Evidence from our research on teachers' bargaining indicates that issues are splintered and redefined through arguments. In the first study (Putnam & Wilson, in press), we employed a hierarchical coding system to analyze the degree of integrativeness present in settling sixteen issues from a teachers' negotiation. Integrative settlements emerged from a significantly higher proportion of arguments on the workability of original proposals. That is, when the two sides clashed on the feasibility and efficacy of initial offers, novel proposals that redefined goals often emerged.

In a second investigation (Putnam et al., 1986), we analyzed argument about the framing of issues. This study centered on the concept of case, or the overall justification that each side presents in support of policy proposals. In tracking cases over time, we observed that the two sides disagreed about both case type (that is, over the definition of an issue) and case fit (that is, argument over the substance of an issue). Frequent argument on case type facilitated issue redefinition and integrative outcomes.

In sum, bargainers often attempt to accomplish multiple objectives that change in priority, substance, and relevance as the negotiation unfolds. Dynamic interaction goals indicate that bargainers may have vague initial objectives, may modify global goals and plans based on feedback from lower levels, may aim to alter their opponent's goals, and may redefine issues and underlying objectives through the process of argument. Because negotiators manage multiple goals that change rapidly, conflict frequently arises among their objectives.

THE CONFLICTING NATURE
OF INTERACTION GOALS

As noted above, negotiation is a mixed-motive activity. Because bargainers compete to maximize individual gain and cooperate to attain joint settlements, they operate within a social interaction system characterized by a dialectical tension (Craig, 1986). That is, the activity of negotiation creates an inherent *intraparty* tension between *incentives* to compete and cooperate. Neither incentive can be avoided; rather, both are present throughout the negotiation.

As an illustration, incentives to cooperate must exist even during a period of escalating attacks, since the parties stay at the table only if they perceive that the benefits of settling are larger than those of failing to settle or of entering into arbitration (Pruitt, 1981; Walton & McKersie, 1965). Alternatively, incentives to compete must exist even when the parties identify "win-win" solutions that integrate most of their seemingly incompatible interparty goals, since the parties usually can maximize their individual gain even more by totally dominating their opponents. Thus neither side can escape this dialectical tension. Indeed, we will argue that each bargaining move creates incentives both to compete and to cooperate.

Bargainers inevitably must manage these conflicting incentives as their interaction unfolds. Craig (1986) observes that "such dilemmas must be worked out in actual behavior, the tug of principles being reduced to degrees of constraint in the selection of plans" (p. 265). The parties usually will not manage the tension by cooperating but not competing, because this risks the loss of their instrumental goals. Compromising between cooperating and competing by finding a middle ground between the parties' objectives typically is viewed as ineffective conflict management in which both parties lose (Follert, 1941). Hence theorists have tried to develop descriptions of how bargainers can merge these conflicting incentives through such guidelines as "flexibility-rigidity," or being flexible on means for accomplishing goals but rigid on the goals themselves (Pruitt, 1983). This approach suggests that negotiation often places participants in the position of pursuing contradictory goals concomitantly.

Types of Goal Conflict

Three pairs of interaction goals often are in conflict. First, bargainers have incentives to be both *firm* in pursuing individualistic objectives and *flexible* in searching for a mutually acceptable settlement (Pruitt, 1981, 1983). These conflicting goals are evident in the following excerpt from a teacher-school board negotiation, in which both bargainers refuse their opponents' proposals but signal willingness to give ground.

> TN: There is room to move. Insurance can be thrown in the hopper. But the board must pay all but $1 on long term disability [insurance] . . .
>
> SN: I cannot give you the all but $1 on this one, but I can compromise on the dollar amount.

Conflict between firmness and flexibility sometimes is apparent even in threats or demands, since they may be worded to leave room for movement. For example, the bargainer specifies two alternative settlements that are acceptable to his constituents within the following threat.

> TN: If we don't get one or the other of these packages, we're willing to say no settlement now or in the future.

Negotiators face a second conflict between *revealing* resistance points to facilitate problem solving and *concealing* them to achieve higher gain for self. Examples of simultaneous revealing and concealing are difficult to decipher out of context, since negotiators are often ambiguous, vague, or deceptive about expectations. In the following excerpt, the teachers' negotiator had just argued that health insurance premiums had increased 120% in four years. Moving away from their original proposal—that the school district pay all but $1 of medical charges—the negotiator offers an alternative:

> TN: There is one other alternative. . . . Could we get the board to reconsider the commitment to Blue Cross. . . . The Board could sign a memorandum to investigate a new insurance carrier within 60 days. We can stop the steamrolling problem if the teachers see that no agency can do a better job for a better rate. The teachers . . . are starting to say dishonest things about the board—kickbacks and such.

Here he reveals his side's resistance point: verifying that the current insurance carrier's premiums are competitive. However, he also deceives his opponent (in that the teachers' actual comments on kickbacks were made in a joking manner), thereby concealing the relative priority of the issue.

Negotiators face yet a third tension between incentives to *support* and *attack* their opponent's face. These conflicting goals are evident when a school board representative (SR1) observes, during a caucus meeting, that incentives exist both to attack the teachers for making unreasonable demands and to avoid attacks that could jeopardize the negotiation.[4]

> SN: They must become convinced that we're not going to achieve a settlement unless they give on salary.
> SR1: We could break off negotiations at this point and claim that we're willing to open them only when the teachers are willing to be reasonable. But we don't want to make an official move that is an insult to them.

Negotiators often pursue conflicting goals, including the simultaneous desires to be firm and flexible, to reveal and conceal, and to support yet attack. Goal conflict can be traced to the interrelationship between integrative and distributive bargaining subprocesses, as well as to bargainers' planning processes.

Rationale for Goal Conflict

Relationship of bargaining subprocesses. Although negotiation theorists concur that interdependence gives rise to both integrative and distributive subprocesses, they disagree about how the two subprocesses coexist during negotiation (Gulliver, 1979; Lewicki & Litterer, 1985; Pruitt, 1981; Walton & McKersie, 1965). In a discussion of separate, phase, and interdependence models of integrative and distributive bargaining, Putnam (in press) argues that an interdependence model grounds negotiation in the pursuit of conflicting goals.[5]

Separate models treat integrative and distributive bargaining as distinct processes enacted through different strategies and tactics. For instance, commitments, threats, and persuasive arguments promote distributive bargaining, while offers, honest disclosures, and concessions promote integrative bargaining. Because tactics associated with one process "drive out" those associated with its opposite, negotiations generally are dominated by one of the two processes. Participants reach integrative agreements by setting aside individualistic goals and focusing on joint gains through problem solving. The separate model is evident in studies of cooperative versus competitive bargainers (Greenwood, 1974; Smith, 1969; Wilson, 1971), as well as in recent perspectives contrasting win-win and win-lose negotiations (Fisher & Ury, 1981; Jandt, 1985; Pruitt, 1981). Putnam (1989) criticizes separate models on several grounds, including that bargaining tactics such as threats and persuasive arguments appear to serve both distributive (Guyer & Rapoport, 1970; Roloff, Tutzauer, & Dailey, in press) and integrative (Pruitt & Gleason, 1978; Putnam & Wilson, in press) functions. Moreover, separate models are inconsistent with dynamic and contradictory interaction goals.

Stage models, in contrast, view integrative and distributive processes as distinct goal/behavior clusters that merge along a temporal dimension. According to one stage model (Douglas, 1957, 1962), distributive bargaining dominates the first phase of negotiation, as participants haggle over agenda items, define issues, and differentiate interests. Integrative bargaining dominates the second phase, as parti-

cipants clarify common ground, generate proposals, and reframe issues. Negotiators return to distributive bargaining during the final phase as they divide
available resources. Unfortunately, stage models imply that bargainers' goals are
determined by a "life cycle" of negotiation, independent of the content and framing
of issues, the perceived intent of opponent and constituents, and negotiators'
personalities. Evidence contradicting these models includes the following: (a)
"Integrative" information-exchange strategies do not vary in frequency across
phases (Bednar & Currington, 1983), and (b) cycles of attack-defense and attack-
attack tactics occur within all three phases (Donohue, 1981; Putnam & Jones,
1982a).

Putnam (1989) proposes an interdependent model of integrative and distributive bargaining. Interdependence creates a "difficult marriage between such op-
posites as cooperation and competition, short and long term gain, and need for both
individual and joint gain" (pp. 3-4). Different tactics are not associated with each
process; rather, any tactic simultaneously contributes to both. Disclosure of intentions, for example, encourages integrative bargaining by facilitating the search for
common ground, but also serves distributive ends by providing information that
could be exploited by the opponent. The degree any tactic contributes to each
process is a function of the tactic's wording, the merger and sequencing of tactics,
and both negotiators' interpretive schemes. Bargainers engage in "opportunistic
interaction," that is, they constantly evaluate their goals and plans in light of their
opponents' perceived intentions. Bargainers reach mutually satisfactory settlements through an argumentation process that uncovers similarities while ferreting
out differences, generates alternatives while attacking and defending dichotomous
positions, conceals resistant points while cuing the opponent to priorities and
intentions, and constantly emphasizes both individualistic and joint goals.

In sum, an interdependent model posits that bargainers simultaneously engage
in integrative and distributive bargaining by using strategies and tactics that
encourage pursuit of both individualistic and collective goals. Pursuit of conflicting goals also can be tied to planning processes.

Bargainers' planning processes. In some instances, bargainers may pursue
inconsistent goals due to the ways in which they plan to achieve those objectives.
Hayes-Roth and Hayes-Roth (1979) contend that people plan in an *opportunistic*
rather than a completely predetermined fashion, and that this opportunistic quality
of planning can lead people to pursue inconsistent goals. As an illustration, these
authors collected think-aloud protocols as people planned to complete a list of 14
errands that varied in priority. Analysis of the protocols revealed that, in contrast
to the predetermined model, people "do not plan in a systematic top-down fashion. . . . [They] frequently plan low-level sequences of errands or routes in the
absence, and sometimes in *violation*, of a prescriptive high-level plan" (p. 294;
emphasis added).

In an opportunistic model, bargainers may pursue local goals in a manner that
becomes logically incoherent with their plan for accomplishing global goals. For
example, in a teachers' negotiation the teachers might set a global goal of persuad-

ing the school administration to pay over one-half of their insurance premiums, when the administration currently pays only 20%. However, in the debate about the causes of skyrocketing insurance premiums, the teachers might become embroiled in discovering why premiums have increased. In this instance, the teachers might accept a proposal to gather competing bids for a new insurance carrier, losing sight of their original global objective of having the administration contribute a sizable increase to their premiums. This example illustrates how discussions of issues can shift attention from global to local levels, and thereby produce incompatibility between local-level planning and original global goals.

IMPLICATIONS AND FUTURE DIRECTIONS

Viewing interaction goals as dynamic and conflicting points to the need for new models and alternative approaches to the study of bargaining objectives. This section explores alternative research methods and presents four directions for future research on interaction goals.

Methods for Assessing Interaction Goals

Future research on interaction goals in negotiation necessitates development of reliable and valid assessment procedures. Two procedures for assessing interaction goals are to infer goals from the negotiation discourse and to collect self-report protocols from bargainers. Both have advantages and limitations, and both require additional testing of reliability and validity.

Scholars who adopt discourse analytic perspectives on negotiation (Donohue et al., 1983; Donohue & Diez, 1985; Neu, 1988) rely on knowledge of linguistic conventions, illocutionary and syntactic forms, conversational context, and relational history between parties to make inferences from messages to goals (see Craig, 1986; Daly, 1988). In like manner, we have used this procedure to illustrate interaction goals throughout this chapter. The procedure of inferring goals from discourse provides clues about global, regional, and local goals; allows for analysis of naturalistic or simulated interaction; and is well suited for studying connections between goals of negotiating opponents.

Relationships between goals and messages, however, are complex and indeterminate, and this creates potential limits on the procedure of inferring goals from discourse. Because bargaining interaction is multifunctional, negotiators may rely on identical discourse forms to accomplish distinct objectives. For example, negotiators might use warnings of future resistance or reprisals to restore their face, but they also might use identical tactics to underscore the importance of an instrumental objective or to assert relational control (Brown, 1977). Moreover, because bargainers edit their message content as a means of managing conflicting goals (Hample & Dallinger, 1987), the best indication of their goals can be what is omitted from rather than what is present in their messages. Hence discourse and contextual features, in isolation, at times may provide insufficient information for inferring goals.

Self-report procedures represent a second approach to assessing interaction goals. These procedures include any method that obtains information from participants about their cognitive states. For example, recent studies have utilized stimulated recall to elicit people's thoughts and feelings during conversation (Cegala et al., 1988; Ickes, Robertson, Tooke, & Teng, 1986; von Cranach et al., 1982). Participants take part in videotaped conversations, view the tapes individually, and list the content of any recalled thoughts or feelings. A second form of self-report data surfaces in caucus meetings, when bargaining teams discuss objectives for upcoming sessions.[6] Think-aloud protocols are a third form of self-report procedure, in which researchers instruct participants to verbalize their thoughts while formulating goals and tactics at various breakpoints in the negotiation (see Thompson & Hastie, 1987). Finally, researchers could administer open- or closed-ended questionnaires to ascertain goals at the outset, during intermissions, and following the settlement of negotiations.

Self-reports offer several distinct advantages. In particular, when messages indicate potential pursuit of multiple objectives, respondents could clarify the purposes underlying their discourse. These methods also can capture dynamic shifts in interaction goals. These advantages must be balanced against potential shortcomings of self-report methods.

The most obvious concern about self-reports is whether people have the ability to inspect, recall, and report their cognitive states (Nisbett & Wilson, 1977). This concern is heightened by our claim that negotiators often form and plan to accomplish interaction goals with low levels of conscious awareness. It is important to recognize, however, that consciousness exists along a continuum rather than being present or absent in an "all-or-none" fashion (Hample, 1987). Even when engaging in scripted sequences, individuals must attend to whether conditions for the script continue to be met and select among possible variations (Abelson, 1981; Bargh, 1984; Benoit & Benoit, 1986). Moreover, people have greater awareness of cognitive states such as their interaction goals under certain conditions, including when behavioral strategies and tactics are initiated, attempts to accomplish goals are thwarted, or multiple goals are in conflict (Motley, 1986; von Cranach et al., 1982). As previously noted, these conditions occur regularly during negotiation. In addition, negotiators generally will have greater awareness of global than of local objectives, since they are more likely to talk explicitly about global goals and to pursue them for longer periods of time (Carver & Scheier, 1982; Hample, 1987).

The available evidence suggests that people should be able to report the content of their global and regional goals (see Benoit & Benoit, 1986; Ericsson & Simon, 1980). For example, Ickes et al. (1986) report several validational studies documenting relationships between people's stimulated recall of thoughts/feelings and their personality, global evaluations of interactants, and (most important) concrete verbal and nonverbal behaviors during natural conversations. The utility of self-reports for assessing interaction goals, especially more transitory local goals, merits future empirical investigation.

An additional concern is that social desirability could influence negotiators' self-reports even when they are able to inspect their goals. Different self-report procedures, however, are affected to varying degrees by appropriateness concerns, and open-end reports appear relatively immune to desirability bias (Burleson et al., 1988).

Future research could compare and contrast data on interaction goals collected by alternative methods to tap diverse levels of analysis and to interpret the findings from a holistic picture of the data. Thus data gathered through different methods are supplementary, and discrepancies in research findings between methods become opportunities for enriched explanations (Jick, 1979; Weick, 1985). Refining the use of inferential and self-report procedures would aid researchers in pursuing three additional directions for future research.

Bargaining Context, Goals, and Outcomes

Interaction goals might provide an explanatory framework for exploring reciprocal relationships between bargainers' perceptions of the negotiation context and their interaction patterns and outcomes. Participants' roles and actions obviously place some constraint on the ways in which bargainers construe negotiation sessions, and thereby influence the interaction. For example, *negotiator accountability*, or the degree to which bargainers must justify actions to their constituents, affects strategies and outcomes. Highly accountable negotiators are more likely to use aggressive tactics, reach impasse, and demonstrate unwillingness to deviate from initial objectives (see Brown, 1977; Roloff & Campion, 1987). Researchers attribute these effects to the impact of accountability on face-maintenance goals, but most studies do not directly assess interaction goals. Thus future research might investigate how the effect of accountability on global goals in turn affects negotiators' regional persuasion and information-exchange objectives, and attempt to differentiate situations in which accountability leads to impasse from those in which it does not. Moreover, a goals focus might help explain why other variables, such as constituent feedback (Organ, 1971) and negotiators' self-monitoring (Roloff & Campion, 1987), can exacerbate the influence of accountability.

Although contextual features place some limits on situational definitions, negotiation sessions frequently are open to multiple plausible interpretations. Neale and her colleagues emphasize this polysemy by distinguishing between bargainers who adopt a *positive frame* — viewing negotiation outcomes as "gains" over present policies — and those who adopt a *negative frame* — viewing outcomes as "losses" from initial offers (Neale & Bazerman, 1985b; Neale, Huber, & Northcraft, 1987). Frames influence bargainers' subjective perceptions of contexts, and thereby affect their objectives in the negotiation. Positively framed bargainers make more concessions and reach impasse less frequently than negatively framed negotiators.

Perceptual frames influence risk-taking propensity, such that negatively framed negotiators are willing to risk failure in reaching mutual goals by holding to initial objectives. Again, research on perceptual frames does not directly assess interaction goals. Future research might investigate how events at local levels can lead negotiators to adopt different frames, thereby modifying their global goals.

Expert and Novice Negotiators

The study of interaction goals might aid researchers and practitioners in understanding the differences between skilled and novice negotiators. Rackham and Carlisle's (1978a, 1978b) studies of 56 sessions with skilled negotiators and 37 sessions with average bargainers indicate that the two types of negotiators form and manage interaction goals differently. In selection of global goals, skilled negotiators focus on common ground between the sides, work within a range of outcomes rather than with fixed limits, and plan strategies for particular issues rather than for a sequence of steps. Although instrumental goals appear to dominate the planning stage, consideration of relational issues is embedded in discussions of common ground and the opponent's perceptions of issues. Average or inexperienced negotiators fail to engage in perspective taking as a way of setting instrumental and relational goals and often conclude that "what makes sense to me, will make sense to them" (Neale & Bazerman, 1983). This failure to differentiate the opponent and one's own perspectives leads the novice negotiator to focus on the details rather than the interpretation of "facts."

Expert and novice negotiators also pursue instrumental goals differently. Skilled negotiators seek and use information through a question-answer pattern; summarize, reflect, and test understanding; give reasons that lead up to disagreements; and present a sufficient but not an excessive number of counterproposals (Donohue & Diez, 1983, 1985; Rackham & Carlisle, 1978a). The timing of tactics, particularly in offering counterproposals and in making concessions, may be directly related to the way bargainers set instrumental goals at the regional level.

Identity and relational goals at the local level play a dominant role in distinguishing between skilled and average bargainers. Expert bargainers are particularly adept at supporting their opponent's face by avoiding words and phrases that "irritate" or "antagonize" without any persuasive effect (e.g., using value-loaded terms such as *fair* or *unreasonable*) (Rackham & Carlisle, 1978a). This identity goal is closely aligned with building and preserving trust. For example, skilled as opposed to average negotiators share motives or inferences on issues and express feelings about the communication between parties. Skilled negotiators might say, "I'm uncertain how to react to what you say. I feel some doubts about its accuracy," while average negotiators would typically call a caucus and remain silent about these apprehensions. In effect, by applying a goals framework to analysis of expert negotiators, we can gain an understanding of how bargainers manage multiple goals simultaneously. Future studies need to center on how negotiators make choices when goals conflict or are contradictory across levels.

Conflict Escalation and Deescalation

Researchers could also study escalation and deescalation from a goals perspective. Specifically, how do changing goals at the local level shape modifications in global goals? Escalation of conflict is usually defined as an attack-attack or defend-defend conflict spiral in which the number of issues, costs, and ramifications of a dispute tend to grow (Putnam, 1984). Escalating conflicts appear to evolve from the mismanagement of distributive tactics rather than from the absence or failure to develop integrative or problem-solving behaviors (Putnam & Jones, 1982a). Specifically, when local goals change from arguing for or defending a position to matching the opponent's tactics, escalation typically results. This matching of tactics leads to modifying instrumental goals toward winning, slanting relational goals toward gaining power and asserting control, and increasing emphasis on attacking rather than supporting face. The expansion of face-threatening directives as a means of exerting relational control also increases the intensity level of the conflict (Donohue & Diez, 1985). As the global goals begin to parallel the local ones, conflict spirals begin to dominate the direction and momentum of the interaction and become self-sustaining. Global goals of winning or beating the opponent often lead the negotiation to a stalemate (Deutsch, 1969).

Negotiators who have a sense that a conflict spiral is developing may buffer cycles with information-giving or integrative tactics that slow down the spiral (Putnam, 1984). When these integrative tactics are reciprocated, pressures to pursue face-maintenance and power-balancing objectives at the global level may be reduced. Conflict spirals are also controlled through treating attacks in an impersonal manner rather than by becoming defensive and engaging in one-upmanship behaviors. Rackham and Carlisle (1978b) have also observed that when skilled negotiators attack, they attack hard and then cease their attack without warning. Thus skilled negotiators might curtail gradual escalation of conflict by altering goals quickly at the local level and keeping them constant at the global level. Average negotiators, in contrast, build up attacks slowly and gradually, triggering a similar pattern of escalation by the opponent. For average negotiators, then, subtle and slow changes at the local and regional levels gradually may increase the salience of global-distributive and face-maintenance goals.

Once again, although some studies mention goals as explanatory concepts, few directly assess interaction goals during cycles of conflict. Future research needs to decipher the role that multiple and contradictory goals, across levels of abstraction, play in the escalation and deescalation of conflict.

CONCLUSION

This chapter has discussed the role of interaction goals in negotiation. We have described a broad range of interaction goals that vary along two dimensions: type and level of abstraction. Both features of negotiation and of planning shape the particular goals that bargainers aim to accomplish. Due to these features, bargainers often pursue multiple, conflicting goals that change rapidly as the negotiation unfolds.

Our discussion has indicated that future research on interaction goals is justified on several grounds. A goals focus could offer insights about the role of communication in a wide variety of negotiation phenomena, including the reciprocal relation between bargaining contexts and outcomes, the escalation and deescalation of conflict, and the development of negotiation expertise. These phenomena can be understood from a perspective that views negotiation as a strategic activity, in which participants manage conflicting incentives and pursue multiple goals within a complex planning environment. A goals perspective also highlights the dynamic nature of negotiation, by emphasizing that bargaining behavior is guided by interaction goals but often reframes those goals.

Understanding the role of interaction goals in bargaining may provide insights for negotiation practitioners as well as for scholars. Specifically, individuals who realize that interaction goals change during negotiations and that local goals can reframe global ones might be less likely to cling to predetermined, ineffectual goals. Bargainers who attribute their opponents' behaviors to relational and identity objectives in addition to instrumental objectives may develop a more accurate understanding of their opponents. Recognizing the dialectical tension between incentives to pursue cooperative and competitive objectives, as well as the contextual features that enhance competitive incentives, would aid negotiators in monitoring the delicate balance between attack-defend interaction and problem-solving communication. Finally, sensitizing negotiators to relations among goals at different levels of abstraction might help them recognize when such local goals as "matching the other party's tactics" begin to alter the salience of those global goals that increase the odds of escalation and impasse. In sum, the negotiation literature would benefit from a broader, more interactive approach to the study of bargaining goals.

NOTES

1. Of course, negotiators at times will manage their impressions with constituents by claiming they have pursued specific interaction goals during prior sessions (Pruitt & Smith, 1981; Walton & McKersie, 1965). But a negotiator's objective in such instances is not to make sense of prior sessions; rather, it is to persuade constituents that the "sense" he or she has made is a valid interpretation of events. Such impression-management objectives are examples of interaction goals.

2. Indeed, Donohue et al. (1983), in the discourse analytic tradition, infer the "purposes" (p. 257) and "objectives" (p. 261) that negotiators are attempting to accomplish through their messages.

3. Work on conversational coherence distinguishes global models of coherence, which assume that discourse coheres around overarching structures encompassing numerous individual turns (e.g., story grammars or scripts), and local models, which assume that discourse coheres around sequencing rules linking single turns (e.g., adjacency pairs) (Goldberg, 1983).

4. Wilson (1989) presents evidence that people pursue both supporting and attacking goals when seeking compliance, another mixed-motive activity. In a series of studies, participants provided open-ended reports of their goals in one of twelve hypothetical compliance-gaining situations. Across the studies, 17% of participants reported *both* face-support and face-attack goals. Moreover, for the subset of participants reporting face-attack goals, 42% also reported face-support goals.

5. Putnam's three models of integrative and distributive bargaining bear some resemblance to O'Keefe and Delia's (1982; O'Keefe & Shepherd, 1987) selection, separation, and integration message strategies for coordinating multiple goals. However, O'Keefe's strategies describe how communicators coordinate conflicting goals within single messages, while Putnam's models present views of how bargainers manage incompatible goals throughout the negotiation. Each of Putnam's models contains assumptions about bargaining goals, issues, strategies, tactics, and outcomes.

6. In a sense, caucus meetings present both self-report and inferential data about goals. Bargainers often report the interaction goals they will pursue at the table during caucus interactions. However, bargainers also attempt to achieve goals pertaining to their constituents during these meetings. Researchers might infer the latter goals from caucus interaction.

REFERENCES

Abelson, R. P. (1981). Psychological status of the script concept. *American Psychologist, 36,* 715-729.

Adams, J. S. (1976). The structure and dynamics of behavior in organizational boundary roles. In M. P. Dunnette (Ed.), *Handbook of Industrial and organizational psychology* (pp. 1175-1199). Chicago: Rand McNally.

Bacharach, S. B., & Lawler, E. J. (1981). *Bargaining: Power, tactics, and outcomes.* San Francisco: Jossey-Bass.

Bargh, J. A. (1984). Automatic and conscious processing of social information. In R. W. Wyer & T. K. Srull (Eds.), *Handbook of social cognition* (Vol. 3, pp. 1-44). Hillsdale, NJ: Lawrence Erlbaum.

Bazerman, M. H., & Carroll, J. S. (1987). Negotiator cognition. *Research in Organizational Behavior, 9,* 247-288.

Bednar, D. A., & Currington, W. P. (1983). Interaction analysis: A tool for understanding negotiations. *Industrial and Labor Relations Review, 36,* 389-401.

Benoit, P. J. (1983, November). *A review and response to criticism of argument.* Paper presented at the annual meeting of the Speech Communication Association, Washington, DC.

Benoit, P. J., & Benoit, W. L. (1986). Consciousness: The mindless/mindfulness and verbal report controversy. *Western Journal of Speech Communication, 50,* 41-63.

Berger, C. R. (1987). Planning and scheming: Strategies for initiating relationships. In R. Burnett, P. McGhee, & D. Clarke (Eds.), *Accounting for relationships: Social representations of interpersonal links* (pp. 158-174). London: Methuen.

Bonoma, T. (1976). Conflict, cooperation, and trust in three power systems. *Behavioral Science, 6,* 419-514.

Brown, B. R. (1968). The effects of need to maintain face in interpersonal bargaining. *Journal of Experimental Social Psychology, 4,* 107-122.

Brown, B. R. (1977). Face-saving and face-restoration in negotiation. In D. Druckman (Ed.), *Negotiations: Social psychological perspectives* (pp. 275-299). Beverly Hills, CA: Sage.

Brown, P., & Levinson, S. (1978). Universals in language use: Politeness phenomena. In E. N. Goody (Ed.), *Questions and politeness* (pp. 56-289). Cambridge: Cambridge University Press.

Bruce, B., & Newman, D. (1978). Interacting plans. *Cognitive Science, 2,* 195-233.

Burke, J. A. (1986). Interacting plans in the accomplishment of a practical activity. In D. G. Ellis & W. A. Donohue (Eds.), *Contemporary issues in language and discourse processes* (pp. 203-222). Hillsdale, NJ: Lawrence Erlbaum.

Burleson, B. R. (1981). On the analysis and criticism of arguments: Some theoretical and methodolog-
    ical considerations. *Journal of the American Forensic Association, 15*, 137-147.
Burleson, B. R., Wilson, S. R., Waltman, M. S., Goering, E. M., Ely, T. K., & Whaley, B. (1988). Item
    desirability effects in compliance-gaining research: Seven studies documenting artifacts in the
    strategy selection procedure. *Human Communication Research, 14*, 429-486.
Carlisle, J., & Leary, M. (1981). Negotiating groups. In R. Payne & C. L. Cooper (Eds.), *Groups at work*
    (pp. 165-188). New York: John Wiley.
Carnevale, P.J.D., Pruitt, D. G., & Britton, S. D. (1979). Looking tough: The negotiator under
    constituent surveillance. *Personality and Social Psychology Bulletin, 5*, 118-121.
Carnevale, P.J.D., Pruitt, D. G., & Seilheimer, S. D. (1981). Looking and competing: Accountability
    and visual access in integrative bargaining. *Journal of Personality and Social Psychology, 40*,
    111-120.
Carver, C. S., & Scheier, M. F. (1982). Control theory: A useful conceptual framework for personality-
    social, clinical, and health psychology. *Psychological Bulletin, 92*, 111-135.
Cegala, D. J., Waldron, V., Ludlum, J., McCabe, B., Teboul, B., & Yost, S. (1988, March). *A study of
    interactants' thoughts and feelings during conversation*. Paper presented at the Ninth Annual
    Temple University Conference on Discourse Analysis, Philadelphia.
Cialdini, R. B. (1988). *Influence: Science and practice* (2nd ed.). Glenview, IL: Scott, Foresman.
Clark, R. A., & Delia, J. G. (1979). *Topoi* and rhetorical competence. *Quarterly Journal of Speech, 65*,
    187-206.
Craig, R. T. (1986). Goals in discourse. In D. G. Ellis & W. A. Donohue (Eds.), *Contemporary issues
    in language and discourse processes* (pp. 257-275). Hillsdale, NJ: Lawrence Erlbaum.
Craig, R. T., Tracy, K., & Spisak, F. (1986). The discourse of requests: Assessment of a politeness
    approach. *Human Communication Research, 12*, 437-468.
Daly, L. A. (1988, March). *The unmasking of underlying goals*. Paper presented at the Ninth Annual
    Temple University Conference on Discourse Analysis, Philadelphia.
Derber, M., Chalmers, W. E., & Edelman, M. T. (1965). *Plant union-management relations: From
    practice to theory*. Urbana: University of Illinois, Labor and Industrial Relations Institute.
Deutsch, M. (1969). Conflicts: Productive or destructive? *Journal of Social Issues, 25*, 7-41.
Donohue, W. A. (1978). An empirical framework for examining negotiation processes and outcomes.
    Communication Monographs, 45, 247-257.
Donohue, W. A. (1981). Development of a model of rule use in negotiation interaction. *Communication
    Monographs, 48*, 262-276.
Donohue, W. A., & Diez, M. E. (1983, May). *Information management in negotiation*. Paper presented
    at the annual meeting of the International Communication Association, Dallas.
Donohue, W. A., & Diez, M. E. (1985). Directive use in negotiation interaction. *Communication
    Monographs, 52*, 305-318.
Donohue, W. A., Diez, M. E., & Hamilton, M. (1984). Coding naturalistic negotiation interaction.
    Human Communication Research, 10, 403-426.
Donohue, W. A., Diez, M. E., & Stahle, R. B. (1983). New directions in negotiation research. In R. N.
    Bostrom (Ed.), *Communication yearbook 7* (pp. 249-279). Beverly Hills, CA: Sage.
Douglas, A. (1957). The peaceful settlement of industrial and intergroup disputes. *Journal of Conflict
    Resolution, 1*, 69-81.
Douglas, A. (1962). *Industrial peacemaking*. New York: Columbia University Press.
Ericsson, K. A., & Simon, H. A. (1980). Verbal reports as data. *Psychological Review, 87*, 215-251.
Ervin-Tripp, S. (1976). Is Sybil there? The structure of some American English directives. *Language
    in Society, 5*, 25-66.
Esser, J. K., & Kormorita, S. S. (1974). Reciprocal and non-reciprocal concession strategies in
    bargaining. *Research and Social Psychology Bulletin, 1*, 231-233.
Fisher, R., & Ury, W. R. (1981). *Getting to yes*. Boston: Houghton Mifflin.
Folger, J. P., & Poole, M. S. (1984). *Working through conflict: A communication perspective*. Glenview,
    IL: Scott, Foresman.

Follert, M. P. (1941). Constructive conflict. In H. C. Metcalf & L. Urwick (Eds.), *Dynamic administration: The collected papers of Mary Parker Follert* (pp. 30-49). New York: Harper & Bros.

Fossum, J. A. (1979). *Labor relations: Development, structure, and process*. Dallas: Business Publications.

Frey, R. L., & Adams, J. S. (1972). The negotiator's dilemma: The simultaneous ingroup and outgroup conflict. *Journal of Experimental Social Psychology, 8*, 331-346.

Goffman, E. (1967). *Interaction ritual: Essays in face-to-face behavior*. Chicago: Aldine.

Goldberg, J. A. (1983). A move toward describing conversational coherence. In R. T. Craig & K. Tracy (Eds.), *Conversational coherence: Form, structure, and strategy* (pp. 25-45). Beverly Hills, CA: Sage.

Greene, J. O. (1984). A cognitive approach to human communication: An action assembly theory. *Communication Monographs, 51*, 289-306.

Greene, J. O., & Lindzey, E. (1989). Encoding processes in multiple-goal messages. *Human Communication Research, 16*, 120-140.

Greenwood, S. G. (1974). Opportunity to communicate and social orientation in imaginary-reward bargaining. *Speech Monographs, 41*, 49-81.

Gulliver, P. H. (1979). *Disputes and negotiations: A cross-cultural perspective*. New York: Academic Press.

Guyer, M., & Rapoport, A. A. (1970). Threat in a two-person game. *Journal of Experimental Social Psychology, 6*, 11-25.

Haire, M. (1955). Role-perceptions in labor-management relations: An experimental approach. *Industrial and Labor Relations Review, 8*, 204-216.

Hample, D. (1987). Communication and the unconscious. In B. Dervin & M. J. Voight (Eds.), *Progress in communication sciences* (Vol. 8, pp. 83-122). Norwood, NJ: Ablex.

Hample, D., & Dallinger, J. M. (1987). Individual differences in cognitive editing standards. *Human Communication Research, 14*, 123-144.

Hawes, L. C., & Smith, D. H. (1973). A critique of assumptions underlying the study of communication in conflict. *Quarterly Journal of Speech, 59*, 423-435.

Hayes-Roth, B., & Hayes-Roth, F. (1979). A cognitive model of planning. *Cognitive Science, 3*, 275-310.

Hobbs, J. R., & Evans, D. A. (1980). Conversation as planned behavior. *Cognitive Science, 4*, 349-377.

Huber, V. L., & Neale, M. A. (1986). Effects of cognitive heuristics and goals on negotiator performance and subsequent goal setting. *Organizational Behavior and Human Decision Processes, 38*, 342-365.

Ickes, W., Robertson, E., Tooke, W., & Teng, G. (1986). Naturalistic social cognition: Methodology, assessment, and validation. *Journal of Personality and Social Psychology, 51*, 66-82.

Jandt, F. E. (1985). *Win-win negotiating: Turning conflict into agreement*. New York: John Wiley.

Jick, T. D. (1979). Mixing qualitative and quantitative methods: Triangulation in action. *Administrative Science Quarterly, 24*, 602-611.

Kellermann, K. (1984, November). *Scripts: What are they, how do you know; and why should you care?* Paper presented at the annual meeting of the Speech Communication Association, Chicago.

Kellermann, K. (1987). Information exchange in social interaction. In M. E. Roloff & G. R. Miller (Eds.), *Interpersonal processes: New directions in communication research* (pp. 188-219). Newbury Park, CA: Sage.

Keogh, C. M. (1987). The nature and function of argument in organizational bargaining research. *Southern States Speech Journal, 53*, 1-17.

Kline, S. L. (1984). *Social cognitive determinants of face support in persuasive messages*. Unpublished doctoral dissertation, University of Illinois, Urbana.

Kochan, T. A., & Katz, H. C. (1988). *Collective bargaining and industrial relations: From theory to practice*. Homewood, IL: Irwin.

Lax, D., & Sebenius, J. (1986). *The manager as negotiator*. New York: Free Press.

Leusch, R. F. (1976). Sources of power: Their impact on interchannel conflict. *Journal of Marketing Research, 13*, 382-390.

Lewicki, R. J., & Litterer, J. A. (1985). *Negotiations*. Homewood, IL: Irwin.

McCall, G. J., & Simmons, J. L. (1978). *Identities and interactions: An examination of human associations in everyday life*. New York: Free Press.

Miller, G. A., Galanter, E., & Pribram, K. H. (1960). *Plans and the structure of behavior*. New York: Holt, Rinehart & Winston.

Morley, I., & Stephenson, G. (1977). *The social psychology of bargaining*. Cambridge, MA: Harvard University Press.

Motley, M. T. (1986). Consciousness and intentionality in communication: A preliminary model and methodological approaches. *Western Journal of Speech Communication, 50*, 3-23.

Neale, M. A., & Bazerman, M. H. (1983). The role of perspective-taking ability in negotiating under different forms of arbitration. *Industrial and Labor Relations Review, 36*, 378-388.

Neale, M. A., & Bazerman, M. H. (1985a). The effect of externally set goals on reaching integrative agreements in competitive markets. *Journal of Occupational Behavior, 6*, 12-32.

Neale, M. A., & Bazerman, M. H. (1985b). The effects of framing and negotiator overconfidence on bargaining behaviors and outcomes. *Academy of Management Journal, 28*, 34-49.

Neale, M. A., Huber, V. L., & Northcraft, G. B. (1987). The framing of negotiations: Contextual versus task frames. *Organizational Behavior and Human Decision Processes, 39*, 228-241.

Neu, J. (1988). Conversation structure: An exploration of bargaining behaviors in negotiation. *Management Communication Quarterly, 2*, 23-45.

Nisbett, R. E., & Wilson, T. D. (1977). Telling more than we can know: Verbal reports on mental processes. *Psychological Review, 84*, 231-259.

O'Keefe, B. J., & Delia, D. J. (1982). Impression formation and message production. In M. E. Roloff & C. R. Berger (Eds.), *Social cognition and communication* (pp. 33-72). Beverly Hills, CA: Sage.

O'Keefe, B. J., & Shepherd, G. J. (1987). The pursuit of multiple objectives in face-to-face persuasive interaction: Effects of construct differentiation on message organization. *Communication Monographs, 54*, 396-419.

O'Keefe, D. J. (1977). Two concepts of argument. *Journal of the American Forensic Association, 13*, 121-128.

Organ, D. W. (1971). Some variables affecting boundary role behavior. *Sociometry, 34*, 524-537.

Peters, E. (1955). *Strategy and tactics in labor negotiations*. New London, CT: National Foremen's Institute.

Pruitt, D. G. (1981). *Negotiation behavior*. New York: Academic Press.

Pruitt, D. G. (1983). Integrative agreements: Nature and antecedents. In M. H. Bazerman & R. J. Lewicki (Eds.), *Negotiating in organizations* (pp. 35-50). Beverly Hills, CA: Sage.

Pruitt, D. G., & Gleason, J. M. (1978). Threat capacity and the choice between independence and interdependence. *Personality and Social Psychology Bulletin, 4*, 252-255.

Pruitt, D. G., & Smith, D. L. (1981). Impression management in bargaining: Images of firmness and trustworthiness. In J. T. Tedeschi (Ed.), *Impression management theory and social psychological research* (pp. 247-267). New York: Academic Press.

Putnam, L. L. (1984). Bargaining as task and process: Multiple functions of interaction sequences. In R. L. Street & J. N. Cappella (Eds.), *Sequences and pattern in communicative behavior* (pp. 225-242). London: Edward Arnold.

Putnam, L. L. (1989). Bargaining. *International Encyclopedia of Communication* (Vol. 1, pp. 176-178). Amherst, PA: Oxford University Press.

Putnam, L. L., & Jones, T. S. (1982a). The role of communication in bargaining. *Human Communication Research, 8*, 262-280.

Putnam, L. L., & Jones, T. S. (1982b). Reciprocity in negotiations: An analysis of bargaining interaction. *Communication Monographs, 49*, 171-191.

Putnam, L. L., & Wilson, S. R. (in press). Argumentation and bargaining strategies and discriminators of integrative outcomes. In A. Rahim (Ed.), *Managing conflict: An interdisciplinary approach*. New York: Praeger.

Putnam, L. L., Wilson, S. R., Waltman, M. S., & Turner, D. (1986). The evolution of case arguments in teachers' bargaining. *Journal of the American Forensic Association, 23*, 63-82.

Rackham, N., & Carlisle, J. (1978a). The effective negotiator: The behavior of successful negotiators. *Journal of European Industrial Training, 2*(6), 6-11.

Rackham, N., & Carlisle, J. (1978b). The effective negotiator: Planning for negotiations. *Journal of European Industrial Training, 2*(7), 2-5.

Rieke, R. D., & Sillars, M. O. (1975). *Argumentation and the decision making process.* New York: John Wiley.

Roloff, M. E., & Campion, D. E. (1987). On alleviating the debilitating effects of accountability on bargaining: Authority and self-monitoring. *Communication Monographs, 54*, 145-164.

Roloff, M. E., Tutzauer, F., & Dailey, W. O. (in press). The role of argumentation in distributive and integrative bargaining contexts: Seeking relative advantage but at what cost? In M. A. Rahim (Ed.), *Managing conflict: An interdisciplinary approach.* New York: Praeger.

Rubin, J. C. (1983). Negotiation. *American Behavioral Scientist, 27*, 135-147.

Rubin, J. C., & Brown, B. (1975). *The social psychology of bargaining and negotiation.* New York: Academic Press.

Schank, R., & Abelson, R. (1977). *Scripts, plans, goals, and understanding.* Hillsdale, NJ: Lawrence Erlbaum.

Schelling, T. C. (1960). *The strategy of conflict.* Cambridge, MA: Harvard University Press.

Schlenker, B. R., Helm, B., & Tedeschi, J. T. (1973). The effects of personality and situational variables on behavioral trust. *Journal of Personality and Social Psychology, 25*, 419-427.

Scotton, C. N., & Owsley, H. (1982). *What about powerful questions?* Paper presented at the annual meeting of the Chicago Linguistic Society, Chicago.

Searle, J. R. (1969). *Speech acts: An essay in the philosophy of language.* Cambridge: Cambridge University Press.

Smith, D. A. (1969). Communication and negotiation outcome. *Journal of Communication, 19*, 248-256.

Spector, B. I. (1977). Negotiation as a psychological process. *Journal of Conflict Resolution, 21*, 607-618.

Srull, T. K., & Wyer, R. S. (1986). The role of chronic and temporary goals in social information processing. In R. M. Sorentino & E. T. Higgins (Eds.), *Handbook of motivation and cognition: Foundations of social behavior* (pp. 503-540). New York: Guilford.

Tedeschi, J., Hiester, D. S., & Gahagan, J. P. (1969). Trust and the prisoner's dilemma game. *Journal of Social Psychology, 79*, 43-50.

Thompson, L., & Hastie, R. (1987). Negotiators' perceptions of the negotiation process. In B. H. Sheppard, M. H. Bazerman, & R. J. Lewicki (Eds.), *Research in negotiation in organizations* (Vol. 2). Greenwich, CT: JAI.

Tracy, K. T. (1984). The effects of multiple goals on conversational relevance and topic coherence. *Communication Monographs, 51*, 274-287.

Trice, H. M., & Beyer, J. M. (1984). Studying organizational cultures through rites and ceremonies. *Academy of Management Review, 9*, 653-669.

Turner, D. B. (1988). *Intraorganizational bargaining: The effect of goal congruence and trust on negotiators' strategy use.* Unpublished doctoral dissertation, Purdue University.

van Dijk, T. A., & Kintsch, W. (1983). *Strategies for discourse comprehension.* New York: Academic Press.

von Cranach, M., Kalbermatten, U., Indermuhle, K., & Gugler, B. (1982). *Goal-directed action.* New York: Academic Press.

Walker, G. B. (1985). Argumentation and negotiation. In J. R. Cox, M. O. Sillars, & G. B. Walker (Eds.), *Argumentation and social practice: Proceedings of the fourth SCA/AFA conference on argumentation* (pp. 747-769). Annandale, VA: Speech Communication Association.

Walton, R. E., & McKersie, R. B. (1965). *A behavioral theory of labor negotiations.* New York: McGraw-Hill.

Weick, K. (1979). *The social psychology of organizing* (2nd ed.). Reading, MA: Addison-Wesley.

Weick, K. E. (1985). Systematic observational methods. In G. Lindzey & E. Aronson (Eds.), *Handbook of social psychology* (Vol. 1, pp. 567-634). New York: Random House.

Wilson, S. R. (1987, November). *Extending O'Keefe and Delia's view of message production: Arguments for a model of communicative goals and strategies.* Paper presented at the annual meeting of the Speech Communication Association, Boston.

Wilson, S. R. (1989, November). *Situational moderators of priming and construct differentiation on interaction goals: A cognitive rules perspective.* Paper presented at the annual meeting of the Speech Communication Association, San Francisco.

Wilson, W. (1971). Reciprocation and other techniques for inducing cooperation in the prisoner's dilemma game. *Journal of Conflict Resolution, 15,* 167-195.

The Structure of
Interaction Goals

PAMELA J. BENOIT
University of Missouri Columbia

> Man is not just a rational animal. . . . It is in the use of symbols that a man differentiates himself from other men as he puts his personally projected world in the kind of order he can live with. Further, it is through symbols that he relates himself with others so that, in his organized system of interdependency, he may satisfy his needs. (Fogarty, 1959, p. 60)

Social action occurs because interactants are often dependent on others to accomplish their goals. Communication is the means by which humans perform behaviors that are believed to facilitate the achievement of such goals. Communication is "action" rather than "motion" (Burke, 1978) and can be explained through "in order to" reasons as well as causes. The marriage of goals and communication theory is a natural association. Wilson and Putnam's essay extends the goals concept into the negotiation context. They describe and illustrate a typology of goals based on the dimensions of type and level of abstraction. They also argue that because goals can be both emergent and complex, interaction goals often conflict.

Because I share many of the assumptions articulated by Wilson and Putnam, this commentary is written from within a goal-oriented perspective of communication. Thus the first purpose of this essay is to reaffirm these assumptions and highlight the contributions made by Wilson and Putnam. In the next section, however, their particular conception of goals is critiqued. The description of levels of abstraction of goals (global, regional, local), based on the length of the interaction segment for which the goal is relevant, is problematic. This difficulty is the impetus for describing an alternative perspective for displaying the structure of goals.

AUTHOR'S NOTE: I would like to thank William Benoit for suggestions on drafts of this commentary.

Correspondence and requests for reprints: Pamela J. Benoit, 115 Switzer Hall, University of Missouri, Columbia, MO 65211.

Communication Yearbook 13, pp. 407-416

INTERACTION GOALS: A REAFFIRMATION

Wilson and Putnam's particular conceptualization of goals includes four properties:

(1) Goals are proactive, prompting behaviors.
(2) Goals are pursued by individuals in situations.
(3) Goals are preplanned and emergent.
(4) Interactants have multiple and sometimes conflicting goals.

Consider first the notion that goals are proactive. Given Wilson and Putnam's attempt to understand the behaviors of bargainers and to generate a pragmatic description of the bargaining context, their concentration on proactive goals is appropriate. Communication is a practical discipline (Craig, 1986; Goodall & Phillips, 1981), and understanding that particular behavioral strategies can be produced and understood as outcomes generated by goals can increase predictability and ultimately improve competence.

Second, Wilson and Putnam's definition of goals identifies this construct as an objective *people* strive to attain (see, for instance, p. 376). For example, a bargainer who feels the loss of power will strive toward maintenance goals, or distributive goals may be more prevalent when a bargainer's face is threatened. Wilson and Putnam's endorsement of individual goals is also apparent in their discussion of self-reports as a means of identifying goals. A contrasting position is articulated by O'Keefe (1988), who argues that "the relevance of a goal to a situation is not equivalent to the relevance of a goal to a person within that situation" (p. 82).

A rational goals analysis directs attention to examination of the situation to understand the goals and behaviors that occur. Situational and individual orientations are also reflected in Craig's (1986) distinction between formal and strategic goals. Formal goals are dictated by the conventional expectations of the situation, while strategic goals assume that "the conversationalists behave strategically in pursuit of their individual goals" (Craig & Tracy, 1983, p. 15). Explanations of goals must consider both form and strategy to "make clearer that neither cooperative nor individualistic motives are ultimately more basic, that all uses of conventional forms are strategic, while even the most individualistic goals emerge from a social matrix that is constituted of conventions" (Craig, 1986, p. 268). Wilson and Putnam's description integrates form and strategy by accounting for the interaction of individual and situational influences on goals. Goals can be predicted to some degree by the type of negotiation (e.g., labor negotiators will have goals concerning salary, insurance, retirement), but individual bargainers are also strategic in ordering goals, modifying goals as the interaction emerges, and accomplishing goals.

A significant contribution of the Wilson and Putnam essay is the focus on emergent goals. They argue that negotiation researchers have typically viewed goals as predetermined, but that planning involves both top-down and bottom-up processes. Bargainers may generate goals and tactics prior to meetings, but the negotiation context is interactive and involves adaptation and rapid planning as the interaction unfolds. Hobbs and Agar (1981) argue that bottom-up processes are more common and may in fact dilute the global goals established prior to the interaction. The concept that interaction is collaboratively developed and thus emergent is familiar (e.g., Delia & Grossberg, 1977), but the extension to goals and the application to the negotiation context is novel and an important development. Pursuing this view of goals will require a careful examination of the procedures used to determine goals. At this point, think-aloud procedures (Ericsson & Simon, 1984) are most promising for capturing the emergent quality of goals, but additional procedures must be developed to identify goals in process. Inferences from behavior must be made cautiously within this framework because retrospective analyses of goals are bound to overestimate coherence among goals and thus favor top-down explanations.

The description of multiple goals and goal conflicts in negotiation is a significant addition to the understanding of the complex context of negotiation. Analysts are beginning to explicate complex situations in which interactants have several, often conflicting, goals and to account for the impact on the discourse (Benoit & Follert, 1986; O'Keefe & Shepherd, 1987). Wilson and Putnam describe common goal conflicts in the negotiation setting and argue that bargainers' behaviors may, but do not always, reflect coordination among their goals. Interesting issues emerge from this line of thinking about goals. The extent to which interactants can recognize, develop, and enact behavioral strategies to accomplish multiple objectives is surely an indication of competence.

DIMENSIONS OF INTERACTION GOALS: A CRITIQUE

Wilson and Putnam's scheme for describing goals varies along the dimensions of type and abstraction. The dimension of type categorizes goals by their function, embracing the distinctions among instrumental, relational, and identity goals (Clark & Delia, 1979) and illustrating its application in the negotiation context.

The second dimension for distinguishing goals is the degree of abstraction, "the length of interaction segments to which they have relevance" (p. 379). Global goals are present for the entire negotiation. Regional goals are present in single sessions or encounters. Local goals are applicable to "small discourse segments" (p. 381). This distinction indicates that some goals are overarching, while others are relevant for briefer periods of time. Unfortunately, the distinction is untenable as presented by Wilson and Putnam. I will argue that (a) there are ambiguities in the descriptions of global and regional goals, and the distinctions between regional and local goals is often abandoned; and (b) the examples of global, regional, and local goals do not support length of the interaction segment as the basis of a distinction.

Ambiguities

First, there are ambiguities in Wilson and Putnam's descriptions of the levels of goals. Global goals are described as pertinent to the entire negotiation. The first example of a global goal involves a preplanning meeting in which an abstract goal is articulated. And yet, because all goals can be emergent, global goals are described as changing as the interaction progresses. Modifications of regional and local goals are seen as one impetus for new global goals. When new global goals emerge, they become relevant for the remainder of the negotiation. Earlier in this commentary, I acknowledged the importance of both preplanned and emergent goals. But it is confusing to define global goals as pertaining to the *entire* negotiation and then to argue that new global goals emerge in the *midst* of the negotiation. A goal of improving grievance procedures would be classified as global if it was operative for the entire negotiation and would receive the same label if it emerged in only the last two sessions of a negotiation. And if it emerged in the last session, it would be unclear whether it was an emergent global goal or a regional goal. The typology of global, regional, and local goals is organized by the principle of largest to smallest interaction segments, but this principle is violated when global goals are not always relevant to the largest interaction segment.

The definition of regional goals is also problematic. My reading of Wilson and Putnam's regional goals is that they are relevant to single sessions or encounters. The first illustration of a regional goal describes a teacher negotiator's strategy for the initial session, and bargainers are also said to use breaks to formulate regional goals. The difficulty with this distinction is the gap that is left between global and regional goals. If global goals pertain to entire negotiations and regional goals only to a single session, where do we place goals that are relevant to several sessions but not to all sessions? A bargainer might determine an opponent's resistance point on a given issue after several sessions and be able to negotiate this issue success-fully across multiple sessions that are prior to the close of the negotiations. Or a bargainer's constituents might decide well into the negotiation that a particular goal is salient, and that goal emerges in several sessions, but the bargainer is able to convince the constituents that it should be abandoned in favor of obtaining some other goal. The definition of global and regional goals is constructed in such a way that there is a gap that excludes goals that occur across multiple sessions but prior to the close of the negotiation.

Analysis of Examples

The remaining criticism of the dimensions of levels is based on a close examina-tion of Wilson and Putnam's examples. If their examples are found to be problem-atic, the foundation on which their conceptualization of goals is built is shaky. Thus a careful examination of the examples is an important element of this critique.

Because Wilson and Putnam's conceptualization advocates three levels of goals, a reader might reasonably expect that some examples would indicate how a given negotiation involved global, regional, and local goals. An example contrasting the three levels would help illustrate differences and justify the distinction. In categorizing each set of examples in the Wilson and Putnam essay, I found that four sets involved a single goal level, while thirteen sets involved a description of different levels. Of the thirteen combinations of goals, only four included global, regional, and local goals. The difficulty is that in each of these cases, regional and local goals were joined together so that it was impossible to determine which goal was at what level. In describing instrumental goals in distributive bargaining, Wilson and Putnam write:

> Parties engaged in distributive bargaining must persuade their opponents to forgo their proposals or make concessions (Gulliver, 1979). Thus both parties have a number of regional *and* local influence goals, including the following: to affect the other party's belief about what is possible in the settlement; to change the opponent's utility estimates concerning possible outcomes, proposals, and counterproposals; to promote one's own objectives as desirable. (p. 382; emphasis added)

We simply are not told which of these goals are regional and which are local. Furthermore, in a description of the goals arising from the labor role, they indicate:

> In general, the labor role takes the offensive, with the negotiator pursuing such global goals as changing status quo policies, improving wages and working conditions, and participating in organizational decision making. Regional *and* local goals associated with this role include demonstration of the significance of harms within the present system, protection and separation of proposals from the management domain, and aggressiveness in probing and advancing ideas. (p. 383; emphasis added)

Again, regional and local goals are not distinguished. In fairness, some examples include both regional and local goals, but global goals are noticeably absent. So while the conceptualization advanced by Wilson and Putnam has three distinct levels, they give no examples that demonstrate the utility or necessity of distinctions among three levels of goals.

The next criticism of the examples for levels of goals is the most damaging. The description of global, regional, and local goals is based solely on variations in the length of the interaction segment for which they have relevance. But virtually all of the examples fail to make reference to time. Consider four of Wilson and Putnam's examples and alternative but equally plausible readings.

First, a consumer's global goal is to buy a product at the lowest price, and his or her local goal is to refute a seller's claim that a product is difficult to obtain. However, a buyer could spend a lengthy period of the interaction attacking the seller's claim that a short supply of the product exists. There is no reason this local goal would necessarily be limited to a brief discourse segment.

In the second example, the global goal in integrative bargaining is to increase the total payoff, while a local goal is to modify excessive demands. But, even in integrative bargaining, it could require more than a brief discourse segment to persuade an opponent to moderate an unreasonable demand. Here again, the local goal need not be limited to a small discourse segment.

Third, management adopts a global goal of defending the status quo, while its local goal is to maintain current policies. Yet management could devote a considerable portion of the negotiation to maintaining current policies. In fact, this goal can even be conceived as one that could dominate an entire negotiation, which, by Wilson and Putnam's definition, would make it a global rather than a local goal.

In the final example, Wilson and Putnam say that an identity global goal is to maintain face, and an example of a regional or local identity goal is to fulfill constituent expectations. But surely fulfilling constituent expectations could pertain to a lengthy interaction segment or the entire negotiation, which would disqualify it from Wilson and Putnam's definition of local and regional goals. Thus each of the goals could plausibly be identified as an instance of a goal at a level different from the one proffered by Wilson and Putnam. The examples they provide of regional goals could be relevant to entire negotiations, while their examples of local goals could be relevant to single sessions or to entire negotiations. In sum, any given goal could be relevant for any length of interaction segment, so a distinction based on length of time is indefensible.

While the functional distinctions among types of goals appear to describe interaction goals adequately in negotiation contexts, the distinction based on level of abstraction is troublesome. Because this hierarchy is not conceptual, it seems that the use of three levels is arbitrary. Why not two levels or five levels? And, most important, the examples fail to make reference to their defining characteristic, length of the interaction segment. As demonstrated above, the examples could easily describe levels of goals different from those advanced by Wilson and Putnam. In essence, length of the interaction segment does not reveal the structure of goals. Any goal can be the focus of a negotiation for any length of time. In short, time is not an indication of level of abstraction, and relationships among goals cannot be examined through the dimension of time. Hence an alternative conception of goals that provides a conceptual distinction for levels of goals is needed.

AN ALTERNATIVE PERSPECTIVE
ON THE STRUCTURE OF GOALS

It is through structure that behaviors are produced and interpreted as coherent, and it is through structure that multiple goals can be organized as interrelated objectives in a plan. Thus it is through an examination of structure that the interdependence among goals can be mapped. The criticisms of Wilson and Putnam's use of length of interaction segments in the last section prompt an alternative perspective for typologizing the structure of goals.

This structural description specifies two types of goals: consummate and contributory. *Consummate* goals are the ultimate objectives desired by an interactant. They are ultimate because accomplishing a consummate goal is to bring a desire to fruition. *Contributory* goals are instrumental. They are believed by the interactants to facilitate the accomplishment of a consummate goal. Notice that this conception of consummate goals directs our attention to conditions that prompt negotiations (unmet goal states) as well as to the termination (successful for achievement of consummate goals, unsuccessful for realization of an impasse in achieving consummate goals).

A labor union may want to achieve an improved benefit package, wage increases, and better working conditions. These can be considered consummate goals because success would result in termination of the negotiation. A parent might want a child to watch less television and do homework before other activities. If, in accomplishing these goals, the ultimate state of affairs is reached, they are consummate goals. Of course, negotiations are interactional, and not all consummate goals will be accomplished. The futility of a particular consummate goal may become clear as the negotiation emerges, and interactants may modify or abandon these goals. Or negotiations may cease if the interactants perceive that there is no movement toward their consummate goals. It is not the actual success or failure of a goal that renders it consummate, but the interactant's perception that this objective is the final state of affairs desired.

Contributory goals are perceived as facilitating the ultimate goal. If labor negotiators adopt a consummate goal of improving working conditions, they may have a contributory goal of convincing management that improving working conditions will improve productivity. If a parent wants a child to watch less television, a contributory goal may be to apprise the child of a number of attractive alternatives. The interactant perceives that the successful completion of a contributory goal or series of contributory goals will achieve the consummate goal. Several outcomes can occur when contributory goals are enacted through behaviors. The contributory goal may be effective in accomplishing the consummate goal; for instance, management may be convinced that better working conditions do lead to increases in productivity and agree to improve them. On the other hand, interactants may accomplish the contributory goal or series of goals but find that the consummate goal is not accomplished; management may agree that working conditions and productivity are related but be unwilling to spend the money required to improve conditions. Alternatively, interactants may fail to accomplish their contributory goals and thus may be unable to assist with the consummate goal. While there are several possible outcomes, it is the perception of the interactant that accomplishing this goal will lead to the consummate goal (and the fact that it could be achieved without reaching the consummate goal) that identifies an objective as a contributory goal. Thus there is an ends-means relationship between consummate and contributory goals.

The structure of the relationship within consummate and contributory goals can also be explored. Most negotiation contexts are complex and interactants have multiple goals of both types. Multiple consummate goals can be structured through priority, the level of importance ascribed to each goal in relationship to all other consummate goals. This prioritization may be explicit or implicit, loosely configured or elaborately detailed, preplanned or emergent. Labor negotiators may initially consider wages to be their top priority, while changes in grievance procedures or health insurance benefits are of lesser importance. As the negotiation proceeds, it could become apparent that more progress can be made on improving health insurance benefits, and the negotiators may attempt to convince constituents to alter their priorities. Thus the organization of consummate goals reflects their importance within a plan.

Types of relationships can also be specified among contributory goals. They may be parallel, hierarchical, or unrelated. A parallel relationship exists among contributory goals if there are multiple but independent means of facilitating the consummate goal. This relationship is consistent with the principle of equifinality, for there are many ways of accomplishing the same ultimate objective. For example, a car salesperson's consummate goal is to sell a car. Contributory goals may be to convince the buyer that a particular car is a quality product or to convince the buyer that the car is affordable. Each of these goals (or a cumulative effect of both of them) could induce the buyer to purchase the car. Contributory goals can also be arranged hierarchically, with each goal functioning as a link in a chain, sustaining movement toward the consummate goal. The seller may adopt a goal of persuading the buyer that he or she is similar to the seller. Accomplishing this goal may assist the seller in obtaining a second contributory goal of establishing a trusting relationship, which may in turn assist him or her in accomplishing the consummate goal of securing the purchase of the car. Finally, contributory goals may be unrelated when they are connected to discrete consummate goals. Combinations of parallel and hierarchical contributory goals can occur with a single consummate goal, while all three relationships (parallel, hierarchical, unrelated) can occur when there are multiple consummate goals.

This typology of goals is not subject to the criticisms leveled at Wilson and Putnam's global, regional, and local goals. The distinction between consummate and contributory goals is conceptual and avoids the difficulties of Wilson and Putnam's approach. Both types of goals can be emergent without altering the definition of their nature. They are not dependent on the length of the interaction segment. The structural description of goals does not leave an unexplainable gap. And these examples illustrate the distinction, in this case, a difference between ends and means. While length of the interaction segment cannot reveal the structure of goals, this typology is able to accomplish this objective.

Finally, there are three implications associated with this alternative perspective on the structure of goals. First, this conceptualization can describe the organization of diverse negotiations. At the simplest level, a negotiator has a single consummate goal and enacts a behavior to accomplish it. At a complex level, a negotiator has multiple consummate goals that are organized according to level of importance. Each of these consummate goals is facilitated by multiple contributory goals that may be parallel, hierarchical, or both. There may be a single level of goal or there may be far more than three levels in complex situations with sophisticated negotiators. It is the conceptual relationship that distinguishes consummate and contributory goals and the nature of the relationships that can exist among multiple consummate and contributory goals that can improve our understanding of the coherence in goal-directed interactions.

The second implication is that this typology of goals reveals the relationships between and among goals. The relationship between consummate and contributory goals is one of ends-means. Consummate goals are organized by priority, while contributory goals can be parallel, hierarchical, or unrelated. A description of the structure of goals reveals how behaviors are produced and interpreted as coherent. It indicates the relationships among multiple goals. Unlike the distinctions among global, regional, and local goals, there is a conceptual foundation for these relationships.

The third implication returns to the argument that this discipline is fundamentally pragmatic. Goals indicate the motivation for behaviors and account for the coherence among behaviors. Competence is clearly an issue. This perspective on the structure of goals generates a number of testable questions about goals and competence. Negotiators able to generate an extensive repertoire of contributory goals may be more effective in the negotiation context. Negotiators able to generate contributory goals to facilitate consummate goals are more strategic and may be more effective in accomplishing their ultimate objectives. Negotiators able to create contributory goals that apply to more than a single consummate goal may be more efficient at accomplishing their ultimate goals. The complexity of the situation and the resistance of an opponent may be important elements that influence the need for multiple contributory goals. Thus some aspects of competence concern how negotiators invent and organize their goals.

Wilson and Putnam's essay is an important contribution to the literature on goals and negotiation. Their description of the properties of interaction goals is commendable. I endorse the basic assumptions proposed in their chapter, but the dimension of level of abstraction, the length of the interaction segment for which goals have relevance, is problematic. Viewing goals as consummate or contributory, however, avoids the criticisms directed at Wilson and Putnam's global, regional, and local goals, and leads to three implications. The first is that negotiations have varied structures, and a set number of levels cannot be specified. Rather, a set of relationships can be established. The second implication is that this typology provides a conceptual foundation for interrelationships among and between goals. And the last implication is that this particular conceptualization of goals generates a series of questions concerning their relationship to competence, an issue of importance to our discipline.

REFERENCES

Benoit, P. J. (1988). A case for triangulation in argument research. *Journal of the American Forensic Association, 25*, 31-42.

Benoit, P. J., & Follert, V. (1986). Appositions in plans and scripts: An application to initial interactions. In D. G. Ellis & W. A. Donohue (Eds.), *Contemporary issues in language and discourse processes* (pp. 239-256). Hillsdale, NJ: Lawrence Erlbaum.

Berger, C. R., Karol, S. H., & Jordan, J. M. (1988, November). *When a lot of knowledge is a dangerous thing: The debilitating effects of plan complexity on verbal fluency.* Paper presented at the annual meeting of the Speech Communication Association, New Orleans.

Burke, J. A. (1986). Interacting plans in the accomplishment of a practical activity. In D. G. Ellis & W. A. Donohue (Eds.), *Contemporary issues in language and discourse processes* (pp. 203-222). Hillsdale, NJ: Lawrence Erlbaum.

Burke, K. (1978). (Nonsymbolic) motion/(symbolic) action. *Critical Inquiry, 4*, 809-822.

Clark, R. A., & Delia, J. G. (1979). *Topoi* and rhetorical competence. *Quarterly Journal of Speech, 65*, 187-206.

Craig, R. T. (1986). Goals in discourse. In D. G. Ellis & W. A. Donohue (Eds.), *Contemporary issues in language and discourse processes* (pp. 257-274). Hillsdale, NJ: Lawrence Erlbaum.

Craig, R. T., & Tracy, K. (1983). Introduction. In R. T. Craig & K. Tracy (Eds.), *Conversational coherence: Form, structure, and strategy* (pp. 10-22). Beverly Hills, CA: Sage.

Cronen, V. E., Pearce, W. B., & Harris, L. M. (1982). The coordinated management of meaning: A theory of communication. In F.E.X. Dance (Ed.), *Human communication theory* (pp. 61-89). New York: Harper & Row.

Delia, J. G., & Grossberg, L. (1977). Interpretation and evidence. *Western Journal of Speech Communication, 41*, 32-42.

Denzin, N. K. (1977). *The research act: A theoretical introduction to sociological methods.* New York: McGraw-Hill.

Ericsson, K. A., & Simon, H. A. (1984). *Protocol analysis: Verbal reports as data.* Cambridge: MIT Press.

Fogarty, D. (1959). *Roots for a new rhetoric.* New York: Russell & Russell.

Goodall, H. L., & Phillips, G. M. (1981). Assumptions of the burden: Science or criticism? *Communication Quarterly, 29*, 283-296.

Gulliver, P. H. (1979). *Disputes and negotiations: A cross-cultural perspective.* New York: Academic Press.

Hawes, L. C., & Smith, D. H. (1973). A critique of assumptions underlying the study of communication in conflict. *Quarterly Journal of Speech, 59*, 423-435.

Hobbs, J. R., & Agar, M. H. (1981). *Planning and local coherence in the formal analysis of ethnographic interviews.* Unpublished manuscript, SRI International, Menlo Park, CA.

Jackson, S. (1986). Building a case for claims about discourse structure. In D. G. Ellis & W. A. Donohue (Eds.), *Contemporary issues in language and discourse processes* (pp. 129-148). Hillsdale, NJ: Lawrence Erlbaum.

Kuhn, T. S. (1962). *The structure of scientific revolutions.* Chicago: University of Chicago Press.

O'Keefe, B. J. (1988). The logic of message design: Individual differences in reasoning about communication. *Communication Monographs, 55*, 80-103.

O'Keefe, B. J., & Shepherd, G. J. (1987). The pursuit of multiple objectives in face-to-face persuasive interactions: Effects of construct differentiation on message organization. *Communication Monographs, 54*, 396-419.

Planalp, S., & Hewes, D. (1982). A cognitive approach to communication theory: *Cogito ergo dico?* In M. Burgoon (Ed.), *Communication yearbook 5* (pp. 49-78). New Brunswick, NJ: Transaction.

Rubin, R. B., Perse, E. M., & Barbato, C. A. (1988). Conceptualization and measurement of interpersonal communication motives. *Human Communication Research, 14*, 602-628.

Schuman, H., & Johnson, M. (1976). Attitudes and behavior. *Annual Review of Sociology, 2*, 161-207.

Wicker, A. W. (1969). Attitudes versus actions: The relationship of verbal and overt behavioral responses to attitude objects. *Journal of Social Issues, 25*, 41-78.

Interaction Goals in Negotiation: A Critique

WILLIAM A. DONOHUE
Michigan State University

MAKING sense of conflict interaction is a difficult business. It is difficult because conflict interaction is very messy. People talk over one another frequently, their contributions dart in all different directions, displaying minimal coherence, and it is often difficult to tell what disputants seek. This appearance is understandable given the emotional purging that often accompanies proposals, issues, and arguments. Because they illustrate these features, our divorce mediation and hostage negotiation transcripts often provoke a response in first-time observers: "What the hell are you going to do with those?"

When I read the title of Wilson and Putnam's chapter, my hope was that it would provide a useful framework for making sense of the often-chaotic negotiation interaction. In part, my expectations were fulfilled; the chapter makes two important contributions. First, Wilson and Putnam's goals framework brings the concept of goals squarely into the interaction analysis perspective. The goals concept enjoys extensive exposure in accounting for such negotiation processes as coordinating on agreement making (Pruitt, 1981; Schelling, 1960) and such interpersonal processes as maintaining interaction coherence (Tracy & Moran, 1983) and information seeking (Kellermann, 1987). However, goals have been largely ignored by interaction analysis research in conflict contexts (see Putnam & Jones, 1982, for a review). The advantage of taking this perspective is that analyzing goals enables researchers to trace how disputants converge toward agreement or diverge toward impasse.

Second, the chapter offers a very thoughtfully developed framework of the kinds of goals individuals pursue in negotiation interaction. This framework

Correspondence and requests for reprints: William A. Donohue, Department of Communication, Michigan State University, East Lansing, MI 48824-1212.

Communication Yearbook 13, pp. 417-427

integrates several key conflict phenomena that traditionally have been studied independently when their integration was clearly warranted. For example, studying instrumental goals independently from relational and identity goals seems rather limiting, because it is difficult to imagine using a highly competitive instrumental strategy devoid of significant relational and identity implications. Threats carry clear relational and identity messages. The Wilson and Putnam perspective recognizes this integrative need and does an excellent job of integrating these ideas into a useful framework for studying negotiation interaction.

While Wilson and Putnam's framework accomplishes two very important objectives, it may fail to achieve its most important objective of providing a full accounting of negotiation interaction processes. To support this claim, this critique will argue, first, that from an interactional perspective, the concept of goal as a retrievable, cognitive representation of an individual's desires places a severe limit on the phenomena researchers might draw upon to understand negotiation interaction. Second, Wilson and Putnam's concept of goals limits opportunities to account for a full range of negotiation contexts. Third, an expanded framework needs more powerful conceptual integration to aid in interpreting interaction results. This critique will begin by discussing the perspective from which the critique will be argued. Each of the three problems of Wilson and Putnam's framework will then be discussed in detail.

THE INTERACTIONAL PERSPECTIVE

This critique will approach the goal construct from an interactional perspective, since Wilson and Putnam seek to use this construct to interpret negotiation interaction. The type of interactional perspective articulated here deals with the quantitative analysis of interaction that involves determining the objective nature of the discourse content or structure. Other approaches to the analysis of communication, such as conversation analysis, may rely upon the subjective judgments of the researcher and are often conducted from a wholly different philosophical perspective.

The main tenet of the interactional perspective is that communication research should focus on the joint accomplishment of the communicators and not only on the communicators as individuals (for overviews of this perspective, see Fisher, 1978; Poole, Folger, & Hewes, 1987). The rationale behind this perspective is that individuals form their essential social awareness as persons through the interaction process. In particular, Blumer (1969) argues that through role-taking individuals develop self-concepts by aligning their social actions with one another and then assessing the confirming or disconfirming nature of that social interaction.

By taking this position, interactionism holds that social interaction and self-concept are inextricably intertwined. This is a very important position for scholars studying interpersonal communication because it argues that the essential qualities of an individual's relational self are revealed through that aligning process. This aligning process can reveal the struggle for relational control (Watzlawick, Beavin, & Jackson, 1967), the negotiation of relational decay (Gottman, 1979), or the development of marital cultures (Sillars, Weisberg, Burggraf, & Wilson, 1987). As a result, studying the interaction gives scholars access to how the relationship is created through communication.

According to Poole et al. (1987), the meaning of social interaction can be examined from both the observer's and the interactant's perspective. Observer meanings focus on how an uninvolved and uninitiated onlooker might interpret the interaction. These observer meanings are divided into those available to everyone from that particular cultural group (generalized observer meanings) and those available only to observers versed in a particular theory or interpretive scheme (restricted observer meanings). Generalized observer meanings focus on features of interaction that are unambiguous and clearly definable, such as vocalized pauses. Restricted observer meanings might include a speech acts analysis of some structural feature of the interaction. The analysis is not particularly interested in how the observers understand the analyses; it focuses strictly on the structural features of the language.

Interactant meanings are those meanings judged to be available only to participants in the interaction. These meanings are also divided into two categories: those subject meanings accessible to members of the subject's cultural group (generalized subject meanings) and those available only to the actual participants in the interaction (restricted subject meanings). Generalized subject meanings represent those used in the role-taking process in which communicators try to interpret what an utterance means to the other person. Restricted subject meanings include those that only subjects themselves can report through stimulated recall or other kinds of self-reports.

Both Wilson and Putnam's chapter and the interactional perspective used in this critique seek to learn about subject meanings. Neither perspective is interested in exploring the structural features of the messages independent of what meaning is attached to them. However, Wilson and Putnam's work and the interactional perspective diverge on the kind of subject-meaning approach they prefer. Wilson and Putnam argue that goals must be understood from a restricted-meaning point of view, while the interactional perspective takes the more generalized subject-meaning approach. Based on this distinction, it might be useful to examine the differences in how goals are explored from both of these subject-meaning approaches.

Goals from a Generalized Subject-Meaning Perspective

The interactional perspective, from the generalized subject-meaning point of view, has always argued that goals are critical for participants in organizing their talk. Schutz's (1962) phenomenology holds that individuals cannot build social realities without attributing motives to one another. These attributions allow communicators to predict how the message will be heard (Tracy & Moran, 1983). Communicators assess one another's messages, attribute motives based on those messages, predict how one another will hear what each speaker wants to communicate, and then continue interacting. The communicators may have individual goals that are at variance with their attributed motives, but the other has access only to the attributed motives. Communicators never have access to the "real" goals because the "real" goals, or those only in the communicators' heads, must be framed in some symbol system to come out. When that happens, then, an attributed motive is made about the "real" goal.

Negotiators, or any communicators for that matter, fold the "real" goal into a much broader understanding about what the other wants to accomplish. For interactants, the "real" goal is not actually distinguishable from the attributed motives, since figuring out what the other wants goes far beyond what they say they want. Communicators risk appearing incompetent by using only the other's substantive goal statements as guidance for predicting how the other will hear the communicator's message. Thus, from an interactional perspective, focusing on attributed motives makes much more sense than focusing only on "real" goals.

Goals from the Restricted Subject-Meaning Perspective

In their chapter, Wilson and Putnam are interested in accessing the restricted subject's meanings for their "real" goals. They conceptualize goals as exclusively cognitive entities. Negotiators are fully aware of them and formulate their strategies around them. Wilson and Putnam generally desire to uncover those psychological states called goals that drive negotiator interaction. They advocate making sense out of negotiation interaction by discovering negotiator goals at various points in the interaction and then demonstrating how those goals drive the structure and substance of the interaction. Thus the framework is intended to be used to uncover psychological phenomena and not to code interaction. This critique will now move to address three concerns about the ability of the Putnam and Wilson framework to provide a full accounting of the negotiation interaction process by taking a cognitive approach to goals.

CONCERN I:
THE COGNITIVE APPROACH'S LIMITATIONS

The first concern of this critique is that focusing only on the restricted subject meaning for negotiator goals exhibits two significant limitations. First, a full accounting of negotiation interaction must be broadened to include those behaviors that individuals may or may not use in attributing motives to one another. Second, very significant portions of negotiation interaction are impulsive, reactionary behaviors that show little evidence of planning. The meaning and significance of both these phenomena are available only from a generalized subject-meaning perspective. This critique now moves to a discussion of these two arguments.

Broadening the Focus

Why broaden the focus of negotiation interaction research from a restricted to a generalized subject-meaning perspective? The primary reason is that focusing on the broad range of behaviors available for motive attribution gives researchers access to understanding how the interaction process influences outcome. To illustrate, Wilson and Putnam focus on two relational goals: power and trust. These goals fit within their framework because it is likely that negotiators would be able to report how their trust and power goals influenced outcome. The research on divorce mediation conducted by my colleagues and me indicates that disputants display many other relational behaviors that interact with outcome, even though these behaviors generally are not retrievable, reportable behaviors (e.g., Donohue, Allen, & Burrell, 1988). For example, husbands and wives in divorce mediation often communicate their desire for physical separation by referring to common property as "my house" or "my child," instead of "our house" or "our child." While these expressions communicate the goal of physical separation, the husbands and wives would probably not associate these statements with that goal. Since we found that such microscopic processes are very significant predictors of outcome, it seems reasonable that they warrant some kind of attention.

At a more macroscopic level, other communicative actions appear very influential in guiding the interaction context that also cannot be accounted for by a cognitive goals model. In accounting for disputants' ability to settle in a community mediation context, Littlejohn and Shailor (1986) focused on the manner in which disputants coordinated on their values dealing with morality, justice and conflict. Through discourse analysis, these authors found that disputants experiencing difficulty coordinating on the substance of their dispute were using very different value foundations for their arguments. One disputant would argue from one moral or justice perspective, while the other would argue from the opposite perspective. Since they were explicitly asking one another to accept their arguments, the disputants were also tacitly asking one another to accept the values underlying their arguments. However, if someone were to ask the disputants if they were trying to impose such values in that situation, they would probably not have any planned sense of doing so. Indeed, the mediators never picked up on the value discrepancies, and the interactions terminated unsuccessfully.

While the failure to recognize the discrepancies may or may not have contributed to the lack of success, it is clear that the disputants maintained a culture-bound perspective that they were seeking to impose on other disputants, but not at an overtly cognitive level. Just like the relational parameters at the more microscopic level, these value conflicts at the more macroscopic level are influential in negotiations. By automatically eliminating such phenomena, the Wilson and Putnam model is less than capable of providing a full accounting of important interactional phenomena in the negotiation context.

Exploring Reactive Phenomena

As suggested above, most of the limitations of Wilson and Putnam's model can be traced to their focus on restricted subject meanings. However, they even further restrict their interest to those prospective meanings interactants use in directing their interaction, that is, their goals. This restriction is further evidenced by their insistence that goals are accomplished through the planning process. The planning process begins with negotiators dividing goals into two categories: final and intermediate. The final goals are intrinsically valued end states, while the intermediate goals fulfill prerequisites of final goals. Next, planning evolves into the creation and implementation of various strategies and tactics capable of accomplishing these two goal forms. If these plans do not work out or are not sufficiently complete, Wilson and Putnam point out that negotiators plan as the negotiation unfolds, as they examine the success of their various strategies and tactics. Thus Wilson and Putnam view planning as both a deliberate top-down process and as an opportunistic bottom-up process in negotiation.

Wilson and Putnam explain that a focus on goals and planning allows researchers to track patterns of escalation and deescalation in highly rational conflict contexts. However, they do not provide for those contexts in which escalation leads to highly spontaneous, unplanned conflictual outbursts. In such contexts individuals' actions evolve mostly as reactions to the other immediate past behavior of others.

Perhaps the best example of these contexts is found again in our divorce mediation transcripts (see Donohue et al., 1988). In divorce mediation, a neutral third party conducts a face-to-face meeting to assist a divorcing or divorced couple to formulate a child custody or visitation plan. In comparing mediator and disputant interaction strategies across ten sessions in which an agreement was reached and ten sessions in which an agreement was not reached, we discovered that the no-agreement sessions exhibited very tense, emotional interaction patterns. For example, attack-defend cycles became quite common. One party would accuse the other of some transgression and the other would react with a defensive comment. In such reactive circumstances, it is difficult to see how such behaviors are planned, goal-oriented activities.

This analysis illustrates that interaction reflecting intense conflict may not exhibit the kind of planning, goal-oriented process described in Wilson and Putnam's model. In intense conflict, individuals focus on the here and now; highly strategic behavior is not a priority. Their reactive behavior may follow from some scripted response they experienced in other conflict situations. The argument I wish to forward is that such reactive phenomena exert an important influence on negotiation processes and ought not be excluded because they are not planned, proactive, cognitively organized phenomena.

CONCERN II: ACCOUNTING FOR A FULL RANGE OF NEGOTIATION CONTEXTS

Clearly, the Wilson and Putnam framework works best in highly cognitive contexts characterized by extensive planning. However, many negotiation contexts offer few opportunities for the kind of rational, cognitive activity typical of the labor-management negotiations for which the Wilson and Putnam framework was designed. As indicated above, disputants in mediation may have fairly general global goals in mind when coming to mediation, but their interaction is often highly reactive and devoid of much planning. To unpack this claim in greater detail, this section will begin by identifying various types of negotiation contexts and then will proceed to assess their capacities for planned, rational discourse.

Types of Negotiation Contexts

Keltner (1987) discriminates among a variety conflict contexts based upon their levels of conflict intensity. The least intense conflicts are termed "mild differences," in which interactants discuss their concerns in an open and friendly fashion through joint problem solving. The next level of conflicts, labeled "disagreements," includes rivals negotiating in an open but relationally strained context. At this level, the parties' goals still involve working together in any final settlement. At the third level, termed "dispute," participants seek goals that do not involve working together in a final settlement. The parties still use many rational arguments, but the communication is limited and tense, and third parties are often needed to help the parties work together. In the final three stages, "campaign," "litigation," and "fight or war," conflict is characterized by more hostile and emotional messages, the emphasis is on winning and losing, and parties seek to exclude or eliminate the other.

Contextual Applicability

Based on the concerns presented above, it seems reasonable to assume that the Wilson and Putnam framework can account for goals, but not necessarily for a full range of interaction processes, at the first and second levels. Once the interaction becomes more intense at the third level and beyond, their framework may lose some of its power. At these levels, the interaction is less proactive and more reactive. Significant conflicts may stem from such macroscopic problems as cultural values that are not thoughtfully processed by the parties. Many other microscopic issues might influence the direction of the disputes also, such as establishing relational distance.

The problem is that once disputes become intense, the predominance of planned, rational problem solving becomes less likely. Even during the kinds of labor-management disputes that Putnam and Wilson have researched extensively, interaction is characterized by both distributive and integrative strategies. In extrapolating to other contexts, it seems reasonable to assume that most negotiations are characterized by these intertwined strategies. As a result, both cooperative and competitive processes are commonplace in most conflict contexts, with the possible exception of mild differences on the one hand and war on the other. The competitive processes that become reactive and emotionally laden may remain more obscure to the Wilson and Putnam model, given their emphasis on rational problem solving.

CONCERN III: THE CONCEPTUAL
INTEGRATION OF GOAL DIMENSIONS

While the Wilson and Putnam framework is limited in both the kinds of negotiation phenomena it can account for and the contexts to which it applies, its value is also limited by the lack of conceptual integration among its three goal dimensions: instrumental, relational, and identity goals. This section will begin with an exploration of the need to integrate these three dimensions.

The Rationale for Integration

Why is it necessary to integrate the goal dimensions provided in the Wilson and Putnam framework? Two reasons seem relevant. First, the potential applicability of the dimensions would increase if their interrelationships were specified. Specifically, the question of which goals drive other goals seems relevant here. Some evidence suggests that, indeed, the dimensions are not independent. For example, Pruitt's (1981) examination of negotiation indicates that implementing competitive goals may influence the kinds of power strategies selected by negotiators and the levels of trust apparent among the disputants. Similarly, Folger and Poole (1984) integrate identity goals and relational goals by defining *face saving* as "members' attempts to protect or repair their relational images, in response to threats real or imagined, potential or actual" (p. 149). Without some kind of conceptual integration it is difficult to separate instrumental from relational from identity goals.

A second reason for providing some kind of integration deals with data analysis. Specifically, can coders look for evidence of all three goals in any given segment or should only one goal be coded for each segment? If the dimensions are somehow interdependent, then it makes sense to examine the data for all three kinds of goals. It is clear from an example used by Wilson and Putnam that this statement contains information about all three goal dimensions: "When we set the money, let's hit them with reduction in force procedure coupled with binding arbitration, or if we cut out binding arbitration, let's go with reduction in force and due process or due process and binding arbitration. How does that sound?" (p. 380). Information about instrumental goals is apparent as the negotiator is deciding what to ask for. Relational information is apparent as he or she decides how to increase his or her power. Identity messages are present as the negotiator plans strategies for managing attacks from the opposition. By specifying how the three dimensions are interrelated, Wilson and Putnam could help researchers and practitioners specify how individual goals overlap in interaction.

A Shift from Goals

While integrating the goal dimensions would be desirable for the reasons specified above, that task is difficult because Wilson and Putnam would need to demonstrate that individuals cognitively and actively try to achieve multiple goals simultaneously. As indicated above, individuals may be hard-pressed to retrieve how their contributions work to accomplish all three goals, particularly when many negotiation interactions are highly reactive and unplanned. Moving to a generalized subject-meaning perspective places researchers in a better position to examine the interrelationship of negotiator behaviors.

Making this statement, however, means that researchers would need to move away from restricted to more generalized subject meanings to focus on interaction *functions* as opposed to subjects' goals. A functional approach to understanding interaction seeks to learn what the communicators' messages work to achieve as opposed to what the speakers seek to achieve. This distinction indicates that messages generally do more than speakers try to do because speakers may not be able to control all dimensions of their messages, particularly in highly intense conflict.

Focusing on messages instead of on speakers has at least two distinct advantages. First, more microscopic phenomena, beyond the cognitive control of the negotiators, can be explored from this perspective (as illustrated above). Since more refined units of analysis can be used, more detailed patterns of interaction can be detected. Second, multiple functions of utterances can be examined. Since utterances always serve multiple functions (Hewes, 1979), this advantage is particularly important. Ironically, the functions approach may be better at accessing communicator goals just because it can code multiple functions of utterances at microscopic levels that go beyond the negotiator's ability to control them cognitively. The relational distance construct used in our divorce mediation research is an excellent example of this phenomenon (see Donohue, in press). In an attempt to understand how disputants use language to negotiate their relationships, we coded each disputant thought unit for evidence of spatial, temporal, implicit, and modified immediacy. More distance is communicated when disputants use language that spatially separates them from one another, deals inappropriately with the past or future, expresses ideas more implicitly to avoid attachment to them, and is highly modified or qualified to avoid commitment to the ideas. By coding these and several other content and strategic functions of each disputant utterance, we were able to understand each utterance from multiple perspectives. It is possible that with such extensive analysis, researchers might be very capable of estimating disputants' global, regional, and local goals.

CONCLUSIONS

Pursuing a restricted subject-meaning perspective may have the intuitive appeal of gaining access to individuals' actual strategic behaviors. If we know the sequence of what they want to do and how they want to do it, we might be able to account more accurately for the structure of interaction. Unfortunately, the trade-off for trying to realize this desire is that it forces the researcher to define phenomena at a level of abstraction that allows negotiators to report on it. Interactionists would argue that the process of communication is best exposed through the examination of more microscopic phenomena. At least beginning at this more microscopic level would give researchers access to a variety of phenomena that are unavailable at higher levels of abstraction. Because these phenomena create the contextual details to which individuals respond when they communicate, it is important to describe them.

It might be useful for the Wilson and Putnam perspective to begin at more microscopic levels to describe those communicative phenomena that are present when individuals report on certain goals. Tying these interactive phenomena in with self-report phenomena might give them more confidence in inferring goals from interaction segments.

REFERENCES

Blumer, H. (1969). *Symbolic interaction: Perspective and method.* Englewood Cliffs, NJ: Prentice-Hall.

Donohue, W. A. (in press). *Communication, marital dispute, and divorce mediation.* Hillsdale, NJ: Lawrence Erlbaum.

Donohue, W. A., Allen, M., & Burrell, N. (1988). Mediator communicative competence. *Communication Monographs, 55,* 104-119.

Fisher, B. A. (1978). *Perspectives on human communication.* New York: Macmillan.

Folger, J., & Poole, M. S. (1984). *Working through conflict: A communication perspective.* Glenview, IL: Scott, Foresman.

Gottman, J. (1979). *Marital interaction.* New York: Academic Press.

Hewes, D. E. (1979). The sequential analysis of social interaction. *Quarterly Journal of Speech, 65,* 56-73.

Kellermann, K. (1987). Information exchange in social interaction. In M. E. Roloff & G. R. Miller (Eds.), *Interpersonal processes: New directions in communication research* (pp. 188-219). Newbury Park, CA: Sage.

Keltner, J. S. (1987). *Mediation: Toward a civilized system of dispute resolution.* Annandale, VA: Speech Communication Association.

Littlejohn, S., & Shailor, J. (1986, November). *The deep structure of conflict in mediation: A case study.* Paper presented at the annual meeting of the Speech Communication Association, Chicago.

Poole, M. S., Folger, J. P., & Hewes, D. E. (1987). Analyzing interpersonal interaction. In M. E. Roloff & G. R. Miller (Eds.), *Interpersonal processes: New directions in communication research* (pp. 220-256). Newbury Park, CA: Sage.

Pruitt, D. G. (1981). *Negotiation behavior.* New York: Academic Press.

Putnam, L. L., & Jones, T. S. (1982). Reciprocity in negotiations: An analysis of bargaining interaction. *Communication Monographs, 49,* 171-191.

Schelling, T. C. (1960). *The strategy of conflict.* Cambridge, MA: Harvard University Press.

Schutz, A. (1962). *Collected papers 1: The problem of social reality.* The Hague: Martinus Nijhoff.

Sillars, A. L., Weisberg, J., Burggraf, C. S., & Wilson, E. A. (1987). Content themes in marital conversations. *Human Communication Research, 13,* 495-528.

Tracy, K., & Moran, J. P., III. (1983). Conversational relevance in multiple-goal settings. In R. T. Craig & K. Tracy (Eds.), *Conversational coherence: Form, structure, and strategy* (pp. 116-135). Beverly Hills, CA: Sage.

Watzlawick, P., Beavin, J. H., & Jackson, D. D. (1967). *Pragmatics of human communication.* New York: W. W. Norton.

SECTION 3

MEDIATED COMMUNICATION: INFORMATION, INDUSTRY, AND CONSUMPTION

9   The Trade Winds Change: Japan's Shift from an Information Importer to an Information Exporter, 1965-1985

YOUICHI ITO
Keio University

This chapter describes the process of Japan's change from an information-importing country to an information-exporting country in the fields of news reporting and popular culture. In addition, the factors and mechanisms of this change are discussed. It is confirmed that there are many factors that caused imbalanced international information flow, and that they differed from one kind of information to another. The influence of Japan's change on Japanese cultural identity is discussed. It is suggested that the Japanese people are more self-confident today than they were in the past and that the problems of cultural identity, including those of historical continuity, seem to be practically overcome. Two existing comprehensive theories on international information flow, the media imperialism and dependency theories and the theory of "free competition in a free market," are examined and their strengths and deficiencies discussed. As an alternative, the influence of political and economic competition among nations on international information flow is analyzed.

ALL countries are interdependent and influence one another; however, the flow of influence is rarely equal. Roughly speaking, larger countries influence smaller countries, stronger countries influence weaker countries, and economically and technologically more advanced countries influence less advanced countries. When the external influences are too strong and the speed of change of influenced countries is too rapid, various social and cultural problems occur in those influenced countries. In order to cope with these problems, we must

Correspondence and requests for reprints: Youichi Ito, Keio University, Institute for Communications Research, 15-45, Mita 2-chome, Minato-ku, Tokyo 108, Japan.

Communication Yearbook 13, pp. 430-465

have an understanding of the international flow of influence so that we can make necessary policies for adjustments.

It is extremely difficult to keep track of the "flow of influence" because influence is invisible and not measurable, especially on a macro level. The flow of influence can be estimated, however, using the "flow of information." It is generally accepted that international information flows (and therefore international flows of influence) in the present-day world are basically one-way rather than two-way. Schramm (1964) has said that international information flows are "as regular as the trade winds" (p. 58). There are two ways of explaining this regularity.

One approach consists of the so-called cultural imperialism, media imperialism, and dependency theories. According to these theories, the world consists of a "center" (economically advanced, capitalist, exploiting countries) and a "periphery" or "satellite" (the economically and politically exploited countries). The former corresponds to the First World and the latter to the Third World. According to these views, the unidirectional nature or imbalance in international information flows is caused by the politico-economic structure of the world capitalist system. The one-way flow of information is a reflection and a result of the domination and exploitation of the Third World by the First World (Beltran, 1978; Beltran & Fox de Cardona, 1977; Frank, 1969; Mattelart, 1973; Salinas & Paldan, 1979; Sauvant, 1979; Schiller, 1969, 1973a, 1973b, 1976, 1979; Somavia, 1976; Wallerstein, 1974). This approach is obviously strongly influenced by the theories of Marx and Lenin.

The second approach to explaining the international flows of information is based on all non-Marxist theories and hypotheses. The common understanding in this diverse approach is that the information flows from strong and rich countries to weak and poor countries are a result of free competition among media enterprises (Read, 1976; Tunstall, 1977). The amount of volume and direction of international information flows are determined by geographical, cultural, economic, and political factors, and not necessarily by domination-subjection relationships (Ito & Kochevar, 1984; Schramm & Atwood, 1981). In addition, this approach holds that imbalance in information flows can be remedied by appropriate policies (Katz & Wedell, 1977).

In these theoretical discussions, Japan provides a unique case because it has changed its status from information importer to information exporter, from "peripheral country" to "central country," during the past twenty years. In the 1950s and 1960s, the pattern of Japan's international information flows was typical of Third World counties. At present, however, there are only three countries in the world where the media coverage of Japan is less than the Japanese media coverage of those countries. These are the United States, the Soviet Union, and China. The coverage of Japan in the rest of the world is either about the same as or more than the Japanese media coverage of those countries. Nowadays, Japan exports three times more television programs to Western Europe than it imports, and the trade of television programs between the United States and Japan is almost balanced (9:7 in favor of the United States).

Japan is also faced with unprecedented complaints about its information balance with the United States and Western Europe. This problem may be called an "access imbalance problem." The Americans and Europeans claim that Japan imports American and European scientific information, adds Japanese know-how, and produces extremely competitive products. U.S. and European information is easily accessible and available, whereas Japanese information is not. According to Europeans and Americans, Japanese social systems and organizations are "so different" and "closed" that it is extremely difficult for them to find out where valuable scientific information is in Japan. In addition, even if they find out, it is written, according to them, in "one of the most difficult languages in the world." They also claim that while Japanese students and researchers can easily live in the United States and Europe and absorb American and European scientific knowledge, it is very difficult for American and European students and researchers to do the same in Japan because of the nature of Japanese society and its language. Some people claim that present-day Japan is a huge "black hole" that swallows international scientific information without providing its own. Although these arguments may sound a little humorous, they represent a serious difficulty in Japanese relationships with the United States and the European community.

Existing theories, whether Marxist or non-Marxist, have not treated Japan in their discussions. A major reason has been that for most of the theories, Japan has been an embarrassing exception. Marxist social theorists still appear to regard Japan as one of the poor Asian countries dominated and exploited by the United States. Non-Marxist theorists are still preoccupied with the image that Western civilization is dominating non-Western civilizations and that non-Western people are suffering from loss of traditional culture and endangered cultural identity. Neither Marxist nor non-Marxist scholars provide a theory that explains the process or mechanism of Japan's change of status from information importer to information exporter. This chapter attempts to describe the process of the change that occurred in Japan, to analyze its causes and examine its consequences for Japanese cultural identity, and to propose a new theory regarding international flows of information.

FLOWS OF NEWS REPORTING

In 1961, the Institute for Communication Research of Stanford University and the Institut Français de Presse of the University of Paris jointly conducted an extensive study on the flows of news among thirteen countries on five continents. They conclude:

> The world flow of foreign news deals chiefly with a group of highly developed countries which are also dominant in world politics. . . . News flows from the highly developed to the less developed countries. It flows from Europe and North America

to the other continents. It flows from the United States and the Soviet Union to all other countries. (Schramm, 1964, p. 61)

Japan was one of the thirteen countries investigated in this study, which found that the coverage of the United States, the Soviet Union, France, and England by three Japanese newspapers (*Asahi, Mainichi,* and *Hokkaido Shimbun*) exceeded their own coverage of Japan by 16:1, 4:1, 6:1, and 4:1, respectively. In other words, the pattern of news flows to and from Japan in the early 1960s followed the typical pattern that is seen in most developing countries at present.

Thirteen years later, the amount of television news flow between Japan and the United States was surveyed. According to this survey, the ratio of the number of programs NHK (Nippon Hoso Kyokai, or Japan Broadcasting Corporation — Japan's largest national network) received from the United States to the number NHK sent to the United States was about 10:1 (CULCON, 1974, p. 5).[1]

By the end of the 1970s, however, many observers pointed out that American and European mass media coverage of Japan had improved remarkably. Armstrong (1982) calculated the number of *New York Times* articles about Japan from 1966 through 1975 and showed that there had been an increase in the coverage of Japan during that period. Armstrong also compared the coverage of Japan and Germany in *Newsweek* and *Time* magazines from 1966 to 1976. He found that before 1971 the coverage of Germany usually had been heavier than that of Japan. However, this trend reversed itself in 1971 and, after that, the coverage of Japan usually exceeded that of Germany.

Armstrong compared the American television coverage of the resignation of Japanese Prime Minister Kakuei Tanaka and that of German Chancellor Willy Brandt in 1976, and found that during the two-month period investigated, Tanaka's resignation produced 18 American television news program reports, whereas Brandt's resignation produced only 11 reports. Furthermore, this survey revealed that, partly due to the Lockheed scandal, in 1976 "Japan stories ran to over ten percent of total international news" (Armstrong, 1982, p. 77).

The Research Institute of the Japan Newspaper Publishers and Editors Association (JNPEA, 1979, 1981) compared the coverage of ten foreign countries by the Japanese newspaper *Asahi Shimbun* with the coverage of Japan in those countries, and found that the coverage of the Soviet Union, the United States, and China by the *Asahi* exceeded those countries' coverage of Japan by 5.8:1, 4.9:1, and 2.7:1, respectively. News coverage between Japan and France (1.3:1), England (1:1), and West Germany (1:1.4) was almost balanced. On the other hand, Japanese coverage of Thailand, the Philippines, Hong Kong, and Singapore was less than those countries' coverage of Japan by 1:4.6, 1:13, 1:23, and 0:30 (Research Institute of the JNPEA, 1981, p. 173).

Furthermore, a content analysis of 29 newspapers in 14 countries and 5 news agencies in 4 countries, including Japan, the United States, and seven Asian and Pacific countries, roughly supported the previous findings (Research Institute of the JNPEA, 1984a, 1984b). Coverage of the United States by the three Japanese newspapers in the study (on average) accounted for 44% of all international news in these newspapers, which was far greater than the coverage of other countries. The average coverage of Japan by the three American newspapers accounted for 8.7% of all international news. This figure was the fourth highest after the United Kingdom (12.9%), the Soviet Union (10.9%), and Israel (10.4%). The coverage of Japan by U.S. media exceeded that of Germany (7.2%, fifth place) and France (6.9%, sixth place). This tendency was more prominent in quality newspapers. For example, the coverage of Japan by the *New York Times* (one of the three American newspapers investigated) was 10.2%, which was the second highest after the United Kingdom (12.6%). The coverage of China by three Japanese newspaper was the second highest, accounting for 11.1% of all international news. The coverage of Japan by two Chinese newspapers (*People's Daily* and *Wenhui Bao*) was the fifth place, accounting for 6.7% of their international news coverage. Japan's newspaper coverage of the United States and China was found to exceed its newspaper coverage of Japan.

The relationships between Japan and the second group, consisting of France and the United Kingdom, are worth examining. Coverage of France and the United Kingdom by the three Japanese newspapers was fourth (8.9%) and fifth (8.3%), respectively, whereas the coverage of Japan by two French and two British newspapers was seventh (8.2%) and sixth (6.5%), respectively. In other words, news flows between Japan and this group were found to be almost balanced.

The third group consists of Asia and Pacific countries other than China and the United States. Let us take Australia, the most affluent country in this group, and South Korea, the closest foreign country to Japan, as examples. The coverage of Japan by two Australian newspapers was the third highest (13.4%), following the United States (44.0%) and the United Kingdom (32.3%). However, Australia was not included in the list of the top ten most heavily covered countries by Japanese newspapers (the percentage is not available). The coverage of Japan in two Korean newspapers was the second highest (18.5%) after the United States (32.0%). However, the Japanese newspaper coverage of South Korea ranked seventh, accounting for only 4.6%. Japanese newspaper coverage of Indonesia, Malaysia, the Philippines, Thailand, Singapore, and Hong Kong is all out of the top ten list. These countries' newspaper coverage of Japan, however, was always in the upper half of their top ten lists.

The relationship between Japan and the rest of the world (i.e., Latin America, the Middle East and Africa) is not clear because of lack of data, but my presumption would be that the coverage of Japan by Latin American, Middle Eastern, and African newspapers would be less than in the three groups discussed above. Even so, it would be greater than the coverage of these areas by Japanese newspapers.

Overall, the results of the two large-scale surveys conducted by the JNPEA Research Institute were almost identical. They confirmed that the international news flows into and out of Japan favor the three political-military superpowers, the United States, the Soviet Union and China; that they are balanced with the major

Western European powers, the United Kingdom, France, and West Germany; and that they favor Japan with the rest of the world.

Analysis

Research on the determinants of international news flows has revealed the factors discussed below to be significant.

Geographical proximity. The data from the Stanford University and University of Paris study cited above indicated that relatively large amounts of news moved between Argentina and Brazil and between India and Pakistan. Later studies have repeatedly confirmed that geographically close countries tend to be mutually covered more heavily than distant countries (Galtung & Ruge, 1970; Idid & Hasim, 1986; Lee & Kang, 1982; Liu & Gunarantnc, 1972; Mulugetta & Miller, 1985; Schramm, 1980; Sparks, 1978; Sreberny-Mohammadi, 1984; Stevenson, 1984; Stevenson & Shaw, 1984). It seems certain that geographical proximity is an important factor determining the direction and volume of international news flows in both developed and developing countries.

Cultural affinity. Based on studies by Galtung and Ruge (1970), Ostgaard (1965), Hester (1973), and Kariel and Rosenvall (1983) analyzed the content of Canadian newspapers and found that French-language newspapers tend to cover France, while English-language newspapers cover the United Kingdom. Idid and Hasim (1986), in analyzing Malaysian newspapers, conclude that Tamil-language newspapers tend to focus on India, English-language newspapers focus on the United Kingdom and the United States, and Chinese-language newspapers concentrate on Singapore and China. A study of Japanese, Korean, and Indian newspapers by Mulugetta and Miller (1985) also confirms that cultural affinity affects foreign coverage by newspapers. The fact that the United Kingdom is usually more heavily covered than France and West Germany in newspapers in the United States can also be explained by cultural affinity (Robinson & Sparks, 1976).

It seems certain that geographical proximity and cultural affinity play important roles in determining the direction and volume of international news flows. However, although these two factors are useful in explaining static patterns of flows, they do not explain dynamic changes in those flows. These factors do not explain why the Japanese news flow pattern changed from being similar to those of developing countries before 1965 to being similar to those of major Western European countries after 1970. The explanation of this change in Japan's news flow pattern must be sought elsewhere.

Existence of powerful news agencies and mass media infrastructure. Along with the development of the Japanese economy, the scale of the Japanese newspaper and broadcasting industries and news agencies was drastically expanded during the period under study. The annual budget of the Japanese Kyodo News Agency at present is more than twice as large as that of France's Agence France Presse (AFP).[2] Despite that, Kyodo is little more than a national news agency, whereas AFP is a major *international* news agency.

The major reason for Kyodo's inability to compete with Anglo-Saxon and French international news agencies despite its scale and financial strength is language. In order for Kyodo to sell news reports in foreign markets, the reports must be translated into English or French. This means higher cost and, more important, delayed distribution. Delayed distribution is fatal in the news agency business.

This lack of an international market for Japanese-language news is the largest reason for Kyodo's inability to become a genuine international news agency. In the case of major international news agencies, more than 20% of their total revenue comes from sales to foreign mass media.[3] Sales to foreign mass media account for only a small percentage of Kyodo's revenue. Kyodo does distribute news in English (mostly on Japan) to foreign mass media, but this service loses money for the agency. Kyodo says that it does not provide its English-language service for profit, but "for the country." [4] Given these factors, any increase in the coverage of Japan by the foreign mass media cannot be attributed to the growth of Japanese news agencies.

Influence on other countries' politics, economy, technology, and military. From the earliest studies of international flows of news, it has been noted that political, economic, technological, and military influences have much to do with the international news flow pattern. For example, Schramm (1964) notes:

> To point out merely that the countries that get the most news coverage . . . are also the ones that own the world news services is far too simple an explanation. The potency of these countries in world affairs; their possession of the nuclear weapon; the strength of their economics, and the relation of these through trade and finance to the economies of all other countries; their eminence in science and industry — all these things ensure that almost anything of serious significance that happens in one of these countries is likely to be of interest or concern to smaller countries throughout the world. (pp. 62-63)

Sommerlad (1977) gives a similar reason for the imbalance of international news flows:

> The imbalance in international news flows, of which so many countries complain is, in the first place, a reflection of world political power. In a world context, more things happen of international importance in centers of power such as Washington, New York, Moscow, London, and Paris, than in smaller countries in Asia, Oceania, or Africa, or for that matter, in any part of the world. As power blocs change so will news flows. That is in the nature of news. (p. 28)

Galtung and Ruge (1970) conducted a content analysis of four Norwegian newspapers. They found that "elite nations" — nations with political and economic power — tend to be covered more heavily than "nonelite nations." Among the four factors discussed as determinants of the direction and volume of international news flows, this fourth factor seems to be the most important. It could be the main reason for Japan's change from news importer to news exporter. Let us briefly review the changes in Japanese influence on other countries after World War II.

Japan lost 75% of its industrial ability by the end of World War II, as well as all the territories acquired after its modernization. The postwar Japanese Constitution, written under the guidance of the American occupation authorities, prohibited Japan from holding any form of military force. Japan once again became one of the many poor, underdeveloped, militarily dependent countries.

Postwar Japanese leaders focused the nation's attention on the goal of "making money." When Prime Minister Ikeda visited France in the early 1960s, President De Gaulle could not remember his name and said to the French press corps, "I have an appointment with a transistor salesman." When Prime Minister Ikeda was asked his reaction to this after he returned to Japan, he said, "I don't mind. While abroad, I consider myself a salesman." At about the same time, Pakistani President Bhutto called the Japanese nation "economic animals." In those days, the coverage of Japan by mass media in other countries was almost negligible. No important news came from Japan at that time.

Now the economic strength of Japan in terms of the gross national product (GNP) is larger than the *total* GNPs of all other Asian countries combined, including China, India, and all the Middle Eastern countries. (The Japanese GNP is about equal to the combined French and German GNPs.) Economic trends and policies of a country of this power cannot help having strong influence on the economies of the areas closely related to Japan through trade or direct investment, such as North America, East Asia, Oceania, and Western Europe. It is no wonder that the increase in the coverage of Japan first occurred in the area of economics.[5]

The expansion of the Japanese economy, however, resulted in Japan's increased influence in other areas, such as the military. Japan's only military forces are its Self-Defense Forces, which were originally organized as the Police Reserves at the time of the Korean War in 1950-53. Japanese governments have traditionally publicized the fact that Japanese military expenditures are the lowest in the world in terms of percentage of GNP. Japan at present spends only 1% of its GNP for the Self-Defense Forces. Recently, however, a Philippino journalist wrote in a Japanese newspaper that the Japanese people should realize that "1% of the Japanese GNP" means "three and half times more than the Philippines' total national budget" ("Gunji ryoku ni ginen nokoru," 1987). Under such circumstances, foreign countries, especially neighboring Asian countries, cannot help being concerned about Japanese defense policies and the movements of the Japanese military forces.

After World War II, Japan hid itself behind the United States and avoided leadership or initiative on the stage of international politics. Postwar Japanese diplomacy was called "low-posture diplomacy" or "all-directions diplomacy." It was designed to avoid political involvement and to concentrate on economic growth. Japan's economic expansion, however, steadily increased Japan's political influence. It became more and more difficult for Japan to stay away from international political issues. Japanese foreign aid, which is now the second largest in the world, after the United States, influences international political affairs. For example, Japan has stopped economic and technical aid to Vietnam and increased aid to Thailand to "punish" Vietnam. At the request of the U.S. government, Japan drastically increased economic aid to Pakistan, which takes care of millions of Afghan refugees, and to Egypt, which tries to bring peace in the Middle East in a "realistic" way (from American and Japanese viewpoints). Japan's political position on economic aid must be a concern for many developing countries.

As mentioned above, Japan now has an "access imbalance" friction with the United States and Western European countries. Information regarding technological development trends and managerial know-how in Japan are now important for these countries to strengthen their competitive position with Japan. Therefore, mass media coverage on these subjects has increased. Furthermore, economic and technological success has increased interest in all aspects of Japanese culture and traditions, including customs, ways of living, ways of thinking, social systems, arts, music, and architecture. Consequently, coverage of Japan in foreign mass media has increased drastically in almost all fields.

Considering the four factors discussed so far as determinants of the volume and direction of international news flows, the fourth factor — that is, the increase of influence on other countries' politics, economy, technology, and military — seems to be the most important reason for Japan's change from news importer to news exporter.

FLOWS OF POPULAR CULTURE

In the late 1950s and early 1960s, a large proportion of the television programs seen in Japan were imported. The peak appeared in the early 1960s, when most of the programs that were popular in the United States were shown in Japan.[6] Imported programs gradually lost popularity, however, and were replaced by Japanese programs after the mid-1960s. When Varis (1973) investigated the percentages of foreign programs on major television stations in 53 countries in 1971, the percentage of foreign programs in Japan broke down as follows: 1% on NHK Educational, 4% on NHK General, and 10% on the average on the commercial networks. At that time, the percentage of imported television programs in Japan was already the second lowest in the world, after the United States.

Ten years later, Sugiyama (1982a, 1982b) investigated the number of foreign television programs on seven Japanese television stations. In 1980-1981, foreign programs accounted for 2.3% of the (112,977) titles and 4.9% of the actual time (47,630 hours) on these seven stations. Of the total amount of broadcast time of all the imported programs, 78.1% was from North America, 19.3% from Western Europe, 1.3% from Eastern Europe, 1.0% from Asia, and 0.3% from Oceania.

According to Sugiyama (1982a, 1982b), Japan exported 4,585 hours of television programs to 58 countries in 1980, compared to approximately 2,200 hours of

TABLE 1

Export/Import Balance of Television Progress by Region (in hours)

	Imports		Exports
Asia	24	<	1,182
Oceania	3	<	41
Middle East	2	<	120
Africa	3	<	41
Western Europe	429	<	1,121
Eastern Europe	31	=	33
North America	1,820	>	1,407
South America	0	<	444

SOURCE: Sugiyama (1982b, p. 34)

programs in 1971. At that time, the levels of Japan's exports and imports were approximately equal (Varis, 1973). Therefore, Japan's export of television programs doubled between 1971 and 1981, while the level of imports remained almost the same. The largest buyer was the United States (1,357 hours), followed by Italy (767 hours), Hong Kong (391 hours), South Korea (284 hours), and Taiwan (185 hours). Table 1 shows the Japanese export/import balance of television programs by region.

Table 1 indicates that the United States is the only country in the world that exports more television programs to Japan than it imports from Japan. However, the export/import ratio is 9:7, and it is possible to say that television program trade between the United States and Japan is almost balanced. Table 1 also shows that Japan exports three times more television programs to Western Europe than it imports from that region. This ratio is unusual because when the international flows of television programs are discussed, the one-way and overwhelming flows from Western countries to non-Western countries have always been emphasized (Read, 1976; Tunstall, 1977). Present-day Japan, however, does not fit that mold.

Similar trends are observed in some other relatively developed parts of Asia. As early as 1975, Tsui, Lau, and Choi (1975) wrote an article titled "Hong Kong's Strong Preference for Local Productions." In this study, the researchers compared the popularity of imported and local information products in the fields of television, newspapers, radio, and motion pictures. Concerning television programs, they conclude: "According to ratings of the past years, the overall pattern consistently suggests the audience's preference for local productions over imports. None of the top ten ratings was for a foreign programme" (p. 118). Results for newspapers, radio, and motion pictures were by and large the same: "It can be fairly concluded from results of this investigation that the situation of 'information imbalance' supposedly existing in a number of developing countries exists only to a very limited degree in Hong Kong" (p. 121).

More recently, Wu (1987) has reported:

In the bygone days of the late 60s and early 70s, Western movies and dramas enjoyed tremendous popularity in Hong Kong on both English and Chinese channels. Not only were the English channel watchers familiar with such series as 'Quincy', 'The Six Million Dollar Man', 'Addams Family', 'The F.B.I.', 'Hawaii Five-O,' 'Mod Squad', but also the Chinese channel viewers as well, as these programmes were dubbed into Cantonese and had received very good ratings.

However, as the television industry flourished and there came great improvement in technology, resources and manpower, TV drama/movies dubbed into Cantonese could no longer satisfy the needs of local viewers. The Chinese channels then tried out locally produced gag shows, variety shows and drama serials. They all proved to be popular. It was in the mid 70s and from thence on, that Japanese/Western movies and series stepped down as primetime programmes. In fact, they are almost nonexistent on the Chinese channels. If they were shown at all, they were only given late night/fringe time slots. (pp. 1-2)

Many other researchers have made similar observations. Based on data collected at the Asian Mass Communication Research and Information Centre (AMIC), Menon (1985), secretary-general of AMIC, states: "A comparison of programming patterns in 1970-71 and 1983 in selected Asian countries shows that the percentage of domestic programmes has gone up in the majority of countries. These include Hong Kong (Chinese channel), Korea, Malaysia, Pakistan, Philippines and Singapore" (p. 66). After studying the situations in Indonesia, Nigeria, Senegal, Algeria, Thailand, Iran, Cyprus, Brazil, Peru, and Singapore, Katz (1977) notes: "Whenever there are measures of popularity, . . . homemade programs outdo the most famous of American imports" (p. 118).

Hong Kong and Taiwan now export many television programs and movies to Southeast Asia, mainland China, Japan, and the United States. Western experts often dismiss these trends with the following argument. Most of the television programs and movies that the United States imports from Japan, Hong Kong, and Taiwan are televised through minor stations with limited audiences, such as cable stations, the Public Broadcasting Network, educational stations, and independent UHF stations. Many of these television programs and movies are seen only by Asian communities living in the United States. Therefore, the influence of East Asian television programs and movies on mainstream American communities is negligible. While this argument is true to some extent, it should be noted that these factors also operate in Japan, Hong Kong, and Taiwan. Most imported television programs are shown in Japan by independent UHF stations, satellite channels, and cable stations or by the English-language channels in Hong Kong. They seldom appear on the major networks.

The preference for domestic programs in Japan is further supported by audience data. A comparison of imported and domestic programs in Japan shows that the ratings of imported programs, particularly entertainment programs, are much lower than those of programs of Japanese origin (Sugiyama, 1982b). The ratings of imported programs exceed Japanese programs only for information and cultural programs (Kawatake, 1982b).

A study of the programs of the seven television channels that were available in Tokyo in 1975 revealed that imported programs appeared only six times during prime time (7:00-10:00 p.m.) throughout the whole month of April 1975 (Sugiyama, 1982b, p. 9). Imported programs are televised in Japan late at night or during the daytime for special interest groups rather than for the general public. Thus imported foreign television programs almost completely disappeared from the prime-time programming of the Japanese major networks by the mid-1970s. As shown by the quotes from Tsui et al. (1975) and Wu (1987) above, this was also the case in Hong Kong. According to my own personal interview surveys, this shift also happened in Taiwan and Singapore, and is happening in South Korea, but not yet in Malaysia, Thailand, Indonesia, or the Philippines.

Programs that disappeared at the earliest stage were domestic comedies, variety shows, and drama series. Those that continue to be shown at the time of this writing are action dramas such as *Airwolf* and *Knight Rider* and police and detective stories such as *Remington Steele* and *Miami Vice*. The ratings of these programs are all lower than 10%. In other words, programs featuring American domestic life, human relations, and humor disappeared at an early stage,[7] while programs featuring war, crime, and violence remain. For this reason, some Westerners living in Japan believe that the Japanese public sees the West through a prism of violence and sex, and that the Japanese are likely to form inappropriate images of the West and its people.

On the other hand, however, the Japan Public Broadcasting Corporation (NHK) imports serious documentary series produced by American, Canadian, and Western European public broadcasting corporations and telecasts them on its educational channel. The ratings of these programs are about the same as those of the imported entertainment programs, and, in this sense, it is possible to say that some kind of balance is maintained.[8]

According to Lyle, Ogawa, and Thomas (1986, p. 17), almost no American programs now appear on Tokyo's television prime- or golden-time "windows," but there are many Japanese programs that look very much like those Americans see at home. This argument implies that, even if Japan exports many television programs, it is exporting pseudo-Western culture and not authentic Japanese culture. Let us examine the export of Japanese animation programs, which account for about 70% of Japanese television program exports.

It is true that the content and settings of some Japanese animation programs are almost completely Western. For example, Sata (1982, p. 64) reports that the animation programs exported by Japan include *The Adventures of Tom Sawyer, King Arthur and the Knights of the Round Table, 8000 Miles to Find Mother, Les Miserables,* and *The Tales of Hans Christian Andersen.* However, some are Arabian (*The Adventures of Sinbad*) and some Chinese (*Sai Yu Ki,* or *Xi You Ji* in

Chinese). On the other hand, some Western television programs and movies have definite Eastern themes. For example, *Kung Fu,* a television series produced in the West and that was popular in East Asia, was like an imitation of Hong Kong movies. It seems appropriate to regard television programs and movies as a kind of industrial product accommodating the market.

Another implication of the study by Lyle et al. might be that the Japanese take ideas from the West and produce television programs that are competitive in domestic and international markets. Maybe this was true ten years ago, but not any longer. The number of cases in which the *ideas* of Japanese programs have been sold to American television networks and stations has increased in recent years. In 1986, the ideas of two popular Japanese television programs, *Wakuwaku Dohbutsu Rando* (a quiz show involving wild animals) and *Fuun Takeshi Joh* (a game show with audience participation) were exported to ABC and 20th Century Fox Television. Although the flows of ideas are still imbalanced in favor of the United States, there are some American programs "that look very much like those Japanese see at home."

Lyle et al. (1986) state:

> In terms of today's cultural whirlpool, what really is "American" and what is actually "global"? Maybe American television, like American English, is so adept at accepting and absorbing innovation and ideas from other cultures that it is achieving a "supranational" character. (pp. 17-18)

I agree with this view as long as it is clear that the word "American" in this statement can be replaced by "Japanese," "Chinese," or the name of any other culture in the world.

Motion Pictures

Japan has the longest history of motion picture production in East Asia. The Kinetoscope (peep-show type), invented and commercialized by Thomas Edison in 1893, was imported into Japan in 1896 and shown to the public. In 1897 the Cinematographe, developed by the Lumiere brothers in France, and the Vitascope, developed by Edison (both screen type), were imported and shown in Japan. Two years later, the first documentary film and the first dramatic feature movie based on a stage drama were produced in Japan and shown in public. In the early 1920s, imported films accounted for 40% of all the movies shown in Japan (Ministry of International Trade and Industry, 1963, p. 121). However, due to restrictive policies against foreign movies since 1938, the import of foreign movies drastically decreased.

The export of Japanese films steadily increased. Table 2 shows the number of long, short, and news films that Japan exported to foreign countries from 1937 to 1957. Table 3 shows the countries to which those films were exported before World War II. This table indicates that the U.S. mainland, Hawaii, China, Manchuria,

TABLE 2
Export of Japanese Films by Year (number of titles)

	Long Film	Short Film	News Film
1937	439	489	1,023
1938	664	535	1,458
1939	426	758	2,023
1940	1,156	1,221	2,045
1947	17	0	14
1948	80	35	102
1949	120	25	55
1950	147	20	106
1951	539	33	228
1952	625	73	408
1953	675	57	303
1954	740	89	325
1955	987	110	427
1956	1,158	112	424
1957	1,107	153	432

SOURCE: Ministry of International Trade and Industry (1959, p. 37).

TABLE 3
Export of Japanese Films by Region, 1937-1940 (number of titles)

	1937	*1938*	*1939*	*1940*
Mainland United States	910	672	663	610
Hawaii	—	357	436	373
Manchuria	81	151	285	1,836
China	170	322	580	965
Germany	142	254	253	118
Italy	57	113	157	101
United Kingdom	71	99	106	56
France	103	166	145	38
Brazil	44	31	47	22
Argentina	1	27	21	10
Philippines	68	90	70	38
India	37	19	85	32
Thailand	—	56	30	14
Australia	13	24	35	16
Others	254	276	294	195
Total	1,951	2,657	3,207	4,424

SOURCE: Ministry of International Trade and Industry (1959, p. 38).

Germany, and Italy were major markets for Japanese films before the war. These data confirm the finding by Ito and Kochevar (1983) that the trade of films has much to do with political and economic relationships.

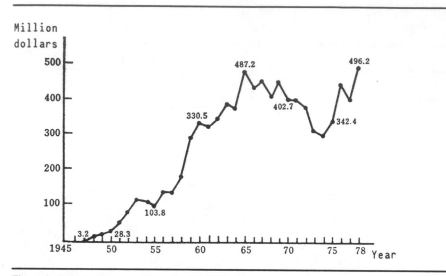

Figure 1. Export of Japanese films after World War II.
SOURCE: Yamamoto (1980, p. 207)

At the end of the war, the export of Japanese films dropped almost to zero. It steadily recovered, however, and in 1956, the number of exports of long films caught up with the prewar peak (see Table 2). In 1954, Japan surpassed the United States to become the largest film-producing country in the world. In 1954, Japan produced 377 films, followed by India (275), the United States (253), and Italy (157). Until the 1960s, when India surpassed Japan, Japan was the largest film-producing country in the world.

In the mid-1950s, several Japanese films were awarded grand prizes at prestigious international film festivals, such as Venice and Cannes; interest in Japanese feature films grew, and the export of Japanese feature films has steadily increased. Japanese movies are very much influenced by Japanese traditional stage arts such as Kabuki, Noh, and Bunraku. They have developed specific techniques and a unique style, and have acquired a strong following in the West.

In addition to specialty art films, Japan has produced many popular movies featuring violence, sex, and horror. Those movies have been exported to Southeast Asia and to Japanese communities in the United States and Brazil. Japanese monster movies (such as the Godzilla series), *chambara* (sword fighting by samurai) films, and pornographic movies were popular in Southeast Asia in the late 1950s and early 1960s.

Figure 1 shows the trend of the export of Japanese movies after the war. Until 1965, film exports increased steadily, but the growth in the number of television sets undermined the film industry and the volume of film production decreased. The size of the movie audience had already started to decrease in 1958 and the number of movie theaters began to decline in 1960. The export of Japanese films

Number of
titles

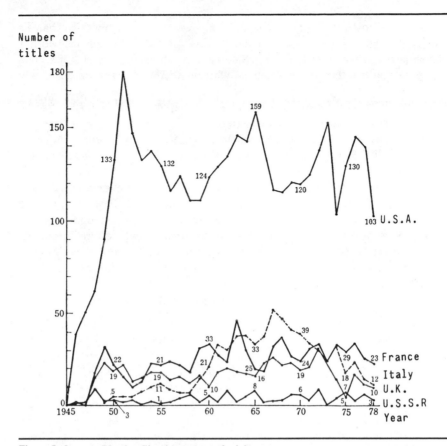

Figure 2. Import of foreign films by country of origin.
SOURCE: Yamamoto (1980, p. 199)

decreased accordingly. However, the size of movie audiences and the number of theaters stopped decreasing around 1974. Since that period the export of Japanese films began to increase again.

Figure 2 shows the trend of foreign film imports into Japan. As this figure shows, the total number of imported films has not changed very much since the 1950s. However, there seems to be a trend toward the diversification of sources. The dominant share of American movies has gradually decreased while the proportion of movies from other countries has slightly increased. According to Yamamoto (1980, p. 198), the share of imported films in the Japanese domestic film market is smaller than in other countries.

In the total amount of international trade of feature films in 1977, 53.7% were imported and 46.3% exported (Ministry of Posts and Telecommunications, 1978, p. 70). These figures mean that the trade in feature films was almost balanced. Compared with television programs, where Japan exports twice as much as it imports, it is possible to say that Japan's movies are less competitive than its television programs. One of the major reasons for this is that in the world's television program market, the United States and Japan have much larger program supply capabilities than other countries, whereas there are many European and Asian countries that produce internationally competitive films. Another reason may be that television programs such as animation programs can be made "cosmopolitan," a move difficult in the case of film.

Of all the feature films that Japan imported in 1977, 76.6% came from North America, 16.7% from Western Europe, 5.6% from Asia, and 1.2% from other areas. This pattern is very similar to the pattern of imported television programs. Of all the feature films that Japan exported in 1977, 52.9% went to Asia, 12.8% to Western Europe, 11.1% to North America, 9.0% to the Middle East, and 14.2% to other areas. This is very different from the pattern of television program export. Japan exports more television programs to North America and Western Europe. As noted, Japan sells "cosmopolitan" animation programs in the North American and European markets, whereas Japanese movies are more difficult to sell in the Western markets because they are more culturally bound.

Popular Music

In traditional Japan, music could be classified into four categories: (a) folk songs, (b) *rokyoku* (a narrative style of singing, telling popular stories), (c)*hogaku* (Japanese classical music, originally used in traditional stage arts such as Kabuki, Noh, and Bunraku), and (d) *gagaku* (orchestra or ensemble music used at formal ceremonies in court). Western music was introduced to Japan in the mid-nineteenth century and had a strong impact on Japanese classical and popular music. The mixture of traditional and Western music led to the creation of many new kinds of music. One of the new genres that became very important in the latter half of the nineteenth century in Japan and the whole of East Asia was *enka* (the original meaning is "stage song"). Enka originally started as political protest songs. The political nuances were gradually dropped and enka became songs to lament sad feelings and the lives of the suppressed.

As World War II ended, the American occupation forces brought with them American popular music. This bright, happy, and rhythmic music, which did not exist in prewar Japan, was attractive to Japanese people, who were experiencing miserable conditions at that time. American popular music came to dominate the Japanese popular music market throughout the 1950s. At that time, most American popular songs were translated into Japanese and sung by Japanese singers. In the mid-1950s, American rock and roll music was introduced and enthusiastically accepted by the younger generation.

Even under the domination of American popular music, enka grew steadily. Before and during World War II, when Japan occupied Korea and a part of China, it had absorbed and become enriched by elements of Korean and Chinese folk songs. It also absorbed American and European elements, and the repertoire expanded from just sad songs to include more forward-looking and cheerful songs. (The development of enka parallels the development of the modern French *chanson*.) Apart from enka, there emerged many Japanized, Western-style kinds of popular music. They were called *wasei poppusu* or "pops made in Japan."

As a result, enka and wasei pops gradually replaced American popular songs throughout the 1960s. By the early 1970s, the domination of enka in Japanese popular music became obvious. According to a later survey conducted by NHK in 1978, the order of popularity was as follows: enka, 31%; Japanese traditional folk songs, 24%; Western-style popular music, 16%; Western classical music, 8%; rock music, 6%; Western songs, 5%; rokyoku (story telling in the form of singing), 5%; and hogaku (Japanese classical music), 2%. According to this survey, the order of popularity differed by region. In seven rural prefectures Japanese traditional folk songs were the most popular, whereas in two urban prefectures, including Tokyo, Western-style popular music was the most popular. In the rest of the 38 prefectures, enka was at the top (Komota, Yazawa, Shimada, & Yokozawa, 1980, p. 97).

In 1976, a record company developed *karaoke* ("sing-along" or "song without words") records. They sold surprising well. As a result, many record companies and audio set manufacturers entered this new market and the "karaoke boom" occurred in the late 1970s. People bought karaoke sets, with which they could sing along with a combo or orchestra band at home. Karaoke bars, where people can drink, sing, and dance (in some places), emerged and rapidly expanded all over Japan. By 1980, the number of karaoke bars in Japan was estimated to have reached 200,000; Tokyo alone was estimated to have 20,000 (Komota et al., 1980, p. 89). The introduction of laser-disk karaoke sets in the early 1980s further accelerated this boom. Most of the songs used in karaoke were enka.

The Japanese karaoke culture was widely exported to the whole of East Asia. As a result, enka has become a dominant popular musical style not only in Japan but also in Korea, Taiwan, and Hong Kong.[9] Popular songs in these regions are now influencing one another, and enka is now having a strong influence on mainland Chinese popular music. It is said in China that Teng Hsiao-p'ing dominates China during the daytime, but another Teng (Teresa, a Taiwanese enka singer) dominates in the evening. Enka is no longer Japanese popular music but Northeast Asian popular music.

Analysis

The balance of information flows from and into Japan in the fields of news reporting and popular culture has shifted back in favor of Japan. However, there are some differences in the meaning of *balance* in these two areas. First, in the case of news flows, balance is considered in terms of the amount of coverage, while in the case of popular culture, balance between export and import as well as balance of shares of the domestic market are of interest. In the case of news flows, the balance changed in favor of Japan because of a dramatic increase in the coverage of Japan by the foreign mass media. In the case of popular culture, the balance changed in favor of Japan because of the significant decrease of foreign products' market share and an increase in exports. In quantity, the import of foreign products has not necessarily decreased during the past twenty years. Therefore, what follows is an analysis of how the market share of imported products decreased and how Japanese exports of popular culture increased.

Decrease of imported products' market share. As discussed above, the percentage of foreign programs in Japanese television significantly decreased in the last half of the 1960s. Imported programs also shifted from major networks to minor stations and from prime time to fringe time. There were two reasons for these changes. One was that higher ratings were earned by domestic programs, and therefore foreign programs became less attractive for programmers. Further, advertising expenditures by big businesses as well as license fee revenues for the public broadcasting corporation markedly increased. Thus it became possible for Japanese television stations to generate more domestic programs. As Japan had rich human resources and experience in the traditional stage arts and film, it was relatively easy to raise the quality of television programs with the increased financial resources. Even if Japanese networks could not finance the same level of production as the major American networks, it was now possible for Japanese program makers to compete with imported American programs in the Japanese market. Thus Japanese programs gradually overcame imported programs and occupied most of prime time.

The second important reason for the drop of ratings of imported programs was the increasing ownership of television sets by the rural population. There were many people in Japanese rural areas, in farming and fishing villages, who had never seen or talked to Western people. Those people often complained about imported programs, especially dramas. They said that they could not distinguish the faces of Westerners ("Westerners' faces all look alike") or remember the names of Westerners. The stories were confusing for them, and they could not enjoy the programs. As these people became a significant part of the Japanese television audience, the average ratings of foreign programs naturally dropped.

The failure of *Dallas* in Japan is a good example. In 1981, a major Japanese commercial network decided to broadcast the American drama series *Dallas* in prime time because at that time *Dallas*'s ratings were extremely high, not only in the United States but also in Europe and Australia. The network invested a great deal of money in a promotion campaign. The program was televised once every week from 9:00 to 10:00 p.m. However, the ratings were so low that the series was canceled in six months. The average rating of 24 episodes televised during the six months was only 4.8%.

A strong tendency to prefer domestic programs to imported programs in rural Asia is reported not only in Japan but also in other Asian countries. For example, Lee (1980) states that in Taiwan

the mass audience favors homemade programs which are not difficult to understand. . . . [An] overwhelming proportion of the low-education mass audience (69%)

liked the indigenous series and serials best compared with the elite audience of college graduates (50%) who preferred imported American films. (pp. 158-159)

This tendency is observable even in much less developed countries in Asia. According to Goonasekera (1987) of Sri Lanka:

> Surveys in Indonesia, Taiwan and Sri Lanka indicate that at least as far as rural audiences are concerned, foreign programmes from the West, which sometimes fill a considerable amount of time, are the least watched. . . . It is the local language programmes that attract huge audiences. This is because of the ease of understanding and the closeness of the events in the programme to the events in everyday life of the local audience. (p. 12)

Many experts have already pointed out that two major reasons for excessive importation of foreign popular cultural products include lack of domestic supply to meet the demand of the general public or inferior quality of domestic products compared to imported products (Katz & Wedell, 1977; Lee, 1980; Mowlana, 1986; Pool, 1977a). Furthermore, Goonasekera (1987) gives three reasons for the predominance of foreign programs on Third World television: (a) the high cost of local productions, (b) the lack of trained staff, and (c) the lack of will and determination of the management and government of Third World countries to increase the level of local productions (p. 12). Therefore, "in this so-called cultural invasion, there is complicity of the government and media professionals of Third World countries" (p. 12).

These arguments all suggest that if the production of domestic programs increases, the quality of these programs is improved, and the rural population become a significant part of the audience, then cultural differences will start working as an effective barrier against excessive import of foreign programs. From this, we can predict that *where there are significant cultural differences*, the problems of "cultural invasion" will be solved naturally as the above three conditions come to be satisfied. Therefore, between regions such as East Asia and the West, the "cultural invasion" problem will be short-lived. However, *where there are insufficient cultural differences*, such as between the United States and Canada[10] or between Japan and Korea[11] or between India and Sri Lanka, "cultural invasion" will remain a serious problem.

Increase of exports. As noted above, Japan's export of television programs more than doubled between 1971 and 1980 (Sugiyama, 1982b, p. 25). Further, as Figure 1 indicates, exports of Japanese films have been steadily increasing. In this section, some conditions that have made these increases possible are examined.

The first factor was the expansion of channel capacities and broadcast time that occurred on a worldwide scale. In the 1960s, many developing countries started television broadcasting, and a large demand for television programs was born. As the largest television-producing country, the United States was the country that could meet this worldwide demand. By 1975, however, Japan had become the second largest television program-producing country, after the United States. Many countries had apparently become cautious about overdependence on American television programs, but not, seemingly, on Japanese programs. Therefore, each time a country introduced a commercial broadcasting system, the export of television programs from Japan increased. Kawatake (1982a) notes: "In Europe, as the percentage of American programs decreased (in the mid 1970s), the export of Japanese television programs drastically increased" (p. 12).

Richeri (1982) writes that as a result of the broadcasting deregulation in 1975, import of television programs drastically increased in Italy, especially among new commercial stations. Richeri comments that "Italy imports the majority of her television programmes" from the United States and Japan, and that "Italy was the largest importer of Japanese animation programmes, having imported more than 25% of all animation programmes exported by Japan" (p. 37).

The second factor in Japan's rising exports concerns the strong interest many newly industrialized countries (NICs) and developing countries in Asia have in Japan's recent economic and technological successes. Their interest is in Japan as a model for the modernization of their own societies and economies. For this reason, governments and/or public broadcasting corporations seek out Japanese drama series depicting the lives of ordinary Japanese citizens in the late nineteenth and early twentieth centuries. They think that their people should be able to learn from the way of life and thinking of the Japanese people at that time.

For example, in 1984 and 1985 the "Oshin fad" or "Oshindrome" occurred throughout East Asia, including mainland China. *Oshin* is a television series named for its title character, a woman born early in this century, the daughter of a miserably poor peasant in a mountain village in the northern part of Japan. This long drama series described her life from childhood until the 1970s, when she retired from the management of a successful supermarket. It showed how she bore many hardships, worked diligently, educated herself, and loved her family. It was not only educational but also quite entertaining, and, even in Japan, where the competition between programs is very severe, ratings were in the 40-50% range. In Japan, this series continued for one year. A 15-minute episode was broadcast every day of the week except Sunday. In many developing countries in East Asia, the ratings were unprecedentedly high. In China and Thailand, it was reported that people disappeared from the street as the program started. In Thailand the word *oshin* was used in daily conversation to mean "perseverance" or "hardship" (Akagi, 1985).

The Polish National Television System telecast this series in 1984. It is reported that the ratings there were as high as 70% ("Saikin warushawa fuuzoku," 1985). The Iranian National Television System started this series in November 1987, and its average ratings were as high as 70%. The program was also shown at movie theaters, which were filled with citizens on Saturday evenings when *Oshin* was telecast ("Oshin," 1988). A producer of the Iranian National Television System reportedly said, "Oshin's spirit of self-sacrifice is what the Iranian people need at this moment" ("Sekai no shakaimen," 1987).[12] So far, *Oshin* has been telecast in 16 countries outside Japan, including non-Asian countries such as Australia, Belgium, Canada, Iran, and Poland (Shimizu, 1988; Takashima, 1988).

The third factor contributing to Japanese exports of popular culture was the conscious export effort made by Japanese television stations, movie companies, television program production companies, record companies, distribution companies, and trading companies. Japan, at present, has a serious trade imbalance with many countries in the world, especially the United States and Western European countries. One of the structural problems behind this trade friction has to do with market size and maturity. The American and Western European markets are *major* markets, whereas the Japanese market is currently a *minor* but *mature* market. While the Japanese market was still underdeveloped, Japanese consumers bought products made in the West. Given cultural differences, they *had to* buy automobiles a little too large for them and refrigerators and washing machines definitely too large for their homes. They had to buy cosmetics, processed food, and electrical appliances with English instructions. They did not have much choice at that time. However, as Japanese manufacturing grew and provided Japanese consumers with exactly the products they wanted, the sales of foreign products rapidly dropped in Japan.

Similar developments, although on a far smaller scale, are occurring in the field of information products. In a mature, non-Western market such as the Japanese market, information products made in the West do not now sell as easily as they did 20 years ago. On the other hand, Japanese producers and distributors of information products study foreign markets carefully. Lyle et al. (1986) report that "the Japanese firms are making a serious study of the American market, its practices and its audiences. The trade publications of the American television industry are carrying an increased number of reports about the efforts of Japanese program salesmen" (p. 15).

According to this report, the Japanese strategy started with the purchase of small cable television stations in Honolulu, Los Angeles, and New York. While these operators initially provided Japanese communities with Japanese programs, they are now making efforts to increase viewers among Anglo citizens. They are marketing Japanese educational, cultural, and serious documentary programs to educational stations, the Public Broadcasting System, and the three major networks, and even producing their own programs for presentation in a network of major markets (Lyle et al., 1986). The result is that Japan, a non-Western country in its basic culture and a member of the Third World bloc before 1920 and between 1945 and 1965, is now trying, although on a far more modest scale, to penetrate the U.S. information market in a manner similar to U.S. firms' penetration of Latin America (a move for which American firms have been condemned; for more on U.S. firms' penetration of Latin America, see Beltran, 1978; Beltran & Fox de Cardona, 1977; Mattelart, 1973; Somavia, 1976).

THE SHIFTING INFORMATION FLOW AND
JAPANESE CULTURAL IDENTITY

An issue that has always been discussed together with that of the imbalance in international information flows is the problem of cultural identity. It is worthwhile to consider what happened to Japanese cultural identity under the situation that changed Japan from an information importer to an information exporter.

A famous slogan advocated by the Japanese government when Japan started modernization was *wakon yosai* — Japanese soul and Western knowledge. Despite the slogan, it was not easy to make a clear distinction between "soul" and "knowledge." As a result, "Westernization" in the early times of modernization tended to be extreme and excessive (for example, see Natsume, 1908, 1911a, 1911b; also see Kitamura, quoted in Sato, 1974, p. 25). In late nineteenth-century Japan, while the elite enjoyed highly "Westernized" life-styles, the masses were left in traditional poverty — -a familiar scene in many developing countries at present. As a result, while leading elites tried to imitate and pursue Western cultures, strong anti-Western feelings, antagonism, and resentment against Western-oriented elites and the West per se developed among the masses. The military took advantage of this atmosphere because, unlike elites in the central government and business, the military was composed largely of people from the rural and lower classes.

After Japan's victory in the Russo-Japanese War (1904-05), Western powers began to regard Japan as a dangerous competitor, and the idea of the "yellow peril" was disseminated in the "White world." In reaction, Japanese anti-Western agitators declared that the Japanese race had a mission to liberate its Asian "younger brothers" from "White colonialism." They claimed that "White colonialism" was the real "peril" in Asia and elsewhere (see Burger, 1974; Hashikawa, 1976). Racial discrimination against Japanese immigrants in North America hurt the proud Japanese immensely. The Japanese public was shocked to realize how much they were looked down upon by the White race, and began to support the cause of the military to "expel the White race from East Asia." Pro-Western views and ideologies were severely oppressed, and Western movies, customs, and even fashions were attacked. Thus the cultural identity problem of the early times of Japan's modernization disappeared as a result of anti-Western policies and a regression to Japan's medieval militaristic tradition.

The sense of continuity of cultural identity through militarism was shattered by defeat in World War II. The American occupation forces brought into Japan new political, social, and economic systems and forced the Japanese to accept them. American popular culture flooded into Japan. There still are many people who feel strong resentment against all or some of these changes that occurred as a result of strong American influence.[13]

However, the situation after World War II has been very different from that of the late nineteenth or early twentieth century. Attempts to cancel "Westernization" after World War II have not gained substantial support from the Japanese public.

As postwar Japan has developed, economically and technologically, more for-ward-looking views and attitudes have developed among Japanese intellectuals. They now suggest that Western civilization is *one* of the civilizations that the Japanese have absorbed and incorporated, as, in the eighth and ninth centuries, Japan adopted much from the Chinese. Even so, they argue, Japan could maintain its own cultural identity while assimilating elements from other cultures.

Western and Japanese observers report, for example, that the Japanese political system, although democratic, is different from Western democracy; the Japanese economic system, although capitalistic, is different from Western capitalism; and Japanese business management, although efficient, is different from Western management. In these delicate differences, Japanese see the combination of Western knowledge and Japanese tradition.

In pointing out these differences, Lee (1982) characterizes Japanese technology as the "technology of miniaturization," and relates modern Japanese electronic technology to the philosophy behind the Japanese garden, *bonsai, hakoniwa* (miniature landscape), *haiku,* and other traditional fine arts. After reviewing many cases of cultural change in modern Japan, cultural anthropologist Ishige (1987) concludes that what happened in modern Japan could be better characterized as "Japanization" of imported Western civilization than as "Westernization" of Japan (p. 46).

THEORIES THAT MAY EXPLAIN
THE JAPANESE EXPERIENCE

In this last section, theories that may explain the Japanese experience described so far are addressed. First, two major theories are presented; I then suggest a supplementary theory about international information flows.

Media Imperialism and Dependency Theories

According to media imperialism and dependency theories, international flows of information in the present world reflect the world capitalist system. Dominant countries send out information as propaganda for indoctrination to maintain the status quo. People in subordinate countries are conditioned to buy news and other media products produced in dominant countries through direct investment in local mass media, dumping, and monopolistic behavior of world news agencies and advertising agencies (Frank, 1969; Mattelart, 1973; Salinas & Paldan, 1979; Schiller, 1969, 1973a, 1973b, 1976; Somavia, 1976; Wallerstein, 1974).

These theories do not explain the Japanese experience very well, or any situation in which a country that used to be heavily dependent on the import of information gradually becomes an information-exporting country. One way to explain this phenomenon is to argue that Japan used to belong to the "periphery" but has grown to a "center status." These theories, however, assume that the center always exploits the periphery, and provide no mechanism by which peripheral countries become central countries.

In order to avoid this difficulty, dependency theorists usually treat Japan as an "exception" in one of two ways:

(1) Compared with countries like India, Indonesia, and China, Japan had few natural resources to attract Western colonialists. Furthermore, the average Japanese before the mid-nineteenth century were so poor that Western capitalists were not interested in Japan as a market. As a result, Japan, helped by its geographical location, was left outside the world capitalist trading system, enabling Japan to pursue its own national development. Frank (1979, quoting Baran, 1957) writes:

> Japan had very little to offer either as a market for foreign manufactures or as a granary of raw materials for Western industry. Consequently the lure of Japan to Western European capitalists and governments came nowhere near the irresistible attraction exercised by the gold of Latin America, the flora, fauna, and minerals of Africa, the fabulous riches of the Indies, or the supposedly bottomless markets of China. (p. 153)

(2) Compared with other non-Western countries, Japan was highly developed economically, militarily, and politically when Western powers reached its shores. Therefore, it was impossible for any Western power to conquer Japan. Japan could pursue its own independent national development based on its already well-developed (for that time) economic structure. Wallerstein (1974), for example, supports this view, arguing that the reason Japan could expel the Spanish and the Portuguese in the early seventeenth century and allow the Dutch to trade with Japan under conditions humiliating to the Dutch was that Japan was economically and militarily powerful.[14]

History would seem to contradict the first scenario and support the second. From the sixteenth century through the nineteenth century, Japan was a major producer of gold, silver, and copper. In the early seventeenth century the amount of silver exported from Japan per year reached one-third of the world's silver production. Chiefly for this reason, the Western powers at that time, especially the Spanish, Portuguese, British, and Dutch, competed to increase their shares in trade with Japan. However, partly because too much gold, silver, and copper left Japan, the Tokugawa Shogunate began to restrict foreign trade, and finally in 1639 it decided to give a license only to Holland among Western countries (Japan continued to trade with China and Korea). The Dutch accepted several conditions that were extremely inconvenient and even humiliating to them because the trade with Japan was so profitable (Yomiuri Shimbun-sha, 1959, p. 132).

The assumption that Japan was not attractive as a market is equally questionable. The population of Japan in the nineteenth century was about 30 million — already larger than the populations of England and France. Personal disposable income of the Japanese masses on average probably exceeded those of the Chinese or Indian masses in the nineteenth century. This difference is reflected in the high literacy rate (about 50% for men and 15% for women in the mid-nineteenth century, close to the rates of most advanced European countries; Ohkawa & Rosovsky, 1965, p. 59; Reischauer, 1977), the existence of mass media for commoners, a consumption economy, and a highly developed market economy in the large cities.[15] Although Japan in the mid-nineteenth century was certainly behind advanced Western European countries, there is much evidence indicating that Japan was not behind less developed Southern and Eastern European countries in terms of military, economy, and especially education (for example, see Horie, 1965; Marshall, 1967; Ohkawa & Rosovsky, 1965; Reischauer, 1965, 1977; for a comparison with China and Korea, see Ito, 1988).

If we accept the second scenario, the following argument in defense of dependency theories is possible. When Japan began modernization in the mid-nineteenth century, it was already different from most of the existing Third World countries. Japan was economically and militarily strong enough to reject interventions by Western powers, to maintain its independence, and to trade with Western powers as equal partners. Dependency theorists use this argument because they assume that the rise of status in international rankings may be possible only for countries that have never been colonized or experienced a peripheral status. Once a country's economic structure has changed as a result of colonization or dependency, the change of status from the periphery to the center is impossible.

Counterarguments can be advanced, however. Some scholars think that Japan rose from the status of periphery or dependence. Tominaga (1987), for example, argues that China and Japan were both "dragged into" the periphery of the Western world trade system in the mid-nineteenth century. Both countries were forced to accept unequal treaties and suffered from disadvantageous trade conditions. Japan, however, fled from that status through various efforts, including the war with Russia.

Dependency theories come under additional attack from the following three modern developments: First, there can be little doubt of Japan's periphery status following World War II. As a result of that war, more than three-fourths of Japan's industrial facilities were destroyed. Japan's per capita income became lower than that of many Latin American countries. The trade conditions for Japan after World War II were the same as those for Latin American countries. If Latin American countries were in the periphery soon after World War II, Japan was also in the periphery.

Second, South Korea, Taiwan, Singapore, and Hong Kong, which were all once colonies of other countries, are now reaching the level of advanced industrial countries. These countries are now building factories in many Southeast Asian countries and are earning significant amounts of surplus money from their trade with Western powers. These countries are very likely to join the "center" in the near future. Japan, therefore, is not the only exception any more. The possibility of change of status through international competition should be seriously considered.

Finally, there are many phenomena that cannot be explained by the media imperialism or dependency theories, which assume an exploitative relationship. For example, as described earlier, two large-scale surveys have concluded that Japanese newspaper coverage of China exceeds Chinese newspaper coverage of Japan. Is that because China is dominating and exploiting Japan? Per capita income of the Chinese is less than one-thirtieth that of the Japanese. Another example: More news and popular culture flow from the United States to Japan than the other way around. Is that because the United States is dominating and exploiting Japan? During the past several years, Japan has been earning a $50 billion surplus every year from U.S./Japanese trade, and the Japanese have been buying American national bonds, stocks, companies, and real estate. I would conclude, and Lee (1980) would suggest, that media imperialism and dependency theories might explain the (present) situation in Latin America, but not that in East Asia.

International Flows of Information
as a Result of Free Competition in Free Markets

Many non-Marxist scholars agree that the fact that international flow of information is very much imbalanced is not a reflection of domination or exploitation but a reflection of the degree of product success in the world market. For these scholars, news, movies, television programs, books, and magazines are all commodities just like any other industrial products that flow from country to country as a result of commercial transactions. News and other information products generated or produced in highly industrialized countries flow to less developed countries because there is a strong demand for them (Kato, 1976; Katz & Wedell, 1977; Kim, 1986; Lee, 1980; Mercado & Buck, 1981; Mowlana, 1986; Pool, 1979; Read, 1976; Tunstall, 1977). This theory implies that if developing countries reach a stage where they can produce attractive information products, their level of exportation will increase and their level of importation will decrease (Pool, 1977a, 1977b).

According to this theory, the flow of news from Japan increased drastically because of the increasing importance of Japan in the world economy and world politics. The export of Japanese popular culture increased because, reflecting the strength of the economy, television stations, movie companies, and record companies spent much more money than before on production. Consequently, the international competitiveness of Japanese products increased.

This explanation may be sufficient for economists, but it is not sufficient for communication scientists. Communication scientists would like to know what kind of needs are satisfied by and what kind of effects are expected from watching these kinds of programs. They would further want to know why the demand for news and mass culture generated in advanced industrial countries tends to be stronger than the demand for news and mass culture generated in Third World countries. It is in the realm of competition, I would argue, that we can fruitfully seek an answer.

International Flows of Information
as a Result of Political and Economic Competition

It was pointed out in a previous section that the reason for the stronger demand for news generated in economically, politically, and/or militarily powerful countries is the stronger influence these countries tend to have on the fates of other countries (Schramm, 1964, pp. 62-63; Sommerlad, 1977, p. 28). It was also pointed out that the export of Japanese popular culture increased because the quality of products improved and private export efforts in Japan became stronger and more systematic. I would like to suggest another basic reason: the influence of international competition on international information flows.

Competition for a stronger military and more political influence among different tribes, groups, nations, or groups of nations has been known since the beginning of human culture and civilization. In ancient times, a strong military organization was a prerequisite of survival and independence. If a tribe was threatened militarily by another tribe, there was no choice for that tribe but to build an equally strong or superior military organization. Otherwise, it would be conquered, destroyed, or colonized by the stronger tribe.

A sophisticated economy and technology have always been the two most important factors necessary to build and support a strong military and, therefore, political influence. The secret of the strength of great conquerors such as Alexander the Great, Genghis Khan, and Pizarro was that they had access to advanced military technologies. The hegemony by Europeans in the eighteenth and nineteenth centuries was, of course, made possible by a superior military organization supported by superior economies and technologies.

After two disastrous world wars in the twentieth century, and for the first time in history, there is a general agreement that every nation in the world has a right to exist and to be independent regardless of its military strength. Military aggression based on ethnocentric motives has been clearly denounced. However, since there is no absolute guarantee of adherence to these principles, nations remain suspicious of one another. Thus military competition continues to flourish in today's world. In addition, a well-developed economy and advanced technology still continue to be the two most important factors necessary for building and supporting a strong military and maintaining strong political influence.

Another feature of the world after World War II is that demands from the public for an improved quality of life have become increasingly intense. The popularity of movies and television and an increase in overseas travel have enabled the general public to see and compare their own quality of life with those in other countries. Lerner (1958) describes how "rising expectations" created by mass media gradually led to "rising frustrations" in the Middle East. Thus since World War II economic strength has been important not only in building and supporting a strong military but also in raising the standard of living and increasing the welfare of the general public. Similarly, post-World War II technologies have been important not only for military applications but also for strengthening the economy and increasing public welfare. Thus the military, political influence, the economy, and technology are the four most important areas in which most nations, if not all nations, cannot avoid competing with each other. These are the same areas in which Japanese novelist Natsume (1911b) suggested 80 years ago that if you don't join the competition, you may preserve your past but you will lose your present and your future.

On the other hand, there are many cultural items that usually do not provoke international competition in this (presumably) postcolonialist era. Religion, language, customs, ways of living and doing things, values, arts, and political and legal systems are examples. In these areas there are only differences, not ranks. It is also in these areas that the concepts of Japanese "modernization" and "Westernization" need to be distinguished. Basically, modernization can be considered the acceptance of a more successful competitive strategy. Westernization is the acceptance or imitation of Western cultural characteristics in noncompetitive cultural areas. In this reasoning, Japan's military, economic, or technological achievements per se are not Westernization. Japan's adoption of Western parliamentary democracy, however, certainly is. Modernization and Westernization are both cultural change, but the two are conceptually different.[16]

International flows of information occur through the following mechanisms:

(1) Each major nation tries to occupy a respectable position in the international ranking in competitive areas of culture.
(2) In efforts to climb the ladder of international ranking in competitive areas, every nation tends to learn from and imitate the countries that occupy higher positions in the international ranking.
(3) Every nation needs information about its competitors or rivals. Surveillance is needed for such countries.
(4) The countries competing for more political influence tend to propagandize their philosophies and policies.

Because of the first and second mechanisms in this list, late starters imitate advanced countries, thinking that some of the cultural characteristics of the advanced countries may be prerequisite to economic and technological development. They imitate more advanced countries, often blindly, not only in competitive areas but also in noncompetitive areas. This is one reason information flows from the countries whose rankings in competitive areas are higher to those whose rankings are lower.

In the third and fourth processes listed above also, information tends to flow from the countries whose rankings in competitive areas are higher to those whose rankings are lower. As discussed above, there are several competitive areas, therefore there are several kinds of rankings. This diversity explains why Japanese newspaper coverage of China exceeds Chinese newspaper coverage of Japan. Japan's ranking is higher than China's in the fields of economy and technology but lower in the fields of political influence and military.

This theory also explains the "access imbalance" problem that Japan has with the United States and the European community. The United States and Western European countries need more information about the latest developments in Japanese science and technology to cope with competition from Japan. But these countries complain that the information they need is not easily accessible in Japan. Whether by design or happenstance, the competitive value of information is recognized in the complaint.

Finally, the theory explains why some Japanese television programs, such as *Oshin*, sold well in Asia and in other countries that have serious economic problems. These programs were considered to be helpful in those countries' economic development efforts.

CONCLUSIONS

In this chapter, the process of Japan's change from information importer to information exporter in the fields of news reporting and popular culture has been described. In addition, the factors and mechanisms of this change have been discussed. It was confirmed that there were many factors that caused imbalanced international flows, and that they differed from one kind of information to another.

In the case of news flows, it was suggested that the most important factor that changed Japan from an importer to an exporter was the increase of Japan's influence on other countries' economy and politics. In the case of flows of popular culture, Japan's change from an importer to an exporter was brought about by a decrease in the import and share of foreign cultural products and an increase in the export of Japanese products. It was suggested that major factors that reduced the share of foreign cultural products were (a) a strengthening of the mass media infrastructure, including the advertising industry, and (b) the existence of cultural peculiarity, which functions as a barrier against foreign cultural products. Important factors that contributed to the increase of export programs were, in the case of Japan, well-prepared strategies for export such as the production of programs specially made for foreign markets, careful market research, investigation of foreign audience tastes, and purchase of, or investment in, foreign television systems.

The influence of Japan's change on Japanese cultural identity was also considered. A cultural identity crisis occurred twice in modern Japan, in the late nineteenth century and immediately after World War II. These two crises, however, were overcome by different processes and approaches — the first by a regression to medieval militaristic tradition and anti-Western policies, and the second by economic and technological development powerful enough to "absorb" and "incorporate" parts of Western civilization into the modern Japanese or East Asian civilization.

Finally, two existing theories on international information flows (i.e., the media imperialism and dependency theories and the theory of "free competition in free markets") were examined, and their strengths and deficiencies were discussed. As a supplement to these theories, the influence of political and economic competition among nations on international flows of information was considered.

Japan has provided many valuable "exceptions" to social theories developed in the West. Instead of treating Japan as an "embarrassing exception," social scientists must face up to and tackle the theoretical implications of historical facts about Japan, because Taiwan, South Korea, Singapore, Hong Kong, and China appear to be following in Japan's path.

NOTES

1. Kitatani (1985) surveyed the coverage of Japan by *CBS Evening News* and the coverage of the United States by NHK *News Center Nine* during the months of December 1980 and February, April, June, and August 1981, and found that NHK aired more than 13 times as many stories about the United States as CBS aired about Japan.

2. Estimations of major international news agencies' annual revenue in 1976 were as follows: AP, $100 million; Reuters, $80 million; UPI, $70 million; and AFP, $43 million (Tunstall, 1981, p. 263). The annual budget of Kyodo News Agency in 1976 was 15,669,270,000 yen (about $62 million at the exchange rate at that time). The budget of Kyodo in the 1987 fiscal year (April 1987-March 1988) was about 31,750,000,000 yen (or about $244 million at the present rate of exchange).

3. Revenues from overseas services in 1976 were about 80% at Reuters and 25% at UPI and AP (Tunstall, 1981, p. 260).

4. This was a statement made by Toshio Horikawa, a former executive director of Kyodo News Agency, at a lecture organized by the Institute for Communications Research, Keio University, on November 13, 1981.

5. Mulugetta and Miller (1985) studied the relationship between the volume of international news flow and (a) GNP of a reported country, (b) the total value of the annual trade between a reporting and a reported nation, (c) the strength of military relationship, (d) geographical proximity, and (e) cultural proximity using multiple regression analysis. They found GNP to be a strong significant determinant of foreign news coverage.

6. At that time, the ideas that underpinned the "New World Information Order" debate had not emerged, and most Japanese were indifferent to excessive importation of American programs. Therefore, Japan did not adopt any policy that restricted the broadcasting of foreign television programs.

7. *Little House on the Prairie* is an exception. Although it was treated as a children's program and telecast during the time band aimed mainly at children (6:00-6:45), average ratings were about 10%.

8. The same kind of balance holds for books and magazines. Japan imports many serious specialized books on science, the arts, technology, literature, and other "high-quality culture" and enthusiastically translates them. At the same time, Japanese editions of *Playboy* and *Penthouse* magazines enjoy commercial success. However, foreign books and magazines, and their translations, that do not fit in either of these two extreme categories are not easily available in Japan. Japan Reader's Digest Co. went bankrupt in 1985 after many years of financial losses.

9. Some people claim that enka originated in Korea. Although this is probably wrong, there is no doubt that traditional Korean folk songs made some contribution to the development of enka.

10. For discussion of "cultural invasion" problems between the United States and Canada, see Lee (1980, chap. 4).

11. For discussion of "cultural invasion" problems between Japan and Korea, see J. Kim (1973), P. Kim (1973), and Shin (1973). These works are in Korean; Japanese translations are in Shibuya (1973).

12. As of February 1989, the Oshin fad still continues in Iran. All kinds of Oshin goods, with pictures of Oshin on them — from socks, rubber boots, and toys to key rings, shirts, and pants — are sold

all over Iran. On a special radio program broadcast on the "women's day" that commemorates the birthday of Mohammed's daughter Fatima, a woman said that an ideal woman for her was Oshin. An interviewer asked her what she thought of Fatima, and she said that Fatima was a woman of 1,400 years ago and could not be an ideal for women of today. Ayotollah Khomeini was offended by this statement and ordered the president of the national broadcasting corporation to punish those who were responsible for the program. A few days later, three program directors and their supervisor were sentenced to four to five years of imprisonment and 50 lashes. However, they were pardoned later (*Asahi Shimbun*, 1989; *Sankei Shimbun*, 1988, 1989).

13. There are a considerable number of Japanese who resent the Westernization of Japanese units of measurement of length, weight, space, and so on, the ways of writing names and addresses (when written in Roman letters), and especially the convention of adding commas to large numbers. Many Japanese feel that they have been inconvenienced as a result of the Westernization of standards, and protests and complaints appear from time to time in newspapers and magazines. See, for example, a newspaper article by Honda (1980) sensationally titled "Prevailing Colonial Cultures: Possible Loss of National Pride" or Nakada's (1982) article titled "Nonsense of Writing Japanese Addresses in the Western Way."

14. For example, the Dutch merchants were confined in a small area on the coast of Nagasaki City called Deshima. The area was surrounded by high walls, and the gates were guarded by Japanese officers. The Dutch were not allowed to bring their wives, although they were allowed to bring in local women. In order for the Dutch to go out of Deshima, they had to get permission. If they went out, they were placed under strict surveillance by Japanese police officers. The Dutch merchants felt like they were in prison, except that the life inside the walls was a little more comfortable than prison life.

15. Japan was probably the only non-Western country that had mass media before influence from the modern West.

16. The noncompetitive area of a culture with a superior competitive area may or may not directly influence other cultures. The imitation of the noncompetitive area of a culture with a superior competitive area in an effort to strengthen one's own competitive area is an example of direct cultural influence. However, at least a part of the noncompetitive area of a culture with a superior competitive area may be assimilated as a result of a natural cultural adjustment to development in the competitive area. Therefore, countries that are more advanced in the competitive area may seem to influence less advanced countries because they both take a similar road to development. Since the goals in the competitive area are by and large the same among different cultures, some cultural traits will be shared by those cultures in competition sooner or later. For example, punctuality and respect for efficiency are results of adjustment to industrialization rather than causes of it. Therefore, it is not appropriate to say that a nation was "Westernized" because people became more punctual and efficiency conscious than in the past. For further discussions on cultural change, see Ito (1988).

REFERENCES

Akagi, O. (1985, July 25). Tai no Nihon buum [Japan boom in Thailand]. *Asahi Shimbun*.

Armstrong, R. E. (1982). The American media and news about Japan and American/Japanese relations. *Keio Communication Review, 3*, 75-86.

Baran, P. (1957). *The political economy of growth*. New York: Monthly Review Press.

Beltran, S.L.R. (1978). Communication and cultural domination: USA-Latin American case. *Media Asia, 5*(4), 183-192.

Beltran, S.L.R., & Fox de Cardona, E. (1977). Latin-America and the U.S.: Flaws in the free flow of information. In J. Richstad (Ed.), *New perspectives in international communication* (pp. 85-127). Honolulu: East-West Center.

Burger, G. M. (1974). Ajia shin chitsujo no yume [Dream of a new order in Asia]. In S. Sato & R. Dingman (Eds.), *Kindai Nippon no taigai taido* (pp. 93-122). Tokyo: Tokyo Daigaku Shuppan-kai.

CULCON. (1974). *Communications gap and mass media: Television.* Report prepared for the Seventh United States-Japan Conference on Cultural and Educational Interchange, Tokyo.

Frank, A. G. (1969). *Latin America: Underdevelopment or revolution.* New York: Monthly Review Press.

Frank, A. G. (1979). *Dependent accumulation and underdevelopment.* New York: Monthly Review Press.

Galtung, J., & Ruge, M. H. (1970). The structure of foreign news. In J. Tunstall (Ed.), *Media sociology* (pp. 259-298). Urbana: University of Illinois Press.

Goonasekera, A. (1987). The influence of television on cultural values: With special reference to Third World countries. *Media Asia, 14*(1), 7-12.

Gunji ryoku ni ginen nokoru [Still apprehend Japan's military strength]. (1987, August 15). *Asahi Shimbun.*

Hashikawa, B. (1976). *Kohka monogatari* [Yellow peril]. Tokyo: Chikuma Shoboh.

Hester, A. (1973). Theoretical considerations in predicting volume and direction of international information flow. *Gazette, 19,* 239-247.

Honda, K. (1980, February 25). Shokuminchi bunka no oukou: Minzokuteki hokori ushinau osore [Prevailing colonial cultures: Possible loss of national pride]. *Asahi Shimbun,* p. 1.

Horie, Y. (1965). Modern entrepreneurship in Meiji Japan. In W. W. Lockwood (Ed.), *The state and economic enterprise in Japan* (pp. 183-208). Princeton, NJ: Princeton University Press.

Idid, S. A., & Hasim, M. S. (1986). *Gatekeepers and audience: Two neglected actors in international news flow study.* Paper presented at the First Canberra Conference on International Communication, Canberra College of Advanced Education, Canberra, Australia.

Ishige, N. (1987). I to shoku to juh to [Clothing, eating and housing]. In T. Sofue (Ed.), *Nihonjin wa dou kawattaka* (pp. 33-48). Tokyo: Nihon Hoso Shuppan Kyokai.

Ito, Y. (1988, March). *International competition and domestic harmony as driving forces of social and cultural change in Japan.* Paper presented at the conference "Japan and Europe: Looking Towards the 21st Century," Brussels.

Ito, Y., & Kochevar, J. (1983). Factors accounting for the flow of international communication. *Keio Communication Review, 4,* 13-37.

Ito, Y., & Kochevar, J. (1984). Terebi bangumino kokusaikan no nagare no kitei youin ni kansuru kenkyuu [A study on the factors determining the international flow of TV programs]. In *Kenkyu hokoku: Hoso ni kansuru horitsu, keizai, shakai bunkateki kenkyuu chousa* (pp. 98-107). Tokyo: Hoso Bunka Foundation.

Kariel, H. G., & Rosenvall, L. A. (1983). Cultural affinity displayed in Canadian daily newspapers. *Journalism Quarterly, 60,* 431-436.

Kato, H. (1976). Global instantaneousness and instant globalism: The significance of popular culture in developing countries. In W. Schramm & D. Lerner (Eds.), *Communication and change: The last ten years — and the next* (pp. 253-258). Honolulu: University of Hawaii Press.

Katz, E. (1977). Can authentic culture survive new media? *Journal of Communication, 27*(2), 113-121.

Katz, E., & Wedell, G. (1977). *Broadcasting in the Third World.* Cambridge, MA: Harvard University Press.

Kawatake, K. (1982a, April). Hoso wo chuushin to suru joho no kokusai koryuu [International information exchange through broadcasting]. *Kokusai Denki Tsuushin to Nippon,* pp. 3-18.

Kawatake, K. (1982b). A week of TV news: A comparative study of TV news in eight countries. *Studies of Broadcasting, 18,* 51-68.

Kim, J. (1973). Nihon shoku no hanran [Overpresence of Japanese culture in Korea]. In S. Shibuya (Ed.), *Minami Chosen no hannichi ron* (pp. 136-148). Tokyo: Saimaru Shappankai.

Kim, J. (1986, October). *The movie industry in South Korea: A Hollywood stepchild?* Paper presented at the Third Communication Forum, Tokyo.

Kim, P. (1973). Shintou suru Nihon bunka [Penetration of Japanese culture in Korea]. In S. Shibuya (Ed.), *Minami Chosen no hannichi ron* (pp. 97-113). Tokyo: Saimaru Shappankai.

Kitatani, K. (1985). A content analysis of television news flow between Japan and the United States: Another one-way street? *Keio Communication Review, 6*, 55-68.

Komota, N., Yazawa, T., Shimada, Y., & Yokozawa, C. (1980). *Nihon ryukokashi* [History of Japanese popular songs]. Tokyo: Shakaishiso-sha.

Lee, C. (1980). *Media imperialism reconsidered: The homogenizing of television culture.* Beverly Hills, CA: Sage.

Lee, K., & Kang, H. (1982). International news flow: Testing the distance hypothesis. *Hanyang Communication Review, 3*, 133-146.

Lee, O. (1982). *"Chijimi" shiko no nihonjin* ["Contraction"-oriented Japanese]. Tokyo: Gakusei-sha.

Lerner, D. (1958). *The passing of traditional society.* Glencoe, IL: Free Press.

Liu, U. C., & Gunarantne, S. A. (1972). Foreign news in two Asian dailies. *Gazette, 18.*

Lyle, J., Ogawa, D., & Thomas, J. D. (1986). Japanese programs in the United States: A widening window on another culture. *Keio Gijuku Daigaku Shimbun Kenkyuujo Nempo, 27*, 1-18.

Marshall, B. K. (1967). *Capitalism and nationalism in prewar Japan: The ideology of the business elite, 1968-1941.* Stanford, CA: Stanford University Press.

Mattelart, A. (1973). Mass media and the socialist revolution: The experience of Chile. In G. Gerbner, L. P. Gross, & W. II. Melody (Eds.), *Communications technology and social policy: Understanding the new "cultural revolution"* (pp. 425-440). New York: John Wiley.

Menon, V. (1985). Information flow in Asia: An overview. *Media Asia, 12*(2), 63-66.

Mercado, O. S., & Buck, E. B. (1981). Media imperialism in Philippine television. *Media Asia, 8*(2), 93-99.

Ministry of International Trade and Industry. (1963). *Eiga sangyo hakusyo* [White paper on motion pictures]. Tokyo: Author.

Ministry of Posts and Telecommunications. (1978). *Tsuushin hakusho* [White paper on communications]. Tokyo: Ohkurashou Insatsukyoku.

Mowlana, H. (1986). *Global information and world communication.* New York: Longman.

Mulugetta, Y. M., & Miller, M. (1985). Government control of the press and factors influencing international news flow: Comparative study of the Indian, Japanese and Korean press. *Keio Communication Review, 6*, 69-84.

Nakada, Y. (1982, June 7). Nihon dewa muimi na gaikokushiki juusho [Nonsense of writing Japanese addresses in the Western way]. *Sankei Shimbun*, p. 8.

Natsume, S. (1908). *Sanshiro.* Tokyo: Iwanami Bunko.

Natsume, S. (1911a). Gendai nihon no kaika [Civilization of modern Japan]. In *Souseki bunmeiron shu* (pp. 7-38). Tokyo: Iwanami Bunko.

Natsume, S. (1911b). Mahdokku sensei no "nihon rekishi" [Professor Murdock's "Japanese history"]. In *Souseki bunmeiron shu* (pp. 227-238). Tokyo: Iwanami Bunko.

Ohkawa, K., & Rosovsky H. (1965). A century of Japanese economic growth. In W. W. Lockwood (Ed.), *The state and economic enterprise in Japan* (pp. 47-92). Princeton, NJ: Princeton University Press.

Oshin: Senjikano Iran de ninki bakuhatsu [Oshin boom in Iran under the war regime]. (1988, January 22). *Hochi Shimbun*, p. 19.

Ostgaard, E. (1965). Factors influencing the flow of news. *Journal of Peace Research, 2*, 45-63.

Pool, I. de S. (1977a). The changing flow of television. *Journal of Communication, 27*, 139-149.

Pool, I. de S. (1977b). Technological advances and the future of international broadcasting. *Studies of Broadcasting, 13*, 17-31.

Pool, I. de S. (1979). The influence of international communication on development. *Media Asia, 6*(3), 149-156.

Read, W. H. (1976). *America's mass media merchants.* Baltimore: Johns Hopkins University Press.

Reischauer, E. O. (1965). *The United States and Japan* (3rd ed.). Cambridge, MA: Harvard University Press.

Reischauer, E. O. (1977). *The Japanese.* Cambridge, MA: Harvard University Press.

Research Institute of the Japan Newspaper Publishers and Editors Association. (1979). Gaikoku kankei kiji ni kansuru shimen chosa [A foreign news survey]. *Shimbun Kenkyu, 340*, 79-91.

Research Institute of the Japan Newspaper Publishers and Editors Association. (1981). *Kokusai joho no hodo jokyo chosa sogo hokokusyo* [Comprehensive research report on the coverage of international information]. Tokyo: JNPEA.

Research Institute of the Japan Newspaper Publishers and Editors Association. (1984a). "Kokusai nyuusu" no hohdoh johkyo: Nichi, bei, asean sougo hohdoh chosa yori [The state of the art of "international news" reporting: From mutual surveys among Japan, the United States and ASEAN]. *Nihon Shimbun Kyokai Kenkyuujo Nempo, 6,* 1-47.

Research Institute of the Japan Newspaper Publishers and Editors Association. (1984b). *Nichi, bei, asean sohgo hohdoh chohsa chuukan hohkoku: Kakkoku shimbun, tuushinsha no kokusai hohdoh johkyo* [An interim report on the research of mutual reporting among Japan, the United States and ASEAN: The state of the art of international news reporting by newspapers and wire services in these countries]. Tokyo: JNPEA.

Richeri, G. (1982). Japanese TV programmes in Italy. In *International Television Flow Project—Japan* (pp. 36-38). Tokyo: NHK Public Opinion Research Institute.

Robinson, G. J., & Sparks, V. M. (1976). International news in the Canadian and American press: A comparative news flow study. *Gazette, 22,* 203-218.

Saikin warushawa fuuzoku [Recent fashion in Warsaw]. (1985, November 30). *Yomiuri Shimbun,* p. 7.

Salinas, R., & Paldan, L. (1979). Culture in the process of dependent development: Theoretical perspectives. In K. Nordenstreng & H. I. Schiller (Eds.), *National sovereignty and international communication* (pp. 82-98). Norwood, NJ: Ablex.

Sata, K. (1982). Animation programme exports. In *International Television Flow Project—Japan* (pp. 63-65). Tokyo: NHK Public Opinion Research Institute.

Sato, S. (1974). Bakumatsu, Meiji shoki ni okeru taigai ishiki no shoruikei [Patterns of attitudes toward foreign countries in the late Tokugawa and early Meiji period]. In S. Sato & R. Dingman (Eds.), *Kindai Nippon no taigai taido* [Attitudes toward foreign countries in modern Japan] (pp. 1-34). Tokyo: Tokyo Daigaku Shuppan-kai.

Sauvant, K. P. (1979). Sociocultural emancipation. In K. Nordenstreng & H. I. Schiller (Eds.), *National sovereignty and international communication* (pp. 9-20). Norwood, NJ: Ablex.

Schiller, H. I. (1969). *Mass communication and American empire.* New York: Kelly.

Schiller, H. I. (1973a). Authentic national development versus the free flow of information and the new communications technology. In G. Gerbner, L. P. Gross, & W. H. Melody (Eds.), *Communications technology and social policy: Understanding the new "cultural revolution"* (pp. 467-480). New York: John Wiley.

Schiller, H. I. (1973b). *The mind managers.* Boston: Beacon.

Schiller, H. I. (1976). *Communication and cultural domination.* White Plains, NY: International Arts and Sciences Press.

Schiller, H. I. (1979). Transnational media and national development. In K. Nordenstreng & H. I. Schiller (Eds.), *National sovereignty and intercultural communication* (pp. 21-32) New York: John Wiley.

Schramm, W. (1964). *Mass media and national development.* Stanford, CA: Stanford University Press.

Schramm, W. (1980). Circulation of news in the Third World: A study of Asia. In G. C. Wilhoit & H. de Bock (Eds.), *Mass communication review yearbook* (Vol. 1, pp. 589-619). Beverly Hills, CA: Sage.

Schramm, W., & Atwood, L. E. (1981). *Circulation of news in the Third World: A study of Asia.* Hong Kong: Chinese University of Hong Kong Press.

Sekai no shakaimen: Iran [Societies in the world: Iran]. (1987, December 15). *Sankei Shimbun.*

Shibuya, S. (Ed. & Trans.). (1973). *Minami Chosen no hannichi ron* [Anti-Japanism in South Korea]. Tokyo: Saimaru Shuppankai.

Shimizu, S. (1988). Terebi dorama wo chuushinto shita kokusai kohryuu [International exchange through television programs]. *Joho Tsushin Gakkai-shi, 5*(4), 54-57.

Shin, I. (1973). Teikokushugi Nihon no seishin shinryaku [Intellectual invasion by imperialistic Japan]. In S. Shibuya (Ed.), *Minami Chosen no hannichi ron* [Anti-Japanism in South Korea] (pp. 159-174). Tokyo: Saimaru Shuppankai.

Somavia, J. (1976). Transnational power structure and international information. *Media Asia, 3*(3), 149-158.

Sommerlad, E. L. (1977). Free flow of information, balance, and the right to communicate. In J. Richstad (Ed.). *New perspectives in international communication* (pp. 22-32). Honolulu: East-West Center.

Sparks, V. M. (1978). The flow of news between Canada and the United States. *Journalism Quarterly, 55*, 260-268.

Sreberny-Mohammadi, A. (1984). The "world of the news" study: Result of international cooperation. In M. Gurevitch & M. R. Levy (Eds.), *Mass communication review yearbook* (Vol. 5, pp. 613-625). Beverly Hills, CA: Sage.

Stevenson, R. L. (1984). Pseudo debate. In M. Gurevitch & M. R. Levy (Eds.), *Mass communication review yearbook* (Vol. 5, pp. 626-630). Beverly Hills, CA: Sage.

Stevenson, R. L., & Shaw, D. L. (Eds.). (1984). *Foreign news and the new world information order.* Ames. Iowa State University Press.

Sugiyama, M. (1982a). Nihon wo chuushin to suru terebi bangumi no kokusai furoo [TV programs coming into and going out of Japan]. *NHK Hoso Bunka Kenkyu Nempo, 27*, 225-269.

Sugiyama, M. (1982b). Television programme imports. In *International Television Flow Project — Japan* (pp. 7-24). Tokyo: NHK Public Opinion Research Institute.

Takashima, H. (1988, February 21). "Oshin" ninki: Nihon eiga to dorama kaigai hankyou samazama ["Oshin" boom: Reputations of Japanese films and television dramas in foreign countries]. *Sankei Shimbun.*

Tominaga, K. (1987). *Shakai kohzoh to shakai hendoh* [Social structure and social change]. Tokyo: Nihon Hoso Shuppan Kyokai.

Tsui, A., Lau, A., & Choi, A. (1975). Hong Kong's strong preference for local productions. *Media Asia, 2*(2), 117-121.

Tunstall, J. (1977). *The media are American.* New York: Columbia University Press.

Tunstall, J. (1981). Worldwide news agencies: Private wholesalers of public information. In J. Richstad & M. Anderson (Eds.), *Crisis in international news: Policies, and prospects* (pp. 258-267). New York: Columbia University Press.

Varis, T. (1973). *International inventory of television programme structure and the flow of TV programmes between nations.* Tampere, Finland: University of Tampere, Institute of Journalism and Mass Communication.

Wallerstein, I. (1974). *The modern world system.* New York: Academic.

Wu, M. (1987, November). *Broadcasting: The question of television drama.* Paper presented at the Fourth Communication Forum, Tokyo.

Yamamoto, T. (1980). Eiga [Motion pictures] In A Yamamoto & A. Fujitake (Eds.), *Zusetsu nihon no masu komyunikeishon.* Tokyo: Nihon Hoso Shuppan Kyokai.

Yomiuri Shimbun-sha. (1959). *Nihon no rekishi* [The history of Japan] (Vol. 8). Tokyo: Author.

The Competitive Theory of International Communication

MAJID TEHRANIAN
University of Hawaii

T HERE seems to be no news in the news that news follows trade and influence. But Youichi Ito's chapter brings a new and challenging perspective to that "common sense." By a detailed examination of the Japanese case in comparative perspective, Ito touches on a wide-ranging set of theoretical, empirical, and policy issues in international communication.

THEORETICAL PERSPECTIVES

Ito's "competitive theory" of international communication attempts to assume a middle ground between the "free flow" and "media imperialism" doctrines. But, as its label suggests, the theory comes closer to the central propositions of the free-flow perspective. In fact, the chapter may be considered a refutation of the main contentions of the media imperialism school.

For the past two decades, international communication scholars and professionals have been polarized in a debate between these two doctrines. The proponents of the "free-flow doctrine" have employed a dual strategy for the justification and explication of the existing world imbalances in information flows. The normative strategy has relied on a commitment to the "free flow of information" doctrine as embodied in the United Nations and UNESCO charters. However, to explicate and rationalize the existing imbalances, the empirical strategy has relied on the classical theory of international trade. As the centerpiece in that theory, the doctrine of comparative advantage is invoked to argue that countries will tend to import those media products that they cannot make as well or as cheaply at home. Ergo, the "media are American" (Tunstall, 1977) because it has historically proved

Correspondence and requests for reprints: Majid Tehranian, Department of Communication, 2560 Campus Road, Room 337, University of Hawaii at Manoa, Honolulu, HI 96822.

Communication Yearbook 13, pp. 466-472

cheaper to import higher-quality U.S. media products than to produce them at home at higher cost and lower quality. Economies of scale, scope, and status in producing for a larger English-speaking world consuming a variety of complementary media products that enjoy a global cultural status have historically given Anglo-American media producers a comparative advantage over other countries. Therefore, government intervention to correct existing imbalances not only goes against the economic laws of supply and demand, it is politically pernicious. In the name of some vague notions of cultural identity and autonomy, government intervention threatens the free flow in the world marketplace of ideas. So goes the main thread of the free-flow arguments.

Ito goes a step or two further in implicitly supporting these arguments. The effective entry of Japan into the world media markets, Ito argues, demonstrates that — contrary to the contentions of the media imperialism school — a periphery nation can in fact become a center nation *culturally* as well as economically. The economic success of Japan has paved the way for such diverse Japanese cultural exports as "management style," television serials (notably *Oshin*), music (notably *enka*), and comic books. Despite the handicaps of an intractable language barrier, Japan is thus exporting its national values of hard work, perseverance, and achievement through these cultural products.

Ito's competitive theory of international information flows provides a key to the understanding of this remarkable phenomenon. By making a distinction between the competitive sector (production of goods and services) and the noncompetitive sector (cultural patterns of identity) of national life, Ito puts forth the following three propositions:[1]

(1) Every nation attempts to achieve world preeminence in its competitive sectors.
(2) Every nation attempts to establish a harmony between its competitive and noncompetitive sectors.
(3) Every nation attempts to borrow those cultural traits of other nations that could contribute to the strengthening of its own competitive sector.

These three propositions are clearly borne out by the Japanese historical experience of modernization. Ever since the Meiji Restoration of 1868, Japan has attempted to achieve preeminence in the competitive sectors of international life by adopting imitations of the West. It has succeeded remarkably well in the economic sector, but it has failed in the political and military sectors and is currently restrained by the memories of that failure. But Japan has achieved its economic preeminence largely by maintaining a balance between increasing its productivity and preserving its unique cultural identity. In the meantime, as Japanese economic successes have become more manifest, other nations have attempted to borrow those Japanese cultural traits that might strengthen their own competitive sectors. The success of Japanese media products is thus due not only to their higher quality and lower cost but also to the messages and values they contain. As Ito shows, this success has proved somewhat uneven. In sectors where language is a barrier, such as news gathering and dissemination (e.g., the Kyodo News Agency), the Japanese have not been as successful as in sectors that are relatively language free, such as audiovisual media (e.g., music, film, and television).

But Ito's "competitive theory" begins to falter when it tries to be a general comparative theory. True enough, some other East Asian countries, such as South Korea, Taiwan, Hong Kong, and Singapore, have already shown an ability to emulate the pattern of Japanese economic and cultural successes at exports. But once we broaden the scope of analysis to the rest of the world, factors other than success in the competitive sector seem to explain cultural exports better. India has been the world's largest producer and exporter of motion pictures not because of any particular economic or military success but because of the economies of scale and low marginal costs it can obtain from film production in its own large market and because of a cultural affinity that it enjoys with the rest of South Asia (Narula & Pearce, 1986). Brazil and Mexico are large-scale exporters of television programs (notably *telenovelas*) to the rest of Latin America fundamentally for the same reasons (Katz & Wedell, 1977; Shinar & Dias, 1977). Egypt is the cultural mecca and the major media exporter of the Arab world not because it is admired for its economic growth or political achievements but because (a) it has been historically the seat of Arab learning, (b) it has the largest population in the Arab world, and (c) it has consequently enjoyed economies of scale, scope, and status in media productions (Boyd, 1982).

More generally in the Third World, we cannot realistically hold the promise of a distant "economic miracle" as bait for the opening of the national gates to an overflow of external messages (Tehranian, 1987). The example of Japan, in fact, demonstrates the compelling need for a period of self-isolation. The foundations of the Meiji Restoration and its modernization program were laid during the preceding two and a half centuries of Tokugawa peace and isolation, during which Japan approached the status of a unified and fairly well-integrated nation. Even the Meiji "opening" to the West was measured and calculated to transfer Western science and technology without endangering Japanese national autonomy and cultural integrity (Tehranian, 1984). The Soviet Union and China have also followed similar patterns of self-imposed isolation. The foundations for Soviet heavy industry were laid under Stalin from 1927 to 1941, during which a desperate effort was made to achieve the status of an industrial socialist bastion to face the threat from the West. Following its communist revolution, China also went into a period of isolation that was further intensified, in the 1960s, by the rupture of its relations with the Soviet Union. Economic self-reliance and cultural autonomy and identity were the chief objectives and achievements of all these national periods of self-isolation.

Although Ito does not suggest it, one possible implication of his competitive theory of international information flows is the recommendation of an open-door policy for the less developed countries (LDCs). If so, then, the theory is flying in the face of historical realities. To open up the gates to global advertising, whether of a direct or indirect kind (via Western TV serials), is tantamount to whetting consumer appetites at a stage of primitive accumulation that requires high national savings and investment. Again, the example of Japan and the newly industrializing countries (the NICs) is most instructive. South Korea, for example, has been saving about 33% of its national income for the past three decades in order to achieve an annual average growth rate of about 8%. Japan's rate of savings is currently about half that rate, but it has been historically high. It is only now, under considerable international pressure, that Japan is beginning to shift from a policy of high savings and investment to a policy of encouraging imports and consumption (see *The Economist*, February 1988). The countries that have followed an open-door strategy of development, such as prerevolutionary Cuba, Iran, and Nicaragua as well as present-day Philippines, Brazil, Egypt, and India, opened themselves up to the social and political contradictions of dualism. In such situations, the development of a modern sector and bourgeoisie is accompanied by the underdevelopment of an increasingly marginalized traditional sector that is the breeding ground for a social revolt against the modern sector and its global support systems.

EMPIRICAL FINDINGS AND POLICY IMPLICATIONS

Ito's empirical contributions are found mainly in his analysis of the Japanese transition from media importer to media exporter. In the process, however, he identifies certain information and cultural policy problems for closer scrutiny. These policy problems may be more explicitly labeled as (a) information flow imbalance, (b) information access imbalance, and (c) cultural influence imbalance. In these three areas, Japan once again proves to be more of an exception than a rule in the total world picture.

First and foremost, much like the rest of the Third World, Japan has historically experienced an information flow imbalance with the West. In 1961, "the ratio between the coverage of the U.S. by Japanese newspapers and the coverage of Japan by American newspapers was about 16:1" (Schramm, 1964, p. 60). Ito argues that coverage of Japan by the Western media has dramatically improved in recent years. While the news flow seems to have reached somewhat of a balance with France, England, and West Germany, Japan continues to have an imbalance with the Soviet Union (5.8:1), United States (4.9:1), and China (2.7:1) (as quoted by Ito from studies by the Research Institute of the Japan Newspaper Publishers and Editors Association, 1979, 1981). Although hard evidence is lacking, the flow imbalance with the Third World appears to favor Japan.

Ito acknowledges the importance of geographic proximity (United States/ Canada, India/Pakistan), cultural affinity (United States/United Kingdom, Japan/ China), and mass media infrastructures, but he argues that the decisive factor in news flows consists of political and economic influence. By this token, Japan's increasing worldwide prominence in news flows should occasion no surprise. But media attention can be obtained by both "positive" and "negative" influence. The

Middle East receives a good deal of world media attention not because of its positive economic and political achievements but because of conflicts generated over this economically and strategically important region. However, the "bad news syndrome" seems to be at work in both the Japanese and the Middle Eastern cases. Neither Japan nor the Middle East would have attracted as much attention from the Western media if they were not posed as threats to Western economic and strategic interests.

Second, Japan faces an information access imbalance problem vis-à-vis the West. Due to its linguistic and cultural barriers, Japan appears less accessible to the West than vice versa. This problem has given rise to bitter complaints in the United States and Western Europe that due to the "closed" nature of Japanese society, scientific and technological information flows have been largely one way — from the West to Japan. It is maintained that this has given Japan an "unfair" competitive advantage. Although Ito does not examine this problem in detail, he suggests that increasing coverage of Japan by the Western media in all fields may redress some aspects of this problem. Access to information is, however, a larger international flow problem. Countries with advanced technological capabilities in information gathering, storage, and retrieval (e.g., satellite remote sensing, large data bases, value-added networks, computer data processing) enjoy a decisive advantage over countries with little or no access to these facilities. The issue of information access imbalance is thus related to both scientific and technological development of a country as well as to the "closed" or "open" nature of society. So long as Japan was considered an "imitator," few complained about the "closed" nature of its society. Now that Japan has achieved the status of an "innovator," information access has become a pressing policy problem.

Third, Japanese exports of popular culture are posing a "cultural influence flow" policy problem. Ito seems to agree with Lyle, Ogawa, and Thomas (1986) that American culture is achieving a "supranational" character. By adopting the genres of American media productions, other countries can also score success. But Ito's own evidence seems to suggest a different interpretation. The "Oshin boom," the popularity of enka music, and the spread of Japanese comics in East Asia suggest that culture is a unique product. Evidence shows that cultural tastes favor local programming or foreign imports of close cultural affinity. The failure of *Dallas* in Japan points to the first truth, while the success of Indian films and Japanese TV shows and comics in South and East Asia support the second generalization. However, homogenized foreign imports often win over local programs because of their ubiquitousness, lower cost, and higher production quality.

The LDCs are thus faced with three fundamental cultural policy options: assimilation, dissociation, and selective participation (Hamelink, 1983; Tehranian, 1989). Assimilation policy is often assumed by default when an open-door policy allows global advertising and foreign cultural imports to nourish the interests and tastes of a rising comprador bourgeoisie at the expense of autonomous development and indigenous culture. This policy is often followed by peripheral capitalist countries in the Third World that have no autonomous cultural policy (most of

Latin America as well as some parts of Africa and Asia). Dissociation policy is often adopted in the pursuit of a major social revolution (such as those in the Soviet Union, China, Cuba, and Iran) — attempting to consolidate the new regime while purging past foreign cultural influence. Selective participation policy is often assumed as a result of internal pressures for maintaining cultural purity (e.g., Saudi Arabia) or political threats of consumer advertising (e.g., Indonesia), or subsequent to a period of dissociation in order to revitalize the economy (e.g., China since the late 1970s) (Tehranian, 1989).[2]

CONCLUSION

As Ito suggests through the words of Natsume Soseki, it is true that countries that do not confront international competition may preserve their past but may lose their present and future. But it is equally true that countries with undiscriminating open-door policies will destroy not only their infant industries but also their indigenous cultures. Without political independence, economic autonomy, and cultural identity (possibly in that order), no country can compete effectively in this extremely competitive world.

Ito's contribution on Japanese cultural trade demonstrates how Japan has achieved all three objectives in an increasingly interdependent world. His competitive theory of international information flows fits the Japanese case rather well, but it cannot refute the realities of a largely dependent Third World still in throes of a continuing struggle for its political independence, economic self-reliance, and cultural autonomy. Nor can it serve as a recipe for an open-door cultural policy. The lessons of Japan are as follows: (a) Every nation should try to excel, (b) every nation should try to adjust, and (c) every nation should try to adopt (Tehranian, 1988).

NOTES

1. To sharpen the argument, I have taken the liberty of rephrasing Ito's formulations, I hope without distorting them.

2. For a look at the different cultural strategies in Malaysia, Thailand, and China, see Adnan (1987), Boonlue (1987), and Fan (1987).

REFERENCES

Adnan, M. H. (1987). *Advertising: Social and cultural implications—a Malaysian case study*. Paper presented at the Fourth Communication Forum, Tokyo.

Boonlue, T. (1987). *The present state and future of television and video systems in Thailand*. Paper presented at the Fourth Communication Forum, Tokyo.

Boyd, D. (1982). *Broadcasting in the Arab world*. Philadelphia: Temple University Press.

Fan, F. (1987). *Foreign advertising and Japanese TV commercials in Shanghai.* Paper presented at the Fourth Communication Forum, Tokyo.

Hamelink, C. (1983). *Cultural autonomy in global communication: Planning information policy.* New York: Longman.

Katz, E., & Wedell, G. (1977). *Broadcasting in the Third World.* Cambridge, MA: Harvard University Press.

Lyle, J., Ogawa, D., & Thomas, J. D. (1986). Japanese programs in the United States: A widening window on another culture. *Keio Gijuku Daigaku Shimbun Kenkyuujo Nempo, 27,* 1-18.

Narula, U., & Pearce, W. B. (1986). *Development as communication.* Carbondale: Southern Illinois University Press.

Research Institute of the Japan Newspaper Publishers and Editors Association. (1979). Gaikoku kankei kiji ni kansuru shimen chosa [A foreign news survey]. *Shimbun Kenkyu, 340,* 79-91.

Research Institute of the Japan Newspaper Publishers and Editors Association. (1981). *Kokusai joho no hodo jokyo chosa sogo hokokusyo* [Comprehensive research report on the coverage of international information]. Tokyo: JNPEA.

Schramm, W. (1964). *Mass media and national development.* Stanford, CA: Stanford University Press.

Shinar, D., & Dias, M.A.R. (1977). Communications policy in Brazil. In M. Tehranian et al. (Eds.), *Communications policy for national development.* London: Routledge & Kegan Paul.

Tehranian, M. (1984). Communication and revolution in Asia: Western domination and cultural restoration in Japan and Iran. *Keio Communication Review, 3*(3).

Tehranian, M. (1987). *Information technologies and world development: Promises, perils, prospects.* Paper presented at the Fourth Communication Forum, Tokyo.

Tehranian, M. (1988, January 31). Japan's emerging peaceful role in international affairs. *Sunday Star Bulletin & Advertiser.*

Tehranian, M. (1989). *Technologies of power: Information machines and democratic prospects.* Norwood, NJ: Ablex.

Tunstall, J. (1977). *The media are American.* New York: Columbia University Press.

News Media: Frontiers
in International Relations

JASWANT S. YADAVA
Indian Institute of Mass Communication, New Delhi

P ROFESSOR Ito's chapter presents a comprehensive case study of the "embarrassing exception" of Japan in the arena of international news and information flow. He has brought together rich empirical data to show how Japan, an information importer in the 1960s, has emerged as an information exporter in the 1980s. From a position of "periphery," Japan has now moved to the "center" of international flow of news and culture.

Professor Ito has marshaled an enormous amount of evidence from a large number of research studies not only to explain the process of shift over the years but to put in perspective the theoretical and policy debates on international flow of information and influence. He has diligently built a case in support of the "free-flow doctrine" and, in the process, by implication, has demolished the media imperialism and dependency theories.

Professor Ito seems to argue that information imbalance between nations is not the result of so-called media imperialism but of competition between and among nations in a situation of a free marketplace of ideas. Further, "center" or "periphery" positions are not fixed; rather, they can change — as has happened in the case of Japan. The policy implication seems to be that, drawing a lesson or two from the Japanese experience, a Third World country can actually change its position from one of dependence upon media material from the developed Western countries to one of independence; it can even become an exporter of news and information. This move can be achieved particularly by improving the country's edge in such competitive areas as technology, economy, military, and political influence.

So far, so good: Professor Ito's analysis is a typical example of using a positivistic approach and deductive logic to present a neat picture and build a

Correspondence and requests for reprints: Jaswant S. Yadava, Indian Institute of Mass Communication, D-13 Ring Road, South Extension Part II, New Delhi-110049, India.

Communication Yearbook 13, pp. 473-477

convincing case. However, the realities of international information flows are much more complex than they are made out by Ito's analysis. The study of international flows of news and information, like any other area of inquiry in social sciences and policy studies, is influenced by the theoretical perspective and methodological approach the scholar adopts for his or her research, and analysis. This influence is true of Professor Ito's study as well. One has no difficulty in following Ito's analysis and being convinced of his "competitive" thesis if one has an a priori orientation and inclination in favor of the doctrine of the free flow of information.

Ito's presentation throws into relief the strength of the doctrine and elaborates upon its propping mechanism, in a historical perspective in the context of Japan. But how about those who happen to have a different orientation? I, for one, although I admire the efforts made in presenting a comprehensive case study, find it hard to accept fully the theoretical position taken by Ito or the conclusion emerging from his study. Without undermining the merit of the study, I have some conceptual reservations.

To begin with, let us face facts. The international flow of news and information is largely one-way, from the developed West (including the developed East — Japan) to the developing Third World countries. The justification and explication of the existing world imbalances in information flows are sought broadly in the two opposed, if not exclusive, theoretical positions. The proponents of free-flow doctrine, like Ito, while invoking freedom of the press as a basic human right, search for rational "universal" patterns of news and information flows across nations. News is news in all media systems, they argue. Their comparative analyses of international news coverage of newspapers and radio and television networks in countries with different political systems and levels of development are undertaken to bring out common or universal factors that influence news coverage.

They suggest that hot spots of conflicts are news for all news media. Factors such as geographical proximity and ethnic/cultural affinity influence the coverage of news and flow of information. Further, detailed analyses of news flows indicate, as in Ito's chapter, that the economic, technical, and military strengths of a country are a relevant consideration in the country's political influence and hence its centrality in the international flows of news and information. And the positions are not static in the face of dynamic realities of international relationships. Thus, as Ito argues (p. 458), international flow of information occurs through the following mechanisms:

(1) Each major nation tries to occupy a respectable position in the international ranking in competitive areas of culture.
(2) In efforts to climb the ladder of international ranking in competitive areas, every nation tends to learn from and imitate the countries that occupy higher positions in the international ranking.
(3) Every nation needs information about its competitors or rivals. Surveillance is needed for such countries.

(4) The countries competing for more political influence tend to propagandize their philosophies and policies.

While the explication of mechanisms of international flows may be acceptable, the inferences of the above formulation are open to question. The implications of the second and third mechanisms are that seemingly every nation has the necessary initiative and control over its affairs to decide things freely in its own best interest so as to improve its international ranking in competitive areas of culture.

The reality seems to be that most Third World countries are weak in the information game and are not in a position to stand up and decide for themselves what they should learn or imitate from whom and to what purpose. Further, it is true that every nation needs information about its competitors or rivals and surveillance is needed. But, again, the initiative is usually not in their hands. More often than not, the job is done for them by the powerful media systems of the Western world — and the job so done is not always in the best interests of the concerned Third World country.

In the information game, Western, developed societies have tremendous advantages over developing Third World countries. The conduits of Western influence and domination established during the colonial period are still operational and are further strengthened by the recent revolution in communication technologies. The imbalance in the flows not only portrays world realities in a distorted fashion but, more important, creates a geopolitical environment detrimental to Third World political, economic, and cultural interests (Yadava, 1984). There has been a strong belief among many Third World leaders that political freedom from colonial rule is not enough in the context of the prevailing world economic and information order. With such realization increasing, there have been strong demands in international forums for restructuring of economic relations between nations and establishment of a New World Information Order. I need not go into the details of the policy debates in UNESCO and International Telecommunications Union (ITU) that encapsulate all the contradictions in the communication world. The developed, industrialized, Western countries maintain policies that regard information as neutral, as technical, as free flowing. Any check or hindrance to the free flow of news and information is viewed as a threat by most Western leaders and media professionals. On the other hand, leaders and professionals in the nonaligned and developing countries usually do not view information as neutral, but as a vehicle of ideas. As Indira Gandhi said while addressing the Media Conference of the Non-Aligned Movement in New Delhi in 1983, "Not only opinion but news has become a weapon to project images, laudatory or condemnatory according to predetermined strategy" (NAMEDIA, 1983, p. 31). Further, the prologue to the same conference declares that "the information and communication systems with ever increasing technological innovations invade the mind with relentless pressure to inform selectively, to misinform cunningly, and hand disinformation mischievously. The world witnesses an impeded and unbalanced flow of information which threatens culture, life values and world views, which threatens societies themselves hoping to find a place in the sun" (p. 22).

While Japan successfully entered the world cultural market on the strength of its economic and technology effects, the path taken by Japan in the process of its shift from information importer to information exporter may not be easy for other Third World, developing countries to emulate. Even though Japan is likely to continue as a unique example for decades to come, the Japanese experience needs close examination. Ito's analysis suggests that improvements in competitive areas like economic growth and technological innovation and progress are likely to give a country a wider political role and greater influence in world affairs and hence will result in greater news coverage of the country by other country's media systems.

Further, a country's success in competitive areas invokes greater interest in noncompetitive areas of its culture, such as religion, way of life, and ethos. The technological and economic success of Japan evoked greater interest in Japanese culture on the part of many countries, including the United States. This interest led to greater exports of Japanese media material, such as educational television programs dealing with management and work styles, television serials like *Oshin*, music like enka, and comic books.

But influence in world affairs is not exclusively determined by the economic, technological, and military power of a country. India, Egypt, Yugoslavia, and Indonesia as initiators of nonalignment as a policy in world relations in the face of cold war and power-bloc politics drew a lot of media attention, including attention from the Western world. In the Schramm (1964) study quoted by Ito, it could be seen that India occupies the fourth position, with 8% of foreign news in American newspapers, after France (20%), the United Kingdom (22%), and the Soviet Union (25%). Indian coverage was comparatively higher than that of other countries, including Japan, which accounted for only 3% of foreign news. India was certainly not stronger in economic or technological development compared to Japan in 1961. Although little empirical evidence is available, I hypothesize that India is covered fairly well by most of the nonaligned and developing countries — at least this is the impression that many of the Afro-Asian journalism students at Indian Institute of Mass Communication have given me over the years. Among other things, the strength of ideas and ideological position also seems to influence media coverage and international flow of news and information. Today also, India, besides being one of the main leaders of the nonaligned movement, is among the front-ranking advocates of the banning of nuclear arms. Thus besides generally acceptable factors such as proximity, affinity, and technical and economic strength, the relevance of or threat from ideology and policy position also influences international flow of news and information. India gets comparatively more coverage than warranted by its ranking in competitive areas perhaps because of the "relevance" of or perceived "threat" to India's ideological position and stand in world affairs.

Finally, though Ito does not state it clearly, he seems to suggest an open-door policy for other developing countries in their search for greater visibility on the world scene. It is true that such a policy has helped Japan to come to the "center" of the world stage, and is facilitating some other Southeast Asian countries in this direction. True, all nations want to excel. But as long as there are nation-states, the decision regarding what policies and strategies should be adopted to excel should remain with each nation. What some of the developing nonaligned countries are asking is limited insulation and not isolation, so that the power of discretion and choice remains with them. Otherwise, with the revolution in communication technologies, communication "winds" or flows become storms threatening to uproot national identities and obliterate cultural diversities. In the ever-increasingly interdependent world, developing countries want to be linked meaningfully and not just sucked in by more powerful ones. To conclude, as a normative principle, Gandhian ideas can show the way to the developing world in areas of communication revolution and international flows. To quote Mahatma Gandhi: "I do not want my house to be walled in all sides and my windows to be stuffed. I want the cultures of all lands to be blown about my house as freely as possible, but [I] refuse to be blown off my feet by any" (Bose, 1957, p. 298).

REFERENCES

Bose, N. K. (1957). *Selections from Gandhi*. Ahmedabad, India: Navajivan.
NAMEDIA. (1983). *Final report*. New Delhi: Author.
Schramm, W. (1964). *Mass media and national development*. Stanford, CA: Stanford University Press.
Yadava, J. (Ed.). (1984). *Politics of news: Third World perspective*. New Delhi: Concept.

10 Media Industries, Media Consequences: Rethinking Mass Communication

JOSEPH TUROW
University of Pennsylvania

This chapter calls for the movement of research on the creation of mass media materials to a more central position within mass communication scholarship. It argues that the study of mass media industries is critical for disentangling a variety of fundamental issues relating to communication and contemporary life, including questions of media consequences. The chapter proposes a definition of mass communication that emphasizes the process of creation and its social potential. It examines theoretical and methodological issues that grow out of the concept, and presents a case study to show how research on the considerations that shape one medium's fare — television's — is critical to suggesting long-term implications of the medium's cultural products.

T HE past several years have witnessed what Clifford Geertz (1973) calls "the rise of the interpretive turn" in various areas of scholarship. Increasingly, the tendency in many areas of knowledge is to approach people's worlds as social constructions that are constituted and reproduced symbolically through interactions. Scholars from across the university spectrum underscore the importance of understanding "culture." They speak about culture as webs of meaning, organized in terms of symbols. They stress that to study culture means to study social significance — how things, events, and interactions are "constructed" to be "meaningful."

Nowhere is the construction of meaning a more fascinating or important area for exploration than in mass media industries. Investigating mass media industries involves examining the creation of stories for large segments of a society. Members of book publishing companies, greeting card firms, newspaper concerns, and other media organizations go beyond continually creating their own organizational

Correspondence and requests for reprints: Joseph Turow, Annenberg School of Communications, 3620 Walnut Street, University of Pennsylvania, Philadelphia, PA 19104-6220.

Communication Yearbook 13, pp. 478-501

realities. They also continually create visions of the world that reach thousands, even millions, outside their interpersonal reach.

And yet, while the construction of meaning is central to the study of communication, many communication researchers, even those who focus on mass communication, reveal little interest in the way media industries participate in society's creation of its reality. This chapter argues the wrongheadedness of this attitude. My call here is for the movement of research on the creation of media materials to a more central position within mass communication scholarship. In particular, it is my contention that the study of media industries is critical for disentangling a variety of fundamental issues relating to communication and contemporary life, including questions of media consequences.

PROGRESS, PROBLEMS, AND POTENTIAL

The preceding comments are not intended to give the impression that research on media industries has languished. To the contrary, during the past two decades, the amount of research on the considerations that shape mass media materials has far exceeded the amount of research on the subject in the two decades preceding them. Moreover, the output has been broadly based. Work has been done in a number of different industries, using a variety of perspectives, across different levels of analysis.[1]

Nevertheless, it must be said that as an area of study the examination of mass media industries is laboring under a number of severe problems that pose formidable challenges for those who care about its future. A basic difficulty is that, particularly in the United States, the field of mass communication research seems to have split among a large majority that studies the uses and consequences of media, a large minority that examines media content, and a much smaller contingent that explores media organizations. Moreover, many mass communication researchers in the first two camps seem to feel there is little need theoretically or practically to understand media organizations.

One long-standing argument against paying attention to mass media organizations stresses that individuals in an audience place their personal interpretations on the messages that reach them. Thus the important question to ask is not how the material was created in the first place or even what "it" says. Rather, the task is to understand (and try to predict) how individuals use the messages, how the uses relate to the people's interactions with media, and why.

This argument has taken on new wrinkles in recent years as the variety of competitive media dotting the social landscape has grown (see Koughan, 1981-82; Maisel, 1973; Ruben & Lievrow, 1989; Turow, 1985). The contention begins with the idea that mass communication means sending messages to huge numbers of individuals who have little in common. It adds that the traditional mass media — television, radio, newspapers — have been the vehicles through which mass communication has taken place. But it suggests, with channel fragmentation and audience selectivity as waves of the future, the idea of calling television, radio, and newspapers mass media — that is, vehicles that reach huge numbers of faceless individuals — becomes more and more suspect.

Questioning Mass Communication

By extension, the term *mass communication* also becomes suspect. The critics urge that the process of mass communication be considered a fading historical stage in the development of more sophisticated technologies that mediate person-to-person communication. By making mass communication obsolete as a description of contemporary phenomena, the critics hope to focus research attention away from the "mass audience," the process of creating media material, and the material itself. Their goal is to justify attention to what they consider most important about media technologies, from the television to the telephone: the way persons use them to cope with themselves and others in everyday life.

A similar emphasis on the power of individuals in the audience and away from the process of production can be found in writings that approach the mass media from a critical tradition. This is a disconcerting development, for thinkers adopting neo-Marxist perspectives were a bastion of support for the study of media process during past decades. Marxist political economists, especially, have insisted on the importance of scrutinizing media ownership patterns in order to tease out the forces that control society's systems of consciousness creation. During the past few years, however, a number of analysts from a variety of neo-Marxist directions have been discouraged by what they perceive to be reductionist approaches toward media creation and consequences by political economists.

Some of these analysts have been influenced by literary scholars who stress the importance of understanding the structure of the text rather than the structure of the industry that created it (e.g., Jameson, 1981). Others have joined the trend within literary studies to designate the individual "reader" a prime creator of "the text" (see, for example, Fiske & Hartley, 1978; Morley, 1980; Radway, 1984). The latter group, especially, has emphasized the ability of individuals to challenge media material, to take manifestations of the "dominant" ideology in news or entertainment and turn it to their own uses. Unlike researchers concerned with the way people cope with media, these writers are interested in discovering whether people from different class backgrounds come to media materials with similar "readings." Yet this research stream has also tended to shift attention away from media industries and to weaken communication researchers' interest in studying them.

For those who study mass media industries, one solution to such neglect is not to care. In fact, it turns out that many studies of the considerations that shape media material come from people whose work reflects little interest in the mass communication research tradition. Rather, their concerns are based in a broad area that has been tagged the "sociology of art," "production of culture," or something similar.[2]

Many of the writings in this vein have made important contributions to the understanding of media situations, yet by ignoring the relevance of their findings to issues of mass communication that go beyond their realm of study (and, instead, seeing their work only in terms of the sociology of art or production of culture) the researchers are implicitly supporting those who argue that mass communication is not a relevant concept. They are signaling that there is nothing about the process of mass communication — its nature, its consequences, or the relationship between the two — worth singling out for sustained attention.

My position in this chapter is quite different. It is that mass communication ought to be viewed as a uniquely important concept for understanding a range of critical issues regarding communication across society. Contemporary scholarly emphases on individual and group differences in interpreting media "texts" should not, I argue, obscure the idea that within contemporary society mass communication is a crucial force for providing a common pool of discussion for large populations.

This realization is especially important because it points to a fundamental way through which power is exercised in modern society. Mass communication serves as a major avenue whereby groups with diverse interests argue over key definitions of cultural life. A social actor's ability to have the most widespread media champion certain kinds of arguments while playing down others holds profound implications for the ability of that actor to control discussion of institutional agendas among large segments of society.

The purpose of this chapter is to show that developing a range of specific suggestions about media consequences from these propositions requires a thorough understanding of the industries that create and distribute mass media materials. To that end, the following pages propose a definition of mass communication that emphasizes the process of creation and its social potential. The chapter then examines implications of the concept, teasing out theoretical and methodological issues that grow out of it. It ends with a case study aimed at showing how research on the considerations that shape one medium's fare — television's — is critical to suggesting long-term societal implications of the cultural products.

Roots of the Concept

The biggest problem with *mass communication* as an umbrella term for various media processes has already been suggested: Traditionally, it has come to mean sending messages to "the mass," which, in turn, has meant huge numbers of separated, anonymous individuals who have little in common. Contemporary observers argue, correctly, that too many aspects of this definition do not fit Western media trends for the concept to hold water. But the term *mass communication* need not accommodate all media issues from all viewpoints to be viable. The real challenge for someone wanting to encourage scholarship via the term is have it resonate with current issues that demand attention via a number of research avenues.

As it turns out, one need not search too far for help in doing this. Ranging over the history of thought about "the mass," it becomes clear that during the first half of the twentieth century two slants on the notion were prominent. One was the now-familiar characterization of the mass as a very large number of normally dispersed individuals who have few, if any, communal bonds. The other, quite different, has elements that suggest a contemporary trajectory for the idea. That slant emphasizes that the mass is a special form of social aggregation, an organic unity that arises when large numbers of people share certain kinds of events cognitively, if not geographically.

Both slants came from the same starting point in the nineteenth century.[3] Early sociologists who wrote about the rise of "the mass" saw it as part of a twofold change in the connection of the individual to society. On the one hand, increased urbanization and occupational specialization had sharpened individuals' disconnectedness by fragmenting the traditional communal bonds (what Ferdinand Tonnies called *gemeinschaft*) that had marked the society in earlier centuries. On the other hand, the new environment seemed to be encouraging people to respond to powerful leaders and events as one — to submerge their individuality periodically in masses or crowds that, like organisms, seemed to take on a power of their own.

At the time, the idea of the mass raised much interest among social thinkers. To observers such as Karl Marx, it indicated the potential power of the proletariat to exert favorable upheavals in society. To conservative intellectuals, the possibility that masses could be mobilized to force collective action indicated one of the worst implications of democracy. Gustave Le Bon (1896), for example, wrote that such social aggregations were by nature irrational and "only powerful for destruction" (p. 18).

In the United States, such concerns affected the reactions of American intellectuals at the turn of the twentieth century to startling changes in the nature of the nation's communications media and the audience for them (see Czitrom, 1982; Jowett, 1976). For the first time, millions were reading issues of daily newspapers and weekly magazines. Millions were listening to phonograph records and watching motion pictures. Moreover, the novel elements that constituted the audience were drawing at least as much attention as its size. Children and illiterate adults were among the multitudes drawn to records and movies, which required no reading ability. And the immigrants who were then flooding the United States from Eastern and Southern Europe were attracted not only to the movies but to records and a burgeoning foreign-language press.

It was around these populations, which had until then been only marginally connected to communication technology, that the most nervous discussions about the implications of the growth in that technology tended to coalesce. One branch of the academic discussion, following the individualistic slant on the mass, asked how particular people (usually children or criminals) reacted to particular messages. The question, in effect, was whether individual reactions to mass media might reflect the pathology of the mass. This is the offshoot that evolved into mainstream mass communication research, along with the commonly accepted notion of mass communication.

The other branch, focusing on the slant that stressed the mass's organic nature, tended to highlight quite different problems and to suggest different solutions. The benign social integration of polyglot ethnic groups in an era of mounting urban tensions was the problem addressed. It explored whether the irrationality of the mass could be countered by encouraging social aggregation based on reason and a positive sense of community.

Major voices of the second approach were John Dewey, Charles Horton Cooley, W. I. Thomas, Florence Zaniecki, and Robert Park, social philosophers and sociologists at the University of Chicago.[4] Park, especially, saw the importance of elaborating this idea. He posited an alternative to Le Bon's version of the mass (or "crowd"), which he called a "public." Whereas the crowd was energized by feeling, empathy, and instinct, the public was motivated by thinking and reason. The modern world, Park (1922) argued, "offered more than the crowd as an alternative to traditional community" (p. 468).

That is where the notion of mass communication came in. To Park and the other Chicago sociologists, it was clear that modern media represented a major change in communication to the masses that could determine whether they would act as crowds or publics. The challenge of the media, Park and his colleagues suggested, was to create patterns of messages that would bind the disparate and potentially disruptive elements of U.S. society into a community of interests based on reason and democratic impulses.

In retrospect, many of their ideas may be considered both naive and paternalistic. Among other points, it is difficult to accept their stress on the rationality of news to the exclusion of entertainment, which they felt appealed too much to the emotions and thus worked against the formation of a functional sense of community. Nevertheless, a number of elements in the Chicago school's approach to mass communication are attractive for a contemporary reshaping of the term.

Foremost among them is the idea that the process influences *large social aggregates* through the dissemination of *patterns of messages*. By "patterns of messages," I mean systematic representations of the world that are created linguistically or pictorially as well as through the medium that is the vehicle for the representations. The emphasis in this perspective is away from the fact that individuals have widely different responses to such messages. Rather, the emphasis is on the realization that when people of a society tune into the same media products, their understandings of the materials converge in important ways. At the very least, for example, they share a starting point that allows them to discuss nuanced meanings of the cultural products and argue over possible social consequences of the materials.

There is, in other words, no reason to associate an insistence on the importance of shared media messages with a simplistic, "stimulus-response" view of people's interpretive powers. As communication researchers as diverse as George Gerbner (in Gerbner, Gross, Morgan, & Signiorelli, 1986), Elisabeth Noelle-Neumann (1981), and Steven Chaffee (1981) have argued, it is perfectly compatible with an emphasis on message sharing to realize that not everyone in the audience may accept media presentations in the same way. This slant on mass communication posits that, whatever their particular interpretations, the dissemination of messages through mass media provides a unique potential for large numbers of otherwise different and unrelated people to orient around similar images of the world.

It should be stressed, however, that the unique potential of mass communication comes not from technology alone. Important thinkers such as Karl Marx, Max Weber, and Robert Park understood that it comes from the use of those instruments by large-scale organizations as they apply standards of mass production to the creation and dissemination of news and entertainment.

A MASS COMMUNICATION PERSPECTIVE

With this orientation in mind, mass communication is best viewed as the industrialized (mass) production, reproduction, and multiple distribution of messages through technological devices. The word *industrialized* means that the process is carried out by mass media complexes or industries—that is, by conglomerations of organizations that interact regularly in the process of producing and distributing messages. It is the industrial application of technology for the production and distribution of messages to various places that provides the potential for reaching large, separate, diverse groups of people. Note, however, that in shifting the primary focus on the word *mass* from the nature of the audience to the nature of the process, this definition prominently avoids setting requirements about the number and nature of people attending to the messages. Whether and how the production process influences, or is influenced by, the size and characteristics of the audience should be a matter of discussion and empirical examination.

Many other issues regarding the activity, content, and consequences of mass communication can cascade directly from the definition just presented. Yet systematic research directions are most likely to emerge by tying the definition to a concept of society—that is, by formulating a perspective on the relationships among the industrial process, the sharing of messages, and the social fabric. One such "mass communication perspective" can be derived by building on a number of works in cultural anthropology (especially Geertz, 1973), industrial sociology (Aldrich, 1979; Touraine, 1979; Weick, 1979), and communication research.

My perspective starts with the proposition that society is a conflicted phenomenon. It is a system of relations in which different "actors" (i.e., organizations and individuals) struggle continuously over resources. The resources are material (for example, supplies) and symbolic (for example, the provision of information and permission to create).

At heart, this struggle is also a battle for control over society's basic orientations toward social practice. Put briefly, these orientations are the society's *model of knowledge* (for example, scientific, religious, secular-humanistic), *approach to resources* (for example, capitalistic, socialistic, and variants along these lines), and way of implementing the first two elements into the forms and structures of daily life (that is, its *cultural model*). Together, these orientations represent a society's definition of itself.

It is through this battle over society's image and the implementation of that image that the society continually produces — not just reproduces — itself. Actors with political and economic power regularly dominate the self-definition process and its implementation in social practice. At the same time, other actors regularly oppose these approaches and try to gain control for themselves over society's basic orientations.

Mass communication is a key vehicle for this self-definition process. Mass media (the technological devices used in mass communication) have the capacity to present cultural models to huge numbers of people in vivid form. These models depict conduct by individuals and organizations along with the consequences of the conduct. Doing that, the models (a) convey rules guiding the basic allocation of resources for society's educational, leisure, medical, economic, media, religious, military, and governmental activities (that is, they depict principles of institutional order); and (b) illustrate preferred ways to employ those resources (that is, they depict styles of production and consumption).

In the process, the media show huge publics certain preferred approaches toward society's resources. The presentations imbue (or reinforce) particular impressions in members of the audience and guide them toward particular activities. They bring people behind the scenes of institutions to show them how professionals work and why. They provide voices for certain issues and concerns, and, in so doing, turn people away from other institutional scenes, issues, and concerns.

Many accept the media presentations as "common sense" or "the way it is," for others, if not for them. But for some people the media images provoke discontent and underscore what is at stake in the battle over society's self-definition. The media images lead them to want to place their version of society alongside the others in the media, to call attention to themselves, and to gain legitimacy for their cause.

One key task of mass communication research, then, is to understand the process of cultural argumentation through the mass media as part of the larger conflict over societal self-definition and self-production. What cultural models get enacted in which media, how, why, and with what consequences? A raft of unexplored and underexplored areas flow out of this basic question.

Organizations, Power, and Messages

Clearly, the process of creating media messages is part of the larger process of creating meaning. But the definition of mass communication presented earlier suggests that, unlike attempts to understand the creation of meaning among two individuals or in a small group, research on the creation of cultural models in mass media industries requires seeing organizations and industries, rather than individuals, as the major units of analysis.

Obviously, organizational processes involve individuals. Organizations are, after all, made up of people. They are, to quote Howard Aldrich (1979), "goal directed, boundary maintaining activity systems." His definition highlights the essentially social nature of organizations, yet it also underscores that organizations are not merely the sum of the individuals that constitute them—their particular personalities and backgrounds. Rather, as he says, they are "products of, and constraints upon, social relations" (p. 4). The roles that people take on as members of one organization tilt them in directions that might well be different from the ones they take on in other contexts.

Aldrich's definition also points to the importance of an organization's environment in keeping the organization going. The environment comprises every person not admitted to participation in the organization (that is, everyone outside its boundaries) and everything not already a part of, or a product of, the activity systems of organizational personnel. Clearly, it is the environment toward which the organization directs the products of its activities. At the same time, it is the environment that provides people for recruitment into the organization; supplies used in the performance of organizational activities; required information, permissions, and services to help the acceptability, or permissibility, of its activities in that environment; and money to pay for it all.

Interdependencies

People, supplies, permission, information, services, money—very broadly defined, they represent the material and symbolic resources that must continually infuse an organization if it is to survive. Organizations are continually in competition with other organizations for resources, especially because resources are not distributed randomly throughout the environment. Rather, they are concentrated in various areas of the environment and are often under the control of other organizations. Awareness that the consequences of this situation are quite broad is what Aldrich (1979) calls the "resource dependence perspective": "The resource dependence perspective . . . goes beyond the idea of simple exchange in arguing that one consequence of competition and sharing of scarce resources is the development of dependencies of some organizations on others" (p. 267).

Here, then, we arrive at the concept of power in interorganizational relations, given that, as Richard Emerson (1962, p. 32) notes, an organization's power resides in another organization's dependence. Power in this framework is the capacity of one organization to control resources so as to restrict the options available to another organization in such a way that the latter takes actions consistent with the former's vested interests.[5]

The point applies clearly to a media production organization. It cannot possibly generate internally all the resources it requires to ensure the viability of its creative and administrative activities. For example, money must be found; talent has to be hired; machines, videotape, or other exhaustible materials have to be bought; the distribution and exhibition services of other organizations have to be contracted; the favorable services of law firms and regulations of government agencies have to be ensured; the inactivity of some pressure groups might have to be ascertained or negotiated; and information about available talent, activities of competitors, and the potential of the public's interest in the planned products has to be presented and evaluated. In other words, to create and distribute its messages, the mass media production firm has to rely on entities in the environment for resources, and those entities might demand substantial recompense for their help.

EXPLORING PROCESS AND CONSEQUENCE

The implications of such organizational interactions are quite important because, as noted earlier, the materials that mass media production organizations create represent cultural models that might carry substantial emotional and intellectual significance for those who come into contact with them. The significance may not be noticed simply by gauging whether viewers or readers react angrily to the output. Many people might feel comfortable with the cultural models presented; for them, the materials may represent what Gerbner (1972, p. 152) terms a celebration of conventional morality. Others may see in the depictions norms accepted by the larger society, even if they disagree with them. They may exercise a public tolerance of the shared models.

But even when there are few loud public complaints about particular media materials, the struggle to control arguments still takes place. Huge outcries and obvious attempts at censorship actually represent only the tip of an iceberg of attempts to influence the public sharing of messages. On a daily basis, a broad gamut of organizations, from banks to advertising agencies to public relations firms to government agencies to labor unions, routinely place pressures on media production firms so as to constrain creators in certain ways and not others.

These exercises of power need not be explicitly related to the materials produced to be considered part of the cultural argumentation process. Interorganizational squabbling over the cost of resources within a media industry often has consequences for the worldviews firms present, since the ability to use certain equipment, to travel, or to hire personnel may lead to certain types of output and not others. Moreover, a number of studies have noted that the range of ideas particular media industries and organizations may champion is typically linked to industry structures — that is, to patterns of roles that organizations have evolved with one another (e.g., see Garnham, 1983; Murdock, 1982; Tuchman, 1983; Turow, 1984).

What this means is that dominant interests within the society have been able to constrain the extent of cultural argumentation in certain media industries by setting the terms and traditions by which resources become available to organizations wanting to produce and disseminate messages. The tendency is clear in any system, whether it be capitalism, state socialism, or a mixed economy. Thus it is inconceivable that the contemporary United States would have its most pervasive media free of corporate, commercial involvement just as it is inconceivable (at least currently) that the Soviet Union would allow commercial interests independent of the government to control its television, radio, movie, newspaper, and magazine complexes.

In the United States, certain media vehicles are more likely than others to pay favorable attention to cultural models that severely challenge basic societal premises. Production firms that rely on getting a great many of their most important resources (money, authority, personnel, services, and the like) from the mainstream of society (government, giant advertisers, powerful advocacy groups, necessarily huge audiences) will likely arrange their activities so as to offend as few of these entities as possible. Conversely, production firms that can rely on resources from areas of society outside the mainstream (for example, nongovernmental bodies, atypical advertisers, specialty distributors and exhibitors, rather homogeneous audiences) might not hesitate to attack the mainstream.

The difference is between what can be called "mainstream" and "peripheral" media output. So, for example, in the United States it is possible to produce novels extolling communist ideologies as a contemporary solution to social problems; the First Amendment to the Constitution prohibits government interference. However, it is extremely doubtful that such peripheral material would be the central theme of a network television series.

Two Major Points

The foregoing comments set the stage for two major points: First, *one of the major consequences of the mass media is the belief by many actors in society that the media have consequences.* Clearly, individuals and organizations that are concerned about TV programs, magazine articles, or records feel they want to have an impact on the ideas that media share with large numbers of people. Second, *the steps that organized actors take toward the media likely relate to larger agendas they have with respect to their society as a whole.*

These points apply to a wide variety of entities, from the Moral Majority to the National Lesbian and Gay Task Force, to Action for Children's Television to the Ku Klux Klan. From a broader standpoint, they also apply to institutions such as medicine, law, education, politics, business, and the military. Institutions are loosely knit sets of organizations (hospitals, bar associations, teacher unions) that hold authority over fundamental aspects of social life. These organizations, in groups or individually, may approach the media with the idea of reinforcing or changing the cultural models that broad segments of the population have come to accept about the institutions and the professionals (doctors, lawyers, teachers) who lead them.

How do they do that? What happens when forces championing different models try to stop them? What possible social consequences derive from such attempts to guide cultural arguments? Answers cannot be inferred only by surveying members of the audience or examining the content. These research tacks must be joined to an understanding of media industries as well as of the way the groups' larger social strategies link up with their actions toward the media.

This realization points to a stream of other basic questions about the role of mass communication in the bid for influence over a society's cultural models. For example: Do certain social actors (organizations and individuals) feel a greater need than others to try to affect certain media — and, if so, why? What strategies do actors with greater or lesser status use to get their ideas into the most pervasive media? How do these strategies connect with their larger social agendas? How do media organizations react to attempts by different kinds of outside forces to influence their decision-making processes? And what social consequences do these interactions have for the reinforcement or negation of certain values, activities, and power relationships within media organizations, within nonmedia groups who try to influence them, and within society as a whole?

Studies to help answer these questions do not abound. The many theoretical writings on media and social power tend to focus broadly on conceptualizing the relationship between the economic "base" and the mainstream "superstructure." Only rarely do they suggest ways to trace how complex social movements or institutions within given economic arrangements have an impact on media material. Also uncommon are studies that actually elaborate approaches to these questions by exploring the process of creation within the media world.

Of the work that does exist, the creation of "news" has been studied most (e.g., Gans, 1979; Gitlin, 1979; Nelkin, 1987; Tuchman, 1979). A good deal less attention has been given to other kinds of nonfiction (for an exception, see Silverstone, 1985), and to fiction. Moreover, with the exception of newspapers, electronic media have been the focus of most of this research. Such key sites for cultural arguments as billboards, greeting cards, the book publishing industry, magazines, and even the music industry have hardly been examined with an eye to these issues. Nor have researchers explored processes that move material across media boundaries. Public relations firms, syndication and creative rights companies, talent agencies, the process services, and advertising agencies act as "linking pins," actively bridging production and distribution channels. So do media conglomerates, that is, corporations with financial holdings in a variety of media industries.

During the past few decades, the lines between mass media industries have become increasingly blurred as producers long involved in one industry convey their material to other symbol-producing and distributing domains. So, for example, products created by "the movie industry" typically run through a gauntlet of distribution "windows" in different industries — starting with theaters, moving through pay cable and home video, and ending in TV syndication.

Research on the organizational decisions that encourage such intermedia exchanges might well point out that while the proliferation of channels may fragment audiences, widespread sharing of perspectives on the world may not diminish nearly as much as the fragmentation would suggest. The reason is that budgetary considerations as well as concerns about corporate positioning in the new media environment are increasingly encouraging media executives to move news and entertainment across media boundaries. Through one form or another, and through one forum or another, the publics for particular depictions of the world may snowball tremendously. Even people who do not see a movie, for example, may share public statements about its basic themes by reading ads for it, hearing reviews on the radio, or seeing interviews with its stars on TV talk shows (see Turow, 1983; Turow & Park, 1981).

One research implication of this phenomenon is that even when studying the process of cultural argumentation in so pervasive a medium as network television, it might be important to understand how comments about the programming played out across other media. How broadly shared were certain interpretations of the TV programming? What were the arguments and cultural models that were extolled or contested? What possible critiques got little or no public play? How might discussions of the programs in the press have influenced the audience's interpretations of the programs? Examining these areas in conjunction with explorations of the forces that shape cultural argumentation within the television industry can lead to new suggestions about the social role and consequences of TV programming.

A CASE EXAMPLE

An investigation that I recently completed on the relationship between the American television industry and the medical institution had this multifaceted approach as its aim (Turow, 1989). I wanted to explore the way powerful sectors within the medical system (commonly termed "organized medicine" or "the medical establishment") try to guide network television's fictional images of their institution. And I wanted to suggest as best I could the consequences that those interactions may be having for the reinforcement or negation of certain perceptions about physicians and health care within the media organizations, the medical system, and society as a whole.

Medicine is an especially interesting area to examine from a mass communication perspective. The medical world today has changed fundamentally from the way it was in 1948, the year commercial television took off in the United States. Of course, the techniques and technologies are different. More significant, however, are the sociopolitical changes. Many of the basic assumptions and structures that guided medicine before World War II and in the decades since have been challenged dramatically by lawmakers, government bureaucrats, hospital administrators, and insurance company executives (Starr, 1982; Turow & Coe, 1985).

The most important philosophical change they instituted was an abandonment of the long-held notion that medicine is an unlimited resource, potentially available to all who need it to the extent they need it. The change came around the turn of the 1970s, when these and other public and private policymakers began to take steps to slow what they considered an alarming rate of increase in the nation's health care costs. To cap the upward spiral of medical spending, they forced enormous alterations in the makeup and principles guiding the nation's health care delivery systems.

Instead of seeing medicine as an unlimited resource, policymakers have acted on the proposition that medicine is a scarce resource that will have to be doled out sparingly, with the ethical and material costs such allocations entail. Their activities have already altered basic relationships among physicians, patients, hospitals, insurance companies, and employers — and there are more changes to come. It is not surprising that the situation has instigated concern and perhaps confusion among some segments of the public.

My interest in looking at the link between the TV industry and organized medicine reflected, then, a desire to examine the way program creators reacted to these critical changes in health care. I also wanted to know whether contending groups within the medical system demonstrated an ability to integrate their political agendas about health care into the programming. And I wanted to track discussions about TV's medical images in a wide range of print media. Doing that, I believed, would allow insight into the extent to which backstage conflicts over medical agendas became part of the ongoing cultural argumentation about the evolving medical institution.

Theoretical and Methodological Considerations

My initial task involved exploring how constraints from inside and outside of the TV industry affected the decision-making processes of the teams directly involved in turning out the programming. To frame the subject theoretically, I drew on Pfeffer and Salancik's (1978) discussion of "the mechanisms by which organizational environments may affect organizations" (p. 229). They argue that the key activities within an organization (for example, decisions about plots for a doctor show) become patterned as a result of executives' attempts to cope with perceived risks of getting proper resources for their work from the organization's environment. Pfeffer and Salancik (1978, p. 229) diagram this flow of influence in the following way:

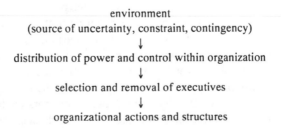

Their model posits that outside forces exert great influence on organizational activities. With respect to a TV production firm's depiction of medicine, the operation of these mechanisms would seem to echo a number of basic tensions that

I suspect are inherent to mainstream storytelling about any powerful sector of American life. That is, a number of considerations would seem to push program creators toward and away from writing their scripts in tune with the medical establishment's concerns.

On the one hand, resource considerations suggest that producers and writers would welcome good relationships with powerful organizations within the institution they are portraying. The medical establishment holds important assets in a TV production firm's environment that could presumably decrease storytellers' risks. One such resource is credibility. There is always a chance that those who portray health topics will be accused of mistakes, sensational dramatics, and bad advice. The help of prestigious medical sources reduces this possibility.

Medical organizations, for their part, often find real public relations benefits in offering TV storytellers free advice, and even free equipment. Gandy (1981) argues that this ability to offer attractive "subsidies" to producers gives wealthy parties the clout to shape media portrayals to their liking. As Gandy points out, these considerations are likely to move storytelling away from antiestablishment inclinations about medicine.

On the other hand, a number of equally important resource considerations would lead to the expectation that interactions between producers and powerful institutional forces outside TV would often be quite strained. One would suspect that the seeming coziness of their symbiotic relationship would be disturbed frequently by resource-related claims on the producer from other quarters of the medical establishment with conflicting agendas to push. Demands on producers from *within* the television industry likely also complicate the situation and make it not at all clear that TV's creators will always toe the establishment's line.

After all, the most direct test of a production firm's utility to a network is not whether it will portray the establishment respectfully, but whether the firm can create popular material on time and on budget. The combination of requirements is nerve-racking. So, to reduce at least some of the enormous tensions involved, network and production personnel have adopted a number of interrelated routines—including the use of formulas (patterned settings, character types, and plot lines)—for choosing and arranging the bulk of TV fare.

But here is precisely where conflicts might develop between production executives and institutional leaders. Many of the former's routines have come about because of requirements within the TV industry. Yet the portrayals that result from those routines might not coincide with depictions that the latter would favor.

Conflicts may take place even if the institution's leaders historically had a strong say about those portrayals, because they may feel the portrayals no longer suit their needs. Sparks may also fly when program creators try to update their settings, plots, and characterizations for contemporary audiences without consulting leaders from the area of life they are depicting. The storytellers may feel that they know how to insert changes into formatted plots so as not to disturb the most important routines that lower their risk, but the people they are portraying may not like the result.

They may also not like watching criticism of themselves on the home tube. The storytellers, on the other hand, may insist that being controversial is important for grabbing and holding viewers. As a result, they may actually be attracted to certain criticisms of the institution's establishment, or they may be interested in depicting certain fringe sectors of the institution in a positive light.

The situation, then, is likely to be filled with a number of competing mandates for the creators of television fiction. How these tensions work themselves out in changing institutional environments, how they affect the competing agendas of competitors within those institutions, and the possible consequences that may have for public understanding of institutions are topics that have hardly been explored.

Doctor Shows and the Public Agenda

In my study of these issues, I focused on the prime-time television doctor show. The doctor show embodies a storytelling tradition that spans the history of commercial network TV in the United States and has its roots in other media before that. A total of 56 drama and comedy series centering on physicians have aired on one of the three major U.S. networks since the start of commercial TV. From the days of *Ben Casey* and *Dr. Kildare* through *M*A*S*H, Trapper John, M.D., St. Elsewhere, Heartbeat,* and *Hothouse,* television doctor shows have reached tens of millions of people almost every year. *M*A*S*H* remains one of the most popular off-network programs in syndication. And *Marcus Welby, M.D., Quincy, M.E., Medical Center, The Lazarus Syndrome, Nurse, Trapper John, The Bold Ones, Ben Casey,* and *Emergency!* continue to make their weekly rounds on local stations and cable systems throughout the country.

My investigation demanded a variety of methods. To follow the actions of the people and organizations who developed the doctor show formula, I interviewed many of the producers, writers, directors, actors, network executives, and medical consultants who worked on the programs over the years. To learn about the public ideas and arguments Americans shared about the shows during four decades, I examined almost 40 years of newspaper and magazine articles. To refresh my memory about the programs themselves, I watched many of them and read scripts of others.

Much of my viewing took place at the Motion Picture and Television Archive at the University of California, Los Angeles. Universal Pictures Television and MTM Enterprises allowed me to view series and TV movies in their studios. I found other shows at the Museum of Broadcasting in New York. The Television Script Archive at the Annenberg School of Communications, University of Pennsylvania, was a valuable place to get scripts of programs I could not view in the archives or studios, or on TV.

I turned to the *Reader's Guide to Periodical Literature, Index Medicus, Business Periodicals Index, New York Times Index,* and the last three and a half decades of *Variety, Daily Variety,* and *TV Guide* for magazine and newspaper articles on medicine and television. In addition, I found a gold mine of newspaper clippings and network press releases in the files of the Television Information Office Library.

Contacting people to interview began by plugging into the relatively small network of producers who have worked on network TV's doctor series. Fortunately, the doctor show is young enough that most of its creators — producers, writers, actors, directors, network executives, medical consultants — are still alive. Most were generous with their time. Their stories led me to the somewhat larger web of people who were influential in the creation of most of the medical series and TV movies that have aired on the home tube. These people, too, were typically helpful, though a number of individuals declined to be interviewed. No one requested anonymity, but four did ask that certain comments not be associated with their names. I interviewed 109 people in all.

Recounting the findings in detail would be impossible here. My purpose is to indicate briefly how an analysis of the forces vying over media images pointed to conclusions about the social consequences of the programming. Accordingly, it should be stated at the start that organized medicine's interactions with TV producers have been part of a conscious agenda by that sector of the health care institution to reinforce and extend the central position of physicians in American society.

During the first two decades of network television, the elements of that agenda were articulated publicly and forcefully by the American Medical Association, organized medicine's most powerful representative (see Starr, 1982; Stevens, 1971). In the AMA's vision of health care, physicians were captains of the medical ship. Hospitals were the physicians' key workplace, a workplace they rightfully controlled. The best kind of medicine was private and entrepreneurial. And medicine was best presented to the public as an unlimited, free-flowing resource that in its most professional aspects was outside the realm of politics and contention.

Clearly, many of these propositions are highly contestable; some were contested even in the early days of television. But during the 1950s, mainstream American medicine was powerful enough, and successful enough, to mute the criticisms. The American Medical Association and its coalition of interest groups guided federal and state legislators toward laws and policies that would shape medicine's growth according to their agenda. By far the most drastic example of their power at mid-century was the way the medical establishment went about burying national health insurance (see Starr, 1982, pp. 285-289).

That power carried over to the clout mainstream medical organizations had with TV's storytellers. Actually, the involvement by physicians predated television. As early as the 1930s, the major movie studios and radio producers hired doctors from large hospitals in Los Angeles, New York, and Chicago to lend authority to their radio programs and photoplays. However, in TV's first decades, the organized influence of medicine came into the picture. Beginning with the NBC series *Medic* in 1954, and through the late 1960s, five of the six prime-time doctor drama series had their scripts directly controlled by special committees of the AMA or its Los Angeles affiliate.

The link between TV and organized medicine was born most directly out of producers' need for the kind of resource subsidy Gandy (1981) has described. James Moser, whose *Medic* series did not have the cash to create elaborate hospital sets, asked officials from the Los Angeles County Medical Association (LACMA) to help him arrange the filming of episodes in real hospitals around the city. LACMA officials agreed to get involved, but only on the proviso that they could have the last say on the accuracy of all the scripts. After Moser assented, he was chagrined to learn that in the eyes of the physician-advisers "accuracy" covered a broad territory, from genuine medical errors to the use of slang by physicians and their drinking coffee while discussing a patient.

The series lasted through 1956. In the late 1950s and early 1960s the American Medical Association took over LACMA's chores on *Dr. Kildare, Ben Casey, The Eleventh Hour,* and other shows. The AMA Advisory Committee's rules were a bit more relaxed than LACMA's had been. The Association's public relations officer in Los Angeles persuaded the physicians to compromise with program creators in the name of "dramatic license" and long-term goodwill.

Still, the AMA's basic agenda implicitly remained a key criterion for program acceptability. While some tension-filled topics such as medical malpractice got past the Advisory Committee, the scripts clearly adopted organized medicine's positions on the issues. Moreover, the shows never discussed such subjects as the power of organized medicine, the inherent limits of medicine as a resource, the diminishing power of physicians in the hospital, or the possibilities of socialized medicine. In fact, the AMA Advisory Committee prevented a number of plot lines that challenged the system from getting produced.

The AMA advisers also took care that TV physicians administered the bulk of proper patient care. Nurses invariably had little to do medically. Clinical psychologists were forced aside: In the early 1960s, insistence by the AMA committee that a psychologist take a clearly subordinate role to a psychiatrist in *The Eleventh Hour* series caused a great argument between the two professions. The public ruckus discouraged TV executives from using clinical psychologists in dramas for years.

I ought to note that battling over major issues was rare. There *was* a consistent undercurrent of tension between the two parties, as producers' desire to charge their plots with conflict, romance, and a touch of contemporary controversy bumped against the physicians' conservative approach to doctors' images, hospital activities, and political concerns. Most of the time, however, producers found ways to compromise with the advisers. One incentive to do that was the desire to keep the AMA's seal of approval. The networks and advertisers liked the seal, and the producers did not want to jeopardize it.

Perhaps a more important reason for the absence of fundamental clashes with advisers was that the producers and writers who worked on the shows felt perfectly comfortable with organized medicine's perspective on health care. In the midst of the most optimistic medical environment in American history (polio had just been conquered, after all), they did not need to be prodded to accept the fundamentals of the AMA's agenda. It was hardly questioned that the physician was the leader of health care in a society where medicine was an infinitely expandable resource judged by its ability to deal with illness in an acute (i.e., quick-acting, immediate-gratification) manner.

Producers' attitudes changed in the late 1960s and early 1970s, when ill will toward several institutions, including medicine, swept through American society. Doctor show creators, wanting freedom from the continual tension of having the AMA Advisory Committee looking over their shoulders, were glad to find network executives no longer insisting on the need to display the imprimatur of a medical organization at the end of their episodes. The desire for separation was mutual among some medical leaders. A number of AMA board members, disgruntled with the romantic posturings of TV's physician-heroes and angry about a few cases of "dramatic license," pushed for removing the AMA seal from shows that did not follow their script prescriptions to the conservative letter.

But even while the AMA lost its direct grip on scripts, doctor shows continued to enact the fundamental perspectives on health care that it championed. One key reason was that mainstream medicine's public approach toward health care had become an integral part of the setting, characters, and plots—the doctor show formula. Television producers, writers, and network executives recognized it as *the* viable way to tell stories about medicine. Certainly, producers and writers were constantly looking for new doctor show concepts. Certainly, in several ways the doctor show changed dramatically from *Medic* and *Dr. Kildare* to *M*A*S*H*, *Trapper John, M.D.*, and *St. Elsewhere.*

Yet, the creators' emphasis on hospital-based, acute-care medicine was pretty consistent through the decades. More consistent, even among those who worked on such maverick series as *M*A*S*H* and *St. Elsewhere,* was a fundamental respect for medicine as a profession, a presentation of the physician as captain of the medical ship, and a message that health care typically ought to be above the government/corporate fray. Simply using variations on tried-and-true plots, the creators acted out the idea that, aside from subjects at the edges of life, medical decisions typically had nothing to do with politics and, in fact, ought to be guided by the principle that people had a right to unlimited possibilities of the best care.

This perspective has held sway even as the contemporary sociopolitical revolution in medicine has taken irretrievable root. The reason seems to be that no one involved with the programming has had an interest in encouraging change in portrayals. Producers, satisfied with their tinkerings with the traditional formula, have been afraid to venture into new dramatic territory with fundamentally different dramatic premises. Their medical advisers, hired at lucrative fees to help with plot ideas and "accuracy," have learned that their advice is much better received if it fits tried-and-true directions.

Pharmaceutical companies, medical equipment firms, and disease foundations such as the American Cancer Society also feed the traditional approach. By suggesting ways to use their technologies and new discoveries in plots, they hope to garner favorable publicity. Like the physician-advisers, they know it is more efficient and self-aggrandizing to shape their suggestions to fit TV's outdated view of the medical world rather than to move against the grain.

As for the American Medical Association, the American Hospital Association, and the many other national, regional, and local members of mainstream medicine, they also have very pragmatic reasons not to encourage network television to revise its views of how the medical system works. During the past decade and a half these organizations have been struggling furiously to maintain the clout of their constituencies against an onslaught of formidable foes. The foes include corporations concerned about rising medical costs, insurance companies wanting to keep costs down, government agencies wanting to cap physician fees as they have been capping hospital fees, and others. The issues are as complex as they are important. There are no simple bad guys and good guys here.

The public and private policies over which these struggles are taking place are still emerging, mostly out of view of the general public. It is, in fact, often in the interest of all the parties to keep their contentions out of the mainstream media, because many of the sensitive issues would flare up if exposed to large-scale inspection and debate. Typically, the contending elites encourage the circulation of their concerns only when acceptable solutions have begun to be worked out, or when issues have gotten to the point where the parties feel comfortable agreeing to disagree in public. Clearly, when it comes to network TV, medical leaders feel that time has not arrived.

Organized medicine's approach to discussing doctor shows in popular print media has been consistent with this strategy. Every now and then, individual physicians have issued angry denunciations to the press about popular TV physicians, saying, for example, that their zealous personalities are causing the public to make unrealistic demands on real-life doctors. But leaders of organized medicine — and AMA leaders, especially — have tended to take a stance in public speeches and interviews that not only has approved of the programming but has lauded its authenticity through a narrow, ambiguous construction of the word *realistic.*

In both medical journals and popular periodicals, AMA representatives have termed doctor shows realistic if they depict the use of medical technology in an accurate manner and if they portray the personality of the physician in a way that coincides with the image of the doctor that organized medicine favors at the time. In addition, they have fed into the star-centered, fan-magazine orientation that most articles about television's doctors have taken. Never has the AMA, or any other branch of organized medicine, commented on the disjuncture between the TV portrait of medicine and the structure that policymakers have been shaping in the real world.

The current claim of AMA officials is that it has never had influence over television's depiction of medicine apart from narrowly conceived questions of accuracy. While clearly false, this assertion of little influence should be read as a protective stance. It distances the AMA from historical responsibility for the consequences of medicine's images. Moreover, it excuses the Association from the responsibility of lobbying Hollywood for portrayals that reflect the policymakers' new realities. The latter excuse would seem useful at a time when medical leaders do not want to bring large publics behind the scenes of medical politics.

By not admitting its role in cultivating cultural patterns along these lines, the AMA also helps to lend legitimacy to those physicians who blame their patients for skyrocketing health care expenditures. Some doctors have argued in the medical trade press that costs have risen primarily because of public demand for the most expensive treatments in the most expensive hospitals (e.g., Honan, 1985; Hunter, 1984; see also Turow, 1989, pp. 273-285). Rising malpractice suits, they argue, are also the result of public demands for (and lawyer encouragement of) virtually risk-free, top-of-the-line care.

What their argument overlooks is the great effort by organized medicine over the years to boost the expensive style of health care among Americans. As this sketch has suggested, an integral part of the medical establishment's attempts to implement its broad social agenda during the past three decades involved encouraging fictional images that hyped impeccable, unlimited, private, high-tech, specialty-oriented health care. Turning public attention away from its role may be convenient self-protection for organized medicine, but it may further confound large publics that currently must deal with radical shifts in their health care experiences without understanding the reasons behind them.

CONCLUSION

My aim in this chapter has been to suggest how broadly designed research on the industrial and organizational forces that shape mass media materials can illuminate the relationship between mass communication and contemporary life, including questions of media consequences. The case study just described indicates that exploring media processes can highlight the way social actors use mass media in their wide-ranging attempts to extend their power. An exploration of the complex historical interaction between the American television industry and the medical system yielded insights about the way organized medicine has exerted influence over the creation of prime-time fiction about itself. The study revealed that prime-time television fiction has been one vehicle the medical establishment's leaders have used consistently to advance their political agendas. And it suggested questions about TV's contributions to Americans' knowledge of medicine *that would be difficult to induce without an understanding of institutional and industrial processes.*

The study of media processes can help inform the study of media consequences in other ways, as well. One important challenge is to elaborate the societal consequences that flow from the media's collective role as a social subsystem unto itself. The media as a group fit the definition of an institution that was presented earlier. They are loosely knit sets of organizations that hold authority over a key area of life; their purview is the creation and dissemination of many of society's most vivid cultural models of themselves and other institutions.

Often, as in the case of mainstream medicine and mainstream TV, particular media and the groups they portray evolve symbiotic relationships that lead to similar approaches to cultural models of concern to both parties. Sometimes their interests do not coincide, however. The political and economic consequences this kind of disjuncture causes for each party have hardly been scrutinized, but they may be profound.

A number of scenarios come to mind. One wonders, for example, what happens when news organizations report on their own clashes with government or corporate entities. How do various sectors of the media institution portray themselves, and how do their competitors portray media/nonmedia struggles? What consequences do the media's power to define situations about themselves to large publics hold for the way nonmedia groups approach the media legislatively or in their corporate dealings?

A related area for investigation involves the ability of certain media to induce social change simply by aiming to depict situations to large publics. One example is the rush by U.S. senators toward legislative activity when they learned that a network TV documentary crew was conducting a critical investigation of fraud in particular federal programs (Cook et al., 1983). In this case, the mere anticipation of public concern resulting from a TV documentary shared by huge audiences led to changes in the political process — even before the documentary was aired. Such "institutional consequences" of media processes deserve a lot more attention.

Exploring the implications of these and other mass communication processes means trying to get a handle on the models of society people share of and through the media, trying to follow the cultural argumentation that takes place as a result of media depictions, and trying to track the ways organizations and individuals attempt to exert control over those depictions. In the end, the issues to be raised in the study of media industries extend to the production and reproduction of society itself. The research avenues are fascinating. Many questions have hardly been examined. There is much to learn.

NOTES

1. For a number of literature reviews, see Ball-Rokeach and Cantor (1986), Gurevitch, Bennett, Curran, and Woolacott (1982), Rowland and Watkins (1984), and Turow (1984).

2. Reviews of this literature can be found in Becker (1982) and Peterson (1976).

3. The evolution of these perspectives as they relate to the development of scholarship is found in Czitrom (1982), Gouldner (1970), and Williams (1976).

4. The first three scholars are discussed in Czitrom (1982, chap. 4).

5. For an elaboration on this idea, see Glasberg and Schwartz (1983) and Turow (1984, pp. 7-38).

REFERENCES

Aldrich, H. (1979). *Organizations and environment.* Englewood Cliffs, NJ: Prentice-Hall.

Ball-Rokeach, S., & Cantor, M. (1986). *Media, audience, and social structure.* Beverly Hills, CA: Sage.

Becker, H. (1982). *Art worlds.* Berkeley: University of California Press.

Chaffee, S. (1981). Mass media in political campaigns: An expanding role. In R. Rice & W. Paisley (Eds.), *Public communication campaigns* (pp. 181-198). Beverly Hills, CA: Sage.

Cook, F. L., Tyler, T., Goetz, E., Gordon, M., Protess, D., Leff, D., & Molotch, H. (1983). Media and agenda setting: Effects on the public, interest group leaders, policy makers, and policy. *Public Opinion Quarterly, 47,* 16-35.

Czitrom, D. (1982). *Media and the American mind.* Chapel Hill: University of North Carolina Press.

Emerson, R. Q. (1962). Power-dependence relations. *American Sociological Review, 27,* 31-40.

Fiske, J., & Hartley, J. (1978). *Reading television.* London: Methuen.

Gandy, O. (1981). *Beyond agenda-setting.* Norwood, NJ: Ablex.

Gans, H. (1979). *Deciding what's news.* New York: Vintage.

Garnham, N. (1983). Toward a theory of cultural materialism. *Journal of Communication, 33,* 314-330.

Geertz, C. (1973). *The interpretation of cultures.* New York: Basic Books.

Gerbner, G. (1972, September). Communication and social environment. *Scientific American,* pp. 153-160.

Gerbner, G., Gross, L., Morgan, M., & Signiorelli, N. (1986). Living with television: The dynamics of the cultivation process. In J. Bryant & D. Zillman (Eds.), *Perspectives on media effects* (pp. 17-41). Hillsdale, NJ: Lawrence Erlbaum.

Gitlin, T. (1979). *The whole world is watching.* Berkeley: University of California Press.

Glasberg, D., & Schwartz, M. (1983). Ownership and control of corporations. In A. Inkeles (Ed.), *Annual review of sociology* (Vol. 9, pp. 311-332). Palo Alto, CA: Annual Reviews.

Gouldner, A. (1970). *The coming crisis in Western sociology.* New York: Basic Books.

Gurevitch, M., Bennett, T., Curran, J., & Woolacott, J. (Eds.). (1982). *Culture, society, and the media.* London: Methuen.

Honan, P. (1985, June 7). M.D. asks, can U.S. afford best medical care? [Letter to the editor]. *American Medical News,* p. 5.

Hunter, W. (1984, March 16). How to boost the cost of health care. *American Medical News,* p. 4.

Jameson, F. (1981). *The political unconscious.* Ithaca, NY: Cornell University Press.

Jowett, G. (1976). *Film: The democratic art.* Boston: Little, Brown.

Koughan, M. (1981-82). The state of the revolution, 1982. *Channels, 1,* 23-27.

Le Bon, G. (1896). *The crowd.* London: Ernest Benn.

Maisel, R. (1973). The decline of mass media. *Public Opinion Quarterly, 37,* 159-170.

Morley, D. (1980). *The nationwide audience: Structure and decoding.* London: British Film Institute.

Murdock, G. (1982). Large corporations and the control of media industries. In M. Gurevitch, T. Bennett, J. Curran, & J. Woolacott (Eds.), *Culture, society, and the media* (pp. 118-150). London: Methuen.

Nelkin, D. (1987). *Selling science: How the press covers science and technology.* New York: W. H. Freeman.

Noelle-Neumann, E. (1981). Mass media and social change in developing societies. In E. Katz & T. Szecsko (Eds.), *Mass media and social change* (pp. 137-163). Beverly Hills, CA: Sage.

Peterson, R. (Ed.). (1976). *The production of culture.* Beverly Hills, CA: Sage.

Pfeffer, J., & Salancik, G. (1978). *The external control of organizations: A resource-dependence perspective.* New York: Harper & Row.

Park, R. E. (1922). *The immigrant press and its control.* New York: Harper & Bros.

Radway, J. (1984). *Reading the romance: Women, patriarchy, and popular literature.* Chapel Hill: University of North Carolina Press.

Rowland, W., & Watkins, B. (Eds.). (1984). *Interpreting television: Current research perspectives.* Beverly Hills, CA: Sage.

Ruben, B., & Lievrow, L. (Eds.). (1989). *Information and behavior.* New Brunswick, NJ: Transaction.

Silverstone, R. (1985). *Framing science: The making of a BBC documentary.* London: BFI.

Starr, P. (1982). *The social transformation of American medicine.* New York: Basic Books.

Stevens, R. (1971). *American medicine and the public interest.* New Haven, CT: Yale University Press.

Touraine, A. (1979). *The post-industrial society.* New York: Random House.

Tuchman, G. (1979). *Making news. A study in the construction of reality.* New York: Free Press.

Tuchman, G. (1983). Consciousness industries and the production of culture. *Journal of Communication, 33,* 330-341.

Turow, J. (1983). Local TV: Producing soft news. *Journal of Communication, 3,* 111-123.

Turow, J. (1984). *Media industries: The production of news and entertainment.* New York: Longman.

Turow, J. (1985). Cultural argumentation and the mass media. *Communication, 8,* 139-164.

Turow, J. (1989). *Playing doctor: Television, storytelling, and medical power.* New York: Oxford University Press.

Turow, J., & Coe, L. (1985). Curing television's ills: The portrayal of health care. *Journal of Communication, 35,* 36-51.

Turow, J., & Park, C. (1981). Television's publicity outlets: An initial investigation. *Public Relations Review, 1,* 15-24.

Weick, K. (1979). *The social psychology of organizing* (2nd ed.). Reading, MA: Addison-Wesley.

Williams, R. (1976). *Keywords.* New York: Oxford University Press.

Organizational Communication, Media Industries, and Mass Communication

CHARLES R. BANTZ
Arizona State University

R ATHER than critiquing or explicating Turow's cogent argument, this essay takes an interpretive perspective to address Turow's point that "the process of creating media messages is part of the larger process of creating meaning" (p. 485). In providing a communicative, cultural reading of the mass communication process, the goal is not to question the validity of a dependency analysis, but to illustrate what a communicative, cultural analysis can contribute.

Turow examines meaning creation at the macrosocial level, suggesting that the industrial production of mediated messages contributes to the societal construction of meaning. In his limited space, he does not extend that argument to media organizations or to their interorganizational relationships, relying instead upon the resource dependency perspective (Aldrich, 1979; Pfeffer & Salancik, 1978). These pages are a communicative commentary that provides an alternative reading of Turow's argument by characterizing media organizations as communicative cultures, suggesting that relationships among media organizations are accomplished communicatively, and speculating on media consequences from this perspective. From this viewpoint, the medium of interorganizational relationships is communication; from Turow's viewpoint the medium is economics. Thus Turow suggests that one must understand mass communication as an institutional process. However, to understand mass communication fully as an institutional process, one

AUTHOR'S NOTE: My thanks to Sandra Petronio for comments on earlier drafts of this essay, and to Dean Scheibel for his continuing exploration of organizational communication cultures.

Correspondence and requests for reprints: Charles R. Bantz, Department of Communication, Arizona State University, Tempe, AZ 85287-1205.

Communication Yearbook 13, pp. 502-510

must take an additional step and understand organizational communication. In adopting this perspective, this argument incorporates Turow's perspective by situating the study of media industries within a broader communicative framework. In such an encompassing communicative framework, the explanation of economic relationships is based upon an analysis of communicative relationships.

The line of my argument involves four connecting claims. First, organizational communication constitutes an organizational communicative culture. Second, organizations constitute their environment, including other organizations with which they interact. Third, in constituting their environment, organizations within a large industry communally create images of each other. This communal creation leads to the development of industrial families. Fourth, viewing media organizations and media industries as communicatively constituted helps explicate media consequences. These claims are briefly addressed in the remainder of this commentary.

ORGANIZATIONAL COMMUNICATION CULTURE

Turow uses the organizational theory literature for his definition of organizations, citing Aldrich (1979), who characterizes organizations as "goal directed, boundary maintaining activity systems." In contrast to such a definition, an organizational communication culture perspective defines organizations as created in communication.

Organizational communication cultures are constituted in communication as members develop and use messages in the process of creating, maintaining, and transforming meanings and expectations (Bantz, 1981, 1989). This approach is founded upon symbolic interactionism (Blumer, 1969) and developed using Hawes's (1974) argument that communication constitutes social collectivities, Johnson's (1977) discussion of communication as involving the creation of meanings and expectations, Bormann's (1972, 1983, 1988) fantasy theme analysis and symbolic convergence theory, Weick's (1969, 1979) theory of organizing, and Pacanowsky and O'Donnell-Trujillo's (1982) approach to organizational cultures.

From this communicative, cultural approach, organizational communication is defined as "the collective creation, maintenance, and transformation of organizational meanings and organizational expectations through the creation and use of messages" (Bantz, 1989, p. 11). The participants in organizations send messages (e.g., write memos, talk) and use messages (e.g., read memos, listen to talk), but the acts of creating and using messages are only the first step. Through the ongoing exchange of these messages, members of an organization create, maintain, and transform collective meanings and expectations.

The fundamental premise in this perspective is that organizations exist in human communication. They are not activity systems; rather, they are symbolic realities. Adopting such a viewpoint makes communicative processes essential to organizing. Symbolic processes are, therefore, the core of organizational life. Because communicative processes are fundamental to organizations, understanding interorganizational relationships necessitates understanding the communicative relationships among organizations. This can best be illustrated by considering the relationship between an organization and its environment.

ORGANIZATIONS AND THEIR ENVIRONMENTS

Turow's approach emphasizes the competition among organizations for scarce resources in their environment, hence the relationship between an organization and its environment is one of need, acquisition, and obligation: "To create and distribute its messages the mass media production firm has to rely on entities in the environment for resources, and those entities might demand substantial recompense for their help" (p. 487). While Turow refers to symbolic as well as tangible resources, the assumptions of the resource dependency model appear to be economic rather than communicative.

Building on a view of organizations as communication cultures and Weick's (1979) conception of the relationship between organizing and the environment, an alternative proposal suggests that organizations actively construct their environments — including the other organizations with which they deal (see Bantz, in press). Thus any dependency relationship among organizations is a mutually constructed symbolic relationship (it may also be an economic relationship).

From this viewpoint, organizations enact their environments as they enact specific entities in their environments. The environments, and the other organizations in the environments, are symbolic constructions that can be seen as the products of organizing activity (Weick, 1979, chap. 6). An obvious example from mass communication is the way news organizations enact events that will then be reported. For example, if a newspaper receives a news release announcing a news conference, the activity of news workers will dramatically affect the extent to which the news conference is part of its environment. If the assignment editor sends a photographer and reporter to cover the conference, the organization co-*enacts* the news conference as information that can be turned into a story.

The enactment of the environment by media organizations occurs not only when creating news stories, but also in other activities. In this view, therefore, a media organization may enact an environment where a certain studio, a certain network, and a certain bank are defined as significant to its reality. If such a studio, network, or bank defines a reciprocal relationship with that media organization, then symbolically constructed interdependency arises. Thus interrelationships that are seen as economic have symbolic origins as interdependencies that are mutually constructed by organizations across time.

For example, there is no law of nature that demands that production companies must sell television programs only to one of the three largest television networks. Those relationships have developed (and are changing) across time through mutual construction by producers, networks, advertisers, and stations. Thus there have been a wide variety of relationships among producers, networks, stations, and advertisers including nearly exclusive relationships between producers and networks (e.g., Aaron Spelling and ABC), networks created by producers (e.g., Fox), and networks created by stations (e.g., TBS). These symbolic interdependencies are dynamically created as organizations enact each other as part of their environment.

As a single organization acts upon the environment, thus constituting various aspects of that environment, other organizations within the environment are doing the same. Organizations that deviate significantly from societal norms appear to understand this process because they act as if they are competing with other organizations in constructing their own environment. For example, organized crime "families" select various sections of the Internal Revenue Code that they enact as legitimate and other sections they ignore. They enact specific aspects of the code based on their enacted assumption that the IRS will be trying to catch them — hence what they enact will be influenced by both what the organization assumes is effective and what is less likely to be discovered. Organized crime organizations seek to enact an IRS that can be deceived by front organizations, skimming, laundering, and other strategies, yet they know that the IRS is simultaneously enacting those crime families as "catchable." Crime organizations are, therefore, defining the IRS (and other organizations) in one manner, while the IRS is defining them in another. This mutual, yet antagonistic, enactment or definition epitomizes the politics of the symbolic construction of societal social reality.

Organizations, such as crime families, that are tightly knit (i.e., "tightly coupled"; see Weick, 1979, chaps. 4, 7) are more independent in their construction of the environment than are loosely knit organizations. By assessing the degree of coupling within media organizations and assessing the effect of that coupling on their environmental relationships, the relationship between media organizations and their environment can be more carefully specified. For example, inasmuch as reporters act as boundary spanners (connecting their home organizations with those of sources) and news employees frequently and easily change jobs, many news organizations appear to be loosely coupled. With such loose coupling, news organizations may be more responsive within their environment than a tightly coupled organization, such as a cell of terrorists.

Since organizations are actively involved in enacting their environments and other organizations that coexist within their environments, the next section assesses the relationship among a group of organizations operating within the same environmental arena.

CREATING INDUSTRIAL FAMILIES

Turow suggests in his chapter that organizations develop dependencies that lead to differential influence and power among organizations (see also Turow, 1984). Media have become more interrelated, as films, broadcast and cable television, books, public relations, and even greeting cards join together to produce, promote, distribute, and sell cultural products. Thus media industries have become a large and interconnected organizational sector. Given the recent emphasis on corporate strategic planning in focusing on a core business, several large mergers highlight the degree of interconnection in the media industries — Warner and Lorimar, Capital Cities/ABC, and Time and Warner. Turow's resource dependency view characterizes interorganizational relationships as economic power relationships.

Instead, a communicative, cultural analysis of interorganizational relationships directs attention to the interplay of organizational cultures and their enactment of other organizations in their industry. Media institutions build interrelationships that are predicated on individual organizational communication culture and their enactment of those related organizations collectively. Media organizations, like all other organizations, develop patterns of collective meanings and expectations that influence their relationships with other organizations. Since organizations are simultaneously involved in enacting their environment, including other organizations, interorganizational relationships are *collectively constituted* by the communicative activity of the organizations within an industry (for an example, see Scheibel, 1989).

The process of interorganizational communication produces an "industrial family," representing organizations that are related to each other by a constitution. An industrial family is created within an industry (such as media) as organizations attend to other organizations. Industrial families, like human families, are created and transformed by choices (adoption, marriage, and divorce may all be seen as choices), and one organization can be the member of multiple families simultaneously. Thus a major advertiser may be a part of several industrial families by virtue of product, sponsorship, advertising, and purchasing (e.g., a company chooses to belong to the tobacco family by virtue of making a product, the auto racing family by sponsorship, outdoor advertising through advertising, and agriculture through purchasing).

Turow's analysis of network television doctor shows illustrates the contrast between his argument and this communicative cultural analysis. His resource dependency analysis suggests that in the 1950s and 1960s production companies followed the AMA line because they needed access to resources (e.g., hospitals) and needed the legitimacy provided by AMA approval.

To analyze the production of doctor shows from the organizational communication culture perspective, it is necessary to identify how the production companies' patterns of meanings and expectations led to the enactment of the AMA and an industrial family. Rather than assuming that the production companies needed the resources of the AMA, the question, instead, is, What in the production companies' and the AMA's organizational cultures led to the development of an industrial family and its culture? What in the organizations and their interorganizational family led to the belief it was necessary to use expensive resources like hospitals and why was the AMA seal of approval important?

While it is very risky to hazard an answer without doing a close analysis of the organizational communication, for the sake of argument consider the possibility that in creating their environment (which includes audiences and the AMA as well as other media institutions), production companies enacted a world that wanted a *hospital drama.*

Doctor shows were located in *hospitals* because medical organizations were communicating with advertisers as well as production companies about the importance of hospitals in "new" medicine. Further, the industrial family includes organizations concerned about profits (e.g., sponsors, networks, banks) and organizations that seek programs with high traditional production values (e.g., studios). It is likely those expectations led to interorganizational communication about the value of the hospital setting, since it has the ease, control, and efficiency of interior shooting.

Doctor shows were *dramas* because in seeking efficiency and high production values the industrial family put a premium on controlled sets, familiar plots, and straightforward writing. In addition, production companies were familiar with the dramatic form and, because of the audience assumed by the companies, felt drama was appropriate for hospitals. The interplay of audience, sponsors, advertising agencies, production companies, and networks created an industrial family that constituted medicine as proper, professional, and hospital-based.

The interorganizational relationships Turow describes involving television medical shows, then, can be seen as *existing in* and *because of* communicative relationships among those organizations. Organizational communication and the resultant *organizational communication cultures* of the AMA, the production companies, the networks, the advertisers, and the commentator organizations all influence how these organizations interacted with one another. The communicative relationships among those organizations influence the individual organizations, constitute the industrial family, and contribute to the creation of media content. The outcome may be dependency for resources (as in the doctor shows), or it may be an antagonistic relationship, where one organization refuses to allow another to use its resources (e.g., the Central Intelligence Agency has sought to prevent the publication of unapproved books, and, in the case of Snepp's *Decent Interval*, 1977, successfully seized royalties).

MEDIA CONSEQUENCES

Turow's essay argues that the consequences of mass communication need to be understood as the product of media industries vying over resources. He exemplifies this by showing how the relationships between the medical establishment and production companies have produced a televised image of medicine that has become part of U.S. cultural understandings. Turow suggests that institutional analysis helps identify symbiotic relationships in a society, makes problematic the relationship between media organizations and social issues, and implies that media organizations may be able to induce social change.

Consider that organizations are communicative cultures, where organizations constitute their environments and interorganizational communication creates industrial families. From this perspective, mass communication consequences are the result of using mediated messages in the construction of cultural meanings and cultural expectations. By considering organizational and interorganizational communication in the creation of mediated messages, mass communication consequences may be illuminated.

A communicative analysis of media institutions provides a rationale for two aspects of media content and their potential consequences: (a) fundamental similarities and (b) superficial differences. Critiques of media content often attack the media for producing programming of a dull sameness that accepts the basic premises of society. At the same time, the specifics of programming vary wildly — locations, occupations, costumes, and so on. The interplay among media organizations provides a common explanation for the two characteristics.

While the complexity and the multiplicity of communication in producing media content may produce superficial differences in content, it is unlikely to vary significantly from society's models of knowledge or resources. Fundamental social knowledge is likely to be reproduced in multiple exchanges among organizations in closely knit industrial families. Thus it is unlikely that a production company would propose a program that challenges fundamental societal values (e.g., acceptance of capitalism in the United States) when part of an industrial family includes strongly capitalistic organizational cultures (e.g., banks, large holding companies, communications conglomerates). Instead, the program is likely to take such values for granted, and communication among the various media organizations will reinforce such assumptions rather than challenge them (e.g., concern for the bottom line).

At the same time, messages produced by media organizations are the outcome of a complex exchange of communication among organizations. They may reflect the diversity of several organizational communication cultures and lack of consensus in the industrial family. Hence those messages may not be unified and harmonious, but may reflect the variation in communicative exchanges among many organizations. A writer, for instance, may propose a television series to be set on a boat (she likes the ocean), but the production company may want it in a hotel for reasons consistent with its culture (e.g., cost, convenience); the insurance companies may want it in a bank because of their culture's concern for security, the network may want it in a hospital because of its cultural concern for consistency, and so forth. The interplay among these organizations will reflect numerous aspects of the organizations' cultures and how they communicate with the other organizations in their industrial family. Such diversity of players involved in industrialized media production will contribute to numerous superficial differences in media content (e.g., is there a significant difference in the settings for the *Love Boat* and *Hotel*?).

The tendency in media content toward presenting fundamental similarities and superficial differences should not be seen as undermining Turow's argument that media can induce social change. A communicative explication of media industries and media consequences makes the analyst consider the dynamic interplay of organizational communication, interorganizational communication, and audience use of media content. Media consequences are assessed by considering how communication among members creates a particular organizational culture, how *that* process influences communication among organizations, how *that* process produces media content, and how this sequence affects the possible consequences of *that* content. By taking such a route, one can view both the innovative and the reproductive consequences of mass communication.

CONCLUSION

By adopting a communicative, cultural perspective, Turow's analysis of resource dependency is incorporated into a communicative framework for explicating the organizational, interorganizational, and social consequences of mass communication processes. In doing so, the economic relationships among organizations are interpreted as arising from communicative action. Furthermore, because economics arise from communicative action, they influence subsequent communicative action. By shifting to a communicative, cultural analysis it is possible to understand both the microprocesses of mass communication (e.g., individual responses to media, decision making in programming) and macroprocesses of mass communication (e.g., social change, interorganizational negotiation) as instances of the same process — communication.

REFERENCES

Aldrich, H. (1979). *Organizations and environment*. Englewood Cliffs, NJ: Prentice-Hall.

Bantz, C. R. (1981, August). *Interpreting organizational cultures: A proposed procedure, criteria for evaluation, and consideration of research methods*. Paper presented at the ICA-SCA Summer Conference on Interpretive Approaches to Organizational Communication, Alta, UT.

Bantz, C. R. (1989). *Understanding organizations: Analyzing organizational communication culture*. Unpublished manuscript, Arizona State University.

Bantz, C. R. (in press). Organizing and enactment: Karl Weick and the production of news. In S. Corman, S. Banks, C. Bantz, & M. Mayer (Eds.), *Foundations of organizational communication*. New York: Longman.

Blumer, H. (1969). *Symbolic interactionism: Perspective and method*. Englewood Cliffs, NJ: Prentice-Hall.

Bormann, E. G. (1972). Fantasy and rhetorical vision: The rhetorical criticism of social reality. *Quarterly Journal of Speech, 58*, 396-407.

Bormann, E. G. (1983). Symbolic convergence: Organizational communication and culture. In L. L. Putnam & M. E. Pacanowsky (Eds.), *Communication and organization: An interpretive approach* (pp. 99-122). Beverly Hills, CA: Sage.

Bormann, E. G. (1988). "Empowering" as a heuristic concept in organizational communication. In J. A. Anderson (Ed.), *Communication yearbook 11* (pp. 391-404). Newbury Park, CA: Sage.

Hawes, L. C. (1974). Social collectivities as communication: Perspectives on organizational behavior. *Quarterly Journal of Speech, 60*, 497-502.

Johnson, B. M. (1977). *Communication: The process of organizing*. Boston: Allyn & Bacon.

Pacanowsky, M. E., & O'Donnell-Trujillo, N. (1982). Communication and organizational cultures. *Western Journal of Speech Communication, 46*, 115-130.

Pfeffer, J., & Salancik, G. (1978). *The external control of organizations: A resource dependency perspective*. New York: Harper & Row.

Scheibel, D. F. (1989, March). *Linking social worlds and organizational cultures*. Paper presented at the Gregory Stone Symbolic Interaction Symposium, Tempe, AZ.

Snepp, F. (1977). *Decent interval: An insider's account of Saigon's indecent end told by the CIA's chief strategy analyst in Vietnam*. New York: Random House.

Turow, J. (1984). *Media industries: The production of news and entertainment*. New York: Longman.

Weick, K. E. (1969). *The social psychology of organizing*. Reading, MA: Addison-Wesley.

Weick, K. E. (1979). *The social psychology of organizing* (2nd ed.). Reading, MA: Addison-Wesley.

Research from Start to Finish

SANDRA BRAMAN
University of Illinois

AKIBA A. COHEN
Hebrew University of Jerusalem

T HE arguments used in Joseph Turow's chapter are bigger than one may initially see. This critique opens with a summary of the broad sweep of his comments, pointing to some diversions from his line of thinking and commenting briefly upon the case study offered. The larger focus, however, is on expanding upon important themes embedded in Turow's piece. The first section will explore and elaborate upon some theoretical issues raised in Turow's chapter and suggest some directions for movement; the following section does the same for the methodological and research issues he raises.

DEFINITIONAL AND THEORETICAL ISSUES

Turow's chapter initially centers on the question of whether or not "mass communication" is still a meaningful concept. Some of the reasons he asks this question are commonly found throughout the literature (e.g., today's audience is fragmented), while others are more novel (e.g., identifying variant meanings for the concept of "mass"). Turow deals with culture from the perspective of symbolic interactionism, and thus finds mass communication inherently of interest in a world built through symbol generation and communication.

Turow's answer turns the angle of the question away from the nature of the audience and toward the message production process. He argues for using the organization as the unit of analysis, and urges a research agenda designed to mine

Correspondence and requests for reprints: Sandra Braman, Institute of Communication Research, University of Illinois, Urbana, IL 61820.

Communication Yearbook 13, pp. 511-518

the ways in which organizations create, exchange, and use messages. (It is a strength of Turow's that he consistently refers to a wide range of media, including greeting card companies as well as newspapers, when he discusses mass communication.)

The dominant image used is organic. For Turow, organizations absorb and process information nutritionally. They need to receive information in order to function, and much of their functioning is the processing of that information. New messages are sent into the environment in the attempt to affect or control that environment — in other words, to exercise power.

It is one of Turow's key points that organizations interact symbiotically, so that in order to understand the message creation process we must examine message flows between and among organizations — information that crosses institutional boundaries. This is a powerful insight that complicates not only the biological metaphor but our research agenda.

Turow offers a definition of mass communication that is both technological and organizational: "the industrialized (mass) production, reproduction, and multiple distribution of messages through technological devices" (p. 484). He understands the term *industrial* to mean a process being carried out by "mass media complexes or industries," although it is not clear how "complexes," "industries," "conglomerations," and "organizations" are to be distinguished from one another. Turow touts as an advantage of this definition that it "prominently avoids setting requirements about the number and nature of people attending to the messages" (p. 484).

His insistence on the organization as the unit of analysis, and particularly his fascination with information flows across institutional boundaries, suggests yet another definition of mass communication that is implicit in the lines of argument developed in this commentary: Perhaps mass communication can be defined as communication that is aimed at *organizations*, rather than *masses of individuals*, as its audience. At its logical conclusion, this approach would imply, then, that the point of television is to serve the linking function suggested. In Turow's case study, this line of analysis suggests, then, that the point of the doctor shows on television is to provide the medical establishment with a relatively accepting and complacent group of patients.

Turow's research agenda would be enriched by greater articulation of some of the most fundamental concepts he uses. Four that we can ruminate on are power, organizational boundaries, mass, and culture. The notion of "power" has recently been an area of great theoretical activity. Lukes (1986) has synthesized the literature and developed a framework that has had a great deal of influence. He distinguishes among three types of power: instrumental, structural, and consensual. Instrumental power is direct exercise of force; structural power is the power inherent in designing the rules of action; and consensual power is power that is exercised in the realm of ideology.

Turow's focus on the role of media organizations in shaping the way in which the mass media are used as a realm for cultural argumentation can be viewed as an attempt to link evidence of two types of power—structural and consensual. His claim is that better understanding of the structural exercise of power, ways in which organizations shape the creation of media messages, will help explain ways in which development of consensual power is demonstrated in message content.

Turow sees organizations as goal-directed, boundary-maintaining activity systems, and defines mass communication as a process that occurs at the boundaries of organizations. He is particularly interested in organizational boundaries, as the domain for cultural argumentation. Both theoretically and in his case study, Turow discusses only *fiction* as the mode of cultural argumentation. But *fact* is also a boundary-defining technique (Braman, 1985). Every locus of consciousness uses fact (a narrative and political device) as a boundary-defining technique; each offers as fact a version of reality that favors its own continued survival. A locus of consciousness can be either biological (a person) or organizational (a corporation).

Operationalization of these ideas in a case study involved comparing Joan Didion's "private" locus of consciousness (her biological unit, using "new journalism" techniques) and the *New York Times*'s "public" locus of consciousness (representing, as newspaper of record, both the ideals of "objective journalism" and the U.S. government) as each reported on El Salvador during June 1982 (Braman, 1985). The survival concerns of each locus of consciousness were clearly evident in the widely differing reports. Didion's terrified biological organism saw chaos where the *Times*, also concerned for the survival of its interests, saw merely stalled bureaucratic procedures, such as elections, and land reforms.

The debate between the two styles of journalism ("new" and "objective") opens and closes on the question of which fact-gathering and reporting methodologies result in the most accurate portrayals of fact. Insertion of the notion of fact as a boundary-defining technique for competing individual and corporate loci of consciousness into Turow's discussion makes the question more vivid: Whose vision of the world will hold—and who will, if they're right, survive as a result?

The notion of "mass," so central to this piece, is treated somewhat inconsistently. Turow goes back to early notions of the mass and identifies two strains of interpretation: A mass could be identified by geographical boundaries (a group of people within a given area) or by cognitive boundaries (a group of people moved to respond to events in the same cognitive manner). This distinction does seem to provide a powerful and potentially fruitful way of thinking about changes in the nature of the audience, including its fragmentation, but unfortunately Turow wanders away from this dichotomization toward another typology. For the bulk of his discussion about the mass, he distinguishes between masses that are moved rationally and those that are moved irrationally. This is quite a different approach. One wonders why he switched from one typology to the other, and how either might have played out had it been used consistently across the range of questions raised.

Finally, the notion of "culture" is itself problematic. While a quote from anthropologist Geertz opens his chapter, Turow seems to draw largely upon social psychology for his notion of culture. There are, however, many other ways of approaching the concept. The fact that it can be approached in so many ways, with wide disagreements as to just what social processes should be included, has, in fact, led social scientists from other cultures (notably Latin America) to discard the use of the term altogether.

Turow himself emphasizes the difficulty in using the term. While he talks about ways in which the same images are disseminated to diverse cultures around the world, he fails to explore the reverse of this phenomenon: People in one place can now be exposed to messages from an enormous variety of cultures simultaneously.

METHODOLOGICAL AND RESEARCH ISSUES

A number of methodological issues are raised in Turow's essay, both explicitly and implicitly. One way of elaborating upon the methodological framework implied by Turow would seek to broaden the study of the way in which organizational structures shape messages by inclusion of cross-cultural research. Turow does not deal with the question of whether or not what he says is universal, or how what he describes is affected by cultural forces or manifested in different cultural settings. Many central research questions of the kind raised by Turow can best be investigated only through cross-cultural or cross-national research that provides the kind of variation necessary for this form of analysis.

A second key direction for elaboration of the methodological framework suggested by Turow is to look at information flows across institutional boundaries in the course of the creation of media materials. The kernel here is the idea that research should look at media messages "from start to finish," and it is based on the assumption that research into one isolated facet of a process will necessarily yield only a partial understanding of the nature of that process.

As a result of both academic specialization and the overwhelming literatures amassed inside these specializations, it is common to find varying degrees of emphasis even among scholars who basically see themselves as engaging in the same general field. This is also true, of course, in the realm of mass communication research. Hence, as Turow suggests, there are those in our field who focus mainly on uses and consequences of media (what he claims is the large majority); others concentrate on media contents (a large minority according to Turow), and there remains a "much smaller contingent," Turow argues, that is concerned with media organizations. While this assessment of the relative strength of the various "camps" may be more or less correct, it seems that more centrally lacking in the area of mass communication research are serious attempts to deal with all three subareas of interest in a more coherent, comprehensive, and unified framework. It is imperative that we combine these three domains of inquiry (production, content, and consequences) in substantial fashion within the framework of broad research projects.

Turow limits his notion of "media process" to the production of messages. He does not examine audience perception of messages in his case study, perhaps overreacting to the imbalance he objects to by overweighting the work in the other direction. However, the notion of media process also accurately refers to phenomena that occur and processes that unfold in message content and the audience. Moreover, an argument for studying audience perception of messages is not necessarily an argument against paying attention to media organizations. Hence true start-to-finish research would look at the process of creating messages, their content, and their perception by and impact upon the audience.

Start-to-Finish Research

Turow's case study is an example of start-to-finish research limited to tracing control over creation of messages and their flows across institutional boundaries. Examples of research that attempts to be start to finish on a comparative dimension can be found in a group of projects on television news by researchers from Israel and other countries.

The first attempt to do start-to-finish research was a study of a then new late-night television newscast, appropriately called *Almost Midnight* (Roeh, Katz, Cohen, & Zelizer, 1980). It was an attempt to strengthen the research links between the organizational/production aspect of the news (or what Turow might term the "industry"), the contents, and the potential and even actual social effects or consequences. The study illustrated how broadcasters can benefit from researchers in formulating their objectives, and how input from the audience at the formative stages of the program can be put to use in advancing those objectives.

Another attempt to look at the three levels of the mass communication process on a cross-national basis (including the United States, the United Kingdom, West Germany, Israel, and South Africa) explored social conflicts in TV news (Cohen, Adoni, & Bantz, 1989).[1] That study examined the possible links between the presentation of conflicts in the news and the perception of conflict by news audiences. It was found that government regulation and media competition factors seem to be less important than were expected, whereas similarities and shared journalistic norms and values in the five countries appeared to be more important in determining the contents of the news. The distinction between foreign and domestic news proved to be especially powerful. It was found, for example, that foreign conflicts in all of the five countries were presented as being more complex, more intense, and more difficult to solve than domestic conflicts.

A third start-to-finish project, still under way, deals with foreign news on television in a variety of countries.[2] It is a study of how decisions are made in a "global" newsroom as well as in the news departments of different countries regarding what foreign news stories will be shown, how they are actually presented in the various countries, and how audiences in the different countries make sense of and interpret them.

This study is being conducted within the framework of the European Broadcasting Union (EBU). The major function of the EBU's News Exchange Service is to facilitate the transfer of news among its members and affiliates. The basic operating premise is that of reciprocity in sharing information and providing coverage of events that would otherwise not be accessible to most of the members due to budgetary and logistical limitations (news sharing is a phenomenon not common among the highly competitive and commercial U.S. television networks).

Each day, two radiotelephone conferences take place in which representatives of the member countries "negotiate" offers and requests for material on stories of the day. Later in the day, satellite (as well as ground cable) transmissions provide the selected news materials to member countries. Most of the items provided include only visual material, but sometimes verbal material, such as interviews, is included. Each country may then choose to use the material in any way it wishes. Member countries pay only for the material they use.

A tentative conclusion of this study is that while there are indeed formal EBU rules according to which items are "accepted" for transmission to the member countries, idiosyncratic criteria are also employed. Further, the interaction among the representatives of the various countries is influenced by country-specific interests and considerations. In any event, as Turow would suggest, it is critical to take such factors into account in trying to grasp the intricacies of the system.[3]

CONCLUSIONS

Turow's chapter is rich in sweeping ideas and provides a fascinating and useful case study. Expansion of theoretical and methodological ideas embedded in the piece leads to a call for designing research agendas that look at communication issues from start to finish—looking at the processes involved in the production, content, and audience response to media messages. In order to tap cultural variables in a number of significant dimensions, research design should be cross-national or cross-cultural. While different methodologies should be used as appropriate for different elements of the research design, the same concepts must be operationalizable throughout.

Such research gains its meaning from what it learns about society in general. Thus it must be based upon a well-developed theoretical and conceptual framework that deals with basic questions about such issues as the nature of the social structure, the role of change and conflict within that social structure, ways in which societies differ along key dimensions (such as level of development, linguistic structure, and legal history), and the nature of power and its exercise in various societies over time. Use of such terms as *society* and *power* cannot be casual.

In this regard, communication researchers should combine work with scholars from other "disciplines" when it is pertinent. Concepts such as "power" have received a great deal of discussion in the field of political science during recent years, while our understanding of the nature of highly articulated social structures has been greatly forwarded by sociologists.

In stressing the role of communications as a boundary-maintaining mechanism, Turow joins a growing stream of researchers working on this function of discourse. He stands between two very different approaches to such issues. On the one hand, there is Foucault (1982) and his descendants (e.g., Davis, 1983; Said, 1981). On the other hand, there are the frameworks being developed by Krippendorff (1984) and others working in the area of cybernetics and its consequences in the social sphere.

The Turow agenda calls for analysis of interinstitutional information flows as mutual support systems; this profound insight into what might be called a social ecology of organizations is pregnant with implications for research. Turow's own work, as demonstrated in the enticing case study, has found an accessible and absorbing route into complex and powerful relationships among key institutions and organizations in society.

NOTES

1. Several colleagues participated in this work: Deanna Robinson, Michael Gurevitch, Jay Blumler, Karen Honikman, Gabriele Bock, Alison Ewbank, and Friedrich Knilli.

2. Colleagues involved in this study are Itzhak Roeh, Mark Levy, and Michael Gurevitch. The countries in the study are Belgium, France, Israel, Italy, Jordan, Luxembourg, Spain, Switzerland, the United Kingdom, the United States, and West Germany.

3. The design of the foreign news study is complex in another sense as well. Whereas in current research aimed at studying how people from different cultures interpret the same content (e.g., the work on *Dallas* by Liebes & Katz, 1988) the focus is usually on a specific episode presented in an identical fashion in the various countries, the rationale behind the present study is to show people in different countries the particular version that their respective television station presented of a given item or story. Thus, by definition, there is more variability in the design itself.

REFERENCES

Braman, S. (1985). The "facts" of El Salvador: The objective journalism of the *New York Times* vs. the new journalism of Joan Didion. *Journal of Communication Inquiry, 13*(2), 75-96.

Cohen, A. A., Adoni, H., & Bantz, C. R. (1989). *Social conflicts and television news: A cross national study of presentation and perception*. Manuscript submitted for publication.

Davis, L. J. (1983). *Factual fictions: The origins of the English novel*. New York: Columbia University Press.

Foucault, M. (1982). *The archaeology of knowledge and the discourse on language* (A. M. Sheridan Smith, Trans.). New York: Pantheon.

Krippendorff, K. (1984, May). *Information, information society and some Marxian propositions.* Paper presented at the annual meeting of the International Communication Association, San Francisco.

Liebes, T., & Katz, E. (1988). *Dallas* and Genesis: Primordiality and seriality in popular culture. In J. W. Carey (Ed.), *Media, myths, and narratives: Television and the press* (pp. 113-125). Newbury Park, CA: Sage.

Lukes, S. (1986). *Power*. London: Macmillan.

Roeh, I., Katz, E., Cohen, A. A., & Zelizer, B. (1980). *Almost midnight: Reforming the late night news.* Beverly Hills, CA: Sage.

Said, E. (1981). *Covering Islam: How the media and the experts determine how we see the rest of the world.* New York: Pantheon.

Turow, J. (1984). *Media industries: The production of news and entertainment.* New York: Longman.

Turow, J. (1985). Cultural argumentation and the mass media. *Communication, 8,* 139-164.

11 Textual Status, the Stigmatized Self, and Media Consumption

VIRGINIA H. FRY
Haverhill, MA

ALISON ALEXANDER
University of Massachusetts

DONALD L. FRY
Emerson College

This chapter develops and explores the interaction among three concepts: textual status, the assumption of media texts, and the way in which an individual's preference for low-status texts such as soap operas may stigmatize the self in communicative contexts where texts are encountered as subjects of talk and not just as objects viewed, heard, or read.

I
N *The Logic of the Sciences and the Humanities,* Northrop (1959) comments on the importance of developing inquiries grounded in a recognition of the *intra*disciplinary character of one's investigation:

Scientific inquiry in any field must begin not with some method taken over a priori from some other field, but with the character of its own field and the analysis of those problems. A subject becomes scientific not by beginning with facts, with hypotheses or with some pet method brought in a priori, but by beginning with the peculiar character of its particular problems. (p. 274)

Operating within an *intra*disciplinary spirit, this essay will articulate a perspective that places the generative power of communication at the center of our concerns.

AUTHORS' NOTE: Each of the authors contributed equally to this chapter.

Correspondence and requests for reprints: Donald L. Fry, Division of Mass Communication, Emerson College, Boston, MA, 02116.

Communication Yearbook 13, pp. 519-544

Our goal is to move toward an integrative theory of communication by exploring the interrelationships among media consumption, textual status, and the stigmatized self as they interact in the production and reproduction of meaning in primary media exposure contexts and in additional communicative contexts. These interrelationships point toward a set of larger issues that are significant for a number of domains of mass communication research.

Specifically, we will argue that mass communication research must extend its research focus beyond the primary exposure context, usually constituted by some direct and immediate contact with media content, and explore a whole series of communication contexts in which texts are encountered through talk and where meanings also are produced and reproduced. Most mass communication research has focused on the primary media exposure context, and has assumed implicitly that what a text means to a media consumer is fixed at that time. By contrast, we are less interested in the primary media exposure context (the initial choice to consume a particular text/genre) than in the other communicative contexts in which individuals reencounter their preferred texts through talk about those texts. In other words, we are less concerned with the *what* and *why* of media consumption — with what particular texts mean to individuals and why they prefer particular texts — than with *how* texts become meaningful.

In maintaining a communicative focus, we must integrate three major aspects of our perspective (media consumption, textual status, and the stigmatized self) and constitute these concepts as a case in point that addresses the larger issue of how texts become meaningful. *Communication*, then, is our overarching term. We will treat consumption as a particular kind of communicative behavior. The object consumed is a text, and the text has a significant status in the culture within which it exists, a status that transcends its particular distinguishing structural features. The relationship between texts and the contexts in which texts are consumed also will be discussed. In developing our notion of the stigmatized self, we will explore the extent to which one's consumption of texts that have low cultural status may "mark" the self in particularly negative ways. Material from a case study of viewers of daytime serials will be presented to illustrate our theoretical arguments.[1] The larger purpose of the study, however, extends beyond textual status and stigma per se. The interrelationship among these concepts allows for an examination of the connection between primary media consumption contexts, communication contexts, and the transformation of texts as they pass from context to context.

TEXT AND CONTEXT

In the past several years, the issue of where meaning is located — in the message, in the audience, in some interaction between the two, or elsewhere — has been significant to researchers in diverse fields. Feeling constrained by the term *message*, which historically has been tied to a linear, transportation model of communication, many researchers have taken up the term *text* as a starting point for their inquiry into meaning. Employing this alternative term has led critics in at least two particular directions—structural and interpretive—as they inquired into the way in which texts become meaningful to audiences. Regarding the text primarily as a container of meaning, structurally oriented critics have tried to identify and enumerate the significant features distinguishing particular texts. Borrowing from Iser (1978), who describes traditionally oriented literary criticism as treating texts as if they contained a meaning just as a carpet may have its own special pattern, Allen (1987) refers to this type of criticism as "figure-in-the-carpet" criticism. Within this tradition, critics have assessed issues as diverse as Freudian metaphors in children's fairy tales, consumerism in sitcoms, and value systems in prime-time programming. In their systematic exploration of the characteristics of texts, these critics have tended to detach texts from the audiences who receive and interpret them. Another approach has treated a text as something that is "read" and thus is somehow different from a message that is transmitted. The notion of audience members as "readers" has been developed to call attention to the active role played by audience members in interpreting texts. Rather than attempting to locate the inherent pattern, or figure in the carpet, this kind of criticism has shifted attention away from determining the "real" meaning of a text to accounting for how audiences make texts intelligible (Allen, 1987). Researchers operating within this perspective have studied works of music, romance novels, and soap operas, among other things.

Although, historically, mass communication researchers have assumed meaning to be in the mediated message itself, today the consensus has shifted to a more audience-centered focus that locates the production of meaning largely in a combination of audience-centered and content-centered factors (Allen, 1987; Eco, 1979; Fiske, 1986; Fry & Fry, 1986; Hall, 1980; Newcomb, 1984; Radway, 1984; Schudson, 1987). For example, Eco's (1979) classification of texts as open or closed is based on the relationship between the structural features of each textual type and the appeal of those features to actual readers. Fiske (1986) argues that a television text is "polysemic" because it allows for "various subcultures to generate meanings from it that meet the needs of their own subcultural identities" (p. 392). In addition to the likelihood of multiple meanings across subgroups, Fry and Fry (1986) comment on the capability of individual audience members to produce multiple meanings by interpreting a given media text in a number of different ways. While emphasizing audience involvement with texts, both Eco and Fiske conclude that a text's range of possible meanings is constrained by the content structures of the text. Whether it is the dominant ideological structure in the text (Fiske) or the author's intention that is translated into either an open or closed textual structure (Eco), most researchers agree that studying meaning requires an awareness of both textual and audience-related factors. Researchers tend to differ on the weight they place on the structural components of the text and on the interpretive act of actually reading a particular text.

Replacing message with text has engendered the significant shift from receiver to reader; this change in terminology, however, has not altered the notion of message or text to the same degree that it has led toward conceptualizing an actively engaged audience. Extending the term *text* from literary studies into other fields has enlarged the notion of text to allow for the treatment of a wide range of communicative activities as texts. Nevertheless, undergirding many of these approaches to text and meaning is a particular conception of text that, though masked by a changed vocabulary, does not differ radically from the transportation view of message.

Although a widely accepted interpretive perspective implies a dialogic and somewhat conversational relationship between a text and its reader, text remains a physically definable entity with specific linguistic, auditory, and/or visual characteristics — an object that can be located physically in time and space. Further, even though researchers have begun to focus on the interpretive activities of individuals and cultural subgroups, there is a general presumption that a text has some specialized and intrinsic content to which readers somehow are drawn at the moment of their encounter with it. Texts are often viewed as having a "preferred meaning" (Hall, 1980; Morley, 1980), a "preferred reading" (Morley, 1981), or "semiotic excess" (Fiske, 1986). The "preferred meaning" arguments grant the existence of multiple textual meanings; in some ways, however, they actually return to the earlier view of the message as a container for meaning.

In summary, while the complexity of the meaning production process has been expanded by these and other studies, we remain limited in our understanding of the production and reproduction of meaning. The implicit force that drives the debate surrounding the relationship between media content and audience is the assumption that meaning can be located somewhere in a concrete and physical way, usually in the text or in audience decodings of a text. Asking "where?" questions presumes that meaning is contained somewhere, that meaning is situated somewhere — in content, audience, or some interaction between the two. This set of presumptions inherently ties meaning to the primary exposure context.

In order to display the limiting features of "where?" questions, it is necessary to develop more complex conceptions of both text and context. We will move in this direction by defining and clarifying several different uses of the term *text* and by linking those uses to the multiple contexts in which texts can be encountered. Though we agree with those who use the term to refer to a definable object that is "read" or encountered by an audience at some precise moment, text should not be reduced to this single usage. Interestingly, the shortcoming of this view of text and context derives from what Allen (1987) has praised as "the common-sense observation that meaning does not occur except through the reading act" (p. 75). By locating the production of meaning in a concrete act of reading, an act that takes place at the moment when a reader encounters a text, other possible ways of thinking about texts and our encounters with them are eliminated.

Our argument is that in addition to being an object with definable and empirically apparent structural characteristics, a text can also be an object of talk. In other words, it is just as possible to encounter a text—a poem, a film, a television program, even a textual genre—through talk about the text as it is to encounter it as a definable physical object. These two usages of the term *text* parallel the two different types of contexts in which a text can be encountered. We use the term *consumption context* (our use of the term *consumption* is discussed in the next section) to describe a reader's engagement with a text as a physical object, and *communicative context* to refer to the myriad encounters one can have with the same text as an object of talk. Consumption and communicative contexts can be linked in complex temporal and spatial ways. For instance, these contexts may be simultaneous, as in the case when one discusses a news story with someone while at the same time watching the story on television. At other times, they may occur in a range of temporally and spatially distinct contexts, either prior to the consumption context (for instance, discussing an event with friends and only then being exposed to media coverage) or after a consumption context. These communication contexts where a text is transformed from an object encountered directly by an audience member to an object of discourse are crucial to the understanding of the production of communicative meaning, possibly more crucial than the consumption context, where the text is encountered as a directly accessible physical object. It should be noted that by distinguishing between consumption and communication, we do not intend to suggest that communication does not occur in consumption contexts; we are suggesting that the phenomenology of the two contexts is different.

This emphasis on additional communicative contexts provides an alternative to the assumptions that historically have guided mass communication research. Media use or exposure traditionally has been placed within temporal and spatial parameters, a primary use or exposure context that presupposes a particular ideal case (a concept borrowed with some modifications from Weber, 1949). An ideal case is an index of the guiding assumptions about how researchers think the phenomenon being studied is constituted. The ideal case in most audience-based mass communication research assumes an individual viewer (reader, listener) positioned before a screen (newspaper, radio, stereo), usually within some private or semiprivate environment. Studies of recall, uses and gratifications, content analyses of various types of programs, and so on, are predicated upon this prototype. Clearly, if one assumes, for example, that an individual's attention is focused on a television text in a primary viewing context, it is possible to argue, as does Jensen (1987), for the study of "concrete contexts of decoding and the *immediate* ways the programs are used" (p. 26; emphasis added).

However, not all television researchers agree that the primary viewing context is that cohesive and highly structured by a text. In fact, some researchers have suggested that primary television viewing may be engaged in as a secondary activity (Bechtel, Achelpohl, & Akers, 1972). Others have argued that effects are mediated interpersonally, by previous experiences with the same or similar texts and by other objects and occurrences within the viewing environment. Bennett (1982) points in this direction when he says that each encounter with a text produces meanings that are "encrusted" with every preceding encounter with the same or similar texts. In noting that all objects in an environment are not equally meaningful, Schudson (1987) contributes to our understanding of the viewing context. Viewing activity may be less structured by the features of the text than by extratextual factors that may lead audience members to make contextual factors differentially meaningful. Thus factors not directly related to the constitution of the exposure context affect the production of meaning.

Although mediating factors certainly add complexity to the ideal case, they fall short of questioning its validity: Viewers are still seen as "using" content to shape their interpersonal interactions, or prior interpersonal relationships are thought to protect viewers from or subject viewers to media effects differently. The ideal case still remains positioned at the point where an individual directly encounters a text.

Interestingly, the ideal case is not challenged by most reader-response critics, who also idealize an individual's solitary encounter with a text. Although individuals may bring to that encounter a particular set of background experiences, including personal history and preferences and a host of prior experiences with similar texts, it is the individual's resources interacting with a text in a consumption (reading, viewing) context that provides researchers and critics with their ideal case. This stance, quite simply, means that the individual's history mediates the effects and the impact of a text; it does not necessarily result in an active audience capable of actually producing texts (this latter point will be elaborated shortly when we present our definition of text).

In summary, the traditional ideal case encourages the typification of a viewer at the point of exposure to a medium; this context is constituted within temporal parameters bounded by the beginning and ending of viewing, reading, or listening and within spatial parameters bounded by where that activity takes place. We think this ideal case is unduly restrictive and simplistic. Although the exposure context is obviously highly complex and significant, we argue that the meaning produced in that context is not necessarily the only fixed meaning for the audience in many cases, or the most significant. A research focus on communicative contexts may be much more crucial in understanding the production and reproduction of meaning because it acknowledges the range and complexity of the different ways in which texts and individuals can come together.

An alternative ideal case positions the individual not only within the media consumption context, but also in numerous ongoing communicative contexts (Alexander & Fry, 1986; Fry, Alexander, & Fry, 1989). This ideal case counters the assumptions guiding mass communication research that the media/audience encounter is a cohesive and well-defined instance and thus capable of being studied within limited temporal and spatial bounds.

The complexity of the relationship between exposure and communication contexts is highlighted through the example of an individual who reads a review of a film or watches a television film review program. In both mediated products, another media product is the content of discourse. As such, these are interesting genres in that they contain elements of the experience both of viewing context in which an individual views a particular television program and of a communication encounter with another media product. More commonly, however, texts encountered in consumption contexts reappear in other contexts where the initially consumed text becomes an object of discussion. For instance, the engagement between Vice President Bush and Dan Rather during the 1988 presidential campaign may well have been encountered in a viewing context. Additionally, it may have been reencountered as a topic of conversation with friends or family, and/or as the focus of discussion in a journalism or media ethics course. In fact, it is quite possible that these communication exchanges might actually precede the media consumption context, or that the communication exchanges may occur without any direct consumption of the actual Bush-Rather encounter. That is, it is clearly possible that some people may never see the actual encounter but, nonetheless, still carry on extended discourse about it in various communication contexts. The meanings that are produced in these various contexts should be expected to vary based on the defining nature of the context (we will return to this point later in the essay).

The communication contexts that will be the concern of this chapter are those interpersonal communicative contexts in which discussions, direct or indirect, take place regarding a medium, a particular media product, or product content outside the viewing, reading, or listening context. These communication contexts are significant, we believe, because the meanings produced in these contexts may differ from those produced during the media consumption context. A good example of the importance of these communicative contexts is provided by Hodge and Tripp's (1986) reproduction of an exchange between an interviewer and a group of 12-year-olds regarding their interpretations of a cartoon shown on television. The children's responses punctuate an important consideration in discriminating between exposure and communication contexts and in determining the relative importance of each:

Interviewer: Were you thinking these things when you were watching that?
All: Yeah.
Interviewer: Were you?
Len: But you don't feel much about it when you are watching but after somebody, anybody asks you what we felt, then you say what happened.
Geoffrey: You don't really take it into consideration.
Interviewer: That's an interesting comment. You don't, you don't feel much when you're watching?
Mark: You don't really think about it if you aren't asked. If you aren't asked, you don't think about it again. (p. 66)

Wren-Lewis (1983) makes a similar point. He argues that audience members who are interviewed about a television program will tend "to construct a more critical reading than they might do otherwise" (p. 196). While viewers understand

and enjoy their exposure to media content, elaborated meaning may not occur unless or until audience members discuss the content in communication contexts. Hodge and Tripp (1986) contend that thoughts and feelings do not really exist until they are made public and visible. We contend that communication contexts are where thoughts and feelings become public and visible.

In his extended essay on the television serial *Dallas*, Ang (1982/1985) suggests that the immediate experience with the program may well deviate significantly from the abstract and rational explanations that are often attributed to television viewing. He notes that the immediate experience for his viewer-subjects was a "'spontaneous' phenomenon: a person enjoys watching it, or otherwise, in some way or other" (p. 82). In essence, the consumption context may be constituted through the simple recognition of the intent of the program or the genre of program (V. Fry & D. Fry, 1987; Nelson, 1985) and a basic reaction of pleasure, excitement, boredom, or the like. The viewer engages the text primarily as a cultural practice that is "directly available, casual and free" (Ang, 1982/1985, p. 84).

Another good example of communicative contexts is provided by the regular viewer of daytime serials who informs another viewer who missed a particular episode of what took place in that program. Picture, also, another discussion between the same viewers: Both talk about how hard it is to find time to view all episodes, of how they try to arrange their schedules in order to see as many episodes as possible of their favorite programs, and, perhaps, of how others in their family react to their serial viewing behavior. In this discussion, viewing behavior rather than the specific content of a text is the subject of the conversation. However, in both communicative contexts, the text — soap opera — is made problematic and becomes the subject of discourse. In our interviews with soap opera viewers, we found that such discussions occur with some regularity, and it is clear that the text — the soap opera — becomes transformed into an object of discussion.

Certainly, a reconstituted ideal case not only includes a number of communicative encounters that traditionally have been outside the domain of mass communication research but also directs us to formulate a fundamental reconceptualization of the term *text*. The examples in the preceding paragraphs point to this altered definition of text. Our argument that discussions in communicative contexts that have nothing to do with textual content should be treated as encounters with those same texts is predicated upon a substantially different conception of text than has heretofore informed literary and mass communication research.

Rather than thinking of a text only as a single identifiable entity, we think the term has a dual usage. These two usages parallel the two contexts in which texts are encountered. For lack of another means of labeling the difference between these two usages of the term *text*, we tentatively will use *text{obj}* to denote the object that is "read" by an individual in a consumption context and *text{subj}* to denote text as the subject of discourse. Given our claim that individuals encounter or consume mediated texts over time and space in both consumption (text{obj}) and communicative contexts (text{subj}), it is important to examine what occurs within those two types of contexts. It is not wise to assume that the meaning produced in a consumption context is merely reproduced with no alteration in communication contexts or that the modes of production are the same in both types of contexts.

Because mass communication researchers already have contributed significantly to our understanding of text{obj} and the consumption context, we will focus primarily on the experiences individuals have with text{subj} in communicative contexts. To clarify our concept, it is useful to think of text{subj} as a fabric that is woven into myriad textured patterns and configurations. Halliday's (1978) discussion of text as a semantic concept, as being continuous and "seamless," and as having no clearly identifiable beginning and ending contributes to elaborating our fabric metaphor. A text, Halliday argues,

> is the linguistic form of social interaction. It is a continuous progression of meanings, combining both simultaneously and in succession. The meanings are the selections made by the speaker from the options that constitute the *meaning potential*; text is the actualization of this meaning potential, the process of semantic choice. (p. 122)

Text{subj}, then, is a "semantic concept," produced through social interaction and resulting from the actual choices made by individuals involved in interaction.

In this sense, text{subj} cannot be reduced to linguistic, grammatical, or visual components; it exists as a generic structure that, while not denying its content components, is capable of standing apart from them (Halliday, 1978, pp. 134-135). Using our fabric metaphor, text{subj} is talk about text{obj}, and as such is a product of social interaction; although it requires the existence of text{obj}, it is not reducible to the content or uses of that text gleaned by a reader encountering it in a consumption context.

Linking our two uses of text with Halliday's definition suggests that text{obj} possesses a "meaning potential" and text{subj} is produced when some aspect of that potentiality is realized through speech in a communicative context. In metaphorical terms, it is possible to make a number of different garments in varied sizes and colors out of the same materials; what is made depends, among other things, upon the inclinations of the tailor and upon the needs, preferences, and wishes of those for whom the garments are being produced. Just as a particular fabric does not become a sweater or skirt simply because it can, the meaning possibilities of a text do not exist simply as inherent textual properties. What texts become has as much to do with extratextual factors, including the context in which they are encountered and produced, as with their intrinsic features.

Since the existence of text{obj} is a necessary, though not sufficient, condition for the production of text{subj}, it is reasonable to assume that the matrix of possible meanings that can be produced as text{subj} is not limited to those suggested by text{obj} or by the consumption context in which it is deployed. In producing text{subj}, individuals may talk about the plot, character, or theme of text{obj} as well as about their experiences with text{obj}, including what family and friends think of their media preferences. Text{subj}, then, is woven from talk about every aspect, use, and implication related to the consumption of text{obj}. At the same time, as a fabric woven through talk or human interaction, text{subj} is not reducible to the boundaries established by text{obj} and the context in which it is consumed. The contexts within which the text is encountered and reencountered will affect materially the meanings that are produced.

The following discussion and example should help clarify this point. To cite Halliday (1978) again, text is

> a continuous process that is involved in all human interaction; it is not unstructured, but it is seamless, and all that one can observe is a kind of periodicity in which peaks of texture alternate with troughs — highly cohesive moments with moments of relatively little continuity. (pp. 136-137)

Although it may be possible to fix text{obj} at the time and space of the consumption context, text{subj} is a carefully woven, highly textured, and seamless fabric that is continuously being produced and reproduced through ongoing communicative action by the weavers of the fabric.

The following example should be helpful in distinguishing between text{obj} and text{subj}. Our interviews with soap opera viewers put us in contact with a number of people who regularly watched this genre of programming (text{obj}). Several of our informants would regularly gather with other viewers of the same program (text{obj}) to discuss and analyze what had happened and what might happen in the future (text{subj}). In this instance, text{obj} becomes transformed into text{subj} through an ongoing analytic discourse. Further, many of our informants encountered people who did not watch soap operas. At times, the informants' viewing habits became the focus of discussion (text{subj}). In such situations, the program (text{obj}) was justified by the informant (text{subj}), but, additionally, the nonviewer also engaged in a discussion of the text (text{obj}) without actually consuming the text{obj}.

As an object of discourse, a text{obj} can be talked about in many different ways, to many different persons, and through many different channels of communication. Each specific communicative context can be treated as a concrete instance of interaction — a stitch in the fabric. When taken together, all contribute to forming soap opera as text{subj}, a concept that is inclusive of all the various ways in which soap opera has been talked about. This inclusive notion of text{subj} encompasses as well the way in which soap opera has been studied by researchers. Scholars are as much weavers of this textual fabric as are viewers, nonviewers, marketing researchers, advertisers, and the performers on the programs.

The implications of this conception of text are substantial. Because encounters with text{obj} and text{subj} occur over time and space in consumption and communicative contexts, it is not wise to assume an isomorphism between the two contexts. An individual's experience with text{obj} in a consumption context may be fundamentally different from when the same individual encounters that text as an object of talk. Not only may the meanings that text holds for the individual vary between contexts, but also how those meanings are engendered may be quite different. The differences derive less from such factors as a text's "preferred reading" and the acknowledgment that individuals can produce a range of readings than from the probability that text{obj} and text{subj} and the contexts in which they are consumed and produced have fundamentally different phenomenologies. Each comes into being and exists in the world in radically varied ways.

Another implication of this altered conception of text relates to the possible connections that can be established between an individual and a text. Granting an actively involved audience makes it possible to treat interactively the individual/text encounter in a consumption context. Individuals are not purely passive receivers of texts, but, instead, based on their own histories, orientations, and preferences, may arrive at interpretations that were not envisioned by the producers of text{obj}. Thus the concept of text{subj} makes it possible to argue (a) that individuals extend textual denotations to produce meanings that were not envisioned by textual authors and (b) that persons engaged in ongoing interaction weave together a textual fabric of their own. This communication produces an ongoing text{subj} that is seamless but, as Halliday (1978) notes, has a periodicity as the individual moves from communication context to communication context.

In this section, we have argued for an alternative to the ideal case that has guided much of mass communication research. This alternative is predicated upon the argument that text and context can be linked in complex ways, an argument that was developed by introducing the notions of text{obj} and text{subj} and the respective contexts, consumption context and communicative context, in which each is encountered and produced.

This new ideal case does not ignore the importance of the consumption of text{obj} in consumption contexts. It does suggest that the meaning produced in those contexts is not necessarily the only fixed meaning, or the most significant. Through communicative contexts in which media consumers must account for and reconstruct their media-related behaviors, meaning is produced, fixed, and reproduced again. In the next section, we will develop the notion of consumption as well as examine the importance of the relationship between textual status and media consumption.

MEDIA CONSUMPTION

Labeling the activity that is constituted through an encounter between media and audience is a significant task that should be undertaken with some care. Different implications are derived from the choices of "watching," "reading," "using," "consuming," and "exposing." Each label calls forth a somewhat different understanding and focuses attention toward a variable range of concerns that make up this complex interaction (see Salomon & Cohen, 1978, for a systematic discussion of different meanings of television viewing). We have chosen the organizing label of *media consumption* (D. Fry & V. Fry, 1987), as has Peterson

(1987), because it opens up the opportunity both to position the media/audience encounter in several particularly useful ways and to enlarge our understanding of consumption.

Before elaborating on our use of the term *consumption*, it is necessary to explain what we do not mean. Our use brackets the term's economic and physiologic connotations. The consumption process has been defined in classical economic theory as one in which the exchange value (price) of an object is turned into some form of use value by the consumer. This conception extends to a discussion of market and other economic factors on one hand, and to a discussion of individually generated consumer needs on the other (Douglas & Isherwood, 1979). From a Marxist perspective, consumption is conceived of as a socialized behavior (Appadurai, 1986; Preteceille & Terrail, 1985) emerging from economic structure, with the means of production seen as the basic criterion for understanding consumption. Although needs are viewed as socially derived, they remain a function of the production system.

Another typical usage relates consumption to physiological processes. Baudrillard (1981) notes that one commonplace way of thinking about consumption is as the "process of craving and pleasure, as an extended metaphor of the digestive function" (p. 85). Eating consumable products such as food and beverages means that the products are used up, digested, and excreted as waste.

While we accept the relevance of the physiological implications and of the factors regulating both the production and distribution of media content and the ideological considerations that drive that production system, we wish to bracket these connotations in favor of a view of consumption as social process that stresses the various levels on which the act of consumption takes places: individual, societal, and cultural. On the individual level, people make decisions to purchase particular consumer products over others; the act of purchase is a physical act. However, consumption is more than merely a physical act; it is motivated social action as well. Both Baudrillard (1981) and Douglas and Isherwood (1979) contribute to the development of this perspective. Baudrillard (1981) notes that "objects are the carriers of indexed social significations, of a social and cultural hierarchy" (p. 37). Arguing much the same point, Douglas and Isherwood (1979) explain that commodities are used to make "visible and stable the categories of culture" (p. 59). They argue that it is less the physical act of buying a commodity than the fact that consumption activity is shared with other fellow consumers that contains the meaning and the joy of consumption. Thus the term *consumption* should not be limited temporally or spatially to the physical aspects of consuming, but must extend to a concern with the set of components that can function to distinguish and confirm class, taste, and social status. As with media consumption, we are arguing that the ideal case for all consumption extends beyond the consumption context to a series of communication contexts in which the consumption act or the goods themselves are transformed from object (text{obj}) to object of communication (text{subj}).

The social and cultural levels of consumptive activity that are inherently communicative in nature possess a range of potential force: incidental force, episodic force, and rhetorical force. Once purchased, the social display of commodities (clothing, jewelry, automobiles, and so forth) communicates messages to others about the consumer's life-style, group memberships, values, and character. This communication can take place casually and incidentally, as we pass people in public places and form judgments about them based on the consumer goods that form a part of the personae they present to others. These observable goods allow us to differentiate among persons. This differentiation can take place in the most loosely or unstructured contexts as we pass people on the street or stand near them in a line. In this fashion, goods can be said to have an incidental social force.

This communicative potential of goods also can be realized in more highly structured communication contexts in which one's consumer choices become the specific object or focus of communication. In these contexts, consumer goods can be said to have episodic force, to borrow, with some alteration, a term used by Frentz and Farrell (1976). In these contexts, we may see the specific and intentional use of a particular commodity to accomplish a communicative goal with another person or persons. Wearing a particular article of clothing, displaying the "right" books in the public parts of one's home or in one's office, having the "right" music on when guests come over, and so on, are examples of how goods can be chosen carefully to accomplish specific instrumental communicative goals. These uses of goods are motivated, intentional — that is, symbolic — acts that can be understood within the structured communicative episodes in which they occur.

Consumption also can have rhetorical force. The symbolic use of consumer goods to accomplish instrumental communicative goals is a means by which individuals identify themselves with others. Burke's (1950) view of rhetoric contributes to our understanding of the episodic and rhetorical force of the particular use of goods. His definition of rhetoric highlights the ways individuals employ symbols, intentionally as well as spontaneously and intuitively, to identify themselves and their positions in society with the ways of life of others. Once identification is established, individuals can be said to be consubstantial in that they act together to preserve a way of life in which they share particular concepts, values, ideas, and attitudes with others in their culture. The symbolic use of a material good in a specific context may be said to have episodic force to the extent that it links individuals with one other in a particular and specific context. These symbolic acts also carry with them a cultural or rhetorical force in that they uphold a particular hierarchical system of ranked and ordered goods. Using ranked and graded goods to identify oneself with others contributes to the continuance of a social and cultural system that provides consumption as the viable means of marking and identifying self in the world. The rhetorical force of consumption, then, includes, but is not limited to, its purely episodic force.

Consumable goods, therefore, can be thought of as social texts. As with our discussion of media texts, the consumable good is an object of consumption (text{obj}) as well as an object of discourse or communication (text{subj}). In the various communication contexts where the consumable good reappears, it carries a force that is related to its nature as an object and becomes part of a social discourse. By treating media behavior as a form of consumption, many more of the complex characteristics of media behavior are made available.

The notion of media consumption organizes one's attention around social meanings; consumption choices are a means of making sense of the social world and of indexing or marking oneself within that world. The car, house, and clothes an individual buys and displays to others perform marking functions in that these goods differentiate him or her from some and integrate him or her with others. So, too, can the choice of one medium over another (print over electronic, film over radio) and of specific texts within a preferred medium (a mystery movie over an Altman film, an action-adventure program over a soap opera) mark a person as being of a certain class or personality type, or as holding a particular set of values, if those media choices become part of public discourse.

Baudrillard (1981) argues that consumption

> is always the mechanism of social presentation which must be recognized in our choice, our accumulation, our manipulation and our consumption of objects. This mechanism of discrimination and prestige is at the very basis of the system of values and of integration into the hierarchical order of society. (p. 30; also see Appadurai, 1986, p. 29, for a similar statement, and Sigman, 1987, for a discussion of this orientation applied to interpersonal communication)

Media consumption also functions as a mechanism of social presentation, or discrimination and/or prestige, with potential positive or negative consequences for the consumer. Thus we begin to move beyond the isolated individual interacting with the media to satisfy internal needs toward an approach that is socially bounded and controlled.

Clearly, using the concept of consumption in this fashion points to a fundamentally different notion of the self that has implications for the self as audience to (or consumer of) media products. It is predicated on the social self, the self in context with others, rather than on the isolated autonomous self positioned before a screen or curled up with a novel. The self indicated by the alternative ideal case discussed in the previous section is an active producer of texts (text{subj}) as well as consumer of texts (text{obj}). Employing the notion of consumption provides a link between consumption and communicative contexts because of the explicit social and cultural implications of consumer choices. The consumption choices made in consumption contexts have incidental, episodic, and rhetorical implications for the self in numerous ongoing communication contexts in which those choices may appear.

Inherent in the use of *media consumption* as a guiding term is the social significance of media consumption choices and the public display and use of media text{obj} in communication contexts (text{subj}). Although the host of reasons that bring a person to a medium may have nothing to do with the public or social world, as one moves from the private to the public arena, the relative cultural status of one's preferred text may well become a factor in communication contexts.

A text or medium acquires its status from its social life more than from its particular textual features. Thus a text or medium does not acquire a status because it has certain characteristics, but because it is imbued with the values and critical stance of the "taste cultures" (for definitions, see Escarpit, 1977; Gans, 1974) that differentially consume it. As with other consumable goods, texts and media function as social markers for those who consume them and allow that consumption to become public. This identification is as true of consumers who select low-status texts (such as daytime serials) and who prefer television news to the *New York Times* as it is of individuals who choose not to consume the high-status texts (news, information, documentaries, and public affairs programs) expected of them. As markers, these media choices are worked out in a range of communication contexts and become integrated into the larger processes of social evaluation, where they may have incidental, episodic, and rhetorical force just as do other consumable goods.

There is little doubt that different media types and media genres are differentially valued and evaluated. Attallah (1984), for instance, argues that in this society television is considered "unworthy." He contends that "the entertainment it [television] provides has long been considered inferior to the entertainment provided by books and films or plays; its information more ephemeral and less substantial than that provided by newspapers, books, magazines, or journals" (p. 224). Nor are all media products evaluated equally. Even though television is "unworthy," watching public station programming may redeem the viewer. Alternatively, even the high value placed on print will not reestablish the status of Harlequin romances. These actions display social placement in much the same way as do more traditional commodities. Commodities are social in function because there is a socially agreed-upon basis for evaluating them.

In addition, most audience members recognize status issues, differentially grade and evaluate the texts that they contact, and through that evaluation admit that others in the society also grade and evaluate them (see Foss & Alexander, 1987; Fry, Alexander, & Fry, 1989; Himmelweit & Swift, 1976; Smith, 1986; Steiner, 1963). McQuail (1987) argues that there exists in any mediated society "discriminations and valuations made in relation to audience use" of media and media content (p. 231). He contends that values, internalized from social interaction, regulate the use and self-report of the actual content consumed, and the amount of time spent with a medium. Both Steiner (1963) and Himmelweit and Swift (1976) report that many of their subjects felt guilt when they consumed large amounts of television and when they watched some types of content. Although this guilt did not necessarily directly affect the individuals' consumption of a particular content, it might have some influence on *overall* consumption patterns (Neumann, 1982). It is not unreasonable to presume that the individual's guilt arises from a realization that his or her media consumption patterns fall within a socially unacceptable range, thus causing the subject concern, even though the consumption patterns continue. Additionally, researchers have long known that the cultural valuation of texts will affect the way audience members account for their media consumption habits. Respondents' tendency to provide "socially desirable" responses to content preference and media use items has long been a problem in audience research. A more pertinent issue, and one that has been less well researched, is the role textual status plays within consumption and communication contexts and the related impact on the production of meaning.

In summary, consumption, including media consumption, is accomplished within social environments (communication contexts) permeated with social values and valuations. The goods that are consumed and publicly displayed are evaluated through the standards accepted by the culture or the relevant subculture. Texts and media become markers of the relative social position of the audience members who publicly display their choices based on the status attributed to the medium or text{obj} by the society or subgroup. As such, an individual's media preferences, if made public, can have incidental, episodic, or rhetorical force. The status of the text or medium within the particular social context of display can function not only to distinguish media consumers from others but also to allow them to identify themselves with others who share their media consumption preferences.

In the next section, we will develop more fully the link between the self as a consumer of text{obj} and the self as a communicator employing specific strategies for the management of the social display of consumption choices in communicative contexts in which those choices become the object of talk. This self is both user and reader of texts (text{obj}) and weaver of the fabric of talk that produces text{subj}.

THE STIGMATIZED SELF

Given our argument that consumption is a social act marked with social valuations, one would expect consumers to avoid public display of inappropriate consumption choices in order to keep others from becoming informed of their private consumption patterns. One of us has had the experience of having a friend visit our home for the first time. After carefully inspecting the home for several hours, the friend asked: "Okay, I give up. Where is the junk?" The response came: "What do you mean, what junk?" "I've inspected all your book shelves and all possible secret hiding places, and all I can find is your good reading material. You know, the literature and academic stuff. Where's the stuff you really read?" The assumption in this exchange is an interesting one: You must be like me, you really must read lighter — and lower-status — fare, and you must be hiding it from public view.

Another way of thinking about this social marking that occurs with both the consumption of low-status texts and the neglect of high-status texts is provided by

Goffman's (1963/1986) work on stigma. In introducing Goffman's concepts, we hope to clarify the relationship between the communicative activities of (a) consuming particular texts, media, or textual genres in consumption contexts, and (b) talking about those choices in communicative contexts in which those choices mark or stigmatize the self in particular ways.

Goffman (1963/1986) notes that an individual can become stigmatized in three different ways: as a result of a physical deformity, illness, or condition; by virtue of some individual shortcoming or flaw inherent to the person's character; and, by extension, because of family lineage, nationality, race, or religion ("tribal" stigmas). Goffman (1963/1986, p. 138) argues that "the normal" and "the stigmatized" are not different kinds of persons, but, rather, are roles or positions individuals assume in actual interactions. This positioning is the case because all persons are potentially "discreditable" for one of the three reasons cited above. Goffman's (1963/1986) distinction between the potentially "discreditable" and the actually "discredited" focuses our attention on the communicative nature of the difference. Though all individuals are blemished and potentially "discreditable," becoming actually discredited requires a communicative situation in which one's stigma is identified and recognized by another.

Goffman argues that we all strive to manage information about ourselves in ways that reduce and/or mask our stigma in order to minimize the likelihood that we will become actually discredited at any point during an interaction. In regard to a person's particular stigma, Goffman (1963/1986) identifies three groups of potential interactants: (a) "one's own" (those who share one's stigma), (b) "the wise" (those who are "normal," but who for some reason are highly sympathetic to one's plight), and (c) all other individuals who are neither like oneself nor sympathetic to one's stigma. When interacting with the first two groups, individuals are not likely to become "discredited" for a particular stigma because they are communicating with people who share and/or are tolerant of their stigma. With the latter group, however, the stigmatized individual always exists in a precarious communicative situation, in which he or she could become actually discredited at any time. To prevent this potential loss of face, the presentation of self to this third group of interactants requires extensive information management in order to avoid becoming actually discredited. In other words, individuals may manage information carefully to prevent themselves from actually acquiring a stigmatized role.

Because the notions of self as normal or blemished arise and exist through repeated interactions, both normal and deviant are necessary to one another. This necessarily communicative relationship between "stigmatized" and "normal" persons requires the investigation of communicative contexts in which "stigmatized" and "normal" are copresent to one another either in conversation or in unfocused gatherings. In other words, since "stigmatized" and "normal" are communicative roles that emerge in and through interaction, of particular interest is the exploration of those communicative contexts in which media consumers are copresent with others who do not share their textual preferences. In such situations, consumers may find that their consumption behavior renders them potentially discreditable persons. The possibility of becoming discredited is most likely to exist when one is interacting with an individual or group of persons who neither share one's textual choices nor are sympathetic and understanding of those preferences.

This focus leads us to an investigation of the ways in which media consumers talk about (i.e., manage information about) their consumption choices, and, consequently, about themselves, in communicative contexts in which their media choices stigmatize them. Of interest is identifying the communicative strategies consumers employ to manage information about themselves and their media activity (a) to avoid being "found out" and discredited and (b) to regain face when they are discredited.

The status of television viewing in general and the consumption of daytime serials in particular provide an excellent illustration of the way in which media preferences can stigmatize individual consumers. Not only is television per se considered "unworthy" (Attallah, 1984) by at least some segments of this society, but certain texts, such as the soap opera, occupy a special low status in American culture. In fact, the soap opera is one of the most criticized of media genres, symbolizing low-level standardized fare to many. Goldsen (1975) charges that the soap opera world "do[es] violence to images of family commitment" (p. 49) and that it trivializes emotions. In her observational study of collegiate soap opera viewing, Lemish (1985) identifies the "challenger," whose hostile remarks are consistent with "stereotypical attitudes toward soap operas, which seem to be laden with misconceptions and negative overtones" (p. 283). And in our phone and focus group interviews, a number of subjects noted that friends and/or family members had criticized them for "wasting" time watching soap operas.

The negative textual status of the soap opera genre may mean that serial viewers risk being discredited in some contexts if they are unable to hide or mask their low-status media consumption habits from those who do not share their media preferences. In our case study, we suspected that denial of viewing or silence in the face of potential opportunities to discredit self by identifying self as a viewer was one strategy used to avoid stigma. This inference derives from observations made by ourselves and others (Lemish, 1985) in which individuals denied watching soap operas but in subsequent conversations revealed considerable knowledge about the characters and plots of various serials.

Of significance here is that when the consumption of a text{obj} becomes an object of communication in another communication context in which the status of the text{obj} is in question, the production of text{subj} will revolve around specific strategies that attempt to account appropriately for the consumption of the devalued text{obj}. For example, in a situation in which one's media consumption habits are questioned by someone who is known to prefer radically different texts, the nature of the social action taking place is likely to be a "challenge" that demands some sort of "defense" from the potentially discredited in order to keep self from being actually discredited in the interaction. By contrast, if one is talking to someone known to share one's preference for soap opera programs, for example, the nature of the action is likely to be supportive and "sharing." To the extent that these varied social actions require quite different communicative strategies, the symbolic organization of these varied social actions differs as well. These differences point once again to Goffman's notion that stigma is best understood as a specific kind of communicative relationship among participants who, from interaction to interaction, alternate in roles being potentially discreditable. This movement also highlights the possible variations in the production of text{subj} based on the nature of the communication context.

By exploring the strategies that viewers use to account for their media consumption, in this case the consumption of soap operas, it is possible to begin to see the reproduction of text{obj} through the conversational production of text{subj}. In part, the transformation from text{obj} to text{subj} is regulated by the nature of the attack on an individual's soap opera viewing and the strategies the individual uses to prevent being stigmatized. These strategies take the form of "lines" that individuals create in order to prevent themselves from becoming discredited and/or to reestablish face when they are actually discredited. In our case study of serial viewers, some individuals claimed they watched soap operas in order to laugh at them. This strategy not only placed the viewer in a superior position to the text{obj} but also described the self as a critic amused by the absurdities of the genre. By implication, this strategy produced a text{subj} that placed the viewers who adopted it in a position superior to that of other consumers of the genre.

Others attempt to negotiate a text{subj} that detaches them from the text{obj} in an indirect manner. A total of 28 individuals in our case study described their viewing as simply entertaining, one adding that everything didn't have to be intellectually stimulating. One noted that soaps were better than prime-time programs because they were less violent, and another viewer stated that her boyfriend watched cartoons and that soaps were "no worse than cartoons." In these responses viewers seem to assert their right to pleasure — that is, entertainment — while simultaneously denying any further importance to the activity. By invoking the value of entertainment and by defending their own entertainment choice, individuals define their viewing as a ritualized use of the medium dependent upon function rather than content. One viewer made this distancing even more explicit with the comment, "I am not an addict." This strategy established the self as somehow different from and superior to those for whom viewing might be out of control. In essence, the text{subj} produced in these communication contexts places the soap opera text{obj} in context with other discredited texts{obj} and argues for equivalence, if not superiority, constructing a comparative framework not present in the text{obj}.

A different class of responses attempted to counter criticism by showing that the texts{obj} were used in some socially valued way. Thus respondents legitimated serial viewing by linking it with wider social values. One such value was "activity" versus "passivity." A total of 16 viewers noted that serials made their lives appear less complicated by comparison. These responses identified a mentally active approach to the genre in which the individual actively compared self to text{obj} rather than depicting self as a passive consumer of the genre. Acknowledging implicitly that watching soap operas is considered a waste of valuable time, one viewer attempted to redeem his image by adding, "I do other things so it's not a waste of valuable time." Though in a somewhat different way from viewers who actively used the programs in their lives, this viewer appealed to the same cultural value of productive use of time. Here the production of text{subj} focuses on relative use-value of the text{obj} and/or of the behaviors during the consumption context.

However, some viewers refused to accept the "stigma" of soap opera viewing, asserting that others had no right to question them regarding their serial viewing patterns. Viewers preferring this strategy refused to acknowledge a negative definition of self (that is, they refused outright to accept that they were discreditable) because of their serial viewing — 12 people reported that they typically responded in such a manner. A total of 5 indicated that they advised challengers to begin watching soaps themselves; 6 noted that they did not care what others thought; and 2 reported on specific ongoing debates with family members, with one indicating that her typical response was, "Mom, leave me alone." Another had whittled down his response to the straightforward rebuttal, "You're a fool." In these instances, text{subj} is constituted through a discourse that not only places the appropriateness of the communication context in question but also denies anyone's right to criticize text{obj}.

It was clear in our interviews that considerable conversational work was required to create an acceptable and appropriate communication context. These conversational strategies should not be dismissed as "mere" justifications or rationalizations of behavior, nor should they be treated as totally distinct from the consumption of the soap opera text{obj}. We argue that the meanings of an individual's textual choices become constituted and reconstituted through a series of ongoing conversational encounters with many different people, some who share the individual's preferences as well as some who do not. The constitutive power of conversation in creating much of what members of a society establish and reify as social reality has been noted by Hawes (1977) and others. The importance of conversation as a communicative mode for engendering meanings leads us to make problematic the set of activities that accomplish this ongoing organization of social reality.

In order to clarify the relationship between the textual status of the soap opera genre and its consumption and communicative contexts, we need to introduce two additional concepts: keying and register. Goffman (1974) argues that a key

> is a set of conventions by which a given activity, one already meaningful in terms of some framework, is transformed into something patterned on this activity but seen by the participants to be something quite else. The process of transcription [or transformation] can be called keying. (pp. 43-44)

It is clear that, as individuals reencounter a text{obj} in communication contexts, a process of keying occurs. During this process the text{obj} is transformed into the text{subj}. The subjects in our case study were caught up in communication contexts where their regular viewing of soap operas was questioned, a communication process having potentially negative consequences for the soap opera viewer. The text{subj} that is then created in these communication contexts "keys" the original text{obj} and one's choice of that text{obj} to meet the needs of the situation. Viewers engage in "keying" in the same ways, in part because the registers of various communication contexts in which text{obj} becomes text{subj} vary. The way a text{obj} is transformed in communicative contexts, then, is contingent on the registers that prevail in specific communication contexts within which the text{obj} is encountered as an object of talk.

Halliday's (1978) use of the term *register* can function to clarify the force different communication contexts may have on the keying process. He defines register as "what you are speaking (at the time) determined by what you are doing (nature of social activity being engaged in), and expressing diversity of social process (social division of labour)" (p. 35). This notion becomes relevant to media consumption because each context within which a text is reencountered has its own distinct register. The consumption context has a register determined by the nature of the function of the media exposure, possibly defined in uses and gratifications terminology. Each reencounter with the text{subj} in communicative contexts also has definable registers based on the social activity and relative role relationships apparent in each context. Register, then, is associated strongly with situation and is easily recognized by the participants in the experience through their social knowledge.

Halliday (1978) further subdivides register into field ("type of social action"), tenor ("role relationships"), and mode ("symbolic organization") (p. 35). These components of register can function as analytic categories in understanding the keying process that takes place in communicative contexts. Mediated texts{obj} have a variety of registers as the texts{subj} are produced in communicative contexts. As an audience member reencounters a particular mediated text{subj}, the field, tenor, and mode of the register present in the communication context in which the text{subj} is produced contributes to the differences in how text{obj} is "keyed" — that is, talked about — in the communicative context. Keyings vary from register to register because the type of social action, the role relationships, and the symbolic organization of the communication contexts may encourage a different set of meanings each time the text {obj} and/or questions related to one's consumption patterns arise.

Our soap opera viewers, particularly those who participated in the focus groups, indicated that they recognized the presence of different registers and that these affected the ways in which their consumption of text{obj} was talked about (i.e., keyed) in communicative contexts. Specifically, our informants acknowledged that they discussed soap operas differently depending on who was involved in the discussion.

In summary, individuals do something far more complex than "use" media texts in communication contexts. When media preferences are challenged, consumers reencounter their preferred text{obj}, and, at that time, must formulate explanations, justifications, and so forth that account for their consumption activity to self and to others (through the formulation of text{subj}). The registers of these accounts vary depending on whether one is copresent with people who share one's media preferences, people sympathetic to those preferences, or people hostile to them. These differences derive from the three major components of registers: the type of social action in which one is engaged, the role relationships of the interactants, and the symbolic organization of the context in which the action takes place. Thus it is imperative that we understand the transformations that occur as the text{obj} of a consumption context becomes the text{subj} in various communicative contexts.

CONCLUSION

This chapter has initiated an exploration into the concepts of consumption, textual status, and the stigmatized self as they relate specifically to an overarching communicative dynamic. Consumption, status, and stigma, then, are fundamental communication activities that, when explored together, provide a means of moving toward a theory of communication processes that relies less on questions and concerns from other disciplines than on an intradisciplinary set of concerns dealing with enhancing understanding of a variety of communicative processes. Additionally, we have offered an alternative ideal case for mass communication research that takes textual meaning to be constituted and reconstituted across a range of different communicative contexts rather than determined and fixed at the exposure context.

The effort to articulate a purely communicative theory is, necessarily, integrative rather than divergent. Rather than assuming and/or reinforcing existing boundaries among mass communication, interpersonal communication, and public communication, our approach has been to see these specific contextual foci as subsets of a larger communicative frame. As such, each may contribute in its own way to the constitution and reconstitution of the meaning of *the same communicative object*, the text {obj}, as it moves from its consumption context into the realm of discourse and communication.

In a more global sense, the interconnection between consumption and communication contexts must be explored through a range of variables beyond textual status and stigma. For instance, much media effects research has been concerned with establishing the linkage between content and impact. Examining mediated content (e.g., children's commercials, pornography, violence), researchers have hypothesized cognitive and behavioral consequences (e.g., product requests, devaluation of women, perceptions of a "mean world"). Factors that influence the linkage of exposure and effects are considered mediating variables, that is, variables that modify the way meaning is delivered to the exposed individual. Within this linear construction of the impact of media on individuals, interpersonal contexts are considered to modify media effect. Our analysis of the communication process demonstrates that texts{obj} also have lives within larger symbolic and communicative contexts. Because texts{obj} can move from an object consumed (watched, read, listened to) to an object produced as talk, it is crucial to understand how selected texts acquire meaning as viewers interact with them during both consumption and communication encounters.

Our perspective suggests that existing research, including this chapter, has only begun the difficult process of illuminating what happens to texts{obj} as they move between consumption and communicative contexts. Although studies of the interactional environment surrounding television viewing are an important first step, they must be supplemented with additional research into other communicative contexts in which media are implicated. Most important, researchers must develop more sophisticated theoretical frames for examining the communicative context, frames that are sensitive to the seamlessness of texts{obj} and texts{subj}. These studies ought to take us beyond scrutinizing texts{obj} for their manifest, latent, preferred, and/or oppositional meanings.

In this chapter we have assumed that consumers of various media and media texts are aware of the differential cultural status of their preferences, and that this knowledge leads to a communicative sensitivity to the need to display their choices in different ways depending on the register of the communication context. The process of appropriately keying text{obj} to communication contexts requires a good deal of social knowledge. In this sense, then, the production of various texts{subj} is in part an issue of literacy. Literacy extends beyond the bounds of properly decoding texts{obj}, where it has tended to be analyzed, to encompass the knowledge of how to produce texts{subj} that resonate appropriately with the register of the communication situation. If we are to understand how variables such as textual status and stigma affect the production of textual meaning, we must learn more about both the literacy required to decode text{obj} and that required to adapt text{obj} to the differential production of texts{subj} in communicative contexts. For instance, this essay is a part of soap opera as text{subj}. The knowledge required to produce this part of soap opera as text{subj} is fundamentally different from the literacy needed to carry on a casual conversation about the soaps. The study of how individuals contribute to producing various texts{subj} and of the cultural and communicative required to perform these tasks is essential.

In conclusion, we hope this chapter will be taken by communication researchers of all specializations as an attempt to articulate the relationships that can exist among varying contexts. In so doing, we hope that we all can move together, beginning with our own specialization and moving outward toward our shared communicative concerns, to build purely integrative theories of communication processes.

NOTE

1. Data for this study were derived from focused telephone interviews, focus groups, questionnaires, and unobtrusive observations of naturally occurring conversations over a seven-month period. Observations concentrated on the social management of soap opera viewing in conversation. These observations were used to refine interview and questionnaire items.

Telephone interviews were conducted with 48 adult serial viewers from urban and suburban areas of Massachusetts. Respondents were asked their serial preferences, time spent viewing, and the perceived strengths and weaknesses of the serial format. They were also asked to discuss interactions with others in which they were questioned about their serial viewing. Respondents indicated the bases upon which individuals had challenged their serial viewing "habits" and their responses. These responses were elicited in an open-ended form and were organized into a category scheme by the researchers. Additional data of the same type but in written form were gathered from students in a communication fundamentals course. Of 60 students, 11 indicated they were regular serial viewers. These data were used in conjunction with the adult viewer data in this analysis.

Two focus group interviews approximately 90 minutes in length were conducted. One group was composed of five college students, both male and female, who watched soap operas at least occasionally. The second group was composed of five adult females who reported regular soap opera viewing. The interviews focused on the social environments that surrounded both the media exposure context and numerous communicative contexts where soap operas and soap opera viewing were discussed.

REFERENCES

Alexander, A., & Fry, V. (1986, October). *Interpreting viewing: Creating an acceptable context*. Paper presented at the Sixth International Conference on Culture and Communication, Philadelphia.

Allen, R. C. (1987). Reader-oriented criticism and television. In R. C. Allen (Ed.), *Channels of discourse: Television and contemporary criticism* (pp. 74-111). Chapel Hill: University of North Carolina Press.

Ang, I. (1985). *Watching Dallas: Soap opera and the melodramatic imagination*. London: Methuen. (Original work published 1982)

Appadurai, A. (1986). Introduction: Commodities and the politics of value. In A. Appadurai (Ed.), *The social life of things: Commodities in cultural perspective* (pp. 3-63). London: Cambridge University Press.

Attallah, P. (1984). The unworthy discourse: Situation comedy in television. In W. Rowland, Jr., & B. Watkins (Eds.), *Interpreting television: Current research perspectives* (pp. 222-249). Beverly Hills, CA: Sage.

Baudrillard, J. (1981). *For a critique of the political economy of the sign* (C. Levin, Trans.). St. Louis: Telos.

Bechtel, R., Achelpohl, C., & Akers, R. (1972). Correlates between observed behavior and questionnaire responses on television viewing. In E. Rubinstein, G. Comstock, & J. Murray (Eds.), *Television and social behavior* (Vol. 4, pp. 274-344). Washington, DC: Government Printing Office.

Bennett, T. (1982). Text and social process: The case of James Bond. *Screen Education, 41,* 1-21.

Burke, K. (1950). *A rhetoric of motives*. Berkeley: University of California Press.

Douglas, M., & Isherwood, B. (1979). *The world of goods: Towards an anthropology of consumption*. New York: W. W. Norton.

Eco, U. (1979). *Role of the reader: Explorations in the semiotics of texts*. Bloomington: Indiana University Press.

Escarpit, P. (1977). The concept of "mass." *Journal of Communication, 27,* 44-47.

Fiske, J. (1986). Television: Polysemy and popularity. *Critical Studies in Mass Communication, 3,* 391-408.

Foss, K., & Alexander, A. (1987, May). *Trashing the tube*. Paper presented at the annual meeting of the International Communication Association, Montreal.

Frentz, T. S., & Farrell, T. B. (1976). Language-action: A paradigm for communication. *Quarterly Journal of Speech, 62*, 333-349.

Fry, V., Alexander, A., & Fry, D. (1989). The stigmatized self as media consumer. *Studies in Symbolic Interaction, 10*, 333-344.

Fry, D., & Fry, V. (1986). A semiotic model for the study of mass communication. In M. McLaughlin (Ed.), *Communication yearbook 9* (pp. 443-462). Beverly Hills, CA: Sage.

Fry, D., & Fry, V. (1987). Some structural characteristics of music television videos. *Southern Speech Communication Journal, 52*, 151-164.

Fry, V., & Fry, D. (1987). Reconceptualizing the encoding and decoding "moments" of the mass communication process. *Research on Language and Social Interaction, 20*, 221-242.

Gans, H. J. (1974). *Popular culture and high culture: An analysis and evaluation of taste*. New York: Basic Books.

Goffman, E. (1967). *Interaction ritual: Essays on face-to-face behavior*. Garden City, NY: Anchor.

Goffman, E. (1974). *Frame analysis: An essay on the organization of experience*. New York: Harper & Row

Goffman, E. (1986). *Stigma: Notes on the management of spoiled identity*. New York: Simon & Schuster. (Original work published 1963)

Goldsen, R. K. (1975). Throwaway husbands, wives, lovers (soap opera relationships). *Human Behavior, 4*, 64-69.

Hall, S. (1980). Encoding/decoding. In S. Hall, D. Hobson, A. Lowe, & P. Willis (Eds.), *Culture, media, language* (pp. 128-138). London: Hutchinson.

Halliday, M.A.K. (1978). *Language as social semiotic: The social interpretation of language and meaning*. London: Edward Arnold.

Hawes, L. (1977, December). *Conversation as sociality*. Paper presented at the annual meeting of the Speech Communication Association, Washington, DC.

Himmelweit, H., & Swift, B. (1976). Continuities and discontinuities in media usage and taste: A longitudinal study. *Journal of Social Issues, 32*, 133-156.

Hodge, B., & Tripp, D. (1986). *Children and television*. Stanford, CA: Stanford University Press.

Iser, W. (1978). *The act of reading: A theory of aesthetic response*. Baltimore: Johns Hopkins University Press.

Jensen, K. B. (1987). Qualitative audience research: Toward an integrative approach to reception. *Critical Studies in Mass Communication, 4*, 21-36.

Lemish, D. (1985). Soap opera viewing in college: A naturalistic inquiry. *Journal of Broadcasting & Electronic Media, 29*, 275-293.

McQuail, D. (1987). *Mass communication theory: An introduction*. Newbury Park, CA: Sage.

Morley, D. (1980). *The nationwide audience*. London: BFI.

Morley, D. (1981). The national audience: A critical postscript. *Screen Education, 39*, 3-14.

Nelson, J. (1985). Soaps/sitcoms: Television genres as situated discourse. In J. Deeley (Ed.), *Semiotics 1984* (pp. 137-146). New York: University Press of America.

Neumann, W. R. (1982). Television and American culture: The mass media and the pluralistic audience. *Public Opinion Quarterly, 46*, 471-487.

Newcomb, H. (1984). On the dialogic aspects of mass communication. *Critical Studies in Mass Communication, 1*, 34-50.

Northrop, F.S.C. (1959). *The logic of the sciences and the humanities*. New York: Meridian.

Peterson, E. E. (1987). Media consumption and girls who want to have fun. *Critical Studies in Mass Communication, 48*, 37-50.

Preteceille, E., & Terrail, J. (1985). *Capitalism, consumption and needs* (S. Matthews, Trans.). Oxford: Basil Blackwell.

Radway, J. A. (1984). *Reading the romance: Women, patriarchy, and popular literature*. Chapel Hill: University of North Carolina Press.

Salomon, G., & Cohen, A. (1978). On the meaning and validity of television viewing. *Human Communication Research, 4*, 265-270.

Schudson, M. (1987). The new validation of popular culture: Sense and sentimentality in academia. *Critical Studies in Mass Communication, 4*, 51-68.

Sigman, S. (1987). *A perspective on social communication*. Lexington, MA: Lexington.

Smith, R. (1986). Television addiction. In J. Bryant & D. Zillman (Eds.), *Perspectives on media effects* (pp. 109-128). Hillsdale, NJ: Lawrence Erlbaum.

Steiner, G. (1963). *The people look at television*. New York: Alfred A. Knopf.

Weber, M. (1949). *The methodology of the social sciences* (E. A. Shils & H. N. Finch, Trans.). Glencoe, IL: Free Press.

Wren-Lewis, J. (1983). The encoding/decoding model: Criticisms and redevelopments for research on decoding. *Media, Culture and Society, 5*, 197-198.

Finding New Models for Mass Communication Research: Notes on Surviving Ferment in the Field

DENNIS K. DAVIS
Southern Illinois University

I T is now commonplace to view our field as one that is in "ferment." Fry, Alexander, and Fry give evidence of this ferment as they combine ideas drawn from semiotics, social psychology, literary analysis, and audience research to create an innovative framework that integrates concerns about personal identity, media consumption, and mass culture. They clearly are optimistic about the possibility of shaping a new research paradigm that will go beyond present approaches. While I share their optimism, I am also aware of the enormity of the task. It will not be easy to shape new paradigms. As critic, I will assess the integrity and utility of the framework they develop. What sort of research is likely to result from their perspective? Through my comments on the Fry et al. essay, I will illustrate some of the theoretical and methodological issues that we will need to face as we seek to move beyond the "dominant paradigm."

There have been several recent essays that discuss possibilities for integrating quantitative and qualitative approaches (Fejes, 1984; Jensen, 1987; Schroder, 1987). They have focused on the utility of integrating textual analysis of media content with empirical research on audience reception of content. In each case, the authors have emphasized the necessity for textual analysis to move beyond content analysis to interview content consumers. *Reading the Romance*, by Janice Radway (1984) is widely cited as a prototype for this sort of research (Schroder, 1987).

My comments will emulate these earlier reviews. However, the Fry et al. approach is not centered on textual analysis; these authors are mainly concerned

Correspondence and requests for reprints: Dennis K. Davis, Department of Speech Communication, Southern Illinois University, Carbondale, IL 62901.

Communication Yearbook 13, pp. 545-553

with adding a new dimension to audience research. Although they do not apply textual analysis to soap operas, they obviously consider it useful. Given their concern with text, it should be easy for them to extend their research to include textual analysis. With such an addition, convergence with other innovative research approaches may be possible. Ideally, dialogue might be opened among researchers whose strength is textual analysis. Fry et al. would seem ideally prepared and situated to engage in such an exchange.

I will begin with an analysis of the Fry et al. essay from a cultural analysis paradigm and consider how their work would fit within this paradigm. I will then discuss how their approach might be developed and broadened to make it more useful.

A CULTURAL ANALYSIS PARADIGM

It now appears likely that the recent era of communication research will be characterized by the emergence of a cultural analysis paradigm. Fry et al. provide evidence of this. As they integrate various theories, culture emerges as a focal point. Similarly, if there is any common theme to be found in recent appraisals of our field (Blumler, Gurevitch, & Katz, 1985; Carey, 1977; Jensen, 1987; Hall, 1982; Schroder, 1987), it is the view that the relationship of mass media to culture must be taken seriously as a focus for research. Culture, it has been argued, must be considered a potentially powerful force for social change. Culture also must be recognized as the foundation upon which any social order necessarily rests. To the extent that media are important in the creation and maintenance of culture, they play a significant social role.

What would be the consequences of making culture a central focus of media research? Clearly, there are several important ways that a cultural analysis paradigm would differ from the minimal effects perspective. If we view culture as potentially dominant in relation to either social-structural factors or psychological states, then any influence that media have on culture will necessarily have significant structural or psychological repercussions. Research concern shifts from measuring short-term attitudinal or behavioral effects to assessing the role of media in creating and maintaining culture. This role can be assessed by several lines of research: (a) studies of how content producers are guided by their culture in their creation of media content (encoding research), (b) studies of how media technology is inherently biased toward certain genres of content and thus encourages development of certain forms of culture over others (channel research), (c) studies of how individuals use culture to guide their experience of content and their creation of personally meaningful interpretations of content (decoding research), and (d) studies of how experiences with media content are integrated into and affect our everyday lives (media frame analysis research).

Such a cultural analysis paradigm views the social world as a much more dynamic but also disordered place than the world envisioned in minimal effects theory. This social world lacks the stability that social institutions and psychological attitudes were assumed to provide. Instead, we must constantly work at defining the world and our place in it. We can take nothing for granted because anything is subject to redefinition. Our experience of people and situations can be transformed by changes in culture. No longer is the average person seen as a "social robot" socialized by remote institutions. Rather, each of us is dependent upon culture in coping with a complex world.

This cultural analysis paradigm would seem especially well suited to developing useful insights into contemporary American society. We need a means of exploring human experience in a social order based on a pluralistic, liberal public culture where there is no Truth, but many truths; where the individual is at least nominally free to choose from among those truths but where many groups compete to promote their ideologies; where a key problem is maintaining sufficient order so that individuals are "free" to pursue activities that they find personally meaningful.

One of the possibilities offered by a cultural analysis paradigm would be creation of a body of research findings that could in turn guide development of more useful public and private cultures. Our current public culture would appear to be in need of considerable reform. The strength of this culture would appear to be its diversity, its pluralism. But it also contains much that is trivial and superficial. Americans consume complex media content much as they consume fast food. They are willing to assume that it is nutritious (enlightening) so long as it tastes good (is entertaining). Television provides easy access to a culture supermarket — with the junk food prominently marketed and the more serious content stocked in less accessible specialty sections. Like a supermarket, television offers no directions for preparing or consuming culture. We are assumed to be independent, competent adults who know what to do with culture.

Goffman as a Cultural Analyst

The perspective that underlies the Fry et al. approach is one ultimately derived from phenomenology and social psychology. In grounding their work on that of Erving Goffman (1963), they have chosen a theorist who was much concerned with the "culture of everyday life." Goffman's view of *everyday life* was heavily influenced by Alfred Schutz (1967). Goffman views individuals as caught up in a complex social world in which one must work to appear to others as "normal." Coping with daily life involves learning how to categorize and act properly toward persons, situations, and objects. To do this, people develop a stock of practical knowledge, an everyday life culture that enables them to cope successfully with a wide variety of everyday life situations.

Goffman was fascinated by the mistakes people make while dealing with everyday life ambiguities. He was convinced that analysis of such errors revealed much about the hidden fabric of social life. In his major theoretical work, *Frame Analysis* (1974), Goffman focuses on how we frame everyday situations and events. He analyzes how we cope when our existing frames prove inadequate, and notes that we can be easily deceived when we rely too much on frames. For example, a con artist succeeds by manipulating victims so that they frame situations to his or her advantage. Once deceived, victims are easily fleeced.

Goffman became known for his book *The Presentation of Self in Everyday Life* (1959), in which he was concerned with how individuals develop social identities, self-definitions that others will understand and accept. In developing such identities, we have many constraints. Though there may be an infinite number of personal attributes that we could possess, we must choose to highlight and present to others a small number that they will be able to interpret. We must also determine which attributes we need to conceal.

The book Fry et al. have chosen for their research, *Stigma*, is an extension of the work in *The Presentation of Self in Everyday Life*. Some persons experience abnormal difficulties in developing social identities because they possess personal attributes that others find objectionable. For Goffman, such difficulties provide an excellent research opportunity. Because these persons have to work at developing and maintaining social identities, they inadvertently provide watchful researchers with insight into the underlying social process. Like the con man, persons with "spoiled identities" must work at deceiving "normals." Goffman (1963) provides the following description of this situation:

> An individual who might have been received easily in ordinary social intercourse possesses a trait that can obtrude itself upon attention and turn those of us whom he meets away from him, breaking the claim that his other attributes have on us. He possesses a stigma, an undesired differentness from what we had anticipated. We and those who do not depart negatively from the particular expectations at issue I shall call the "normals." (p. 5)

The problem of coping with a stigma is fundamentally a cultural rather than a personal one. The individual as manager of his or her personal identity must determine how to live with others who have learned cultural definitions that label certain attributes negatively. Because the stigmatized person has typically been socialized to the same cultural definitions, he or she must decide how to cope with them.

> One phase of this socialization process is that through which the stigmatized person learns and incorporates the standpoint of the normal, acquiring thereby the identity beliefs of the wider society and a general idea of what it would be like to possess a particular stigma. (Goffman, 1963, p. 32)

> When in fact his is a discreditable . . . person, then the second main possibility in his life is to be found. The issue is not that of managing tension generated during social

contacts, but rather that of managing information about his failing. To display or not to display; to tell or not to tell; to let on or not to let on; to lie or not to lie; and in each case, to whom, how, when, and where. (Goffman, 1963, p. 42)

Thus, by focusing on the problems facing stigmatized persons, Goffman is able to consider how people construct and project personal identities when they live in a culture that is biased against them.

Stigmatization of Soap Opera Viewers

Fry et al. argue that soap opera viewing is a negative personal attribute that could lead to stigmatization if others became aware of it. Thus, like the person with a criminal past or the secret drug addict, a soap opera viewer finds it useful to develop strategies that enable projection of a misleading personal identity. Their concern with stigmatization leads Fry et al. to focus on what they label secondary consumption of media content—talking about media content. The soap opera viewer must be judicious in talking to others about what he or she has viewed. Viewing can be fully shared with other soap opera fans, of course, but nonviewers may need to be misled.

In certain respects, soap opera viewing provides Fry et al. with a useful way of investigating secondary consumption of media content. Because individuals are forced to defend themselves from possible stigmatization, they appear to have reflected more on both primary and secondary consumption of soap operas. When interviewed by researchers, they have had insightful stories to tell about how they cope with the threat of stigmatization. If viewing were less problematic and talking about it less of a threat, viewers may not have had much to remember. Certainly, two decades of television audience research has taught us that people are singularly unreflective about their use of this medium. Thus the choice of soap opera viewing may have been a very practical means of beginning to investigate secondary consumption.

But there appear to be some rather severe limitations that the choice of soap opera viewing imposes on the Fry et al. research. How universal is the stigmatization of soap opera viewers and how serious is this stigmatization? If it is not very serious, most viewers may feel free simply to ignore it. Some may even take it as a badge of courage to defend—their right to view what they want. It would appear unlikely that such stigmatization would have any important negative consequences for most persons. If the stigmatization of viewers had more serious consequences, more elaborate schemes would be developed to hide viewing, and more viewers might band together to share their addiction and find a haven from censure.

If stigmatization as a result of media use is of central concern to Fry et al., why not choose consumption of pornography, extremist political propaganda, or even romance reading? All of these would seem more likely to stigmatize users and might reveal more about coping strategies. On the other hand, these persons might be harder to find or less willing to cooperate with researchers.

TOWARD DEVELOPMENT OF
A CULTURAL ANALYSIS PARADIGM

I would encourage Fry et al. to consider developing a more comprehensive research approach. Stigmatization based on media consumption would be only one facet of this approach, just as stigmatization is but one aspect of Goffman's perspective. It provides a convenient starting point for research, but it would not be the only or even the most important site for research. In the early portions of their essay, Fry et al. appear to be moving toward development of a comprehensive approach. Then, by focusing on stigmatization, they seem to pull back from broader concerns, and they do not return to them. Above, I briefly described four lines of research that might be part of a cultural analysis paradigm. Stigmatization research would fall under media frame analysis. It would be possible for Fry et al. to adapt their approach so that it would guide research on encoding, channels, and decoding as well.

I was especially intrigued by the analogies Fry et al. draw between material consumption and media consumption. This comparison permits them to generalize from theories of material culture that speculate about the social implications of consuming goods or services. Clearly, consumption of certain media content does carry status implications. Audience research has found that educated persons tend to overestimate their consumption of news and to underestimate their consumption of entertainment. Less educated persons generally provide more accurate estimates of media consumption, presumably because they have little to gain or lose from such reports.

The choice of Goffman as a theorist has an important drawback when it comes to construction of a broader theoretical framework. Goffman confined his research to observation and description of everyday life; he was very reluctant to generalize much beyond these observations. Even in his most abstract and macroscopic work, *Frame Analysis* (1974), he confines himself to analysis of how people cope with things as they are. He rarely offers perspective on the broader cultural context in which such coping takes place. He accepts the existence of various stigmas and finds their existence useful in developing his theory. He does not ask why such stigmas exist and only briefly considers their implications for the social order. In my rereading of *Stigma*, I found the following quote to be representative:

> Social deviants, as defined, flaunt their refusal to accept their place and are temporarily tolerated in this gestural rebellion, providing it is restricted within the ecological boundaries of their community. Like ethnic and racial ghettos, these communities constitute a haven of self defense and a place where the individual deviator can openly take the line that he is at least as good as anyone else. (p. 145)

Goffman expresses little concern here for the plight of ghetto dwellers, and he does not question the morality of a prejudiced culture.

Creation of Social Identity Through Media Consumption

An issue briefly touched on by Fry et al. is the extent to which individuals use media content to develop social identities. This aspect of their framework might be particularly useful to develop. If they did so, they could link their work quite directly to research growing out of textual analysis. This development could also be a way of extending their framework so that it encompasses decoding research. For example, social identity is considered by Radway in her development of her explanation of how women experience romance novels. She argues that through involvement in a mediated fantasy, readers may be able to imaginatively take on identities that a patriarchal culture has socialized them to value. Given the limited life options available to them, the women she studied had no hope of ever realizing these identities in their everyday lives. Thus reading romances may provide important support for patriarchal culture. Not only does such decoding reinforce the values of this culture, it also provides some women with a nondisruptive means of experiencing these identities.

Might similar explanations be found for soap opera viewing? With what sorts of soap opera characters might viewers be likely to identify? The answers to these questions are likely to be quite complicated given the variety of soap opera characters and the heterogeneity of the viewing audiences. Development of such research questions would require careful analysis of soap opera content, perhaps patterned after Radway's analysis of the content of romance novels. To what extent does identification with soap opera characters permit sanctioned social identities to be imaginatively enacted?

Once such questions about social identities have been developed, they could be explored through conversations with soap opera fans. Because Fry et al. have a strong interest in secondary consumption of soap opera content, one way of collecting data would be to attend meetings of groups of soap opera fans. Program experiences reported by members of such groups could be contrasted with experiences of solitary viewers. Persons who regularly engage in secondary consumption of media content with groups of other persons would seem likely to have experiences that are very different from those of solitary viewers. Such research might begin to establish how secondary consumption shapes primary consumption and vice versa.

Developing a Perspective on Public Culture

Fry et al. do not discuss the implications of their perspective for research on soap opera production or consider why television may be uniquely suited to delivering the form of culture represented by soap operas. A comprehensive research approach would need to encompass content production and transmission as well as consumption. To undertake this effort, it may be necessary to develop a broader theory of public culture, in which soap operas represent just one subcategory of content. Then it would be possible to discuss organizational constraints or channel biases that favor production and transmission of some forms of content over others. The work of the British cultural studies researchers provides some indication of the utility of such research (e.g., see Glasgow University Media Group, 1976, 1980; Hall, Hobson, Lowe, & Willis, 1980).

If these issues were addressed, Fry et al. might be able to develop a truly comprehensive explanation of how consumption of soap operas fits into public culture as a whole. My own research suggests that it may be very useful to compare how people experience, consume, and learn from various forms of content. I have focused on a quite different form of television content — news. Specifically, I have been concerned with assessing how and what people learn from television news (Robinson & Davis, 1988). It is quite clear that television is not a very effective means of delivering news. Typical news stories are too brief and contain too little background information to facilitate long-term learning. Though people appear to take in passively quite a bit of information from their exposure to news, very little of this information is ever stored in long-term memory. Thus average viewers are not well served by television news, but there are some who do seem to benefit. These are persons who regularly use newspapers to cue recall of televised content and who also are stimulated to reflect on news because they frequently discuss news with friends (Robinson & Davis, 1988). Thus television news viewing has very different consequences for different viewers, depending upon the context in which it is consumed.

Cultural analysis research might reveal that mass media institutions make certain forms of culture consumption easier and more pleasurable than others. This would in turn affect what Fry et al. call secondary consumption. Social groups may form around consumption of the most accessible and attractive forms of content. Such groups would further enhance primary content consumption. It is possible that with the growing availability of specialized media content we might observe a rapid proliferation of groups devoted to enhancing their members' consumption of media. If content is sufficiently complex, such groups may be essential. Like groups of soap opera fans or persons who regularly talk about news, such groups would enable their members to cope with content.

We may already be observing phenomena that foreshadow future developments. For example, it is clear that televangelism has transformed some people's experience of religion. Some churches may now serve primarily as places that facilitate secondary consumption of televised content. Within some denominations, televangelism has become quite important. By comparing such denominations with others in which televised religion is unimportant, some conclusions might be drawn about what happens when television becomes a significant medium for culture. If we understood more about such differences we might better understand the followers of Pat Robertson. Why has television proved such a successful medium for fundamentalist religion but so ineffective as a vehicle for formal education? Perhaps educators have not paid enough attention to secondary consumption. We might find that our structure is suited to the consumption of books but not to the consumption of television.

The utility of a cultural analysis paradigm seems clear. Its practicality, on the other hand, is still open to question. Schroder (1987) has pointed out that current approaches to textual analysis are both diverse and opaque. It may be impossible to adapt any of the existing forms of textual analysis to the research objectives that Fry et al. have outlined. Similarly, practitioners of textual analysis may find little in Fry et al. that could be adapted to their purposes. Thus, while we may be witnessing some convergence of research traditions, it is not at all clear what the outcome will be. It now seems unlikely a single research community can be formed given the diverse concerns and backgrounds of the persons now drawn to cultural analysis. But perhaps we can strengthen the existing communities through increasing dialogue.

REFERENCES

Blumler, J. G., Gurevitch, M., & Katz, E. (1985). Reaching out: A future for gratifications research. In K. E. Rosengren, L. A. Wenner, & P. Palmgreen (Eds.), *Media gratifications research* (pp. 255-273). Beverly Hills, CA: Sage.

Carey, J. (1977). Mass communication research and cultural studies. In J. Curran, M. Gurevitch, & J. Woollacott (Eds.), *Mass communication and society* (pp. 409-426). London: Edward Arnold.

Fejes, F. (1984). Critical communications research and media effects: The problem of the disappearing audience. *Media, Culture and Society, 6*, 219-232.

Glasgow University Media Group. (1976). *Bad news*. London: Routledge & Kegan Paul.

Glasgow University Media Group. (1980). *More bad news*. London: Routledge & Kegan Paul.

Goffman, E. (1959). *The presentation of self in everyday life*. Garden City, NY: Doubleday.

Goffman, E. (1963). *Stigma: Notes on the management of spoiled identity*. Englewood Cliffs, NJ: Prentice-Hall.

Goffman, E. (1974). *Frame analysis: An essay on the organization of experience*. New York: Harper & Row.

Hall, S. (1982). The rediscovery of "ideology": Return of the repressed in media studies. In M. Gurevitch, T. Bennett, J. Curran, & J. Woollacott (Eds.), *Culture, society, and the media* (pp. 56-90). London: Methuen.

Hall, S., Hobson, D., Lowe, A., & Willis, P. (Eds.). (1980). *Culture, media, language*. London: Hutchinson.

Jensen, K. B. (1987). Qualitative audience research: Toward an integrative approach to reception. *Critical Studies in Mass Communication, 4*, 21-36.

Radway, J. (1984). *Reading the romance: Women, patriarchy, and popular literature*. Chapel Hill: University of North Carolina Press.

Robinson, J. P., & Davis, D. K. (1988). *Television news and the informed public: Not the main source*. Manuscript submitted for publication.

Schroder, K. C. (1987). Convergence of antagonistic traditions? The case of audience research. *European Journal of Communication, 2*, 7-31.

Schutz, A. (1967). *The phenomenology of the social world*. Evanston, IL: Northwestern University Press.

Toward an Integration of Diverse Communication Contexts

STUART J. SIGMAN

State University of New York at Albany

[Life] is constructed by human beings through active ratiocination, by the same kind of ratiocination through which we construct narratives. When somebody tells you his life . . . it is always a cognitive achievement rather than a through-the-clear-crystal recital of something univocally given. (Bruner, 1987, p. 13)

The research program underlying Fry, Alexander, and Fry's chapter is a timely one. It parallels the movement toward interpretive and naturalistic research in interpersonal and organizational communication (Craig & Tracy, 1983; Pearce & Cronen, 1980; Putnam & Pacanowsky, 1983) and forms part of the larger social scientific movement toward actional and nondeterministic theorizing (Geertz, 1983; Gergen 1982; Harré, Clarke, & De Carlo, 1985). The chapter represents a rediscovery of, and a reasoned commitment to, the disciplinary concern for "meaning." In the process, it provides a focus that may serve to unify currently disparate research programs.

Specifically, Fry et al. argue for a dissolution of the distinctions between and among interpersonal, mass, and public communication. They do this by developing a theoretical framework that is general enough to apply across communication phenomena and contexts, yet is sensitive to the situated processes of meaning creation. Communication as the continuous social activity of meaning generation and negotiation is accomplished in interpersonal, telemediated, and organizational *moments* (see Sigman, 1987a). The authors offer a basic disciplinary vocabulary for conceiving of the semantically based relations among various message "exposure" contexts.

I characterize Fry et al.'s thesis as the development of a *social semiotics* of human communication (see Halliday, 1978; Sigman, 1987b). This term is intended to highlight (a) the societal roots of meaning generation processes and (b) the

Correspondence and requests for reprints: Stuart J. Sigman, Department of Communication, State University of New York, 400 Washington Avenue, Albany, NY 12222.

Communication Yearbook 13, pp. 554-563

existence of behavioral (sign and symbol) systems that guide and regulate these processes. Such a concern for the "how" of meaning production as embedded in social situations differs from more traditional disciplinary foci that take the priority of messages for granted and that view individuals as reactors to messages rather than interpreters and generators of meaning and information. I am myself overwhelmingly sympathetic toward social semiotic models, and, although I offer some criticisms and extensions of the Fry et al. program, am in strong agreement with its basic thrust.

INITIAL IMPLICATIONS

Fry et al.'s theoretical work serves the important function of laying bare notions about reality and the symbolic mediation of reality. Indeed, *mediation* may not be the best word to describe this process because of the implication of a fixed reality that is mediated (conveyed) through communication, rather than created and constituted by it (see Carey, 1975). One suggestion in the authors' present work is that there do not appear to be clear monosemic messages transmitted by mass media products (and, more generally, by all communication products). Whatever it is that the mass media provide — and a good term for it does not as yet exist — it is not *a* message or *an* information bit. The media provide etic behaviors or signs whose meaning at any one time rests upon social actors' interpretive and practical activities, as these encounter and interact with the structures (structural appearances) of texts. However, such a theoretical position need not be taken to imply that meaning resides in the heads of "receivers" rather than "senders." [1] Rather, it suggests that meaning is always tentative, negotiable, or "up for grabs," even though it may be treated by persons as relatively exact and fixed at any one moment. Donald Fry and I previously demonstrated — admittedly in an experimental situation and for a limited audience (public school teachers) — that the media do not contain or transmit singular messages, but rather that "content" is constructed by audience members as they interact with media products and the semiotic principles organizing a particular encountered product (Fry & Sigman, 1984; Sigman & Fry, 1985). The "same" text can be assigned different significances depending on the interpretive procedures employed by different persons in primary contexts. Similarly, there is a "life history" to media products and messages — that is, a course of meaning from primary to secondary contexts — that involves communicators in negotiating (Blumer, 1967), transforming (Goffman, 1974), and formulating (Heritage & Watson, 1979) products and messages.

Communication in this view is no longer a neutral vehicle on which (or, through which) information is carried. Instead, it is the activity constituting the information *of* the social world (Carey, 1975; Pearce & Cronen, 1980; Peters & Rothenbuhler, 1987; Sigman, 1987a). In this respect, Fry et al. are correct in intimating that such questions as, What is real? Where is reality (meaning) located? Whose reality (e.g., media agency's versus audiences') is the accurate one? are less important to research than questions concerning the mechanisms of meaningful reality constitu-tion — *How* is something meaningful?

In a useful paper by Peters and Rothenbuhler (1987), both mediated events and everyday face-to-face occasions are seen as "fictions," that is, makings or fabrica-tions of reality. They write:

> The essential insight of media events studies . . . is to deny any hierarchy of reality to fictions. . . . There is simply no privileged rock bottom out there somewhere that we can appeal to in order to find out what really happened. (p. 12)

This suggests to me that the accuracy of meaning is less important than the *potency* of interpretation. That is, who has the power to impose meaning on which others? And which contextual meanings are considered by various persons to be more real or significant?

This leads me to add a point that is developed in more detail below, but that requires mentioning here, namely, my rejection of possible solipsistic interpreta-tions of the Fry et al. thesis. In specific, the fact that *the* meaning does not exist, that it resides neither in the medium nor in the text but rather in their uses and appropriations by social actors, does not require us to see meaning as subjective or personal and the processes that render something meaningful as random or idio-syncratic. Without denying the creative and proactive aspects of meaning construc-tion (communication), I nevertheless believe that there is some evidence for the existence of rules for textual interpretation and use. While meaning in an absolute sense may not exist, constraints and limitations may be placed on meaning in any specific social context.

CRITIQUE AND ASSESSMENT

This section is concerned with providing a critical perspective on Fry, Alexander, and Fry's chapter. Although I endorse the general social semiotic movement advanced by their work, I believe that a number of specific pronounce-ments by the authors would benefit from more careful scrutiny. It is in the spirit of clarifying and extending the initial effort made by Fry et al. that this discussion is advanced.

The "How" of Communication

Fry et al. are primarily concerned with studying the *how* of the meaning-generating process. However, since human communication is rarely or never content free or context free, I question whether the *how* of communication can realistically be disassociated from the *what* and *when/where* of communication.

The authors assume that communication scholars can (and indeed should) study the attributes of the meaning-generating process without equally examining the social situations in which this process transpires. They write: "We are less concerned with the *what* and *why* of media consumption—with what particular texts mean to individuals and why they prefer particular texts—than with *how* texts become meaningful" (p. 520).

An emphasis on the *how* of interpretation, however, would be unable to address a feature of continuous social communication that is at the heart of the Fry et al. program, namely, the societal historicity of the evaluative statuses assigned to various media and texts. In order to understand social actors' efforts to acquiesce to or disclaim stigmatizing attributions, it seems necessary to study not only the verbal techniques for carrying this out, but also the historical self-concept each participant brings to the encounter, the dimensions of respective power (see above) assumed by the participants, and the dimensions of the social situation leading to context-specific expectations for preferred and dispreferred status presentations.

The Focus on Stigmatized Identity

It is not clear why Fry et al. have limited themselves to the potential for stigmatized identities in secondary contexts as related to primary context consumption. They delimit the former contexts in the following manner: "When media preferences are challenged, consumers reencounter their preferred text{obj}, and, at that time, must formulate explanations, justifications, and so forth that account for their consumption activity to self and to others" (p. 540). Additional meanings about self and media products are presumably produced and reproduced in these secondary contexts.

However, I want to suggest that the limiting case of stigma management, that is, control over the information that potentially discredits one, is a poor operationalization for the overarching conceptual framework. It does not seem to me that information control in secondary contexts does or can radically transform or reprogram the primary consumptive experience. While there are certainly occasions when individuals misperceive the social significance of particular media encounters—this misperception being brought to the original audience members' awareness by some "confrontation" with cointeractants in secondary contexts—nevertheless, I would suggest that audience members are just as likely (perhaps even more so) to recognize the stigmatizing/nonstigmatizing features of their media encounters *during* and *within* the spatiotemporal boundaries of the primary context. The interview data presented as a case study in the chapter seem to support my contention. Fry et al. indicate that soap opera viewers are aware of the low value placed on the soap opera genre and on their viewing activity. The authors' literature review similarly leads them to conclude that television viewing generally and soap opera viewing specifically "occupy a . . . low status in American culture" (p. 536). While it may be the case that individuals in interview situations and related secondary contexts are bound by self-presentation rules, it is less clear-cut that implementation of these rules in the aforementioned face-to-face encounters results in (or requires) alteration of the primary context experience and the primary context meanings. The interviewees' reports signify for me that the stigmatizing potential of soap opera viewing is something that audience members "carry around" with them and does not emerge from critical or hostile interpersonal encounters.

Fry et al.'s work seems prepared to handle this objection rhetorically but not empirically. For example, they write: "These conversational strategies [of avoiding stigmatization and/or aligning conversation subsequent to stigmatization] should not be dismissed as 'mere' justifications or rationalizations of behavior. . . . We argue that the meanings of an individual's textual choices become constituted and reconstituted through a series of ongoing conversational encounters with many different people, some who share the individual's preferences as well as some who do not" (p. 538). In this manner, "meaning" and "social value" are not separated, for "meaning" is seen *as* or *through* "social value." Their data (see p. 537-420, for example) provide no insight into the meanings generated at the primary viewing site or into the transformative or formulative relationship between the primary and secondary encounters.[2]

Although Fry et al. have an extremely rich theoretical alternative to offer communication scholars, the case study they use to illustrate it is insufficient to the task. I find myself in the curious position of endorsing wholeheartedly the overarching theoretical structure being developed by the writers, while at the same time remarking that their data as currently collected and analyzed do not mirror the power and contribution of the theory. Thus I urge readers to look beyond the case example to the major perspectival features.

Formulations, Transformations, and Invocations

In the present discussion, I offer an understanding of the kinds of interpretive and interactional resources available to social actors when confronted by challenges in secondary communication contexts. The potential responses to challenges can be divided into two broad categories: *conscientious responses* and *refusals*. Included in the first category are remarks that accept the legitimacy of secondary context criticism and that redress the self-stigmatizing potential of the criticism. Included in the second category are remarks that deny the legitimacy of the criticism and/or the critic. Of interest here is the relative similarity of these responses to "accounts" and "aligning actions" (Buttny, 1987; Scott & Lyman, 1968; Stokes & Hewitt, 1976), that is, those behaviors that social actors employ in warding off the status implications of untoward conduct and in acknowledging the existence of social expectations.

Self-presentational and stigma-reducing activities must, however, be seen as subsidiary to those activities that directly restructure and resemanticize meaning. Two terms employed by Fry et al. — "formulation" and "transformation" — can be developed here to describe the comprehensive interpretive procedures involved in the reencountering of texts from primary to secondary contexts. The two terms are not synonymous, however, and may not be appropriate to all cases of secondary contexts.

Transformation represents the alteration of an item with clearly identifiable properties and meanings into something that is phenomenally similar yet semantically different (Goffman, 1974). An example of such transforming occurs when communicators parody soap opera stars (e.g., Joan Collins) by donning look-alike costumes for Halloween or affecting their speech styles and favored expressions.

In contrast, *formulation* is a momentary attempt to establish and/or confirm meaning for an item. According to Heritage and Watson (1979), who develop the concept with regard to conversational topics, this attempt occurs when actors articulate or produce some summary for an item or items of behavior. Formulations are not definitive, for different interactional participants may offer competing gists of their conversation. An example of a secondary context formulation was presented to me at a recent dinner party I attended that included talk on the controversial Dan Rather television interview with Vice President George Bush and whether this encounter should be viewed as a "setup" (and victory) by the broadcaster or the politician's staff.[3]

It should be noted that in both examples above there is "active" (re)negotiation of textual meaning and that this effort exists apart from stigma/status conferral. Formulational and transformational behaviors can thus be seen as general, textually oriented interpretive procedures. They constitute two pieces of the larger interpretive process that continuously produces and reproduces social meaning. They are not in principle equivalent. Therefore, research attention can be directed toward (a) the differential contexts in which each procedure is deployed, and (b) the differential outcomes of deploying each procedure in particular contexts and for particular social identities, especially with regard to resulting textual meaning. The "life history" of social behavior can be charted according to the transformations and formulations of meaning across time and place.

By emphasizing the concept of formulation, I am not merely borrowing a term from the conversation analysis literature. Rather, and more important, I am attempting to point to a structural similarity between the handling of telemediated and nontelemediated information, a similarity hinted at by Fry et al. but not fully developed in their chapter. I propose that all life experiences (or, more precisely, all the social informational features of life experiences) are subject to negotiation, renegotiation, formulation, and reformulation. A personal example can be found in the various ways I have formulated my earliest teaching experience at an Appalachian university. Despite my relatively positive feelings toward the place at the time, I find myself referring more and more today (especially with "big city" friends) to the "hick" aspects of the experience. These conversations *have* altered the meaning of that early experience for me and represent the continuous interactional construction of my biography.

The divisions between mass and interpersonal communication become far less exact as scholars acknowledge that information from either "source" may be subject to *narrative conventions and conversions* across contexts (see Bruner, 1987). That is to suggest, focus on the *continuous* constitution of the life world breaks down the distinction between public and private, mass and interpersonal communication, because each of these is seen to provide partial constituents of the life world on an ongoing basis, and because each may modify or elaborate on meaning from the other. Formulations, to take but one such activity, may occur (a) for both nonmedia and media experiences, (b) immediately during a conversation or media contact, and (c) over an extended period of time removed from the original conversation or media event. This potential suggests that studies of interpretive mechanisms by themselves will eventually need to be augmented by research on the *progression of social meaning and content across multiple communication contexts.*

Having articulated this claim, I should reiterate my belief that information negotiation does not occur in random fashion or result in essentially unique reformulations. I do not believe that the social world is that uncertain or unpredictable (Sigman, 1987a). Thus I would urge Fry et al. to articulate a set of principles that explain the organization of the negotiation processes and the patterning of the negotiation outcomes or results.

The constraints, or situational modifiers, associated with meaning formulations may relate to a number of features of the "mass communication" primary experience: (a) the medium to which a given unit of information is attributed (for example, information from TV is denigrated, while the "same" information from radio is not); (b) the "channel" within a medium from which information is derived (for example, just as folk wisdom teaches the lay public to trust "body language" over spoken language, persons may accept information from PBS but not from CBS); (c) the personal and sociodemographic characteristics of various "users" of the medium (Dan Rather versus a local newscaster on issues of global geopolitics; our mothers versus our fathers on matters of family history); and (d) the genre or tone (Hymes, 1974) of the message, which is itself not static but subject to social actors' reformulations (television sitcoms versus public service announcements about AIDS). In brief, we need to study the rules of the language game(s) involving the situated creation and use of media messages.

Fry et al. counter these suggestions by writing:

> Asking "where?" questions presumes that meaning is contained somewhere, that meaning is situated somewhere — in content, audience, or some interaction between the two. This set of presumptions inherently ties meaning to the primary exposure context. (p. 522)

The present proposal does *not* inevitably place meaning in primary communication contexts, but it does suggest that processes of meaning creation and re-creation *are* always located in sociocultural space-time. This proposal is not limited to primary contexts, for it simply encourages examination of situational constraints *wherever* meaning processes occur. Fry et al. are probably correct when they assert: "A text or medium acquires its status from its social life more than from its particular textual features" (p. 533). And it is the *structural features of that social life* that I am emphasizing here.

There is one additional interpretive activity to describe. This discussion is prompted by the question in the preceding section regarding whether there is always a *change* in textual meaning from primary to secondary contexts or an *invocation* (Sigman, 1987a) of one of the multiple available textual meanings.

A somewhat state-oriented approach is evident in some of Fry et al.'s writing, particularly with regard to their interest in the cultural status of texts. The authors suggest that the relative ranking of media and media products can serve as a defining indicator of selfhood. They write:

> The notion of media consumption organizes one's attention around social meanings; consumption choices are a means of making sense of the social world and of indexing or marking oneself within that world. The car, house, and clothes an individual buys and displays to others perform marking functions in that these goods differentiate him or her from some and integrate him or her with others. So, too, can the choice of one medium over another (print over electronic, film over radio) and of specific texts within a preferred medium (a mystery movie over an Altman film, an action-adventure program over a soap opera) mark a person as being of a certain class or personality type, or as holding a particular set of values, if those media choices become part of public discourse. (p. 532)

This implies that the relative prestige of media and media texts is known by social actors and is essentially stable, that is, that there is some *semantic historicity* to texts.

When an individual encounters and consumes a media product in a primary context, he or she may be aware of the multiple meanings of the text *at that moment*, as well as the likely textual statuses of the text vis-à-vis various reference groups and the most efficacious strategies for handling interactions with these others. This perspective does not reduce interactants to the role of passive agents of already established meanings; rather, it enables us to see persons as active manipulators of societally delimited ranges and variations of meaning.

Fry et al. use the concept of invocation. For example, they write about one strategy for detaching the self from stigmatizing viewing: "By *invoking* the value of entertainment and by defending their own entertainment choice, individuals define their viewing as a ritualized use of the medium dependent upon function rather than content" (p. 537; emphasis added). Referring to a different respondent, they write: "This viewer appealed to the . . . cultural value of productive use of time" (p. 538). In other words, there is a set of socioculturally available explanations for and evaluations of media behavior; uses of these explanations and evaluations in either primary or secondary contexts, while they may alter meaning in the *immediate* moment, also call upon and thus reproduce prior sociocultural understandings. The largest set of such understandings represents a socially available, yet contextually discriminable and exploitable, repertoire of behaviors. It is a repertoire of a priori values and meanings that, as noted above, is differentially available to persons for invocation.

We must develop analytic vocabularies that recognize both (a) the relative stability of information and textual status over time and (b) the possibility of change and renegotiation of information and textual status. *Invocation* and *transformation/formulation* may thus serve jointly to capture these two functions.

CONCLUSIONS

As Fry et al. move the discipline toward a conceptual integration of mass and interpersonal communication phenomena, we are forced to reckon with the multi-channel and multimedia contributions to persons' construction of their social identities and to their knowledge of the social world. Persons are seen as "marked" as the kind of persons who do or do not exhibit particular media consumption habits and particular verbal and nonverbal interpersonal displays. As Peters and Rothenbuhler (1987) have also recently remarked: "The difference between mass communication and face to face speech is not in terms of 'mediation' so much as structural possibilities" (p. 18). So there is a question that at some point will need to be addressed: What is peculiar and especially "marketable" about media products, especially in comparison with other communication modes (e.g., clothing or automobiles)? Relatedly, what is the differential significance of having one's identity established (or contradicted) by one medium over another?

What we specifically learn from Fry, Alexander, and Fry is the following: The fullest embodiment — although by no means the final or complete embodiment, for there is no such thing — of media messages occurs through acts of interpretation and interaction by persons, and, I would add, within the conventions and constraints set down by social context. To expand ever so slightly on the social semiotic model advanced by Fry et al.'s chapter, I suggest the following three areas for research: (a) the rules and procedures for the production and reproduction of meaning, (b) the ideological functions or social values of the media and interpersonal coding conventions and outcomes, and (c) the societal distribution of the rules, procedures, and values associated with meaning-generating processes.

NOTES

1. In the theory of continuous communication presented here, there are, strictly speaking, no "senders" and "receivers." Instead, there are "participants" who invoke the social semiotic system of meaning and who contribute to the continuity and/or alteration of particular meaningful components (see Birdwhistell, 1970; Carey, 1975; Sigman, 1987a).

2. Neither do the present data evidence Fry et al.'s claim that distinct "registers" (Halliday, 1978) are employed by audience members in primary and secondary contexts, and across various secondary contexts.

3. I am grateful to Anne Donnellon for informal discussion about this commentary, which resulted in the two examples of meaning negotiation used here.

REFERENCES

Birdwhistell, R. L. (1970). *Kinesics and context.* Philadelphia: University of Pennsylvania Press.

Blumer, H. (1967). *Symbolic interactionism.* Englewood Cliffs, NJ: Prentice-Hall.

Bruner, J. (1987). Life as narrative. *Social Research, 54*(1), 11-32.

Buttny, R. (1987). Sequence and structure in accounts episodes. *Communication Quarterly, 35*(1), 67-83.

Carey, J. W. (1975). A cultural approach to communication. *Communication, 2,* 1-22.

Craig, R. T., & Tracy, K. (Eds.). (1983). *Conversational coherence: Form, structure, and strategy.* Beverly Hills, CA: Sage.

Fry, D. L., & Sigman, S. J. (1984). Newspaper language and readers' perceptions of news events. *Newspaper Research Journal, 5*(3), 1-11.

Geertz, C. (1983). *Local knowledge: Further essays in interpretive anthropology.* New York: Basic Books.

Gergen, K. J. (1982). *Toward transformation in social knowledge.* New York: Springer-Verlag.

Goffman, E. (1974). *Frame analysis: An essay on the organization of experience.* New York: Harper & Row.

Halliday, M.A.K. (1978). *Language as social semiotic.* London: Edward Arnold.

Harré, R., Clarke, D., & De Carlo, N. (1985). *Motives and mechanisms: An introduction to the psychology of action.* London: Methuen.

Heritage, J. C., & Watson, D. R. (1979). Formulations as conversational objects. In G. Psathas (Ed.), *Everyday language: Studies in ethnomethodology* (pp. 123-162). New York: Irvington.

Pearce, W. B., & Cronen, V. E. (1980). *Communication, action, and meaning: The creation of social realities.* New York: Praeger.

Peters, J. D., & Rothenbuhler, E. W. (1987). The reality of construction. In H. Simons (Ed.), *Perspectives on the rhetoric of the human sciences.* London: Sage.

Putnam, L. L., & Pacanowsky, M. E. (Eds.). (1983). *Communication and organizations: An interpretive approach.* Beverly Hills, CA: Sage.

Scott, M. B., & Lyman, S. M. (1968). Accounts. *American Sociological Review, 33,* 46-62.

Sigman, S. J. (1987a). *A perspective on social communication.* Lexington, MA: Lexington.

Sigman, S. J. (Ed.). (1987b). Multichannel communication codes [Special issue]. *Research on Language and Social Interaction, 20/21.*

Sigman, S. J., & Fry, D. L. (1985). Differential ideology and language use: Readers' reconstructions and descriptions of news events. *Critical Studies in Mass Communication, 2,* 307-322.

Stokes, R., & Hewitt, J. P. (1976). Aligning actions. *American Sociological Review, 41,* 838-849.

NAME INDEX

ABOUT THE EDITOR

JAMES A. ANDERSON (Ph.D., University of Iowa) is Department Chair and Professor of Communication at the University of Utah. A Past President of the International Communication Association, he currently edits the ICA's prestigious *Communication Yearbook* series. He has published extensively in the field of communication. His most recent works are *Mediated Communication: A Social Action Perspective* and *Communication Research: Issues and Methods.* His research interests focus on the communication structures and practices of social action routines, political campaigns, media literacy, and family ethnographies.

ALISON ALEXANDER (Ph.D., Ohio State University, 1979) is Associate Professor of Communication at the University of Massachusetts. Her research interests are concentrated generally in the area of media and society, with specific interests in the importance of mass media in interpersonal contexts, and television and the family.

CHARLES R. BANTZ (Ph.D., Ohio State University, 1975) is Associate Professor and Acting Chair of Communication at Arizona State University. His studies of television news, organizational communication, and mass communication audiences have been published in *Communication Research, Communication Monographs, Journal of Broadcasting and Electronic Media, Quarterly Journal of Speech, American Behavioral Scientist,* and *Western Speech Communication.* His current work includes a cross-national team research project investigating social conflict and television news, developing an approach to understanding organizational communication cultures, and the uses of communication in organizations.

WAYNE A. BEACH (Ph.D., University of Utah, 1981) is Associate Professor in the Department of Speech Communication at San Diego State University. His research interests involve both casual and institutional conversational activities. His current studies involve the initiation, pursuit, and avoidance of blame in interaction, and judges' techniques for moving cases along in municipal court.

PAMELA J. BENOIT (Ph.D., Wayne State University, 1979) is Assistant Professor of Communication at the University of Missouri — Columbia. Her current interests focus on the collaborative development of discourse in interpersonal relationships and conversational memory.

FRANKLIN J. BOSTER (Ph.D., Michigan State University, 1978) is Associate Professor in the Department of Communication at Michigan State University. His research interests include small group decision making and compliance-gaining message behavior.

SANDRA BRAMAN (Ph.D., University of Minnesota, 1988) is Research Assistant Professor of the Institute of Communications Research, University of Illinois. Her major interest is international information policy, exploring the theoretical, conceptual, and legal issues facing policymakers and policy analysts. A second stream of research, converging with the first in the domain of the sociology of knowledge, involves the evolution of narrative form. She has published articles in *Telecommunications Policy, Journal of Communication Inquiry, Journalism Quarterly,* and elsewhere.

MARY HELEN BROWN (Ph.D., University of Texas at Austin, 1982) is Assistant Professor of Organizational Communication in the Department of Speech Communication at Auburn University.

AKIBA A. COHEN (Ph.D., Michigan State University, 1973) is Associate Professor of Communication and Director of the Communication Research Institute at the Hebrew University of Jerusalem. His major interest is television news. His books include *Almost Midnight: Reforming the Late Night News* (Sage, 1980) and *The Television News Interview* (Sage, 1987). Forthcoming, with several colleagues, is *Social Conflict and Television News* and an issue of *American Behavioral Scientist* that he is editing on various aspects of research on TV news. He is on the Editorial Board of the *Journal of Broadcasting* and *Electronic Media, Communications: The European Journal of Communication,* and the *International and Intercultural Communication Annual.*

CHARLES CONRAD (Ph.D., University of Kansas, 1980) is Associate Professor in the Department of Speech and Theatre, Texas A&M University. His primary research interests are in the areas of organizational power relationships and the application of critical theory to organizational analysis.

WILLIAM R. CUPACH (Ph.D., University of Southern California, 1981) is Associate Professor of Communication and Codirector of the Personal Relationships Research Group at Illinois State University. His research interests include interpersonal conflict, communication competence, relationship development and dissolution, and impression management. He recently coauthored the *Handbook of Interpersonal Competence Research* (with B. Spitzberg).

DENNIS K. DAVIS (Ph.D., University of Minnesota, 1973) is Professor of Speech Communication at Southern Illinois University. He is coauthor of books on political communication, mass communication theory, and learning from television news. Currently he is conducting research on the 1988 French and American presidential elections.

STANLEY DEETZ (Ph.D., Ohio University, 1973) is Associate Professor in the Department of Communication at Rutgers University. He is coauthor of *Managing Interpersonal Communication* and editor or coeditor of four other books. He has published more than 25 essays in scholarly journals and books regarding research methods, critical studies of organizations, and philosophy of communication. He is the incoming editor of the *Communication Yearbook* series, a member of the Board of Directors of the International Communication Association, and Chairperson-Elect of the Organizational Communication Division of the Speech Communication Association. His current research projects include a book on the politics of everyday life and an empirical analysis of power and the suppression of conflict in organizations.

WILLIAM A. DONOHUE (Ph.D., Ohio State University, 1976) is Professor of Communication at Michigan State University. His conflict-related research interests focus on three areas: (a) communication strategies in labor-management bargaining to discover the ways in which negotiators intermix relational and substantive information in bargaining, (b) communicative competence in divorce mediation settings that seeks to describe how mediators increase cooperativeness among divorcing couples, and (c) the management of hostage negotiation situations to describe the varieties of communication strategies negotiators use to gain control and ultimately resolve various terrorist activities.

ROBERT J. EDELMANN (Ph.D., Birkbeck College, 1981) trained in clinical psychology at the Institute of Psychiatry, London. He has worked as a Lecturer in Psychology at the University of Sheffield, U.K., and is currently Lecturer in Clinical Psychology at the University of Surrey. His major research interests include embarrassment and blushing, and the psychological aspects of infertility. He is the author of *The Psychology of Embarrassment* (1987) and is author or coauthor of more than 40 journal articles and several book chapters.

DONALD L. FRY (Ph.D., Ohio State University, 1981) is Assistant Professor of Mass Communication at Emerson College. His research interests include the areas of audience-text interaction, semiotics, and political communication.

VIRGINIA H. FRY (Ph.D., Ohio State University, 1982) has research interests in language, semiotics, and media.

CONNIE J. G. GERSICK (Ph.D., Yale University, 1984) is Assistant Professor of Organizational and Strategic Studies at the Graduate School of Management, University of California, Los Angeles. Her research interests include group effectiveness, creativity, and change process in human systems.

H. L. GOODALL, Jr. (Ph.D., Pennsylvania State University, 1980) is Associate Professor in the Department of Communication at the University of Utah. His most recent book is *Casing a Promised Land: The Autobiography of an Organizational Detective as Cultural Ethnographer* (Southern Illinois University Press, 1989) and his interests include interpretive and field study methods, organizational communication, and ethnography.

DENNIS S. GOURAN (Ph. D., University of Iowa, 1968) is Professor and Head in the Department of Speech Communication at Penn State University. He is the author of two books and numerous articles on decision making in groups. He is past editor of the *Central States Speech Journal* and has served as an associate editor of several national and regional journals in communication. He is a Past President of the Central States Speech Association and is President-Elect of the Speech Communication Association.

LARRY E. GREINER is Professor of Management and Organization in the School of Business Administration at the University of Southern California. He holds an M.B.A. degree from the Harvard Business School. He currently serves on the editorial boards of the *Academy of Management Executive, Organization Dynamics, Journal of Group and Organization Studies, New Management,* and *Consultation.* In addition, he is on the Board of Directors for the MAC Group in Cambridge, Massachusetts, and CAST in Milan, Italy. He is the author of numerous publications on the subjects of business strategy and organization change, growth, and development, including the classic *Harvard Business Review* article, "Evolution and Revolution as Organizations Grow." He is coauthor of *Consulting to Management* (with Robert Metzger; Prentice-Hall, 1983), and his most recent book is *Power and Organization Development* (with Virginia Schein; Addison-Wesley, 1988).

BETH HASLETT (Ph.D., University of Minnesota, 1971) is Professor of Communication at the University of Delaware. She has published a book, *Communication: Strategic Action in Context,* as well as numerous articles and book chapters. Her major research interests are in discourse and conversational analysis, organizational communication, and developmental communication. She is particularly interested in using discourse analysis to assess corporate culture and in assessing the relationship between national and corporate cultures.

ROBERT HOPPER (Ph.D., University of Wisconsin, 1970) is Charles Sapp Professor of Communication at the University of Texas at Austin. His areas of interest include language and conversation, and cross-cultural communication.

YOUICHI ITO is Professor in the Institute for Communications Research at Keio University in Tokyo. He obtained his degrees from Keio University, School of Public Communication at Boston University, and the Fletcher School of Law and Diplomacy at Tufts University. He is Director of International Relations of the Japan Society for Studies in Journalism and Mass Communication, a member of the Research Planning Committee of the Japan Society of Information and Communication Research, and a member of the Liaison Committee of the International Communication Association. He served as Head of the Secretariat for the four Communication Forums, international symposiums held in Tokyo during the past four years under the sponsorship of the Japan Society of Information and Communication Research. He has organized and implemented several other international symposiums held in Tokyo, Seattle, Vancouver, and Singapore.

GARY L. KREPS (Ph.D., University of Southern California, 1979) is Professor, Director of Graduate Studies, and Coordinator of the Corporate Communication Resources Network in the Department of Communication Studies, Northern Illinois University. He is also a member of the University Gerontology Program Faculty. He is author or editor of several books, including *Organizational Com-*

munication; *Health Communication*; *Applied Communication Research*; *Investigating Communication: An Introduction to Research Methods*; and *Models of Communication Research*. He is also the author of many articles and chapters concerning communication, health care, management, information science, and education.

JENNY MANDELBAUM (Ph.D., University of Texas, 1987) is Assistant Professor of Communication at Rutgers University. She is interested in the organization of conversation in interpersonal relationships and activities. Her recent research has examined the interactive organization of storytelling and its interpersonal outcomes.

JILL J. McMILLAN (Ph.D., University of Texas at Austin, 1982) is Associate Professor of Speech Communication at Wake Forest University. Her teaching and research interests include organizational communication, rhetorical theory and criticism, and institutional discourse. She has been especially interested in the study of the organization as corporate rhetor.

SANDRA METTS (Ph.D., University of Iowa, 1983) is Associate Professor of Communication and Codirector of the Personal Relationships Research Group at Illinois State University. Her research interests include deception in close relationships, communication and sexuality, language and gender, and beliefs about relationships and how they influence relational outcomes.

RENEE A. MEYERS (Ph.D., University of Illinois, 1987) is Assistant Professor in the Department of Communication at the University of Oklahoma. Her primary research interests include small group argumentation and decision making, and organizational communication. Her writings have appeared in such journals as *Human Communication Research, Communication Monographs, Communication Education, Journal of Applied Communication,* and *Communication Research.* Recently, she was the recipient of the 1987 SCA Distinguished Dissertation Award.

DENNIS K. MUMBY (Ph.D., Southern Illinois University, 1985) is Assistant Professor of Communication at Purdue University. His research interests include the study of power in organizations and an examination of how power is mediated discursively and ideologically in organizational contexts. In addition, he writes in the area of philosophy of communication, with particular attention to relationships among discourse, knowledge, and human identity formation. His published works include articles in several communication journals and a book, *Communication and Power in Organizations: Discourse, Ideology, and Domination* (Ablex, 1988).

SANDRA PETRONIO (Ph.D., University of Michigan, 1979) is Associate Professor of Communication at Arizona State University. Her overall areas of interest are in family communication, with particular focus on managing private information and on divorce adjustment.

LINDA L. PUTNAM (Ph.D., University of Minnesota, 1977) is Professor of Communication at Purdue University. She teaches courses in negotiation, conflict management, and organizational communication. She is coeditor of four books and author of more than 45 articles appearing in publications such as *Human Communication Research, Communication Monographs, Communication Yearbook,* and *Small Group Behavior.* Recently she served as guest editor for two issues on conflict in organizations in *Communication Research* and *Management Communication Quarterly.*

SONJA A. SACKMANN (Ph.D., University of California, Los Angeles, 1985) is Dozentin at the MZSG Management Zentrum St. Gallen and the University of St. Gallen, Switzerland. She teaches, conducts research, and publishes in the areas of organizational culture, organizational development and change, decision making in nonroutine situations, leadership, and human resource management. She has taught at the Graduate School of Management at UCLA and in the Department of Business Administration at the University of Vienna. She was Research Associate in the Department of Management, UCLA Extension, and the Center for Human Environments at the City University Graduate Center, New York. She serves on the Board of the Standing Conference of Organizational Symbolism (SCOS), and is a member of the AAM and GWG.

SANDRA SANFORD (B.A., University of Alabama, Huntsville, 1987) is a technical writer and computer consultant in Huntsville, Alabama. She has been awarded a writing fellowship at the University of Utah beginning in 1989.

DAVID R. SEIBOLD (Ph.D., Michigan State University, 1975) is Professor of Speech Communication at the University of Illinois, Urbana-Champaign. His research interests include interpersonal influence processes, group argumentation and decision making, health communication, and program evaluation methods. He has published widely, and he serves on the editorial boards of several communication publications. He is the former chair of the Interpersonal Communication Division of the International Communication Association.

STUART J. SIGMAN (Ph.D., University of Pennsylvania, 1982) is Associate Professor of Communication at the State University of New York at Albany. He is the author of *A Perspective on Social Communication,* and of articles in *Critical Studies in Mass Communication, Human Communication Research,* and *International Journal of Aging and Human Development.*

PATTY SOTIRIN (M.A., San Diego State University, 1985) is a Ph.D. candidate at Purdue University. Her research interests include issues of rhetoric, power, and gender in organizations. Her current project involves the critical-rhetorical analysis of contemporary labor activism among women clerical workers.

CYNTHIA STOHL (Ph.D., Purdue University) is Associate Professor in the Department of Communication at Purdue University. Her research interests focus primarily on formal and emergent communication networks and worker participation programs. Her work has appeared in several journals, including *Management Communication Quarterly, Journal of Communication, Communication Quarterly, International Journal of Intercultural Relations,* and *Peace and Change.*

MAJID TEHRANIAN (Ph.D., Harvard University) is Professor of Communication and Director-Elect of the Institute for Peace at the University of Hawaii. His chief areas of teaching and research include communication and development theory, intercultural and international communication, and telecommunication policy and planning. He also specializes in Middle Eastern and Asia-Pacific affairs. Dr. Tehranian has served on both national and international organizations as well as on the editorial boards of several publications, including *Iranian Studies, Communication Theory, Progress in Communication Sciences,* and *International Encyclopaedia of Communications.* His publications include *Socio-Economic and Communication Indicators in Development Planning: A Case Study of Iran, Technologies of Power: Information Machines and Democratic Prospects,* and *Dependency and Dialogue: Communication and International Development.*

JOSEPH TUROW (Ph.D., University of Pennsylvania, 1976) is Associate Professor at the University of Pennsylvania's Annenberg School of Communications. A former Head of the Speech Communication Association's Mass Communication Division, he is a member of the editorial boards of *Critical Studies in Mass Communication, Journal of Broadcasting and Electronic Media, Journal of Communication,* and the Sage *Annual Review of Communication Research.* His most recent book is *Playing Doctor: Television, Storytelling and Medical Power* (Oxford University Press, 1989).

STEVEN R. WILSON (Ph.D., Purdue University, 1989) is Assistant Professor of Communication at Michigan State University. He teaches classes in interpersonal communication, persuasion, and conflict and dispute resolution. His research focuses on relationships between communication and cognitive processes during conflict and social influence episodes. He has authored articles appearing in *Human Communication Research, Central States Speech Journal,* and *Management Communication Quarterly.*

JASWANT S. YADAVA (Ph.D., Delhi University, 1968) is Director of the Indian Institute of Mass Communication, New Delhi. From 1971 to 1987 he was Full Professor and Head of Communication Research at the Institute. His specializations are international communication, political communication, and development communication. He has undertaken many research and consultancy assignments from UNESCO, UNICEF, UNFPA, and ESCAP, and has served on committees on media for family planning, health, and family welfare of the government of India. He has published 150 research and popular articles in professional journals and magazines and five communication series from the Institute, and has edited two books. He has participated in a large number of seminars and conferences in India and abroad.